of Representation

Gilles Deleuze
and the Ruin of Representation

Dorothea Olkowski

University of California Press
Berkeley Los Angeles London

University of California Press
Berkeley and Los Angeles, California

University of California Press, Ltd.
London, England

Library of Congress Cataloging-in-Publication Data

Olkowski, Dorothea.
Gilles Deleuze and the ruin of representation / Dorothea Olkowski.
p. cm.
Includes bibliographical references and index.
ISBN 0-520-21691-1 (alk. paper).—ISBN 0-520-21693-8 (pbk. : alk paper)
1. Kelly, Mary, 1941– —Criticism and interpretation. 2. Feminism and art.
3. Psychoanalysis and art. 4. Deleuze, Gilles—Contributions in logic. I. Title.
N6537.K42O44 1999
1119.85—dc21
98-38667
CIP

Manufactured in the United States of America

08 07 06 05 04 03 02 01 00 99
10 9 8 7 6 5 4 3 2 1

The paper used in this publication meets the minimum
requirements of ANSI/NISO Z39.48-1992 (R 1997)
(*Permanence of Paper*). ♾

This book is dedicated with love to my mother,
Wanda Krawic Figurski

Contents

Illustrations

Acknowledgments

It is not easy to know how to properly acknowledge those who have helped me to complete this book, for there is no exact starting point for delineating the inspiration and assistance they have provided. I can say, however, that this book got fully underway through the confidence that my editor at the University of California Press, Edward Dimendberg, showed in my writing and my ideas. I greatly appreciate his steady and calm approach. In the actual writing I was animated again and again by the essays and translations of my friend, Constantin V. Boundas, who seems always to be thinking through the knots in Deleuze's work and who reads the texts so purely. I would also like to thank Todd May, who graciously read a draft of the early chapters and provided me with the critical assurance I so much needed. Marjorie Hass guided me through the intricacies of symbolic logic. Jane Drexler discussed many issues with me and Gail Weiss provided encouragement. Students, especially Karla Finelli, gave me the motivation and opportunity to discuss and work through Mary Kelly's art. My colleague Abby Ferber listened to many ideas and arguments and affirmed the concrete social situations that philosophical ideas often ignore. My husband, Kurt Laetz, and our son, Max, surprised me with their steady confidence in my project and were generous, good-humored, and loving about the huge amounts of time and life that writing consumes.

Elizabeth Grosz encouraged me to apply for an Australian National University Fellowship at the ANU in Canberra, where I began working on chapter 1. She also gave me the opportunity to test-run parts of chapter 3 by inviting me to speak at the "Becomings" conference at the University of Richmond. Patrick Burke gave me a forum in which to present the critique of phenomenology. Kerstin Behnke invited me to present parts of chapters 4 and 5 to her Northwestern University literary studies colloquium, which helped me to gauge the effect of the work. John McCumber gave me the opportunity to develop a large view of Deleuze's work for the *Routledge Encyclopedia of Philosophy.* The University of Colorado at Colorado Springs granted me sabbatical leave in the spring of 1997, during which time most of the manuscript was written. The University of Colorado's Committee on Research and Creative Work provided me with a grant that covered many of the expenses of producing the manuscript.

Part of chapter 1 was published in David Michael Levin's edited collection, *Sites of Vision: The Discursive Construction of Vision in the History of Philosophy* (Cambridge, Mass.: MIT Press, 1997), as "Difference and the Ruin of Representation in Gilles Deleuze." It benefited greatly from his careful and demanding editing. Parts of the Nietzsche interpretation scattered throughout the book appeared first in *Gilles Deleuze and the Theater of Philosophy,* edited by Constantin V. Boundas and Dorothea Olkowski (New York: Routledge Press, 1994). I thank all who directly or indirectly affected the production of this book. Hélène Cixous directly inspired me to write; her words and example came along at an important moment in my efforts. I am especially grateful to the artist Mary Kelly, now chair of the art department at the University of California, Los Angeles, for her courageous, articulate, and creative work and for the two volumes that first came my way, *Interim* and *Post-Partum Document.* My encounter with her art—which I first read about only in a review that inspired me, by the power of the images reproduced there, to search out more of her work—let me make the connection between the ruin of representation and the philosophy of Gilles Deleuze. Finally, Deleuze's work is always there as an image of thought but more, for me, as affective reflection, both passion and understanding. For this I thank him and, with many, deeply mourn his passing.

1
Women, Representation, and Power

Difference Itself

If I begin this book by writing about difference or announce that I am interested in the question of "difference," this is hardly a startling statement. If I write that I think difference, as it is understood in contemporary philosophy, is almost always tied to a system of iconic or imagistic representation and discourse about that representation, this too is hardly startling. If I write that the notion of identity (including the identity of the "I" who speaks or writes) is also a key aspect of what I am trying to analyze, no one would be surprised. And if I conclude that all these concepts in some way contribute to a philosophy that is conceptually and practically interested in how representation has contributed to the subordination of women to men, I still have concluded very little. Given the multiplicity of ethnic, economic, social, and sexual minorities around the globe who are calling out for recognition, it is no longer enough, even or especially for a feminist philosopher, to speak about the subordination of women as if only women are subordinate or as if subordination as a structure of social organization and philosophical thought is not found throughout the world. In its deepest and most profound ontological and epistemological conceptualizations, philosophy is at a point where it must once again consider its own participation in and contribution to systems in which the poor have been subordinated to the wealthy, the immigrant has been subordinated to the citizen of generations, workers have been subordinated to capital, sexuality has been subordinated to Oedipal values, and creative force has been subordinated to objectified representation.

This means that it is not enough to provide a social and political analysis of existing conditions or to rely on empirical or contingent explanations. What interests me instead is linking the analysis of existing conditions to the critique of the structure of representation to produce the ruin of representation, the ruin of hierarchically ordered time and space. With this ruin underway—with static structures of time and space, of life and thought, disassembled—a philosophy of change becomes viable. This is a philosophy that is more abstract than the static structures that undergird representation and that produces more than just "women" as oppressed by social structures; it considers oppression and dominance in their ontological determinations and representative functions. Simultaneously, it is a philosophy that is more particular, discussing not identities or even communities, but attempting instead to focus on specific practices, engaging the particular in the sense of "this" woman here and now, this situation of impoverishment, this sexuality, this particular site of creation and/or oppression and this so-called I, the self that each of these situations produces. Still, it is probably difficult to make sense of why such an approach, at once more abstract and more particular, might produce useful analyses, especially because the roles of women and minorities, particularly in western societies, are closely associated with a system of linguistic, social, political, iconic, or imagistic representation. The system of representation, whether in the realm of philosophy, psychology, social and political theory, ethics, or aesthetics, operates by establishing a fixed standard as the norm or model. The very meaning of minority is associated with falling below the standard of that norm, failing to represent that standard in all its perfection and completeness. Feminists in particular have been sensitive to the function of the representational norm, but many attempts to analyze the representation of women have fallen short. This is, I will argue, because these analyses have operated with categorical generalizations: concepts neither abstract enough nor particular enough, which represent women merely in terms of pre-established, even naturalized, standards. It hardly seems fruitful to continue down the path of general statements about objectified looking or about which social contexts women or minorities are or are not allowed to participate in.[1] Such representations do no more than register a complaint against the norms of language, images, and social and political structures.

This conclusion has provoked me to search for concepts and transformational structures characterized by an abstract but fluid ontology that can make sense of difference by accounting for the reality of temporal and spatial change on a pragmatic level while providing appropriate theoretical constructs in whose terms change can be conceived. This sort of approach to the problem of the representation of women and minorities as deficient in relation to the social and political norm or standard has not been attempted by the majority of theorists concerned with these issues in the contemporary setting. And where it has been attempted, it has not been well understood. Such an ontology, insofar as it delegitimizes the primacy of the model and its exact repetitions or copies by undermining the stability of representational categories, would also serve as a guide to the creative aspects of minority status. Minorities are recognized as minorities because they deviate from representational norms, sometimes to the extent that they seem to make no sense at all. This has proved to be the case with respect to long-established markets like those of art or literature, let alone in politics and philosophy. Additionally, in order to assure that the particular "this" of minority orientation is carefully considered, all analyses, insofar as they are analyses of the social world, must be firmly grounded in that world, in real practices. To the extent that theory does not arise out of and in terms of social practices, it risks irrelevancy and oblivion. But the crucial matter here is: how does this happen?

Although the work of Gilles Deleuze has become central to my inquiry into the power, the authority, and ultimately the ruin of representation, Deleuze was not the first to draw my attention to the ascendancy of representational thinking. My interest came from work in two seemingly separate fields: feminist theory and the visual arts. In the former I found persuasive the epistemological critique of objectified representation coming from contemporary feminist legal theory. Catherine MacKinnon writes so compellingly about the relationship between objectification and representation that I was drawn to study her ideas.[2] With respect to the visual arts, I have often written about painting and the history of art. In that work what aroused my attention was the relation between objectification and single-point perspective, which I came to define as the paradigmatic norm of visual representation.[3] More recently, I have been attentive to the work of one particular artist, Mary Kelly, who challenges the norms of representation in art and the representation of the signifier as promulgated by Jacques Lacan. Although MacKinnon provides an opening for a feminist theoretical approach to practical issues, it is an opening that principally serves the forces of destruction necessary for the approach the rest of this book will develop. Kelly, however, does much more. Her work is no mere "example"; it is a process through which the ruin of representation is effected and carried out. Thus, Kelly's art is simultaneously practice and concept, socially actual and theoretically real. Kelly's art will be addressed in chapter 3 and throughout this book. For now, I focus on that aspect of MacKinnon that critiques representational objectification and ties this feminist concern to Deleuze's indictment of organic representation.

For many contemporary feminists, the work of feminist legal theorist Catharine MacKinnon will be an odd, even unpopular choice of text with which to begin to make my point. MacKinnon is noted, at best, for expressing strong if not rigid ideological bias with regard to social relations between men and women, and at worst, for making alliances with the far right and promoting censorship of sexually explicit materials in a way that many take to be antisex with regard to women.[4] To a certain extent, these often-discussed features of MacKinnon's work make it practically impossible to seriously consider other aspects of her writing. The standard approach to MacKinnon is to denounce her quickly for her dogmatic or negative vision and to move on to others, although there are also theorists who provide a more comprehensive critique.[5] Few feminist readers appear to be able to make much use of MacKinnon's most radical work, her critique of liberalism and of the liberal individual whose right to rights is defined by a system of objective representation.

I would like to take up the facet of MacKinnon's work that begins with her critique of liberalism and its accompanying ideology of the individual and ends with her epistemological critique of objectivity.[6] I choose this course because in this text MacKinnon clearly enumerates the shortcomings, in theory and practice, of objectified representing, shortcomings that derive from "generalizations" defining the individual. She exposes the "individual" as a generalization that excludes anyone who can be defined as a woman or as a member of a minor group, that is, as "different" or unrepresentable. In her critique of liberalism and liberal feminism, MacKinnon argues that for liberalism, the individual is always taken to be the "proper unit of analysis." Therefore, "sexual inequality" turns out to be an arbitrary and irrational division by law and custom that restricts individual human potential. So, she argues, sexism is taken to be just incidental and not a "system of subordination," that is, a system in which some "individuals" are represented as subordinate to other ideal individuals.[7]

In the state of Colorado, for example, an anti–gay/lesbian rights bill, "Amendment 2," was held up in the courts and never put into law while the state and then the federal supreme courts determined whether the amendment merely affected individuals who just happen to be engaged in the practices of a gay/lesbian "lifestyle" or whether it was aimed at those practices themselves and attempted to subordinate them to another sexual practice, one dominant in heterosexist society.[8] That is, for anti–Amendment 2 forces (gay and lesbian rights activists), this law is a matter of what MacKinnon calls hierarchy, social and political domination, and the systematic and cumulative result of heterosexist male power. Supporters of the amendment (principally members of the religious right) presented its passage as necessary to keep any individual or individuals from being given rights not available to the rest of the community. There was no admission or recognition from advocates of the amendment that their own hegemony was what they were seeking to maintain. They obscured their general claim of dominance behind the liberal language of individual rights, just as political theorists obscure the hegemony that representation dictates behind theoretical claims for equality.

MacKinnon targets J. S. Mill and Harriet Taylor's 1869 *The Subjection of Women* as one of the earliest as well as most complete statements of a liberal feminist argument for women's equality.[9] Mill and Taylor argue that the only real differences between men and women are individual differences; woman is man's equal in nature, so she must become his equal under the law in order to become his equal in society as well.[10] They conclude that sexual inequality is irrational because it is a group quality, not an individual quality. Mill and Taylor's objection to the physical force men may exercise over women is that, regardless of his class, *any* man may exercise power over any woman: "The clodhopper exercises, or is to exercise his share of the power equally with the highest nobleman."[11] One may recognize here certain moral and aesthetic concerns such as those Kant addresses in his consideration of men of good taste.[12] The "clodhopper" presumably does not have the good taste or the moral goodness that would make it possible for him to exercise such authority appropriately. According to MacKinnon's account of the liberal theory of equality, "What contemporary feminism terms 'sexism' is in Mill a form of unjust authority that restricts the free development of each woman. Distorting her character to fit her subordination, inequality violates her nature, constrains social efficiency, and obstructs human happiness."[13]

What equality presupposes (and this is the definition of individualism) is that each person is a unique individual who defines him/herself as separate and distinct from all others. Such a presupposition entails others, for in this definition lies the kind of generalization I warned about above: it either makes the term one that excludes women or renders it meaningless. The definition also presupposes naturalism: that "her" nature is fixed and knowable; it is a thing, such that, "[i]n this view, body originates independently of society or mind . . . it undergirds social relations, limiting change."[14] Otherwise stated, the fixity of the natural, material world is the ground of the fixity of the social world. For liberalism, fixed and knowable nature guarantees hierarchical order and grounds representation and truth. This assumption still haunts feminism and will be subject to criticism throughout this book, beginning with the discussion of Aristotle below. Liberal equality also assumes idealism in the sense of a belief in reason's efficacy, such that, "independently of surroundings, advocacy, or audience," rational persuasion and argument are assumed to be or guaranteed to be the "engine[s] of change," even while they act to guarantee uniformity.[15]

In addition to this there is moralism, an aspect of the naturalism and idealism that follows from the guarantee of reason to persuade. If nature is fixed and knowable, if "transhistorical logic" or reason provides the method for knowing, then it is clear that nature and reason must also provide some clues for acting. Right and wrong mean, as Taylor and Mill affirm, "conforming to rules that are abstractly right or wrong in themselves" though the place of this "in themselves" remains to be negotiated.[16] Ultimately, MacKinnon concludes, liberalism implies the morality of volunteerism, the idea that "social life is comprised of autonomous, intentional, and self-willed actions."[17] Naturalism (or materialism), idealism (or rationalism), and moralism; each of these aspects of the system of objectification will be subject to radical critique by the ruin of representation and will be shown to be implicated in the system of subordination that MacKinnon exposes.

As Merle Thornton argues, even though Mill and Taylor make use of this agenda to seek women's higher development, because they lack any standard other than the male standard (what MacKinnon refers to as objective science), the equal freedom of women can only mean "equal contract in marriage up to the standard of men; property rights like men's; access to occupations now reserved for men; granting political rights such as men have; equal access to the education men have."[18] The problem with "similar" standards is that they presuppose that whatever attempts to be "like" the original or to "represent" the original is always degraded with respect to it, for the copy is never a perfect "equal" of the original. Thornton observes that Mill and Taylor do give "equivocal intimations of a possible *different* but equally valuable nature for women," namely "the capability they have for tying the general to the particular."[19] However, they simultaneously fail to recognize the extent to which this is not merely a question of "nature," of a fixed, natural ability that women might will to use: "This serious deficiency stems from the power of abstract individualism in their thinking. Too committed to the idea of members of society as individual contractors and choosers, they are unable to think through the implications of the sexual division of labor for women as a social category."[20] In addition, it is highly problematic to take biology as fixed or unsuited to social influence because at the very least, "some types of biological engineering could prove more feasible than some types of proposed social engineering."[21] Contraceptive devices, for example, are the product of biological engineering and biological management. They have resulted in great social change in situations that have been highly resistant to educational campaigns and social engineering alone. Recent experiences, for example, with providing third-world women with small bank loans to establish their own businesses have taught us that biological engineering is much more effective in combination with economic and social empowerment. Nevertheless, presuming the fixity of nature (male or female), the universal efficacy of reason, and the prejudice of morality attached to the correct use of reason (what is called good sense), liberal theory suggests that the individual and only the individual can act on the basis of reason. But such an individual is no one, for "it" is by definition so general as to account for any natural, rational, human being who thinks and acts on an extremely limited basis (good sense), a basis that by definition excludes having a body as well as any accompanying bodily sensation.[22]

MacKinnon argues that, as an idealism that believes in the power of the individual to willfully make changes in society in accordance with universal standards of right and wrong as determined in fixed nature, such objectivism seriously underestimates the realities of power and social determination.[23] I would add to this that under the conditions liberalism assumes, it is virtually impossible to make sense of how there can be agency at all. The ideology of individualism takes social issues to be questions of individual taste, value, and interest or, worse, misrecognizes them as questions of fixed and knowable nature. As Thornton expresses it, if there is a possibility of distinctive excellences, potentialities, or natures for the sexes, developed human beings would embrace these distinctions without a structure of similarity. But such a claim is always incompatible with the claim of individual equality irrespective of sex.[24]

What is crucial for this book is that any theory of women's liberation beyond equality must certainly abandon the belief that nature is immutable and fixed; otherwise, no liberation is possible. Otherwise, women's (and some men's) bodies are taken to be not just the justification and rationalization for their oppression; they are seen as its root, even its cause.[25] Social relations, MacKinnon reminds us, are man- (and woman-) made.[26] Feminists such as Adrienne Rich argue that the culture's pervasive "heterosexism" is the social relation that oppresses both men and women.[27] Once heterosexism is made the focus of a social critique of power and control, Rich enumerates other kinds of practices that bring women together to create provisional and even formal groupings that decrease their reliance on modern liberal heterosexism. Less visionary, MacKinnon takes the very social structures that women are most likely to value to be the site of their greatest oppression: "Feminist theory sees the family as a unit of male dominance, a locale of male violence and reproductive exploitation, hence a primary locus of the oppression of women. . . . [C]apitalism expresses the same authority structure as does the family, through its organization, distribution of wealth, and resource control."[28] The link between these sources of oppression—family, capitalism—and others such as race, class, and gender is that they express an "authority structure," and this authority structure, I maintain, is the structure of representation whose ruin is imminent. This is why women cannot be defined solely in terms of the class status of their "men": fathers, husbands, sons, or lovers. Feminism, as MacKinnon wishes to define it, finds women oppressed *as a sex*. MacKinnon thinks that feminism has developed a unique epistemological practice that can account for women's oppression as a sex and that this is what differentiates feminism from all other critical practices. MacKinnon gives this epistemological practice the somewhat dated name *consciousness-raising*.[29]

Significantly, MacKinnon takes consciousness-raising to be principally not a discursive practice but a social practice arising out of the actual activities of women. For her this means that consciousness-raising is a mixture of thought and materiality insofar as consciousness, and specifically women's consciousness, is not a conglomerate of individual/subjective ideas, but is rather constituted as an effect of real social relations.[30] MacKinnon does not specify the precise organization or structure of this "mixture" of the mental and material, and this is a serious deficiency in her work, leaving her wide open to the attack that she formulates the world in terms of oppositions. That is, if women's material reality is so constituted that "mere" discourse leaves no mark upon it and does not participate in the opening up of any heresies or differences, then the world is truly constituted out of a kind of static and hierarchized dead matter and no change is possible. When MacKinnon maintains that women's subordination is social, not natural and not individual, that it is the effect of a division of power in society, and that while consciousness-raising makes women aware of their situation, it does nothing to alter it, I am inclined to agree; yet MacKinnon has not been able to offer any effective account of how change can be produced. If women are to create themselves or anything else, they need to be specific about what kind of materiality they have to work with. Yet MacKinnon's statement that in society the division of power is maintained by a system of *representation* produced by the scientific stance called objectivity operated as a wake-up call in my search for an ontology of change.

As a scientific stance, objectivity is justified by an epistemology with two primary characteristics: first, sufficient visual distance from what is viewed so that the viewer is no longer limited by "his" position as material being; and second, aperspectivity so that the viewer can observe the world from no particular place or time, but rather from all places and times.[31] In short, the observer presumes that "he" is no longer part of the process and also assumes that what "he" sees is essential to the object and not merely incidental to it. MacKinnon also argues that this epistemological stance produces gender inequality (indicated by the masculine possessive and pronoun in quotation marks). This is because objectivity is assumed to be neutral when in fact it is the point of view of men, men with the power and authority to enforce it. The standpoint taken by men becomes the standard for measuring any other; women and minorities can never meet this standard because it excludes their points of view. In other words, "gender is socially constructed as difference epistemologically."[32]

Such a way of seeing the world both assumes and produces spatial and temporal homogeneity, and in leaving out the impact of the point of view of the observer, it produces knowledge of the world defined neutrally as a copy of reality, as representation. The effect of this epistemology is to constitute the world without a knower and without a point of view.[33] There is an assumption that any situatedness with regard to human life would undercut the truth value of the knowledge produced. MacKinnon's version of feminist practice implies the possibility of an analysis that locates the actual site from within which one knows, as well as the "standpoint and time frame of that attempting to be known."[34] A methodology that is generated from this kind of analysis may direct us toward the more particular knowledges I discussed at the beginning of this section, especially insofar as analysis of the site of knowledge is neither representation nor misrepresentation, but rather a response to the world from what MacKinnon still refers to as a "consciousness" in the world, and what I would prefer to call a point of view, a particular temporalization and spatialization.

Still, the question here remains something like: Who is the oppressor? If MacKinnon has been successful (as I think she has been) in detaching feminism from liberal theories of the individual, she may well be less successful in keeping feminism from sliding back into ideological absolutism—that is, in MacKinnon's case, a position according to which women are identified so closely with their oppressed social position that change is impossible. And so it is important to know if she is constructing sexism as a material structure that, in spite of its supposedly social basis, remains impenetrable, or if she is attempting to construct a philosophy that does not insist upon the identity of the male sex as oppressors and the identity of the female sex as oppressed. She writes that white, upper-class (straight) men may argue against "rights" and a rights approach to questions of sexual difference. They may claim that rights are liberal, individualistic, useless, and alienating, but this is because they *have* rights.[35] The questions MacKinnon raises here cannot be ignored. Can the notion of "individuals" who have "rights" be maintained apart from liberalism's objectified representation of the world? What would it mean to reformulate the legal or social system from a minoritarian point of view—the perspective of "the subordinated, disadvantaged, dispossessed, and silenced"? And finally, what is the relation between such a reformulation and the ruin of representation?

Feminism has tended to look at women as constituting a group that is characterized by a certain shared reality, but it is not enough just to say, as MacKinnon does, that although no female escapes the meaning of being a woman within a society that defines human beings in accordance with their sex, nonetheless all women are not the same.[36] Something else is needed here. Not only are all women and especially all minorities not the same, but no points of view can possibly be the same. MacKinnon's materialist approach does address the question of the generalized representation of women through its comprehensive critique of the notion of objectivity, but it does not and cannot recognize the multiplicity of "particular" perspectives and points of view of those who see in "difference" not just the status of an outsider with regard to the dominant culture, but those who in some manner practice "difference" and who value this practice.

For some feminist theorists (and I include myself in this group), as well as theorists who may not specifically be working from a feminist point of view, the only solution seems to be to pursue what Michele Montrelay has called "the ruin of representation."[37] Even objectivity—that is, distance and aperspectivity—has specific social roots and implications, as MacKinnon reminds us; but I would go further, for MacKinnon ties these implications to history, which is much too general. MacKinnon is not alone among contemporary feminists in looking to contingent (historical) factors to explain social and political inequality; nonetheless, I will remain focused on her position. When the view from inside and within the social order is devalued, when views conflicting with epistemological objectivity are declared unreal or irrational, then historical evaluations are not enough and we must work on a more abstract level. However, when MacKinnon points out that the detached observer is precisely the one science needs to validate its non–point of view, that science creates a reality conforming to its own image, and that men use science to maintain their power, she is heading in the direction of an abstraction that is not simply an historical analysis. When liberal theory makes use of the objective scientific point of view to attribute not just woman's feelings but her very experience, not to her place in the organization of the socius, but instead to the woman as an individual, the woman "in there," opposed to the world "out here," then the question is: Where do we look for forms of expression and forms of content that both document women's oppression and lack of power, and operate to create new realities?[38] Is it by individualizing women's point of view that liberal society excludes women?

This is where the work of Mary Kelly comes into play, for it is both a critique of objectified representation and the creation of new points of view. Kelly's forms of expression are a new orientation in life for herself as a woman, an orientation she creates in works of art through the organization of images, objects, and words. Kelly's forms of content, the materials she uses in her work, are borrowed from the context of the psychoanalytic schema, from the naturalist's world, from the social world of a woman-theorist-artist, as well as from the stock of art supplies and images available to anyone working in the arts. Kelly transforms these forms of content by resituating them in non-representational series or forms of expression as opposed to fixed social and psychological schemas. Her work, I think, not only ruins the hierarchical order of representations discussed above and below, it acts as a creative memory of something that will not be represented even though it is produced in images. To see in Kelly's art not just the destructive force but also the creative force of difference, it might help to first make sense of the difference between a logic of difference and a logic of representation. To do this, I would like to make use of two analyses, one (by Iris Marion Young) that shows how power and knowledges might be distributed everywhere once the logic of representation is robbed of its authority; and one (by Deleuze) that connects categorical representation to the logic of identity.[39] I now turn to these distributions.

The Logic of Difference

Iris Marion Young's political philosophy has taken up the kinds of social, political, racial, gendered, and class exclusions MacKinnon and others are concerned about. In an essay that strikes at the heart of what I take to be the difference issue, Young maintains that there is an enormous diversity of interests in contemporary culture based on privilege, oppression, race, gender, ethnicity, age, sexuality, and ability, each with the potential for creating division among people. Any political movement that wants to address the truly disadvantaged has to differentiate between the dissimilar needs and experiences of those who are relatively disadvantaged and persuade the relatively privileged of the justice in recognizing the claims of oppressed peoples as groups.[40] The question is how to accomplish both tasks. Young recognizes immediately that there is a logical problem, and that a single logic (that derives from one specific ontology) has dominated our thinking about minorities and rights. What she proposes is a change of logic that, I would maintain, entails a change of ontology, more specifically, an ontology of change.

Historically, Young argues, group-based oppression and conflict has been most extreme when it is grounded in a conception of difference as otherness and exclusion. This, in turn, presupposes a "logic of identity" according to which groups' natures are defined as essential and/or substantial.[41] For example, men and women have been stereotyped as rational or emotional, public or private, and one group makes use of these essential or substantive differences to subjugate the other group. The obvious problem with the logic of identity is that whatever group tends to dominate, to have the most privilege and power, will represent themselves as active human subjects and represent everyone else as "others," not up to the level of the original, until and unless they find a way to conform to the definition of the individual or the citizen established by the dominant group. The long, sad history of colonialism and racism attest to this disparity and conformism. The "others," those who have been colonized or enslaved, have found themselves judged "lacking" in relation to the dominant group: "The privileged and dominating group defines its own positive worth by negatively valuing the Others and projecting onto them as an essence or nature the attributes of evil, filth, bodily matter; these oppositions legitimate the dehumanized use of the despised group as sweat labor and domestic servants, while the dominant group reserves for itself the leisure, refined surroundings, and high culture that mark civilization."[42]

Such severe hierarchical relations of privilege and oppression may be the extreme, yet Young concludes that as long as the logic of identity operates to differentiate groups in terms of "otherness," the heterogeneity of peoples—their experiences, culture, and language—is reduced to merely accidental qualities of their existence as human beings. To the genus "human being" are attributed only so many specific differences. That which does not conform to these categories is placed under the genus "nonhuman." Even within the genus "human being," differences have been ordered hierarchically. In western nations, the white bourgeois male is taken to be the norm and model for the female and for all minorities; against this standard all other humans are considered lacking and deficient.[43] Additionally, within this schema, mind is given priority over body, reason over emotion, activity over passivity. In each case the valued member of the pair is valued absolutely. Thus, any variation or contextual valuation of differences is denied or repressed. Any attributes of specific groups that do not fit into the schema of genus, species, and differences must be either assimilated to one of the accepted categories (as inferior copies) or denied and suppressed.

Young acknowledges that capitalism as a sociopolitical system contributes to this in several important ways. The need to have a ready labor force gives way to the demand that there be a group or groups of so-called despised persons ready to be hired when they are needed, and fired when overproduction threatens, and generally available to do the dirty work privileged groups do not want to do, or at least do not want to do cheaply.[44] In the United States we tend to turn a blind eye to immigrants who do farm labor or factory labor as long as they do not wish to stay in the country or send their children to American schools. Oddly enough, they are seen as not contributing to the economy, not paying their way. But the United States is not alone. All the major European nations and many booming Middle Eastern and Asian economies have the same "problem" with immigrants.

To challenge the logic of identity and the conception of group identity as essence or substance, Young proposes something very much like what we will find in the work of Gilles Deleuze. That is, she proposes a logic of relation that is less a relational arrangement than a conception of difference that begins with the fact of heterogeneity and the interrelation of groups. I would prefer to call this a logic of difference, since it must be stressed that *relation* in this case does not refer to some notion of relativity, and that Young is not arguing for relativity. Conceiving of groups on the basis of a logic of relations or a logic of difference means that different groups can no longer be evaluated in terms of the categorical definitions demanded by the structure genus, species, and difference, for this leaves the nonprivileged groups with the designation of merely contingent "other," or even with no designation at all. Rather, Young argues, groups have to be seen as overlapping, constituted in relation to one another, yet as formed out of the experience of particular and often diverse ways of life and forms of association, even within the same society, even within the same group.[45]

Ultimately, Young suggests, "social movements of oppressed or disadvantaged groups need a political vision different from both the assimilationist and separatist ideals . . . a politics that treats difference as variation and specificity, rather than exclusive opposition."[46] Practically, she maintains the necessity of a political system in which different groups accept the fact that they must participate in the same society, and that because this is so, all groups must expect that the interactions between groups will often produce conflict, division, privilege, and oppression. The point of political interaction will be to ameliorate these problems. It will thus be one of the responsibilities of governments to find ways for different groups to meet and discuss policies that can be accepted as legitimate by all. But this means that all groups must have roles in government and the points of view of repressed or disadvantaged groups must be respected and legitimized. This will only happen if significant numbers of minorities can participate in political practices to the extent that they have real political influence.[47]

Young provides examples of both failed (in Eastern Europe) and successful (among New Zealand's Maoris) attempts by minority groups to exercise real political influence, thereby ascertaining the extent to which such aims are realizable or at least conceivable. I want to add that a change in the basic presuppositions of western political systems such as Young is proposing is no simple thing. That this is a significant change must be clear from the discussion of political liberalism and MacKinnon's critique. Young (to her credit) develops a political logic based on successful practices, whereas MacKinnon does not take her positive analysis beyond the act of consciousness-raising, though she does attempt to make it clear that there are significant epistemological and ontological issues.[48] A change from a logic of identity to a logic of difference arises in practice but must be formulated with concepts that differentiate differences and that undermine the "representation" of such differences as merely specific differences belonging to a single genus. To do this, I have suggested, calls for a new ontology, an ontology of change as opposed to an ontology of static hierarchies and objectified structures.

To begin with, there must be a critique of representation defined provisionally as the hierarchical ordering of categories that produces an objectified state of affairs. Further, the task will be to create an image of difference that sweeps away the metaphysics of being and identity and their representation, so as to practically and conceptually acknowledge the stuttering practice of an ontology of becoming. To accomplish this reorientation of thought and practice, I am making use of the philosophical thought of Gilles Deleuze. I have been reading Deleuze and using his critiques as well as his creative rethinking of philosophy since my graduate studies. Gradually, I found that my own concerns about philosophy as a regulative practice rather than a creative one could be concretized and theorized with the help of Deleuze's work, not as a fixed philosophy but as an ongoing practice. Deleuze has problematized philosophy with a certain conception of the philosopher and philosophy. From its high days as queen of the sciences, Deleuze pulls philosophy down to the surface. From the depths of materiality and the body, Deleuze brings philosophy up for air. On the surface between material depths and transcendent heights, Deleuze proposes that philosophy is stuttering. Stuttering is what happens in language when the language system is in motion, in "perpetual disequilibrium," so that the entire language system stutters, murmurs, mumbles, and breaks up in a heterogeneity of time and space.[49] Without a homogeneous system, whose terms and relations are constant, to fall back on, language quickly breaks up; it bifurcates because the elements of its syntax have to respond dynamically to other linguistic elements, creating new linguistic orders. In philosophy, this means that there are no constant terms supplied by a homogeneous system of reference, but rather the radical insistence that philosophical conceptions do and will vary in every one of their terms, depending upon the point of view of the philosophy, depending upon the concrete practices out of which and in terms of which it arises.

So there is a sense in which Deleuze, in problematizing philosophy, is setting it in motion, making no claims about the nature of the world, providing no taxonomies or hierarchies of its inhabitants, no claims about what is or is not true. When philosophy no longer erects a new order of fixed thought in the place of the old, then philosophy has become stuttering. But in order for an ontology of becoming to continue in disequilibrium, another aspect of practice and thought might need to be called upon; this aspect of life and thought might be called "spiritual" or simply creative. To find this aspect will take more than a critique of the metaphysics of being and objectified representation, though that is where it starts. It will take an investigation into the most profound aspects of temporalization, life and death, without which no life and no thought becomes. That it is not easy to characterize this dimension of life and thought goes without saying. It will be a painstaking process to produce this as ongoing, though many thinkers have tried and just as many have fallen into the numerous systematic and representational traps laid out by philosophy. So to become engaged with the creative surface of thought, we will need good guides, guides who cannot lead us anywhere final but who, through their stuttering process, set time and space in motion so that stuttering differences can be created from every point of view.

Difference and Organic Representation

At the beginning of *Difference and Repetition,* Deleuze is primarily interested in discovering a way to think the notion of difference apart from the Aristotelian metaphysical framework in whose terms it was originally conceived, at least among western thinkers.[50] In doing so, he seems to have recovered the philosophical underpinnings of representation as the dominant mode of seeing and thinking of the world, regardless of which historical conception of time and space obtains at any given moment. The discovery that Deleuze makes is that representation has been constituted, in western philosophy, in terms of the Aristotelian framework. This discovery may be why, following *Difference and Repetition,* Deleuze engages in numerous efforts to analyze representation as a particularly restricted form of acting and thinking; thus it may also be the case that this first analysis remains the heart of all his other thinking on the question.[51]

For Deleuze, the bias that has constructed representation as the standard and norm for images and thought is not merely part of an historical moment. It is grounded in something more profound, whose persistence and effects I have alluded to in the feminist critique of representation, but whose cause may well lie in philosophy's answer to the question: What is difference? In asking this question, Deleuze is clearly not interested in empirical differences or in things insofar as they are already distinguished from one another and so remain outside the notion of difference; he wants to ask about difference itself. Deleuze's description of this notion is so evocative and creates such a strong image that it merits quoting at length:

> Let us imagine something which is distinguished—and yet *that from which* it is distinguished is not distinguished from it. The flash of lightening for example, is distinguished from the black sky, but must carry the sky along with it. . . . One would say that the bottom rises to the surface, without ceasing to be the bottom. There is, on both sides, something cruel—and even monstrous—in this struggle against an elusive adversary, where the distinguished is opposed to something which cannot be distinguished from it, and which continues to embrace that which is divorced from it.[52]

A number of considerations can be discerned in this analysis. Consider the norm for all visual representation, single-point perspective. In his treatise "On Painting," Alberti laid out the rules of representation in painting. The image must appear within the boundaries of a rectangle or framed window that maintains the image at a distance from the viewer who views it as if through a window.[53] The canvas itself is divided geometrically so that the illusion of three dimensions can be produced on the canvas by establishing an infinitely receding horizon in the center of the flat surface. This ordering of the canvas constitutes a hierarchy in terms of the proportionate sizes of the objects that appear within the grid. Those objects closest to the viewer appear largest, those furthest removed appear smallest, and objects become smaller as they recede toward the infinite horizon. Within this space, the figures are carefully modeled with light and shadow, furthering the illusion of depth and three dimensions. Drawing is emphasized over color insofar as it meets the demand for planar, symmetrical, and conceptual surfaces conveying more intelligible and less optical images.[54] Numerous Renaissance scholars attest to the fact that although Renaissance artists battled against the restrictions of the theorists, preferring the living quality of images in *movement* to the mirrored perfection of nature, nonetheless this more static conception prevailed in the end and became the very definition of representation.[55]

We find it, for example, in the work of Nicolas Poussin (1593–1665), who wrote that the highest aim of painted imagery is to represent noble and serious human actions, shown in a logical and orderly way—not as they actually happen, but as they would happen were nature perfect.[56] In

Poussin's painting, the impressions of nature are ordered according to laws of visibility that create the topographical exactitude required for idealized landscapes. Figures are frozen in the moment of action in landscapes that are hierarchically ordered spaces. But if we follow Deleuze's prescription, we must think about the bottom of such images rising to the surface, that is, the background rising up onto the surface of the image. The result is distortion of the image, a distortion that decomposes the planar and symmetrically arranged bodies and objects. When, as Deleuze says, the bottom rises to the surface, the grid is effaced, modeling is defeated, and form is destroyed. This is the monstrosity, the cruelty of difference in the image. Such cruel or monstrous distortion of the hierarchically composed representational image, the three-dimensional illusion, and the plastic technique of relief produces irregular and sometimes disturbing images.

Goya's *Executions of May 3, 1808* offers a grey wall of soldiers that forms a solid, nearly undifferentiated plane, each soldier a repetition of the next, while the surface of the canvas becomes a site of murder and carnage. In William Blake's primal scenes of awe, terror, or creation, an emblematic figure blazes in the center of a depthless surface. These paintings and drawings manifest no respect for norms of proportion or sense, the key elements of perspectival visual representation. Such distortion is not limited to the nineteenth century, that is, it is not tied to a particular historical era in the West. Giotto's fourteenth-century Arena Chapel interior likewise articulates a highly differentiated kind of pictorial space that sharpens the viewer's awareness of the picture surface. In the scene of hell, in particular, there is a total collapse of hierarchized space: shattered architecture, a completely flat surface, fading and disappearing color and bodies.[57] In none of these cases does what appears on the surface correspond to any account of progressive or contemporaneous technological or historical ideas about space.

In each case, form is destroyed, relief is renounced, and a determination is made. Far from being the materialization of irrationality and chaos, what emerges in these images is a profound and difficult kind of vision in which, as Deleuze notes, "determination is made by dint of [*à force de*] supporting a precise and unilateral relationship with the indeterminate."[58] The bottom rises, the form dissolves, yet a determination is made, perhaps the most important determination of all: one that has been routinely and without thought compromised by the categorical orientation of western philosophy since Aristotle, who articulated the demand for coherence and hierarchy in the organic representation and who, according to Deleuze, inscribed all difference in a general concept.

Although the detour through Aristotle is complex, it is absolutely necessary for insight into how hierarchical conceptual representation came to be established as the single and authoritative source of visible intelligibility and political stabilization. According to Deleuze, it is Aristotle who, to a far greater degree than Plato, refused to recognize difference and who is thus accountable for the establishment of the hegemonic reign of representation and the social and political practices that it rationalizes. For on the level of practice, when the system of organic representation is taken to be the only intelligible regime of thought and visibility, then hegemonic and rigid social and political practices embrace representation to justify their existence.

For Aristotle, Deleuze states, terms differ through the mediation of something else, but there are degrees of mediation, and thus degrees of difference. True difference, in Aristotle, is located only in the greatest of these, but not so distantly that there is no basis for comparison:

> That contrariety is the greatest difference is made clear by induction. For things which differ in *genus* have no way to one another, but are too far distant and not comparable; and for things that differ in *species* the extremes from which generation takes place are the contraries, and the distance between extremes—and therefore that between the contraries—is the greatest.[59]

Merely material contraries would of course be accidental; generic differences are too great and cannot even be considered together; individual differences are too small.[60] Only the genus is divided by specific differences; specific differences modify the subject in its form such that the genus remains the same for itself (identical), yet becomes other in the differences that divide it.[61]

Aristotle is completely unwilling to count as differences those differences that are merely other and do not differ in a particular respect, that is, do not begin with something in common. This is why the organic unity of the representation of a genus in a concept is what is at stake for him: "For . . . that which is different is different from some particular thing in some particular respect, so that there must be something *identical* whereby they differ."[62] Difference is only allowed to exist in terms of identity with regard to a generic concept. What gets constituted in Aristotle is thus the very ruin of *difference* itself. There is and can be no concept proper to difference, for difference is always inscribed within the genus, the concept in general, and difference is no more than difference within identity. The result is that "one confuses the determination of the concept of difference with the inscription of difference in the identity of an indeterminate concept."[63]

While this approach provides coherence and intelligibility through the hierarchy imposed by identical generic concepts and their specific differences, it restricts difference to the status of a predicate of concepts. But the restriction is not absolute, for precisely at this point something happens that amounts to a "crack" in thought through which another notion of difference will emerge. Genera are, in Aristotle's account, "ultimate determinable concepts [categories]," so they are not conditioned by a higher-level concept or meta-genus common to them all. Aristotle insists: "But it is not possible that either unity or being should be a single genus of things; *for the differentiae of any genus must each of them both have being and be one.*"[64] Differences *have being;* differences themselves *are,* they are not merely predicates of concepts. Yet, in the same breath Aristotle also maintains that no genus can be predicated of its differentia. The point to note here is that if differences *are,* if they exist as differences, then the genus should be able to be predicated of or attributable to its differences. But as I will make clear, Aristotle's overall framework makes this impossible.

In Aristotle, being subsists as an identical or common concept that functions distributively and hierarchically.[65] This means that being is not a genus whose species would be the categories; such a division would make being *univocal,* which, for Aristotle, it is not. Rather, the unity of being is that of an *analogy.*[66] Franz Brentano has clarified the first point:

> Thus *Metaphysics* V.10 claims that, since being is said in several ways, the same follows for all other concepts which are attributed to it, so that the identical, the different, and the opposite ought to be recognized as something different for each category. . . . Similarly, *Metaphysics* V.28 states peremptorily that whatever belongs to different categories does not have a common genus and that the categories can be reduced neither to one another nor to a single higher entity.[67]

As for the unity of being lying in *analogy,* Aristotle states that unity comes from number, species (those whose definition is one), genus (those with common attributes), or analogy (those that are relative to one another).[68] Since, as Brentano points out, the unity of being cannot be derived from number, species, or genus, this leaves only analogy. Analogy, Brentano argues, operates specifically in relation to "one definite kind of thing."[69] In Aristotle's examples, all that is healthy is relative to health and all that is medical is relative to the medical art. Aristotle writes: "And that which is medical is relative to the medical art, one thing being called medical because it possesses it, another because it is naturally adapted to it, another because it is a function of the medical art. And we shall find other words used *similarly* to these."[70] In the specific case of being, *being* refers primarily to substance, and all other categories only have being in reference to or by analogy to substance.[71] Or, as Deleuze states, being is hierarchically primary and distributively common to all categories, thus insofar as it operates analogically, being is equivocal in Aristotle and will *never* give us a proper concept of difference.[72]

Specific difference determines difference only in the identity of the concept in general, while generic difference is no more than analogy. Between these two kinds of differences a bond of complicity is formed in *representation.* Thus, what we are witnessing is the very formation of representation, the *logos* of representation described above, which is composed of two elements. The first consists of the differences (conceived in terms of analogy) between species that are subsumed under the *identity* of a genus, or it consists of the genus that stands in relations of *analogy* with other genera. However, this abstract representation, in order to be a representation, insofar as it subsumes species, must also rely on what constitutes them, a second element, namely *resemblances* that presume the continuity of the sensible intuition in a concrete representation.[73] The effect of this dual system of classification is to erase *difference* as a concept and as reality. This occurs, of course, in the process of reflection, the *judgment* according to which these determinations are made and according to which difference is made to submit to representation: "In the concept of reflection, indeed, the mediatory and mediatized difference submits itself fully to the *identity* of the concept, to the *opposition* of predicates, to the *analogy* of judgment, and to the *resemblance* of perception. Here we rediscover the necessarily quadripartite character of representation."[74] Deleuze characterizes representation as "organic" insofar as it is constituted in terms of this four-part judgment, in accordance with which difference is excluded from representation. If difference were to show itself at all as a concept and reality, it could do so in this model only as a crack, a catastrophe, a break in resemblance or as the impossibility of claiming identity, opposition, analogy, or resemblance where reflection demands that they should occur.

It is clear to Deleuze that in most political, social, artistic, ethnic, economic, scientific, linguistic, and philosophical practices, the Aristotelian model of organic representation—organized around identity, opposition, analogy, and resemblance—dominates. This development is motivated by the intelligibility and simplicity of organic representation as revealed in political and visual practices. As Poussin discovered, organic representation perfects vision and idealizes the real; and as the Italian Renaissance attests, organic representation offers visible intelligibility and coherence. These effects are magnified by Aristotle's conception of time, for as he works through the problematic of temporality, nuanced as his reading is, it nevertheless contributes to the substantive and static nature of representation.[75] In the *Physics,* Book IV, Aristotle begins by claiming that movement and time are experienced together, whether it is by movement in the mind or movement through the body.[76] Time must in some way belong to movement, since it is clearly not the same as movement. This would seem to augur a fluid conception of time, except that movement, Aristotle immediately decides, also goes with magnitude, so it is necessary first to decide what operates to unite them.

When something moves, it moves from something to something through a continuity that is magnitude. The continuity of magnitude makes the movement continuous. The continuity of movement makes for the continuity of time as well. The principle of resemblance in experience is at work guaranteeing continuity at each step, or perhaps it is analogy in thought.[77] The distinctions "before" and "after" are derived in the same manner. First, they are qualifications of magnitude, then we apply them to movement, then we apply them to time, since time and movement always correspond.[78] Unlike magnitude, however, time does not exist, for in order to claim that something exists we must be able to say that it "is" and that it is "now."[79] But time does not appear to be such a "now." Keeping in mind that only the experience of motion actually gives us time, it is necessary to ask: What is this motion that is "together" with time? For it is likely that if time is connected with motion, is given only with motion, and is not given in a static representation, there will be a crack in Aristotle's theory of time that will provide an opening through which a non-representational account of time may emerge.[80]

That time is given "together" with movement explains why, when we perceive time, we perceive that one part of time "has been" and so "is not," while another part of time is "going to be" and so also "is not."[81] Thus, time consists of what "is not" in relation to which the "now" serves as a boundary, a boundary to the past or future; the "now" is the intermediary between "before" and "after" when we perceive "before" and "after" in motion. But what does this mean? Time as what "is not" is nothingness and can only be thought of on the basis of the past and future modes of time. However, if the "now" is a unit of measure that distinguishes "before" and "after" and allows movement to be determined only on the basis of the "now," then the "now" as actual (as being *in act*) is opposed to movement. For Aristotle, being and movement are opposites. This indicates that in Aristotle's conception of time, the "now" is nontime, it is being *in act,* and "before" and "after" are qualified as time but only insofar as they are diminishing affectations of the "now." But when being is actual and "before" and "after," no-longer and not-yet, are nothing, what sense does it make to speak of time? Or how do we come to speak of time, to make sense of time, to say that something takes a certain amount of time to go from one place to another?

Time, ultimately, can only be made sense of as what is counted. But since "before" and "after" are nothing, what we count is the "now." So we should not be surprised to read that the "now" is a subject that accepts different attributes. Aristotle tells us that we count the "now" in succession, and each "now" is different but "its substratum is an identity."[82] So it is a genus with species, each "now" of succession is a species of the "now" as substratum. This makes of "before" and "after" nothing more than specific differences, which, as differences of a subject, are only accidental (they are not-being) and not difference in itself. Rather than characterizing actual being or motion in an immanent sense, time ends up being an external measure. For the "now" corresponds to a body that is carried along, as time corresponds to motion, so that as a body is carried along we become aware of "before" and "after" by means of the motion. And if we "regard these as countable we get the 'now.'" Hence in these also the "'now' as substratum remains the same (for it is what is before and after in movement), but what is predicated of it is different; for it is insofar as the 'before and after' is numerable that we get the 'now.'"[83] Ultimately, whereas that which is carried is a real thing, Aristotle affirms that the motion is not real.[84] Although Aristotle concedes that without time there would be no "now" either, nonetheless insofar as he represents the now as a substrate, as a subject, and time as a magnitude, a multiplicity of now-points, the limit of the representation of time is that a line of "nows" is a multiplicity of immobilities, a multiplicity of successive arrests that do not give us motion or change and so do not give us a conception of difference (in this case, motion) as real. So Aristotle's conception of time fully complements his conception of organic representation.

Two key questions emerge out of the Aristotelian problematic: First, under what, if any, conditions is difference a concept and real? Second, what accounts for the domination of the occurrence according to which difference is made to submit to organic representation? Is it a choice made in favor of certain historical constructions, or is representation part of some other more determined and less contingent structure? Beginning with the first question, to conceptualize real difference the model of judgments must be abandoned, for it is by means of judgment or "good sense" that difference is lost. Foucault has remarked on this specifically: "But *what* recognizes these similarities, the exactly alike and the least similar—the greatest and the smallest, the brightest and the darkest—if not good sense? . . . And it is good sense that reigns in the philosophy of representation."[85] Deleuze suggests that an appropriate though *contingent* replacement for judgment is the proposition. This is not to insist that the conceptualization of difference as real can only emerge in linguistics. Difference is not principally linguistic either in scope or origin, for as I shall make clear below, the linguistic formalization is only one expression of the science of multiplicities.[86] However, the propositional model explains multiplicities in a rather simple manner, which can serve as an introduction to other kinds of social multiplicities that, themselves, implicate language. Deleuze offers the well-known example of "evening star—morning star." He writes: "The distinction between these meanings is certainly a real distinction, but there is nothing numerical about it, and much less anything ontological: it is rather a formal, qualitative, or semiological distinction. . . . The important thing is that we are able to conceive of several formally distinct meanings, which nonetheless are related to being as to a single, ontologically one referent."[87] Not only is being the ontologically one referent, but it is in no sense equivocal; this means that it cannot be determined on the basis of identity with regard to a generic concept, what differences have in common. Nor is being distributed by analogy as in Aristotle's example of the medical: one thing being called medical because it possesses the medical art, another because it is naturally adapted to the medical art, another because it is a function of the medical art. Each of these exists only by analogy to the substance "medical." Whereas when being is expressed in *one and the same sense* in each of its (numerically) distinct expressors, we can begin to conceive of differences as real, as existing, and not only as referring to being by analogy. In this case, being is (ontologically) one and the meaning of *being* is ontologically one.

In this crucial shift of expression, being is not said in several ways; being is expressed in one and the same sense of each of its (numerically) distinct designates (*les designés*), yet each difference has its own essence—they do not have the same meaning.[88] If being speaks with a single voice in the proposition, and being is "said" of difference itself, then being is not equivocal; it is univocal and being is said of differences, none of which have the same meaning. The effect of this is to conceptualize difference as real, to conceptualize it differentially, and, as Foucault adds, not to submit it to representation, which always searches out the common elements underlying difference. Of course, mere univocity with respect to being does not guarantee that individual differences are not somehow the same or equal, that they do not have the same meaning. Everything depends on how the distribution is governed. In Aristotle, entities have different degrees of being, as if there were only so much being available for distribution. This occurs because "[t]here is a hierarchy which measures beings according to their limits, and according to their degree of proximity or distance in relation to a principle."[89] That is, this manner of measuring and distributing being amounts to a certain kind of law or regulation of being while the being of difference is another.

Having found the crack in thought in Aristotle's notion of being, Deleuze proposes to articulate this crack, and he lays out a different kind of law and measure for the "being which is said of difference." The articulation of this kind of "monstrosity" (monstrous in relation to the fixed hierarchies of organic representation) is yet another thought and practice (in addition to the proposition above) of difference, one that is more easily related to social and political practices. It would be more comfortable to imply that there is nothing out of the ordinary in what Deleuze is suggesting here; however, insofar as this is not the case, I do not want to domesticate this concept. While Deleuze's logic and semiotics are enormously sophisticated, still there is an element of danger in what he is suggesting. The monstrous nature of difference in the face of the stability and hierarchy of representation is undeniable. Consequently, it is not a safe way to act or to think, because in the judgments of what Deleuze calls "state power," difference is heretical and must be scapegoated. In the eyes of state power difference *is* monstrous, and the empowerment of minorities, which Iris Marion Young, for example, is proposing, is highly disruptive to the hierarchical rule of liberal governments. Thus, I want to make use of this word that Deleuze introduces in *Difference and Repetition* because it reflects what is at stake in Deleuze's work and in the ontology of change.

The sort of measure Deleuze proposes to account for monstrous difference is the "*nomadic nomos,* without property, enclosure or measure. . . . an allocation of those who distribute *themselves. . . .* in a *space without precise limits.*"[90] Such a "wandering distribution" is not the Aristotelian space (adopted by Renaissance perspectivism) that is divided, shared, and hierarchized in accordance with the principle of proximity to being and degree of being. It is easy to see that the "fixed and proportional determinations" of Aristotelian hierarchies correlate very well with the fixed and proportional determinations of objectified and perspectival representations, whether those of the Italian Renaissance or those of state power. And what emerges from this analysis is the realization that difference, what is, when it is thought and practiced differentially, is not subject to historical interpretation, even though the absence of difference is certainly a reflection of the prevailing forms of social and political life.

I have noted above that the great Renaissance artists opposed the demand for planar, symmetrical, and conceptual images, and that they did so, perhaps surprisingly, for the sake of movement: "As has been said, illusion was partly realized in the simple creation of virtual three-dimensional forms [*rilievo*], in convincing relationship (perspective). But surpassing these . . . was the representation of movement."[91] Yet in Aristotle, organic representation, as discussed above, is distributed hierarchically around "one center, a sole and elusive perspective," analogous to Aristotle's distribution of being. Thus representation "mediates everything, but mobilizes and moves nothing."[92] Movement, however, accords with the nomadic *nomos* insofar as it involves a plurality of centers (of differences, each of which *is*), superimposing and mixing perspectives and points of view and effecting the distortion of representation in the social field. Such an effect is not the product of the multiplication of representations: "The infinite representation includes precisely an infinity of representations, whether it ensures the convergence of all points of view on an identical object or an identical world, or whether it creates the properties of an identical Self from different moments. But, in this way, it keeps a single center which gathers and represents all the others as a unity of a series that orders, that organizes, once and for all, the terms and their relations."[93] In the system of hierarchical distribution, regardless of the number of representations, the conceptual form of the identical, the concept in general, subordinates all differences. In order for there to be movement and mobility, the nomadic *nomos,* distortion must destabilize representation, representation must be torn from its center and from the identity of the concept, as well as from the perfect hierarchy of distribution that Aristotle establishes.[94]

For Deleuze, Aristotle's conceptualization does not simply create hierarchies of thought; rather it serves to legitimate or justify certain visual, linguistic, social, and political practices that developed around the demand for intelligibility, rigidity, and hegemony. Therefore, merely reconceptualizing difference is not enough to restore difference as difference; rather, the ruin of representation can be accomplished only on the level of actual practices. This is why Deleuze claims that the modern work of art, more than anything, "tends to realize these conditions," the conditions effecting representation's demise. Painting and sculpture distort visual representation so that we have to combine the view from above with the view from below, or we have to go up and come down in space.[95] And as I have tried to show, these distorting tendencies (distorting in relation to the rigid hierarchies of representation) have always been present in selected works of art and, to some extent, even in the work of representational artists, as the crack or the catastrophe that emerges in the midst of representation.

Along these same lines, art historian Svetlana Alpers points out that under the influence of Aristotelian cosmology, Italian artists were normally unwilling or unable to sacrifice either the authority that single-point perspective attributes to the viewer or the unity that it provides to the image. Italian artists, she continues, turned away from individuation for the sake of general human traits and truths, and resemblance to ideals of appearance and action. Alpers contrasts this with the work of Dutch artists such as Samuel von Hoogstraten who urged young artists to be humble and to paint the diversity of things in the world, where each face is created different.[96] She cites an illustration of Jean Perlerin's (called Viator) geometry: "One plate, 'Perspective' shows a multiplication of distance-points leading the eye to a variety of views up and down, in and out of an empty room, *adding* on views of the moving eye."[97]

Perlerin's illustration makes possible the construction of a mobile image. Deleuze and Guattari offer their own mobile image. In the visual work of art, difference refers to other differences that never identify but only differentiate it, such that each difference stands in relation to other differences, all of which are without a center and without convergence, both in relation to themselves and in relation to one another. In this way each work of art is "a true *theater,* made of metamorphoses and permutations. . . . The work of art leaves the domain of representation in order to become 'experience,' transcendental empiricism, or the science of the sensible."[98]

The second question that I posed above remains to be addressed. Why has representation succeeded in dominating difference? The question is difficult to answer directly without falling into a trap that once again submits difference to identity by positing the answer (which has two faces) in terms of contrariety, as Aristotle does. One approach might be to concentrate on the nomadic *nomos* as an anarchic organization of elements.[99] Another approach, one I find preferable and closer in spirit to Deleuze's own writing, might be to explore the nomadic *nomos* as ethical and aesthetic variations without a theme.[100] In later chapters, I will argue that Bergson's radical analysis of time as duration functions in precisely this way. But here, given Deleuze's claim that practice is what realizes movement, a practical formulation may serve as the best guide to envisioning the nomadic *nomos* in Deleuze's work and explaining why there is a tendency for representation to dominate both the practical and the conceptual fields.

Deleuze and Guattari recognize the existence of a double articulation that takes into account both Aristotle's hierarchical distribution of being and their own preference for difference. This double articulation will appear again when the whole question of movement is addressed. These two articulations, alone and in combination, produce an unlimited number and kinds of organization of elements. *Representations* are produced by a certain organization of elements in the assemblage—any collection of molecular or quasi-molecular elements (see below). The production of representation is a second-level articulation that establishes functional, compact, and stable forms (objects) that simultaneously actualize in molar compounds or substances.[101] The resultant stable, functional structure is the type that represents differences as different only in relation to identity. Thus objectification, as discussed above, also refers to the second level of articulation. It is both a matter of reification and making or taking something to be an object, that is, static, inherently necessary, the product of a judgment. The nomadic *nomos,* on the other hand, is constituted in the *first* articulation, *on which* the second, that of representation, is based. It begins with substances that are molecular or quasi-molecular elements—assemblages—and imposes upon them a form that consists only of connections and successions.[102] "Assemblage" (*agencement*) sounds chaotic, though clearly this is not the case. In an assemblage, there are two divergent orientations: "[T]here are lines of articulation or segmentarity, strata and territories; but also lines of flight, movements of deterritorialization and destratification. Comparative rates of flow on these lines produce phenomena of relative slowness and viscosity, or on the contrary acceleration and rupture. All this, lines and measurable speeds, constitutes an assemblage. A book is an assemblage of this kind, and as such it is unattributable. It is a multiplicity."[103]

An assemblage is a multiplicity. If it is "territorialized" and "stratified," it is organized according to the principles of categorical reflection. Such an assemblage is slow and viscous—that is, stable—and makes possible "a kind of organism, in the sense of an organic whole, a signifying totality, or a determination attributable to a subject."[104] As such, it is representational. Turned toward lines of flight that are *movements* of "deterritorialization" and "destratification," that is, of destabilization, the assemblage is dismantled as an organism. This means that it is not an organic representation attributable to a subject; it is the monstrosity.

As noted above, complete and total destratification or pure becoming, pure differentiation without limit, is not the goal of destratification. This is the life of submolecular unformed matter, chaos, void, and destruction, and as has been the case with so many revolutionary movements in politics and even in the arts, insofar as they are wildly destabilized, they are able to be reclaimed even more easily by organic representation.[105] Thus, while the assemblage cannot be identified as either a subject or an object (only representation does this), neither is it the indeterminate chaos of unformed matters. Rather, it is a configuration of speeds (thus movements), intensities (qualitative variations), and varying distributions of its elements. Such an image of thought is necessary to the articulation of difference thought differentially and to the realization of mobility.

So while the first articulation of the assemblage does order elements, it does not do so in the same way as the second articulation; for in the first, the elements remain "supple," while the latter centers, unifies, integrates, hierarchizes, and finalizes its elements.[106] Substances and forms constitute both articulations, so clearly they form no opposition to one another. As Deleuze and Guattari point out, substances are always already *formed matters* and forms always indicate that some coding, some organization of the field, is taking place. Any assemblage (whether it be a work of art, a painting, a book, a subject) is subject to double articulation. This means that organic representation is more than a historical phenomenon; it is an effect of the double articulation that operates everywhere. This is not to say that the choice that double articulation opens up to us is not historical. The choice of perfection over movement, stability over nomadism, and viscosity over flows does seem to be historically—that is, politically—motivated. Functionally, there is a choice between the stability and immobility of identity in the concept in representation with its hierarchic distribution and something that is not its opposite but simply the first level of articulation, the level of multiplicity. The level of the first articulation is what I have referred to in this chapter as monstrosity, making the determination that is difference: the mobility and therefore distortion of the perfected representation.

On the political level, Deleuze and Guattari connect the second articulation that produces representation to the hierarchical distribution of power that characterizes the state apparatus. By this they do not mean to imply that all state governments are somehow corrupted and anarchy should reign. *State apparatus* is merely the name they give to the most static and stratified organization of power, an organization that makes use of representation's intelligibility and rigidity to rationalize its existence: "Undoubtedly, the great collective bodies of a State are differentiated and hierarchical organisms that on the one hand enjoy a monopoly over a power or function and on the other hand send out local representatives."[107] Functioning according to a vision that imposes the order of representation, the state is an *organism* that appropriates a military war machine to serve its political needs; regulates bands or clans as conquerors imposing law on the conquered; reduces the investigation of problems and accidents that condition and resolve them to a model based on the distinction of genus and species or essence and properties; defines thought as either the *imperium*—that is, the "whole" as final ground of being—or as the "republic"—that is, a system in which the "sovereign" subject figures as legislative and juridical ground. The hierarchical and static articulation of representation is, according to this analysis, a function of a state apparatus and state power. State power, as Deleuze and Guattari define it, is made visible in the game of chess: "Chess is a game of State, or of the court: the emperor of China played it. Chess pieces are coded; they have an internal nature and intrinsic properties from which their moments, situations, and confrontations derive. They have qualities; a knight remains a knight, a pawn a pawn, a bishop a bishop."[108] Chess pieces act only biunivocally with one another so that the war they enact is institutionalized, regulated, and coded. It takes place in an arranged, closed space; the hierarchized space of the Aristotelian cosmos and organic representation.

Deleuze and Guattari compare this representational game of centralized and rigidly hierarchized states to the game of Go. The game pieces in Go are anonymous and collective "its": "It could be a man, a woman, a louse, an elephant."[109] Their properties are subject to continuous change depending on what sort of configurations appear on the board. Go is a game of pure strategy, since by itself a single Go piece can synchronically destroy a whole constellation. Alphonso Lingis has beautifully characterized the difference between these two types of organization in his essay "The Society of Dismembered Body Parts."[110] In this essay he describes the practices of the Quechua people, who live in the Andes, and discovers the simultaneous existence of a nomadic *nomos* and a representational power structure: "You can wander the high Andes and, by night, hear the murmurs of the people around the fire, hear their Quechua tongue without understanding it, hear the light, subtle, supple tripping of their sounds, hear their intonations and their murmurs, hear it as the very resonance of their substance, their gentle, unassertive, vibrant, sensitive way of vocalizing together."[111] Here Lingis focuses on the first articulation, the nomadic *nomos* where the voices of the tribesmen distribute themselves in time and space: voices speak and are heard by others who respond, but unevenly, with murmurs, pauses, silences. But when the second articulation asserts itself, the voices can be represented:

> But if you were to drink some magic potion, some cocktail of coca tea and whisky, and suddenly understood their language, and abruptly understood that they are speaking about "transporting cocaine into the hands of the Colombian agents," then abruptly you have subjected yourself to the codings of imperial society; you have suddenly related their sounds not to their own throats and substance but to the international code established by the reigning barbarian empire in Washington and Bonn and Tokyo, where cocaine means the same thing—crime.[112]

Represented under the category of "crime," the murmurs of the Quechua become subject to the international code; they are criminals, identified as outlaws in accordance with the laws of the hierarchic institutions of capitalist nations.

Thus, for Deleuze and Guattari, what is at stake *politically* is historical. There are always particular historical persons acting according to the contingent circumstances of their era. Yet, in the case of the smuggler, a particular assemblage—that of the state apparatus—judges that any element it cannot organize according to its hierarchized demands must be guilty of heresy or treason. From the standpoint of the state apparatus, the nomad is always deterritorialized, always a heretic or a criminal. The nomad, who only ever moves, whose very home is mobile, is distributed in a space without borders or enclosure, and so creates what Deleuze and Guattari call a "war machine," not an army or a guerrilla force, but a mode of organization that is exterior to any "state apparatus," outside what I have been referring to as hierarchized representations.[113]

However, double articulation does not limit the types of political or social regimes to two. In fact, for Deleuze and Guattari, double articulation in the organization of assemblages effects a multiplicity of different regimes which, following a semiotic model, they refer to as regimes of signs. Although I do not want to discuss this in depth here, I do want to make clear that these "semiotics" or organizations of assemblages are *mixtures,* mixtures of presignifying, countersignifying, postsignifying, and signifying elements: "Assemblages determine a given people, period, or language, and even a given style, fashion, pathology, or minuscule event in a limited situation can assure the predominance of one semiotic or another," and there is no limit to the number of these social and political assemblages.[114] The mixed quality of the social assemblage may explain why even while the New Zealand Maoris employ traditional methods in the dispute over land, they continue to engage in other forms of patriarchal state power.

My point here is to show how social and political practices are organized on the basis of mixtures of signifying regimes. That this is a more abstract level of thinking than the historical is, I hope, clear. Exactly how social and political life is constituted cannot be entirely arbitrary, simply a matter of contingent historical choice; but neither is it limited by a single dominant *logos.* Rather, the double articulation that operates in all strata makes it necessary for us to reformulate not only our notions regarding the construction of representation but also our ways of thinking about all social and political life. Regimes of signs are not merely chance events, but assemblages organized in accordance with certain practices specific to a culture or way of life. They have neither the status of historical contingency—which may be explicable after the fact but remain contingent—nor that of an unalterable *telos* in nature. They are fluid structures with efficient causes. As Deleuze and Guattari conclude, "we are not, of course, doing history: we are not saying that a people invents this regime of signs, only that at a given moment a people effectuates the assemblage that assures the relative dominance of that regime under certain historical conditions."[115]

I have noted above that, for Deleuze, only designifying practices effect the ruin of representation. The political representation of the law is just another aspect of the organic representation that dominates life. So to break with this representation, to find ways to bring about the "ruin of representation," is intrinsic to the practice of artists and nomads. Ultimately, double articulation is a function of the practical and ethical level: it is a question of life itself and the value of life. The point is that there is a political and social impetus organizing our modes of thinking and making, living and constructing. And because, for Deleuze and Guattari, this impetus is neither teleologically preordained nor radically contingent history, but part of a grab for power based on irrefutable conceptual claims for intelligibility, coherence, and hierarchic distribution, it is Deleuze and Guattari's project to realize other ways to see, to open up our thinking and practices to the nomadic *nomos* that creates wandering distributions of assemblages, distributions whose plurality of centers mix perspectives and points of view and open up power to create new social and political institutions not yet envisioned by our current democratic practices.

2
Can a Feminist Read Deleuze and Guattari?

Cosmic Empiricism

In a text that introduced many American feminists to the work of Gilles Deleuze, Alice Jardine forcefully lays out her view of the status of Deleuze and his sometime collaborator Félix Guattari in contemporary philosophy and linguistic and literary studies.[1] Largely ignored in the early 1980s by most academics, Deleuze and Guattari had found an American audience consisting, she claims, chiefly of a "vocal [male] student minority."[2] The largely male character of this audience extended, not surprisingly, to France, to the point that, even in France, where Deleuze and Guattari publicly supported the feminist movement, by the mid 1980s only one feminist made extensive use of their work.[3] In the intervening years, Deleuze and Guattari had ceased to be ignored or dismissed by American academics and were beginning to be not merely read but also celebrated in France.[4] However, their audience continued to be chiefly male, and Jardine argues that it should remain so.[5] Let me begin by examining her arguments carefully. It is of great importance to do so insofar as Jardine's essay has been extremely influential in (American) feminist circles.[6]

To begin with, Jardine sees no direct relation between Deleuze's "earlier and academic" historical and aesthetic philosophy and the broadly social and political books he produced with Guattari. She assumes and/or implies that feminists have read little of Deleuze's "philosophical" work because there is no need to do so; instead, with rare exceptions, feminists have directed their studies principally, if not exclusively, to the two volumes of *Capitalism and Schizophrenia* that she critiques. Additionally, she argues that there is little in Deleuze and Guattari that reflects American feminist interests in discourse, particularly in the "putting into discourse" of either "woman" or "the feminine"—that is, the creation of feminine spaces that challenge traditional conceptual boundaries.[7] Jardine names this process *gynesis,* the "valorization of the feminine, woman, and her obligatory, that is, historical connotations as somehow intrinsic to new and necessary modes of thinking, writing, speaking."[8] The failure to put woman or the feminine into discourse rests, in part, on a third factor: that Deleuze alone or Deleuze and Guattari together abandon the familial-psychoanalytic and even the academic-textual point of view for a cosmic vision of the world that is more likely to address "[s]ea animals, computers, volcanoes, birds, and planets than the bourgeois family hearth and its books."[9] In short, nothing in Deleuze and Guattari seems to correspond to the immediate focus on textuality, family, state or religious power, bodies, gender, and what I would call the psychological, that mixture of biographical subjectivity and history filtered through psychoanalysis that characterizes much feminist theory, and which is epitomized for me (not Jardine) in the fiction of a writer like Henry James. It is this last point that appears to disturb Jardine the most, for initially she claims that Deleuze and Guattari do away with "*any* concept of the body."[10] In the end, however, she moderates her judgment and concludes that their attention to the cosmic empirical leads to "denaturalized Bodies of all kinds—and most especially the human one," culminating in the notion of the "body without organs," that body emptied of fantasies so as to make way, not for a new body, but for new processes of production.[11]

Jardine calls upon the authority of Luce Irigaray to assist in her critique of the body without organs. Irigaray is a powerful ally insofar as she has insisted upon the necessity of recognizing sexual difference as the most compelling issue of our time. Irigaray argues that the multiple sexuality of the body without organs (as opposed to the ambiguous but apparently dual sexuality of sexual difference) once again denies to women pleasures that are specific to women's bodies.[12] Wouldn't women end up miming men once again? Is not the body without organs already the historical condition of women's bodies, the emptying of their desire in their bodies? Isn't this concept a repetition of the use of "stereotyped genderizations and images of women" that Jardine finds in Deleuze and Guattari's work, and also in that of their male followers?[13] Irigaray's questions and criticisms deserve the same serious consideration as Jardine's; however, given how complex the question of sexual difference is, I would like to return to Irigaray after some of the parameters of Deleuze's philosophy have been established. The questions she raises cannot be addressed quickly or easily, especially since it is not my purpose here to defend Deleuze and Guattari against their critics—indeed, such a defense would be pointless. After all, if Deleuze and Guattari's cosmic empiricism can contribute to feminist pragmatics, then it will have to show itself within the context of that pragmatics or not show itself at all. No immediate definition-explanation-defense can accomplish this. Among Jardine's conceptual reservations, perhaps the most potentially devastating is her critique of the concept of "becoming-woman." Jardine argues that this notion takes the place of Deleuze and Guattari's earlier notion of "desiring-machines" (which has nothing to do with either the western philosophical and psychoanalytic notion of desire as lack or with mechanics).[14] Although becoming-woman is only one of a multiplicity of such desiring-machines (or "assemblages," as Deleuze and Guattari eventually refer to them), Jardine takes becoming-woman to be emblematic of an impersonal, involuntary, automatic, and arranged (*machiné*) "*agencement*"—that is, an arrangement, configuration, or assemblage. Cosmic empiricism seems to be operating here to abstract and depersonalize "woman." Such *agencement* remains, for Jardine, part of a project to denaturalize the sexes in a *post*-signifying era, that is, a world in which there is "no hidden order, intentionality, or goal in view. . . . no panopticon from which to interpret, plan, or even map that movement."[15] Without a personal, voluntary subjectivity, without a point of view that is God's or god-like—even if it is only something to react to—what sense can we make of our world, and what sense can we make of "woman"?

Thus Jardine insists on reading becoming-woman through a psychoanalytic screen, even though she recognizes that Deleuze and Guattari do not: feminine *jouissance,* becoming-maternal, or writing-woman must, in her account, play a central role in any philosophy that offers insights into and for women. These are the feminine spaces that Jardine finds in Derrida and Lacan, but not in Deleuze and Guattari. Jardine rejects Deleuze and Guattari's insistence that becoming-woman is not part of the western binary machine.[16] "Becoming," for Deleuze and Guattari, is not a metaphor, not a matter of acting like something or imitating something; it is a *deterritorialization,* which involves more than simply undermining or doing away with hierarchy. To deterritorialize is to turn toward "lines of flight" so as to dismantle the subject, disorganize the body, or even to destabilize the state. But even to speak about subjects, bodies, and states—let alone deterritorialization and lines of flight—as if they are clearly understood and unproblematic presupposes a great deal. Even while Deleuze and Guattari claim that a book like *A Thousand Plateaus* can be read starting anywhere, Deleuze also explicitly cautions that it remains necessary to read the history of philosophy as well as the notable commentaries on and interpretations of that history. Given that philosophy has participated in the repression of thought over the centuries, no one is more susceptible to this repression than those who ignore its history: "The history of philosophy has always been the agent of power in philosophy. . . . A formidable school of intimidation which manufactures specialists in thought—but which also makes those who stay outside conform all the more to this specialism which they despise."[17]

My point is that making sense of Deleuze and Guattari's positions and concepts might well demand an examination of Deleuze's "earlier and academic" historical and aesthetic philosophies, for without this study we may find ourselves trapped in the power of the very philosophy we seek to reject. Still, within the context of the two volumes of *Capitalism and Schizophrenia,* Jardine forces us to ask: Why is it that all becomings "begin with and pass through becoming-woman"?[18] "Why then do D+G privilege the word woman?"[19] Indeed, is the introduction of the concept "becoming-woman" a privileging, if the word *privilege* means "a right, immunity, benefit, or advantage granted to some person, group of persons, or class, not enjoyed by others and sometimes detrimental to them"?[20] What sense would there be in an act of deterritorialization that grants advantages to some group or class over others? Jardine's concern is, nonetheless, well placed: it is the concern that if woman must first become-woman "might that not mean that she must also be the *first* to disappear?"[21] What is woman's future if, as Jardine claims, she remains, for Deleuze and Guattari, "caught in a whirling sea of male configurations"?[22]

Deleuze and Guattari write that "[w]oman as a *molar* entity must *become-woman,* so that the man also becomes- or can become-woman."[23] Yet becoming-woman may not be a matter of privilege, of the first and second, of woman's disappearance, insofar as Deleuze and Guattari acknowledge that this has already happened under the Oedipal regime and condemn it: "The girl's becoming is stolen first, in order to impose a history, or prehistory upon her. The boy's turn comes next, but it is by using the girl as an example, by pointing to the girl as the object of his desire, that an opposed organism, a dominant history is fabricated for him too."[24] Nonetheless, the threat of a world "without any women at all" looms large over Jardine's reading of Deleuze and Guattari;[25] to ignore this threat would be careless in several ways, since not only is the theoretical disappearance of women of enormous concern to feminist readers, but the threat must be canceled if feminists interested in Deleuze and Guattari's work are to be able to proceed at all.

Jardine's critique proceeds from here to a critical reading of Deleuze's "exemplary" fiction, *Vendredi ou les limbes du Pacifique* by Michel Tournier.[26] Briefly, Jardine argues that in Tournier's retelling of the Robinson Crusoe tale, as well as in Deleuze's recovery of it, the same exclusion of *gynesis* that she argues is operating throughout Deleuze and

Guattari's collaborations is at work. She takes the narrative to represent a series of metamorphoses. Robinson, the master, metamorphoses into Robinson, the lover of the island, Speranza, who metamorphoses into Robinson, the twin of Vendredi, who finally metamorphoses into the galley boy-child, who is the apotheosis of all of Robinson's metamorphoses. In these metamorphoses there is no room and no place for new becomings of female bodies.[27] Such a conclusion is inevitable, given the exclusively male cast of human characters in Tournier's novel and given Jardine's belief that becoming-woman ushers in the disappearance of woman to make way for the cosmic sea of male configurations. Indeed, there seems to be something particularly blind in Deleuze's choice of novels and writers, for with a few notable exceptions (such as Artaud and Genet), Deleuze draws on male writers who are, as Elizabeth Grosz has commented, "notoriously phallic and misogynist."[28]

Yet as Constantin V. Boundas has argued, putting one's faith in the supposition that an understanding of narrative structure will elucidate the structure of the subject is fraught with difficulties.[29] In fact, Jardine's own account of Tournier's narrative, as well as her treatment of Deleuze and Guattari's philosophy, participates in the phenomenological supposition that the subject of the narrative constructs a self, which then carries out various actions and projects. The problem, Boundas argues, is that such an assumption does not question the "ideal" of the unified self, nor can it account for the fragmentation of personality and the multiplicity of narratives except as pathologies. Thus Boundas is right to question such an approach by asking: "How would such a narrative structure help decide among competing narratives in those cases in which we strongly suspect that the narratee is the victim of self-deception, trapped in distorted communication, or systematically blinded by ideological prejudices?"[30] Boundas concludes that narrativization, for Deleuze, is not phenomenological but a "veritable serialization" that "depends upon an originary disjunction"—that is, Deleuze's analysis of narratives proceeds along at least two simultaneous but divergent series that he creates as he reads.[31] This procedure arises out of Deleuze's logical analysis of series as constituting sense or the event that arises at the surface of bodies as the effect of their pragmatic and social relations, but also their physical, chemical, and biological mixtures.[32]

In the case of Deleuze's analysis of Tournier's novel, Boundas concurs with Jardine's assertion that the "Other" disappears but that Deleuze reads Tournier in order to discern what "Otherness" is and what the effects of the loss of others might be. What is at stake here is complicated. I have noted above that the phenomenological conception of subjectivity presupposes a unified subject and a unified narrative. However, once we dispense with these presuppositions, something else becomes available for thought. In his account, Deleuze notes that in Daniel Defoe's *Robinson Crusoe,* the problem of isolation is poorly posed. Defoe's Robinson, he demurs, not only is presented as asexual, but also constitutes himself as an origin that merely "reproduces an economic world similar to our own [when] one should have led an asexual Robinson to *ends quite different and divergent* from ours, a fantastic world which has itself deviated."[33] In spite of (or because of) the elimination of sexuality, Defoe produces the rigorously economic world of Robinson, a world that is not all that different from our own, governed by capitalist economies. Thus, Deleuze argues, rather than posing the question of Robinson's "origin" on the island, Tournier re-poses isolation as a question of ends: not how to start reproducing western economy, but rather, where does isolation take Robinson? what are the effects of the absence of Others? what is an Other? and what does it mean for the Other to be absent?

Given her concern with woman's disappearance as well as the conclusion of feminist theory that woman has been defined as "Other" within a sociopolitical system dominated by men, Jardine's interest in what happens when the "Other" truly disappears is far from unwarranted. But what happens does not happen at the beginning of Robinson's tenure on the island, when there are no women around him, as Jardine argues; rather, it happens in the process of his isolation, isolation as a process that constitutes subsequent layers or levels of memory even as the memories producing the structure "Other" lapse. Insofar as this is the case, it makes no sense to speak of the "character" Robinson, for one of the first things that becomes apparent is that there is no such character. Robinson is completely determined by the collapse of the structure of "Otherness," and thus the collapse of any possibility, including his own.

Philosophy has misconstrued the problem, Deleuze maintains, and reduced what is Other to an object or a subject; it has forgotten that in order to even have objects and subjects, we must first have "Other" as a structure of the perceptual field, the expression of a *possible* world that comes to be *actualized* by real characters. Deleuze writes:

> Let it be understood that the possible is not here an abstract category designating something which does not exist: the expressed possible world certainly exists, but it does not exist (actually) outside of that which expresses it. The terrified countenance bears no resemblance to the terrifying thing. It implicates it, it envelops it as something else. . . . When I, in turn and for my part, grasp the reality of what the Other was expressing, I do nothing but explicate the Other, as I develop and realize the corresponding possible world.[34]

The terrified face is an effect of the "other" terrifying thing or, rather, an expression of that Other insofar as it determines the one with the face as she or he realizes a corresponding possible world. The impact of Deleuze's structuralist reading of the perceptual field is that the structure-Other and not the ego is what organizes the perceptual field.

Taken in this light, Tournier's "adventure" is a narrative not of the disappearance of the feminine subject but of that which precedes subject and object: the structure-Other. This structure-Other does not disappear immediately, at the "origin" of Robinson's isolation, but gradually and eventually over the years so that by the time Crusoe encounters "Friday" the event does not take place within the structure-Other. It is not Robinson who initiates metamorphoses; it is the perceptual field. If Robinson metamorphoses, it is because of the structure-Other, the expression of a possible world, whose principle effect is to make a distinction between consciousness and its object. Thus, for example, the Sartrean "look," by means of which an other becomes an object for me or I become an object for her, is the effect or the actualization of this structure, which must be defined independently of the look.[35] What the structure-Other ensures is a temporal distinction between consciousness and its object:

> Before the appearance of the Other, there was, for example, a reassuring world from which my consciousness could not be distinguished. The Other then makes its appearance, expressing the possibility of a frightening world which cannot be developed without the one preceding it passing away. For my part, I am nothing other than my past objects, and my self is made up of a past world, a passing away of which was brought about precisely by the Other.[36]

If the structure-Other passes away, so does the past and so does error *and* the ability to verify; for without the Other, consciousness coincides with its object in an eternal present that defies Defoe's Crusoe, who meticulously counts the days and years by making a mark for each day spent on the island. Instead, Tournier's Robinson ceaselessly relives the same day or, more accurately, does not measure the days against one another or take each one to be part of some larger and more important plan or destination. Likewise, things affirm their own worth and desire ceases to be "personal," a desire *for* someone or something without which life is empty and lacking. Thus even the so-called inanimate island asserts itself as a complex site of forces, an *assemblage* and not an object. This is much less a "surpassing" (as Jardine characterizes it) of subject and object and of the structure-Other than a "collapse" of this structure and its effects.[37] This is an important difference, insofar as surpassing carries the idea of bringing subject and object along, while collapse precludes any such possibility and amounts to a de-structuration in which both dissolve into other elements.

In articulating this de-structuration, Deleuze uses terminology that can certainly be read as Jardine reads it—as evoking the disappearance of the feminine—if we insist upon a phenomenological and narrative reading. He writes: "*L'île déserte entre dans un redressement, une érection généralisée.*" (The deserted island begins a straightening out, a generalized erection.)[38] However, if—and only if—we approach this material with a de-structuralizing orientation as marking de-structuring and collapse, how is this phrase operating in relation to the text? The structure-Other is "the grand leveler," flattening out all life and action, imprisoning elements within the limits of bodies, making even the earth a body. What is more, it makes these bodies into objects that relate to one another only transitively, "each one was closed onto itself, or opened onto other objects, only in relation to possible worlds expressed by Others."[39] When this collapses, it does not collapse into a misshapen or pathological imitation of bodies and their relations—indeed, such a reading is possible only when things are measured against one another or taken to be part of some larger and more important plan or destination, whether that of history or God. But when things affirm their own worth and desire ceases to be "personal," a desire *for* someone or something without which life is empty and lacking, then the simple narrative reading clearly misses what is created in the collapse (and this is important: something is created in the collapse). This is the "uprightness" Deleuze announces, the straightening, the erection of a double that does not resemble or imitate in a pathological state but is the "pure phosphorescence of things in themselves."[40] Clearly a paradox is operating here insofar as erection is the mark of a collapse, a paradox that must be affirmed as that which denies good sense (temporal progression) and common sense (the unity of body and/or soul).[41]

Tournier's Robinson cannot simply live through this collapse by mourning the loss of the subject-object relation, but must create his way out of it; otherwise the destructuring of the structure-Other is nothing but the disintegration of the world: chaos instead of objects, loss instead of plenitude. So when Robinson climbs out of the mud or emerges from the cave, his return to the surface is ontological. That is, he engages in a creative evolution, not a metamorphosis, arising out of his current, real existence, his memories of life without the structure-Other, rather than the recreation or imitation of European economy. This, as we shall see in the chapter on life itself, is an ontological rather than a narrative move, and to reduce it to narrative is to reduce all creation and novelty to representation.

Negative Desire

Though Jardine first brought Deleuze to the attention of American feminists, it is Judith Butler who voices perhaps the strongest objections to his work—strong because they are grounded in a thorough account of the history of philosophy and in a philosophical perspective that takes politics into account but does not formulate concepts solely on behalf of political ends. It is not surprising that Butler takes on one of the most important issues in Deleuze's early historical philosophy, desire. She comes to this concept in the course of the development of her own radical and original feminism, which arises out of her articulation of the relationship of Hegel to contemporary theory, in particular to the concepts of identity and difference.[42] Butler draws our attention to theories of desire in order to affirm Hegel's instantiation of dialectic and negativity; thus she construes Deleuze's conception of desire to be a misunderstanding of the true nature of desire as negation or lack as well as an erroneous promotion of a "normative ideal" for desire as affirmation.[43] Although it is not my intent to give a full account of Butler's philosophical positions, her position on Hegel is central to her reading of Deleuze's notion of desire; thus, some explanation of the former is not only useful but necessary if we are to comprehend the latter.

What characterizes Butler's reading of Hegel is, I think, the extent to which she personalizes Hegel (which is *not* the same as reading anthropocentrically) and ties Hegel's philosophy to everyday common sense, or what she calls experience. Two key points guide her reading. First, she embraces a certain kind of phenomenological method by requiring that desire be found in ordinary experience. That is, for Butler, phenomenological method affirms that the subject who desires must experience what it desires in such a manner that what it desires is what it seeks to know. Second, the satisfaction of desire results in the making and remaking of identity: "[W]hen we desire, we pose the question of the metaphysical place of human identity—in some pre-linguistic form—and in the satisfaction of desire, the question is answered for us. In effect, desire is an interrogative mode of being, a corporeal questioning of identity and place."[44] Desire is a mode of being, a corporeal questioning of identity and place—but in such a way that each subject takes this mode of being and questioning of identity into herself and makes it her *own.* This occurs through the experience of what is other than the subject, what is "strange, different, novel, awaited, lost," and so is already saturated with its own negativity.[45] The satisfaction of questioning desire occurs through the transformation of what is different into what is identical, and so with the reemergence of what was absent or lost to otherness. Each new desire opens up the negative—that is, the experience of loss of identity—

and in doing so produces not hopelessness and tragedy, but an entirely new point of view for the subject, a new "fiction," which in its turn will be swept away in the next tide of experience.[46]

So for Butler the importance of negativity lies in its identity-making and remaking function, a function that only negativity, through the action of corporeal desire, can carry out. This is possible insofar as consciousness is *internally* related to what it seeks to know, inextricably caught up in the hermeneutic circle of the knower and his (*sic*) sensuous world of experience.[47] Thus the relation between a consciousness and his other is neither logical nor metaphysical; it is first rhetorical, then phenomenological. Consciousness only becomes itself through its articulation of what is other, but in the moment of that articulation, via the experience of desire, the other comes back to consciousness as its own fullest self.[48] Or, as Butler eventually expresses it, "the sensuousness of desire becomes its [consciousness's] access to the sensuousness of the world."[49] Rhetorical self-consciousness is the process by means of which consciousness conceptualizes the sensuous and perceptual world. It is only at this point that pre-linguistic, corporeal desire makes an appearance. Desire shows itself as the "sensuous articulation" of self-consciousness; it reenacts the rhetorical articulation on the sensuous level, without, however, affecting the ontological difference between self and other.[50] What does change is the way that otherness, difference, the absent or lost, is conceptualized. After the sensuous articulation of self-consciousness by desire, otherness is conceptualized as gaining a more expansive and expanded identity.[51] The field of objects alters at the point of their intersection and interaction with rhetorical articulation and phenomenological-experiential desire. In this sense, desire *is* the activity of Hegelian *aufgehoben,* it is supersession, and Hegel's task in the *Phenomenology* is to describe the alterations of desire from the point of view of consciousness.

Less satisfactory, though still useful to Butler, is Merleau-Ponty's phenomenology of desire: useful insofar as Merleau-Ponty argues against naturalistic accounts of forms of desire and sexuality and argues for a conception of sexuality as coextensive with existence.[52] So Butler reads Merleau-Ponty's concept of desire as one that makes the body into a dramatic structure within a field of historical possibilities. This view of desire and the body unfortunately gives way, Butler argues, to a failure on Merleau-Ponty's part to recognize any sexuality except that of heterosexual males. The result of this is that Merleau-Ponty models the sexual relation between men and women on the model of master and slave by reifying cultural relations between the sexes. Additionally, Merleau-Ponty does not make gender a relevant concern, whereas for Butler, any concrete description of lived experience must ask "whose *sexuality* and whose *bodies* are being described," since, without being situated in concrete social and cultural contexts, sexuality and bodies remain abstractions.[53] In spite of these problems, Butler believes that a feminist appropriation of Merleau-Ponty is called for; it proceeds by means of concrete descriptions of lived experience in order to make sexuality the scene of cultural struggle, improvisation, and innovation, where the intimate and the political converge.[54]

A series of questions, if not contradictions, arises at this point. It is at least odd that prelinguistic sensuous desire arises initially only in the midst of rhetorical articulation, so that conceptual articulation gives rise to corporeal questioning. Why this should be the case is never made clear. What keeps corporeality or desire in check until this moment? I do not mean to argue over the priority of language and corporeality so as to oppose them to one another; my point is different. According to Butler's argument, desire's power to assimilate and unite consciousness and its other gives desire its preeminent role as the basis of experience, and yet desire, along with corporeality, can only be recognized after the emergence of conceptualizing self-consciousness. If desire only shows itself at a certain stage in the process of the development and growth of identity, then it seems that desire has not actually "been there all along," but rather that desire as such is constituted by culture or by self-consciousness (which may turn out to be the same thing).[55] Additionally, there is a certain optimism, or good sense, to this sort of characterization of desire and otherness, for even though consciousness, on its path toward subjecthood, assumes that the world is different, other, and alien to itself, that "alien" world is nonetheless a "natural world, spatiotemporally organized, exhibiting discrete empirical objects."[56] Such a description of the world hardly meets the criterion of "alien"; these absolutely mundane, commonsense parameters are exactly the sort of designation knowing subjects use to talk about their world in everyday terms. The introduction of the idea that movement between consciousness and its other (inner difference) prevails over stasis does little to alter this, since movement itself has an illusory quality in the following sense. Desire is the experiential basis of the *Phenomenology* insofar as "it has as its highest aim the assimilation of all external relations into relations of inner difference."[57] If desire assimilates whatever is "external" into internal relations, it seems obvious to ask to what extent there ever are any external relations at all, for movement between inner differences is never absolute; it is only ever relative to what are always, in truth, internal relations.

Butler begins her account of Deleuze's philosophy by noting that Deleuze makes desire "the privileged locus of human ontology," an ontology that is not historicized.[58] There is no question that the absence of specific social and historical conditions qualifying Deleuze's conception of desire leads Butler to conclude that desire is an "ontological invariant," "a universal ontological truth" that Deleuze has managed to release from an interminable period of suppression. Butler refers to Deleuze's notion of desire as "emancipatory," "a precultural eros," "an originally unrepressed libidinal diversity," and "an ahistorical absolute."[59] Such qualifications are damning in Butler's assessment, since in her estimation it is principally the willingness to locate desire in purely social and historical terms that elevates the work of Michel Foucault above his (approximate) contemporaries Deleuze, Derrida, and Lacan. Given Butler's only slightly revised Hegelianism, it would seem that it is only to the degree that historicization takes place that philosophy can effect its break with the Hegelian system that always already accounts for any rupture with itself. Of course, in response to the charges of universalization, one may always respond that desire per se has been central to Western philosophical conceptions since Plato, but obviously this is not enough to justify Deleuze's refusal to historicize desire.[60] Although it is not my purpose in this preliminary exposition of feminist readings of Deleuze to provide a complete exegesis of Deleuze's ontology, I would like to begin by examining some of the problems that Butler reports in her account.

In *Nietzsche and Philosophy,* Deleuze makes use of Nietzsche to "disjoin desire from negativity, and to account for the genealogy of the Hegelian position in terms of slave morality."[61] According to Butler, an alternative "model" of desire is constituted that is based on the plenitude of life rather than its negation. It is Nietzsche's "slave morality" that represses this desire, just as later, in Deleuze and Guattari's *Anti-Oedipus,* "the coercive force of capitalism and the ideology of psychoanalysis . . . repress life-affirming desire."[62] Although much of her analysis of Deleuze is couched in terms of his use of Nietzsche, Butler is absolutely right to point to Spinoza as the "affective source of revolutionary change" in Deleuze's work.[63] This is of no small import, for Butler has already launched the attack on Spinoza early in her defense of Hegel's dialectic when she notes that Spinoza "fails" to include human negativity in his metaphysical system.[64] For Spinoza, she argues, desire is a modality of substance as well as the fundamental modality of human existence—in other words, substance, the self-actualizing agency, is specified in human beings as desire. Hegel's critique of this position is that Spinoza's thought is only the expression of a more powerful agency and that human subjects require obstruction (negation) in order to have the individual, not the universal—that is, in order to gain recognition of a self by an other.[65] Consequently it is no surprise that Butler attributes universalization to Deleuze as well.

What, if anything, can be said here in Deleuze's defense to mitigate this criticism? There is no point in denying the "dehistoricizing" of Deleuze's approach; this is central to everything Deleuze alone and Deleuze and Guattari together write. I have already argued (in chapter 1) that for Deleuze and Guattari historical contingency is not the point. To repeat: "We are not, of course, doing history: we are not saying that a people invents this regime of signs, only that at a given moment a people effectuates the assemblage that assures the relative dominance of that regime under certain historical conditions."[66] What I will attempt to do here, albeit briefly, is to read some Deleuzian concepts otherwise, to give a preliminary indication of how and why no universal, original desire is being proclaimed.

From the very beginning of his work Deleuze has played with and upon the notion of desire. Such play almost always turns upon a conception of the body. In *Nietzsche and Philosophy,* Deleuze articulates a multiplicity of connections involving the body, the notion of force, and desire. He writes: "What is the body? We do not define it by saying that it is a field of forces, a nutrient medium fought over by a plurality of forces, for in fact, there is no medium, no field of forces or battle. There is no quantity of reality, all reality is a quantity of force."[67] The body is not a medium and *body* does not designate substance; *body* is a term that expresses the relationship between forces. It is precisely because the relationship between forces is not constituted out of some kind of pre-existent medium or reality that, although forces are subject to interpretation, they are never known. With the term *body,* Deleuze is not simply referring to the psychophysical bodies of human beings but to body in its broadest sense. Bodies may be chemical, biological, geographical, topological, social, or political, and the distinction between these modes is neither ontological nor historical. If anything, it becomes, for Deleuze and Guattari, semiological, a function of different "regimes," different organizations of social, political, cultural, and economic life among living beings.[68]

Ultimately, "body" is too general a concept for Deleuze and so is in need of greater articulation on a practical level. Even in this context, the Nietzschean forces that constitute a body are already differentiated by Deleuze as quantitative and qualitative. The difference in quantity between two forces is their "differential"; this is the quantitative element of difference between two forces that generates a qualitative element of a force, the force as active or reactive. Without quality in addition to quantity, bodies would simply be motionless and dead. This is why forces must be constituted differentially; no force can be quantitatively determined apart from its relations with other forces. Yet, unlike in Hegelian dialectics or Saussurean linguistics, each force is wholly positive, and there can be no such thing as *equal* forces of any kind because equality consists of the elimination of any qualitative determination of force at all. Deleuze thus argues that "[d]ifference in quantity is, therefore, in one sense, the irreducible element *of* quantity."[69] Difference generates quality as something absolutely different than quantity, but then it is also necessarily the case that difference in quantity is "the element which is irreducible *to* quantity itself."[70] Difference remains; it is never resolved.

The question arises as to how this conception of the body as a multiplicity of forces is related to desire. Citing Plato's *Gorgias,* Deleuze draws on Plato's discussion with the Sophist Callicles to introduce the notion of desire.[71] Deleuze appeals to Callicles' arguments to support Nietzsche's contention that whatever separates active force from what it can do should be characterized as "law"; thus law, for Nietzsche, always designates the dominance of the reactive over the active. Plato, however, refuses to recognize the distinction between what Nietzsche calls active and reactive. Deleuze points out that for Callicles, as for Nietzsche, the weak cannot generate a stronger force simply by banding together. Instead, reactive forces can only stop active forces from doing what they do by confronting them with law, with an upside-down image, an upside-down mirror that reverses the meaning and force of Callicles' and Nietzsche's positions. Accordingly, Nietzsche does not simply use the term *slave* historically; rather, he uses it philosophically. A slave is someone enslaved to reactive forces, for the slave does not cease to be a slave when he is triumphant, and the slave is triumphant only by means of "law." However, for Callicles, who quietly repeats himself but does not press his points as Socrates does, "from the point of view of nature, concrete force is that which goes to its ultimate consequences, to the limit of power [*puissance*] or *desire.*"[72] It is probably useful to note that *puissance* is not indicative of power over something; it is the capacity to carry out some activity, so that a force (or forces) that goes to the limit of its power has both the capacity to carry out something and the greatest capacity to be affected. But active force or power is not a physical capacity; in Deleuze's reading, it is ethical.[73] Socrates misunderstands Callicles' definition of desire as the limit of power. Socrates comprehends desire as nothing other than an experience of pain followed by an experience of pleasurable satisfaction—hence, in Nietzschean terms, as reactive, as the property or symptom of reactive forces.

For Deleuze, however, desire is the *limit* of power (and not its law) in the sense that "every body extends its power as far as it is able," and "the smallest becomes the equal of the greatest as soon as it is no longer separated from what it is capable of."[74] Such desire is what Nietzsche calls "will to power," desire that experiments with forces.[75] Therefore Deleuze draws on Nietzsche to create a concept of desire as an active force. So it is true, as Butler argues, that for Deleuze (following Nietzsche) "the Hegelian subject can be understood as a product of slave morality" or, as Deleuze expresses it, the agent of reactive forces.[76] But it does not follow that Deleuze proposes an emancipatory model of desire, as Butler claims, or that this model is built upon "the reification of multiplicitous affect as the invariant, although largely repressed, ontological structure of desire," an "insupportable metaphysical speculation."[77] In Nietzsche's analysis of slave morality, as Butler points out, the noble and powerful, the high-minded, call themselves good. In so doing, they create "good" as a value. The high-minded and powerful call what is common and lowly "base," signifying a critique of all that is common. For Nietzsche, evaluations carried out on the basis of a "noble" way of life carry the value "good."[78] But Deleuze does not concur with Nietzsche's valuations; rather, he draws the conclusion that valuations derived from a mode of being, a way of life, are critical and creative—that is, ethical and aesthetic—and that they are constituted as difference at the origin, the result of active force. Most evaluations are, in fact, not active; most can be traced back to revenge, and thus they are reactive. This is *not* the result of repression from the outside, whether that of Christianity or the coercive force of capitalism and psychological repression; it is really a matter of a base way of living. Deleuze begins *Nietzsche and Philosophy* with the startling claim that "we have the beliefs, feelings and thoughts we deserve given our way of being or style of life."[79] And Deleuze and Guattari argue in *Anti-Oedipus* that fascism is not only a state organization of power, but it is also quotidian, local, and molecular; in other words it is a way of being, a style of life.

This approach is evident in Deleuze's critique of Kant in *Nietzsche and Philosophy.* Because Kant's critique of pure reason is carried on from the outside, from the point of view of conditions that are prior and external to the conditioned, Kant never provides a genealogy of reason, understanding, and its categories. That is, Kant never asks: Who wants this kind of reason? What forces dominate it? Such questions are fundamental to Nietzsche's genetic and plastic principles, which "give an account of the sense and value of beliefs, interpretations and evaluations."[80] Instead, like a theologian, Kant installs the priest and legislator *in us,* a move that only serves to justify current knowledge, morality, and religion. "When we stop obeying God, the State, our parents, reason appears and persuades us to continue being docile because it says to us: it is you who are giving the orders."[81] Active force or desire is not a matter of freeing oneself or being freed from an oppressive state, religion, or family. It is not something always already there in every body; it is there to a lesser or greater degree depending on the history of the forces that have taken hold of that body (and so constitute it) and the struggles between those forces for possession of it. Reactive modes of being do not arise out of the oppression of active force; no such organization of life is even possible except from the point of view of the upside-down mirror of reactive forces. Only genuine critique, or in Deleuze's terms active ethics, lets us look at the forces that have actually taken hold of something. If a force dominates, it does so not by means of negation but by affirming and enjoying its own difference from other forces: difference at the origin.

It would be true to the Deleuzian orientation to state that no account of Nietzsche's philosophy is final. Yet I have proceeded in order to provide some insight into the orientation of thought operating in Deleuze's work and to prepare the way for a more thorough account to follow. Nevertheless, in response to Butler's challenging and important critique I have tried to point out that the "body" may be too large and clumsy a concept to rely on for the conceptualization of desire and that desire is not, for Deleuze, simply a question of good but oppressed desire as opposed to bad power. As Nietzsche has made abundantly clear, everything has or is power; it is just a matter of how active or reactive that power is and what a body can do.

Nomadism

The work of Rosi Braidotti has also played a major role in feminist Deleuzian studies. Her essays and books have, curiously enough, agreed with and extended the criticisms of Jardine, Irigaray, and Butler. In *Patterns of Dissonance* Braidotti writes that her purpose is "to work towards new formulations of the question of women and philosophy as a singular multiplicity of related issues," and to do so in a "philosophical style" that she characterizes using the Deleuzian term *nomadism.*[82] Braidotti defines nomadism in terms of a nonsystematic theory, a discontinuous line, a mere collection of points, which "intersects" at times with sociopolitical realities and is "confronted" by potentialities for action.[83] This definition does not yet make clear the relation between theory and praxis in the sense of articulating where theory arises in relation to sociopolitical reality and action, something that needs to be clarified in order to see if Braidotti's nomadism is proximate to Deleuze and Guattari's. What is clear is that in her earliest work, Braidotti believed that it was not yet possible to form a systematic feminist philosophy out of the multiplicity of points of view feminists are registering, so that the most one should expect is a prephilosophical discourse. Thus, to avoid falling into what she takes to be the trap of homologation—that is, disappearing into the master's or the other's text—or into the other extreme, the void, Braidotti intends to proceed not only nomadically, but also with an ear to dissonance: "woman and philosophy—patterns of dissonance, a polyphonic play, a game of multiplicities, that may collapse into cacophony and even shock some sensitive ears."[84] Practically this strategy operates in her text in terms of the multiplicity of feminist viewpoints she incorporates into her prephilosophical and eventual philosophical discourse. Potentially there is a place in Braidotti's account of feminist theory for even the most disparate and oppositional viewpoints, or even ontologies. Whether or not this strategy is successful remains to be seen, particularly insofar as Braidotti's openness to all positions does not amount to a lack of positions and presuppositions on her own part.

Braidotti's initial approach to Deleuze is a by-product of one of *her* central concerns: the challenge to philosophy from psychoanalysis. This challenge arose in conjunction with the rejection, in France, of the primacy of consciousness and reason, as well as the unitary knowing subject. Much of this challenge came from Jacques Lacan, who, she argues, shows that the Cartesian subject of knowledge "has to do with obsessionality and desire for mastery," insofar as "it sees and sees itself in the act of seeing," and erroneously assumes that this seeing is the source of its transparency and reflective power, when in fact it is enunciation that constructs the subject, though in an existential mode rather than as a unity of thought.[85] As such, the subject is the effect of a chain of linguistic signifiers—that is, the effect of what it says (the assumption here is that language is both socially constructed and prior to any given subject)—such that a claim to authority on the part of self-reflection is only a result of the power of its internal logic.[86] The Cartesian subject's desire to know produces the illusion of mastery and the rejection of any notion of an unconscious truth, since for such a subject, truth only arises out of its reflective power. This is why in the history of thought, theoretical structures, especially philosophy, coincide with the rejection of "libidinal, unconscious material which [for Braidotti] is the source of all thought."[87]

What this appears to mean is that Braidotti takes libidinal, unconscious material to be the origin of both the subject and its thought; there is both a desire for knowledge and a desire for mastery—the first constitutes philosophy and the second produces a subject as *cogito*. The problem for psychoanalysis, as Braidotti sees it, is that there is no way to move from that which affects the body to verbal and written accounts of it except by "theorizing the body to be a written text, traversed by codes and affects."[88] That is, the physiological and physical semiotic of the body can only be made sense of by reducing it to the semiotic of language. Braidotti accepts this as inevitable and does not challenge the primacy of linguistic systems. Her concern is a different one. Once psychoanalysis attempts to theorize its clinical insights, she worries, it is subject to the same rules and norms as any other theoretical enterprise, including philosophy; she argues that this is something that Freud effectively avoided whereas Lacan did not. For Freud, Braidotti claims, "there is no separation between affective and intellectual life, between, on the one hand, thought, and on the other, dreams and fantasy."[89] In this account, thinking is nothing but bringing into play "the different registers of experience and representation which structure the subject. No more, no less."[90]

Unfortunately, to claim this is to say practically nothing about bodies, languages, and thought. Although Freud developed several kinds of theoretical accounts of how unconscious drives are translated into thought and action, Braidotti does not.[91] In her analysis of the relation between body and thought, neither term is defined and clarified. Because Braidotti wishes to emphasize *process* over psychical and psychic substance, she is understandably unwilling to address bodies and thoughts as if they are "entities" that can be defined or explained. However, I want to claim that it is not enough simply to describe various bodily, linguistic, and theoretical processes or to point to examples of them, for (as my analysis of Jardine suggests) when we depend upon such phenomenological descriptions, we can always be mistaken about what we are seeing, so that our descriptions may distort or conceal rather than clarify or reveal the "real." Additionally, there seems to be an assumption operating that we know what we mean by "body" and "thought" and, further, that simply connecting the two through libidinal drives is adequate. What I will have to show in the chapters that follow is that this is not adequate and, further, that articulating bodies and thoughts as extremely complex processes that often incorporate incommensurate elements does not exempt us from making sense of them conceptually and theoretically, even if we can only do this provisionally, by explaining how bodies and thought are constructed as processes and how they function in a variety of concrete circumstances. Finally, I will maintain that conceptualization does not necessarily commit philosophy to articulating bodies and thoughts as entities.

The clash between psychoanalysis and philosophy also motivates Braidotti's enthusiasm for the work of Foucault, insofar as he, like Freud, questions the order of rational thought. In *The Order of Things* Foucault asks: "What is man's being, and how can it be that that being, which could so easily be characterized by the fact that 'it has thoughts' and is possibly alone in having them, has an ineradicable and fundamental relation to the unthought? A form of reflection is established . . . a form that involves, for the first time, man's being in that dimension where thought addresses the unthought and articulates itself upon it."[92] Whereas Foucault characterizes the "unthought" in terms of language, labor, and life, Braidotti continues to privilege the psychoanalytic unconscious because of her conviction that it pushes the critique of the knowing subject to the extreme, "bringing to the surface the set of rules, conflicts, and conditions of enunciation underlying the register of subjectivity," such that it undoes even the idea of "man" that the human sciences (including psychoanalysis) study as their object of knowledge.[93] Thus implicated in the very critique it makes possible, psychoanalysis cannot replace the philosophy of the knowing subject with a philosophy of the desiring subject, since, Braidotti argues, psychoanalysis functions precisely to undo the subject.

What psychoanalysis does do, however, is to bring into the foreground and "play around with" the concept of the "feminine."[94] Of course, this second concept arose out of Freud's work with women whom he diagnosed as "hysterics," and it is, as Braidotti points out, the interaction between the "master" and "his women" that constitutes the discourse of psychoanalysis. Yet this fact does not dampen Braidotti's enthusiasm for psychoanalysis, even though the so-called feminine character of psychoanalytic discourse did not prevent Freud from distancing himself from that same discourse in order to construct femininity as a problem and a mystery. In spite of Foucault's argument that modernity demands a break with interiority that will allow thought about man (*sic*) from the outside, and that interiority is only a myth for modern man, Braidotti notes the simultaneity of Foucault's emphasis on language, life, and labor (including especially the analysis of the body) with "the appearance of the discourse of modernity on the unconscious and on the splitting of the subject [especially in Lacan]," and she argues that this must result in a redefinition of discourse on the maternal feminine.[95]

What such a redefinition might accomplish or how it would be structured in order to coincide with Foucault's assertion of the necessity of a philosophy of exteriority and his argument that interiority is a myth is not clear. Foucault's method does seem to be quite specific: he looks to the relation between thought and the outside. What, if anything, psychoanalysis contributes to this method is questionable. Braidotti suggests that the feminine might be one of these exteriorities, but nothing in the psychoanalytic project suggests this, since "[i]n an analytic perspective, thought is always thinking of sexual matters. . . . All thinking turns on and around the essential thought, the only one that really 'matters': Where do I come from?"[96] Even if this thought has to do with the relation to the mother, who is presumably "outside" or "exterior" with regard to the child, the "essential" question of origins certainly does not qualify as thinking *from the outside;* it is still unitary and interior.

In the essay "Towards a New Nomadism: Feminist Deleuzian Tracks, or Metaphysics and Metabolism," Braidotti again addresses the issues of interiority and exteriority by asking the question of how to reconcile historicity and agency with "the political will to change, which entails the (unconscious) desire for the new, which, as Deleuze teaches us, implies the construction of new desiring subjects."[97] Although the assertion that Deleuze teaches (us) that the unconscious desire for the new implies construction of new desiring subjects is highly problematic, I will not address it in this chapter, since it requires not only a preliminary critique of Braidotti's position but also a thorough discussion of Deleuze's. Instead, I will turn my attention to the role of women's desire. Like Butler, Braidotti believes that desire is "what is at stake in the feminist project of elaborating alternative definitions of female subjectivity"—that is, women's desire to "become" is either liberated or constituted when women escape the dominant system of representation and are able to constitute "nonlogocentric modes of representation."[98] This desire, Braidotti argues, must be ontological and not "just" libidinal; it is "the tendency of the subject to be."[99] Thus, it appears that Braidotti has moved beyond her earlier prephilosophical position into ontology proper, an ontology of woman's being.

In the first place, Braidotti finds Deleuze useful to her feminist project for "de-essentializing the body, sexuality, and sexed identities, [because] . . . . [t]he embodied subject is a term in a process of intersecting forces (affects), spatiotemporal variables that are characterized by their mobility, changeability, and transitory nature."[100] Corresponding to this new conception of subjectivity is a new conception of thought as the multiple connections between these intersecting forces. The consequence of this is that the interiority Braidotti had earlier sought to maintain seems to have diminished if not disappeared. However, this may not be the case, insofar as Braidotti continues to characterize this process of intersecting forces—what Deleuze and Guattari call the assemblage—as an "embodied subject," as if the concepts of lived experience and subjectivity could continue to be thought within the framework of phenomenology without a thoroughgoing critique of traditional phenomenological categories. It also appears that Braidotti believes that Deleuze proposes some sort of phenomenological lived experience to be the basis of thought, a position implied, though not explicitly stated, in her earlier work, which overlooks the anti-phenomenological stance of Deleuze's work on Bergson and Foucault.

Following Deleuze, Braidotti refers to the "embodied subject" as the affective foundation of the thinking process, which she characterizes as "beyond" or "behind" the propositional content of an idea. But if affectivity serves as a foundation that is beyond or behind, then the interiority Braidotti claims to have overcome appears to remain. Thus, in her explanation of this new kind of embodied subject and its thought, Braidotti may well reintroduce a dualism of inside/outside. Nor can she claim that the newly configured, embodied subject that she attributes to Deleuze, and which rests on the interconnection between "lived experience" and thought, the activity of the critical, theoretical mind, necessarily eliminates dualism. For unless and until the parameters of such "interconnection" are spelled out, there is no way of knowing how it operates.[101] Although dualism may well be unintended on her part, nonetheless it operates in her text.

Perhaps this dualism, along with the attribution of a phenomenological embodied subject and the claim that there is a tendency of the subject to be, is what leads her to postulate that Deleuze is caught in a contradiction, insofar as he introduces a "general" becoming-woman that fails to take into account the historical and epistemological specificity of female feminist standpoints and forgets that gender dichotomies result in asymmetrical relations between the sexes. Although it is true, as I have previously admitted, that Deleuze is not "doing" history, he is not doing it because he insists upon philosophical and concrete specificities, whereas history demands generalities. Deleuze proposes no generalities at all, but undertakes a radical critique of generalization as a mode of conceptualization. Furthermore, it is Braidotti who clings to conceptual generalization when she writes, "the point is to radicalize the universal, not to get rid of it."[102] For Deleuze, the point is to radicalize the universal to the extent that it disappears.

Braidotti, like Jardine, Butler, and Irigaray, focuses her criticism on Deleuze and Guattari's concept of "becoming-woman." Elsewhere Braidotti argues that although "the becoming–minority/nomad/molecular/woman is posited as the general figuration for the new philosophical subjectivity, . . . not all the forms taken by the process of becoming are equivalent."[103] It is, she continues, as if all forms of becoming are equal but becoming-woman is more equal because Deleuze maintains that there is no becoming-man, since man determines the norm according to which woman is positioned as "other" and because becoming-woman is the key to all other becomings.[104] According to Braidotti, Deleuze faces the problem of "how to free 'woman' from the subjugated position of annexed 'other,' so as to make her expressive of a different difference, of pure difference, of an entirely new plane of becoming, out of which differences can multiply and differ from each other."[105] The question of how to achieve such a conception of difference is central to the project of this book, but it is entirely divorced, I think, from existing postmodern analyses. But Braidotti ties "pure" difference to deconstruction in her conclusion that "it is unthinkable that the question of the deconstruction of phallogocentrism could be disconnected from the concrete changes taking place in women's lives."[106] The notion that a Deleuzian concept should embrace, or is mistaken in not embracing, a deconstructive argument or method may be at the root of Braidotti's claim that Deleuze uses the concept of becoming-woman to critique feminism for not dissolving the subject "woman" into a series of transformative processes associated with a "generalized and 'postgender' becoming," insofar as the "feminine" is a restrictive concept that should be replaced with an "impersonal, multiple, and machinelike structure," ostensibly through deconstructive means.[107]

Braidotti does adopt what she claims to be Deleuze's view of an embodied subject as a term in a process of intersecting forces (affects) and spatiotemporal variables that are characterized by their mobility, changeability, and transitory nature. At the same time, she wishes to hold on to sexual difference as Luce Irigaray defines it. This move coincides with Braidotti's realignment with her interpretation of Deleuze's notion of the unconscious as opposed to the Freudian notion that she previously embraced. Deleuze, she claims, does not take the unconscious to be the source or origin of thoughts or acts; rather, the unconscious "marks the structural noncoincidence of the subject with his/her consciousness."[108] Although such a notion of the unconscious is commensurate with Irigaray's critique of the western logic of solids, which gives the woman no place of her own even while it constructs itself upon this nothing (see chapter 3), it does not accurately delineate what Deleuze takes the functioning of the unconscious to be. The positive aspect of this redefinition, for Braidotti, is that she no longer has to argue in terms of unconscious drives. However, Braidotti still maintains that desire, now understood as "ontological" desire, is the intersubjective basis for a new common plane of experience among women, even though desire "transcends" every subject. Accordingly, the subject is a gendered "unity" inextricably connected to the "other," and given this, the thought or theory of sexual difference follows from the collectivity of female subjects driven by their intersubjective ontological desire. According to Braidotti, "the thought of sexual difference as the expression of the ontological desire of the female feminist is a project that implies transformation of the very act of thinking, of its structural frame and not only of its images or content. . . . High theory or philosophy in its traditional inception is nothing more than the power of/in discourse."[109] So we are back to where we began with Braidotti: both bodily and as a thinker, the "subject" is constituted as discourse. Additionally, the phenomenological notion of a subjective, gendered "unity" seems to present barriers to the conceptualization of difference as difference. In the end it seems that what Braidotti wants to incorporate into her work is Deleuze's conception of the body, not as a natural biological materiality but as the play of forces and a surface of intensities. Further, there is the formation of thinking that is not a function of an interior self-reflective activity but the process whereby a multiplicity of impersonal forces establish connections with one another. Ultimately eschewing the polarizations of feminist debate, Braidotti hopes to bring a Deleuzian conception of nomadism into feminist practice even while recognizing that "woman" has been excluded from masculine systems of representation, including what Braidotti takes to be Deleuze's representational system.[110]

A Thousand Tiny Sexes

Perhaps no contemporary feminist theorist has worked harder to present an accurate and fair account of Deleuze's relation to feminist theory than Elizabeth Grosz, especially in her essay "A Thousand Tiny Sexes: Feminism and Rhizomatics." Addressing the rarity of any discussion of Deleuze and Guattari in feminist theoretical texts, Grosz asks if this is because they are thought to have little to offer feminism, because of the difficulty of accessing their peculiar language and interests, or simply because of chance. She concludes that all three factors are operating and she proceeds to look more closely into Deleuze and Guattari's "possible value for feminist concerns; their potential for contesting and reorienting feminist commitments; and their utility or otherwise for feminist methodologies."[111] Grosz acknowledges the reservations put forth by both Jardine and Irigaray; however, she opts to "temporarily suspend critical feminist judgment in order to 'enter into' the project(s) articulated in Deleuze and Guattari's *A Thousand Plateaus.*"[112] What is at stake at this preliminary point is whether or not what Deleuze and Guattari call "rhizomatics," which Grosz takes to be a form of pragmatics, is concerned with what can be done.[113] She wants to know how rhizomatics can function as a positive theoretical aid in the task of making feminist challenges to dominant philosophical paradigms, methods, and assumptions. As I stated at the beginning of this chapter, Deleuze himself has urged the careful study of the history of philosophy insofar as philosophy has participated in the repression of thought over the centuries, and no one is more susceptible to repression than those who ignore its history. So the question is: To what extent can the concepts provided by Deleuze and Guattari assist feminists in overcoming the virtual erasure of women and women's contributions from cultural, sexual, and theoretical life?[114]

By Grosz's evaluation, Deleuze and Guattari's conceptualizations can begin to do this in terms of how they position systems of thought. That is, they posit such systems, not as causal factors, but as the mere effects of other kinds of processes, such as social, political, cultural, and linguistic practices, which are themselves deeply sedimented and interrelated so that they function in provisional alignments with one another to form a working whole (which is always altering). This would have the effect of deflating the power and authority of thought systems. Why? Because the purpose of this reorganization is to change thought systems if sedimented modes of life are changed. Thus, Grosz concludes that even if the cosmic empiricism that Jardine deplores does not thematically affirm or support struggles for women's autonomy and self-determination, it does sweep away metaphysical frameworks that keep women from devising their own knowledge and accounts of themselves.[115]

Grosz also recognizes what I take to be one of the principal advantages of Deleuze and Guattari's work: their interest in the question of difference formulated independently of the rule of equivocal being or, as Grosz calls it, the "regime of the One, the self-same, the imaginary play of mirrors and doubles, the structure of binary pairs in which what is different can be understood only as a variation or negation of identity."[116] And to this end Grosz acknowledges the necessity of conceptualizing difference outside of identity, opposition, analogy, and resemblance in order to produce a concept of multiplicity that is not just the pluralized identity of liberal political conceptions of pluralism. This means that, like Iris Marion Young, Grosz acknowledges the importance of defining groups as everchanging, as interconnected with other groups, and thus as having indeterminate borders, overlapping interests, multiple points of connection with one another, and an always open relation with the outside that deterritorializes and de-defines groups. In a sense, it appears that Deleuze and Guattari have borrowed some tactics from feminist and minority politics without recognizing this, insofar as the affirmation of multiplicities without hierarchies and without models is already a form of political action among many grassroots minority rights movements.

Given all this, there is still another, and by far the most important, point of interest for Grosz: Deleuze and Guattari's creative reconceptualization of the body, a reconceptualization that has its points of contact with key figures in the history of philosophy, notably Spinoza and Nietzsche. From Spinoza, Deleuze and Guattari wrest a perspective that does not make of the body either a subject or an object but asks: What is a body capable of? For Spinoza this is a matter of how much joy and affirmation or sadness and decomposition a body can endure in its various relations with other bodies. The passions and actions of the body replace the system of genus, species, and its differences and the hierarchy of mind-body dualism. Questions about the body lead, in the end, to questions about desire. The entire tradition of western philosophy since Plato has participated in maintaining this connection, and it has become a particular concern and interest of feminist philosophers. Rather than following the dominant strand of the tradition that characterizes desire negatively as an ontological lack in being (which seeks to be filled by attaining the object but which, in reality, will never be filled), Deleuze and Guattari propose a radical alternative. Grosz points out that Deleuze and Guattari, following Spinoza and Nietzsche, conceive of desire not as longing for something but as that which creates connections and relations. This characterization of desire is a major reversal, an overturning of the Platonic tradition of desire as lack. If desire aims at nothing in particular and seeks only its own proliferation and expansion, by assembling singularities into provisional entities and breaking down so-called objectivities into singularities, then desire is productive of the real.[117] Feminist theorists should take an interest in this conception because in the history of western thought and on the social and political level women have been situated as the personification of (male) lack and have been imprisoned by this placement in the role of the "other."

Finally, Grosz discovers in the work of Deleuze and Guattari an attunement to ethics that is perhaps surprising to anyone not familiar with their work. This arises, in many respects, out of the reconceptualization of the body and desire on an affirmative and productive basis, as opposed to the old conception predicated on the negative and on lack, as well as out of the recognition of multiplicities irreducible to metaphysical unity. Among feminists and theorists concerned with minority points of view, it is absolutely necessary to "rethink relations between dominant and subordinated groups, oppressor and oppressed, self and other, as well as between and within subjects."[118] This new understanding of ethics is one Grosz has been actively involved in creating in her theoretical work. It is an ethics that arises out of and in terms of concrete practices, not moral imperatives; it is thus actively political rather than isolated from political concerns. This is an ethics that starts with the questions: What can a body do? And what can desire create? As such, it is an ethics that is concerned with links between persons and the creation of new possibilities on a multiplicity of cultural, social, and political levels. If we were to posit this in terms of the western political notion of rights, this ethics searches for ways to extend and expand rights and the definition of rights. This ethics therefore creates a willingness and opportunities to continuously reconfigure such rights and the various groups or assemblages to whom these rights apply. In short, ethics is never static; it is an ongoing process.

Although she never identifies herself with "Deleuzians" or even with the supposedly more radical "Guattarians," Grosz nevertheless draws on Deleuze and Guattari's analyses and reformulations of ontology, the body, and ethics throughout her later work. *Volatile Bodies* rearticulates the importance of Grosz's earlier reading of rhizomatics but extends the issue considerably by "making use" of the difficult concept of the body without organs (BwO), a concept formulated by Antonin Artaud and used extensively by Deleuze and Guattari:

> Unlike psychoanalysis, which regards the body as a developmental union or aggregate of partial objects, organs, drives, orifices, each with their own significance, their own modalities of pleasure which, through the processes of Oedipal reorganization, bring these partial objects and erotogenic bodily zones into alignment in the service of a higher goal than their immediate, local gratification (the ultimate goal being reproduction), the BwO invokes a conception of the body that is disinvested of fantasy, images, projections, representations, a body without a psychical or secret interior, without internal cohesion and latent significance.[119]

Indeed, for reasons I will articulate in later chapters of this book, Deleuze and Guattari describe the body in terms of speeds and intensities, productive flows of forces seeking to escape the authority of unity, organization, and hierarchy, what they refer to as stratification. Thus, BwO (their abbreviation) refers not to a body that is literally without any organs, but rather a body that is not determined, not ruled or structured by those organs, whether sexual organs, heart, or lungs.

In opposition to this, Grosz argues, society constructs stable or what Deleuze and Guattari call molar unities: classes, races, and sexes—precisely the groups that are the concern of feminist and minority theorists. Rather than undermining these groups or downplaying the oppression they experience, the BwO is an attempt to render *more complex* the character of the kinds of oppressions these groups endure while simultaneously offering greater opportunities for construction of an escape route. Race, sex, class—these groupings are too fixed, too stable to give way to reform and rethinking. It is only by first breaking up each of these molar unities into a "thousand tiny" races, sexes, or classes that we can begin to undermine their authority and regroup ourselves on a pragmatic level.

Ultimately—and I agree with Grosz on this—a selective reading and use of Deleuze and Guattari may benefit from valuable methodologies, questions, and insights. The shift from a psychoanalytic to a semiotic perspective, the pragmatics that allows thinking to arise out of and in terms of actual practices rather than seeking metaphysical grounds, the critique of binarism as hierarchical, the breaking down of massive social and political structures into microentities, the refusal of any single explanatory paradigm and any single philosopher or philosophy, and finally the positive account of bodies and desire, all seem to Grosz to be specific advantages that Deleuze and Guattari offer to philosophers and to feminist and minority theorists. Although her own philosophical interests range widely, although she considers a full spectrum of contemporary and historical philosophical figures, although she makes considered and strategic use of Deleuze and Guattari in her work, Grosz nonetheless creates a context within which a feminist can and should read Deleuze and Deleuze-Guattari.

Of course there are other feminist thinkers who have read or are beginning to read and "make use" of Deleuze and Deleuze-Guattari (Moira Gatens is an obvious candidate); I make no pretence here of addressing them all.[120] My purpose here is to point out that if there has been resistance to Deleuze and Deleuze-Guattari, it can be addressed, perhaps not in a manner that will satisfy all philosophical persuasions, but at least in a way that can differentiate a "Deleuzian" usage from that of others. In this chapter I have tried to address the criticisms generated by feminist theoreticians. My project in the rest of this book is to move on to what in Deleuze and Deleuze-Guattari I can make use of in my own work.

3
Against Phenomenology

Feminist Narrative

In spite of their many theoretical and practical differences, each of the feminist thinkers examined in the previous chapter shares some commitment to phenomenology as well as to psychoanalysis. It varies from person to person, with Grosz, perhaps, maintaining the highest level of skepticism toward or distance from both phenomenology and psychoanalysis.[1] In my refutation of Jardine, specifically, I began to point to certain objections to a phenomenological approach to feminist concerns in particular and philosophy in general. I cited the arguments of Boundas, who cautions that the phenomenological supposition that the subject of a narrative constructs a self that proceeds to carry out various actions and projects assumes that the unified self and the unified narrative are desirable and real. This assumption makes pathologies of fragmented personalities and narratives while providing no criteria by which to evaluate the amount of self-deception, distortion, or prejudice a narratee is caught up in. Feminist philosophers such as Grosz, Butler, and Iris Marion Young have more specific criticisms, and even Simone de Beauvoir, arguably the founder of feminist existential phenomenology, anticipated some of these concerns without having a language or perhaps a commitment with which to fully express them.

In an early review appearing in the journal *Les temps modernes,* Beauvoir praises Merleau-Ponty for the phenomenological insight that for human beings existence is expressed in terms of our embodied spatial milieu, our embodied history and even prehistory, and finally, in our faith that perception opens subjects up to the world.[2] Likewise, Beauvoir's *The Second Sex* discusses woman from the point of view of the phenomenological lived world.[3] Yet here, as well as in her account of society and individual transcendence in *The Ethics of Ambiguity,* Beauvoir clearly makes use of the Sartrean existentialist notion of the absolute freedom of independent subjects who are in competition with one another to dampen enthusiasm about the phenomenological intersubjective world.[4] In the latter text Beauvoir recognizes that some situated and embodied human beings are subject to loss of freedom as a result of the extreme oppression they endure; and in the former text she specifies that women are a group with no control over their bodies and lives, and thus their embodiment remains a matter of oppression and reduction to object status.

It is precisely this line of thought that contemporary feminist philosophers have followed in criticizing phenomenology in general and Merleau-Ponty in particular. In her important essay "Throwing Like a Girl: A Phenomenology of Feminine Body Comportment, Motility, and Spatiality," Iris Marion Young argues that Merleau-Ponty describes the lived body of masculine existence without any recognition of a body specific to women.[5] While accepting her assessment that women are defined by society as mere objects, Young also criticizes Beauvoir for tending to blame women's physiology for their oppression. Butler's argument against Merleau-Ponty's phenomenology is similar to Young's, although she more narrowly (or perhaps more broadly) targets his account of sexuality. Merleau-Ponty does place sexuality in the lived body of experience and takes it to be coextensive with existence, yet he does so from an unremittingly heterosexual, not to mention voyeuristic, point of view that forecloses the possibility of alternative forms of sexuality.[6]

Citing the work of Irigaray, Grosz points out—with regard specifically to Merleau-Ponty—that phenomenology privileges vision over all other perceptual relations and tacitly ascribes feminine attributes to the idea of flesh or being even while ignoring all aspects of maternity.[7] Phenomenology's failure to provide any account of women's bodily experience even while surreptitiously making use of "feminine" attributes in concepts has, of course, been roundly criticized by feminist theorists. Yet beyond this, and in a manner reflected in Boundas's criticism of the unified subject, Grosz cautions that blind acceptance of the concept of "experience" as the point of view from which knowledge is constructed is dangerous. The acceptance of experience as an unproblematic criterion for the assessment of knowledge overlooks the fact that experience is already determined by the cultural and theoretical milieu, and thus is not ideologically free. Further, as both Grosz and Butler have pointed out in different ways, rather than taking experience as a starting point for discovery, too many feminists naively take it as unquestionably true, as a kind of pure irrefutable truth, no matter how distorted it may be.[8] I would argue that taking the phenomenological perception of lived experience as the basis of knowledge is even more problematic than Grosz and Butler assert.

Luce Irigaray is often cited as the principal feminist who maintains a phenomenological method while criticizing Merleau-Ponty's analysis insofar as it fails to recognize sexual difference. However, contrary to expectations, a closer look at Irigaray's critique of Merleau-Ponty, as well as Irigaray's philosophy in general, might well open the way, not only to an avoidance of phenomenology's sexist tendencies, but to the creation of a fissure so large between Irigaray's goals and those of phenomenology that no reliance on the latter is possible at all. It is my supposition that the manner in which Irigaray constitutes this fissure leads directly to Bergson and to the Bergsonian anti-phenomenology of Deleuze. For Irigaray's critique of phenomenology and of western philosophy is also a critique of representation that I take to be commensurate with Deleuze's ruin of representation.

To begin with, although it is important to look specifically at the critique that Irigaray expressly addresses to Merleau-Ponty—that is, her rereading of Merleau-Ponty's *The Visible and the Invisible*—I believe that it is necessary to pay attention to other aspects of Irigaray's work as well.[9] For even though in that essay Irigaray cites passages from Merleau-Ponty's text and appears to offer her approval of phenomenology, I would maintain that her agreement with Merleau-Ponty is less centered on phenomenology than may generally be supposed. Irigaray writes: "We must go back to a moment of prediscursive experience, recommence everything, all the categories by which we understand things, the world, subject-object divisions, recommence everything and pause at the 'mystery, as familiar as it is unexplained, of a light which, illuminating the rest, remains at its source in obscurity.'"[10] Irigaray's statement that we must return to prediscursive experience has generally been taken as an affirmation of Merleau-Ponty's phenomenological method, but Irigaray's return will not necessarily turn out the same as Merleau-Ponty's. Her concern, Irigaray explains, is to bring the maternal-feminine into *language,* but not, I think, at the level of what Merleau-Ponty refers to as the mystery of language.

Merleau-Ponty, by his own account, is seeking a language that creates itself in its expressive acts.[11] He wishes to grasp language at the moment when the word "takes possession" of the reader, writer, or speaker, and a new signification, like a bodily fluid, is secreted.[12] For Merleau-Ponty, just as perceptions take us from our body to the things themselves, this mysterious kind of language projects us beyond our own thoughts, which are steeped in institutionalized language, to the other's linguistic body, the other's meaning, the other's "linguistic gesticulation."[13] Thus, for Merleau-Ponty expressive language in all its manifestations arises only out of and in relation to the body.

I do not think that this is exactly what Irigaray has in mind when she looks to the "living references" to bring the maternal-feminine into language at the level of theme, motif, subject, articulation, and syntax. For while her essay examines Merleau-Ponty's exorbitant language of visibility in order to uncover the maternal bodily flesh underlying all of his phenomenological descriptions—a maternal bodily flesh that he never acknowledges, indeed is totally unaware of—there is something more profound taking place as well. From Irigaray's perspective, since speech, for Merleau-Ponty, bears the silence of visibility into sound, his phenomenology of the body makes speech into "an almost carnal existence of the idea, as well as . . . a sublimation of the flesh."[14] As I have argued previously, Merleau-Ponty anticipates that the carnal idea may constitute a kind of "depersonalized I"—that is, "the capacity to allow oneself to be pulled down and rebuilt again by the other person before one, by others who may come along, and in principle, by anyone."[15] The problem, as Irigaray registers it, is that of "catching sight of each other." Merleau-Ponty claims that an individual "I" builds up in its own body an expressive organism. Accordingly, the depths of the body are transformed into language and inside becomes outside, sentient and sense are one as speech declares itself in us. Or as he expresses it in *The Visible and the Invisible,* given how the human body sees and hears itself, in its reversibility "the structure of the mute world is such that all the possibilities of language are already given in it."[16] If all the possibilities of language are given, how, Irigaray asks, will *I* ever catch sight of *you?* "Within this world, movement is such that it would take extraordinary luck [*hazard*] for two seers to catch sight of each other, find each other on the track of the same circle and cross paths, or look at each other as they walk in parallel lines."[17] Whether by intent or chance, the French word *hazard* can also carry the meaning risk, danger, or hazard. What risk or danger is there, for Merleau-Ponty, in moving through the mute world? While professing the utmost care with regard to the intertwining of subject and world, Merleau-Ponty's subject never even enters the world because there is no "spacing or interval for the freedom of questioning between two."[18] Two seers would have to inhabit the same world in the same way in order to encounter one another; and even if they did, what would guarantee that one would not overwhelm or destroy the other? In this sense Irigaray's conclusion carries tremendous power, for she asks if it is possible at all for philosophy to give birth to wild meaning (*un sens sauvage*) without first *changing the foundations* of language. The change of foundations, let us recognize, cannot be accomplished without what she refers to as the interval of a temporal bridge between retroaction and anticipation.[19] It is this change of foundations that interests me, for the phenomenological world view cannot introduce this change, but the interval may. A closer look at Merleau-Ponty's and Irigaray's conceptions of space will serve to clarify this.

Irigaray avows that in life, language, and philosophy, women have been women only in relation to the determinations made for them by men. These determinations can be characterized in terms of a system of oppositions: "virginal/deflowered, pure/impure, innocent/experienced."[20] The effect of this system is to displace women from any situation they might establish for themselves, on their own terms. In place of the system of oppositions, Irigaray muses that there could be some kind of "improper" language that expresses multiplicity and fluidity. The reasons for this are social and political, but they are also, and fundamentally, ontological. If we were to examine the properties of fluids, she argues, we would discover that as a physical reality, fluids resist adequate symbolization and serve as a constant reminder of the powerlessness of the logic of solids to represent all of nature's characteristics. It is not insignificant that Irigaray expresses this in a positive manner with regard to fluidity and negatively with regard to symbolization or logic. This makes it clear that for her, symbolic or logical representation are the sites of lack with regard to their representative function, and fluidity is what is real. These modes of representation, unable to alter or reform themselves or to admit that they are incapable of conceptualizing fluidity, have tended to respond to the fluid features of reality by idealizing them. Idealization of this type creates and maintains the relationship between rationality and solid mechanics insofar as solids conform to the normalizing and universalizing judgments of a subject who mathematicizes the idealizable characteristics of fluids, thereby conferring upon them an approximate relation to reality.[21]

Mathematicization, about which I will have more to say later, amounts to the conceptualization of fluids as solids. Solids, in turn, are understood to consist of homogeneous and identical quantities, which are divisible and measurable, and which can be represented clearly in language insofar as each one is unchanging, identical, and common to all who observe it. Thus isolated, the object can be named. Those objects whose characteristics are the most common, or conventional among a group of objects, can even be designated as genera; those that are slightly less common are called species. As we have seen (in chapter 1), Aristotle developed a precise schema for differentiating such objects, arguing that any genus must remain the same for itself (identical) even when differences modify the subject in its form to constitute species. All differences must begin with something in common: the genus.[22] Even when differences are said of a subject, stability and homogeneity reign since "that which is different is different from some particular thing in some particular respect, so that there must be something *identical* whereby they differ."[23] It is clear as well that this conception must conform to traditional Aristotelian logic, in which a subject and a predicate are combined in a sentence, which, if it is true, is supposed to represent a fact in the world. But this point of view is not confined to logic or to an ancient view of the world, for we find similar sentiments expressed even in the diacritical linguistics of Ferdinand de Saussure. For Saussure, the only real object of linguistics is the normal, regular life of an existing idiom.[24] This is no doubt related to the relative stability of the signifier. Both the individual and the community are powerless with respect to the signifier, which is always bound to the *existing* language system, not to language users who remain by and large unaware of language laws and satisfied with the existing idiom: insofar as it is arbitrary, there is no motive to change the sign. Given also the seemingly unlimited number of signs involved and the fact that language as a system is ruled by *logic,* the very complexity of language makes it immutable.[25]

Nonetheless, it is frequently argued that insofar as language as a whole can change, it is ambiguous and unsystematic, and linguistic expressions combine with a shifting multiplicity of meanings to produce concepts that can never be delineated sharply. Even for a logic of solids, the problem has been that the meaning of the concept shifts and the judgment of the truth value of propositions cannot be made with absolute certainty. No doubt it is the slippage inherent in the relations of concepts to subjects that has given many innovative thinkers hope that room can be found for a logic of multiplicities within the Aristotelian framework.[26] It is perhaps also part of the reason why Irigaray is commonly thought to have adopted a position similar to that of Jacques Derrida, who maintains that writing is the supplement of spoken language, but an original supplement that confounds our attempts to make a word mean any one thing or to insist upon the identity of what that word denotes.[27] In her work on Irigaray, Grosz argues that Irigaray opposes logical formalization because it commits language to singular meanings and limits the free play of terms, what Derrida calls *différence.*[28] Butler's focus is slightly different in that she takes Irigaray to believe that the feminine "sex" is a point of linguistic absence insofar as it cannot be determined grammatically as substance—substantive being—but rather is "a relative convergence among culturally and historically specific sets of relations."[29] Presumably this is because, as Butler argues, within pervasively masculinist, phallogocentric language, women are unrepresentable; they are linguistic absence and opacity. Chanter makes a similar point, it appears, when she singles out the silences at the level of utterances as indicative of Irigaray's concern for how such silences mark woman's place in philosophy.[30] How these positions relate to formalization is not clear, for the question remains: What about representation itself and the universal signification it implies? Is it possible to claim, as Butler does, that culturally and historically specific sets of relations operate as an absence within representational hegemony? If so, according to what logic?

Even Derrida's own texts seem to be aiming at something else. In his account of the supplementarity of writing vis-à-vis speaking, Derrida observes that according to the grammarians of the eighteenth century, writing requires that a visible signifier separate itself from speech and supplant it. Still, other needs prevail—in particular, the economy of written communications. Citing Warburton, Derrida agrees with the claim that books, libraries, and the proliferation of knowledge produced the demand for economic writing, which, when carried to its extreme, is algebra, but rejects the consequence that writing anticipates the nonphonetic, universal writing of mathematics.[31] Derrida contests interpreting the movement of writing in this manner, for pictography is no less universal than algebraic phonetics; the latter merely operates so as to repress the pictographic or hieroglyphic signifier only in order to master it more thoroughly: "one then believes one is protecting and exalting speech, one is only fascinated by the figure of the *techné*."[32] But for Derrida writing also functions as the death of desire, a death at the very origin of language, since writing is originarily supplementary with respect to speech and presence.[33] Furthermore, the effacement of speech in economical writing produces the greatest possible freedom for language and for life. If writing is present at the origin of language, language is no longer tied to the immediate presence of the spoken word, to the bodily manifestations of sound, to the moment in which something is said, and especially to the presence of the object in its identity. The effect of writing-speech (writing at the origin of language) appears to make metaphorical slippage the norm, and the presence of sound, body, and object are all already ameliorated.

Yet for Derrida there is another side to this that takes him far from Irigaray's pursuit, a side that overrides the supposed freedom of the supplementarity. Given the increasing economy of writing as it moves from pictograph to phonetics to nonphonetic algebraic universals (think of shorthand, the typewriter, and the computer), it is startlingly clear to Derrida that history becomes the history of knowledge or philosophy, that what is not writing-speech is nothing and has no name. This leads Derrida to conclude that the greatest possible freedom offered by writing-speech is the greatest possible mastery over not only language but also over life itself, over what is named and what is nothing.[34] More profoundly, although alphabetic writing maintains its tie to the voice and so can be *enjoyed* as that which brings the voice (of the loved one, of the actors, of oneself) back to oneself, when writing reaches the point where it breaks radically with phonetics, "it no longer responds to any desire or rather it signifies its death to desire," to that enjoyment of voices, bodies, breath.[35] Death lurks at the door of language. In Derrida's account, language may be the site of metaphorical slippage, but only insofar as it is first and foremost the privileged sphere of mastery and death. To have a language—to speak, to read, and to write—is already to witness death installing itself in the midst of life. This strikes me as a position not far removed from Freud's, a position that I will discuss later in this book. If Irigaray has encountered and recognized the function of mastery and death in granting metaphorical slippage to representation, or even if she has not, these are the things from which her critique turns away. Derrida has posted the warning; Irigaray searches for the escape route. This means that she does not merely repeat Derrida's gestures—she is not obsessed with death—but orients her thinking in a new direction.

It is my position that Irigaray is not content with metaphorical slippage, for if this were enough there would be no reason to pass over this flaw in representational modes in order to examine formalization more carefully. Instead, she takes up a serious although brief interrogation of Frege's mathematical logic because in it there has been a shift from attempting to establish clear definitions of terms to an analysis of relations among terms.[36] The shift, if fully played out on the logical level, would constitute not merely an elision of substance or subject but rather an entirely new orientation for thought. Initially, Irigaray hopes that the turn to Fregean functional analysis—in place of subject-predicate analysis—will work to the advantage of a theory of fluidity because she is interested in the shift from an analysis of terms (subjects or substances and predicates) to an analysis of relations among terms. Frege makes this shift in a manner that does not merely subvert relations to terms, since by his account, to state that a relation holds between two terms means that the characteristic of "relation-holding" is as much an objective property as any other.[37] When Aristotelian logic is replaced by functional logic, a sentence no longer expresses the relation between two separate terms but instead expresses a constant relation between two quantities without recourse to ontologically suspect entities such as substances or universals.[38] 'Socrates is mortal' can be restated as: 'If anything is Socrates, then it is mortal,' a statement that "is logically true in any interpretation in which everything in the interpretation is either not Socrates or is mortal."[39] Irigaray, I believe, approves of not having to have recourse to ontologically suspect entities such as substances or universals, because fluid mechanics cannot be posited in terms of substances or universals, since the latter are solids. If Irigaray's goal is to discover a logic in which there are no ontologically valid substances or universals, we cannot hypothesize that the slippage inherent to them that makes language ambiguous or nonsystematic is part of her plan. Marjorie Hass has elaborated this point by arguing that Irigaray opens the way to a systematic critique of modern symbolic logic when she posits negation as limit, not contradiction. That is, for symbolic logic negation is reversible because the negative is only a structural position; but as Hass points out, for Irigaray, according to the demands of sexual difference, one's sexual limits (or differences) cannot be overcome by adopting the structural position of the other sex; difference is not interchangeability, negation is not structural.[40] Something else must be operating.

Irigaray also announces that she is interested in the Fregean equivalence between numbers and concepts (if the logical extensions of two concepts are equal, then their numbers are equal). This may be because, according to Frege, equivalence begins with nonidentity; the number "0" belongs to a concept not identical to itself—that is, its logical extension is zero. It carves no objects out of the universe of numbers operating only as a functional symbol. The problem, however, is that if concepts start at "0," at a point where they have no logical extension at all, and "1" is defined as belonging to the concept identical with "0": "We need to ask . . . how it gets from zero to one."[41]

Irigaray concludes that functional analysis—as much as propositional logic—does not succeed (no doubt ever sought to succeed) in symbolizing the properties of real fluids (internal frictions, pressures, movements, their specific dynamics): "Considerations of pure mathematics have precluded the analysis of fluids except in terms of laminated planes, solenoid movements . . . spring-points, well-points, whirl-wind points, which have only an approximate relation to reality."[42] In this, claims Irigaray, what is silenced is the real: fluidity, which is the language women speak. For Irigaray, when woman speaks, she does not do so as *identical* with herself (as substance) or with any other standard, so she does not speak as a formal subject, but as fluid. From this point of view the problem of language is to know how to speak and how to listen to what is continuous, compressible, dilatable, viscous, conductible, diffusible, to what does not participate in good form(s).[43] The place to start, however, is not with perception, perhaps not yet even with a body, or not a body in the phenomenological sense. The place to start, according to Irigaray, is with the *affective.* "Be patient," she cautions, and "begin with what you feel, right here, right now."[44] This is not exactly the body. Affectivity, what you feel here and now, hardly adds up to any standard conception of the body. Perhaps in a certain sense there is never a body, insofar as woman is never complete. Irigaray suggests to women a "morpho-logic" appropriate to their bodies;[45] however, if morphology refers to structure or form and that structure or form is fluid, then bodies are not determinable; they are not essential. Bodies, beginning with affectivity, what is singularly here and now, are not genera. They do, however, provide fluid images of something real that we may begin to work with in life and in thought. Fluid structures are not lacking; they are part of an ontology of change. And, even accepting the fluid morphology of woman's image, women can and do embrace themselves as whole. How to account for this strange paradox?

It cannot be accounted for without disengaging from the projections and mastery of the concepts that determine women, the systems of oppositions that constitute women in terms of the idealizations conducive to formalized metasystems of language and logic. Following the logic of these systems, anything that exceeds formalization is rejected as "beneath or beyond the system currently in force."[46] So "woman"—but certainly not only "woman"—only makes sense when subject to the idealizing intervention of a system in which whatever pertains to her can only be characterized negatively. So the virgin is "not yet penetrated, possessed by them," and woman remains a "kind of reserve for their explorations, consummations, exploitations. The advent of their desire, not of ours."[47]

This query remains part of an ongoing critique of philosophy, but it never turns into a trap for Irigaray. That is, critique is not simply a negative or reactive response to the harsh reality of women's daily existence, nor is woman completely absent from philosophy. Even in western philosophy, woman can find herself, not necessarily in the theoretical constructs, but in its processes of production, the conditions and images that are foundational to all theory. Irigaray writes: "Woman ought to be able to find herself, among other things, through the images of herself already deposited in history and [in] the conditions of production of the work of man, and not on the basis of his work, his genealogy."[48] Regardless of how philosophy conceptualizes woman, woman lives as folds of affectivity, "our all touching itself . . . [wherein] top and bottom, inside and outside, in front and behind, above and below are not separated."[49] Such bodily differentiations are not a matter of a phenomenological bodily integration but rather of the affectivity of bodily connections that are not remote from one another, not out of touch, not one inside and another outside, conforming to the alien order of the degraded representation. When the woman's body is represented as without affectivity, not touching itself, woman is exiled to the outside where she can only imitate in face, form, and language each new power that comes to dominate her, each master she perceives. Yet even under the condition of being subject to mastery, it is possible to keep the "inside" silent and virginal; it is possible to keep the affective connections of the inside for herself.[50]

If, in spite of this subjection to mastery, women are women from the start, as Irigaray maintains, and women's holiness and profaneness have never been dependent on the logic of solids with its systems of linguistic and logical formalization, then the distinction between inside and outside loses its authority: "*Between us,* there's no rupture between virginal and nonvirginal. No event that makes us women. . . . Your/my body doesn't acquire its sex through an operation. Through the action of some power, function, or organ. . . . There is no need for an outside: the other already affects you. It is inseparable from you."[51] In short, the other is not just a perception of what is outside my bodily inhabitation, it is also an affection, an invitation to act. How does this operate?

The Origin of the Work of Art

We can see in the work of art the kind of conflict between how woman is conceptualized within philosophy and the auto-affection Irigaray describes. In her review of the New Museum of Contemporary Art's 1984–1985 exhibition "Difference: On Representation and Sexuality," critic Joanna Isaak writes: "Historically, the moment of feminism in the west has been defined in terms of access to individualism. . . . In the 'Difference' exhibitions, however, the aim is not to have women gain access to an individualism in decay, or one that perhaps never did exist. . . . Rather, the aim is to investigate the means by which the subject is produced and . . . to effect 'the ruin of representation.' "[52]

The phrase *the ruin of representation,* which I have adopted and reconfigured for this book, was coined by Michele Montrelay. In Montrelay's work it refers to the unconscious representation of castration, which, unlike conscious representation (which she claims is imaginary), "no longer refers to anything but the words which constitute it. Taken out of reality, it no longer refers to anything other than its form. . . . [T]he unconscious representation is only a text."[53] It may be the case that the difference here is less than Montrelay thinks; nonetheless, the point is that if such representation is ruined, its castrating effects disappear and the representation circulates "emptily." That I have chosen to pluck this phrase out of its Freudian-Lacanian context is in part due to the limits of what I hope to accomplish here, and in part due to my belief that the Freudian-Lacanian approach will not accomplish the ruin of representation after all. Let us see.

The work of American-born artist Mary Kelly that appears in the exhibition Isaak is commenting on is titled *Menacé* (French for "threatened" or "disturbed," and also calling up the surrealist painter Max

Ernst's *Two Children Threatened* [*Menacés*] *by a Nightingale*). *Menacé* is part of a larger project called *Interim,* though it also appeared in book form with other images and texts belonging to *Corpus* following exhibitions of the work. *Interim* as a whole project documents a series of Kelly's conversations with women in a variety of social settings, and groups them under the categories of body (*corpus*), money (*pecunia*), history (*historia*), and power (*potentia*).[54] The images and conversations of the category "body" that appear in the book version of *Interim* are related to the five passionate attitudes of the hysterical women photographed by Jean Charcot, Freud's Parisian mentor, who treated hysterics with hypnotism.

As Kelly has written, this placement of images gave her a chance to refer to the "founding" moment of Freud's theory, the moment of Charcot's creation of a certain kind of visibility that Freud could not or would not see, a moment usually lost in the frantic rethinking of Freud along purely discursive lines.[55] Charcot, who, Freud notes, described himself as a "*visuel,* a man who sees,"[56] emphasized the visible symptoms of nonorganic nervous disorders, creating a spectacle, a theater of hysterics that was, as Kelly's brief but insightful account claims, "a play dedicated to the production of unreason as a tangible event."[57] When the language-based analysis of Freud overtook the theater and spectacle of Charcot's creation, the visual took on a "compensatory value"; it was relegated to the realm of the "unrepresentable, the monstrous, even the sublime."[58] These are the terms of the debate that interest me. When images become monstrous, even sublime, then something is happening that cannot be reduced to organic representation.

Even Charcot, however, falls prey to social norms, for he never photographed male hysterics, and the passionate attitudes are strictly reserved for young women. Even more interesting, from the point of view of norms, is the contrived nature of Charcot's hysterics, which Kelly does not mention but which makes her singular images even more striking. In the first place, according to Pierre Marie, a colleague at the Salpêtrière clinic, many of the hysterics' symptoms came from their being housed with epileptics: "The results of such promiscuity could not fail to be noticed. While the fits of the unfortunate epileptics were not in any way modified, it was quite different as far as the hysteric fits were concerned."[59] The hysterics were reportedly adept at embellishing their performances of the major hysteric crises, which it turns out were quite artificial. The hysterical symptoms were enactments or performances of the seizures suffered by the epileptics whom the hysterical patients helped care for. Charcot recognized the role of emotion and imagination in hysteria, so as a cure he recommended isolation of the patients from one another and from their families as well as "persuasion reinforced by physical therapy and electrotherapy."[60] Because he was able to produce hysterical symptoms through hypnotic suggestion, the emotional and imaginative elements, the "intentional malingering," the simulation by which means patients exaggerate symptoms or create imaginary symptoms, became definitive of hysteria for Charcot.[61]

So Charcot's own photographic images of hysterics were profoundly influenced by his patients' contacts with epileptics. What relation do Charcot's photographs bear to the contemporary advertising Kelly analyzes, advertising that makes full use of images of women "posed in an infinite variety of passionate attitudes," advertising whose size and shape she repeats in the four feet by three feet dimensions of her own bus-stop billboard works of art whose images also repeat the passionate attitudes of Charcot's images?[62] If the original impetus for many of these advertising poses can be located in the images of Charcot's patients' exaggerations of the symptoms of epileptics, the entire production of hysteria in visual terms has been mediated by this nervous disorder characterized by convulsions, seizures, and unconsciousness. Yet precisely these characteristics have been attributed to women as visual representatives of otherwise invisible passions.

In this way, Kelly writes, through a creative repetition in her own artwork of hysterical bodies and passionate poses in advertising (poses that are a creative repetition of epileptic bodies), an entire network of unrepresentable, monstrous, and even sublime signs and senses gets produced. The qualities that make such a presentation sublime will be discussed in a later chapter of this book. For now, we can see that it makes sense that Kelly does not locate her own reading of hysteria with that of Freud or Lacan, both of whom shift hysteria away from a strict tie to feminine repressed sexuality to a generalized hysterical subject or to the hystericization of discourse itself. She is more interested in what Luce Irigaray has to say, for it is more closely tied to the cultural identification of hysteria with Charcot's photographs of women in passionate poses. For Irigaray, the hysteric (woman) founds this discourse and sustains it as the exchange between male theorists, even as she is excluded from it.[63] The tactic here is for the woman to take what had been marginalized by psychoanalysis and make it central. Images of the kind Kelly produces do this in a powerful and immediate way.

Kelly conceives of the networks she creates as primarily historical, but I would say they are both more particular and more abstract than that. For as she notes, there are many poses; none is representative, each is specific to "this" particular woman and, in Kelly's work, to "this" particular image: her leather jacket, her boots, her nightgown, her white dress. "There is not *one* body, there are many"; some of these bodies are human flesh, some are leather jackets.[64] And so she opens up many kinds of connections involving the passionate attitudes: bodies in commercial advertising, the covers of romance novels and the passions of their discourse, and even the passion of a woman of the *école freudienne,* scapegoated, branded heretical, driven out on a line of flight.[65]

In *Menacé,* Kelly's own black leather jacket casts a dark shadow on a pinkish ground. It faces a text, one of the many conversations Kelly participated in and compiled for this process, this ongoing event. The conversations are themselves patterns constituting thought and speech, the way we talk casually to one another in sudden intensities, our energy accelerating and slowing, building and falling: "'You look great,' she says kissing me on both cheeks, 'haven't changed at all,' then Anne mocks us, but affectionately, 'well preserved.' She smiles. We laugh. I am content."[66] Amazingly, these words and images have been read negatively, as representations of women trapped by sexism and misogyny. Joan Copjec, for example, takes them to be "images of hysterical women, images of dysfunction in the representation of drives, images which menace knowledge, confusing categories of real and unreal illness."[67] Yet, given Irigaray's advice, it seems to me that they can be read in terms of a more revolutionary ruin of representation, and not as a series of images and texts in which established verbal and/or visual codes are fragmented, limiting representation or producing a confusion of real and unreal. Such a reading implies a resentment concerning the absent plenum or presence, a resentment that the world should be fully present but is not. By contrast, another use of these images and statements finds, even in their pathos, a sudden intensity, an accumulation of qualities followed by something like their release, in short, life given in the mobile images of the existential dimension, not a plenum, but a site of events; not an absence, but the intensification of images, the collapse of representation as generalization so as to make room for the emergence of this and that image, this and that particular field of light, the evidence of a life, the events of art.

In the same exhibition, the work of artist Victor Burgin was roundly condemned for being a "representation" of women that comes across as fetishism. Burgin is called to task for "remaining the man behind the camera who interjects himself occasionally in a scene."[68] Burgin's photographic remake of Eduard Manet's *Olympia* (1982) and a detail from his *Zoo* (1978) (interestingly enough, this was reproduced in all the reviews as well as in the catalogue) are particularly subject to scathing attacks. The former image is largely self-explanatory; the latter, described as "reconstituted woman-as-sexy-animal scenes" juxtaposed with quotations from Michel Foucault's *Discipline and Punish,* seems to be an obsessive reduplication of oppression, and neither image, in the critics' eyes, goes far enough toward questioning, let alone deconstructing, the pornographic

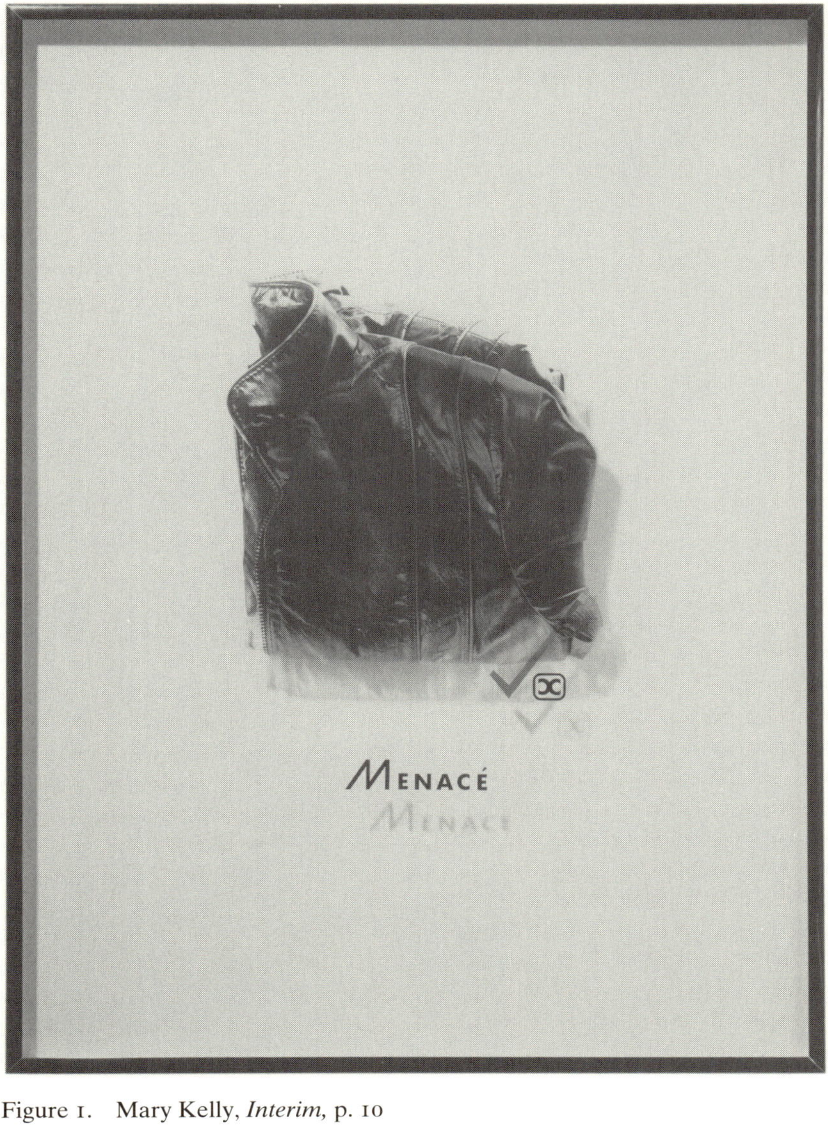

Figure 1. Mary Kelly, *Interim,* p. 10

Figure 2. Mary Kelly, *Interim,* p. 11

poses they imitate.[69] A certain question however, lingers unformulated: Under the circumstances, and given the nature and organization of representation itself, could such an image ever serve to do more than redisplay the detachment of even the sympathetic male observer in his regime of disembodied image-making?

In his written work, Burgin attempts something other than deconstruction of the representational image—that is, the image as overdetermined by the subject-object organization of signs, that organization championed by male artists and philosophers insofar as it produces the beautiful. In his essay "Geometry and Abjection," Burgin points to the "reductive and simplistic equation of looking with objectification" that underlies our current reception and recognition of images.[70] The problem with this "way of seeing," notes Burgin, is that it is drawn from Euclidean physiological optics and cannot adequately describe the changed apprehension of space that corresponds to postmodern life. Euclidean geometry, Burgin tells us, was based on visual evidence, on what could be seen rather than on technical or even practical considerations. Thus, it appeals to classical Greek cosmological models that emerged forcefully in the Middle Ages as the scene of human action: a sphere with a center and a circumference where each being was assigned a place preordained by God.[71] In Aristotle's version, each body is located in a continuum of actual and potential places that constitute space. And even though Newton later conceived of space as absolute, similar, and immovable, the Aristotelian conception remained as a representation of social and/or political localizations within an absolute space. As such, for humanist-derived political philosophy, human beings come to rest, with varied privilege, within social space in accordance with their inherent social and/or natural qualities.[72] In spite of Burgin's plea that space has a history, the Renaissance seems to have first established and contemporary culture continues to maintain a system of space in which socially inscribed human beings are deployed in a more or less uniform space-in-itself.

Burgin is interested in delimiting the history of space, and he does so in terms that historians have created. Thus he claims that premodern space is organized by location; modern space by Euclid's infinite, extensible, boundless geometry; early modern space by the humanist subject; late modern space by industrial capitalism's imperative to disperse, displace, and disseminate; and postmodern space by monetary capitalism's imploding and infolding. In spite of this history, he finds that "psychoanalytically inspired theories of representation have tended to remain faithful to the Euclidean, geometrical-optical metaphors of the modern period, organized in terms of a model, I might add, also invoked by the liberal political theory of the individual.[73] The Italian Renaissance chose to conceive of the picture plane by combining the medieval notion that space has a center (now occupied by the mercantile man who wanders the globe) with Euclidean optics, according to which seeing is produced in a "cone of vision" that the picture plane intersects.[74]

Feminist film theory has, of course, revitalized the cone of vision model to theorize the path of light emanating from the camera's eye that is thrown up against the flat plane of the screen as it intersects the cone. The cone of vision model, however, insofar as it is adopted from the Renaissance, operates to deny the key feature of Burgin's "postmodern" space: the notion that space is not geographical but governed by the electronic speed of the computer and the video. Having admitted that theorizers of space do not seem to adhere to the space of their history, I wonder how Burgin can possibly maintain that space has a history at all except in the purest, most positivist scientific sense. Did he think that when we look at the image of naked women he photographed in *Zoo* we would see postmodern space, imploding and infolding space that follows the path of monetary capitalism? Burgin's failure here and, by contrast, Mary Kelly's success, can be understood, from one point of view, as an effect of the recognition of or failure to recognize sexual difference, but there may be much more at stake in this.

Moira Gatens has argued, and I would agree with her, that at the very least, sexual politics demands the recognition of sexual difference as necessary to the rethinking of women's status and role in philosophy and society. Without a theory of sexual difference, it would be all too easy to pretend that "women's bodies and the representation and control of women's bodies were not a crucial stake in these [political] struggles."[75] Conceptualizing sexual difference is an important and politically necessary way to approach fluidity. Conceptualization of sexual difference necessitates a revolution in thought and ethics that involves a reinterpretation of "everything" concerning the relations between subject and discourse, subject and world, subject and the cosmic, the microcosm and the macrocosm.[76] And although there is a problem getting language to express sexual difference, a problem apparently exacerbated by logic, this may be because there are factors that Irigaray posits as conditions even of logic and language: "To think and live through this difference we must reconsider the whole problematic of *space and time*."[77] In cosmogony and philosophy, the division of the universe into space and time is also the site of the introduction of sexual difference. In western creation myths the gods begin by creating space. The elements are separated into earth, air, fire, and water. Time is introduced only secondarily to serve space, but its origin is in God. God is time, time is God, who exteriorizes himself in the activity of creating space. With respect to ontology or metaphysics, the subject reenacts and takes up the activity of temporalizing, ordering the exterior space of objects. Such is the case with Kant, who makes temporality the interiority of the subject and space its exteriority. And with respect to sexual difference, the masculine is *experienced* as time, the feminine is *experienced* as space.[78] But in relation to what is this gendered experience generated?

Reconsidering Space and Time

I want to proceed by examining Merleau-Ponty's phenomenological account of space and time in order to begin to answer this question. It will not be my goal here to provide a thorough critical account of Merleau-Ponty's bias with regard to women, nor do I seek to defend him from such a critique. My point is to be found elsewhere. Although historical, social, and political factors play the foremost roles in determining to what extent a thinker works from the point of view of a privileged position with regard to what have been called subjugated or minority positions, those lacking in the power to determine what constitutes truth and knowledge, what appeals to me as critical is the hierarchical and hegemonic organization of thought that makes privilege possible.[79] It is this that I will look for in Merleau-Ponty's accounts. In Merleau-Ponty's famous descriptions of space and time we discover that he, like Irigaray, begins by referring to Kant on the same point regarding the nature of temporality. Merleau-Ponty embellishes his argument, noting that Kant attempted a strict delineation between space as the form of external experience and the things in it; thus space is a kind of power or force that enables things or objects to be connected.[80] Unreflectively, living among things, we regard space as the setting or common attribute of objects. But reflectively, we seek the source, which means we seek the subject underlying these relationships, sustaining them. The first conception Merleau-Ponty characterizes as physical space, while the second is a homogeneous, pure position.[81] These spaces account for unreflective life and reflective life, respectively—though what this "physical space" may be is not entirely clear. Merleau-Ponty only describes it as the perception of things in concrete relations, perhaps a kind of naive and uninterested mode of existence. But if, as Merleau-Ponty suggests, we consider neither the perception of things in space nor the conception of space as a system of unification, but instead focus on something else (which he calls the primacy of perception) we may uncover a third spatiality.

In an experiment that produces spatial inversion by means of glasses that invert retinal images, "the whole landscape at first appears unreal and upside down."[82] At the end of six days or so, particularly when the "body" is active, the landscape appears normal, though right has become left and left become right and sound cannot be located unless its source is within the field of vision. Merleau-Ponty accounts for this with the presumption of an absolute within the sphere of the relative, a "space" that survives even this extreme disorganization. Traditional Intellectualist accounts assert that up and down are relative positions, but this fails to make sense of the experience of something being "upside-down," since one cannot stand outside of the relativist position to have an actual perception of space. Empiricist accounts are no more helpful, for although they recognize the validity of perception, they go too far in taking it to be the perception of a real space and real objects representing their orientation in the world; thus, the world would have to have altered in six days. For Merleau-Ponty, there must exist a system of possible actions and a virtual body whose place is defined according to its task and situation, such that this body with its systemic possibilities can even take over for the actual body when the things situated around the body assert a direct power over it.[83]

But there is more to it than this. For, Merleau-Ponty continues, if we happen to look at someone lying down on a bed from the head of the bed for a long while, at least past the point where we think about going around to the bottom to see a "normal" face, we begin to see something unnatural, even terrifying. What makes the expression of this face so frightful is in part due to how we generally perceive faces, but mostly due to what for Merleau-Ponty is a fact: "To invert an object is to deprive it of its significance."[84] To this we need to add: its significance for perception, a system of possible actions and a virtual body whose place is defined according to its task and situation. Merleau-Ponty's own description of this horror is fascinating: "The face takes on an utterly unnatural aspect [*devient monstrueux*], its expressions become terrifying, and the eyelashes and eyebrows assume an air of materiality such as I have never seen in them. . . . [I]n front of me I have a pointed, hairless head with a red, teeth-filled orifice in the forehead and, where the mouth ought to be, two moving orbs edged with glistening hairs and underlined with stiff brushes."[85] What terrifies is the bizarre materiality of the unnatural aspect. The unnatural position of the face, Merleau-Ponty believes, has the effect of depriving its features of significance in a way that ordinary perception never does.

Although much has been said about Merleau-Ponty's philosophy of ambiguity—that is, that the system of significations, insofar as it is embodied, remains ambiguous—nonetheless, Merleau-Ponty very clearly posits for that body a system of possible actions, outside of which the experience of the unnatural and designified materialization of the face terrifies. The face is given to us, by Merleau-Ponty's account, in the space of a gaze that does not correct the upside-down image beyond a certain point, introducing terror when recognition fails: "My gaze, which moves over the face, and in doing so favors certain directions, does not recognize the face unless it comes up against its details in a certain *irreversible* order, and that the very significance of the object—here the face and its expressions—must be linked to its orientation."[86] There is little indication here that as living beings we are open and available to a multiplicity of significances, since what is "possible" is already determined by the "actual" field of perception. The subject of perception can only recognize and be conscious of the face as an *object* when perceiving the "general direction" of the face, which is not a contingent characteristic. As I will argue, this is perception already severed from temporalization, for what distinguishes the face as an objective reality is that it is already detached, like a picture, represented in isolation from other images. Temporal flow, what precedes and follows, has been suppressed insofar as the living perceptual being has no interest in it, but only in the "object."[87]

So when Merleau-Ponty concludes that space, in this sense, is neither a container nor a unifying activity but an open field of possibilities, there are at least two limits to this conception—one that Merleau-Ponty may have been aware of and one that he could not have known. The first comes from Henri Bergson and the second from Irigaray. For Bergson, Merleau-Ponty's primacy of perception is already spatial because it presumes exactly what Bergson thinks the work of philosophy should uncover: the utilitarian work of the mind, the refracting of pure duration into space that creates a separation between us and our own psychic states. For Bergson, perception divides up matter in a manner entirely subservient to our needs, to the actions we will take; thus, perception is in need of continual revision because the representation it provides us with is so provisional, so much a matter of the needs and interests of a particular situation. That is, when we assume that an inverted face is without significance, that a face that is inverted offers us nothing but horror, this is because we imagine that our perception is unrelated to our psychic states and that perception is only a matter for possible action.

In disregarding the separation he has imposed between the spatial perception of the face and the interests of the subject, Merleau-Ponty is not as distant from Kant as he would like to be. To avoid this fate, one cannot assume in advance the spatiality of the body and of the face, what is normal and what is horrifying; categories of thought would have to be engendered, generated by following the introduction of extension into our living existence.[88] Bergson argues that if we follow out the genesis of our categories of thinking, "[e]xtensity [not space] is the most salient quality of perception. It is in consolidating it and subdividing it by means of an abstract space, stretched by us beneath it for the needs of action that we constitute the composite and infinitely divisible extension."[89]

Thus our so-called perception of space is a conception that conceals the immediate knowledge we have of extensity.

The appeal to Bergson might seem arbitrary except for a trait that Bergson shares with Irigaray, which I will discuss below, although before we proceed, it will help to lay out the second limitation. The second limitation comes from Irigaray. If femininity is not to be defined as a container and masculinity is not to be identified with the unifying activity that also determines time, then even while Merleau-Ponty seeks to make a start on the project of a new perception of space and time, there is much more to be done. Merleau-Ponty's insistence upon clear perception and assured action in oriented space as well as his certainty that being is synonymous with being situated, while freeing him from Intellectualist and Empiricist presumptions, nonetheless leads me to ask: *Who* is thus situated and what kind of organization makes this situation possible? What are the temporal and spatial presuppositions of this situated being?

With regard to the question of "who," Iris Young demonstrates that contemporary feminine bodily comportment exhibits a great deal of tension, if not contradiction, between Merleau-Ponty's account of spatial experience and being an object. Feminine motility in women (more than girls) is often characterized by "ambiguous transcendence," such as not engaging the whole body in physical tasks; "inhibited intentionality," such as waiting for and then merely reacting to an oncoming ball in games; as well as a "discontinuous unity" with their surroundings, such as hesitating before leaping a ditch in order to measure the potential bodily harm of a miss. If the world is understood phenomenologically as a system of bodily possibilities, too often women take their own bodies to be the object of action and not the originator of acts within that system.[90] Such determinations, Young stresses, have to be seen as part of women's social situatedness, their oppression in society; thus nothing about these descriptions is necessary, let alone desirable. Girls and women, she argues, must be given the opportunity to fully engage their bodily capacities as well as to develop specific bodily skills. I agree with Young that there is nothing necessary to women and girls about their social situatedness, yet I think that there is still some kind of determination at work that is more than social contingency. I would argue that within this same structure, it is not only women who fail to see themselves as the originators of acts within a system of bodily possibilities. The poor and minorities also seem to have become socially situated in the same kind of structure.

In his book *The Undeserving Poor: From the War on Poverty to the War on Welfare,* Michael Katz describes the "problem" of black unemployment and asks what specific factors are operating in our perceptions of this problem. Not surprisingly, a failure that I would attribute to spatialization figures among the factors relating to the unemployment of black youth. Like women, black youths tend to take their own bodies to be the objects of action, not the originators of acts within the social and economic system. Black youths want the same possibilities for action as whites, but since they confront the economic system from the point of view of what would be for whites its "unnatural aspect," that is, inverted to the point where the low-paying, dead-end jobs available to blacks are not even within the range of perceptibility to whites within that system (except as horrors), the spatial experience of black youths is declared to be invalid. Like women, black underemployed youths do not perceive space in terms of an already constituted set of possibilities. The right-side-up experience of the good job in an interesting field with a future is a spatiality by and large denied to black youths, and *the spatiality of their own experience is judged unnatural and nonsensical.*[91] What is astonishing, Katz comments, is that we know very little about how poor people throughout the history of the United States have actually survived from day to day. Nor is it certain what kinds of complex, intersecting networks of family, neighbors, and institutions providing labor, food, and housing have supported the poor, especially since so many of these networks have disappeared with urban redevelopment and the demise of local inner-city businesses.[92]

Even though Irigaray continues to examine how this kind of judgment (that certain points of view are nonsense) is applied to women exclusively from the point of view of her demand for sexual difference on an ontological level, much can be gained by following out her arguments. For Irigaray, breaking down the traditional assumptions about femininity, masculinity, space, and time calls for disrupting precisely the kind of assumptions Merleau-Ponty makes about situated being. To do this, Irigaray calls for a transformation of the relation of matter to form and the *interval* between them, in which interval operates the concepts of power, act, force, energy, and desire. Irigaray argues that there has to be a change in the interval, which she identifies as relations of nearness and distance between subject and object, and thus also a change in the economy of desire, a different relation between man and gods, man and man, and man and woman.[93] That is, in calling on the interval and conceptualizing it as the moment in which all traditional metaphysical relations are transformed—not only matter and form but also power, act, force, energy, and desire—Irigaray must recognize, even though she does not usually posit this as an aspect of sexual difference, that other relations than those between man and woman are at stake here, too, and that the interval is a crucial element in transforming situated spatiality in a manner that *exceeds* the body and even a morphology of the body.

With the concept of the interval Bergson is drawn backward, as it were, into Irigaray's analysis of phenomenology. Merleau-Ponty has argued for action on the basis of possibilities inherent in bodily situatedness. However, for Bergson, living beings and the actions of living beings are not a matter of realizing one of several possibilities, for what is a possibility? We conceive of it, according to Bergson, as something less than what is real, for the possibility of things appears to precede their existence, and so they could be thought of before coming to be.[94] However, it is only because we insist upon the representation of reality, the isolated perception of what interests us, that we come to such a conclusion. Bergson recounts that toward the end of World War I he was asked about the future possible directions of literature following the war. He replied with some irritation that if he knew the great literature of the future, he would be writing it! Were we to consider the totality of concrete reality and the world of life, including that of the temporal flow of what Bergson calls duration, then we would discover that "the possible is only the real with the addition of an act of mind which throws its image back into the past, once it has been enacted"; thus, at most the literature of the future *will have been possible,* retroactively; when something is already created, and only then, does its possibility arise.[95]

Reality, Bergson insists, is created as unforeseen and absolutely new, such that one can never speak of the actualization of possibilities but only of the actualization through differentiation of the virtual, that is, the real but unactualized multiplicity. If we find this unacceptable or inconceivable, it is only because we do not understand how the poor, women, and other minorities have been represented within a framework that judges their experience to be nonsense rather than attempting to make sense of it from the point of view of becoming. Like Merleau-Ponty, we imagine that perception is already severed from temporalization; that the perceptual object is already detached, like a picture, represented in isolation from other images; and that temporal flow, what precedes and follows, has been suppressed insofar as the living perceptual being has no interest in it, but only in the object and the actions it dictates. Having said this, it is clear that a number of elements have entered the picture, among them Bergson's conception of creation—a concept that in the coming chapters will be clarified as another way of making sense of becoming. Although a full account of these concepts will be offered in these later chapters, I would like to engage in a preliminary exposition of some of these key ideas in relation to Irigaray and Merleau-Ponty so as to elaborate the role of the interval and its difference from Merleau-Ponty's phenomenology.

Interval

Having argued that possibility is a concept determined in advance by what is actual, Bergson turns to an elucidation of the moment of unactualized multiplicity. Such a moment arises in what Bergson calls the "interval" between a received stimulus and an executed movement—that is, in the interval of duration between excitation and reaction. By Bergson's account, the interval is the moment between two movements: (1) a stimulus received, and (2) a movement executed in response to the call for action of the stimulus; thus the interval lies between excitation and reaction. This moment takes place in the intersection of matter and memory and in this context can be called recollection. As the intersection between two contrary movements, recollections must be capable of two simultaneous motions, two kinds of becoming. There is a becoming that orients itself toward what Irigaray refers to as the outside—that is, toward matter, perception, and objects—and thus toward the spatialized representation of objects. Additionally, there is a becoming that orients itself in accordance with memory, recollection, and the subject—that is, in accordance with affectivity.[96] On one line of becoming, the affective temporality (called a subject) perceives, that is, pays attention only to what interests it in the moment of the interval. On the second line, the subject becomes conscious of a recollection as an image that corresponds to its perception and that is adopted by that subject according to its interests. According to Bergson, each recollection or interval is actualized not as its own present, but as freedom, as a new present, as a moment of creation. Thus, the interval is the movement between affective temporality and active extensionality, a new conception of space and time that radically reconstitutes relations of nearness and distance between subject and object, and thus institutes a change in the economy of desire, a different relation between man and gods, man and man, and man and woman. As such, the "interval" between perception and memory, intelligence and social life, is decisive for humans, according to both Irigaray and Bergson. And if sexual difference is to matter on an ontological level, it has to be conceived of in relation to the interval.

Regarding this, Merleau-Ponty appears to have little to say. Sexuality, he asserts, must lie in relations and attitudes and not in biology or in anatomical or physiological conditions. Yet he maintains that frigidity is always a refusal—of orgasm, of femininity, of sexuality—that in turn is a rejection of the sexual partner and "his" destiny—as if femininity were in service to "his" destiny.[97] There is certainly no mention of "her" destiny or of the interval in which she acts. There is no consideration at all of Irigaray's dismay over formulas like Merleau-Ponty's in which "woman always tends *toward* without any return to herself as the place where something positive can be elaborated. In terms of contemporary physics, it could be said that she remains on the side of the electron [a negative charge], with all that this implies for her, for man, and for any encounter between them."[98] What is missing is her own affective temporality and thus the kind of active extensity that would exclude woman's disintegration and decomposition and would make everything possible: speech, promises, alliances.

In fact, it is clear that in Merleau-Ponty's chapter titled "The Body in Its Sexual Being," the body in question is the body of a man, perhaps even inscribed with the name of the author of the *Phenomenology of Perception.* Merleau-Ponty writes: "Insofar as a man's sexual history provides a key to his life, it is because in his sexuality is projected his manner of being towards the world, that is towards time and other men."[99] Judith Butler has pointed out that at least Merleau-Ponty does not reduce sexuality to a mode of existence,[100] nor does he reduce sexuality to organs and desire to instinct so that all existence could only be made sense of through its sexual substructure. And yet, let us examine Merleau-Ponty's account of destiny: for an embodied being whose place is defined according to a system of possible actions, an open field of corporeal possibilities, and thus a space that survives even the disorganization of appearances, a manner of being is projected. This manner of being pivots to temporality from spatiality, from what Bergson would call the representation of isolated objects that are perceived solely in accordance with spatial corporeality's interests and cut off entirely from the temporal flow of becoming—that is, from duration—so as to artificially derive living affective temporality from space, something that Bergson avows cannot be done.

So it is no wonder that in Merleau-Ponty's analysis of a young woman's hysteria, she is perceived as having no time of her own, and thus no place, no envelope. The young woman's mother forbids her to see the man she loves. She stops eating, sleeping, and talking. She enacts an oral fixation that manifests itself as a refusal of communal existence. She breaks with life, she is unable to "swallow" food, unable to swallow her mother's dictum.[101] Nothing positive, nothing creative is attributed to her. There is no insight that perhaps this action was chosen in the interval between recollection and perception, or that it could emerge from the intersection of mind and matter. She is understood to have surrendered to the negative that she "is," and is thereby shut off from her own time, her own future, as well as the outside. If she is discussed at all, it is only through the representation of her as an object from the point of view of the interests of the perceiver.

In fact, it is not simply the young woman who is subject to this kind of mental or psychological alienation that manifests itself in a return to mute stasis. For Merleau-Ponty, all psychological disturbances are explained by means of this spatial paradigm. Nor can he generate affective becoming out of static spatiality. Cut off from the future, from time, such a situation "sets bounds . . . to the immediately available mental field . . . [and] what collapses is the whole field of possibilities."[102] Merleau-Ponty provides numerous descriptions of this collapse into muteness: "when the hysterical fit has reached its climax . . . even if the subject plunges into it as a place of refuge . . . with every minute that passes, freedom is depreciated and becomes less probable."[103] Psychological disturbances represent "a refusal of the future torn from the transitive nature of 'inner phenomena,' generalized, consummated, transformed into de facto situations."[104] And the patient-victim's own body participates in this double-cross; the body transforms the inner phenomena, the temporal delineations, into a de facto situation. In and of itself, the body-matter is factualized even if not fully reified. It is without act, interval, energy, or desire; it is mute.

Traditionally, Irigaray argues, woman represents a sense of place for man. She becomes a thing and she is also used as a kind of envelope to help man set limits to things. In Aristotle Irigaray finds the following: "for the natural substance of the menstrual fluid is to be classed as 'prime matter' (*proto hyle*)."[105] Although for Aristotle each living being finds its specificity in the form given to it by the male parent, the first matter, the body of the mother, and the "becoming-flesh" within the body of the mother have no form. Any such "bodilyness . . . has no movement of its own, has yet to divide up time or space, has, in point of fact, no way of measuring the container or the surrounding world or the content or relations among all these," and even its elements are not defined; same and other have not yet been separated out.[106] It is boundless, eternal, and perfect. The activity of the form located in the being of the father is constituted as plenitude in action so as to require no movement, no extension that might somehow entail its bodily relation to mother and matter.[107] The first matter, although radically lacking all power or *logos,* radically mute, nonetheless serves as the absolutely necessary and thus all-powerful soil upon which *logos* grows.[108] This is why Irigaray thinks it is dangerous for there to be no third term—no interval, act, force, or desire enveloping temporality, matter, and form, a limitation of matter from within matter—that can be transposed into a formalization of the mode of expression.

As it stands in philosophy, woman's own development has only been named by an other who possesses a *logos,* an other to whom mother-matter (woman perceived from the outside) affords the means to realize "his" form in time. The problem, for Irigaray, is that given this conceptualization, "theoretically there would be no such thing as a woman."[109]

For, following Bergson's critique, we find ourselves once again at the point where philosophy imagines that matter is cut up along the lines of action, yet it is simply deducing a priori the categories of thought. In this schema, if woman can be pointed to or differentiated (theoretically), she is simply in the gap between beings, that from which beings have taken care to detach and separate themselves through the realization of their form.[110] In this sense, Irigaray writes, if woman exists at all, she undoes the work of the philosopher by distinguishing herself from both the envelope and the thing. But remembering that woman can and ought to rediscover herself precisely in the images of herself in history and in the conditions of the production of philosophy, remembering that woman can be reborn from the traces of culture and works produced by the other, we can follow Irigaray in finding the place of the woman in the gap, the so-called void, wherein she has been placed, a place that is, of course, no place, insofar as she serves as the unrecognized foundation for the other who cannot separate himself. It is in this gap that she would create her sexual difference, her salvation on an intellectual level, "distinguishing herself from both the envelope and the thing, ceaselessly creating there some interval, play, something in motion and un-limited which disturbs his perspective, his world, and his/its limits."[111] She produces a complete change in our conception of space and time.

This is the interval. This power in the sense of act is desire, what Bergson calls "life," the necessities of living, that is, acting. The interval is a dynamic force whose form changes and so cannot be predicted. Such a dynamic force carries its own formalization along with it, a dynamic potential that would replace the separation between negatively charged matter with no place of its own and positively charged form that acts by refusing the positing of space as the container within which one acts. The interval is a double-desire. In the history of philosophy, the positive and negative poles have, according to Irigaray, divided themselves between the two sexes "instead of establishing a chiasmus or a double loop in which each can go toward the other and come back to itself."[112] Each side of the loop is both positively and negatively charged. If positive and negative elements are not chiasmatic, one remains in motion and has no place of its own and the other will always serve as the pole of attraction.

It is, of course, Merleau-Ponty who introduces the notion of the *chiasm* in *The Visible and the Invisible,* though he previously spoke of *carrefours,* the intersection, and of doubled crossings over. Merleau-Ponty calls forth this conceptualization not in the context of the body and its sexual being but in that of the intertwining of visibility and tangibility.[113] He writes, "There is a double and crossed situating of the visible in the tangible and the tangible in the visible; the two maps are complete and yet they do not merge into one. The two parts are total and they are not superposable."[114] *Chiasm* is also the relation between or the orientation of seer and the seen, touching and being touched, such that these lived experiences are no longer taken to be negative and positive poles. Instead, a seer is also looked at by the things she sees; the toucher feels herself being touched by things. To accomplish this, Merleau-Ponty posits flesh, a thickness, between or among seer and seen, and a reversal: seer becomes seen, seen becomes seer. "It [flesh] is their means of communication."[115] What is crucial is that flesh does not simply unify. The body is not a thing but is *sensible* for itself. The body is not an envelope but a connective tissue. But, as Merleau-Ponty notes, the problem is how the body can be thought.

I would say that Merleau-Ponty's formulation of the question is caught up in the spatialization of the body that I have critiqued, a spatialization that materializes the body to the point of objectifying it. The problem could be expressed differently: How can a discourse emanate from each bodily point of view, how can each one speak and act? Merleau-Ponty is right that we need to reexamine the *cogito.* There must be a gap or interval in which a choice is made and action taken, in which their relation to one another is chiasmatic. These contractions of time in memory and their commensurate expansions into the world meet and intertwine to the point of being, at times, indistinguishable, even while remaining particular in themselves and retaining their own integrity.

Perhaps Merleau-Ponty is right to say that seeing and being seen, touching and being touched, are like two mirrors facing one another, an infinite series of images set in one another, a couple more real than either. Yet this description remains too much from the point of view of an original subject. Even Merleau-Ponty notes that the mirrors must be slightly decentered with regard to one another, yet, according to Hubert Damisch, two mirrors guarantee nothing but more perfect perspectival representation.[116] What is needed is a schema according to which the seer is not just being-seen, the seer is the sight from the point of view of other seers, other worlds: sexual difference, salvation on an intellectual level. This is the gap, the necessary interval, the third thing between woman and man. In this sense, the *chiasm* is not narcissism, as Merleau-Ponty suggests, for that comes too close to eliminating difference, unless narcissism can be radically refigured as something creative.

Language at the origin is the residue that Irigaray insists upon. The sexual act consists not in the consummation of space by time, its total division and subjection to control. Since woman and man cannot stand in for one another, since they are incommensurable (each one being but one angle of the *chiasm*), woman and man differ. The gap between them, sexual difference, which is not simply a void, does not and cannot seize something as its object, but it is the site of life and language. That we do not yet have such a conception of sexual difference is evident even as we look for its "strange advent." As Irigaray writes: "But, in order for an ethics of sexual difference to come into being, we must constitute a possible place for each sex, body, and flesh to inhabit. Which presupposes a memory of the past, a hope for the future, memory bridging the present and disconcerting the mirror symmetry that annihilates the difference of identity."[117] Sexual difference remains in reserve, but, at least with a conception of the interval as positive, creative act, such a point of view can be generated as a moment of freedom. Yet as we will see, even the interval as positive and creative act will require another level of support. Not just the interval, not just becoming, but also the being of becoming will have to be thought in order to generate the non-sense of multiple perspectives and so to realize freedom.

4
Bergson, Matter, and Memory

Order-Words, Common Language

In *Bergsonism,* Deleuze organizes his reading of Bergson around the constitution of the rules of what he calls Bergson's strict method. First, he argues, no problem can be properly resolved, for Bergson, unless it has been properly stated. In philosophy, but also in the rest of social life, problems come to us in the form of ready-made language. Language transmits the society's "order-words" and, in them, the ready-made problems that society seeks to force us to solve.[1] So there is a sense in which in order to even begin to address the issues of the first three chapters—issues surrounding the authority of representation—we must first ask if the problems raised are the right problems or if they are unresolvable in the language in which they are posed and have to be thoroughly reconceived. How do we go about achieving this? My approach to Deleuze-Bergsonian problematics does not call for a full account of Deleuze's theory of semiotic systems; nevertheless, a brief discussion may be of use in clarifying these initial inquiries.[2] In *A Thousand Plateaus,* Deleuze and Félix Guattari reject the claims of structural linguistics, including any claims that valorize language above all other semiotic systems. Their efforts are directed toward the creation of a transformational semiotic. Thus, they maintain that language is *not* informational and communicational, that language is not a synchronic set of constants, that there are no universals in language constituting it as a homogeneous system, and finally, that there is no standard or major language. The theory of order-words arises largely out of the first claim. "The elementary unit of language is the order-word"; thus, so-called information is only the "strict minimum necessary for the emission, transmission and observation of orders as commands"—that is, what is transmitted is simply what has first been heard, making of language in its most elementary form nothing more than indirect discourse.[3] The schoolteacher, they argue, neither gives students information nor communicates with them; rather, her job is to "insign," to impose on her students semiotic coordinates—that is, "she gives orders and gives order, she commands because every order-word arises only in terms of previous orders."[4]

Incorporating J.L. Austin and a reformulation of the work of Émile Benveniste, Deleuze and Guattari conclude that language can be defined as "the set of order-words, implicit propositions [doing in speaking] or speech acts [doing by saying] current in a language at a given moment."[5] When we speak we merely transmit what has been heard, what is wholly social and in no manner expresses the ideas, thoughts, wishes, fears, or desires of an enunciative subject insofar as the words used are taken from the common stock available to all in that society. From this point of view language is always a social and political matter, and as such, semiotic systems or regimes of signs (as Deleuze and Guattari call them) are always being constructed in the context of social and political conditions, though never with any purity; they are always the result of mixtures of different semiotics. The force of regimes of signs arises out of their being made and remade in terms of the pragmatic, everyday life of a society and not in any hypothetical or idealized derivation from purely linguistic factors.

This view of language as consisting chiefly of order-words is expressed in terms of spatiality in Bergson's account. Ready-made ideas, those which are most easily expressed in words, Bergson claims, are external and social, organized only by association or perhaps some logical formulation (itself an effect of spatialized thinking), either of which would always be the aspects of the drive toward homogeneous spatiality. Words relate to one another without at all expressing the affective temporality of the self. As Bergson articulates it:

> But mark that the intuition of a homogeneous space is already a step towards social life. . . . Our tendency to form a clear picture of this externality of things and the homogeneity of their medium is the same as the impulse which leads us to live in common and to speak. . . . [T]he current which carries our conscious states from within outwards is strengthened; little by little these states are made into objects or things, they break off not only from one another, but from ourselves.[6]

Finally, Bergson concludes, a second self is produced in addition to the affective temporal self; it is one whose existence consists of distinct moments, objectified on the basis of homogeneous spatiality, and easily spoken insofar as words reflect what is common, social, and ordered. Were we to reflect upon the ontological unconscious, to delve deeper into passive synthesis, we would find a personality that is original and creative, but the self, for convenience as well as simplicity, takes up its position in this socialized part of ourselves, on the surface among other exteriorized personalities.[7]

Accordingly, we can begin to take in the import of Bergson's claim that in philosophy, the first matter is simply to find the real problem, since so many philosophical problems are handed to us in common words, in the order-words of social language, which as common—as the words of the socialized self—too often distort the real problem that needs to be resolved. Yet, once a problem is properly stated, then its solution exists, though it may be hidden or covered up. What is unusual here, which I shall develop through the remaining chapters of this book, is that stating a problem correctly and not simply in terms of the order-words handed down to us requires invention. Invention, neither actual nor virtual, gives being to what does not already exist.[8]

But the very existence of a false problem, whether badly stated or simply nonexistent,[9] implies something even more disturbing, something that helps to explain why the whole dilemma of representation has been so intractable, so unresolvable. "The very notion of a false problem indeed implies that we have to struggle not against simple mistakes (false solutions), but against something more profound: an illusion that carries us along, or in which we are immersed, inseparable from our condition."[10] As Deleuze argues so intensely, what is intriguing in considering the false problems produced by social order-words is not just that we make mistakes—no, the stakes are much higher. For what we have to struggle against is that in which our mistakes are rooted: "an *illusion* that carries us along, in which we are *immersed,* inseparable from our condition" (emphases added). We are so deeply and profoundly immersed in the illusion producing false problems that the illusion and the problems alike are inseparable from our condition. In this way they become our condition; we become the agents of our own suppression, our own misery, our own lies. This is the dark thought I have had about representation for so long; we are immersed in it and it has become inseparable from our condition. It has created a world, a cosmos even, of false problems such that we have lost our true freedom: that of invention.

So, how are we to proceed? Following Deleuze-Bergson, there is a second rule that, like the first, is more nomadic *nomos* than dictate. It is simply to struggle against this illusion, to continue to search for differences in kind and the articulations of the real by means of our critical ability, what Bergson calls "philosophical intuition," a term whose meaning should not be assumed and whose importance is so great that without some sense of this critical method we might never discover the illusions within which we operate. Bergson himself provides an illustration of intuition. Reading the philosophy of Berkeley, Bergson discovers two images of matter, one visual, "scarcely indicated by Berkeley himself," the other "often evoked by the philosopher, which is only the auditory transposition of the visual image."[11] What is important in reading Berkeley, whether one agrees with him or not, is to keep these simple images in view. Each is an image of God expressing himself (*sic*) through matter, an image that, Berkeley complains, the philosophers and metaphysicians immediately distort so greatly that they can no longer see or hear God. These kinds of images must be respected, Bergson argues, because if they are not the intuition that generates Berkeley's philosophy, then they are immediately derived from that intuition.[12]

Given that all we have at our disposal are intuitions/images and concepts, the more clear and precise the concepts, the farther away they are from the intuitions and the more "superlatively insipid and uninteresting . . . banal in the extreme" the intuitions/images become.[13] This is good for our purposes as well as unfortunate: unfortunate because even the most creative philosophy can be reduced to banal, common language, and those that are not creative are nothing but banalities; fortunate insofar as each thinker does not have to begin with the pre-existing ideas that structure philosophy and society and attempt to revise them so as to produce some slight variation. Philosophy begins, rather, with intuition. This is the force of its creativity and innovation. How does it come about? Deleuze casts Bergson's method of intuition as the method of division, whose critical and strict rules point to the discovery of differences in kind where we have presumed there are only differences of degree.[14] Or, as Deleuze also expresses it, intuition divides what has become mixed together into two "tendencies," that is, into what differs in nature or in kind.[15]

Deleuze explores this fully in his first work on Bergson, "La conception de la différence chez Bergson," which begins with the distinction between quality and quantity that I will take up in a moment, but locates the issue more broadly in the problem of internal versus external difference.[16] In Bergson, Deleuze maintains, thanks to the idea of the virtual, a thing differs from itself first and immediately, whereas according to Hegel, the thing differs first of all from what it is not, and this has the effect of making difference into contradiction.[17] With this, we would be forced to posit that duration is the synthesis of unity and multiplicity, something Bergson explicitly denies, since the synthesis of contradictories lacks difference itself and so the force of internal differenciation through divergence. We can see this confusion operating, Bergson claims, with regard to time and space, which throughout the history of philosophy have been placed on the same level and treated as the same in kind: "The procedure has been to study space, to determine its nature and function, and then to apply to time the conclusions thus reached."[18] This is the case even with Kant, who posited time as a homogeneous medium whose moments are situated spatially—that is, side by side—and susceptible to the same causality as the outer world.[19]

It is toward the end of critically uncovering differences in kind between time and space that Bergson carries out the intuitive method in *Matter and Memory:*

> We will assume for the moment that we know nothing of theories of matter and theories of spirit, nothing of the discussions as to the reality or ideality of the external world. Here I am in the presence of images, in the vaguest sense of the word, images perceived when my senses are open to them, unperceived when they are closed. . . . Yet there is *one* of them which is distinct from all the others, in that I do not know [*connais*] it only from without by perceptions, but from within by affections: it is my body. I examine the conditions in which these affections are produced: I find that they always interpose themselves between the excitations that I receive from without and the movements I am about to execute.[20]

Working only with images, without knowledge of theories of matter and spirit or mind (*l'esprit*), Bergson can still examine the *conditions* in which sensory images are produced. He finds that while most perceptions are perceived from "without," there is one (the body) that is also given to him "within," meaning through affections, and that every affection is conditioned by a dual movement that itself contains a multiplicity. Each and every affection is situated at the "interval" between a multiplicity of excitations received from "without" and the movements about to be executed. The movements about to be carried out arise because each affection contains an invitation to act as well as the permission to wait to act, or not to act at all. Within affectivity, there is nothing constraining choice. Feeling and sensation affirm this, for they are activated whenever the human being takes the initiative and they fade when behavior becomes automatic. Affectivity thus arises in the interval between excitation and action, but not only for human life.[21]

Everywhere in the organic world, every living being with the power of mobility exercises this dual function of sensibility and choice, leaving Bergson to conclude that the power of affectivity serves as an indication of innovation or creation, the addition of something new to the universe. This conclusion is in many respects central to every aspect of Bergson's method and indicative of his attraction for Deleuze and his importance in undermining organic representation. The intuitive method is conditioned by life as a process of creation extending from the least organic level to that of complex vertebrate life.

Interpretation and Force

In many respects, Deleuze-Bergson's strict method of condemning false problems and struggling against illusion to discover differences in kind or articulations of the real carries out the program of Deleuze's evocation of Nietzsche's critical method. There the false problem and the illusion are discussed in terms of the interpretation of force. For Nietzsche, the history of a thing consists of the forces that take hold of it and the struggle between forces for possession, a history that is obscured by the functions that the winning force imposes on the thing. In this respect, the history of a "'thing,' an organ, a custom, becomes a continuous sign-chain of ever new interpretations and adaptations."[22] This is why Nietzsche considers the form of a thing to be fluid, but the meaning to be even more so.[23] Deleuze takes this to be an account of phenomena, the effect of critique or of the strict method that interprets phenomena as signs, interpretations whose meaning is found only in an existing force or in the struggle(s) between forces. A critique of the force that has overtaken a given sign then amounts to the Bergsonian program of casting aside false problems and illusions. As Todd May has clearly argued, for Deleuze the point is not to arrive at the truth—meaning at how the world is or is not. This attempt holds little importance for Deleuze's philosophical pragmatics even though Deleuze recognizes that science generally believes this to be crucial to the development of its thought.

Nor is Deleuze advocating that philosophy concern itself with nothing but fictions, contingencies, or fantasies. The scrupulous attention to scientific research in geology, biology, mathematics, and chemistry found especially in the two volumes of *Capitalism and Schizophrenia* certainly belies such an aim. The point in creating an ontology or a concept of becoming is to take up a viewpoint on the world that arises out of life itself but that also affirms living in certain ways; in other words, how we conceive the world is absolutely relevant to how we live it.[24] If, as in feminist and much contemporary social theory, one is seeking to alter real patterns of control and domination, then one must have concepts that make that possible, that do not undermine or ridicule pragmatic experiments and experimental modes of life. Here I am arguing that the concepts that much of social and political philosophy has embraced (including feminist and minority philosophies) make change impossible insofar as they are static and rigid representational concepts that lack the fluidity that is conducive to conceptualizing change.

We are mistaken, then, when we expect philosophy to provide us with a model or a regulating rule from which we may deduce answers to all the problems we have determined, and equally mistaken when we determine what possibilities such a rule or model entails. Such concepts can be marketed and displayed, promoted as the products of their creator, as the key to finding answers to difficult and important questions.[25] But Deleuze finds this entire program repugnant, antithetical to philosophy as life-enhancing and pragmatic. For Deleuze-Bergson, the counter to marketing concepts begins with stating the problem without the crippling impact of order-words. This is the first creative act, the first act of interpretation whose usefulness, not its truth, is at stake.

In *Bergsonism,* Deleuze writes that the meaning of philosophy consists in opening human beings up to what is inhuman and superhuman—that is, to "durations inferior and superior to our own"—but we should not do this by seeking concepts that define the conditions of all possible experience in general, as Kant did and science continues to do.[26] Here Deleuze is practicing a philosophy of life, an attunement to the cosmos—to the "inhuman" and "superhuman"—yet it seems to me that it is for the sake of the real, which is as much the human as the inhuman real. For if we are seeking the conditions of real life with its peculiarities, "we do so only in order to find the articulations on which these particularities depend," and these articulations, these conditions of the possibility of real life, are "less determined in concepts than in pure percepts," so that even concepts that are modeled on percepts will account for real life with its particularities, since if a concept is modeled on each particularity, it will be no broader than what it must account for.[27] So let us keep in mind that the concept of the particularity is not business as usual, but neither is it a dismissal of human concerns. By turning away from the generalizable, from common sense and good sense, Deleuze brings our attention again and again to the particular, the remarkable, the interesting, and even the useful.

So for Bergson, the false problem of the nervous system that lives apart from the organism must be restated in order to create a more useful interpretation. If the brain is conceived of as simply one image among others, it is part of the material world and so cannot produce that material world as its representation.[28] Image, for Bergson, means something more than what an idealist calls representation and something less than what a realist calls a thing; matter is an aggregate of images, a multiplicity of images.[29] Even the body must consist of an image that is a multiplicity of affections, choosing now this and now that movement in response to the many it receives. As Bergson explains it, external objects disturb afferent nerves and that disturbance is passed on to the nerve centers, theaters of molecular movements whose being affected can only come from objects. If the objects change, so does the disturbance—what Bergson refers to as the "interior movements of my perceptive centers" as opposed to "my perception," which, as we shall see, is not the same thing.[30] Perceptions, however, do not inhabit a separate world, so they must also vary with the molecular movements, for the molecular movements themselves are inseparable from the material world that produces them. Bergson conceives of the universe as a system of images that exist and influence one another through movement and for which the image of one's own body occupies a central position, but only because everything else changes as the body moves.

The entire universe, insofar as it is available to any living creature, is available as images. Everything is an image: afferent nerves (transmitting disturbances to nerve centers), efferent nerves (conducting disturbances from the nerve centers to the periphery to set some or all of the body in motion), bodies, the brain. All function without ever producing a single representation of the material universe. Rather, external images influence the "body" image by transmitting movement to it. The body image responds by bringing about changes in its surrounding images and giving back movement to them, choosing how it returns what it receives. With this, Bergson strikes his first blow against the idealists or internalists, who to this day proclaim the brain to be the condition of affection and movement, thereby excluding the universe and reconnecting with it only through some clumsy mechanism such as Kant's unity of the faculties of sense and understanding. Likewise there are the realists, who also isolate the brain from the rest of the material universe as if it were not also matter, and thereby make perception the accident of an epiphenomenal consciousness.[31] For both, perception pictures the states of our nervous system as if it lived apart from the organism. For Bergson, this is a prime case of posing a false problem: asking if the universe exists only inside our thoughts or only outside our thoughts is putting the question in terms that make it insoluble.[32]

An important result of Bergson's recasting of materiality in terms of images that transmit movement is that perception cannot be construed as knowledge, for it operates even in the simplest mass of protoplasm. Indeed, for Deleuze, there appears to be some degree of perception even at the level of simple molecules. This is of consequence because in addressing the question of what exactly perception is, the perceptual capacity of the molecular makes it necessary to recognize that all life is open to the influence of external stimulation; all life perceives and so is open to the outside. The openness to the "outside" of living beings makes of duration and memory something real; they are not simply psychological.[33]

Given that the material world is a system of closely linked images ranged around a center of real action (living matter), perception occurs. In lower organisms, perception can hardly be distinguished from mere touch followed by necessary movement (all the more for earth, it will be shown), active and passive at once. In higher organisms there exists a greater "zone of indetermination" that allows the plethora of images to be sorted though and perceptions to take place. The zone of indetermination is that area of affectivity within multidimensional duration in which the organism selects from among the multiplicity of the images that each and every material image is bound up with in order to perceive what is of interest to that organism's various functions, or it lets that flow of images proceed unimpeded because they are of no interest to it. The effect of this is that when any material image is perceived—that is, when this "existence" or "duration" moves in the direction of perception—the material image is transformed into what Bergson calls a representation (and this appears to be something like organic representation as I have previously defined it, although its representational nature is due to its isolation rather than to the force of intellectual categories). Rather than being a part of its surroundings—part of existence and duration constituted in the flow of images—in the zone of indetermination, the thing detaches from them as a picture.[34] Far from being manufactured by the brain and so being added to the object, perceptual representation, by Bergson's account, is the object *minus* everything else; is it the object created by the process of separating it out from everything that does not interest that duration. So while Bergson's perceptual representation seems to have a basis in life itself, in the flow of unimpeded duration, still it is related to choice and action. Consequently, perceptual representation is a highly selective mode. It will be necessary to move beyond the Bergson of *Matter and Memory* in order to make this point. For Bergson, though they are the effect of the same kinds of external influences as all other images, perceptions presuppose a suppression of all those images toward which one is currently indifferent.

Any unconscious material point has infinitely greater and more complex perceptions than human perception, for the former gathers and transmits upon itself, whether directly or indirectly, all the influences of all the points of the material universe. Though the human body is an image, it is one that reflects others and in so doing analyzes them according to the actions it can exercise upon them.[35] Thus external objects are *perceived* where they are as objects of virtual action. Perception (what Bergson also calls consciousness, which does not refer here to conceptual knowledge of any sort) consists specifically in the power of discernment and choice, and yet it impoverishes—although the impoverishment is produced by movements transmitted to a being from the world, since there is no image without an object and the nervous system merely transmits movement.[36] If any part of the nervous system is damaged, perception is diminished since some objects or parts of same will be unable to transmit their motion and make their appeal. Equally diminishing are habits; their motions are ready-made responses and not created replies to questions posed by the universe, that is, to movements transmitted from objects.[37] The degree to which habit dominates affective perception will turn out to be of great relevance in the relations between the organism and the world.

I have focused at length on perception, in part because it is an aspect of Deleuze and Deleuze-Guattari's work that is generally not given much attention, so that the connections between molecular life, animal life, and human life are also ignored; and in part because of the claim that only phenomenology is attuned to questions of the lived body, questions that feminism especially has propelled to the front of the stage, yet struggles with both for and against itself. Furthermore, perception involves, in Bergson's account, separating some images out of the multidimensional flow of images because the organism is most interested in them. This appears to make perception something like organic representation but, as will become clear, it does not become part of categorical representation until and unless habit or intellect detaches it completely from what I would call the creative aspect of life. The organization and functioning of this creative line is therefore decisive in enacting the ruin of representation. As I indicated in the previous chapter, in posing the problem of life the elements of perception, matter, and space are only part of the composite; they are one direction in which life moves. The other element in the composite, the other *kind,* is affection, recollection, and duration. Why? Because perceptions present organisms with discontinuous views of the universe. The perception of pain is proof of this to Bergson. Although the body as a whole can move away from a source of pain, the sensitive element is immobile in relation to the body. The damaged element attempts to set things right; pain is the result, but such pain is always local. What is the point Bergson is making here?

The living body as a center of action receives the action of some of the objects surrounding it, objects whose movements, when transmitted to the body, might even destroy it. The experience of pain shows that the body "does not merely reflect action received from without; it struggles, and thus absorbs some part of this action. Here is the source of affection."[38] Although originating in a perceptual image, pain itself is pure affectivity, "the impurity with which perception is alloyed." The perception of an object insofar as it is separate from the body itself is the expression of a virtual action; perception expresses the phenomenon that any future actions of the body with regard to the object are real but unactualized. Affections or *affective states* are real action. Affective states are the body's "actual effort upon itself different in kind from perception and, as in the case of pain, whether a toothache, a burn, or a phantom limb, affective states are localized in their own way from the very beginning.[39]

The analysis of perception so far has focused primarily on "pure" perception, not perception as it actually occurs. One "line" has been traced out; it links perception with the object and finally with matter. But we are beginning to see that all along the way affectivity has been a major aspect of the discussion of perception, though it is not yet fully articulated. Thus, there is a second line, which interpenetrates with the perception-object-matter line but is different from it in kind. This line constitutes a subjectivity without which perception would be irrelevant. The second line is that of affectivity, different in *kind* from the first line, interpenetrating with it, as Deleuze writes, but also its condition. The two differ in kind insofar as one line moves from the living being to perception and to matter while the other moves from affection to memory to mind, thereby reinstating the role of memory in perception. Without affection, however, the body would be only this first line, the one that moves from perception to objects and matter, a purely impersonal existence, since the totality of perceived images subsists even if the body disappears.[40] It is to the analysis of affection that we must now turn.

The Earth Screams; Life Itself

As it turns out, this is the level of analysis that Jardine has judged mostly irrelevant to feminist philosophical interests: protoplasm, geology, life itself. But this analysis, for Deleuze, is at the basis of the constitution of time and memory, which I will show are surely not inconsequential for the ruin of representation and for the concerns about power and domination central to feminist theory. In other words, a theory of change demands concepts that are made from real change and that make change real. And, I will argue, it is only by conceiving life, including duration and subjectivity, in the image of flows that such a conception of change in the subject and in the cosmos can come to be realized.

Bergson argues that we must follow "external perception" in monera (nonnucleated protoplasmic bodies without any organization or structure) as well as in higher vertebrates. When we do, we see that even a simple mass of protoplasm is irritable and contractile, open to the influence of *external stimulation,* to which it responds with mechanical, physical, and chemical reactions.[41] Throughout his work, Deleuze echoes the thought that at the most elementary levels, a sensed quality blends with the contraction of elementary excitations. We are, Deleuze argues, contracted water, earth, light, and air, not only before recognizing them or representing them, but even before sensing them. Deleuze's enthusiasm for the drama of life that is implicated in Bergson's move comes to the fore in *Difference and Repetition:*

> Every organism is, in its receptive and perceptive elements, but also in its viscera, a sum of contractions, retentions and protentions. At the level of this vital, primary sensibility, the lived present already constitutes in time a past and future. This future appears, if need be, as an organic form of protentions; the past of retention appears in the cellular heredity. Moreover, these organic syntheses, as they combine with the perceptive syntheses piled upon them, redeploy themselves in the active syntheses of a psycho-organic memory and intelligence. . . . All this forms a rich domain of signs, enveloping the heterogeneous each time and animating behavior. For, each contraction, each passive synthesis, is constitutive of a sign, which is interpreted or deployed in the active syntheses. The signs by means of which the animal "senses" the presence of water do not resemble the elements which its thirsty organism lacks.[42]

So when molecules of earth, air, fire, or water join one another, substances are formed; they are connected and ordered successively according to physical or chemical or biological properties, which from the point of view of the human world we call natural laws.

Insofar as, following Bergson, we take perception to be that which we call "materiality," the joining together of molecules is, therefore, perception. But these so-called original substances themselves are already formed matters, for earth, air, fire, and water are already "territorialized," already incorporated into a reorganization of functions and a regrouping of forces.[43] In their first articulation, that is, as formed matters, they are "strata." From the point of view of various uses or regimes, strata are acts of capture because they code the singular elements (the substances) into relatively stable systems organized by resonance, the excess or surplus value that is the sympathetic vibration of each element for the next that produces molecules both large and small, and redundancy, contracting or folding those molecules into larger molar aggregates.[44] Thus strata territorialize whatever they are able to seize, and in the process of a second articulation the body is made into an organism through a continuous folding of the outer over to the inner, a continuous contraction and transmission of movement. This is how such elements may be organized in terms of mythical principles or natural laws until another use for them is devised, until, for example, earth is subjected to developers, air to particulate counts, fire to a curse for destroying housing, and water to natural resource allocations. Each then takes on a new function and is subject to a new set of forces.

The capture of elements into strata and their reinterpretation in accordance with whatever force captures them for use are part of the grab for political and social power that operates everywhere in life. We know that it makes a huge difference if such strata are taken to be part of mythical culture, natural law, natural resource allocation and supply, economic theory, environmental degradation, or art. We know that formed substances usually participate in more than one stratum at once, but that the political game with earth and air, as well as with bodies and genders, is one of capture. Already the elements involved here are so complex that they may appear opaque. The elements of sensibility of every living thing constitute what I will later describe as the first level of temporality, a passive synthesis. And each passive synthesis, a sum of contractions, retentions, and protentions, is a sign, a point of interpretation, not a representation. Still, these indications of a link between life itself, affectivity, and primary temporality must be further unraveled to be of any use to the ruin of representation.

A Thousand Plateaus brings us into the central nervous system of this complexity by starting with the earth. Arthur Conan Doyle's story "When the World Screamed" becomes the setting for the articulation of the contraction and response of the earth itself, the "giant Molecule," permeated by unformed and unstable matters and flows in all directions.[45] When Professor Challenger, ridiculed by his peers for his unorthodox scientific ideas, succeeds in piercing the earth's crust eight miles under the surface with a rod otherwise used by an artesian well-digging operation, the response is immediate. The earth howls in pain, anger, and menace, like a thousand sirens in one. Not only that, it blasts out a vile, tarlike substance, and blasts into the sky the fourteen elevator cars that had conveyed the diggers and machines. The part of the earth that has been pierced under the crust in Professor Challenger's experiment is matter, but let us be clear what this means. This matter is the unformed, unorganized, nonstratified or destratified body of the earth with all its flows of subatomic and submolecular particles. Deleuze and Guattari call it the plane of consistency, the body without organs—that is, the body of the earth, of protoplasm, even of human life that is not subject to an organizing principle, to a sign, to a force that orders it.[46]

Simultaneous with this flow, there are stratifications; these are layers of geological formations, not simply flows, in which matters that occur in flows are given form. The process according to which they are formed is not without complexity. In geological formations, the first articulation of matter is known as sedimentation. Sedimentation is formed when one grain is joined by another, A then A. While the original joining is by chance and arbitrary, it is not completely so. Influenced by external stimulation, something characteristic of a bit of sand—of its size, weight range, or chemical properties—calls for another bit.[47] Deleuze refers to this as resonance; one element, a bit of sand with specific properties, resonates on the basis of these properties with another and another to form a series; then one series resonates with another to form systems. The first linking of one bit of sand with another is already a contraction, an *affectivity;* positing it assumes that a body is something and has volume in space. It especially assumes that a body is something other than a mathematical point.[48] The affective contraction is followed by a perception, that is, from out of all the grains sliding down the hillside only certain ones are selected. A selection is made of metastable molecular or quasi-molecular units, which are given a statistical order of connection and succession.[49] This means only that there, in that particular site under those particular conditions, are certain characteristics of these formed substances actualized in the connections that have taken place.

These formed substances are still not fully stratified, not fully stabilized. The first articulation "A" exhibits a double articulation "B of A" or simply "BA." A second articulation constructs molar compounds, stable functional structures are established, and sediment hardens into sedimentary rock. Thus in the second articulation phenomena are unified, totalized, integrated, and hierarchized. If we look at cellular chemistry we find the same double articulation at work. First, hundreds of chemical reactions produce a limited number of small compounds. Then small molecules are assembled to produce larger ones. The first articulation forms compounds that exist temporarily through a series of different reactions; the second constructs stable products by repeating the same reaction.[50] Such double articulations are everywhere where life is organizing itself, that is, on every stratum, leading Deleuze and Guattari to refer to them, not without humor, as God.

The foray into geological first and second articulations seems to have taken us far afield from the affectivity that conditions Bergsonian intuitions. It is the theory of signs that brings all these elements together, for human beings as affective beings are also subject to double syntheses. Deleuze's claim that we are contracted water, earth, light, and air, not only before we recognize or represent them but even before we can sense them, is not a metaphor. It is a claim about the processes of production that constitute life itself, processes that we share with the simplest protoplasm and with the earth. Likewise, we can find Bergson claiming that protoplasm replies to external stimulation with mechanical, physical, and chemical reactions, while animal nerve cells appear and diversify, grouping themselves into systems that are first and second articulations. Distinctions between automatism and voluntary acts, spinal cord and brain, are only differences of degree; since the brain is simply a central exchange, it analyzes and selects a movement to execute but adds nothing to what it receives.[51] Biologists studying contemporary genetics echo this Bergsonian claim when they argue that "[t]he information which is passed on and, due to the capacity of the 'DNA-RNA-Protein computer' [popularly known as the DNA molecule], increases gradually in structural refinement, is a product of matter; . . . [O]ne may say that matter is transforming itself into an 'alien' thing—information. Or to put it another way, matter shows its non-material potentiality . . . and the *élan vital* of Bergson expresses the same thing."[52]

Affections are, then, only one element in the line of subjectivity, only the point of intersection between matter and memory. Concepts that allow us to theorize about life begin here as well, with movements that effect change. I am arguing that life itself is a process of production, the creation of the new. Bergson describes this in *Creative Evolution:*

> Of phenomena in the simplest forms of life, it is hard to say whether they are still physical and chemical or whether they are already vital. Life had to enter thus into the habits of inert matter, in order to draw it little by little magnetized, as it were, to another track. The animate forms that first appeared were therefore of extreme simplicity. They were probably tiny masses of scarcely differentiated protoplasm, outwardly resembling the amoeba observable today, but possessed of the tremendous internal push that was to raise them even to the highest forms of life. That in virtue of this push the first organisms sought to grow as much as possible, seems likely.[53]

The simplest phenomena are simultaneously physical, chemical, and vital. But we cannot say that life is simply the effect of environmental circumstances, whether those circumstances are characterized by inert matter or social systems. Yet this "push" that Bergson describes is, by his own account, not some mysterious inner force or magical power that was invoked under the name of vitalism; it is what Bergson evokes and Deleuze describes as the contraction, the folding in of what is outside, the passive synthesis. As Bergson points out, if life arises merely as the product of environmental factors, whether inert or social and historical, then life would be nothing more than a mechanism, the adaptation to accidental circumstances, to mere contingencies. He notes that materialists always reduce consciousness to nothing but the interplay of material elements, but that what stymies them is that these material elements are supposed to be able to create the elementary facts of consciousness.[54]

Idealism, on the other hand, simply trades in matter for mind. The qualities matter invests in perception are, for idealism, reduced to subjective appearances; matter itself is a mystery.[55] Both approaches fall into the error of the false problem, specifically, the badly analyzed composite that arbitrarily groups things that differ in kind as if they differed only in degree.[56] This is why Bergson is not claiming that life is determined by a plan, representable prior to its realization. For life creates not only life forms but also the concepts by which means we come to understand it, and if creation is not operating on the level of ideas and concepts as well as with respect to life forms, then there is no creation.[57] This means that neither dialectics nor instinctual drives have any advantage in Bergson's view. What advances life is the contraction, the passive synthesis that is followed by the impulsion to grow and scatter, not merely to divide. As Bergson describes it: "The evolution movement would be a simple one, and we should soon have been able to determine its direction, if life had described a single course, like that of solid ball shot from a cannon. But it proceeds rather like a shell, which suddenly bursts into fragments, which fragments, being themselves shells, burst in their turn into fragments destined to burst again, and so on for a time incommensurably long."[58] At no level is the world static. Creation, the always and ever new, is an ongoing process of contraction, folding in what comes along on the outside, exercising only partial control over what is contracted; thus, the stability of each articulation is only relative in the sense that it is never complete or final.[59]

Duration and Memory

The all-important result of this view is one that philosophy has ignored to its detriment. As Bergson puts it, "questions relating to subject and object, to their distinction and their union, should be put in terms of time rather than space,"[60] and time begins with pure duration. The problem, as Bergson argues, is that even when philosophers believe they are providing an ontological account of temporalization, they base this account on a pre-given understanding of static and homogeneous spatiality from which they derive their interpretation of time. For Deleuze-Bergson, given the affectivity of the body, the nervous system is open to a "succession" of *qualitative* changes, which are not clearly laid out one after the other but melt into one another, permeate one another, are without precise outlines, without any tendency to externalize themselves in relation to one another; thus they do not serve as the measure or number of movements: pure duration is pure heterogeneity, difference, and becoming.[61] Deleuze calls this "time unhinged," insofar as it is temporality freed from subordination to the succession of objects that succeed one another in time in order to be the immutable form of everything that changes and moves. And Deleuze attributes the insight into time as immutable form to Kant, who recognized the inner difference between being and thought and so argued that the "I think" as spontaneous undetermined existence can be determined only *within time* as the existence of a phenomenon, of a passive, receptive phenomenal subject whose thought is exercised in and upon it but not by it.[62]

Bergson's prototype of the pendulum clock brings the "I" whose thought is passively constituted to the fore. He argues that if we count each of the sixty oscillations of a clock's pendulum beating out one minute, by excluding the recollection of the preceding beats we screen out any experience of duration, for we remain always in the present of each beat—a static arrangement in which each beat is without relation to what has come before. If we picture the sixty beats all at once we likewise forfeit any sense of duration in exchange for a spatialized homogeneous representation. But if we retain the recollection of the preceding beat along with the current one, perceiving each permeating the other like the notes of a tune, they form a "qualitative multiplicity," the image of pure duration.[63] What matters here is that we do not substitute quantity for quality. In space as measured by science, we count simultaneities; each stroke of the clock on the wall is a homogeneous unit; nothing of the past position of the hand remains in the new position. But for a self, for some being that endures, the past remains in the present, movement but no externality.

In *Difference and Repetition,* Deleuze proposes a reading of Hume to reinforce this point. Deleuze argues for Hume's thesis that "[r]epetition changes nothing in the object which is repeated, but it changes something in the mind which contemplates it."[64] Hume's example is stated slightly differently than Bergson's and already reflects the immediate creation and influence of what Hume calls "imagination," a power of contraction:

> 'Tis plain, that in the course of our thinking, and in the constant revolution of our ideas, our imagination runs easily from one idea to any other that *resembles* it, and that this quality alone is to the fancy a sufficient bond and association. 'Tis likewise evident, that as the senses, in changing their objects, are necessitated to change them regularly, and take them as they lie *contiguous* to one another, the imagination must by long custom acquire the same method of thinking . . . [and] that there is no relation, which produces a stronger connexion in the fancy, and makes one idea more readily recall another, than the relation of cause and effect.[65]

With regard to each of the three forms of association, when A appears, we expect B; beyond Bergson's beating of the clock, we have a more complex difference at work in the difference between A and B. In the repetition of instants, imagination contracts the so-called successive independent instants in one another to constitute the passive synthesis that is the living present: "It is in this present that time unfurls. It is to time that both the past and the future belong. . . . Past and future do not designate instants, distinct from a supposed present instant, but the dimensions of the present itself as it contracts the instants. The present does not have to go out of itself in order to go from past to future. . . . Time is subjective, but it has the subjectivity of a passive subject."[66]

Recalling the argument above that every being is the contraction of elements—thousands of contractions, in fact—the effect of contractions, retentions, and protentions on the vital and primary plane of sensibility, we can follow Deleuze's claim that on the plane of life itself, every being is a living present that already constitutes a past and future.[67] This makes of duration not a psychological principle but the point of departure for an ontology that takes into account the thousands of contractions, the double articulations, and the strata that inhabit the universe and create life itself. While duration becomes, for Bergson, the "location and environment of differences in kind," space is constituted as the other direction of complex being, "the location, the environment, the totality of differences in degree."[68] Thus, when Bergson describes pure duration as perhaps nothing but a succession of qualitative changes, this is the beginning of the constitution of a radical ontology of heterogeneity and of true difference, difference in kind. In fact, duration is not even a succession, for if time unhinged is no longer subordinated to spatiality, it is released from its subordination to succession as well; it no longer serves space as the measure or number of movements of objects in space. Time or pure duration is "the form of everything that changes and moves, an immutable form that does not change, not an *eternal* form, but the form of that which is not eternal, the immutable form of change and movement."[69] Disengaged from its subordination to spatiality and the representation of objects in space, time is the form of change.

At this point, however, I have only provided an image of the pure form of time, the passive synthesis. It remains to be seen how the passive synthesis of the passive subject is transformed into an active synthesis. Again, the explanation benefits from a return to Hume. Given, first, that for Hume ideas are always derived from impressions, and second, that when these impressions disappear, something is left, an idea that "returns upon the soul" to produce "impressions of reflection," which are again copied or repeated, passions as well as understanding are, for Hume, an effect of reflection, contemplation.[70] Let us briefly examine both. Living beings reflect on impressions of pleasure or pain, but the original impressions from which reflections arise always and only come from "natural and physical causes," only from the outside, from the contraction, the folding of what is outside to the inside, from impressions such as hunger, cold, thirst, and heat.[71] And as the effect of the repetition of pleasure and pain, there arise desire, aversion, hope, and fear. When impressions of reflection that resemble one another are connected, grief and disappointment connect with anger, envy, malice; joy conjoins love, generosity, pity, courage, pride. The association of ideas and that of impressions intertwine, generating an even more violent "double impulse" of the passions.[72] Impressions are connected solely by resemblance; consequently no hidden inner impulses need be formulated to do the work of ontology, which, we have seen, is always already at work. Nor do we revert, however, to mere mechanism such that passions are the effect of purely material forces.

The result of this must be that intellectual faculties of living beings are not ready-made or preformed, nor can they be attributed to a mechanical associationism. Reason, as the association of ideas, the system of understanding, is an "affection of the mind," though it is no different in beasts than in humans; it is instinct, habit, nature, "the wonderful and unintelligible instinct in our souls, which carries us along a certain train of ideas, and endows them with particular qualities, according to their particular situations and relations."[73] Given that all ideas originate with impressions, the mind is not constant, and it is "impossible for the mind to fix itself steadily upon one idea for any considerable time; nor can it by its utmost efforts ever arrive at such constancy."[74] The mind is constantly in motion, but it is not pure contingency because, "however changeable our thoughts may be, they are not entirely without rule or measure in their changes. The rule by which they proceed is to pass from one object to what is resembling, contiguous to, or produced by it."[75] That is, once ideas are repeated often enough to give way to association (resemblance, contiguity, cause and effect), by association a single idea takes on the role of standing in for all those it associates with through resemblance to produce a general idea; or a group of contiguous ideas are united by imagination to produce the complex ideas of substance or dispersed by imagination to produce simple ideas of modes; or finally, when two ideas are placed together and compared, we get a variety of relations. These principles of reason, such as the relation of necessary connection, are also impressions of reflection for, as Hume argues, it is the observation of a number of instances of resembling conjunctions that determines the mind to carry our thoughts from one object to another, from cause to effect. As nothing sensible produces this idea, it must derive from some "internal" impression of reflection.[76]

Deleuze employs the Humean explanation to point to the mind *affected* by these dispositions, tendencies, or principles, and so to become the subject. Hume confirms that "[e]xperience is a *principle,* which instructs me in the several conjunctions of objects for the past. Habit is another *principle* which determines me to expect the same for the future; and both of them conspiring to operate upon the imagination, make me form certain ideas in a more intense and lively manner than others, which are not attended with the same advantage."[77] Thus, in the search for ultimate principles we discover that the connection between one idea and another lies in the determination of the mind, a qualification of the mind that constitutes and subjects the subject. Impressions of sensation are the origin of the mind, but principles of association by which means we make the transition from an object to its usual attendant, from the impression of one to the lively idea of the other, are what give a nature to the mind; they qualify the mind.[78] Likewise, impressions of reflection produced by passions and understanding are qualifications of the mind and the effect of principles in it. And so the mind is not *the* subject; it is *subjected* in the passive synthesis of contraction.[79]

This is absolutely critical to any attempt to establish a sense of the "self." Like every idea, the idea of a "self" must also be traced to some impression, but in the case of the "self," Hume argues, self or person is not one impression but several because no impression is constant and invariable, because pain, pleasure, grief, joy, passions, and sensations succeed one another.[80] The problem, given Hume's theory of impressions, is that such a "self" appears to be nothing but a collection of shifting perceptions to the extent that "there is properly no *simplicity* in it at one time, nor *identity* in different."[81] The identity we claim for a self, whether it is an identity we attribute to a distinct object supposedly invariable through time or personal identity ("the concern we take in ourselves"), such an identity is perhaps the most profound manifestation of the illusion that carries us along, in which we are immersed, and which is inseparable from our condition. The former arises from a determined lack of attention to the succession of related objects given in our impressions. Insofar as the impressions of these objects have "almost the same feeling, . . . [t]he relation facilitates the transition of the mind from one object to another and renders its passage as smooth as if it contemplated one continued object."[82] It is our "custom," our habit, to make the transition. Resemblance, contiguity, and causality produce this illusion; they are our habitual ways of organizing impressions. So powerful is the illusion into which we have fallen that in spite of our unremitting attempts to not make the inference, we yield to this bias; we skip over the diversity, we flee the logic of "relation" that Irigaray has recommended to us (see chapter 3), and we plunge into the illusion of sameness. Soul, self, substance, unity, and identity are the disguises we then attribute to objects.

Having gone this far, it is an easy step to fantasize the constant identity of a simple personal self. Although it is true for Hume that, having constituted identity for the object, the "smooth and uninterrupted progress of the thought along a train of connected ideas" strengthens the fantasy of personal identity, nonetheless there are two important differences between the identity of an object and personal identity: (1) contiguity—that is, spatiality—has no role to play in the consideration of personal identity, since contiguity is a characteristic of impressions of objects that belong to the external world, but not of the self and the diversity of impressions that constitute a self; and (2) the addition of habits of memory provides the greatest possible impetus to this error. It is, again, as with all double articulations, all stratifications, both fortunate and unfortunate. A certain aspect of memory that appears in the guise of habit or custom resurrects the images of past perceptions and places them in a chain of thought. This habitual memory thereby produces the relation of resemblance, leading to the assumption of identity in the place of diversity. Memory-habits also provide us with the chains of cause and effect and even allow us to extend them beyond what we can personally remember to what is only generally remembered, what we suppose by inference to be the case. And the self, writes Hume, by means of causal relations, takes on the character of a commonwealth whose members are united by the reciprocal ties of subordination and governance; an unaltering order structured in hierarchies of subordination, which even while changing members, laws, and constitutions nevertheless remains united in its (artificial) identity. Such an image should not be passed over lightly. Insofar as the constitution of a hierarchically ordered commonwealth may provide social and political stability, it is important that we not delude ourselves regarding its legitimacy.[83] It is precisely the legitimacy of this image that Hume's entire philosophy can be counted on to undermine and replace. Nonetheless, the role of memory is not limited to this unfortunate consequence; thus a proper concept of memory, one that is useful for change, is central to this project.

Memory and the Second Synthesis of Time

Hume is resigned though cautious regarding the tendency to use custom and memory-habits to create stable identities, nonetheless custom and memory do extract something new out of the repetition of impressions; they give us the association of ideas and resemblance among passions. This is why Deleuze argues that while the first synthesis is the synthesis of habit and the founding (*fondation*) of time (constituting time as a present), there is something which makes the present pass such that it is not eternal. This something is memory, "the fundamental (*fondamentale*) synthesis of time which constitutes the being of the past; that which makes the present pass."[84] Contraction or passive synthesis constitutes time as a living present whose dimensions are the past and future. We find an example of this synthesis in Bergson's swinging pendulum, insofar as we retain the recollection of the preceding beat along with the current one, but not successively, rather perceiving each permeating the other like the notes of a tune and forming the image of pure duration, a qualitative multiplicity. This means that the past does not function as the old present—custom or habit are the present and never cease to be the present—yet at every present, past images mingle with the present, completing and enriching present experience.[85] Former and actual presents are not two successive instants on a time line; the actual present calls up the past on the basis of its usefulness: "The actual present is not treated as the future object of a recollection but rather as that which reflects itself at the same time as it forms the recollection of the old present."[86] Active recollection of the old present and the simultaneous reflection or contraction of the actual present are constitutive of the second synthesis of time, the active synthesis of memory.

On this basis, the past is not constituted after having been present but is simultaneous with the present it has been. This should not be construed as lack. The trauma produced by a tragedy in childhood should not be construed as a sign of a past wound; it is a present fact, that of having had a tragedy, having been wounded. This will be of increased importance as we proceed. As we shall see, "[t]he entire past coexists with the new present in relation to which it is now past. . . . This is the Bergsonian idea that each actual present is nothing but the entire past in its most contracted state."[87] Bergson's innovation, according to Deleuze, is to conceive of a pure past that is not perceived in the present in relation to which it is past. This past is truly preserved in itself existing in various degrees of expansion and contraction, thus at various levels. It is *virtual*—that is, real but not actualized in space—insofar as it can only be actualized by the perception that attracts it and materializes it. This is why the memory image is an image; it subsists as a virtual object among virtual objects rather than as an actual object that is material and external to the living being.[88] Between matter and memory there is always a difference in kind, yet there is a point at which the two always intersect and the passage between them is effected.

Bergson's famous rendering of a cone is instrumental here. The totality of recollections in memory, rather than stretching out from left to right, past to future on a time line, can best be imagined in the form of a cone. The point of the cone, standing for the present that is continually becoming in the flow of present duration, contracts the outside in upon itself in the fold of affectivity. As Bergson understands it, it contracts movements coming from objects into duration and memory. The body, as the center of action, is concentrated right at the point of the cone, though extending above it as well, while the cone as a whole stands for the open totality of recollections in memory. This whole of memory swells and grows with the flow of becoming; it is always available as a whole to serve what we will call active or bodily memory and to answer the appeal of the present and present action. Likewise, any slice through the cone produces an entirely different repetition of psychical life, one of greater or lesser scope depending on whether it is a more recent or an ancient contraction of memory.[89]

We tend to think of the present as the instant just gone by, but this is not the present under consideration here. Rather, there is a real, live, concrete present that occupies a duration. Because duration is the contraction and affectivity of a being, in the concrete present the immediate past is perceived as a sensation, an order of vibrations, the transmission of movements. But because duration is the perception of sensations, it is also sensory-motor, for as the recipient of images and the center of action, the body acts on the basis of its sensations. This system of sensations and movements is what has been described above as the body's materiality. As Bergson interprets this process, the received impressions intelligently choose (by means of the association of ideas) the path that they will follow to transform themselves into movement so that there is a single system of sensations and movements, the actual state of a being's becoming or duration.[90] This is why one's own body always occupies the center of action; it is the moment when the present is continually becoming and the site where the system of sensations and movements occupies actual parts of the body's surface; thus it is the materiality of existence and the boundary between duration and matter. So, Bergson argues, sensation is extended; it is localized as the source of movement and as the materiality of our existence, while pure memory is different in kind, thus not localized but unextended and latent.[91]

The past, it must be recognized, survives in two distinct forms. First, there is the memory preserved in the body's motor mechanisms, which react to external stimuli. The living body, its nervous system, and even the so-called cerebral process (the brain) are, as Bergson contends, channels for the transmission of movements. Since the brain is nothing more than the effect of such transmissions, it is in no way either the source or the site of representation—that is, the brain is not the cause of memories and does not produce representations; it *transmits movement.* As the effect of the transmission of movements and a transmitter itself via the nervous system, the brain must be conceived of as an instrument of action, not of representation.[92] Thus, concludes Bergson, it is a strange hypothesis to claim that memories are somehow stored in the brain and that they are to be brought to consciousness by some astonishing but unknowable process. The second manner in which the past subsists is in the form of independent recollections requiring an effort of the mind to seek them out. Bergson examines this in detail, noting that too often this second process is confused with the first, with bodily memory. The result of such confusion is that the choices of active memory are reduced to those of habitual bodily memory so that the stratified bodily habits of the latter are confused with conscious recollections requiring effort.

Of course, we can easily investigate how readily the two may be confused. For example, we could memorize a poem or a speech, paying attention to what happens all though the procedure. The process of learning the poem demands repetition of the same efforts, in the same order, in the same length of time, as well as the evocation or production of particular passions: pain, stifled feeling, grace:

> O wind, rend open the heat,
> cut apart the heat,
> rend it to tatters.
>
> Fruit cannot drop
> through this thick air—
> fruit cannot fall into heat
> that presses up and blunts.
> the points of pears
> and rounds the grapes.
>
> Cut the heat—
> plough through it,
> turning it on either side
> of your path.[93]

In short, a closed system is created until the order of words becomes habitual, simply a habit that can be called upon. Nonetheless, to recall the memory of this poem I have to live it and act it. It is an action; it is part of my present, a present that *is* not but which *becomes* and so acts. It does not end here. I find myself at a dinner with friends with whom I have gone through a difficult event together, the death of a friend. We speak of how the event left us all unable to move forward, how it stopped up our emotions and our hearts. Someone at the table speaks about her pent-up feelings following the death, and someone else follows it up with a story of her own suppressed emotions, and someone else. . . . I listen fully as within the body:

> A series of mechanisms . . . react to [these] external stimuli [the stopped up emotion, the story, the group]. . . . [I] become conscious of these mechanisms as they come into play. The consciousness of a whole past of efforts stored up in the present [which] is [for me at that time and for those who hear it] also a memory. . . . It is bent on action, seated in the present, and looking only to the future. It retains from the past only the intelligently coordinated movements that represent the accumulated efforts of the past. It recovers those efforts, not in memory images which recall them but in the

> definite order and systematic character with which the actual movements take place. It no longer represents the past, but it acts it.[94]

So I act; I start to softly speak words I have learned, words memorized in this or another context of seeking release; I murmur: "O wind, rend open the heat, / cut apart the heat, / rend it to tatters. . . . " In spite of the emotional character of the situation, if memory images intervene at all in this habitual bodily memory, it is only to provide an association of ideas, the events that occurred just prior to or just after the initial act of memorizing the poem.

Learned memories, even when they consist of a memorized poem, must be severely differentiated from what Bergson calls "events" or memory images, and the failure to make this distinction distorts memory in a reductive manner. The memory of the act of memorization and the memory of the recitation of the poem at the dinner are memory images, events in life that bear a date, that will never occur again.[95] What passes between these two forms of memory is that I remember the poem because I recall the poem insofar as I know how to use it for this occasion; through the repetition of the poem, of its words, its nuances, its rhythms and moods, the nervous system has built up a motor habit linked with certain sensory stimuli. It is a consolidated system of movements insofar as it resists any attempt on my part to change or improvise the poem I have learned. In recalling the poem, I act before I think. Meanwhile, if I make use of the memory image to recall the moment of memorizing the poem, I must withdraw from the stimuli of the gathering, from the emotions, the stories, the fellowship, to another realm, which is useless, which is the realm of dreams. What this means is that bodily, learned memories are habitual motor tendencies and they do not account for our past psychical life insofar as they are actions, always in the present. We must look elsewhere for psychical life.

If there is such a thing as primary repression, it lies in the active motor habits of the body, "the practical and useful consciousness of the present moment, that is to say, . . . the sensory-motor equilibrium of a nervous system connecting perception with action," that binds us to the fascinating present.[96] And although it is the case, for Bergson, that we are acted upon—fascinated—far more frequently than we act, it is also true that, since affective sensations are qualitatively multiple, there are always fissures and cracks in the system of active habitual memory. When such fissures appear, psychical memory in the form of memory images inserts itself in the fissures, but not without some effort on the part of the living being. Without this effort, however, the whole of psychical life, the entire complexity of living beings, which we will discover in the multiple levels of virtual coexistence, and the ontological basis of change, life itself, would dry up and be lost to us forever. In this process, attention, a manifestation of the body's movements, the engagement of the nervous system—not the mind—in present perceptions, is crucial.

Whatever sense we make or can make of present perceptions relies on interpretation from the point of view of memory images selected by the reflection of attentive perception.[97] Attentive perception is, to recall the words and images of Luce Irigaray, a circuit of positive and negative charges holding one another in tension. As a circuit, every perception, every movement coming from objects and transmitted to the perception of a living being, continues the circuit through consciousness, memory, and back to the object. Such attentive perception arrests the movements of the body while psychically there is an enormous expansion and augmentation of the intellect, whose effect is to shake up the entire psychical organization of the being. When perception is attentive, every perception becomes an act of creation in which the perception opens as many circuits as there are memory images attracted by this new perception, making of every perception a qualitative multiplicity. Emphasizing the expansion of memory, Bergson writes: "It is the *whole* of memory, as we shall see, that passes over into each of these circuits, since memory is always present; but that memory, capable, by reason of its elasticity, of expanding more and more, reflects upon the object a growing number of suggested images—sometimes the details of the object itself, sometimes concomitant details which may throw light upon it."[98] The remarkable outcome of this process is that each perception is a complex multiplicity that includes not only the object perceived but also the expanded circuits, the deeper and more distant regions of memory, given virtually with the object, making possible perception as a "deeper stratum of reality."

In the "interval" between passive synthesis and active synthesis, between affection-action and affection-attention, the present perception and thus "psychical life" itself (which is always only present) can be and is repeated endlessly at different levels of virtual memory, from the most precise, dated and localized personal recollections that form the "envelope" least likely to be reflected because they demand such a specific bodily attitude, to the most vague and impersonal recollections, the envelope most likely to be reflected because the bodily attitude necessary to call them up is so nonspecific. So it is a virtual, and thus ontological and nonpsychological, memory that stands as the condition of the passage of every particular present in the movement from temporal expansion to the contraction in the present duration wherein we act—that is, from the pure ontological form of time to perception wherein an expanded, virtual region of the memory is actualized and so comes to have psychological existence.[99] This is true to the point where memories and perceptions can no longer be distinguished as the reflection—that is, literally, the projection of an actively created image identical with or at least "echoing" the perceived object.[100]

Association of Ideas and the Unconscious

To give up the sensory-motor functions that inaugurate perception would amount to abandoning action and the habits of a life. At the same time, this would be literally *dis*placing ourselves, leaving behind any motive for implementing an attentive life. It would launch us into the time of memory, the time of dreams in the ontological unconscious, where we would drift among useless or indifferent infinite recollections bearing no relation to present duration, to becoming, to life. Each memory image is a particular, an event with a date, a time, and a position in space whereby what is evident is principally its difference from everything else. In a life freed from present perception, truly deconstructive *différence* would be given full freedom, for without the demand of the present for memory images that resemble the current perception "anything can be associated with anything else."[101] Fearing this, philosophy has not been very interested in investigating ontological memory and the being of difference. Radical ontological heterogeneity is passed over because it is mistakenly identified with the dream, the limit of intelligibility, making it possible for representation, the spatialized, homogeneous, and hierarchical identity of selves and objects, to replace becoming as the true foundation of memory and action, and to replace the event as well, even though the event is what makes each present act truly innovative and new. Thus, it is usually the case that no attention is given to the body, that special image in the midst of a cosmos of images, the body as a section of *universal* becoming, a part of the whole. Or, if the body is considered, it is reduced to pure mechanism, pure habitual material. In either case, what is forgotten is that as a section of duration in the flow of the whole of duration of the whole world, the body is guided by contiguity and the echoes of images in calling up this or that spontaneous memory, the ontological memory that gives to the sensory-motor body the recollections it needs to fill each perception.[102]

In exchange—for they are not two separate systems—the sensory-motor functions of the body are the only way unconscious memories can materialize; they must respond to the appeal of perception. In the actual state of the becoming of a living being, duration is growth, but in the continuity that is becoming, bodily memory, consisting of the sum of sensory-motor systems organized by habit, serves the present, that quasi-instantaneous section or cut in the flow of duration. The bodily center of action in the flow of duration responds to the things in the material world that act upon it. The section is an instantaneous view of the flow of duration and therefore immobile.[103] Like all second articulations, bodily memory stabilizes and orders the body. As the references to Hume imply, this articulation feeds the illusion of objects as substances and selves as identical but, for Bergson, it also acts as a principle of choice for spontaneous and multiple virtual memory.

But habits, the second articulation, can also cut us off from the multiple sections of the ontological unconscious. In this there can be loss, sadness, even self-destruction. As Hume has pointed out, in the name of custom we replace diversity with simplicity, and, as Bergson and Deleuze imply, we are thereby cut off from the very form of creation. Swayed by habits, committed to constant action, we find ourselves trapped in an endless repetition in which each new situation forgoes its novelty and is merely repeated on the model of a previous bodily habit. Accordingly, in place of novelty, we produce representations. Under such conditions, without any reflection on difference, we discover nothing but resemblances wherever we turn and live among universals without being able to think them since, as Hume makes clear, we form general ideas by seeking a resemblance among several objects and applying the same name to them all; but even to seek resemblances demands qualitative difference.[104] We find ourselves restrained by a custom whose source of power and efficacy we have yet to examine. Perhaps this is even one and the same with the illusion we are immersed in. Under such conditions, we might find ourselves in the same situation as Ryder, the pianist of Kazuo Ishiguro's *The Unconsoled.*[105] The novel's unrelenting monotony comes, in part, from the disconnected responses of Ryder. He may or may not be married, he may or may not have a son, he may or may not have made promises to support certain members of the community and to carry out certain acts of goodwill. Ryder acts habitually, responding vaguely and thus badly to the demands made on him at every turn. What is amiss is that he is completely without creative memory. He cannot even initiate practicing the piano before the great event he has been brought to the town to inaugurate. He makes a fool of himself, though no one pays any attention, indicating that this is a cultural or social malaise and not just personal folly. Yet he simultaneously (and to some extent knowingly) disappoints and alienates those who depend upon him emotionally, indicating that affective life is not totally dead but is instead somehow cut off by habitual behavior.

Such a wild and extreme lack of connection to life indicates that something crucial is not operating or is blocked. Bergson argues that normal psychical life must oscillate between pure memory and pure action:

> In other words, memory, laden with the whole of the past, responds to the appeal of the present state by two simultaneous movements, one of translation, by which it moves in its entirety to meet experience, thus contracting more or less, though without dividing, with a view to action; and the other of rotation upon itself, by which it turns toward the situation of the moment, presenting to it that side of itself which may prove to be the most useful. . . . Everything happens then, as though our recollections were repeated an infinite number of times in these many possible reductions of our past life.[106]

What is particularly interesting in the contraction and expansion of the various levels of ontological memory is that although, as I have pointed out, in some instances former perceptions set up a complex motor apparatus that responds immediately to the appeal of an echoing perception, it is still the case that under the conditions described above the unconscious itself intervenes and extends itself into movements adopted by the current perceptions.

This is of interest because, as Deleuze asserts, it makes possible the emergence of a psychological unconscious distinct from the ontological unconscious. Whereas the latter is pure memory, virtual, inactive, and in itself, the former is the movement of virtual memory into memory images in the course of becoming actual. And as Deleuze also insists, when such memories seek to become actualized, to become embodied, repressions originating in present action and attention to life are the only ways to ward off any useless or dangerous memories that may also emerge.[107] This problem is the opposite of that of Ishiguro's Ryder, who either lacks or cannot connect with the ontological unconscious. Here, if any aspect of the nervous system or the sensory-motor system is damaged, it may prove impossible to keep useless or dangerous memories out of perception. Likewise, to the degree that the living being does not act, to this same degree such memories may invade. What is interesting is that the ontological unconscious is both the condition of perception in action and the condition of its failure, of what psychology likes to call pathology, the creation of a psychological unconscious that does not respond to our interests or needs. These are the aspects of the development of matter and memory I will begin to investigate in the next chapter. And there is one more aspect of life that is too often forgotten or undermined: if we seriously utilize the conception of virtual ontological memory, accepting that it is engaged as a whole in each perception, then what slips through the crack in the sensory-motor articulation of the body and the attention to interests and needs may prove to be of more interest and importance to philosophy and to life than we ever imagined.

5
Creative Evolution: An Ontology of Change

Tendencies, Not Oppositions

In the previous chapter, the Deleuze-Bergsonian interpretation of memory as ontological unconscious was placed at the intersection connecting human life and intelligence to the life of the cosmos. I wanted to propose that the psychic component of human life is intimately connected with the cosmos as a whole and to suggest that it is an aspect of the first articulation in its many occurrences. The contraction and folding over of the outside to the inside operates among the single-celled creatures as well as in complex human life, from the flows of the body without organs called earth to all forms of life itself. Out of contraction, this real event, duration, memory, and psychological existence are brought into being for humans. From flows and contractions arises the affectivity of all life, those qualitatively multiple durations of earth, of single-celled creatures, and of intelligent human life that, in the latter case, generate a concept of the self that, in the strictest sense, is never an identical self. Any self, any "I," is the flow of duration as well as of the past, wholly brought along in the infinite levels of ontological memory. This means, also, that our human accounts of phenomena must carefully consider that the objects and beings of the world have a history and a temporality that connects with our own and with the cosmos as a whole.

Additionally, I wanted to foster an awareness of the relation of philosophy to science. Although philosophy need not and cannot ignore the data of science, it would be a mistake to confuse philosophy itself with that data. For philosophy, if it proceeds according to the method of intuition, is a process of creation out of memory, out of the ontological unconscious, and not a process of modeling concepts on the data of science. Now, what is absolutely crucial with respect to memory is that it consists of multiple, perhaps infinite, virtual levels or regions, each of which contains the whole of the past in a more or less contracted state. Out of this more or less contracted whole, by a process that dissociates and diverges, increasingly complex structures are produced. When, for example, memories are actualized as memory images, this is not a simple motion; for such actualization can only occur through dissociation and divergence. The memories, each of them repetitions of a whole past life, are expanded or contracted depending on how near or far they are from the present. This movement of the *whole* past into each present is called "translation" by Bergson, and in translation each level of the past, the ontological unconscious, must contract to some greater or lesser degree (more contraction if it is deep memory, less if not) in order to meet the present moment, the flow of duration.[1] The effect of contracting the past into the present, into the sensory-motor perception image and the moment of action in the world, is to make the present the most contracted level of the past and thereby achieve the decisive ontological as well as real connection between matter and memory.[2] Memories contract into the present when they respond to the demands of present perception oriented toward action. Among the many memories and the many levels of memory qualified by the association of images, there is a "rotation" in which each and every level or region of the whole of memory presents that aspect of itself most suited to the present perception. Many, many memories answer the call. This is why the contraction of memory into present perception and action is not a reduction of memory, for "if this perception evokes in turn different memories, it is not by a mechanical adjunction of more and more numerous elements which, while remaining unmoved, it attracts around it, but rather by an expansion of the entire consciousness which, spreading out over a larger area, discovers the fuller detail of its wealth."[3]

What we take to be merely the association of one image with another is preceded by something that conditions it and makes it possible: a dissociation and divergence, a creative force constitutive of life itself, which arises out of and in terms of the actual life of the living being. Since dissociation and divergence are the creative forces of life, we must be able to see them at work in the direction or tendency toward memory as well as in the tendency to action and matter of the preceding paragraph. Memory consists of an infinite number of different planes, though Bergson believes that we have certain dominant memories around which others gather, organizing themselves according to the personality of each subject. So, for example, trying to remember something specific, such as the name of a former acquaintance, demands localizing one of these dominant planes, then expanding, spreading out the confused mass of each plane, until by disassociation and divergence from the mass the name is given. This is not a simplification or reduction of memory; rather, it is an expansion of memory. Even in cases of amnesia, a specific memory can be obtained through hypnosis if it has simply slipped to another plane of memory and the act of hypnosis is able to locate that plane by expanding the search over more and more levels of memory.[4] The point here is that the process of expansion through dissociation and divergence is one that memory shares with matter (movement in the direction of action). Movement, whether in the direction of action or in the direction of memory, is neither two separate and unconnected movements nor an after-the-fact reunification; rather dissociations are constitutive of all life in both directions. For Bergson, each movement is a tendency (each usually containing some elements of the other) of life, tendencies that expand by dissociation and divergence and affirm the reality of a genuinely growing world in which authentic novelties emerge into actuality from virtual memory.[5]

Expansion and increasing complexity are the great forces of life, and creation through dissociation and divergence can be found to figure the constitution of the subject and of time. To conceptualize how the strata that make up a subject and the process that is time are realized necessitates beginning with the real and complex processes that constitute the intermixture of the psychic and material tendencies of life. The problematization of the intermixture may only succeed insofar as it begins with an elaboration of the processes by which duration is creation and life is change. Following Hume-Bergson-Deleuze in describing and theorizing the processes by which matter and memory are created has necessitated investigation into numerous areas of philosophy, science, and especially research into creative processes. This should be no surprise given the diffuse and divergent tendencies of life that have given birth to matter and memory by separating them out of the heterogeneous flow into divergent orders. Still, we have really just started, for many "problems," in Bergson's sense, remain. That is, in order for there to be two directions or tendencies and their intermixture, certain conditions must be met. We must be able to show how the tendencies or directions that life takes make sense when change and creation are their conditions, and that change and creation are the real though virtual conditions of life. By this means an ontology of change, an ontology of creation and becoming, of life itself, will no longer be impossible to conceive of and, more irrefutably, to live. And if, in such an ontology, the ruin of representation has been effected and thus the ruin of time subject to movement and organic hierarchies, then in place of social and political representations—

that is, conceptions of social and political hierarchies—we may start to conceive of as well as to create the monstrosity of singularity and multiplicity that is change.

I would like to begin turning in the direction of exploring psychic states by venturing further into duration, for as Deleuze develops this notion, duration is what differs from itself; thus it is difference in kind, the tendency to differ in kind, where finding differences in kind is one crucial element of the method of intuition.[6] "Pure duration is the form which the succession of our conscious states assumes when our ego lets itself *live,* when it refrains from separating its present state from its former states. . . . [I]n recalling these states, it does not set them alongside its actual state as one point alongside another, but it organizes them with itself [*avec lui*], as it happens when we recall the notes of a tune, melting, so to speak into one another."[7] To interrupt the melody, to hold a note too long, or to play out of tune all result in a qualitative change in the entire melody. We have seen that in Hume's account, the mind has a principle that produces the subject. This is no less the case for Bergson. For the interconnection, the intimate contact of elements of duration, operates such that each one is a contraction of the whole and can only be separated from it by abstraction. And this whole is made greater by the action of memory in each and every perception.

Opposed to this richness and depth are the demands of socialization, to which we acquiesce insofar as they complement duration; they are our other *tendency,* which moves us toward action and matter, a tendency that does not make intimacy with our own duration easy to achieve. The impact of this is that there is and can be no prescientific intelligence, only the two directions, the two tendencies always changing, always in motion. For Bergson, the existence of opposing yet complementary tendencies that are often found mixed together is characteristic of all life. He explicitly rejects the view of animal and vegetable life forwarded by most philosophy since Aristotle, a view that claims that instinctive and intelligent life are successive degrees of development. Even in Merleau-Ponty one finds the impersonal, instinctual existence of animals linked to their sensory-motor capabilities, whereas human intelligent behavior is linked to signification. The ability to signify is, in Merleau-Ponty's account, a different degree of behavior from the instinctual, not a difference in kind. Consequently, animals cannot, for the most part, manipulate or imaginatively vary their situations as can intelligent human beings.[8] Bergson demurs that insofar as instinct and intelligence are tendencies that have evolved by dissociation and divergence from a rich and multiple tendency that gave way to differences in kind, they always can and do intermingle, but differentiation or "differen*c*iation" is that explosive force producing divergent lines of evolution.[9] If at times plant and animal are not easily distinguished, this is precisely because tendencies do intermingle and one or the other dominates from time to time, even in the same species. This argument is reminiscent of Simone de Beauvoir's claims in *The Second Sex* that in certain plant and animal species sex is not easily distinguished.[10] Is it not because, as tendencies that differ in kind from one another, both are present in all species, though now one and then the other of these tendencies will dominate depending on the conditions? In effect, even though sexual difference arises as all differences do, empirically, out of the contraction and folding over of the outside to the inside, nevertheless, this would make of sexual difference a difference in kind and not, as too many contemporary thinkers would have it, a difference in degree.

As animal and vegetable have diverged, so too have instinct and intelligence, and likewise, intension and extension—that is, duration and matter. At each divergence the whole—that is, a virtual whole—moves in each direction; thus each direction must carry some or even a great deal of the other direction within it virtually.[11] What we perhaps fail to realize is that what gets actualized from out of the virtual by means of action does not follow the rules of representation, but has its own rules. Those rules are rules of difference, dissociation, and creation. Since the actual is no more than what gets realized in the image and likeness of the possibility it represents, its rules are the rules of representation. However, when the virtual is actualized, this actuality in no way resembles or represents the virtuality it materializes, and this is what opens the way to creative evolution or, better said, creative explosion.[12]

What Bergson calls instinct is neither a material nor a conscious inner drive; it is simply the tendency to organize, a tendency that is never without its complement, intelligence. Yet the functions instinct produces should not be assumed to be subject to some other hierarchizing order. Instinct just organizes the instruments that it finds at hand and whose structure tends to be invariable; thus, it is not subject to overdetermination. One might in fact claim, with no distortion, that the process of organization is in the instinct that has to use the organ.[13] It is "machinic."[14] In *Anti-Oedipus* Deleuze and Guattari elaborate upon this conception to characterize desire, which is simply another way of referring to what I have called here "life itself." That is, desire is machinic; it makes connections, as productive, unconscious desiring-machines are "the domain of free syntheses . . . [of] endless connections, nonexclusive disjunctions, nonspecific conjunctions, partial objects and flows."[15] Unconscious desiring-production proceeds along a variety of paths unless it is "subjected to the requirements of representation" and must yield to the representation of something like Oedipus, the despotic signifier, where production is no longer the production of the real, but only of some imaginary thing, the "unconscious expression."[16] This is the point at which the machine is overdetermined because it is subject to intelligence. For Bergson, even though machinic connections do not exclude intelligence, the pleasure of such connections is that they are destined for a directness in their functioning, a specialization that precludes their being subject to an organizing signifier. Machinic connections pursue a definite and singular relation. When instinct is conscious in the living being, the latter hesitates before choosing from among several different connections, but chooses only one nonetheless. When instinct can be said to reflect an unconscious intelligence (as when the baby takes the mother's breast, revealing knowledge of a thing it has never seen), it does so as something acted, not as something thought.[17]

Under the influence of the secondary articulation that organizes and stabilizes the body, the opposing but complementary tendency, intelligence, aims at getting matter to act on matter, constructing tools whose specific functions are indeterminate and thus open up an unlimited field of activity. In this sense, intelligence can be defined by the activity of taking something intended to carry out one function and using it to accomplish something else, a definition that Deleuze has put to use in every field from literature to politics in the construction of minor literatures and nomadic politics. Intelligence operates by transferring functions from one activity to another not because intelligence is the only and true province of creation but because at certain points in social and political life, this is the only option open. Under the rule of a dominant and hierarchical state power, a major language, or any system of fascistic order, such a motion is the only free act available. Acting freely, intelligence constructs its own useful machinery; this is already a complex stage in the organization of intelligence, but one that has creative advantages in the midst of practical spheres delimited by major (stable) languages and hierarchic politics.[18]

What intelligence knows, strictly speaking, according to Bergson, is relations, but only relations of a certain type. It relates an object to an object, a part to a part, by processes that connect like to like, cause to effect, attribute to subject. Intelligence can operate to relate one homogeneous point of space to another or one material object to another. What is striking however, is how quickly intelligence, which constructs relations, succumbs to treating everything it places in relations like inert matter, unorganized solids, thus leaving fluidity unnoticed and without consideration. Why? Because duration is movement and continuity, whereas in order to carry out its task, intelligence chooses what is not real, discontinuity. Beginning with immobility, intellect seeks to create motion out of a string of immobilities stuck together and so attempts to *represent* duration and change as this string of immobilities. Of course, it cannot. Fascinated by objects and action, intelligence moves in the direction of its own externalization in homogeneous, spatial representations and forgoes the qualitative multiplicity that necessarily remains uncounted and unhinged from any subservience to objects. Yet intelligence tries to capture duration, too. What happens to pure duration, heterogeneity, and difference when the forces of externalized intelligence capture them? Heterogeneity and difference are profoundly modified; intelligence separates them and represents them in homogeneous space for the sake of clarity and objectification; they are represented. For Bergson, this refracted self is but a shadow of our personal conscious states, our fundamental self (*moi fondamental*), but broken to pieces as it is, its adaptation to social life and, in particular, to language, cannot be denied.[19]

Here we find repeated the distinction Irigaray makes between a logic of fluids and a logic of solids: fluid conditions are represented and solidified in homogeneous space. Perceptions, emotions, sensations, and ideas, when represented, are clear and precise but common, impersonal. Irigaray has said as much: that in life, language, and philosophy, women have been women only in relation to the determinations made for them by men, a system of oppositions. The effect of this system, she proclaims, is to displace women from any situation they might establish for themselves in terms of their own duration; but now, in addition, I would say that the system of solids is an attempt to refute the fluidity of duration, which, though it is a confused because rich multiplicity, is by no means hopeless chaos. It is to Irigaray's credit—and I agree with her in this—that she believes in an "improper" language that expresses multiplicity and fluidity, for (as Bergson argues) as a reality, fluids resist adequate symbolization and serve as a constant reminder of the powerlessness of representational concepts and their logic to account for all of nature's characteristics. Thus Bergson, Irigaray, and Deleuze would apparently share the view that symbolic or logical *representations* (any conceptualization based on homogeneous and hierarchized units) are the sites of lack with regard to their representative function, and that fluidity, as virtual multiplicity, is what is real. It is no accident that the method of philosophy that Bergson endorses is the method of "intuition" (discussed in chapter 4), for intuition is related to instinct. It is an inquiry that refrains from fixation on use by attempting to state the problem correctly by searching for differences in kind and the articulations of the real. Instinct is that tendency that grasps differences in kind and the real, whereas intelligence, driven by action to externalize its activities, articulates differences of degree in the common language of order-words.

From Bergson's point of view, time and space have been collapsed by intelligence into a badly analyzed composite, since in our thinking concrete extensity, which we perceive, is confused with space, which we merely conceive. The latter is a symbolic mental diagram that covers up the immediate knowledge we have.[20] To undo the blunder, Bergson proceeds on several different fronts: he carries out an analysis of matter, he reinvestigates the relation between our personal duration and that of the world, and he carefully examines how space and language—which he takes to be intimately connected—are constructed. To open up the domain between Irigaray's feminist ontological concerns and Bergson's cosmic ontological concerns, let us begin with the last, the construction of space and language. Where do we start? Let us remember Irigaray's words: "Be patient," she cautions, and "begin with what you feel, right here, right now."[21] The place to start, according to Irigaray, is with affectivity.

Duration and Space

"For example, an obscure desire gradually becomes a deep passion. . . . Little by little it permeates a larger number of psychic elements, tingeing them, so to speak with its own color. . . . How do you become aware of a deep passion once it has taken hold of you, if not by perceiving that the same objects no longer impress you in the same manner?"[22] What has taken place? An image has penetrated through perception, through affectivity, into the whole of memory itself, and now colors all perceptions. An intense, deep passion is born. It is a change of quality, but we interpret it spatially as a change of "magnitude" because, Bergson ruefully exclaims, we like simple thoughts, because our language is a poor companion to the subtleties of psychological analysis.[23] But since the same state of affairs exists and applies equally to muscular efforts, we might begin to be a bit more skeptical about magnitude.

Extend an arm forcefully, point the forefinger. What you feel is a complex afferent sensation: contracted muscles, stretched ligaments, compressed joints, immobilized chest, closed glottis, knit brow, clenched jaws. The greater the effort, the greater the number of muscles contracting in sympathy—that is, more and more of the body is affected. "Intensify" any gesture and what occurs? A fist is clenched or hands are thrown up in protest, lips are pressed together; you can only clench your hand so much and your arms only reach so high, your lips press together only so tightly. You cannot bring your body to the point of exploding like a cartoon character. What you experience in your hand, arms, lips remains somewhat constant; what increases is the participation of the rest of your body in the action. Your face and neck grow taut, your arms and legs stiffen, your back may begin to strain. The only change in the hand, arms, or lips is one of quality; they do not explode, they begin to feel tired. So the intensified gesture amounts to a simultaneous feeling of increased peripheral sensations and a change in quality. But again we "tend" to resort to an interpretation based on magnitude. We localize the entire gesture with all its resonating sensations to the exact point where it yields a useful effort, and we focus on the task we are attempting to accomplish.[24] Yes, you have stopped the approaching menace, you have objected powerfully to social injustice; but have you increased the magnitude of effort in any one part of the body? Bergson's unequivocal reply is that you have experienced a combination of a qualitative increase up to a limit point accompanied by an increasing number of muscles and parts of the body. This is the creation of an intensification; it is intensity.

What about sensations whose cause appears to lie in something outside of ourselves? How do we define intensity with regard to heat, weight, or light? Do we resort to the spatialized metaphor, that is, to magnitude? A more intense heat, such as that of the tropical summer sun, is different in kind—that is, different in quality—from a feeble heat, such as that of a Chicago winter. As Bergson argues, "A more intense heat is really another kind of heat."[25] Following from this, there must be no contradiction between the claim that the greatest difference in kind is the difference between intense heat and intense cold and the claim of physiologists that, nevertheless, some points on the body are predisposed to feel heat and others are predisposed to feel cold, for these too are qualitative differences, differences in kind. A pressure of greater and greater intensity against the body, such as one experiences when lifting a weight or carrying a child, is likewise a matter of qualitative differences, differences in kind: first mere contact, then pressure, then resistance, even pain, extending further and further through the body. The increasing pressure is not, therefore, an increase of sensation but rather, focusing on the immediate affection, *a sensation of increase,* a different sensation, a difference in kind.[26]

Reducing the difference between heat and cold to magnitude, whether by moving closer to or further from the source of the heat or cold or because different parts of the body perceive heat or cold somewhat exclusively, is the effect of our tendency to externalize the sensation. Likewise, when we perceive a sensation of increasing resistance and pain because of a heavy object, we reduce this perception to magnitude under the influence of the notion of a homogeneous—meaning continuous and uniform—movement in a homogeneous space. This prejudice extends to all aspects of perception. It is a mark of our imperceptibility that even though we know that changes in light produce remarkable changes in quality with respect to how sharply objects appear, as well as changes in their hues and colors, yet we insist that each and every object has its own particular color, hue, and outline.[27] In each and every case, when we talk about the sensation of increase, we tend to reduce it to merely an increase of sensation.

By this means the qualitative heterogeneity of fluidity is eliminated and what is inserted in its place is a logic of solids characterized in terms of homogeneous spatial units of increasing magnitude. Irigaray has claimed that the denial by philosophy of a way to conceptualize and speak of fluidity has dire consequences for women because women have been socially and historically excluded from the objectified hierarchies of solid logic and so do not and never will have a place in its order. Irigaray suggests that, having been excluded from the domain of solids, the woman's body—not just the maternal body but the affective body of multiple and layered pleasures with woman's "specific sensitivities" as a cluster—has no way of being "known" because morphological fluidity, which is constant change, cannot be conceived using the concepts produced by the logic of solids.[28] So it is of import to follow Bergson in determining how the logic of solids is formed and how it comes to organize the entire field of perception, affectivity, knowledge, and language, for by this means we can see to what extreme this tendency of human beings develops and how it comes to the position where it overwhelms the other tendency, which moves in the direction of memory and also fluidity. This is of great importance not only for language but also, as we will see, for an understanding of social and psychological processes.

What we fail to distinguish, according to Bergson, is the difference between what is immediately given in duration and the physical effect of passion, gesture, movement, color, sound, light, weight. A complex feeling or movement as well as an image, sound, or physical force contains many simple affections which, taken as duration, are neither perfectly clear nor perfectly realized. Any psychic state, any duration affected by these many elements, is fluid becoming and not static units, so the psychic state is changed as soon as the feelings, movements, images, sounds, and physical forces are perceived. This, notes Bergson, is not how we usually talk about something like a body.[29] What, then, do we mean by "body"? Generally, we think of material objects localized in space, able to be divided up in parts of space that can be counted or measured. When something is numbered or counted, we consider it to be a collection of identical units pictured either in succession or repeated, juxtaposed in space. Yet because we are accustomed to abstractly counting numbers that we have learned by counting things in space, we mistakenly assume that number is built up in duration. In fact, what we have done is to transfer points in space onto moments of duration as if the moments were separable material entities. In duration, a succession can be perceived but not counted since each moment is inextricably bound with what precedes and exceeds it. Yet, in the case of numerical units, we go in the opposite direction and subdivide them into fractions. This we could not do if we did not presume that each number is an extended object even while our intuition of it is a simple act of the mind.[30]

Given this presumption, Bergson asks if it is reflected in the manner in which we diagram numbers. We draw each as a mathematical point separated from the next point by an empty space, which is to say, we represent them. In this, what is the role of the mind? Unlike a complex feeling, which includes a large number of elements that do not stand out and when distinctly perceived are perceived from the point of view of an already changed psychic state, there is no change in the general appearance of a body. So even though the psychic process of successive attention to different parts of space proceeds without division, still we perceive actually—that is, as localized in space (and so not virtually)—the subdivisions of what is not divided. Not surprisingly, Bergson argues, we call this perception that mathematics has taught us "objectivity."[31] Unlike mental images, that is, purely affective psychic states, the perception of material objects is localized in homogeneous units in space. If we wish to count affective states (feelings, sensations, ideas), we can accomplish this only by means of a symbolic spatial representation of homogenous units stripped of qualities and separated by empty intervals.[32] This is the meaning of objectification and objectivity, according to Bergson, and we can observe that it coincides with MacKinnon's analysis of objectification as distance and aperspectivity (discussed in chapter I).

Of course, the representation of objectivity is possible only insofar as the intellect is a tendency that is concerned with relations, with the association of whatever parts are presented to consciousness. But association itself is, in the Humean construction made use of here, part of the system of understanding only because we are first capable of the perception of affective qualities, qualities that are given in duration, not extension, qualities that coexist as inextensive sensations and themselves give rise to space. Qualitative, intensive heterogeneity can be interpreted as quantitative, extensive homogeneity, and this gives way to the conception of space that we presume comes first. Thus, Bergson maintains that whereas all that is given is given as affective sensation, qualitative heterogeneity can be represented, through an effort of the mind, as homogeneous space, and, I would add, this is the only way it can be represented, since this is representation. What, Bergson asks, in the qualities themselves gives way to this? Is there among human beings some kind of reaction to qualitative perception, a reversal of quality and heterogeneity? The homogeneous conception of time is of succession, that of space is coexistence, though time seems to be simply the "ghost of space" as it haunts reflection.[33] This must mean that in addition to pure duration, to this life of the ego that endures, there is something else. To find it we must break the barrier between the unextended and the extended and between quality and quantity.

The Dominance of Action

For understanding, mind at first stands over against matter as a pure unity facing a divisible multiplicity; that is, perceptions apparently composed of heterogeneous qualities stand opposed to the homogeneous and calculable changes of matter. So we begin with the "double antithesis" between unextended and extended, quality and quantity. This is because materialism, Bergson complains, always tries to derive duration from matter, whereas idealism uses the same model to construct matter from mind. But if we were to recall that our body is an image among images and that our intellect is a faculty of distinguishing one thing from another and so does not create, then we would recognize the futility of either move. We would realize that perception takes place in the world among images and memory is the beginning of any action, not its ground.[34] Given that pure memory unites with the perception of the body in action, can we not say that the difference between unextended and extended, quality and quantity, has to do with whether or not heterogeneity is highly concentrated and dense or highly diluted and attenuated? In short, between quality and quantity, memory and matter, there is a difference in tension. We can recover this difference by examining the utilitarian work of intelligence in the service of action.

Pure intuition is duration, an undivided continuity, yet it continually appears to us to be broken up into discrete words from the side of consciousness and independent objects from the side of the world. This is due, we have seen, to the demands placed on intelligence to serve action—that is, embodied life.[35] The surprising conclusion that Bergson is leading to is that our knowledge, our most abstract and theoretical knowledge, has been too much under the influence of our surface and acquired habits, our actions, our embodiment, the omnipresent necessity to choose based on what is most useful. And what has been most useful for human beings who are both fascinated by their own action and driven to continue to act is refracting pure duration into space, reducing its fluidity to a static, impersonal, and public form whose elements are dissociated and juxtaposed and which can be spoken about in the common language of society.[36] Personal durations all have their own unique "coloring." If, as Bergson would have it, I am feeling confused or depressed, elated or joyful, there are a thousand different elements that dissolve into and permeate one another without precise outlines. Even more, these feelings and ideas are developing and changing; they are those of a person who lives. These elements assemble a feeling that is entirely original to me, but in order to discuss these feelings and ideas I separate them, giving each a name borrowed from the common stock of publicly used words. Now I can report that I am "happy" or "depressed." Either way, the coded words are colorless, lifeless, without any creative or original character. What I have done, observes Bergson, is replace the living and original feelings with a juxtaposition of thoroughly lifeless states that can be easily translated into words expressing the common, impersonal ideas and feelings thought and felt by everyone.[37]

This is the so-called universal story that novelists and poets are praised for; these are the order-words that we repeat because they are the ones society has taught us; this is the language that differentiates in terms of oppositions. Once the ready-made ideas are spread out, exteriorized in relation to one another, and configured on the model of space, they can be organized by a variety of logical and psychological maneuvers. Given the unrelenting drive toward action of human beings, intellect moves at this stage in the direction of fabrication, treating everything it encounters like inert matter. Whatever is fluid is gone; everything, even the fluid duration of an ego, is projected into homogeneous space and so transformed.

Even though these operations distort duration, fluidity, and continuity, still, as we have seen, they are one of life's own tendencies:

> Let us note, in passing, that it is this power that we affirm when we say that there is a *space,* that is to say, a homogeneous and empty medium, infinite and infinitely divisible, lending itself indifferently to any mode of decomposition whatsoever. A medium of this kind is never perceived; it is only conceived. What is perceived is extension colored, resistant, divided according to the lines which mark out the boundaries of real bodies or of their real elements. We project the whole of these possible decompositions and recompositions behind real extension in the form of a homogenous space, empty and indifferent, which is supposed to underlie it.[38]

So our power over matter is to decompose according to any law and recompose according to any system. The same drive toward fabrication, action, and manipulation operates with respect to language. For instance, Bergson finds the hypothesis that the sign adheres to the signified much too restricted for human life. Instead, he maintains, the word is free and transferable from thing to memory to image to idea. However, even as it extends freely to many different types of entities, language ultimately does not respect their unique qualities. Language converts them all to things by applying forms meant for material objects. Even concepts are thought of as outside one another so as to constitute an intelligible world resembling that of solids. So rather than images, concepts are symbols.

Logic is a complete set of symbols whose rules express the most general relations among solids. In this view, the relation between geometry, which takes solid bodies as its object, and logic, which is modeled on the relations discovered by geometry, begins to be clearer.[39]

Geometry and its product, logic, in turn produce deduction, modeled not on the mind, as we generally believe, but rather on homogeneous matter and on the geometry of solids suggested by the most general and immediately perceived properties of solids. Draw a triangle. The relation between the definition and its consequences, the various geometrical-mathematical properties of a triangle, are all given in the drawing. No deduction of any other kind of concept ever matches that of the geometrical solid for perfection. Yet the logic of deduction ends up being applied to all nongeometrical concepts and so to qualities, even though it derives from a degradation of the geometry fully applicable to the solid and material world alone.[40] Induction, too, implies that qualities do not alter, that they are like magnitudes, and that there is no fluid duration. The same objects in the same relations will produce the same results. Everything remains exactly the same as qualitative differences resolve into the homogeneity of space that contains them until they conform to geometry at the ideal limit of induction as well as deduction—that is, until today's triangle of two specific sides is imposed over yesterday's and produces the same result, the same third side.[41]

For creation and novelty, Deleuze argues, the inverse motion is needed, even in the midst of highly organized languages. "Oppose a purely intensive usage of language to all symbolic or even significant or simply significant usages of it. Arrive at a perfect and unformed expression, a materially intense expression."[42] When duration contracts, its moments are given over to intension, to quality, the unformed expression that deterritorializes the symbolism and significance of the common language. When duration relaxes its tension it extends itself, reterritorializing—that is, reforming and restabilizing—language. This second tendency, Bergson contends, is the interruption of the creative process; it takes an interruption to let mathematical order and inflexible determinism capture the intensive force of duration. In this way physical laws express a negative tendency, the relaxation of the intensive duration into extensive materiality, liberty into necessity, leading the way toward space.[43]

What ontology is at work here? Contraction and expansion seem to coexist in a single duration. Deleuze argues that there is a difference in kind between matter and memory but memory tends, then, to take all differences in kind upon itself, whereas differences in degree fall to matter. Duration consists entirely of qualitative, sensory-motor differences until it relaxes so much that it extends itself. Matter is difference in degree to the point where it becomes space, the schema of an indefinite divisibility. That these transformations occur without dualism is due to the virtuality of all degrees and levels or kinds of duration. Coexistence in duration is virtual. All the levels of expansion and contraction coexist in a single time that is virtual.[44] How can this be? Watch a violinist play a single note that takes up the entire motion of the bow from frog to tip. From the point of view of duration, the bow moves from frog to tip as an indivisible whole passing over the string. From the point of view of space whose every point is fixed, the bow consists of an infinite number of indivisible points, so each point on the moving bow must have passed over the string an infinitely short period of time.[45]

So which is it, a whole duration or a geometrical line? Because mathematics defines position in terms of distance from points of reference or axes, and movement by the variations of distance, this could mean indifferently that the axis is displaced in relation to a point or a point in relation to an axis. Movement, in this sense, is just a change of position. But real movements are not just changes of position.[46] Real movement is grasped affectively as a change of quality. Bodies present themselves to us as systems of qualities; thus between our internal muscular sensations and the external sensible qualities of matter there is movement. Movement and motion connect duration absolutely with matter. One's own body and that of others are first distinguished as zones of action, zones of movement, distinct material zones, from within the continuity of the universe: "Our needs are, then, so many searchlights which, directed upon the continuity of sensible qualities, single out in it distinct bodies. . . . To establish these special relations among portions thus carved out from sensible reality is just what we call *living*."[47] But it is our fascination with our own material interests that has led us in the wrong direction, for the study of bodies does not explain matter at all. Living, as we do, a moving continuity, we follow our needs; we adhere to the supposition that the representation of solids bumping into other solids reflects how we act on the world, and we dissociate movement from the whole that moves. The result is a conception of bodies representing permanence and homogeneous movements in space representing movement.[48] This "habit" hinders our thinking again and again, rendering motion an accidental change of relations between solids.

But there is a solution, Bergson insists, for movements are far from being made sense of as merely changes of quantity. Billions of vibrations are contracted into the narrow duration of a perceived color, which, motionless on the surface, vibrates in its depths. Why can there not be some homogeneity within qualities, a slight homogeneity within heterogeneous qualities? When physicists construe atoms as a vortex or as lines of force, they do so only because these are convenient symbols for their mathematics, but is there not something in their notions of changes of tension and energy to make use of?[49] Ultimately, the problem is not space, since space is merely a representation, a mental diagram; the problem is creating a conception of duration that recognizes its multiple rhythms, the many virtual memories, each of which reflects the whole, each of which when actualized in a perception has greater tension or relaxation. It is a problem of attaining a vision of matter apart from the daily needs and interests that drive us to conceptualize bodies in space; it is the problem of envisioning and creating on the basis of the rhythms of life. To do this, we may have to take the investigation beyond even Bergson. We may have to ask, more profoundly than Bergson, about the ontology of becoming, the being of becoming. The first and second syntheses of time are the movements of affection and action, life and creation. But we have found ourselves stymied. Directed by action into the sphere of objectification and spatiality, how can we recover fluidity? In other words, is there another temporalization, a third synthesis, at work to think the logic of fluidity and the reality of duration? Or is representation the only means available to us to make sense of the world?

Spiritual Life

In the previous chapter I made use of Hume's account of the qualification of the mind to explain how we move from the first to the second temporal synthesis. Let me briefly retrace this argument in order to prepare for Deleuze's articulation of a third temporal synthesis. Experience, for Hume, is a principle that introduces the various conjunctions (and . . . and) of objects for the constitution of the past. Habit is another principle that organizes the mind to expect the same kinds of habitual formations in the future. Together they affect the imagination so as to form certain ideas in a more intense and lively manner than others. What Hume lets us think in place of *a priori* principles is the notion that the connection between one idea and another lies in the experiential and habitual determination of the mind, a qualification of the mind that constitutes the subject. So when Boundas, for example, concurs that empiricists, like Hume, "begin with the mind as a theater without a stage," then proceed to ask how the mind becomes a subject, he affirms this creative empiricism.[50] By such means Deleuze's intervention in Hume was put into circulation: impressions of sensation are the origin of the mind, but principles of association, by which means we make the transition from an object to its usual attendant, from the impression of one to the lively idea of the other, are what give a nature to the mind; they qualify the mind.

From this point, I proceeded to Hume's argument that ideas are always derived from impressions and when these impressions disappear, something is left; what is left is an idea that "returns upon the soul" to produce "impressions of reflection." Impressions of reflection are then copied or repeated so that passions as well as understanding are, for Hume, an effect of reflection or contemplation. When living beings reflect on impressions of pleasure or pain, the original impressions from which reflections arise always and only come from natural and physical causes, which Bergson refers to as motions. This emphasizes the relation to or from the outside and the process of contraction, the folding of what is outside to the inside. It assures that the qualification of the mind giving rise to pleasure and pain derives from impressions such as hunger, cold, thirst, heat. And as the effect of the repetition of pleasure and pain, more complicated passions such as desire, aversion, hope, and fear begin to play upon the scene. This, I noted, is due to the connection of impressions of reflection that resemble one another: grief and disappointment connect with anger, envy, malice; joy conjoins love, generosity, pity, courage, pride. When the association of ideas or that of impressions connect ideas or impressions they are additive, but they are more than that. Idea intertwines with idea, impression with impression; they generate a violent double impulse of the passions. Impressions are connected only by resemblance, which operates such that no hidden, inner, psychological or facultative impulses need be formulated to do the work of empiricist ontology, for which the contraction of outside to inside and the qualification of the mind is always already at work. Nor, however, do we revert to mere mechanism such that passions are the effect of purely material forces. In this way, Hume opens up a new territory for thought, though he does not venture beyond the violent and powerful double impulses of the connected impressions of reflection.

Likewise, Bergson's full attention seems to be focused upon the heterogeneity of duration and the homogeneity of space. And even though duration produces memory as multiple, virtual levels of heterogeneity, each of which interprets the whole, nevertheless it is Deleuze who pushes on deep into memory and deep into the passionate creativity memory actualizes. Deleuze makes his way through Hume and Bergson, through the qualifications of the mind, through fluid virtual multiplicity, to the repetitions in life that make it "*une vie spirituelle.*" Life in this sense is spiritual but this is something more like "spirited life," the movement toward new creations born out of conclusions incommensurable with their premises.[51] Once again, Bergson's cone-shaped diagram has the advantage of offering an image of memory that is multilayered and simultaneous, ever increasing upon itself like a snowball rolling in the snow.[52] Each section of the cone is not so much a different memory as it is a different view of the whole of memory. All the levels of the pure past coexist virtually. Freedom consists of choosing the level; it is the actualization, in becoming, of an entire life emerging as various degrees of the contraction or expansion of a past that has not become past by first being present.[53] Likewise, every object, plant, and animal has its own duration. The duration of the cube of sugar melting in a glass of water coincides with the duration of my waiting, and is indicative of how the entire universe endures, continually elaborating and creating itself anew.[54] So the universe must be a gigantic cone, an ever-rolling snowball in which each and every life chooses its level. Freedom, I have noted, operates here with respect to choosing the level that contracts into the present perception. Such freedom has nothing to do with willing, for this is a freedom realized only insofar as it is connected with what is deeper, the whole of life, the virtual coexistence of all the levels of the pure past, each with its own color, as Bergson says, there for the subject to draw on.[55] Contracting the whole in each present, each present takes up another level of the whole, and each life takes up another life, which is also at another level. So it is that "the philosopher and the pig, the criminal and the saint, acted out the same past, at the different levels of a gigantic cone. . . . Each one chooses his pitch or his tone, perhaps his words, but the tune is certainly the same, and under all the words, in every possible tone, and in every pitch, the same tra-la-la."[56]

Deleuze wishes to enter the whole of virtual memory, along with world memory, in a way that Bergson hints at but does not develop, in a way that Hume anticipates but does not or cannot theorize. Bergson accepts the tendency of human beings that moves in the direction of clarity and definition in language, mathematical measures and calculations in science. This is the tendency that makes possible major languages as well as the minor literatures that are conditioned by "great (or established) literature."[57] But if there is an ontology of change in Bergson's philosophy, if it is possible to create life and concepts on the basis of memory, duration, and virtual multiplicity instead of only on the basis of homogeneous spaces that must be apportioned hierarchically and represented, then it makes sense to push beyond where Bergson has left us. Deleuze takes this analysis to the next layer. He wishes to live the being in itself of the past, to enter the in-itself of memory without realizing it in the present for action. In this sense memory undergoes a passive rather than an active synthesis, a synthesis of reminiscence, neither the present it was nor the actual present it could be; it is the form of a past that has never been present.[58] This is, of course, Proust's Combray, but much more is at stake here than the fading taste of cookies. Nor are we, Deleuze hastens to assert, returning to childhood and its loves, neither womb nor breast. What has *never been lived* is beyond object choice and the mother, even while it coexists with them where they are: the pure past is erotic. Eros always accompanies Mnemosyne.[59] What can we make of this?

For Bergson, the past as virtual memory coexists with itself as a whole at various levels and in various degrees of contraction and relaxation. The present is the most contracted degree of virtual memory among an infinity of levels and an infinity of degrees of relaxation and contraction. The entire past, from a particular point of view, is contracted into each present and the qualification of the mind by experience and habit constitutes a kind of subject, a receptive being who does not initiate the activity of thought but who experiences it for the most part in terms of its effects. This being is subjected by the flow of presents of duration, each of which includes a different level of the whole past.[60]

To actualize a level of memory in the present is to actualize a level of freedom by contracting the whole of the past into duration. Yet in so doing, memory participates in the active synthesis in which memory is subordinated to the actual present in reflection and the resemblance of the old in reproduction. Let us ask, for a moment, what would happen if memory were to be withdrawn or unavailable for present perception? What happens when we abstain from the contraction and so the tendency to act and seek out memory where it is in itself? This is not dreaming, for Bergson has argued, contrary to common sense, that the dream is the most relaxed past of the mind, in which the self is scattered and the recollection that is a whole is broken up into thousands of recollections external to one another.[61] Or if taken in its other direction toward extensity, the most relaxed past expands into matter, into objects that are externalized in relation to one another and situated in homogeneous space. But in taking up memory as memory, yet also as involuntary, a passive rather than an active synthesis of memory, memory rises up in the form of a past that has never been present, the in-itself of memory.[62] This is time out of joint, no longer in service to Platonic circular time, to God, to law, not even to movement, not serving as the measure or number of that movement. If the pure form of time is freed from the circularity of representation of the Idea in the present and if memory is freed from all contents, what is left? The pure order of time. Is this time the being of difference, or is it the time of the being of difference? Given that Deleuze embraces the Kantian critique because it succeeds in separating time from being and thought, I would have to say that for Deleuze it is the latter, the time of the being of difference. Nonetheless, this is one of those points in Deleuze's text where his meaning becomes so obscure that it dismays. Can we push further into this?

Deleuze has turned to Kant to clarify the relationship of the being of difference to time, for even with the Humean notion of "qualification" it is not clear what made it possible for there to be a subject separate from being, separate from impressions and ideas derived from those impressions. Kant's singular contribution to philosophy was to insist that there must be an internal form under which the undetermined subject is determinable. As Deleuze writes, Kant breaks with Hume not because he objects to Hume's empiricism—that is, Kant agrees with Hume that phenomena affect us because we are passive and receptive subjects; the problem for Kant becomes how we can go beyond what is given to us.[63] Hume's principles of association do not go far enough, for even Deleuze's reading of Humean association as *qualifying* the mind so as to make it active cannot guarantee that there would not be an infinite regress of times succeeding one another.[64] The association of ideas and reflection upon association operate so as to qualify the mind and to make it active, but in accordance with what form or organization? What is there in Hume's account beyond simple succession that can put the mind in motion and guarantee qualitative duration as the mode in which we are affected in perception as well as the mode in which we act in the world? In other words, when Irigaray insists that sexual difference calls for a change in our conception and perception of space and time, she may be saying even more than she expects, for her own analysis is deeply mired in the dominant spatial images of the history of philosophy. To realize an ontology of change (see chapter 4), a form must be guaranteed that ensures that the ego will be a phenomenal, receptive, and changing ego; this form is time.

Deleuze argues that Kant takes up Descartes's famous phrase "I think, therefore I am; I am a thing which thinks" and objects that the determination "I think" implies the undetermined "I am," yet Descartes offers no means by which the "I am" comes to be determinable by the "I think." There must be some form under which the undetermined is determinable. Deleuze concludes that Kant's discovery here is the creation of the concept of a transcendental (here operating as only what is formal and fixed) but inner difference, by which means the "I think" and the "I am," thought and being, are related a priori to one another without the interference of God, as the latter would introduce a purely external determination.[65] The implications of this are tremendous. The receptive ego (*moi*) is in time, thus constantly changing, and the I (*je*) is an act, an act that carries out the synthesis of time and of what takes place in time. The I, as the force of internal difference, emerges in the present and divides all time into past and future at each instant, so that ego and I are split, differentiated always in every act of thought by the form of time.[66]

The pure form of time is an inner difference that gives the passive ego its own thought, yet splits it from its thought. Thus I is an Other and the subject "lives it like an Other within itself."[67] For Deleuze, time as the inner difference between ego and I means that ego and I, passive and active "self," can never be integrated; to do so would be to stop the flow of time and make the subject into a representative of God or Platonic memory. So Deleuze calls the subject a "cracked I," since thinking takes place only when the passive ego feels the effects of an active thought exercised upon it. This is the manner in which the mind affects itself or qualifies itself as the affectivity of a passive ego, not the activity of an actor/agent/thinker. The fault or crack in the I is time, the form of interiority that splits the subject. It is of consequence to Deleuze that the pure form of time signifies the death of God insofar as, instead of God guaranteeing the identity of the I am, the pure form of time constitutes it, though not as identity but as split subject. Deleuze faults Kant for resurrecting the dead God in the form of law, which contains a subjective rule to which we must conform. That is, we must act on maxims that can be thought of as formally universal without contradiction.[68] This is why Deleuze also rejects the Platonic formula for introducing memory into thought. Platonic memory is time conceived as unfolding into a representation of the Idea whose being and truth demand the greatest possible degree of resemblance. In this formulation, the Idea is represented in a present as a mythical present, ordering all presents in accordance with their greater or lesser resemblance to the ideal. So the Idea remains entirely relative to the representation of presents, thereby locking memory into an infinite circle of repetition of the same and the similar, but creating nothing new.[69]

This allows us to make greater sense of Deleuze's claim that the pure order of time is an empty formal order, a totality, and a series. Formally, as the cracked I, the pure order of time distributes itself on either side of the crack as the series constituting the past and the series constituting the future, not the empirical and dynamic past and future of the first and second syntheses of time, the passive contractions and active choices. Emptied, like the form of time, of contents and movement, past and future are here purely formal and fixed as well. The necessity and import of this move can also be elucidated in terms of the discussion of Aristotle in chapter 1, where the ontological proposition that being is univocal was raised. Deleuze writes, "being is univocal . . . from Parmenides to Heidegger, it is the same voice which is repeated, in an echo which forms by itself along the entire deployment of the univocal."[70] Thereby, we can explore more completely the ramifications of Deleuze's insistence that being is not a genus. For this brings Deleuze (among other moves) to replace Aristotle's model of judgment with the proposition. Several propositions may have the same referent, but they never have the same meaning, and further, such formally distinct meanings are not themselves ontological but they relate to being as to their single, ontologically one, referent. Being cannot be said to be equivocal, as Aristotle claims; rather it is expressed in one and the same sense in every (numerically distinct) designate. So although being is ontologically the same for each designate, these designates (*les designés*) do not themselves have the same meaning; rather, being is said of differences, each of which has its own meaning.

In *Nietzsche and Philosophy* Deleuze elaborates this same point in a way that brings us back to the empty form of time of the third synthesis. Nietzsche's image of the game of chance provides a clear elucidation of the metaphysics of flux. For Nietzsche, each body is a relation of forces, that is, qualities, and every difference between forces of a body is pure chance.[71] The chance nature of qualities and their relations is what makes existence innocent, a game of chance. So Zarathustra announces:

> [I]f ever I have played dice with the gods at their table, the earth, so that the earth trembled and broke open and streams of fire snorted forth:
>
> for the earth is a tale of the gods and trembling with creative new words and the dice throws of the gods.[72]

Existence is a game of chance, but there must be something determining it to this, something guaranteeing that chance is not merely an anomaly that may never recur or an event that can be integrated into an overall process. This guarantee is the necessity of chance. Above the earth's table and the dice game there is something more.

> Above all things stands the heaven of chance, the heaven of innocence, the heaven of accident, the heaven of wantonness,
>
> that you are to me a dance floor for divine chances, that you are to me a gods' table for divine dice and dicers![73]

The game of chance is played out on two tables, one on the earth among qualitative differences and one in the heavens, the cosmos as a whole, even though there is only a single dice throw at a time. The single dice throw with regard to earth is the affirmation of becoming, but in the heavens it is the affirmation of the being of becoming. On earth the dice throw affirms chance; in the heavens the dice throw affirms the necessity of chance. Ontologically, making of chance a necessity is the only way to assure the affirmation of creation and multiplicity, to assure that we do not fall back into the hands of the law or the representation of memory. In the earlier Deleuzian reformulation of Aristotle, being is no longer said in many ways but is univocal and is said of each and every difference; here time is the unchanging form of the univocity of all change.

Each of the three syntheses of time can be seen to take place, guaranteed by the empty formal order of time that gives rise to multiplicity, to past, present, and future, each of which comes to be experienced in the image of action, since it is only in the present "interval" between affective reception and active response that virtual memory is called upon by the need of the moment to create the future. So Deleuze asks: What images call up the a priori past? The image of action as "too great for me" is the response, though it will take a moment for the import of this claim to manifest itself. Taunted by a Corinthian youth, the young Oedipus goes to the Delphic oracle to ask his future: "'Away from the shrine, wretch!' the Pythoness cried in disgust. 'You will kill your father and marry your mother!' Since Oedipus loved Polybus and Periboea, and shrank from bringing disaster upon them, he at once decided against returning to Corinth."[74] Oedipus shrinks from the action that he is already condemned to and in the midst of, and as soon as he shrinks from it he meets Laius on the road from the oracle and murders him in a dispute over authority. Hamlet, too, finds his task too great and asks of himself:

> Am I a coward? . . .
> But I am pigeon-livered and lack gall
> To make oppression bitter, or ere this
> I should 'a' fatted all the region kites
> With this slave's offal. Bloody, bawdy villain!
> Remorseless, treacherous, lecherous, kindless villain!
> O, vengeance—[75]

Each is thrown back into the past, the past of Laius's vexing of Iocaste doomed by fate and the past of Claudius's act of murder and Gertrude's complicity. Like so many pasts—that of the abused child, that of impoverishment, that of the illegal immigrant, that of the woman, or even that of the artist (Mary Kelly) who is working with the stock of images of women in society—for all of them the image of action out of the a priori past is experienced as too great. The hold of the past is too great for Oedipus to search for the truth behind the taunting to which the Corinthian youth subjects him, for Hamlet to believe the ghost and save himself, for the abused, the poor, the illegal, the gendered-other, the artist to experience the image of action as anything but too great, too much, unbeatable. Too often they fall back into the Idea.

But if an image can be contemplated and drawn from memory the past will be repeated, except as something totally new, the virtual emerging into the actual. If the whole of memory can be contracted into an image for action and into the interval between receptivity and responsiveness, then we have arrived at the present as it moves to the future, the interval that is the capability for action, the "becoming" capable, which is only an instant. No memory becomes action until the third synthesis is called into play, though it is not always clear in Deleuze how to separate the second and third syntheses. In the becoming capable of the third synthesis the future is "discovered," the I is cracked and time surges forth between ego and I. In this positive and creative upsurge, time is out of joint, unhinged; God or the father is dead; the artist, genius, emerges; the "too much for me" of the past is transformed; all these "symbols" of the totality of time come into play. Oedipus and Hamlet, the abused, the impoverished, the illegal, the othered, and the artist act. But in every case, this is not the act of an ego. Event and act—which is to say, virtual memory and present perception—conspire; the ego is in this way *subjected* and remains passive, a receptive affectivity. If the ego has gained on present and future, event and act, it is only in order to be actualized out of its multiple virtuality, and so, differentiated in the Bergsonian manner, "as if the gestator [*gestateur,* both bearing and giving birth to] of the new world were being swept along and dispersed by the shattering of that which it gave birth to in the multiple."[76] Cracked I and divided self never give rise to identity, and to constitute an integrated ego in the shattering brilliance of the dispersion of time amounts to an impoverishment of ontological and psychic forces, of the qualitative dimension of duration and memory, and the explosive movement of the pure form of time.

When the artist looks to her childhood or to the stock of social images to discover some historical material that corresponds to her current creation, does she find anything there other than similarity or analogy? They are of little to no use. In a devastating critique of Freud and Plato, Irigaray argues that the similar or the analogue are logical modes requiring no distinctions on the material level. One thing is like another, two parallel lines that never meet, between which there is no connection possible, like but separate. In his own accounts of Plato's Ideas, Deleuze exposes the similar and the analogue as copies "authorized by resemblance" to the Idea, operating fully within the system of representation. Their claims, by analogy and under the principle of identity, posit the historical event as a kind of Idea, of which this repetition of the historical past is taken to be a degraded version, bearing a resemblance but never up to the standard of the past.[77] The Platonic Idea reemerges in all appeals to similarity and the analogue, and so we must take great care, having escaped habit, not to fall into Mnemosyne. When the artist leaves her black-leather-coated friends behind her to join her husband in taking their little boy to Disney World, she writes:

> The white dress is part of the plot to escape. . . . I refuse to wear a coat even to the airport in anticipation of the happy metamorphosis that will inevitably take place when I emerge eight hours later. And it does. The air is hot and thick. . . . What's more today is Easter Sunday. Naturally! I'm wearing the white dress. . . . Then my angelic son tells every one "Look at my Mommy." The riddle solved. I am transported in a halo of fluorescent light to the land of "good-enough mothers."[78]

She plays in this drama, not to imitate or resemble her mother, or the good mother she never had, but her repetition is itself the "historical condition under which something new is actually produced."[79] In Mary Kelly's book *Interim,* this particular text is faced with an image of a simple white dress, something old, worn many times, with bits of embroidery, folded, though not neatly, as if packed, except that the belt is tied as if someone were still wearing it. On top of the photographic image there is a small grid drawn in just under the left side of the collar, clearly not a part of the worn dress but something marking it perhaps as an object of a certain type. The word *Extase,* ecstasy, rapture, is set below as a label as though by a printer. *Extase* is ecstasy, rapture, a being put out of place by emotion or joy; a being beside itself, time out of joint. Perhaps this too can be a material intensification of the ego cracked by time and the new.

Indeed, solely by conceiving of the work of art in this way is Kelly's nearly bizarre mix of events even imaginable, so that arriving at the amusement park's resort she anticipates that "the Seven Dwarfs will play the Brandenburg Concertos and . . . you will live happily ever after."[80] If there is any resemblance between the new present and the old historical past, it is only insofar as before becoming capable of action, of the work of art, the artist begins repeating in the mode of a specific past. The previous image of the same dress shows it still folded but already being pulled out of shape, though with just the top showing. Here, it is pulled open on one side and the awkward opening is traced over the image as if with pen while two arrows set together like clock hands point to each side of the opening. It is labeled "Fig. 2" but also "*Extase.*" There are three photographs of this dress altogether in the book, three of a gauzy, dark night dress, three of work boots, three of a sling shoulder bag, and three of the artist's black leather jacket; an excess of repetition given their dimensions as well as that of the printed texts (48 in. × 36 in.).

The text of the second dress image refers to the artist's mother:

> Call the doctor, say it's urgent! He agrees to an appointment. . . . I am afraid, afraid her fear will be contagious. Then, in spite of everything, she insists on getting dressed the way she always has as long as I can remember, "to the teeth." Her auburn hair immobilized with spray, brown eyebrow pencil, lipstick-coral pink, the crisp white summer dress. And the stilettos. I protest. . . . More than mere appearance. I can see that now, it's to do with heroes dressed for battle, *willing* to go on.[81]

"It is first for themselves," Deleuze writes, "that the revolutionaries are determined to live like 'Romans come back to life,' before becoming capable of the action that they began by repeating on the mode of a specific

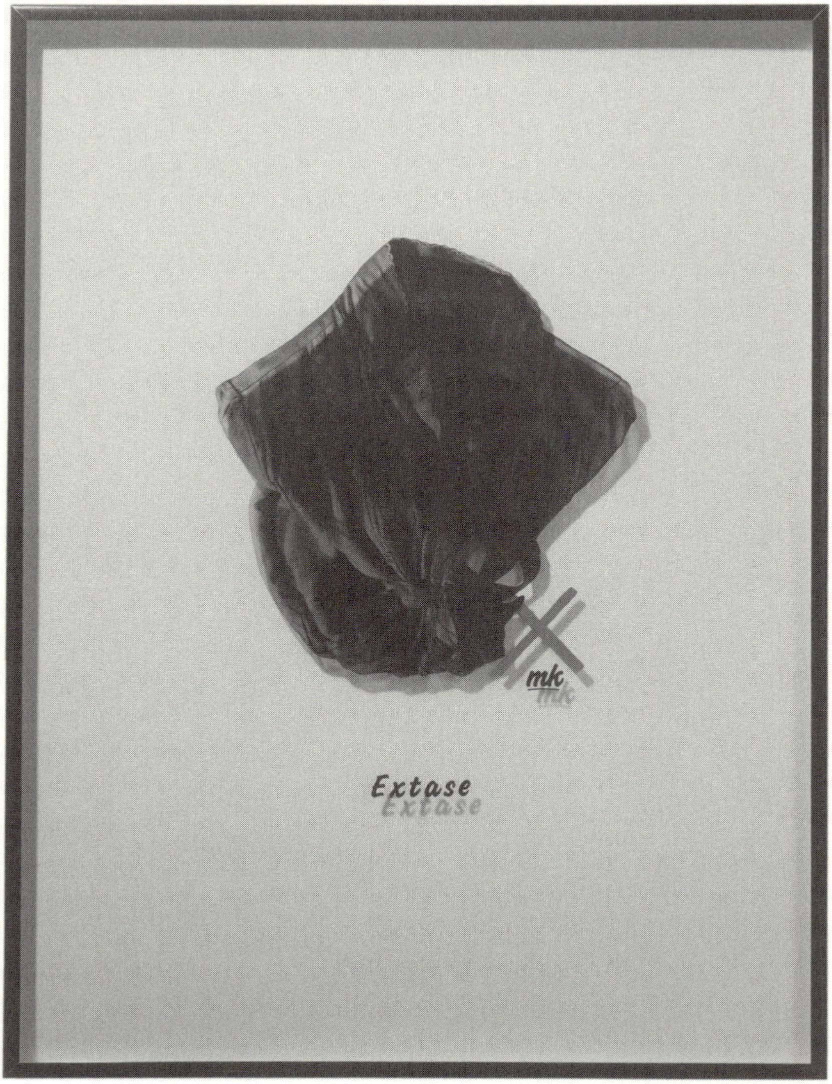

Figure 3. Mary Kelly, *Interim,* p. 38

Figure 4. Mary Kelly, *Interim,* p. 39

past, in other words, under conditions in which they necessarily identified themselves with a figure of the historic past."[82]

The artist, this new revolutionary, is becoming capable by identifying with a figure of the heroic past, but only in the mode of repetition of ontological memory. Then she produces this mode anew, as the absolutely new, in the present of the metamorphosis, the repetition through excess of the future. Deleuze relates this to Nietzsche's eternal return, a repetition that exceeds the virtual past it repeats and, importantly, the present in which it emerges. When Bergson testily exclaimed that if he knew what to expect as the literature of the future he would be writing it, this was precisely his point. So if we were to insist upon clinging to the coherence or the identity of the ego, we would produce nothing new at all. And worse, what is called health, integration and identity, amounts to an atrophy and putrefaction of life, a malady all the more infectious insofar as it is celebrated as well-being. In its place, it appears that creation under the empty form of time and the cracked I seeks collapse. It may never be announced by battle cries of insurrection or by major shifts of power within hegemonic states. Creative becoming sometimes requires the artist's precise attention to what is theoretically most familiar, that which repeats itself excessively, or sometimes to the political activist's wrenching of the discourse on poverty out of the discourse on morality and authoritarianism within contemporary conservative politics.

So we need to pay attention also when Michael Katz addresses the "first major book to justify big government in conservative terms," that of social policy analyst Lawrence Mead.[83] Although Mead is concerned more with society than with the traditional liberal focus on the individual and individual rights, nonetheless, Katz worries, Mead's interests have to do with the maintenance of social order and an end to what Mead takes to be permissive social policy. Mead's ready solution is to force the poor to work. Katz argues that Mead's position rests on an interpretation of the history of American social reform as eliminating barriers so as to advance competent citizens who made use of these opportunities with little or no government assistance. If people need anything, goes Mead's now all too familiar refrain, they need to be taught to help themselves. Katz concludes that Mead's distortion of history as a stable progressive movement has resulted in a distorted view of the present as similarly stable and barrier-free. In short, we have already arrived at the future; it resembles the past so as to represent it in an organic growth of one and the same thing. Nothing new under the sun.

For Katz, however, no matter how competent or hard-working they are, minorities and the working poor cannot reduce discrimination or improve wages or working conditions without recognizing the power of the state, the always new and creative obstructions it produces even as it removes others.[84] Progressive reforms of the past addressed specific events of the past. The right of labor to organize freely, Katz reminds us, came about not as the result of a benevolent government reducing barriers, but as a result of work stoppages, strikes, and battles between labor and capitalists. Finally Congress gave in to the unrest. Since the inception of the Wagner Act (1935), federal and state legislation has done much to undermine this right to organize, and unforeseen conditions have arisen in the form of new immigration, women's rights, civil rights, gay and lesbian rights, the growth of minorities to majority status, the stagnation of wages, and the rise of two-income families and single-parent families. We have a new series of needs and events and even a different kind of state power. Only action in the present, continuous and ongoing action, the recognition that the job of reform is never over, will reverse the steady erosion of workers' rights.

What matters in each case, for the artist, the activist, the thinker, is that the third synthesis, the future, expels any so-called agents as well as the conditions of production in favor of the work of art or the work of political activism or the work of thought; each of which can then be seen as the absolutely different, difference in itself. These creative and pragmatic lives need languages, need concepts that differentiate and produce in order to support their actions. In a time when even the most moderate guarantees of social and political reform are shunned, when the poor and minorities are scapegoated, when artists and writers are censored, when books, paintings, sculptures, compositions, studies are reduced to "content" for information providers, then perhaps the need for a conception of the future and change as a *necessity* is all the more urgent. But we have not yet gone far enough in this analysis, for so much has come to depend upon the political and psychological notion of the individual that without first undoing this, we may not be able to rethink anything else. Let us first turn to this "problem."

6
Beyond the Pleasure Principle

Biopsychic Life

Let me begin here by repeating some points made in the previous two chapters, for now we can bring them to the fore in thinking about biopsychic life. I have argued on the basis of a wish to avoid both what can be taken as an idealist position and a pure empiricist position in philosophy. In order to do this I have followed Bergson in criticizing the usual problematic of perception and action, as well as matter and thought. That is, I have recognized that the usual idealist and empiricist approaches to these issues are snared in the language of badly analyzed composites. It was necessary to make this point—that I am proposing neither an idealist nor a traditional empiricist approach—in order to move in the direction of the reality of an order and organization of life itself that does not exclude the very real conceptual reality of events and interpretations. Thus, I am preserving certain empiricist convictions and I take this to be an act of the highest importance. This is why I began by reasserting Hume's principles that (1) ideas are always derived from impressions; and (2) when these impressions disappear something is left, an idea that "returns upon the soul" to produce "impressions of reflection," which are again copied or repeated. In this way passions, no less than understanding, are for Hume an effect of reflection and contemplation. I argued that in this interpretation of Hume, living beings reflect on impressions of pleasure or pain, but the original impressions from which reflections arise must themselves arise out of "natural and physical causes." Thus they come first from the "outside," but not without the responsive activity of the entity, the effort of contraction, the folding over of what is outside to the inside, effecting impressions such as hunger, cold, thirst, and heat. But at the next level or synthesis, desire, aversion, hope, and fear are produced as effects of the repetition of pleasure and pain, for as Hume views the process, when impressions of reflection that resemble one another are associated, grief and disappointment combine with other impressions such as anger, envy, and malice, whereas joy intermixes with love, generosity, pity, courage, or pride. The association of ideas and that of impressions intertwine and provoke an even more violent "double impulse" of the passions; passions intensify.

Given the synthesis producing passions, the question Deleuze raises is whether we can follow Freud in making of pleasure a principle. Does pleasure exercise a regulatory function with regard to the events of mental life, as Freud claims? Is there a lowering of tension, a negation of discomfort or malaise that is called pleasure?[1] For if we read Freud's own account, it appears that what is at stake for Freud is what he interprets as a disturbance. Pleasure and discomfort are "quantities" of excitation present in the mind but not yet in any way "bound"; they are unattached, not associated with anything else, so qualitatively they remain differentiated. Since they are unbound, Freud assumes that they are disruptive. The task of pleasure as a principle, however, is not to produce these unbound pleasures or pleasure of any kind; indeed, for Freud, it cannot. The task of pleasure, for Freud, is to bind difference, to attach it and invest it, to capitalize it such that one can move from a state of scattered resolution to one of integrated pleasures and pains so as to get on with the work of organizing the psyche.[2] This is the second synthesis or habit.

This articulation in which stable structures are formed is, I have argued, both fortunate and unfortunate. It is needed in order for the contractions of earth, air, fire, and water to bind their elements and organize into life's structures. Deleuze argues that "[a]n animal forms an eye for itself by causing scattered and diffuse luminous excitations to be reproduced on a privileged surface of its body. The eye binds light, it is itself a bound light."[3] The reproduction of light on the surface of the body forms a habit that organizes the eye. Organs are habits, the consequence of ubiquitous reproduction. Yet Hume has shown that the activity of reproduction is by no means the only outcome of the processes of repetition; to repeat, the association of ideas and that of impressions intertwine and provoke an even more violent "double impulse." This time, the repetition does not end in an organ or in a habit; rather, when what is provoked is the double impulse of the passions, passions intensify. But what is the operation of intensification when exercised among the passions? Recall Bergson's analysis: intensify a gesture, a clenched fist or hands thrown up in protest, lips pressed together. What happens is that you can only clench your hand so much and your arms only reach so high, your lips press together only so tightly. What you experience in your hand, arms, lips cannot greatly increase; what does increase is the participation in the action by the rest of your body. More of it becomes involved, though in a specific manner. Your face and neck grow taut, your arms and legs stiffen, your back begins to strain and ache. The principle change in the hand, arms, or lips is a change of *quality;* they grow tired. The increased intensity generates a feeling of increased peripheral sensations and a change in quality, that is, increased difference. Is it not this newly produced difference that Freud's conception of the pleasure principle seeks to capture and bind?

Deleuze takes the discomfort of unbound excitation to be something else entirely. Specifically, it is the reflection on the first passive synthesis, the reflection on the heterogeneous flow of duration, on qualitative differences, difference itself. Let us then ask what happens when heterogeneity and difference, instead of being bound, follow the parameters of Hume-Bergson's analyses of psychic development. Returning to Hume, recall how he has provided us with the tools to exercise caution regarding the illusion of constructing a self. Again, for Hume, impressions of sensation are the origin of the mind, but principles of association by which means we make the transition from an object to its usual attendant, from the impression of one to the lively idea of the other, are what give a nature to the mind; they qualify the mind.[4] Likewise, impressions of reflection produced by passions and understanding are qualifications of the mind and the effect of principles in it. In this manner, the mind is "subjected" in the passive synthesis of contraction.[5] Insofar as it is an idea, the idea of a self, in order to be an idea, must be traced to some impression; but, as Hume makes it possible to conceive of this, the self or person is not one impression, it is *several.* For no impression is constant and invariable, impressions of pain, pleasure, grief, joy, passions, and sensations succeed one another; they are not steady.[6] What we call a self appears to be nothing but a collection of shifting perceptions with neither simplicity in it at one time nor identity in different times; thus it cannot be an idea. When we claim identity for a self, whether it is an identity we attribute to a distinct object supposedly invariable through time or personal identity, "the concern we take in ourselves," such an identity is a manifestation of the illusion that carries us along, in which we are immersed: identity, inseparable from our condition, yet subject to this very critique and so to radical reformulation.

Yet we have this *habit* of connecting the succession of related objects given in our impressions in accordance with resemblance, contiguity, and causality, and these three forms of connection produce the illusion of a self. These relations facilitate the transition of the mind from one object to another and render its passage as smooth as if it contemplated one continued object.[7] When it comes to the creation of a personal self, one form of memory encourages our commitment to making this error. The memory that we call habit or custom resurrects the images of past perceptions and places them in a chain of thought. Memory-habit produces the relation of resemblance that, in turn, leads to the illusion of identity in the place of diversity. Memory in the guise of habit supplies the chain of causes and effects and habit-memory encourages the extension of such causal chains beyond personal memory to what we infer to be the case. And if we can recall Hume's words regarding the commonwealth state as the illusory model of the illusory self, let us be on guard against an image of the self that is an unaltering order, structured in hierarchies of domination and subordination, which, even while changing members, laws, and constitutions, nevertheless remains united in its false identity.

For Freud, on the other hand, in addition to the external stimuli, which Hume maintains are the only stimuli, there are internal perceptions that arise from a deep stratum of the mental apparatus. They are primordial and elementary and involve the pleasure-discomfort series. This is a crucial difference: not all impressions are traced back to external sensations; this view is inimical to Hume's empiricism. These internal sensations are multiple and even contradictory, and they behave like repressed impulses to such a great extent that the repressed becomes the prototype of the unconscious for Freud. This primordial and elementary stratum that absorbs the repressed behaves "as though it were unconscious"; it is the Id.[8] But given Hume's and Bergson's accounts, the organization of the Id (*le Ça*) must be habit. The contractions of the first or passive synthesis are repeated and they qualify the mind so investment is made in certain habits, certain reflections that Freud designates as drives or bound excitations. For Deleuze these drives, like the pleasure principle, are the effects of the temporal synthesis that produces the present; they do not condition it, they are produced *by* the passive synthesis and arise out of it. If this conclusion is applied to the formation of a self, we could say that out of the qualifications of passive synthesis an ego is formed in the id. Remembering Hume's prudence regarding establishing identity, and Bergson's analysis of duration as an interlinking, heterogeneous flow, as well as the passive and active syntheses and intensity, it has to be the case that "the Id is inhabited by local egos," multiple and partial egos that make the present for the id in active synthesis when they are produced by it in every present perception.[9]

As in Freud, there is an acknowledgment of unconscious memory, but Deleuze-Bergson claims that it is an ontological unconscious established empirically from the first passive contractions of the elements; neither repression nor internal perceptions derived from original drives contribute to it. The ontological unconscious is virtual memory with its layered sections, each of which is an image of the whole from a particular point of view, each of which may contract into a present so as to create the future, not as Freud would have it, a future modeled on the past, but a future that is absolutely new because it is actualized out of the virtual. Habits are operative in the body and they do stabilize it but they also cut the living being off from the multiple sections of the ontological unconscious so that in place of the flow of duration, there would be projected a spatialized image of a unified self (Hume's constitutional model); in place of the multiplicity of local egos emerging in present perceptions, we would find a representation of an identical self. To fall into the trap laid by habits is to find ourselves in the endless repetition in which each new situation forgoes its novelty and is merely repeated on the model of a previous habit. This is what psychoanalysis seems to believe is health, or at least its basis: conforming to habitual modes of activity and thought, even on the affective level. But is it not this tired repetition of behaviors, of certain phrases or clichés, even if they are poetry or great prose, of such typical habitual behaviors, rigid and rooted, that actually prevents anything new from happening?[10] Even if it is possible to succeed in living empirically in this purely habitual mode, in the order of temporal syntheses, past and future always emerge from the synthesis of the living present; time cannot be rehinged, the I is an Other, pleasure is and can only be an instant, an effect of the passive and active syntheses. Even the intensification of pleasure or pain is a change in quality in the instant, thus it is difference and not a bound or fixed excitation that precedes such an instant.

Freud has, to some extent, discovered the passive and active syntheses, though he makes strange use of them. In his description of the little boy (a grandnephew) playing the game of *fort-da* (gone-there), Freud writes that the boy throws a string-pull toy and coos "gone," then pulls on the string to retrieve it, joyfully exclaiming "there." Freud comments: "At the outset he was in a *passive* situation [that of his mother leaving him behind]—he was overpowered by the experience: but by repeating it, unpleasurable though it was, as a game, he took on the *active* part."[11] Freud attributes this activity to the twin desires for revenge (against the mother) and mastery (over reality). Yet from the point of view of Bergson's analysis of duration, no one can prevent the passive moment or the active moment; they are the necessary components of the pure form of time and all Freud has succeeded in doing is providing an interpretation of them, not even a very good one, given the inevitability of passive and active syntheses. Much closer, perhaps, to the inevitability of active and passive synthesis is the Freudian "compulsion to repeat." Freud identifies repetition compulsion as a function of the unconscious repressed since it brings to light activities of repressed instinctual impulses, producing discomfort not only for the ego but often for the id as well.[12] The repetition of past, painful actions indicates, Freud declares, that no lesson has been learned from the past; the child and the neurotic produce their own misery. The implication remains that they could stop if they would just learn the lesson and that psychoanalysis is a method for ensuring that they do eventually learn the lesson.

This is remarkably different from Deleuze's insistence that the true object of the repetition of the game would be to raise the passive synthesis to a qualification of the mind, otherwise said, to "raise the passive synthesis to a power from which the pleasure principle and its applications *future and past* ensue."[13] The inescapable conclusion of the Deleuze-Bergsonian methodology must be that the repetition-producing habit, the passive synthesis, is "beyond the pleasure principle," which is to say, passive synthesis is more primitive than the pleasure principle and the pleasure principle is its aftermath.[14] In this account, the moral imperative has ceased to operate with regard to the living being's contemplation of repetition, since only by succeeding in contemplation of the repetition can something new be created. Rather than stopping the repetition, we must continue to repeat. However, in order for something new to be created, repetition will not be merely repetition of something habitual that conforms to the expectation of mother, father, or society; for while passive synthesis is the basis of habit and action, it also deepens in contemplation so as make real the virtual object, whose aftermath is pleasure, Hume's intensified passion. It is this conception of repetition in the contemplation of passive synthesis, a repetition that is creative because it arises out of the multiple levels of ontological memory rather than out of the reproduction or representation of habitual modes, that produces a complete reconception of repetition.

What must also be emphasized here is the importance of recognizing that even though the first synthesis is passive, through repetition (as opposed to reproduction, which is habit), the efficacy of the ontological unconscious is increased. Repeating the various levels and perspectives of virtual memory (ontological unconscious), the living being gains the force needed for becoming active. As I argued in the previous chapter, if the ego has gained on present and future, event and act, it is only in order to be actualized out of its multiple virtuality, that is to say, differentiated as the gestator (*gestateur*) of the new world, swept along and dispersed in an expansion of creative energy. But the active synthesis, for Deleuze, is established on the foundation (*fondation*) of the passive synthesis and proceeds by relating the so-called bound excitation (the drive that is the effect of that synthesis) to an object posited as real and as the goal of our actions. Here, I will conform to the practice of psychoanalysis (which Deleuze also follows in this matter) and refer to the *actual and the actu-*

alization of the virtual in space as the real object. The discussion of Freud's reality principle and, later, Lacan's concept of the "Real," opposed to the "Imaginary" and the "Symbolic," invites this gesture. Yet it is important to remember that the virtual is real, but it is not a real object. An object is spatial and therefore actual in addition to being real. Now if it is a matter of acting on or even producing real objects, need is at work. Between excitation and action, need operates in the choice of image for the sake of action. Otherwise said, the passive synthesis of reproduction gives way to the synthesis of recognition. The ego gathers together all its passive constituent and contemplating egos out of the flow of duration and in a kind of global integration of itself plunges into activity. This is the closest the ego ever comes to being integrated and it happens only in action and only in answer to the demands of need and interest. But in the realm of creation, as we shall see, such integration is unnecessary, since it will not be need that prompts the ego to create.

Freud also claims that the ego, driven by self-preservation, replaces the pleasure principle with the reality principle, whose ruling is that pleasure should be postponed, discomfort should be momentarily tolerated, and the road toward pleasure should be indirect. The Freudian ego's complicity in redirecting pleasure indicates its proprietorship of the reality principle. The ego has the dual task of submitting mental processes to a temporal order as well as to the testing of reality.[15] Temporalization arrives late and in a mechanical form, as an effect of reality. In Freud's thesis, time is not the making subject of a self, but an aspect of exterior reality. It is obvious that Deleuze must reformulate these ideas in terms of the Humean-Bergsonian analysis. Rather than limiting and deflecting the activity of the ego, reality-testing is what mobilizes and inspires action, drawing together a practical ego for this purpose.[16] Contracting all the little reflecting egos into the present perception, incited by excitations, the ego prepares to act. The reality principle, then, is not conceived of as something that sets itself up in opposition to pleasure; it merely determines the active synthesis on the basis of need, though the latter is always necessarily grounded in the preceding passive syntheses.[17]

What is so compelling in this version of events is that it is Bergson, vilified and accused so often of vitalism and subject-object dualism, who makes clear the connection between passive and active syntheses and so between the virtual that is real and real objects, the goals of activity. Simultaneously, in the upsurge of the present instant, while the practical ego gathers local egos toward active synthesis and the reality principle, Bergson acknowledges the reality of the other direction as well, the reality of the continual passive synthesis. In Freud, movement is unidirectional, even though various drives apparently oppose one another at crucial points; ultimately (we shall see) everything moves in the direction of death. But for Bergson-Deleuze, there is a profound asymmetry in life insofar as active synthesis could never proceed without the persistence and deepening of passive synthesis, a deepening into a second passive synthesis.[18] If the little boy seeks "in reality" his mother's return, he simultaneously "constitutes" another type of object: a virtual object that is constituted for contemplation in a deepening of passive synthesis. The boy throws the toy and pulls it back; he regards the entire situation from the point of view of this virtual object, which in this game takes on the function of virtual mother. The second passive synthesis deeply engages ontological memory and the creative *éclat* bursts into the creation of virtual objects, creative responses. Proust's Combray appears "in a splendor which has never been lived" and Mary Kelly dons a white dress and will have been the "good-enough mother."

Each of these little creations, these virtual objects, is a pure past that reveals the double irreducibility to the present it was and the actual present it could be.[19] Extracting difference from repetition is the role of imagination and understanding (Hume) or mind (Bergson) that contemplates. This is our existence; we exist by contemplating-contracting that from which we proceed and if pleasure is a principle governing psychic life and not simply an impression of sensation, then it must exist as the emotion of the contemplation that contracts itself in the repetition of passive synthesis. Pleasure is the emotion of contemplation, though we never contemplate ourselves:

> The lily of the valley, by its existence alone, sings the glory of heavens, of the goddesses and gods, that is, of the elements which it contemplates as it contracts. What organism is not made of contemplated and contracted elements and cases of repetition—contemplated and contracted water, nitrogen, carbon, chlorides, sulfates—intertwining in this way all the habits through which it is formed?[20]

Deleuze returns us again and again to the world, the cosmic, to elements, rocks, flowers, animals, to life itself. It is in the world among contemplated and contracted elements that sense is produced as the effect of contemplation of each passive synthesis. Everything is made of contemplation-contraction. The repeated game of the child yields a virtual object for contemplation and a deepening of the passive synthesis: memory in itself. Contemplation in the active synthesis is, as Bergson has so clearly shown, only for the sake of action. When the mother is contemplated in active synthesis, she is perceived to be the object of action and the standard for the success of that action, given the need of the acting being. This would be an instance of the child seeking to measure up to the mother's demands or expectations, motivated by those demands and expectations. The active synthesis then moves in the direction of real objects, while simultaneously the deepened, reflected, and second passive synthesis moves in the direction of virtual objects. They are concurrent and it would be precipitous to assume we can do away with either. Each requires the other: habit needs spontaneity, spontaneity needs habit, while both require the first passive synthesis, the synthesis of life itself, of existence. Most important, neither in any way resembles the other, neither is the model for the other, representation in no way interferes to establish its hegemony. Actual and virtual are the double series flowing from the pure form of time, producing a crack in the I, the self that is always several, not only empirically, but in the upsurge of time, ontologically as well. And the cracked I can never be a unified ego. Freudian claims about the child's mastery or narcissism, the overestimation of the power of wishes and mental processes, necessarily corrode as the double series surges and repeats.[21] For it should be clear that the virtual is no fantasy and not a similitude, neither a dream nor a degraded copy; it is no less real than the actual, it is merely not actualized. Deleuze calls both series objectival (*objectales*) and elliptic in relation to one another. This would situate the ego in the midst of the flow from one synthesis to the other, at the crossing of a figure "8," where the two intersecting but asymmetric circles cross, that of actual (real objects) and that of virtual objects.[22]

According to Freud, the deflected pleasure principle, once swept aside by reality testing, finds refuge in the sexual instincts, which display the same tenacity toward refusing to learn from the past as that attributed to patients in the matter of compulsive repetition. Once again, the pleasure principle often "overcomes" the reality principle in spite of the latter's drive for self-preservation, thereby (in Freud's view) harming the organism as a whole.[23] Finding little of value in science (excepting one tenuous example), Freud derives the sexual instincts from the comic poet Aristophanes' account of human nature in Plato's *Symposium;* there Aristophanes describes how the gods have cut women and men in half from their original spherical dimensions so that now they are condemned to misery as each searches for its other half.[24] The gods threaten to cut them down to bas relief if they are not humbled enough by the first cut. Freud accepts this, venturing the hypothesis that living substance was, at its origins, torn into fragments and is seeking to reunite with itself, and that the sexual instincts are the vehicle for this. Freud takes the desire for completion to its extreme by declaring that the ultimate return would be to the quiescence of the inorganic world. Sexual instincts, he believes, contribute to the return to inorganicity in any way they can, to the point of serving the death instincts.[25]

Dominique Grisoni has traced the philosophical history of negative concepts of desire beginning with Plato, whose treatment of desire has set the stage for all subsequent philosophical accommodations of this concept. Plato's manipulations of desire are grounded in his hypothesis that "[m]an is not perfect *because* his Being is incomplete."[26] It is clear that a presupposition of this kind must likewise be implicit in Freud's acceptance of Aristophanes' version of Eros. Yet for Plato, desire also assumes positive characteristics: desire propels man (*sic*) toward full, complete Being, which, Grisoni argues, Plato identifies with reason: culture, civilization, the city, and so on. This may be because, as we have seen, for Freud there is always a moral element. Desire is aligned with power in the *Symposium;* man climbs the ladder of Diotima in search of Being, "and so *submits himself to the laws* directing him towards this goal."[27] Grisoni concludes that once Plato established this "circuit of desire," moving from lack to reason and Being, it remained immutable. And so, as Grisoni records these events, it was picked up and augmented by Freud, who interpreted the relation of desire to power as a set of oppositions designated by good desire (life instincts) or bad desire (death instincts), though both operate within the context of the ever-present primal lack, that is, our hypothesized original fullness or completeness and the immediate and devastating fragmentation that followed it.[28]

Grisoni draws our attention to something else of great import, which turns desire away from lack and returns us to Bergson's discussion of the interval. Her argument is that there is a vital difference between desire and need. Need comes into play in the interval between an excitation and a response. An image is chosen from the infinite memory images available on the basis of need and living beings act to satisfy the demands of the need. Need tends to dissolve, Grisoni asserts, though not because its object is realizable as she claims; rather, need dissolves because a virtual image that is already real is chosen and actualized in action in the world. Nevertheless, her point stands: need dissolves but desire, Eros, follows other trajectories, those of the virtual object. On such a basis, the whole Freudian enterprise starts to look tired. If we wish to continue to use the language of preservation drives and sexual drives we can do so, but only with great care. This is because the terms foster the illusion that there can be a single schema for all psychic development, a single explanation of future behavior based on the presupposition that everyone, every living being, has the same mnemonic organization, the same habitual organization, the same response to need, the same development of Eros.

Deleuze takes these drives to have a series character rather than a specific, fixed schema, whether biological or linguistic, and he separates the two series of drives along the lines of the two temporal syntheses. Self-preservation drives are aligned with the reality principle, active synthesis, and the global ego, so that they are concerned with real (what in the Bergsonian context we called actual) objects, their gratifications and dangers. Sexual drives are aligned with the deepening of the passive synthesis, the constitution of virtual objects and the passive ego.[29] This does not appear to be the case for Freud, who maintains that when sexual instincts first emerge they do so by "supporting themselves upon the instincts of self-preservation, from which they only gradually detach themselves, [and] in their choice of object also they follow paths indicated by the ego-instincts."[30] It is not surprising, therefore, that Freud claims that sexual instincts are always active first, and their passivity is a reversal of content, a narcissistic corruption that Freud equates with homosexuality and other forms of "perversion." Even the infant manifests a primary narcissism because the standard and norm for instinctual behavior is always and only the active instinct.[31] Such judgments do not trouble Deleuze, who has no problem reformulating narcissism in terms of the complex processes of the deepening of the passive synthesis, the constitution of virtual objects and of the multiple egos of passive synthesis. We have seen in what way passive syntheses are, in the first instance, commensurate with life itself, and here, in their second phase, we will see why they are commensurate with what comes to be called spiritual, that is, purely creative life.

Given the double irreducibility of passive and active syntheses under the pure form of time, it is absolutely clear that when Deleuze theorizes the sexual instincts, his diagram in no way resembles Freud's. Recall the asymmetry in the pure form of time according to which when there is no actualization of the virtual past that will answer the need of the little boy to retrieve his mother, a connection is made in the persistence and deepening of passive synthesis. That is, as the little boy seeks "in reality" his mother's return, he sympathetically "constitutes" a virtual object for *contemplation* in a deepening of passive synthesis; this is his narcissism. What is important in this reading is that, rather than attributing a sense of moral or intellectual degradation to the character of the patient, narcissism is the condition of creation, a condition that transforms the child from a pathetic, revengeful "patient" into a life artist, a creative and reflective spirit. The boy creates, he throws the toy and pulls it back. Along with the activity of constituting the virtual object, the child is simultaneously passive, but in a deeper sense than that of the first passive synthesis. The boy contemplates the entire situation from the point of view of the virtual object, and the virtual object (here, the virtual mother) is created on the basis of a real object that conforms to the series of the real and to reality testing.

All virtual objects are created from real (spatial) objects: Proust's Combray, Kelly's photographs and journals, Katz's portraits of poverty and race. But in each case, what is taken from the real (actual) to create the virtual object is only the qualitative aspect of the real object, for only as qualitative and heterogeneous can anything be contemplated in passive synthesis (see chapter 4). Deleuze identifies the virtual object with Melanie Klein's partial object, since it cannot be identified with the globalized whole or real object. Bergson has already informed us that passive synthesis consists of duration, that intertwining of moments that are pure heterogeneity and pure qualities. But insofar as our other "tendency" is to expand quality into the homogeneous units of spatiality that go to make up identical units of quantity, we can say that these partial objects will be found everywhere, among both heterogeneous qualities and homogeneous units.

This returns us to the discussion at the beginning of chapter 5. There I began to make the connection between what Bergson refers to as instinct (distinctly not the same as Freud's drives), and what Grisoni and Deleuze (with Guattari) call desire. Recall that instinct, for Bergson, is neither a material nor an unconscious drive; it is mostly the tendency to organize, though it is nonexclusive, such that intelligence, the complementary tendency, will be found there, too. Thus, while instinct and intelligence are tendencies, they are never found in a pure state. The figure of the "8" is also appropriate here as a diagram of the instinct-intellect relation. Instinct and intellect intertwine in the two intersecting but asymmetric circles that cross one another in the form of the figure "8." For Bergson, instinct organizes things whose structure tends to be invariable. But this does not alter the basic fact, for Bergson, that instinct is what Deleuze and Guattari call "machinic"—meaning, it makes connections, linking one thing with another.[32] This facility of making connections is precisely what Deleuze and Guattari mean by "desire." Desire is not that which, as a result of the view that extends from Plato to Freud and beyond, we have come to call instinct, the unidirectional, mechanical drive seeking to integrate partial instincts into a global whole. Rather, insofar as they are productive, ontologically unconscious desiring-machines, "instincts" are "the domain of free syntheses . . . [of] endless connections, nonexclusive disjunctions, nonspecific conjunctions, partial objects and flows."[33] The qualitative passive synthesis continues to make connections unless it is forced by representation to globalize, to integrate all its connective elements into a hierarchized whole, in which case it is no longer machinic.

I have pointed out that Deleuze and Guattari object to the fact that Freud subjects the free-flowing syntheses of unconscious desiring-machines (Bergson's instinct) to the representation of Oedipus, a despotic signifier that demands that an imaginary thing, the "unconscious expression," be produced in place of the virtual object.[34] And I have noted that, in Bergson, even though machinic connections intertwine instinct with intelligence, the force of machinic connections lies in their simplicity of functioning. That is, machinic connections connect one element with another and that is all. Their mode of operation is a specialization that precludes their needing or seeking an organizing signifier that would subject them to its signifying schema while destroying them as machinic connections. Although there are often objections to the term *machine* from readers who take the term to mean "mechanism," given the sense of "connective desire," *machine* remains a convenient designation for desire, since it does not trouble us much with a long conceptual history in the philosophical tradition as other designations for desire might. Nothing about the term *machine* commits us to mythical representation. Machines are immediate, they can be unconscious, making "instinctual connections" in Bergson's sense, or they can be conscious, hesitating and choosing from among several different connections. The baby takes the mother's breast, the boy throws the toy, the boy retrieves the toy, the artist's eye connects to the camera lens, the fingers grasp the pen, the hand inscribes paper, Proust reminisces Combray; each and every partial object is connected and contemplated again and again; none are categories, genera, species, laws, or universals.[35]

Deleuze is not denying the existence of preservation drives and sexual drives, but he is radically redefining them and their functioning by relating preservation drives to the active synthesis and sexual drives to the passive synthesis. This would make of the preservation drives something actual, inseparable from need and the reality principle, while it would make sexual drives virtual, inseparable from the constitution of the contemplating, passive ego, which is a narcissistic ego, contemplating what is virtual. One can see then quite easily, given the organization of the two syntheses, the two drives, into a figure "8," that they are not separate from one another, that they borrow from one another and enrich one another. Specifically, virtual objects that are contemplated in the deepening passive synthesis of the passive ego arrive via the real object; they are an effect of actions, choices, needs, reality testing, even while these real (actual) actions, choices, and needs take their shape based on the contribution of virtual images rotated and translated (to use Bergson's terminology) from virtual memory. Nevertheless, what returns to passive synthesis as a virtual object is never the whole real object; necessarily, it is only its qualitative aspect, what can be affectively perceived in the flow of duration. Thus Deleuze ventures the conception that the virtual object of contemplative passive synthesis is a partial object, partial because it necessarily leaves homogeneous quantitative aspects out of the flow of duration; it leaves out a part in the realm of real objects (what Bergson calls actual). More important, virtual objects will always be partial objects; there is no integration into a whole set up and waiting for them as an effect of the process of contemplation. The contemplation of virtual (partial) objects will always be untotalizable, such that partial objects split, fragment even further, and dissipate themselves in a grand *éclat* whenever they are contemplated. Watching infants, we see that the mouth sucks, the hand grasps, the arm caresses; each of these motions is related to a bodily function necessary to life. According to Freud, they promote the life-preserving drives.[36] But insofar as they also produce pleasure, each of these machinic connections assumes the function of an erogenous zone. This "pregenital" phase is filled by early oral, then later sadistic and anal components, though active and passive component instincts and their objects do not, in Deleuze's view, converge into a single object. In addition Freud contends that there are partial impulses or drives, those for looking, showing off, and cruelty, which are, at this stage, separate from the erogenous zones.[37] These partial objects and partial impulses should be considered as virtual foci, according to Deleuze, poles of sexuality related to sexual drives.

Simultaneously, however, virtual objects are incorporated into real objects and by this means are related to preservative drives and reality (the actual): the mouth sucks the actual breast or the thumb, the hand grasps an actual ear, the arm caresses actual skin. Freud calls this "incorporation," and although this term may simply indicate that in sucking, grasping, and caressing, the infant's virtual objects are part of the drives for self-preservation and so correspond to her own actual body, the actual mother, or an actual person, this correspondence is neither an identification of virtual and real nor introjection of the virtual into the real.[38] Freud separates incorporation into at least two distinct acts. The sexual instinct initiates the infant's sucking, but very soon the instinctual act separates into nutritive and sensual sucking, with the nutritive function breaking away. The sensually driven sucking first gives up an external object and replaces it with its own body (what Deleuze would take to be a virtual object), but then it incorporates, introjects, or identifies the "replacement" back into or with the real object.[39] Accompanying this, of course, Freud claims that the infant's ultimate goal is always to unify the various objects of the separate instincts into a single unitary object, and Melanie Klein places the many partial objects in the mother's body. I would argue that we should not accept this interpretation of incorporation as integration. Incorporation into the real object (the actual) always exceeds the so-called subject but does not result in greater integration of the subject nor in the completion of the virtual in reality. The child already has the virtual object to contemplate; what motivation is there for the constitution of an imaginary one through the identification of the virtual with the actual? Only institutional (including familial) and political demands for Oedipal signification could produce this. Deleuze insists that "[w]hatever the reality into which the virtual object is incorporated, it is not integrated into it; it is rather planted, stuck into it, and does not find in the real object a half which makes it full, but, on the contrary, testifies in this object to the other virtual half which it continues to lack."[40]

The virtual is always the complement of the real (again meaning the actual), but it remains its own object, whereas for Klein in particular and psychoanalysis in general, the life instinct attaches itself to an external object (the so-called gratifying good breast), which when introjected forms an important part of the ego, reinforcing the power of the life instinct working within it. For Klein, who developed the concept of the partial object to a greater extent than any of the psychoanalytic figures Deleuze addresses, the "bad devouring breast," the first external representative of the death instinct, which the newborn supposedly feels as persecution, is likewise internalized and, together with the good breast, represents the ego in its struggle between life and death instincts. Ultimately, Klein maintains that under the influence of the life instincts the ego tends toward integration of itself and synthesis of the different parts of the object.[41] Deleuze desists. If the maternal body "contains" these many virtual objects, as I noted, for Deleuze they are simply planted in it and not integrated into reality as a totality. To see them as parts filling the whole amounts to ignoring and/or rejecting the critique of negative desire, separating life into good desire (life instincts) and bad desire (death instincts) with respect to the ever-present primal lack, that is, our lost original fullness and the fragmentation resulting from it. To accept this is the equivalent of reintroducing God and the I, which Kant's critique of Descartes removed from our horizons. If we are not inclined to reintroduce God and the I along with negative desire and need, if we find this reintroduction to be of little or no use socially and politically, not to say ontologically, then the process of incorporation is the means by which the active synthesis of memory can relate sexuality to real (actual) objects and also integrate sexuality (passive synthesis) into the reality principle, but this can occur without totalization of the numerous "local egos" and without synthesis of real (actual) objects.

Let me repeat the conditions (fully articulated in chapter 4) according to which Deleuze's reading of the reality and pleasure drives is here construed. The relations between past and present that Bergson institutes give us a temporalization in which, Deleuze argues, the past as a whole coexists with the new present in relation to which it is now past. Corresponding to this, then, each actual present is the entire past in its most contracted state.[42] Bergson's innovation, Deleuze reminds us, is a conception of the pure past that is not perceived in the present in relation to which it is past. This is the past as truly preserved in itself, though existing in various degrees of expansion and contraction, thus at an infinity of levels. Such a past is virtual, that is, real but not actualized in space, insofar as it can only be actualized by the perception that attracts it and in which it can be materialized. Until and unless this happens, memory subsists as a virtual object among virtual objects rather than as an actual (and real) object that is material and external to the living being.[43] What this makes clear is that virtual objects are part objects; they are a point of view on the past and so they are *past.* Their memory images (the contracted past) form a circuit with perception images (the present instant) of whose present they are not the past; together they constitute the active synthesis. The pure past is, as a whole, simultaneous with each and every present and contracts with each of those presents so as to generate a virtual object, the whole past from a certain point of view contracted into the perception.

The Purloined Letter

In a radical disruption of the Lacanian rendition of Edgar Allan Poe's "The Purloined Letter," Deleuze exhorts us to consider the virtual object in this manner as an "it was." By doing so, Deleuze attributes to Lacan a position it is less than likely the latter would admit to, yet Deleuze does not do this because he is blinded by the imaginary; he does it as a repetition of the virtual object that Lacan takes to be material. According to Deleuze, Lacan succumbs to the position that real objects (Bergson's actualities) are subject to the reality principle and so must either be or not be somewhere. They may not break the law of noncontradiction. Virtual objects, however, are not so subject. As an "it was" that never is a present, the virtual object is free of any past, present, or future adherence to the reality principle, and thus may both be and not be in the "place" where it is. It is not subject to the law of noncontradiction. The real is always there where it should be, but only the virtual—what Lacan calls the symbolic—is missing from where it should be. This is the predicament of the Queen's unmistakably disastrous letter, which the police cannot find, no matter how often they search and no matter how certain they are that it must be in the Minister's study.[44] We have seen that for Deleuze-Bergson the virtual object is the past that has never been present and is called upon by a present perception to provide a memory image for that perception. On the other hand, for Lacan symbols are a schema that "envelop the life of man in a network so total that they join together, before he comes in the world, those who are going to engender him 'by flesh and blood'; so total that they give the words that will make him faithful or renegade."[45] Given the authority of the symbolic, the life of "man" is enveloped by a destiny so totalized that he is already determined by it; he is faithful or he is renegade.

The dark and demonic as well as the deterministic aspects of this pronouncement are fascinating; they are part of a creative ambush, a snare set for the creative. But the ambush is undermined by Deleuze's reading, which is not conducive to Lacanian mastery at the symbolic origin. For Lacan the scenario of "The Purloined Letter" acts out repetition of the same. But for Deleuze the virtual object, as contemporaneous with the present that is, is never where it is supposed to be: neither the past to come nor the past of a present that has been, the pure past comes to exist (rather than subsist as virtual) only as a point of view on the whole contracted into the instant, a fragment of itself that makes quality change, makes the present pass in the series of real objects, and thereby assures repetition of the *new*.[46]

Deleuze's subversion of Lacan and the symbolic should not shock us, given what appear to be Deleuze's interests. He is interested, I maintain, in the being-in-itself of the past, and he begins by entering the in-itself of memory without seeking to actualize it in a present for action, thus without need or choice. The core of Deleuzian memory is what undergoes a passive rather than an active synthesis: a synthesis of reminiscence; it is the form of a past that has never been present.[47] What matters here is that what has never been lived, what is purely past, is beyond object choice and the mother even while it coexists with them where they are: the pure past is Eros accompanying Mnemosyne, Eros (passive synthesis and sexual drives) tearing virtual objects out of Mnemosyne (memory) and giving them to us to live with.[48] By contrast, given Lacan's totalizing presuppositions concerning the symbolic, it is essential to his thinking that the partial (virtual) objects, those "objects" that have never been lived, should be able to be subsumed under a symbolic organ. The phallus is certainly oppressive enough as a symbol, while simultaneously, because it is situated within the slipperiness of the signifying chain, it can come to stand for anything. Yet it does not signify simply anything. Deleuze inventories its modifications: "To bear witness to its own absence, and to itself as past, to be essentially displaced in relation to itself, to be found only as lost, a forever fragmentary existence which loses its identity in the double—since it can be sought and discovered only on the side of the mother, and has as a paradoxical property the changing of place, not being possessed by those who have a 'penis,' and yet being *had* by those who do not, as castration shows."[49] For Lacan, as for Deleuze-Hume, one does not become a subject, one is "subjected." But for Lacan language subjects in a schema that is unyielding, whereas in the reading provided by Deleuze-Hume and Deleuze-Bergson one is "subjected" by the syntheses of time. Here the comparison ends, for it seems to me that Deleuze finds in Klein, in Freud, and in Lacan the attempt to carry out repetition in the series of the real—that is, in the actual present and in a supposed old actual present. The latter would be the original (in "The Purloined Letter" the Queen, the King who sees nothing, the Minister who exchanges his letter for the Queen's) and the actual present is its repetition (the Minister who has the letter, the police who are blind, Dupin who exchanges his letter for the Queen's).[50] This kind of repetition is "crude and naked" material repetition of the same predicated on an original, material reality that can never be perfectly repeated due to the shifting nature of the signifying chain. Where perfected repetition of the original fails, representation is put in place, with the result that the imperfect repetitions are always lacking in relation to the original. This means that "[t]he traditional theory of constraint of repetition in psychoanalysis [and thus psychoanalysis itself] remains essentially realistic, materialistic, and subjectivistic or individualistic."[51] Let us think this through.

Lacan claims to repudiate Melanie Klein in favor of Freud because Klein advocates prelinguistic psychic structures. For Lacan, even if they exist they are of no serious import insofar as, given the illusions of the imaginary and the authority of the symbolic, all attempts to make right the subject's relations to reality are hopeless and misdirected. Instead, in repetition automatism, writes Lacan, Freud discovers that "the displacement of the signifier determines the subjects in their acts, in their destiny, in their refusals, in their blindness, and in their fate."[52] The very automatism of this process makes it, from Deleuze's point of view, unremittingly mechanistic. Instincts, according to Freud, always seek to restore earlier states, and if the environment did not force changes on "elementary" living entities, they would constantly repeat the same course of life. Even so, whatever modifications are forced on the living entity are stored up and repeated as paths toward the same and ultimate goal. The point of all repetition is to reach the same old state of affairs, the origin that has never ceased to serve as a model regardless of trauma (external excitations) or repression (of instinctual drives). Even the drive for satisfaction is simply a repetition of some primary experience of satisfaction.[53] In *Beyond the Pleasure Principle* Freud attributes repetition compulsion to the unconscious repressed; infantile sexual wishes are incompatible with reality and thus doomed to extinction, that is, repression. Adults, Freud notes with some amazement, repeat unwanted situations and painful emotions derived from their unsuccessful childhood search for love.[54] Lacan's innovation was to link repetition compulsion and the unconscious repressed to the authority of the signifying chain, by which means the unconscious subject, the only true subject, seeks expression. Nonetheless, the ultimate and original term, whether instinct or signifying authority, serves as the model for repetition; if imagination intervenes to displace or disguise the original terms, this is merely a pretense and in no way intervenes in the action of the instinct.

In Lacan's version of "The Purloined Letter," the Minister's action repeats and so represents that of the Queen. Both the Queen and the Minister are subject to the letter as a material entity; neither knows what to do with it, and in that sense each is dependent upon it. Each turns the letter over, each takes on a certain "feminine" passivity; both are subject to the letter's authority when it falls out of their hands. Dupin, too, repeats/represents the Minister. Each has green eyes (lynx or englassed), each deflates the prestige of the person from whom he takes the letter, each leaves a letter of his own in place of the Queen's. The materiality of the signifier, however, is subject to the symbolic schema; thus it need not proceed in accordance with a perfect mechanism. Except for the matter of the authority of the symbolic, the latter is all-encompassing; the structure of the first present determines all. Hence, in all respects, Deleuze concludes, the circumstances of the drama attempt to repeat according to an underlying rule of crude, automatic repetition that is profoundly materialistic. In all respects, the repetition of the signifier is realistic because it takes place in a new present on the model of the old. In all respects, the repetition is subjectivistic, even solipsistic, because the repetition of the old present is taken to be a representation of the subject, whether that subject is conscious or unconscious. The Minister, Lacan argues, is *obliged* to take up the role of the Queen, for the unconscious is the language through which knowledge about truth is represented. The unconscious represents itself, especially through speaking, and all maneuvers such as distortion, condensation, and displacement, as well as fantasies and daydreams, do nothing to recreate or remake this representation negatively or positively; its representative character remains sacred. The new present is then precisely a representation of the old present; it is an effect of the Aristotelian organic hierarchy at work.[55] "The entire theory of repetition is subordinated, in this way, to the demands of simple representation, from the point of view of its realism, its materialism and its subjectivism. One makes repetition subject to a principle of identity in the old present and to a rule of resemblance in the actual."[56] In short: no virtual memory, no creative *éclat.* In the psychoanalytic view, the old present is the original term that remains in its place and exercises a power of attraction; it provides something to repeat, conditioning the entire process even while remaining independent of it. It is the "primal scene," and the primal scene is what must be repeated.[57] Any new elements, deformations, disguises, or displacements are explained away as not really belonging to the repetition, merely superimposed from the outside. Whatever differences one may discover between the King and the police, the Queen and the Minister, the Minister and Dupin, whatever novelty there may be in the repetitions are irrelevant in the face of the naked repetition.

Perhaps we need to ask how else to think of repetition. The child and the adult, the first scene of the purloined letter and the second scene, the first time and the second time, the original and the copy—each occupies a present, not in relation to one another but in relation to the virtual object, which as virtual (real but not actualized) is free to circulate in whatever presents it may press itself upon. Thus between child and adult, one scene and another, there is no repetition; there is repetition only in relation to the virtual object as a result of which the two presents each form a series, coexisting with one another. The virtual is thus the principle of repetition, which displaces itself within the various series of presents each time, producing an absolutely new present, not a mechanical repetition but the absolutely new. The virtual as immanent displacement within each present produces repression and is not its effect. It produces what Freud called primary repression, the disguise, if you will, of the present, within each present, produced by the immanence of the virtual as principle of displacement, production of the new. Though Freud makes of this "displaceable energy" something negative and even destructive, the displacement of virtual memory guarantees that neither the first nor the second series, neither the child nor the adult, neither the first theft nor the second can be designated as the original or the copy.[58] To do so is to return to the Freudian economy of fixed presents (derived from the Platonic Idea) and subjects (primordial infantile aggression and the ego for Klein, the symbolic order and the unconscious for Lacan), by comparison with which all change can be taken to be some degree of madness (what eludes the present, what eludes the action of the Idea or registers it only very poorly).

Thus we must forget about the original and its copy as much as about the determining material organic hierarchy and its genera, species, and differences; we must forget about finding and holding an ultimate term. In *Anti-Oedipus* Deleuze and Guattari admit that the great discovery of psychoanalysis was the production of desire, by which they mean productions of the unconscious, what I have here called the displacement and circulation of the virtual object. So it is with dismay that they articulate the subversions of this great innovation, lamenting: "But once Oedipus entered the picture, this discovery was soon buried beneath a new brand of idealism: a classical [Oedipal Greek] theater was substituted for the unconscious as a factory; representation [the image] was substituted for the units of production of the unconscious; and an unconscious that was capable of nothing but expressing itself [as subject]—in myth, tragedy, dreams—was substituted for the productive unconscious."[59] But if we again inquire into the creative work of artists and thinkers, we find that for Mary Kelly's art, there is no ultimate good mother to represent; for Michael Katz, there is no model of individual behavior to emulate or avoid in order to cease being poor or avoid falling into poverty.[60] And even in the Freudian family romance, Deleuze adds, the parental characters are far from being the ultimate terms for the subject; they are "*middle terms* of an intersubjectivity, the forms of communication and disguise [in this new immanent sense] from one series to another, for different subjects, as these forms are determined by the circulation of the virtual object."[61] The illusion, then, lies in the pretension to mastery of the person who would unmask something or someone while the virtual object continues to circulate and to produce the repetition that Bergson has called spiritual, the motion toward new creations born out of conclusions incommensurable with their "premisses."[62]

At the beginning of chapter 4 I took the position, with Bergson and Deleuze, that too often in philosophy we make use of badly analyzed composites and fail to come to any satisfactory insights regarding philosophical problems. I advanced the position that the existence of a false problem implies something even more disturbing, that we are struggling not against simple mistakes (false solutions) but against something more profound: an illusion that carries us along or in which we are immersed, inseparable from our condition.[63] When I think about the power and authority wielded by psychoanalysis in contemporary feminist theory as well as in contemporary philosophy and literary theory, and even among political theorists, I see that psychoanalysis expands the dominion of this illusion to the point that it has become extremely difficult not only to oppose its diagnoses but also to question its theoretical basis, for the enemies of psychoanalysis too often share that theoretical basis. This is the effect of our immersion in the illusion. Its success can be measured by the extent to which it has successfully produced false problems and controlled the rules not only of its own production but also of the production of any other point of view. No wonder that if we begin with psychoanalysis, even if it is our intent to condemn it, we become the agents of our own suppression, our own misery, our own lies. Immersed in the authority of representation, we have perhaps abdicated the recuperation of creation.

From his earliest work, Deleuze has sought to find ways to release life and thought from these illusions, to generate concepts and to generate a machine for generating concepts always and anew. As for the future of psychoanalysis, is there anything left? It can no longer serve as a schema, or even as a theory of normalized psychic development. As a science, psychoanalysis can no longer promote itself as a science of "man." Its only hope, as I see it, is to give up its name and its claims to truth and to recreate itself as a science of the singular, a science of the singular paths of unconscious desire that most certainly can no longer be called psychoanalysis. And what about desire? Does it still make sense to speak of desire, or is this, too, a left-over conceptual labyrinth, a remnant of philosophical illusion? It has long been an important aspect of Deleuze's rethinking of philosophy. I have written on this elsewhere, but it bears going into briefly here, especially since feminist philosophy in particular and contemporary continental philosophy in general have made desire and the body so central to their view of contemporary philosophy.[64]

From my point of view, Deleuze makes good use of the Nietzschean context to radically rethink the question of desire. I have pointed to *Nietzsche and Philosophy,* where Deleuze problematizes the forces that constitute a body as quantitative and qualitative. That is, as Deleuze points out, Nietzsche believed that science demands that we measure our knowledge in terms of quantities, since any other values (qualities) might entail bias. Yet, like Bergson after him, Nietzsche cannot shake the certainty that quantity is purely abstract, and thus incomplete, and as a result ambiguous. Quantities are the tools of mechanistic interpretations. Thus, Deleuze-Nietzsche concludes, if we insist on measuring forces by quantity, there must always be differences in quantity between two forces because quantity cannot be equalized. Difference in quantity is irreducible in two senses: (1) difference in quantity between two forces is their "differential" element, and (2) the quantitative element of difference between two forces makes up the qualitative element of a force, that is, the force interpreted as active or reactive. An active force reaches out for power "creating forms by exploiting circumstances . . . primary in relation to adaptations," whereas reaction can be grasped on the basis of such active forces.[65] Without conceiving bodies in terms of quality as the difference between quantities, bodies (chemical, biological, social, or political) would simply be motionless and dead. So forces are constituted differentially and no force can be quantitatively determined apart from its qualitative—that is, active or reactive—relation to other forces.[66]

Clearly, a force that actively dominates in one situation may well find itself dominated by other stronger forces. In other words, in struggle, forces do not equalize, quantities do not return to or create states of equilibrium. What Nietzsche struggled against, maintains Deleuze, is the conservation of energy, the interpretation of quantities of energy as having a constant sum and as canceling out difference.[67] In the Freudian context, unconscious phenomena appear to be in relations of conflict and opposition, and although there appears to be a dualism operating between the forces called life and death instincts, in the end differences between instincts are canceled. Deleuze, it seems to me, is offering two radical innovations to the theory of the unconscious: (1) he argues that repression is produced as an effect of the circulation of virtual objects, produced as a repetition immanent to new presents, which does not represent a former present in any respect, but which innovates; and (2) he brings the notion of "forces" into consideration in order to begin to develop a more complicated and productive notion of unconscious processes. When bodies are reactive, they can *act* only by reacting to other bodies. Previously I argued that when Deleuze comments on Plato's *Gorgias,* he argues that in his discussion with the Sophist Callicles, Plato introduces a negative conception of desire based on the quantitatively derived assumption that the weak can somehow grow strong by banding together. But qualitatively, a slave does not cease to be a slave when he is triumphant, "from the point of view of nature, concrete force is that which goes to its ultimate consequences, to the limit of power [*puissance*] or desire," and which consequently has the strongest capacity for being affected.[68] Socrates, however, cannot agree with this and insists upon making desire a reaction, the property or symptom of reactive forces. What happens to this schema if, rather than being a reaction, desire is the limit of a power, "that point from which it [a thing] deploys itself, and deploys all its power" such that "the smallest becomes the equal of the greatest as soon as it is no longer separated from that which it is capable of"?[69] What happens if desire is an immanent principle that experiments with forces? For Freud, as for Plato, the negative serves a double purpose: limitation and opposition. It reactively attempts to limit the forces of other bodies by opposing its own force to theirs through the negation of their force. Whereas for Deleuze, even though the unconscious is desire through and through, it finds in the virtual object not need (for that is the reality principle), not negation (which presupposes a system of the limitation of force), and not opposition (which presupposes dualism). As aligned with the infinity of virtual objects that virtual memory can generate, unconscious desire is the force for searching, questioning, and problematizing; it consists of living acts that will outlive the provisional and partial state of all answers and solutions.[70] Questions, Deleuze maintains, are far more important than answers and solutions, for they arise through the displacement of the virtual object and make it possible for series to develop. If the phallus plays a role in these movements it is not, as psychoanalysis maintains, because of the authoritative power of its representations but because it, too, is a virtual object, intertwined with riddles and enigmas, assigned to the place where it is not, the madness of falling below the level of the Idea, which allows two series to be generated without contradiction. If everything starts with a question, then the phallus is not an absolute schema and Irigaray is right that there can be a language that expresses sexual difference. Even before the opposition of the sexes, determined by the having or not having of a penis, the question of the phallus as virtual object emerges immanent to each series, emerges differentially, emerges in the differential position of sexual individuals.[71] So what about pathology? What about the neuropaths and psychopaths, the hysterics and the schizophrenics, the paranoids and the addicts, the anorexics and the bulimics? Their lives are lived, claims Deleuze, in an altogether exemplary fashion; for they do not live at the level of solutions and answers, but rather where Bergson suggests we all must live, within the posing of problems and questions. Psychological passion and pain, severe mental disorders, extreme destructive and antisocial behaviors have not magically been swept away. What is being suggested here, however, is that the nostalgia dedicated to mourning perpetual unfulfillment and lack is without a basis; the thrill of denial is as illusory as the global Ego. Civilization's discontents can be separated from the erotic fantasy of completion and reproblematized. If we have found in drives the differential arrangements of forces dominating and being dominated by other forces, any victors in this struggle are temporary, authoritative only until a stronger force able to dominate them emerges. Thus they give way not to truth or unmasking, but to eternal unmasking of all masks, eternal displacement of all claims to some place that dominates or orders all others. For as Bergson has pointed out, the claim to occupy a "place" from which perpetual domination is possible is a badly analyzed composite. Such homogenous spaces are the expansion of duration, the development of a tendency, but not in themselves authoritative. For like each duration, whose past it has always been, the unconscious is wholly heterogeneous and differential. For those who ask, "Why do this? Why sacrifice the regressive pleasure of longing for the terrors of creation?" the answer is this: without practices and theories that make change real and theorize real change on the ontological level, life is death, social change illusory, and domination inevitable. Is this not the force behind Foucault's claim that this era will one day be called Deleuzian?[72] Such an occurrence, if it comes about, will also pass; but if it comes about, it will redefine any account we can now give of what it means to be revolutionary and to think change.

The End of Eros

The first passive synthesis produced the pleasure principle, affirming the value of pleasure and filling the passive ego with narcissistic images of itself; otherwise stated, in the passive contemplation of repetition the first machinic connections are made, the first virtual objects produced. The second passive synthesis, that of Eros-Mnemosyne, repeats and supersedes the first by placing the virtual within the present as immanent displacement within each present and producing what Freud called primary repression, the disguise within each present, produced by the immanence of the virtual as principle of displacement, production of the new. As such, Deleuze concludes, the pleasure principle may serve as a "law of general reality" in two directions. In one, the first passive synthesis, that of the present, exceeds itself in the direction of active synthesis and an active ego. In the other, the pleasure principle deepens into the second passive synthesis, the synthesis of the past and of the narcissistic ego that gathers its satisfaction in relation to the contemplation of virtual objects.[73] The first extracts difference from the repetition of presents and the second finds difference in the repetitions of the displacement of the virtual object that disguises the real objects into which it is incorporated. The force of repetition of Eros is derived from memory (Mnemosyne), difference itself, fragments of the pure past creating virtual objects. So it is clear that as the drives are constituted in the active and passive syntheses, the force of repetition in the sexual drive derives from memory and only from memory. Eros—the sexual drives, the production and introduction of new differences—draws its force from Mnemosyne, the ontological unconscious, which, as virtual and infinite, produces heterogeneity and difference.[74]

And yet, that this is the case has not always been so easy to see. In Freud's dualist, materialist, and mechanist model, something else takes place, something that substitutes space for time, homogeneous units for intensity and extensity, and a mechanized death drive for Eros. From the point of view of the first passive synthesis of habit, the series that forms the real or actual presents and the series that forms the virtual past diverge and figure two arcs, two divergent series. But in relation to what Deleuze renames the "object = x," the immanent limit of the series of the virtuals, which series acts to displace the real object (Bergson's actual) as the principle of the second passive synthesis, there is enough ambiguity in the manner in which the two series develop that they are no longer so clearly differentiated. For someone like Freud, for psychoanalysis in general, bound by mechanist and materialist, realist and subjectivist principles, the two series are not differentiated at all. Because the virtual displaces itself and disguises the real, in the present, the role of the virtual is forgotten, introjected, and identified, and the successive presents of reality seem to form the only elements of the cycle. In the circuit of the figure "8," active and passive, real (actual) and virtual are confused.

The second passive synthesis merges with the successive presents of reality as if the pure past is no longer pure past, a past that was never present. Moving along the same trajectory as the real, the pure past appears to be but an old present, a mythical old present like Oedipus, the original present from which new presents are derived and which they are condemned to repeat as unalterable habits. Then Eros, the sexual drive of the pure past, is lived as an element of the old present and, in the same circuit, is opposed to Thanatos, the death drive, insofar as for Freud life and death drives came into being with life itself, with the transformation of inorganic substances into organic substances. Given that the pleasure principle serves the death drive, and that in its efforts to return to an earlier state of affairs the death drive ends up binding otherwise free and mobile energy, it seems that for Freud Thanatos is the original and ultimate drive encompassing itself and its opposite.[75] Life and death, love and hate, construction and destruction, attraction and repulsion in the same old present, the same old myth, the same old unconscious, returning by means of representation, into the circuit whose foundation it is, drowning spiritual life, the new and the rare.[76]

According to Freud, when the sexual drives are withdrawn from the outer world and turned back onto the ego, narcissism is the result. Megalomania, the overestimation of the power of wishes and mental processes, is the infantile precursor of the later, more "immoral" form of adult narcissism. The more a drive is focused on the ego, the less it is turned on objects. The great amounts of drive directed to the object would have found their highest expression in love, whereas the great amounts of drive directed to ego result in self-love and reach their acme, not surprisingly, in the paranoiac end-of-the-world fantasy. By Freud's account, in narcissism it is no longer possible to distinguish ego-drives from sexual energy and difference collapses.[77] This is precisely my point, and I take it to be Deleuze's as well: that according to Freud the sexual drive is taken to be the former present of the new present. This emerges as a representation of what Freud theorizes as the individual's double existence: sexuality is one of the person's own ends, but also it serves some possibly immortal substance of which the individual is merely the mortal vehicle. Ultimately, Freud reverts to the mechanistic explanation, that special chemical processes control the operation of sexuality and the continuation of the individual life among the species, so we only have to substitute special forces in the mind for these chemical substances, with the result that sexual energy is only a product of the differentiation of some other energy generally at work in the mind.[78]

As I have read it, for Deleuze narcissism is movement; it is the deepening of passive synthesis, the constitution of virtual objects as well as of the multiple egos of passive synthesis, since passive syntheses were, in the first instance, commensurate with life itself. To theorize narcissism it is not necessary to embrace Freud's moral message. In its second phase, passive synthesis is commensurate with spiritual life, a creative force in which virtual objects are displaced and real objects disguised, such that the passive ego becomes narcissistic as it experiences *itself* displaced in the virtual object and disguised in the real object. These displacements and disguises are the ego's narcissism, its own sexual drives affecting it and producing its modifications; it is a mask of masks, a travesty of travesties.[79] To call it "ego" without considering its originally multiple nature is to imply that it is something it is not and never could be, something unified and integrated, something signified by some ultimate myth or symbol. However, in the Freudian reading the entire import of the third synthesis fails to be recognized, with the result that "on ne saurait exagérer l'importance de la réorganisation qui se produit à ce niveau, en opposition avec le stade précédent de la seconde synthèse" (one could not know how to exaggerate the importance of the *reorganization* which is produced at this level. . .).[80] Let us not, then, fail to "exaggerate" the importance of the "reorganization."

The passive ego *becomes* narcissistic, but the reorganization that Freud produces at this level must be thought. Why? Because thought *is* sublimated energy, and sublimated energy *is* desexualized libido, desexualized Eros. Freud has developed a view of the instincts as dual. There are the sexual or life-preservative instincts, designated as Eros, and the death instincts that pilot organic life back to its original inanimate state. But characterized in this way, life and death comprise a distinction without much difference, and certainly without difference in kind. For even though Eros is engaged in complicating and preserving life, it too is classified as conservative, aiming at the inanimate state. It is no surprise that between love and hate, construction and destruction, there is ambivalence; one of them (Eros) proceeds to turn into the other (Thanatos), and even though it is by indirect means such as displacement, ultimately passive and active are fused together and the presupposition that they run in opposite directions, that time moves in two directions at once and that difference is maintained, collapses. Nietzsche's warning about the quantification of forces would have been timely here, for in the end the difference between forces is equalized and difference is lost.

In Freud, sexual instincts do not have their own synthesis and are not distinguished by their own qualities. Instead there is a rather nonqualitative displaceable energy, indifferently sexual or destructive, active in both id and ego, yet designated as "desexualized Eros." Yes, Freud is right: Eros is more plastic; virtual objects displace and disguise; but in Freud they do so only by giving up their own qualitative "color," with the result that displacements can be quite haphazard: revenge against the wrong person, for example. This displaceable energy is desexualized libido, sublimated energy. This is why Freud concludes that "[i]f thought processes are to be included among these displacements, then the activity of thinking is also supplied from the sublimation of erotic motive forces."[81] Narcissism, when the ego takes over the libido from the id's first objects, is the first desexualization. The others follow from this. "By thus getting hold of the libido from the object-cathexes, setting itself up as sole love-object, and desexualizing or sublimating the libido of the id, the ego is working in opposition to the purposes of Eros and placing itself at the service of the opposing instinctual impulses," that is, those of the death drives.[82] In Freud's account, the ego is guilty for withdrawing Eros from objects back onto itself; it has not learned from its failures.

Although the passive ego experiences its narcissistic transformation, the activity must be thought. But what kind of thought do relations like displacement and disguise, disappearance and clownish burlesque qualify? In the ambiguity of displacing the virtual object into the present moment so as to disguise the present, the narcissistic Ego passively experiences an "I" exercised upon it like an "Other." But because the two instincts of life and death fuse, and because the displaced energy is qualitatively neutral, when the sexual energy taken from objects is redirected upon the ego, the libido of the id as well as that of the ego is desexualized or sublimated. When the narcissistic ego takes the place of virtual (partial) and real (actual) objects, displacing the first and disguising the latter, it does not replace one content of time with another.[83] For Freud, the infantile narcissistic ego is still a real *extension* of the id, though not yet fully developed, for it is weak; it repeats under the form of the id, which is the form of lack. It is lack because the id seeks objects. But for the undeveloped ego, the image of its action is "this action is too big for me." The experience of the ego, Freud protests, is to feel overpowered. It, too, lacks because it attempts to substitute the reality principle for the pleasure principle that reigns in the id, but more often than not failing, the ego ends up transforming the id's "will" into action in place of its own.[84] The ego's second repetition, in the form of becoming-equal, is the establishment of an ego-ideal to which love is directed and which serves as the measure of the ego, determining its self-respect on the basis of how much repression it is able to engage in. The "ideal" ego receives the love that had been previously directed to the "real" ego. The ideal, we might say, is a disguise created by the displaced sexual drive. It is a disguise of the narcissistic infantile ego, a substitute for lost childhood narcissism.[85] This could be a creative disguise, but for Freud it is not. Something else is driving it; something else is controlling the sexual drives. The transformation of object-libido into narcissistic libido, notes Freud, implies the abandonment of sexual aims and though the formation of an ego-ideal is often not enough to guarantee sublimation, it seeks it. The abandonment of sexual aims is the point of all sublimation and integral to Freud's conception of the death drive.[86]

The third repetition, that of what comes after, is that of the superego. Since Freud does not always distinguish between the ego-ideal and superego, Deleuze makes it a point to do so, for the latter does not limit itself to prescribing what the ego should do, but determines absolutely what it may not do. *After* the Oedipus complex, a prohibition is initiated by the "forming of a *precipitate* in the ego," according to which the ego confronts these "other" contents (those formed by the Oedipus complex) and "succumbs" to repression of that complex.[87] At last there is thought. In this thinking that takes place only when the passive ego feels the effects of an active thought exercised upon it, in which the mind affects itself with its own sublimated energy, Deleuze discovers the prediction of the superego that id and ego, its condition and agent, will be annihilated. "For the practical law signifies nothing other than that empty form of time."[88] But surely this empty form is of another order than that of the upsurge of past, present, and future Deleuze first laid out. The before, during, and after of the narcissistic ego corresponds to the static and homogeneous spatialization of time that Bergson cautions against.

Psychology, Bergson advises, proceeds like all other sciences: it analyzes. The self that is given in a simple intuition is broken up into component parts such as sensations and feelings, which it then studies separately.[89] Yet every psychical state is either a moment of duration or a section of memory that reflects the entire personality; to separate it into states established as independent entities is to neglect its special coloring, to reduce it to common terms. For the real and internal organization of a psychic state, the psychologist substitutes an external and schematic *representation.* "So that, on the whole, his sketch corresponds to an observation of the object from a certain point of view and to the choice of a certain means of representation."[90] The psychologist's analysis of the isolated psychical state is likewise an attempt to begin an artificial construction. But without an intuition of the whole personality, the isolated state is meaningless. Empiricism, laments Bergson, is convinced that by putting together all its diagrams of isolated psychical states, it can reconstitute the personality, which it then takes to be a hopelessly fragmented ego. Rationalism tries to unite these states in the unity of an ego but hopes to constitute this unity out of its analyses, whereas such a unity can be nothing but a form without content.[91] In the end, both approaches spatialize the ego: empiricism makes it a place constructed by the endless addition of psychical states, whereas rationalism makes it a place where those states are lodged, a space with no content of its own, filled to infinity with states.[92]

The latter move is Freud's. In Freud's hands, the unity of the ego is a form without content, and past, present, and future are made static and spatialized as lack, becoming-equal, and annihilation: before, during, and after. After all, Bergson writes disdainfully, nothing is easier than to say that the ego is multiple, or that it is a unity, or that it is a synthesis of these; but these kinds of unity and multiplicity are nothing but representations chosen from a heap.[93] In the third synthesis of the ambiguous, narcissistic, Freudian Ego, Bergson's "real" empiricism, in which the contraction of a section of virtual memory into the present—the distribution and displacement of virtual objects in the real—occurs, is not only abandoned, it is never even part of the Freudian conception. What is broken, finally and completely, is Eros and Mnemosyne; memory no longer surges forth out of Eros. The upsurge of time in the figure "8" is broken and time unrolls into a static and formal straight line; it is the spatialization of Eros and Mnemosyne. This is certainly time empty and out of joint in its most horrendous aspect. The straight line leads straight to the death instinct, not flowing in the erotic-mnemonic figure "8." "Our speculations have suggested that Eros operates from the beginning of life and operates as a 'life instinct' in opposition to the 'death instinct,' [however] the pleasure principle seems actually to serve the death instincts."[94] In place of Eros and Mnemosyne, we are left with "a narcissistic Ego without memory—a great amnesiac—and a loveless and desexualized death instinct."[95] In place of the erotic and reminiscent ego whose memory repeats and so creates the world anew in each moment, Freud leaves us with a "dead body."[96] The project of the next chapter will be to begin with an analysis of this dead body in order to consider the alternatives to it—that is, to posit in its place a living, creative science of the singular that invents a creative narcissism by dissolving the place of the desexualized death instinct, returning it to duration.

7
The Ruin of Representation

The Dead Body

In the Freudian etiology of the narcissistic ego, mechanistic death always has the last word. The transformation of erotic libido into ego-libido (narcissism) has a decisive repercussion: the abandonment of sexual aims. Desexualization or sublimation of unconscious desire (what Freud calls the id's sexual drives) already places the ego in opposition to Eros and puts the ego in service to the death drive. Do not imagine that this is desire for death; it is the death of desire. Desire is dead; the id and ego are desexualized because in Freud's conception of narcissism Eros is "turned back" upon the ego, withdrawn from the world, desexualized, sublimated, emptied out of all energies until desire is dead and the mechanical death instinct has a free hand for accomplishing its purposes.[1] Displacement and disguise, the libido that informs them, the creative energy of the death drive of the third temporal synthesis as well as of eternal return are denied any existence at all.

But why, inquires Deleuze, does Freud posit the death drive as existing prior to the ego's desexualization and independently of it? Certainly the vulgarity, the commonness—in Bergson's sense of the word—of Freud's conceptualization of the death drive has something to do with this. First, whereas Thanatos always is differentiated from Eros, Eros cannot be differentiated qualitatively from Thanatos but is always reducible to it; difference in quality fails, implying that difference itself never pertained to this state of affairs. Second, the Freudian death drive is a return to an inorganic state, mere dead matter, making repetition or the third synthesis conform to homogeneously spatialized, material repetition, mechanism and representation. No wonder the ego is loveless. But an ontology of becoming produces something else. The empiricism of Hume, the contractions and expansions of Bergson's concepts of duration and extensity, and the temporal syntheses of Deleuze enact a repetition that is neither mechanical and quantitative nor homogeneously material; rather it is heterogeneous, differential and qualitative, an effect of the pure form of time surging up as the cracked I, producing simultaneously the series of passive and active syntheses. In short, as I began—repeating Deleuze—repetition changes nothing in the object that is repeated but it changes something in the mind that contemplates it.

This being the case, for Deleuze death—conceived of as an indifferent, inanimate matter to which all life seeks to return—purely and wholly confutes the contraction and expansion that constitutes life itself. If life is machinic and connective, qualitative and differentiated, in order for there to be death, how can it suddenly emerge as perfectly inanimate and mechanistic, since without qualitative heterogeneity and the contraction or connective first synthesis there would be no life, no formed matters, nothing? Or to state it in Bergson's terms, differences in quantity can never produce differences in quality; the latter do not emerge out of and then "return" to quantity, having had their quality somehow sapped out of them. Quality is the more encompassing order of life. And if there is death and it operates with the force of a principle, then it has to occur within the range of qualitative differentiations. This is why Deleuze confirms that death does not conform to dead bodies but, free of all mechanism, death "corresponds" to the pure form of time; it is, in fact, the third synthesis. It is important to note the way Deleuze uses the term *corresponds* (it is the same in French). He never uses it to mean that one thing *is* another thing, or that one thing represents another, he uses it to indicate that one thing is complementary to another. What corresponds to the pure form of time, according to which passive and active syntheses surge forth, is death. Neither the negation of life by matter (quality by quantity), nor the opposition of immortal (God and the I) and mortal (matter), death is the final form of problematizing.

This entire issue and its relation to language has been of the utmost importance throughout this book. Recall what I wrote earlier (in chapter 4): that many philosophical problems are handed to us in common words, in the order-words of social language that, as the words of the social self, distort the real problem by stating it in terms that can never lead to a resolution (and for Bergson are specifically derived from homogeneity). Yet once a problem is properly stated, that is, problematized, then its solution exists, though it may remain hidden since its language is not that of the common point of view. What is important is that stating a problem correctly—and not simply in terms of the order-words handed down to us—requires invention; it gives way to something new, in this case to the intuition of the being of becoming that must exist as (non)being.[2] This is why Deleuze writes that "[d]eath is rather the last form of the problematic, the source of problems and questions, the mark of their permanence above all answers, the Where and When which designate this (non)-being where all affirmation is nourished."[3]

The living present is the ground of the first or empirical passive synthesis, by which the living being, insofar as it is an affective being, contracts the world and folds the outside over into the inside. In this first synthesis of life itself, pleasure is an empirical principle, constituted along with the unconscious on the basis of the passive synthesis of affectivity. In this synthesis as well, time, as the passive flux of affectivity, structures the mind; what had been a flux of ideas, a mere collection of atoms, becomes the structure that is time, organized only insofar as it has become habit.[4] The second synthesis is that of the pure form of time, according to which the pure past that has never been present, the infinite sections of virtual memory are the foundation (*fondation*) that connects the passive synthesis of the pleasure principle to an ego. But this is neither the Freudian pleasure principle nor the Freudian ego; it is Hume's and Bergson's, since, as we discovered, for Deleuze the repetition of the passive synthesis is "beyond the pleasure principle"—meaning that it is more primitive, that the pleasure principle comes after. The task of the pleasure principle is not to produce pleasure but to bind difference and get on with the work of organizing the psyche.[5] The second synthesis of habit (what Deleuze and Guattari call strata) also constitutes the id as habit. Out of the passive synthesis as well an ego is formed in the id, but it is an id inhabited by local egos, multiple and partial egos that make the present for the id in active synthesis.[6]

A third synthesis, a further creation and invention, arises. There must be a groundless third not synthesized into the pleasure principle or habit. When virtual objects are displaced and real objects disguised such that the passive ego becomes narcissistic as it experiences *itself* displaced in the virtual object and disguised in the real object, these displacements and disguises are the ego's narcissism, its own sexual drives affecting it and producing its modifications. This is "desexualization" inhibiting the pleasure principle's application to objects. "The complementarity of the narcissistic libido and the death drive define the third synthesis as much as Eros and Mnemosyne define the second."[7] The effects of this synthesis are disconcerting. While it brings all the syntheses of time together, even if only to rob them of their capacities by inhibiting the erotic drives (which, after all, are bound energies as opposed to freely flowing connections) as well as all habits, it is precisely by doing this that it provokes the reorganization of the temporal syntheses. Erotic drives and habit (id) are cast aside and in their place the ego ideal defines the present. Perhaps the most important result of the death drive is that the third synthesis makes it possible to announce the destruction of past and present, id and ego—that is, the habitual organization of the living being is "deterritorialized," destabilized and disorganized to such a great extent that the organizational strata collapse. But the third temporal synthesis, the death drive, disrupts habit and bound libido; it thereby creates a disorder of all the senses, or in Kantian terms, an "unregulated exercise of all the faculties."[8]

This phrase recalls Rimbaud's poetic formula according to which he wills himself to become a seer by a long, vast, and reasoned *derangement* of all the senses.[9] Deleuze argues that the philosophical intuition of derangement is Kant's. The relationship between the faculties of imagination and reason reaches discord, even contradiction, when reason's demands conflict with imagination's power in an intuition of the sublime. This clash produces the pleasure of imagination exceeding its own limits, though it is mixed with pain, the pain of imagination representing to itself the unattainable rational idea. The image of the sublime is untamed, chaotic nature in its wildest and most irregular disorder and desolation; thus it is free of natural laws governing nature as mechanism as well as free of all constraints and rules.

In any intuition of the sublime, imagination cannot apprehend in a single intuition the absolutely (infinitely) great and so suffers the pain of this inadequacy. Yet the effort of intuiting all at once what requires an infinite and thus unimaginable time does violence to temporality and breaks up the unity of the faculty. That is, what should be given in a succession is given all at once, annihilating time, annihilating mathematical and dynamic succession, annihilating even the *representation* of time as homogeneous units.[10] What is left is the impossibility of representing this intuition, for as given all at once, it cannot be represented. With the death drive, the third synthesis, the derangement of the faculties, defeats (Freudian) representation, the repetition of the drive toward the inorganic, toward an end that is the same as the origin, toward representation. Although Kant may recover from the momentary collapse of the faculties by positing respect for the Idea that prescribes the comprehension of every intuition as an absolute totality, Deleuze does not.[11]

However, the repercussion of the disintegration of the living being's habitual and temporal order is not necessarily chaos and madness, for in being synthesized by the living being itself, the death drive reveals eternal return, which is affirmation of the multiple, of chance, of those connections that are, for Bergson, at once instinctive and intelligent: the mouth to the breast, the eye to the eyepiece, the fingers to the pen. What dies in the synthesis of the death drive is identity, negation, representation.[12] In Deleuze's reading of Nietzsche, eternal return is the thought of pure becoming and the recognition of the infinity of past time since, as Nietzsche asserts, if the world were truly capable of "being," all becoming would long since be over.[13] For Nietzsche, the present moment is a passing moment, a moment of duration that qualitatively intermixes present, past, and to come. Thus what never starts becoming or finishes becoming, what is always becoming, never being, is eternal return, and necessarily, what returns is never the same. Only returning is affirmed as diversity and becoming, since there is no "being" to return.

Of equal importance to Deleuze in the elucidation of Nietzsche's eternal return is that in addition to the affirmation of the being of becoming—which he also refers to as (non)being and the gods' heavenly and earthly dice game (see chapter 5)—there is the idea that the affirmation of becoming involves a selective ontology. As Deleuze states it: "whatever you will, will it in such a way that you also will its eternal return."[14] Of course, it is not possible to will this or that particular to return again and again, for eternal return means that what is becomes, and no thing returns, yet the affirmation of what becomes remains an important and necessary characteristic of eternal return. The second aspect of selection makes it clearer why. I have briefly discussed the role of active and reactive forces in the interpretation of bodies (see chapters 3 and 6); when this is combined with Deleuze's critique of Freud for championing a philosophy of mechanism and being (the unified ego, for example), it is clear that it is quite possible to will reactively, to will negation and denial. This makes a more radical selection viable and necessary.

It must be possible to will "nothingness," negation of negation, the active destruction and negation of all reactive forces. To will nothingness to its limit is to will the destruction of negation and its transmutation into affirmation. In the context of Eros and Mnemosyne, and of narcissistic displacement and disguise, it must be possible to will the active destruction and negation of fixed subjects and fixed objects, of integrated egos, and objectified entities (mother, father, baby). The death drive is the only sure means of willing the complete negation of these fixed entities and thereby willing the affirmation of creation:

I, Antonin Artaud, am my son,
    my father, my mother
    my self;
  leveller of the imbecile periplum rooted
    to the family tree:
    the periplum, papamummy
    the infant wee,
                crud from the ass of
                        granmummy

much more than pa and ma
. . . .
I speak
from above
time
as if time
were not fried,
were not this dry fry
of all the crumbles
at the beginning
setting out once more in their coffins.[15]

Speaking from above time, above the fried and crumbled and dead time of reactive force, is much more than "pa" and "ma"; it is the creation of "myself," but a creation that necessitates a great leveling of at least the family tree, and perhaps more, the rule of nature as mechanism and the Idea as law, the subjective rule to which we must conform. In the third synthesis, the synthesis of the death drive, no personal self ever dies and not even suicide reconciles the death of the "one" (*on*), the impersonal being, with that of the personal self.[16] Artaud's poetry and prose affirm suicide in this impersonal sense: "If I commit suicide, it will not be to destroy myself but to put myself back together again. . . . I free myself from the conditioned reflexes of my organs."[17] Each of these conditioned reflexes is a stratum, God's double pincers, and as I have tried to indicate from the beginning, strata stabilize and strata are inevitable, but derangement, the death drive, is always available to us in the paradox of pleasure-pain and desexualization. Free of id and ego, habits, memory, even Eros, something else can emerge.

The Theater of Terror

In *The Logic of Sense* Deleuze makes strange use of what he refers to, with great good humor, as Melanie Klein's "theater of terror."[18] From a certain point of view, Klein's descriptions of the nursing infant's drama are astounding. She argues, for example, that "[t]he clearest instance of transformation of unsatisfied libido into anxiety is, I think, the reaction of the suckling to tensions caused by physical needs. Such a reaction, however, is without doubt not only one of anxiety but of rage as well. . . . [T]he tension caused by need merely serves to strengthen the sadistic instincts of the infant." And further: "As can be seen, the sadistic tendency most closely allied to oral sadism is urethral sadism. Observations have confirmed that children's fantasies of flooding and destroying by means of enormous quantities of urine in terms of soaking, drowning, burning and poisoning are a sadistic reaction to their having been deprived of fluid by their mother and are ultimately directed against her breast." And finally:

> Every other vehicle of sadistic attack that the child employs, such as anal sadism and muscular sadism, is in the first instance leveled against its mother's frustrating breast; but it is soon directed to the inside of her body, which thus becomes at once the target of every highly intensified and effective instrument of sadism. In early analysis, these anal-sadistic destructive desires of the small child constantly alternate with desires to destroy its mother's body by devouring and wetting it; but their original aim of eating up and destroying her breast is always discernible in them.[19]

Of this history of depths (bodies) Deleuze observes that in Klein's unforgettable picture the breast and body of the mother are split into a good and a bad object, but then "they are aggressively emptied, slashed to pieces, broken into crumbs and alimentary morsels. . . . [I]ntrojected morsels are like poisonous, persecuting, explosive, and toxic substances threatening the child's body from within and being endlessly reconstituted inside the mother's body."[20] Reading these lines and others like them aloud, I have a sense that Deleuze in some manner enjoys this recitation of horrors because he does not perceive in them, as Klein does, the striving of the infant or child for something else, something that would be more complete and perfect, something that could be represented as good. In fact, he concludes his first description of the child's phases by claiming that his comments are intended to sketch out "orientations" only; what interests him and draws him to Klein's work are the variables, the shifting coordinates and dimensions, the geography and geometry of living dimensions: depths (bodies), heights (Platonic forms), and surface (events of language). This "adventure of humor," as Deleuze refers to it, is a dismissal of heights and depths for the sake of the surface, where one finds pure events that are, in a phrase that should resonate now with Bergson's affect, "always already in the past and yet to come."[21]

In the end, the consideration that Oedipus is innocent, full of good intentions that fail, along with the various psychic developments outlined by Freud and Klein, can be read as movements between the depths of bodies and the surface of language. After all, as Deleuze implies, the supposed significance and dominance of the Oedipal structure in our lives could just as well have been designated as the Heracles complex, after the Greek hero who was abandoned by his father and mother, suckled by the Goddess Hera (who had sought to prevent his birth because Heracles was an illegitimate child of Zeus). After all, Heracles' behavior was often so vile and insolent that even the Greeks attributed madness to him, especially in the matter of child sacrifice.[22] Oedipus or Heracles, would it really matter which story psychoanalysis chose? If it is the movements of bodies and language that interest Deleuze, and not the Greek theater, then rather than developing Deleuze's text in *The Logic of Sense* as a pychogenesis, the question of how infants begin to think, of how bodies enter directly into thought, as Philip Goodchild has suggested,[23] I would like to distance myself from a psychoanalytic perspective and interrogate Klein's impulse from the point of view of the ruin of representation.

Still, in the matter of how bodies enter into thought, it remains critical to an ontology of change and becoming to properly analyze the problem and to avoid the common language of order-words. So, to make it clear that all life is engaged in the problem of thinking and living difference, it is Deleuze's empiricism and embrace of duration that yields a viable problematic. If psychoanalysis enters the picture at all, it will be as a social disease or a political crime, not as a personal, mental malady. The judgments of psychoanalysis are perfectly accurate from a particular social and political point of view, but totally unable to be thought or lived from the point of view of an ontology of change and becoming because anyone can recognize in them the order of "being," of what does not change but organizes life in terms of static hierarchies of genus, species, and their differences or in homogenous spatial units. Psychoanalysis belongs to stratifications that will not be undone, that impose their negative valuations on all social interactions and that, ultimately, are mechanized and materialized so that they preclude the third synthesis of the death drive—that is, affirmation of eternal return—even though they attempt, though miserably, the repetition of the same. Ultimately, they are stratifications embraced by fascistic and capitalist regimes of power because they are useful to those regimes in maintaining that power and control over social groups. Against this, eternal return affirms all chance except the chance of subordination to the one, the same, and necessity, making death the affirmation of all that acts and dies once and for all.

In the Aristotelian framework of chapter 1, when being refers primarily to substance and all other categories only have being in reference to substance, being is hierarchically primary and distributively common to all categories, thus, insofar as it operates analogically, being is equivocal and will never give us a proper concept of difference.[24] Specific difference determines difference only in the identity of the concept in general, whereas generic difference is no more than analogy. This is, I noted, what is meant by representation, for representation consists of differences (conceived in terms of analogy) between species subsumed under the identity of a genus that itself stands in relations of analogy with other genera. Representation subsumes species by means of resemblances that presume the continuity of the sensible intuition in a concrete representation.[25] The effect of this dual system of classification is to erase difference as a concept and as reality and to subsume all difference under the one, the same, and the necessary. Ultimately, it is in reflection, not in the contemplation of impressions, that the judgment is made that makes difference submit to representation.

There is also an alliance of death with the future. Here the Platonic model establishes the standard against which the pure form of time and the death drive work. Memory of the Ideas requires that any "true" thing measure up to the Ideas as the standard and model. This requires measuring, counting, weighing, calculating, and limitation in all its forms. A proper representation of an Idea must fall within certain limits, that is, it must measure up to the rule of the equivalent, the same, or at the very least it must be similar.[26] What can never measure up to the standard is rejected as imitation, as false, as evil simulacrum. In the Platonic model, time is repetition of the same and the equal; time unfolds as the representation of the Idea, and there is nothing new in the world, for truth is resemblance. Yet for Deleuze eternal return is linked relentlessly to simulacra, "for it is in the eternal return that the reversal of icons [good copies of the Ideas] or the subversion of the world of representation is decided."[27] Recall Plato's ire at the Sophists, who make their audiences think that the same objects are both like and unlike, both one and many, both at rest and in motion. This is the sophistic joy of affirming chaos and opposing it to the hierarchical order of representation. Eternal return demands the chaos of the virtual object, whereby every movement toward sameness ends in a divergence and every recognition of the similar opens its eyes to the disguise that shows it to be a simulacrum, a copy of a copy of a copy, below the level of the icon, mere imitation and evil, when measured against the standard of fixed time, fixed memory, fixed Ideas.

First, second, and third articulations or syntheses change the living being, its actions and passions, the organization of its life and thought. But if we continue, as Deleuze implies, to analyze the child from the point of view of the stratified adult, the organic representation, or the reminiscence of the Idea, then we are likely to find in the child's motions and creations something as strange and horrible as Klein's sideshow of infant freaks. Living beings are constituted in duration's qualitative and heterogeneous movements as passive egos, mere "larval" subjects, "cracked" by the pure form of time, oriented by passive and active series, temporal and spatial tendencies, connective couplings, intensive aggregations. It is not the case that if we determine that there are resemblances, identities, analogies, and oppositions (the Aristotelian categories) we are self-deluded, but rather, as Hume has shown, these are the effects of the system of differences, the qualification of the mind by empirical principles.[28] If, however, following the critique of Aristotle, difference *is,* then differences relate directly to one another and without having to be represented by genus or its emissaries, identity, similarity, analogy, or opposition. Our delusion arises from taking these relations to be something more than and prior to habits, and bad habits at that. Identity, similarity, analogy, and opposition are nothing but "surface effects," no longer anything but effects of the first difference and its differen*c*iation (the process of actualizing such a structure of differences), overall or surface effects characteristic of the "distorted world of representation."[29]

At this juncture Deleuze asks a crucial question, which has been too quickly glossed over, I think, in the rush to make political statements and social reforms, to criticize what we think are the symptoms of underlying cultural conflicts but too often turn out to be false problems, effects of order-words and badly analyzed composites. Deleuze asks: Is there a difference between these two systems, that of representation and that of differen*c*iation? Or are they two interpretations, incompatible and of unequal value, that is, one changing nothing and one changing everything?[30] Deleuze answers that when the in-itself of difference, the differen*c*iating of difference is hidden, that is the moment when difference falls under the authority of representation. There are, as Bergson has taken pains to show, two "tendencies" or, as Nietzsche would have it, two forces in a struggle of interpretations. According to what organization does difference differen*c*iate without threat of representation? One, answers Deleuze, is that of the series. Any series is constituted by the differences between each of the terms that enter into it and two or more series can constitute a system. Thus, rather than representation by means of resemblance, identity, analogy, and opposition, the system of series is a differen*c*iating of differences by means of the coupling of heterogeneous series (whose elements are already heterogeneous). Such differential elements are "intensities," which—as we have seen in Bergson—indicates that they are constituted by a difference that refers to still other differences, more heterogeneity. The three syntheses of the psyche can be translated into such series. Passive synthesis couples affective excitations forming the basis of habit. Eros, the second or active synthesis, designates the "internal resonance," that increase in qualitative differentiation that occurs when impressions of reflection are associated; when, as I have argued, impressions of grief and disappointment combine with anger, envy, and malice, or joy intermixes with love, generosity, pity, courage, and pride, and the association of ideas and that of impressions intertwine to provoke a violent "double impulse" that intensifies passions. And finally, with the third synthesis the death drive merges with the movement of life itself and by necessity overflows all series, opening them up eternally to chance and chaos.[31]

From the point of view of series, "phenomena" do not look or act the same as from the point of view of representation by resemblance, identity, similarity, and opposition. The resonance of the couplings between series in a system composes a dynamism unthinkable in the system of representation. Artaud proposed such a "theater of cruelty" in the realm of the audible: words become incantations, extending the voice to vibrations and other qualities, wildly stamped rhythms, pile-driven sounds that exalt, benumb, charm, and arrest sensibility, a long and vast derangement of the senses.[32] By these series that form differenciated systems, Artaud wanted to create a new lyricism. Artaud is not simply thematizing theater, which would still be a manner of representing. Artaud is really finding a new manner of living and another order, insofar as a theatrical system-series includes techniques for making the theater "function" as the connective series between dreams of eroticism, obsession, savagery, fantasy, every utopian image the brain generates, and the real life of beings. To this end the physical and perceptible element is of the utmost importance, and the theater, rather than thematizing moral or personal crises, must find a way to thematize immediate affectivity: the cries, groans, apparitions, tricks, magical costumes, dazzling lighting, incantatory voices, harmony, rarity, colors, rhythm, masks, surprise objects, heat and cold, as well as haphazard motions, such that all these things themselves become the scenes and the language, the music, the lighting, the costumes, the stage and props and sets. It is a theater of Bergsonian immediacy, of intensities, series of heterogeneous qualities.[33]

This is the way for the death drive to exceed the basic series themselves. Artaud believed that the very same public that thirsts for news of accidents, earthquakes, revolution, war, love, valor, and fearlessness can be brought to the theater of cruelty and engage in it. And certainly in the rowdy dance halls and cabarets, such theater was still available to even the most ordinary of citizens. But "serious" theater, the classical theater, poetry and prose, instead of offering the immediacy of affectivity, presents itself in terms of the moral injunction (like Freud's regarding narcissism) to learn a lesson, to contemplate a fixed and dead expression, to conform to standards of perception that are constituted by a restrictive social norm. Such conformity does not merely bore the public, it substitutes for the affective immediacy of spectacle the representation of ideals, in order to then judge the public for not living up to the standard of those ideals.[34] Rather than being challenged with what exceeds even their most intense series, the public is given stale models of resemblance, identity, analogy, and opposition; the public is given representations of violent acts, representations of vicious acts, representations of sexual acts, representations of courageous acts, representations of virtuous acts, actualizations that by definition exclude the possibility of what Deleuze has called humor. And so people respond the only way they can: like Freud's narcissist, they do not learn; at best (and this is a horrible and corrupt alternative) they act out or represent to themselves degraded copies of these acts. They kill or they live model lives, and in either alternative they represent but cannot create; most often they are not even given access to the basic tools of creation, and those who are have no idea what to do with them.

If we were to take the construction of series and system-series and turn again to psychic life, we discover that what the embryo or the infant undergoes would destroy the stratified adult. "Already, the truth about embryology is that there are vital, systematic movements, slidings, twistings, that only the embryo can tolerate; the adult would come out of them torn to pieces. There are movements with respect to which one can only be the patient, but the patient can only be a larva."[35] The larva is the early form of *any* animal before it becomes an adult; the patient is a person or thing receiving impressions from external agents.[36] So the systematic movements, slidings, and twistings of the infant are those of the infant alone; no adult could endure them, but this does not stop adults from judging them to be depressive, paranoid, and full of rage. If this is the case for the embryo and the infant, why not for the thinker? Thought, too, Artaud has shown us, is thought of these terrible movements, this theater that only a "larval subject," a dynamic, heterogeneous, and local subject, can endure. The system-series of the constituted subject consists of such larval subjects; they are the patients of the dynamic series that express them.[37]

Why should series resonate to form systems? Is it because they resemble one another? Is difference ultimately reducible to what it resembles in relation to some ultimate identity? Are we back in the sphere of organic representation? Or can we say that Hume has provided the empiricism by means of which resemblance and identity melt into mere effects of the reflection on impressions producing habits? And even though the second (active) synthesis stratifies such reflections and stratifies the larval subject, nonetheless such a synthesis can be undone in the second passive synthesis that brings the subject into the theater of dispersal, displacement, and disguise. From the side of series, Deleuze posits the "object = x" as the differen*c*iator of heterogeneous series, putting them into contact with one another while differen*c*iating them, but it is an object that is always missing from its place—that is, as the whole, it displaces and disguises itself in the series, and so does not unify and cannot be identical with itself. This displaced and disguised object = x, "the disparate," is the displaced and disguised being in differen*c*iation and thought of differen*c*iation whose various differences are constituted out of series differing with respect to intensity.[38] Representation is its distortion, its garbled repetition in the static rather than the dynamic mode. This places representation always on the outside of any series or system-series, whereas difference, we have seen, in Bergson is internal or immanent.[39]

A Science of the Singular

A question now presents itself: What, if any, kind of psychology is left to us? The ontology of becoming undoes the authority of representation through the valuing of creation and becoming. What *is* serves representation with its fourfold order of resemblance, identity, similarity, and opposition, along with the mechanistic return to inorganic matter. What *becomes* is of another order, a fluid intensive series that organizes in accordance with strata, the double pincers of God, but which, following the principle of humor, opens upon creative displacement and disguise: the death drive, eternal return, differen*c*iating difference. However, having mobilized the ruin of representation, are we free to develop a new philosophy of the psyche out of its creative differences and differen*c*iations? In part yes, in part no. There are two directions, each of which must be considered carefully: (1) there is what I will call the science of the singular, a philosophy of becoming and creation, a "science," if you will, of singularity and affectivity; but (2) with just as much urgency, there are the social and political forces of fascism and capitalism, which make use of all the powers of representation for their own ends. Because the latter are perhaps among the aspects of Deleuze's and Deleuze-Guattari's thought that have been most studied and articulated, I would like to investigate principally the first direction, beginning with the psychic impact of an ontology of becoming.

Psychoanalysis operates by means of immobilization, whereas philosophical intuition operates by placing itself within the mobility of duration, and it is from this perspective, Bergson suggests, that any concrete psychology must begin. What is real, experienced, and concrete is variable, whereas the symbol, such as the phallus, is a motionless view of a reality that is otherwise in motion.[40] What psychoanalysis has not recognized is that one cannot reconstitute fluid and concrete reality out of static analysis. Given the succession of qualitative moments, each of which contains what precedes and announces what follows it, psychology resolves duration into separate states—sensations, feelings, and ideas—and studies these separately. Yet Bergson's method insists that every so-called psychic state contains the whole virtual past as well as the present of the being, so that separation into states is a distortion of concrete being.[41] The psychologist, Bergson despairs, begins by isolating the person from the "coloring" duration and memory produce so as to leave behind what cannot be expressed in common language. This allows the psychologist to erect independent facts, certain states that may be symbolized as "ego," for example. But a psychology that is a "true empiricism" must, for each and every living being it studies, cut out for the being a concept that is appropriate to that being alone.[42] Bergson is skeptical about the ability of concepts to manifest the singularity of this being, insofar as he takes concepts to "represent" the common, what is similar, the homogeneous and quantitative, rather than the unique, the singular and qualitative. Even though in *Matter and Memory* Bergson appears to have reconciled quantity and quality by means of extensity, the greatest degree of expansion of quality, we need not only look to Bergson to wrest such a science.

Roland Barthes's *Camera Lucida: Reflections on Photography* provides a rich philosophical intuition from which to create not a philosophy of psychology but a philosophy of flows, series, and system-series of unconscious desire, virtual memory and creation, Eros, Mnemosyne, and death, a philosophy that is singular in every respect, that opens the way to Deleuze and Guattari's conception of schizoanalysis.[43] What better image for the creative human mind than that of a work of art? Every aspect of Barthes's work contributes to this image. Singling out Barthes in general and *Camera Lucida* in particular for guidance in generating a philosophical intuition of becoming may seem, to say the least, to be going against the grain. The literature on Barthes is vast and his place in the history of literary criticism would appear to have been clearly established. By his own account as well as that of his readers, Barthes found Lacan "useful," though I would maintain that it is a limited usefulness, one that establishes a schema to be undone by Barthes's own work.[44] Indeed, this appears to me to be Barthes's relation to most of the ideologies and theoretical schemas through which he has passed; that is, like the reader of the text in his essay "From Work to Text," Barthes has relaxed his Imaginary and become a "fairly empty subject" who sees things as "multiple and irreducible," proceeding from known codes combined in a unique way.[45] It has also been argued that *Camera Lucida* is an elucidation of trauma in photographs, thus making it a text of morbidity as well as a text about the Imaginary and all its problematic lures.[46] Although recognizing the contextual reasons for these claims, I deliberately turn away from them in order to read Barthes otherwise. I want to keep in mind that the book is an homage to Sartre, who abhorred psychoanalysis, and that Barthes's "cynical phenomenology" of an art that is essentially contingency and singularity may lead to the creation of its own terms of encounter apart from those of the traditions he has passed through.

So it is significant that Barthes begins not with photography but with photographs. And at the very beginning of his encounter with photographs, Barthes finds himself looking into the eyes of Jerome, the youngest brother of Napoleon; Barthes is astounded by the concrete reality that "I am looking at eyes that looked at the Emperor."[47] And so the realization of eternal return, that the photograph reproduces by mechanical means as many times as one wishes what can never be repeated existentially as the same, what occurred only once; for no matter how much one manipulates the image, one cannot repeat its referent as the same. This makes of the image that constitutes the photograph an absolute particular, a "sovereign contingency," the "this," the real that evades the discourses of sociology, semiology, and psychoanalysis for the sake of a new science for each object; a *mathesis singularis,* a science of the singular, a science of what is entirely disordered.[48] Moreover, what appears in the photograph is inseparable from the photograph. There is no ideal photograph, no ultimate image, no model or standard; in each and every case the signifier is the signified. So to make sense of the photograph, neither formal-aesthetic considerations (composition, characteristics of the materials) nor analysis (social, political, and cultural circumstances) will do. We must rather look at a photograph we love, look at the desired object, the beloved body. Can we say the same of unconscious desire as it manifests itself and synthesizes time through the living being? If the matter at hand is how not to reduce psychic development to a system of interpretation, then perhaps a philosophy of becoming must also begin with the desired object, the beloved.

Or perhaps we should consider another work by Mary Kelly, *Post-Partum Document,* a series of objects that Kelly created from the time of her son's birth until he reached the age of five, recreated as a book several years after being exhibited.[49] Both book and exhibit, photographs and written text (rather than material sensuous works visited bodily), *Post-Partum Document* works against representational organicity, systems of interpretation, formalization, and preformed ideas of politics and culture to create its own images, senses, assemblages, and politics. Lucy Lippard remarks that when she first saw this work in its initial incarnation, hanging in a London gallery in 1977 (four years in the making and still incomplete), she liked it formally for its melancholic delicacy and visual parallels to motherhood's quick passage. Theoretically and politically, she liked the rigorous (linguistic and psychoanalytic) analysis applied to the intimate mother-child relation, the juxtaposition of creation and procreation in the life of a woman, the mixed masculine and feminine roles.[50] But Lippard eventually realized that these are the very categories that Kelly's work undermines. As the work expanded in complexity and size, Kelly distinguished it from exactly this kind of "generalized feminist art," whose purpose is to define or question the designation "feminist art," the social and political context into which such a work appears to belong. Instead, Kelly leaves these fields open to the suggestion that *Post-Partum Document* is a specific practice that *problematizes* via a work of art and puts into question the badly analyzed composites of so-called "feminist practices."[51] The book form, with its photographic images of artistic objects, and the fact that Kelly in no way wanted photographs incorporated into the works of art that constitute the gallery exhibitions work against what she—following Barthes—has called "the pleasure of the text," which, she explains, means the pleasure of the objects themselves. There is no way around this except Barthes's suggestion that you have to start with a photograph you love. "You can't make art for everyone," in Kelly's terms.[52] So if neither Barthes's photographic choices (the son remembering the mother) nor Kelly's choices of objects (partial objects, virtual objects, the mother's memorializing the son) incite the reader of this text to participate in the debate, if you do not or cannot love them, then as a philosophy this may not work for you. Not all thought is for everyone. "You can't make art for everyone." In essence, photography is a science of the singular. This is another way of saying that a philosophy of unconscious desire can only be a schizoanalysis. Each of these creations, flows, series, and system-series operates at the exterior limit of capitalist society, Oedipal signification and order-words, but they do so without reterritorialization, without overcoding (excessive stratification, higher levels of organization especially under the impetus of the demands of capital).[53]

In transposing her work from the gallery to a book, Kelly worries that she will lose the "viewer's *affective* relation to the visual configuration of objects and texts";[54] yet affectivity can still be found in the "texture" and "sensibility" of the black and white photographs, in their association with "mnemic" traces, or, it might be said, in their role as partial objects, displacing and disguising both the mother's so-called fetishism and the works that had hung in the gallery. In Freud's account of female narcissism, the mother fetishizes the child by dressing and feeding her/him even when s/he grows too old for such attentions, or she simply has another child. Kelly has apparently worked from this situation, making works of art that question the attribution of fetishism by taking it to its extreme. For the book, the works themselves were removed from the frames in which they were shown in the gallery, making the book into its own work of art, displaced and disguised in relation to the gallery version, and in no way a representation of art objects. The gallery exhibition, then, is one system of series; the book is another.

Barthes's book also contributes to this problematization of the work of art. Barthes problematizes the "essence" of photography through its non-representational aspects when he singles out three bodily practices, which he also associates with emotions and intentions. First are the bodily practices of the photographer or operator (to do), then those of the spectator (to look), and finally those of the referent or target (to undergo), which last corresponds to the "little simulacrum," the *eidolon,* the view that the object emits like an afterimage or "the return of the dead."[55] Caught by the lens, Barthes takes the photograph to be the advent of himself as "other"; he is transformed into an object (the referent). But even this is more complicated than it first appears, for there is the "I" he thinks he is, the "I" he wants others to think he is, the "I" the photographer thinks he is, and the "I" the photographer exhibits in her art. All this makes of the referent a subject in transit, on its way to being an object as dead and unchanging as Freud's mechanistic death drive.[56] But Barthes and Kelly find something else, to which Barthes calls attention as he slips from subject to object: he never loves all the work of a single photographer; there is a vast disorder of the specter. Do not assume, warns Kelly, that *Post-Partum Document* is simply about child-development or the artist's relation to her son and the events of their life together: weaning, learning to speak, going to school, writing. Rather, a problem is posed and there is no resolution reached, for desire is eternally transitive, it resists normalization, ignores biology, disperses the body.[57] What is most vital in Kelly's work is that in order to reach this resolution of continual passage and process, the problematic is posed outside of the framework of order-words. This is the case even though, as Kelly writes, the specificity of the labor of child care (that it is the mother's job) is essential to the reproduction of the relations of production, for the mother-child relationship is the basic structure of adult socialization. Thus it is not only the child's but also the mother's personality that is formed in the reciprocity of socialization.[58]

So profoundly does Kelly's text resonate with Barthes's that the two series call up a third. The Other, Deleuze has argued, is neither an object in my perceptual field nor a subject perceiving me. Returning to the essay on Tournier and the world without others, we find Deleuze evoking the great advantage of "the Robinson hypothesis" for exploring the problematic of the structure-Other: that a human being is isolated on an island.[59] Like Barthes's photographs, Tournier's novel operates according to the "principle of adventure": What will happen in a world without others? Indeed, what do we mean by others? Do we know them by their effects?[60] Deleuze's thesis in this case is of extreme importance for all I have written in this book:

> The first effect of Others is that around each object that I perceive or each idea that I think there is the organization of a marginal world, a casing or ground [*fond*], where other objects and other ideas may come forth in accordance with laws of transition which regulate the passage from one to another. I regard an object, then I divert my attention, letting it fall into the ground. At the same time, there comes forth from the depth a new object

> of my attention. If this new object does not injure me, if it does not collide with me with the violence of a projectile (as when one bumps against something unseen), it is because the first object had already at its disposal a complete margin where I had already felt the preexistence of objects yet to come, and of an entire field of virtualities and potentialities which I already knew were capable of being actualized. Now, such a knowledge or sentiment of marginal existence is possible only through other people.[61]

So when I only perceive part of an object, Deleuze continues, I nonetheless "totalize" it by positing the rest as visible not to myself but to those Others. It is others who constitute the "depth" (*profondeur*) in which objects encroach upon one another, guarding and protecting the perceiver from what she cannot perceive, such that without the other the meanness of things shows itself fully. In the case of Tournier's Robinson, that the ship's dog goes wild and runs away in what seems like a remarkably short time is a mark both of the extent of the treachery of things and the ordering power wielded by the structure-Other. As Moira Gatens has written, by the end of Tournier's novel Robinson is no longer a "man": "His relations with the various bodies which populate Speranza have recomposed his body, changing both his speed and slowness, his rhythms of motion and rest, his affects and his powers."[62] Robinson even makes it clear that he has not desired to sodomize the native boy, Friday, for by the time Friday appears, Robinson's relations with the world have been so radically altered that his sexuality has ceased to be European and has become elemental, a vital energy, "feminine," he says, in "human terms," but since such anthropomorphisms are meaningless to describe this cosmological force, this "solar coitus," Robinson abandons them for astronomical descriptions.[63] It is a changed world.

But prior to his transformation Robinson lived as we do, so let us not reduce the structure-Other to either a particular object or a particular subject. It is the expression of a possible world whose effect is to distinguish consciousness from its object, thereby relegating consciousness to the realm of the past, to an "I was." In such a world, in order to make room for the object consciousness is annihilated. The problem with Defoe's Robinson Crusoe, from this point of view, is that he remains materially in contact with the structure-Other, literally the European world, through the various material objects he saves from the sinking ship. He hunts, fishes, farms, builds, plows, sows, reads, and domesticates, all of which activities keep him from discovering what Bergson calls the resources of a deep inner life, the second passive synthesis and the wounding that creates.[64] So there is no harmonization of world and consciousness for Defoe's Crusoe, only a profound splitting and the emergence (as Klein has warned) of a terrifying, annihilating world that he fears.[65] And given that the structure-Other is the absolute within which specific others appear, it must also be the case that desire, like perception, passes through the others. This was precisely the critique aimed at Merleau-Ponty's phenomenology early in this book: that for him desire becomes only what can be "seen, thought, or possessed by a possible Other."[66] Given the annihilation of consciousness by the structure-Other, the question that will be opened up by the work of Barthes, Kelly, and Deleuze is: What happens on the philosophical, visual, artistic, and ultimately psychic level when the structure-Other collapses, when the subject no longer suffers annihilation because she has found the crack in the system of representation of the world that otherwise structures all life?

In Roland Barthes's investigation of photography, the disorder of the world manifests itself in the specter/image in the realization that not all the photographs of a single artist are desired. This incites Barthes to reject Sartrean "fascination" for strong-arming the subject into passivity, as well as Kantian interest, which turns out to be a passing fancy. In their place, Barthes happens upon the "principle of Adventure," barely a principle in the usual sense of universal rule, but in its place something highly particular that emerges when the structure-Other, the world as an expression of possible Others (the only possible Others, since we know possibility is derived from the actual) is broken up by the disorder of the specter. The element of adventure is heterogeneity, as in the co-presence of two discontinuous elements in the photograph, such as the press photograph depicting soldiers and nuns on the same torn-up streets of Nicaragua in 1979. As a "structural" element (can we say here ontological?) heterogeneity animates even photographs in news magazines.[67] "In this glum desert [of indifferent images], suddenly a specific photograph reaches me; it animates me, and I animate it. . . . The photograph itself is in no way animated (I do not believe in 'lifelike' photographs), but it animates me: this is what creates every adventure."[68] Unlike the ideal circumstances of the Robinson hypothesis, in all photographs there is the structure-Other, the *studium,* one's cultural participation in the figures and faces in the images, their gestures or actions, their average effect, the field of unconcerned desire, what one likes, what is comfortable, desire conditioned by the Other. Here the whole realm of the photographic active synthesis operates to inform, to represent, to surprise, to cause, to signify, to provoke desire, to reconcile the photograph with society by any of these means.[69] As *Anti-Oedipus* eventually conceptualizes it, the active synthesis codifies the whole field, thereby constituting "races, cultures, and their gods," but within such socially constructed fields there is always *both* a segregative and exclusive organization (where one proclaims oneself part of the superior race or culture) *and/or* a nomadic and polyvocal crack in the structure-Other (where one finds the outsider and becoming).[70]

The second element that Barthes's spectator discovers in the photograph is one that functions not as what codifies culture but as the narcissistic wound that collapses it. The *punctum* is the sting, the cut, the little hole, the narcissistic wound that displaces and disguises the object; an accident, a pure contingency that pricks and bruises, yet remains poignant insofar as only through the narcissistic wound does death show itself as eternal return.[71] That is, even though there is a structural heterogeneity in all the photographs that animate Barthes the spectator, the photographs that wound "Roland Barthes" are not necessarily the same ones that puncture any other spectator. As a science, that of photographs is then notably singular. It is the *punctum,* the narcissistic wound that creates singularity and fractures the general cultural functions and codes of the photograph. Perhaps the narcissistic wound and the singularity it creates for both the living being and for the photograph are what brings Barthes to connect photography not to its representational precursor, painting, but to another series, that of the theater: "but if Photography seems to me closer to the Theater, it is by way of a *singular* intermediary (and perhaps I am the only one who sees it); by way of Death."[72] Around the world, the first actors participated in the cult of the Dead, designated themselves as a body at once living and dead: the totemic whitened bust, the painted face in China, the No mask in Japan, the Katha-Kali of India.[73] The dead return in the body of the actor: eternal return is this primitive theater, though if we are only interested in the (death) mask as a cultural signification, a generalization, this does not go far enough for Barthes.[74] The general cultural meaning lacks critical power and authority; it cannot crack the *studium.* What can?

Mary Kelly introduces *Post-Partum Document* with a series of photographs of her infant son's tee-shirts (with no frames or other markers that identify them as photographs, except that they are in a book). The shirts are inscribed in a generative manner, starting with horizontal lines of data printed on the cloth and ending with mirror-image triangles that constitute the developing Lacanian symbolic order, called the "Schema L." The tee-shirts are of a peculiar kind, with little ties to hold the shirt closed; they are the kind of shirts that only infants or invalids might wear. The heterogeneity of the infant shirts and the Lacanian schema is marked; it is marked by the general cultural *studium* in which the infant's personality as well as the mother's "feminine psychology" are produced developmentally by the structure-Other, the encounter of the infant's imaginary relations with the symbolic, linguistic structures orienting the mother's world. If this were all, the critical element would be too weak to crack the symbolic structure. For the shirts are a theatrical mask in Barthes's sense, designating psychical and social development as well as the mastery of the linguistic structure-Other. To crack this structure, something much more destabilizing is needed, something that wounds, something that is singular.

Beyond the introduction, *Post-Partum Document* consists of six types of "Documentation" (*Experimentum Mentis* I–VI). Documentation I confronts the spectator with its immediacy and with no delicacy. There is, in fact, a great deal of humor in the meeting of Kelly's "Analyzed fecal stains and feeding charts" (inciting a furor in England when they were exhibited), as well as her highly revised Lacanian schema, with the serious tone of Lacan's own work. The immediate and materially real effect of weaning from the breast is that one has to confront dirty diapers for the first time, something which, if Lacan knew, he certainly did not include in his schemas. In this first Documentation, Kelly puts together two series of infantile development that are the most critical to life, to the child's physical well-being; but apparently they are far from the aesthetic or even sociopolitical concerns of most contemporary art. Even in photographs, these particular images are not beautiful; they are an obsessively detailed quantitative analysis of the infant's daily food intake at specified times of day as it corresponds to the quality of his stools, on a scale of "01" to "05," constipated to diarrhoeal. Each day's analysis is documented on a stained diaper liner. Not the stuff of great social movements? And yet, "[t]he introduction of solid foods is a dramatic event insofar as putrefactive organisms are consequently introduced into the essentially sterile intestinal tract of the newborn infant."[75] The absolute failure of any correlation at all between what the infant takes in and the quality of what it excretes is part of the joke. Equally important, as Kelly states, it undermines the notion of the mother's natural capacity for mothering.[76] Would it not then hold that the failure of correlations undermines the Lacanian schema, too? Is it not the mother who is judged through the child? If she were a schematically better mother, a "good" mother, would the food and the stains correlate? Kelly's epigram is, thus, "What have I done wrong?" Is there nothing anyone could love in these images?

Documentations II and III quickly move into the realm of language. In II, the transition from single words to syntactic speech is recorded daily in twelve-minute sessions over five months and schematized according to utterance or identifiable phonemic content as gloss, or the mother's supposition of the grammatical translation of the child's utterance; function, which defines the utterance's function to indicate existence, nonexistence, recurrence, or rejection; and finally, the child's age in months and days, allowing for a record of the child's speech events from the point of view of development. These are offered at the top of each image in a crude print on white paper produced by small rubbery blocks of letters put together to form words; the actual letters are placed above but in a mirror image, so they are backwards. Both printed words and blocks of letters are in small wooden holders that appear to have been constructed to hold the rubbery blocks. On the lower half of the image are typed "interactions" between mother (or her surrogate) and baby (the baby's are spelled out phonetically). Everything is aligned as symmetrically as possible, and the image again is rather crude, rather simple.

At the end of the documentation, Kelly asks, on a page that repeats without representing the Lacanian sign (S "over" s, signifier dominating signified), "Why don't I understand?" That is, the words are printed above a small "s" (the signified) as the signifier, which, for Lacan, represents the subject for another signifier. Kelly explains that this repetition functions as an image of the "contingency of the 'natural capacity' for maternity,"[77] even, one supposes, if that natural capacity is an effect of the structure-Other. But the documentation also undermines the complementarity of the mother's desire that the child be her "phallus" and the child's desire to be what the mother wants her/him to be. The child speaks a word; the mother interprets it as a conceptually complete sentence. Is not the issue here, for Kelly, that misfire between these two, between the capacities of the child and those of the mother, between the child's passive and connective syntheses and the mother's far more intense (in Bergson and Deleuze's sense) syntheses? For Kelly as mother is operating at the level of spiritual life, the movement toward new creations born out of conclusions incommensurable with their "premises," whereas the child expresses Kleinian rage.[78] What happens when the mother makes this misfire between the child's world and her own into a work of art, producing a new series out of it, creatively constituting a new series rather than attempting to compensate for the misfire? Does such an act turn the Oedipal world inside out, the world in which, hypothetically, the father seeks to be in the child's place (object of desire), the mother wants to be in the father's place (structure-Other of the child's desire), the child wants both father's place (Other of the mother's desire), and the mother's place (signifier of the father's desire)?[79]

In Documentation III the images become more elaborate. The child is entering nursery school, and is it any wonder that the images are more carefully crafted, given that the mother has more time? Here, on what appears in the book to be a sheet of rough paper with a torn edge, Kelly prints out in a column condensed transcripts based on recorded conversations between the child and mother beginning with the child's entrance into nursery school and ending some three months later when he has "adjusted." Then, in a second column she types out reflections that occur to her later in the day, and finally, in a third column, handwritten "perspectives" from the point of view of a full week later. The columns correspond,

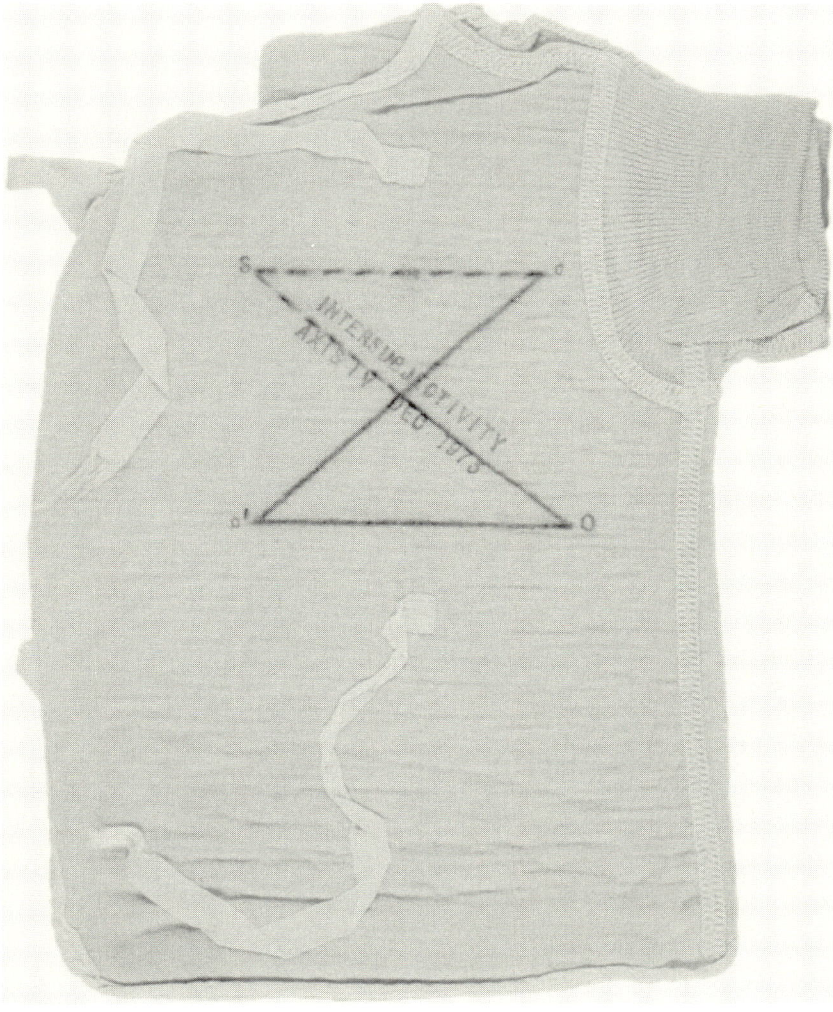

Figure 5. Mary Kelly, *Post-Partum Document,* p. 6 (Introduction)

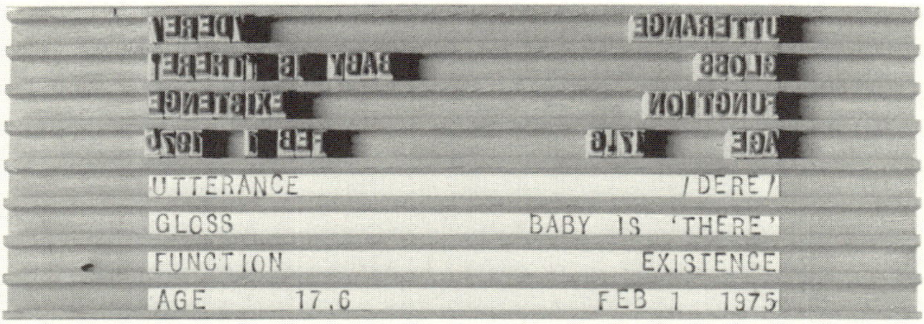

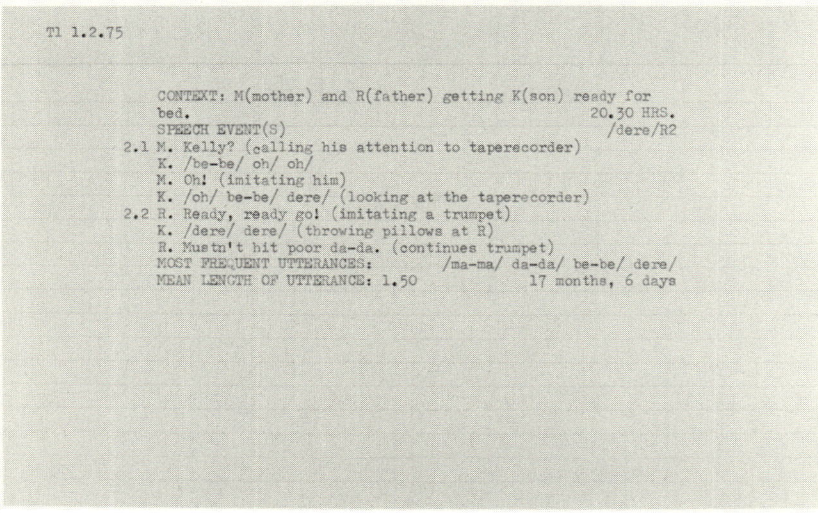

T1 1.2.75

CONTEXT: M(mother) and R(father) getting K(son) ready for bed. 20.30 HRS.
SPEECH EVENT(S) /dere/R2
2.1 M. Kelly? (calling his attention to taperecorder)
K. /be-be/ oh/ oh/
M. Oh! (imitating him)
K. /oh/ be-be/ dere/ (looking at the taperecorder)
2.2 R. Ready, ready go! (imitating a trumpet)
K. /dere/ dere/ (throwing pillows at R)
R. Mustn't hit poor da-da. (continues trumpet)
MOST FREQUENT UTTERANCES: /ma-ma/ da-da/ be-be/ dere/
MEAN LENGTH OF UTTERANCE: 1.50 17 months, 6 days

Figure 6. Mary Kelly, *Post-Partum Document,* p. 48 (Documentation II: Analysed utterances and related speech events)

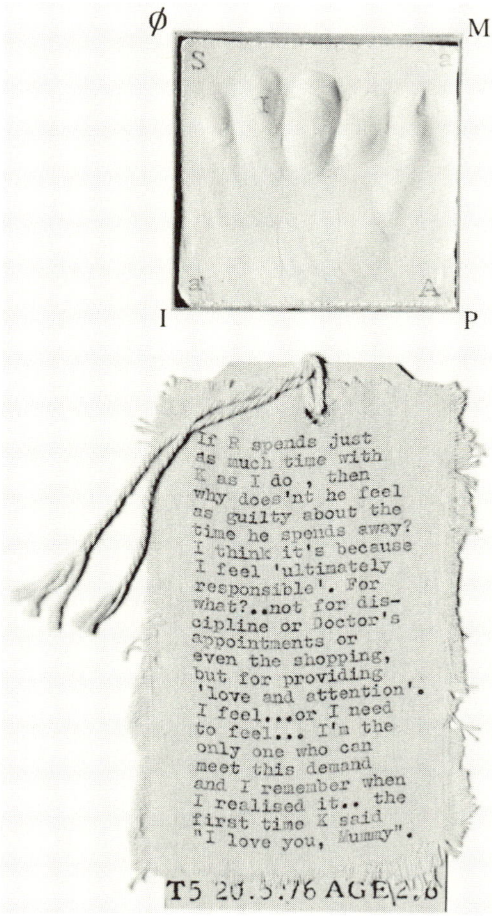

Figure 7. Mary Kelly, *Post-Partum Document,* p. 102 (Documentation IV: Transitional objects, diary and diagram)

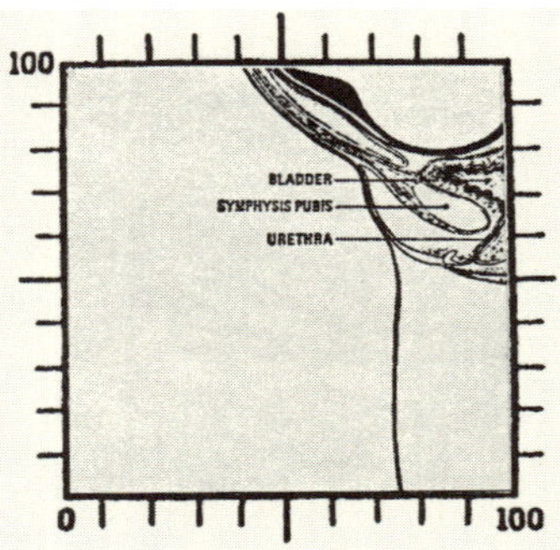

Fig. 2b

L2. INDEX B   Homo sapiens (F)

BABY, BACKACHE, BEARING DOWN, BIRTH CANAL, BIRTHMARKS, BLADDER, BLEEDING-after intercourse, in pregnancy, in labour, intermenstrual, post-menstrual, BLOCKED DUCT, BLOCKED TUBE, BLOOD GROUP, BLOOD PRESSURE, BLOOD TEST, BOTTLE FEEDING, BREASTS-breast abscess, breast cancer, breast feeding, breast fluid, breast milk, breast swelling, BREATHLESSNESS, BREATHING TECHNIQUES, BREECH DELIVERY, BREECH LABOUR, BROW PRESENTATION, BUCCAL PITOCIN.

Figure 8. Mary Kelly, *Post-Partum Document,* p. 121 (Documentation V: Classified specimens, proportional diagrams, statistical tables, research and index)

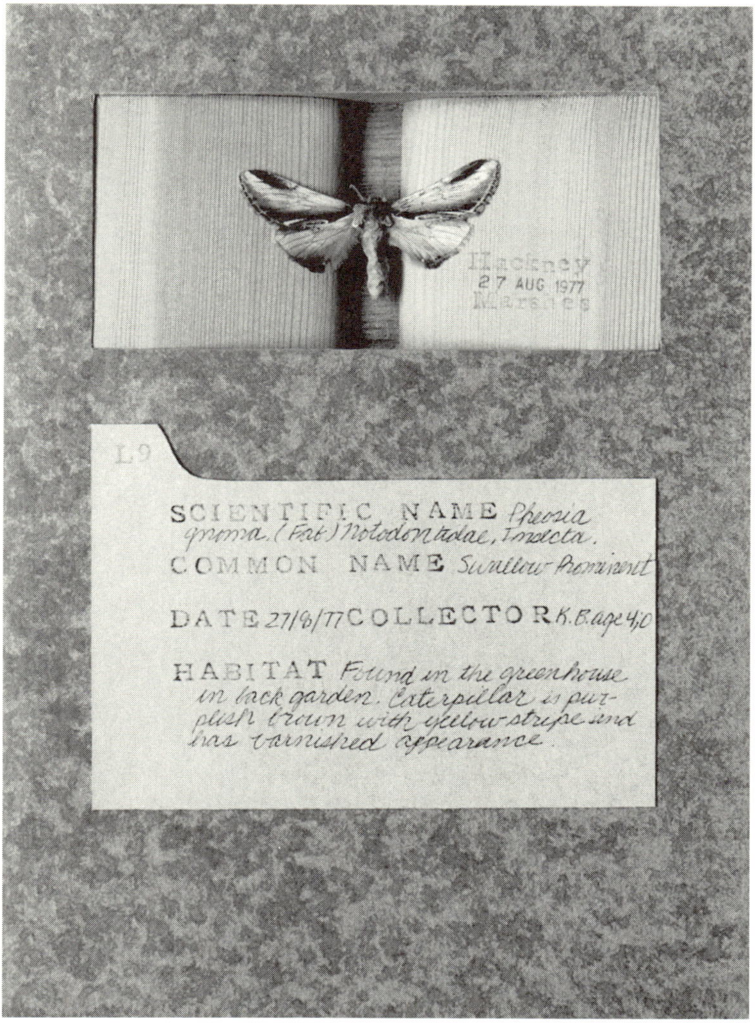

Figure 9. Mary Kelly, *Post-Partum Document,* p. 147 (Documentation V: Classified specimens, proportional diagrams, statistical tables, research and index)

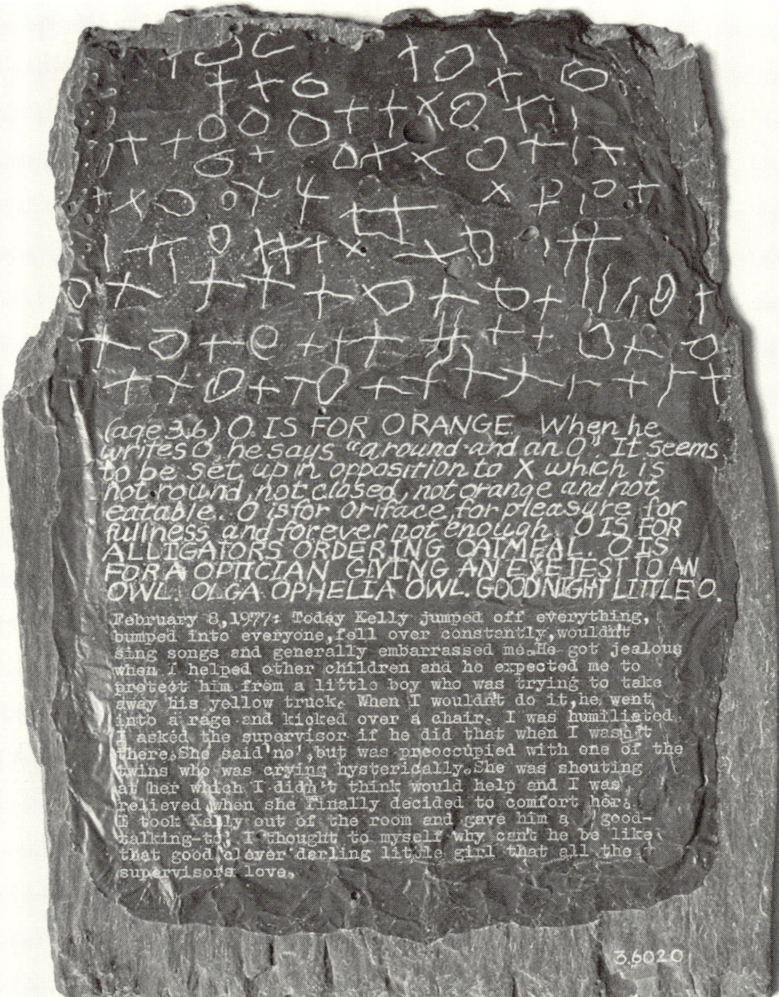

Figure 10. Mary Kelly, *Post-Partum Document,* p. 171 (Documentation VI: Pre-writing alphabet, exerque and diary)

left to right, to the "Real," the "Imaginary," and the "Symbolic" realms. Over it all, her son has scribbled whatever lines and shapes he can with crayon, making it particularly difficult to read the mnemic traces. Kelly measures the placement of the marks on a scale she has composed based on what parts of the paper he has covered. The standard against which the child is measured is that of his level of preparation for visual symbolization, but in two respects: first, the child is measured against the ability to represent the signifying system of written language, the symbolic realm wherein he will play his allotted role and so fulfill his destiny; and second, we see that as a correlate to this, his scrawls are measure against the privileged system of single-point perspective (see chapter 1), that system established by Renaissance theorists to "perfect" the real, a perfection that amounts to doing away with the real so as to put into its place the symbolic realm of repeatable signifiers whose intelligibility and order of importance are assured. Thus the perspectival notion of the vanishing horizon of the real conveys at least a double sense, that of the demand that the real (the scrawls of the child that do not conform to expectations) be given up or lost, and that of "lack," the "lack of object" inserted by the father into the "dialectic of the Oedipus complex."[80] At last, a clear connection has been made between the visual and linguistic demands for intelligibility, substance, hierarchy, and order. As usual, dates and age are carefully recorded.

Thus, only apparently does this documentation present the intervention of the dominant symbolic structure according to which the mother represents the father's authority (Lacan's "Word of the father").[81] The odd thing is that if you read the columns, the father's word and authority leave the room in the very first image and more or less stay away. The documentation then turns its attention to the child's increasing ability to do things and the mother's various affective responses to these doings. Thus, the epigram "Why is he/she like that?" (over a small "s") is less an instance of the boy's transgression of the mother's narcissistic aim in order to be like his father than it is a chronicle of the mother's affectivity, something real that should also have been lost in the transition of the woman to motherhood, but which stubbornly remains.

Documentations IV, V, and VI are quite beautifully crafted. In IV, each image includes a plaster cast of the boy's hand, below which is a printed text on a piece of old blanket belonging to the boy torn into neat rectangles, but torn nonetheless, thereby emphasizing its materiality. It is one of many so-called transitional objects for the child's and the mother's comfort. Another Lacanian schema frames the plaster square, the "Schema R" representing the subject's (the mother's, not the child's) states within the imaginary, symbolic, and real. The symbolic framework is unchanging, the real is unrepresentable, and the imaginary fluctuates wildly from image to image. Kelly records her reflections on her child's behavior, reflections full of emotional ambivalence concerning her child's growth and independence. Remember that for Lacan, such schemas have the force of absolute authority, that symbols are a schema that "envelop the life of man [*sic*] in a network so total that they join together, before he comes into the world, those who are going to engender him 'by flesh and blood'; so total that they give the words that will make him faithful or renegade."[82] If so, how is it that Kelly is so ambivalent, wondering about her own "belief in what I'm doing as a mother . . . as well as an artist. I feel I can't carry on with it."[83] The "it" is deliberately indefinite; it what? Mother? Artist? If the Lacanian regime were absolute in the way Lacan insists upon, what would be the point of even asking such a question? Could such a question even be framed?

Documentation V consists of three different elements: specimens of leaves and bugs, mounted on wood blocks set in what looks like marble, with taxonomic information giving the scientific name, date of collection, and habitat of each specimen neatly scripted below it on a card; proportional photocopied reproductions of the same specimens set out in a proportional diagrams used in the study of plant and animal morphology; and finally, photocopied fragments of women's reproductive system and other affected organs during a full-term pregnancy, accompanied by statistical data that pathologize the mother's body in spite of her own experience of it. This relates, writes Kelly, to the fact that "female" is defined taxonomically only by elements relating to reproduction, thus the heterogeneity of her sexuality is effaced.[84] This documentation consists, then, of images of the scientific and "natural" world that the child is entering, but so also is the mother, through her pregnancy and her artwork. Both child and woman ask: "What am I?" even while the work of art subverts the biological determinism it confronts.

Documentation VI, on alphabetic writing, is the mother's diary printed into the bottom of a roughly shaped rectangular black slate surface. On top, the child's own alphabetic scribblings, one letter or mark to a stone, and in the middle, the mother's comments on her child's writing. In each case the multiple heterogeneity of the series cracks the Lacanian Symbolic and Freudian biological frameworks that continue to attempt to circumscribe and order the relationship between the mother and child. Commentators on Kelly's work who are familiar with the Lacanian context that Kelly sabotages often miss this point. However, some, such as Paul Smith, notice, as he says, that the juxtaposition of the child's conversations or emblems or writing with that of the mother's inner-voice commentary and her secondary reflections (in Documentation III) are not only the mother's analysis of the child, but also the child's analysis of the mother. All this leads Smith to conclude that "our language is never total, never the homogeneous commodity of a unified subjectivity, never wholly rationalized: as the language, so the political structures and strictures. So there are moments of transgression and loss when it is possible to desire to speak and to dare to change."[85]

So the mother's final question, "What will I do?" is already being answered, has been answered from the very beginning of this project. She is making art through the displacement and disguise of libido and in so doing breaking up the power and authority of the social and political structures that are attempting to force their structure-Other upon the multiple relationships this work creates, the system-series it traces. If from a Deleuzian point of view *Post-Partum Document* arises as a synthesis of reminiscence, then the mistake of psychoanalysis would be to forget that such reminiscence is the form of a past that has never been present. It is especially important to remind ourselves in this context that what is purely past is beyond object choice and the mother. Though the pure past coexists with any object choice and with the mother, the pure past is Eros accompanying Mnemosyne, Eros (passive synthesis and sexual drives) tearing virtual objects out of Mnemosyne (memory) and giving them to us to live with.[86] By contrast, given Lacan's totalizing presuppositions concerning the symbolic, it is essential to his thinking that the partial (virtual) objects, those "objects" that have never been lived, should be able to be subsumed under a symbolic organ as if they were representations of the social schema and not creations.

Margaret Iverson has expressed precisely this concern, that the psychoanalytic reading of Kelly's work, which supposedly plots the mother's narcissistic involvement in her child and her subsequent "castration" or loss of the child, thereby returning the mother to her inferior status within phallocentric culture, is a reading that eclipses Kelly's considerable artistic practice.[87] Iverson focuses on Kelly's refusal to represent the female body because femininity is not a pregiven (biological or psychological) entity, but also on Kelly's critique of formalism by means of the work of art. Opposed to the image of art as self-reflexive, Kelly's "pleasure of the text," arises in part from the manner in which she addresses the extra-artistic realms of literature, science, knowledge, and pleasure, an expansion that "problematizes" the assumptions of political thought, psychology, epistemology, and semiology, at the least.[88] Avoiding any traditional "iconic" representation (based on resemblance or similarity), Kelly gravitates instead toward the "index," with its causal or existential links to an object, and the symbol, which takes advantage of a conventional rule, as well as mixtures or juxtapositions of these signs set up in "montage-like" images.[89] Thus, Kelly's work is more filmic than pictorial in the sense that it signals the motion and change of both the child's and the mother's experience and the insufficiency of a single stabilized or stratified framework for making sense of this art. In nearly every image we find the intensely private and personal, the deep reflection on passive synthesis, alongside the scientific, psychological, or statistical abstract languages of knowledge, the common languages of social life and conventions.

Kelly's work, as I interpret it, is a profound image of the fluid and multiple organization of the psychic. It is exactly the sort of image and interpretation that I am proposing in this book; that is, the manner in which Eros and Mnemosyne conjoin to produce the virtual object is intensely private and therefore singular, each system and system-series establishes its own directions, its own sense, even though it lies within the political and economic order of capitalism as well as capital's subsidiaries, such as Oedipus. Whether Kelly the mother is socialized into accepting the schemas of Lacan or not, Kelly the artist creates enough new series, virtual objects, and affirmations of becoming by means of her art to convince me that the Lacanian system is a trap from whose immediate and encompassing authority she has escaped, as Artaud finally escaped from the "care" of various mental institutions, including that directed by Dr. Jacques Lacan.[90]

And Barthes? Looking through some photographs after his mother's death, with no hope of "finding" her or of finding a photograph he loves, Barthes's muses with humor over someday writing a little bit about her (the humor is that he has written an entire book). He has no hope of finding her in these photographs because recognition is "differential." Like the *punctum* recognition is a partial object, a detail of such a kind that "to give examples of the *punctum* is, in a certain fashion, to give myself up."[91] To reveal the virtual objects one creates for oneself, one's own psychic functioning, coloring, and layering, along with the whole of virtual memory from certain points of view would demand converting them into something common, even universal. The pure pasts that have never been present are singular and intensely private; to make them actual is part of a choice and part of where one finds oneself, what one has to respond to in the world. Certainly, looking at photographs of the beloved body places one in the most personal of situations. A representation would attempt to integrate these partial objects into the common language of cultural homogeneity and organicity, but this would be a misfit. Barthes would then cite his sorrow and grief, perhaps his loneliness, but no narcissistic wound. For *puncti* have the power of expansion, they become more than the photographic medium that bears them so that what you see, what is created, what is thought is no longer a sign within a symbolic system but becomes the thing itself.[92] Photographs have a particular quality that perhaps no other art form shares; in a photograph (barring digital and darkroom manipulation) one can never deny that the referent has been there. Reality and the past are superimposed upon one another. In ordinary photographs, this remains unremarkable, but in certain photographs, those that are loved, the fact that the photograph is literally an emanation of a real body, that light is the carnal medium, that the image is extracted, mounted, expressed by the action of light and the body touches me with its own rays, attests to the fact that what I see is a reality and not the product of any schema.[93]

The force of Kelly's images, even though she takes such great care not to announce them as photographs, is precisely this: the photographed bodies (assemblages) in her books, the collages in the *Document* exhibitions, and the laminated, photopositive, silk-screen, acrylic on Plexiglas of *Interim* touch the viewer with their own luminosity. Barthes's *Winter Garden Photograph* is precisely this "treasury of rays" that emanated from his mother as a child. Kelly's *Post-Partum Document* is another system-series of such a treasury, keeping in mind that not all emanations are for everyone. There will not be a single art defining all arts, nor a single desiring-machine defining all desires. This is why I have to be committed to the concept of "a science of the singular." While the ontology of becoming guarantees a peculiar sort of "science," an orientation within which the being of becoming is thought, nevertheless with respect to the series and systems of series that become, we must be able to address each one in its singularity. It is never a matter of calling up a past that has been present; rather, there is a pure past that has never been present but which we acknowledge is reality. This is why the date on the photograph is the date of an event; a real but virtual past that leads ultimately to oneself as viewer and referent of every photograph; the one who sees what "has been"; through this we arrive at our own radical finitude. And this is also why it is useless to speak of a "style" with regard to all the work, the virtual objects, of a single photographer, a single artist, a single human being. While these series may resonate in relation to one another, there is no genus or species drawing them together as the unitary style of an integrated person. No wonder psychology resorts to determinative schemas and internal drives; for the acuity, diligence, and love involved in producing such a science for each series or system-series require the kind of interest and attention, aesthetics and ethics in the creation of concepts that Barthes and Kelly devote to their subjects.[94] It is not that such a science has no logic, for we have seen that the ontology of becoming follows a complex logic, but insofar as there is always a "spiritual" element, the creation of what has no conditions, then that logic must be continually adapted to the realities of the deepening passive synthesis and so can never be finished. This must also be the case, I think, for language. In the final chapter I will examine the language of the science of singularity. My interest there is in maintaining that language does not and cannot dominate all other semiotic systems. Although Kelly has creatively thwarted the authority of Lacanian schemas in the production of objects from her own reflections on her own passive synthesis, and thus through the creation of images and assemblages, a question remains regarding the relationship of all images and assemblages to language. Can the language system and the chain of signifiers not rise up, as language, to dominate all other semiotic systems? That is, will not the demands for intelligibility and clarity in social language align with the insistence upon true syllogisms and the sheer force of words, the potency of language, to override, restrict, and so replace the creative *éclat* of virtual, ontological memory with the banal, measured, and orderly words of common sense?

8
The Linguistic Signifier and the Ontology of Change

Signification or Sense?

The claim I am making in this book will be interpreted cynically or worse if it is distorted by being placed back in the framework of representation's organic hierarchy and static order. That is, it will be embraced or rejected as a kind of idealism or fantasy. For many contemporary thinkers, for numerous artists and writers, representation is inevitable and the conception of a kind of thinking and a series of practices that constitute the ruin of representation is nonsense. However, from the point of view of an ontology of change and becoming, fluid series and system-series, creative practices, and what might be called transformational practices (including psychologies) are real. Only as an ontology of becoming is the "spiritual" element, the creation of what has no conditions, the production of the new out of a deepening passive synthesis, found to occur in the domain of living beings and their practices. However, there may still be serious objections to the relevance of this position for Barthes's examination of photographs. For it is true that Barthes decides that the photograph, insofar as it authenticates what *has been,* must be without a future. Without a future, the photograph cannot possibly be productive and creative; in fact, Barthes decides that photographs are the incarnation of pathos and melancholy.[1] Yet the very trait of the photograph that produces pathos, the trait of flowing back from presentation to retention, is the melancholy trait of the second passive synthesis, that of Eros-Mnemosyne, without which the creation of what is without conditions, schemas, or codes cannot even be contemplated. The photograph violently asserts itself, filling the sight by force, attesting to what Barthes calls a "second *punctum,*" to what has been, in the upsurge of the moment of Death between the clicking of the camera and the development of the print.[2] Does this element of the photograph disqualify it as a system of signs that can participate in the discovery of the creative unconscious of the spectator, that particular "coloring," as Bergson calls it, that is hers and hers alone? Every photograph, laments Barthes, is this same catastrophe, the announcement of impending death, a second *punctum* deepening the first. But for whom? Insofar as the photograph is the epitome of the copy of the copy and no photograph actually resembles the person it refers to, whose death is announced? The photographic copy of a copy makes identity, Barthes comments, an absurd legal affair or nothing more than likeness among family members, a perversion of their fundamental differences.[3]

However, this trait, this simulacral identity, is of great value to the creative aspect of the photograph, for what is left when identity dissolves is only the *punctum,* the personal and private element of the photograph, singularized in the spectator, simultaneous with the displacement and disguise of the virtual that produces the new. And since the flatness of the photograph makes it into a surface, the image has no hidden inner being and so no hidden signification; it can participate, if it is not subverted, in the figure "8" that creates the future. That the photograph authenticates the existence of the being it pictures and creates the wound, the personal and private element, that singular coloring of the spectator's durational flow, fully indicates the importance of the photograph to the spectator's creative evolution. It may be that, insofar as the photograph is the outstanding pictorial exemplar of our modernity, announcing the modern age and emblematic of it, its melancholy is that of our own nostalgia for myth, identity, and certainty, for God and the I. If the photograph does not give us the future, this is because the new must be created *without any conditions* except those of Death's upsurge, an upsurge that cracks time and identity.

I am aware, however, that both Mary Kelly's art and Barthes's photographs evade a serious problem: they are images, not language. Kelly does make use of language, but I have not really clarified its role in her work. Even in my analysis I have subordinated the language to the image because the language in her work does not assert itself apart from the images. Yet there is no doubt that her work exemplifies a particular tension between images and words, language and things, and that this relationship needs to be discussed. Is it the case, as Barthes maintains, that only images—and for him perhaps only photographs—can authenticate the existence of human beings as contingent realities? For, unlike photographic images, whose flat surfaces tell us nothing—that is, they express no subjectivity and represent no objectivity—language, Barthes writes, is a kind of fiction, which means, he explains, that it is a matter of general ideas, of genera or signification.[4] Attempts to make language more than fiction, he continues, end with logic (static formalization) or morality (a Freudian or Lacanian absolute schema). Having elided the Lacanian schema and its claims to absolute authority, what is left to us? A virtual world of creation and discovery that has no language or that does not include language among its creations or creative machines? Does language fail to say anything about the singular creation that emerges out of virtuality, the ontological unconscious, because it is regulated either by logical formulations or the common and thereby mundane grammar and syntax of homogeneous spatiality? This seems to be the question Luce Irigaray poses when she proposes a fluid language of sexual difference. Although Irigaray has provided important critiques of both the logic and morality that dominate western languages, in this book she has served, as well, as a guide toward something else, even if it is a something she might not altogether embrace.

Certainly, we need to be warned, as Félix Guattari has warned us, against the degradation of ethologial, ecological, semiotic, economic, aesthetic, corporeal, and fantasmatic elements and semiotics through the reduction of all of these systems to a semiology of language.[5] For the reduction of all sign systems to informational and communicational linguistic systems presupposes the very definition of language that I have opposed throughout this book. However, given the ruin of representation, in all its forms, that this book proposes, if anything should be clear, it is that the language of representation is ineffective with respect to the being of becoming, the ontology of change. The point is of tremendous consequence to my project. Thus, I will elaborate in what follows by means of Deleuze's critique of representational language. Deleuze takes the opportunity to approach this problem from yet another point of view, though one that overlaps with the project of the ruin of representation and the collapse of determinative schema.

In the *Logic of Sense,* the problematic of language is central to the major theme, the creation of sense. In this text Deleuze is again critical of Plato, this time for the Platonic distinction between limited and measured things with fixed qualities, which presuppose fixed presents and subjects and pure becoming, without measure.[6] Deleuze argues that pure becoming is entirely without measure or limit, to the extent that not only does it never rest, but it also moves in two directions at once, an infinite identity of both directions or senses at the same time, causing future and past, too much and not enough, more and less, and so forth, to "coincide in the simultaneity of a rebellious matter."[7] What is interesting is that this dualism, as Deleuze calls it, is not what we expect. We expect such dualism to take its place in the distinction between the Idea and matter or

Ideas and bodies; between the rational intellectual world and that of sensible materiality. However, it does not. As conceptualized by Plato, it is a dualism *within bodies* themselves. The dualism exists between that which receives the action of the Idea and that which does not and so is very poorly realized (the copy of the copy of the copy). Thus, for Plato it is a dualism between legitimate copies and false simulacra.[8]

Matter within simulacra, insofar as it does not receive the action of an Idea, is pure unlimited becoming. Limited things, on the other hand, are the matter within legitimate copies subject to the action of Ideas. If pure becoming is the simulacrum that does not receive the action of an Idea, then its relation to language must be quite specific, for language does not affect the simulacrum and speech simply flows over its referent.[9] Unless . . . there are two completely different kinds of language: one that designates that which is fixed by the Idea, and another expressing becoming. Is it enough to leave it here? Can we simply say, fine, some bodies are fixed into limited things by the Idea and some are not, and some language designates bodies that have received the action of the Idea and some simply flows unimpeded? A dualism within bodies and a second dualism within language? Obviously, we are pained to ask how language intersects with bodies or why it does not when it does not. Or is a body simply another linguistic construct referring to something symbolic but never accessible as real?

To begin to answer this, Deleuze leads us away from the Platonic problematic toward a different kind of problem and a different kind of solution, those of the Stoics. The Stoics made several distinctions that Plato does not consider and for reasons that Plato could not entertain. On the one hand, there are bodies characterized by physical qualities, actions, passions, and corresponding "states of affairs." Bodies are not Platonic simulacra, awaiting the action of an Idea; bodies do have characteristics of their own. All of these bodily characteristics are, according to this conceptualization, determined strictly by bodily mixtures, such as metal cutting skin, or water mixing with oil, or the emanation of light from bodies that constitutes the photograph. In addition, however, all bodies are causes of certain effects that are *not* bodily. In a radical reversal of the Platonic scheme, the Stoics claim that although bodies form mixtures with other bodies, they are the *causes* of "incorporeal entities" only, that is, of "logical or dialectical attributes," which are certainly not things or facts. They are, however, strictly related to Bergson's duration; they are events.[10]

Here, following Deleuze, we begin sketching out the extremely complex relation between bodies and language, a relation whose complexity is certain to be underestimated. Bodies that mix and are causes are certainly said to exist; they are, after all, bodies with physical qualities, actions, and passions. Events, however, as the effects of bodies, do not *exist;* they do not have the same physical qualities; they are effects and so are said only to *subsist* or inhere in relation to bodies.[11] As such, it would be inappropriate to say that events are *substantives* (they are not things; they do not exist) or even *adjectives,* which characterize and predicate substantives. Events are verbs, infinitives such as *to speak* or *to eat,* which inhere or subsist in bodies, the results of the actions and passions of bodies; they are becomings always eluding the present of perception and action, instead splitting into past and future. Deleuze quotes the French historian of philosophy Émile Bréhier, who explains this as follows: when a scalpel cuts through flesh, one body cuts through another body *producing* an attribute, that of "being cut." The attribute is in no way *real* (or what Bergson calls actual); it is *virtual,* something produced at the limit or at the surface of corporeal nature.[12] By now it should be clear that there is more than a passing relation between this Stoic conception of bodies and incorporeal entities or logical attributes and Bergson's view of time as duration. To elucidate this, we can examine how Deleuze further defines events in relation to unlimited becoming, which divides itself infinitely into past and future while eluding the present. That is, there is the time of living bodies, bodies that act and are acted upon, or more finely, bodies consisting of forces acting on one another.[13] We have already seen that forces that constitute bodies always act and are acted upon in the present, for the present is the moment of perception and action, the moment of choice. But there is also the time of becoming, the upsurge of time that Deleuze has defined as dividing each present into past and future; this is the time of the virtual, of the event and the incorporeal.[14]

The Stoic distinction between mixtures of bodies in depth and surface events that are the effects of bodies allows for the formulation of clear distinctions between the properties and characteristics of bodies and the properties and characteristics of certain morphological aspects of language (verbs). Physical bodies have depth, what earlier in this book was referred to as extensivity: metal cuts the skin, mucous fills the placenta, light is absorbed by a photosensitive medium. These mixtures determine qualitative and even quantitative states of affairs, that is, states of bodies. But when we utter the words *to cut, to fill, to mix,* these events are the result of and so caused by the mixing and coexisting of bodies, but they are not themselves bodies, forces, or mixtures. They are incorporeal events at the surface of bodies, they are the Idea relegated to the realm of effects and evicted from the realm of causes; Ideas do not cause things; bodies cause the Idea.[15] This conception that bodies cause the Idea is an aspect of Deleuze's transcendental empiricism but also his pragmatism, his radical reformulation of the Platonic scheme. The accusation of dualism will immediately be levied here, and perhaps a kind of dualism is at work, but as Deleuze comments, it is one that "entails an upheaval in philosophy."

We are accustomed to the dualism inherent in the categorical philosophy of Aristotle, where "all categories are said of Being" but substance is primary. Other categories (notably genus, species, and difference) exist as accidents of substance, which is primary Being. Stoic philosophy, on the other hand, recognizes a higher term; it recognizes that "something" subsumes both being and *nonbeing,* the existence of bodies and that of virtual events. Being is restricted to bodies, with their qualities and quantities, actions and passions, their states of affairs. Nonbeing encompasses the "sterile, inefficacious, . . . *the ideational or the incorporeal,*" which is an effect of bodily mixtures.[16] And even though there is a dichotomy between bodies and events, dualism has lost its efficacy, and thus its meaning in this context. All bodies, not just false copies (simulacra), but all bodies with their depths and mixtures always and entirely *elude the action of the Idea.* What this implies in terms of representation is that bodies with depths and mixtures also elude representation totally. They are not measured by the distribution of being in the Idea; they are neither a true nor a false copy of an original. Instead of the Platonic false copies, what is produced are the effects of bodies; the virtual objects that can be "sonorous, optical, or linguistic effects and [that] . . . form the entire Idea."[17] The "unlimited becoming" that Plato attributes to that which fails to receive the action of the Idea, to that which is not representable, now characterizes the event; unlimited becoming is not a physical property but a logical attribute of propositions, the sterile and inefficacious Idea.[18]

I have noted that events are characterized by means of the infinitive form of the verb: *to absorb, to cut, to fill.* It is in the infinitive that the "unlimited becoming" of events is expressed. Infinitives clearly are not living presents; bodies act and are acted upon in the present, while their incorporeal effects are simultaneously becoming. Each infinitive, *to cut, to fill, to absorb,* divides itself infinitely and without limit into past and future, always eluding the present in self-differentiation, thus always reversible. As what Deleuze calls the pure form of time, the event in the infinitive form of the verb is the form of the synthesis that constitutes the virtual past and the virtual future; it has both already happened and is about to happen but never is that which is happening.

To summarize: Stoic logic operates in accordance with a set of presuppositions different from those of the Platonic and Aristotelian logic with which western philosophers are most familiar. For the Stoics there are also two orientations at work, two planes of being: not the usual western dualism of body versus mind, but rather the dualism of bodies that are causes and the incorporeal attributes of those bodies. Bodies, in accordance with this way of thinking, are "beings" in depth; they are real, existing in space, and temporally in the present. In the "depths" of bodies, one body penetrates another and they coexist with one another in all their parts. They form mixtures, they intermingle "like a drop of wine in the sea," or like a poison that spreads throughout the body.[19] Such mixtures determine the quantitative and qualitative states of bodies: the red of fire, the blue of the sky, the amount of poison in the body. On the other plane we find incorporeal acts, which Deleuze and Guattari call the formalization of expression because "what we mean by the words 'to grow,' 'to diminish,' 'to become red,' 'to become green,' and their organization is something entirely different from the real, spatial, temporally present intermingling in the depths of bodies."[20] Expressions are not states of affairs but incorporeal events at the surface of bodies. Mixtures deep inside bodies are the causes of incorporeal events that are meanings: becoming green, becoming poisoned, which becomings are the effects of those bodies. To state that "the body becomes poisoned" is, then, to express what Deleuze calls an event and what Deleuze and Guattari together call an "incorporeal transformation," the expressed element of statements that are attributed to bodies.

If we accept the notion that the infinitive is the event and the event is the effect of the actions and passions of bodies, there still remain many questions about how the event as the infinitive form of the verb is related to language, and how (and whether) language intervenes in the actions and passions of bodies. I would like now to begin to articulate this relationship, although it cannot be accomplished simply or with a few convenient or familiar phrases. To begin with, let me make it clear that this discussion is not about the origins of language. The presumption operating is that language is a social phenomenon into which we are inserted. Were there no language, there would certainly be nothing at stake in discerning the differences between bodies, Ideas, and language. So for Deleuze, "[i]t is the characteristic of events to be expressed or expressible, uttered or utterable, in propositions which are at least possible."[21] However, given the many relations inside a proposition, which ones obtain? Deleuze points to three specific relations that Bertrand Russell has designated as commonly acceptable: denotation, manifestation (the statement of desires or beliefs), and signification.[22] Of these three, for reasons that will become clearer, manifestation is primary.

Manifestation is the relation of the proposition to the person who speaks, she who expresses herself. It is the statement of beliefs or desires that are causal *inferences* that correspond to the proposition.[23] "Desire is the internal causality of an image with respect to the existence of the object or the corresponding state of affairs. Correlatively, belief is the anticipation of this object or state of affairs insofar as its existence must be produced by an external causality." That is, belief is an inference from an anticipation to an externally caused object or state of affairs, and desire is an inference from something caused internally to the existence of an object or state of affairs.[24] The basic manifester is "I" because the domain of the personal functions as the principle of all possible denotation. The example of Descartes has been primary in this respect; he shows how the I, manifested in the *Cogito,* grounds the judgment of denotation by which the wax is identified, so he is not at all looking for what dwells in the wax, but is concerned with the realm of the personal.[25]

Denotation is the relation of the proposition to an external state of affairs that is individuated; it includes bodies, mixtures of bodies, qualities, quantities, and relations. Denotations function through the association of the words themselves with particular images that ought to "represent" a state of affairs. From all the images associated with a particular word in a proposition, we select those images that correspond to the given whole and express this in the form of "this, that, it, here, there, yesterday, now, etc." These words are formal particulars, they function as pure "designators." Logically, designation has the true and the false as its criteria. *True* signifies that the denotation is effectively filled by the state of affairs, that the indexicals are realized or the correct image has been selected. *False* signifies that a denotation is not filled due to either a defect in the selected images or the radical impossibility of producing an image that can even be associated with words.[26]

The third relation inherent to propositions is that of signification, in which the word stands in relation to universal or general concepts, which in turn are concerned with syntactic connections. Specifically, "we always consider the elements of the proposition as 'signifying' conceptual implications capable of referring to other propositions, which serve as premises of the first. . . . Thus, 'implies' and 'therefore' are essentially linguistic signifiers."[27] *Implication* is a sign that defines the relation between premises and conclusion, and *therefore* is the sign of assertion that defines the possibility of affirming the conclusion as the outcome of implications. This relation of inferences and conclusions between propositions is an indirect process, whereas denotation is a direct process of demonstration.[28]

Although this discussion clearly involves syllogistic or even mathematical processes, demonstration also has a physical sense (of probabilities actualized) and a moral sense (of promises and commitments asserted in the conclusion); however, Deleuze maintains, the logical value of demonstration or signification is not truth (impossible in the hypothetical mode of the implications) but the conditions under which the proposition "would be" true. The conditioned/concluded proposition may be false if it denotes a nonexisting state of affairs or is not directly verified. Signification does not establish truth without simultaneously establishing the possibility of error.[29] Thus, truth and error are not opposed to one another; they are opposed to that which is without signification, that which may be neither true nor false and so is designated absurd.[30]

Now, for reasons that I will try to make clear, Deleuze advocates the necessity of adding a fourth dimension to the proposition. The fourth dimension is sense, which, he insists, cannot be localized in any of the three traditional dimensions. Rooted in the *Cogito,* from the standpoint of speech (*parole*), manifestation or expression of the "I" is absolutely primary in relation to all denotation as well as to signification, for signification remains implicit. However, from the point of view of the language-system (*langue*), a proposition appears only as a premise or conclusion, signifying concepts prior to manifesting a subject or denoting a state of affairs. Deleuze writes: "It is from this point of view that signified concepts, such as God or the world, are always primary in relation to the self as manifested person and to things as designated objects."[31] Thus, the relation between a word (its acoustic image) and a concept is a necessary relation upon which manifestation and denotation depend. An unchanging signified concept is the condition that makes it possible to vary the images associated with the word (denotation) based on a claim in the form of "this is not that, it's that." Without the stability of concepts that give desires and beliefs signification, the manifestation of desires or beliefs would degenerate to the level of needs or opinions, and desires would amount to demands and duties, while beliefs would be nothing more than the product of inferences.[32]

All this becomes a matter of some interest when Deleuze is brought to the conclusion that the proposition is circular insofar as the primacy of signification over denotation is problematic. When we state the conclusion of a proposition, Deleuze argues, we make it the object of an assertion. That is, in concluding something, we set the premises aside and affirm the conclusion, thus relating it to the state of affairs that it denotes. We can only do this, of course, if the premises have been posited as true (already a departure from the "pure order of implication" insofar as we relate the premises to a denoted state of affairs that we presuppose).[33] But there is a more disturbing vein of thought at work in the syllogism. Affirming the conclusion is possible only insofar as we can affirm the truth of the premises, but such an affirmation amounts to another proposition ("the conclusion is true only if its premises are true"), which in turn relies on an additional proposition that affirms this newest proposition that "the conclusion is true only if its premises are true," and so on to infinity.[34] Such is the regress at the heart of syllogistic logic.

In short, "the conclusion can be detached from the premises, but only on the condition that one always adds other premises from which alone the conclusion is not detachable."[35] Thus, the process of making inferences does not ground denotation except by providing itself with denotation in the premises and in the conclusion. The proposition is circular and so demands, from within itself, the addition of a fourth dimension, that of sense. This demand lies in Deleuze's claims that, given the arbitrary nature of denotation, all denotation presupposes sense, that beliefs and desires are founded on the conceptual stability of signification, and that the identity of the "I" is guaranteed only by the permanence of the signified's "God" or "world." If these stable significations are lost, so is personal identity.[36]

Deleuze argues that by defining signification as the condition of truth, we give it a characteristic that it shares with sense; in discussing the conditions of truth we raise ourselves above the true and the false, because a false proposition also has sense or signification, but we err when we define the conditions of the true and the false solely as the *possibility* of the proposition's *truth.* In short, the condition of possibility of the true and the false is the *form of possibility* of the proposition, whether it is a logical, geometrical, algebraic, physical, or syntactic proposition. But this makes of signification, in its role as foundation, the "possibility of the conditioned."[37] We have already seen what possibility means: something is already actualized, then conceived of as possible. What emerges as somewhat peculiar in this context, though not unexpected, given what we have learned from Bergson's critique of "possibility," is that what is conditioned remains independent of the operation that is supposed to found it, though not in any creative sense. The condition does not affect the conditioned since the move from conditioned to condition returns us to another conditioned: it is circular. For Bergson this means that they are differences of degree when what is called for are differences in kind. Denotation remains external to the order that conditions it; the true and the false remain indifferent to the principle that determines the possibility of the one (true or false), and so allows it to subsist in its former relation to the other. "For the condition of truth to avoid this defect, it ought to have an element of its own, distinct from the form of the conditioned. It ought to have *something unconditioned* capable of assuring a real genesis of denotation and of the other dimensions of the proposition."[38] So the condition of truth is no longer defined as the form of conceptual possibility, as signification, that is, the condition of any possible denotation and manifestation, but as sense, the event that arises out of the mixtures of bodies, not in general, but in particular.

Thus the need for positing sense is revealed. Sense, understood as the *expressed of the proposition* is an incorporeal, complex, and irreducible entity at the surface of things; it is the pure event that inheres or subsists in the proposition. Sense would not be reducible to individual states of affairs, particular images, personal beliefs, or universal or general concepts. Sense is neither a word nor a body, but even more, it is neither a sensible nor a rational representation. As Deleuze notes, "It is difficult to respond to those who wish to be satisfied with words, things, images, and ideas," for sense has neither physical nor mental existence (it is not psychological), and clearly does not satisfy those who insist upon those things.[39]

So, finally, what is the status of sense? The expressed of the proposition, sense does not exist outside of that expression. Its "objectality" (*objectité*) in no way merges with the manifestation, denotation, or signification of the proposition. A qualitative predicate is attributed to the subject of a proposition, "the beloved body of the photograph wounds," but the sense is the event expressed by a verb (*to wound*) and is attributed to the thing denoted by the subject or to the state of affairs denoted by an entire proposition (*it wounds*).[40] The logical attribute does not and cannot mix with bodies, with the physical state of affairs, or with its qualities or relation (thus neither nouns nor adjectives), so as a noun *the wound* designates a mixture of bodies like light mixing with a photosensitive material, whereas *to wound* is not a quality of bodies but an attribute that is *said* of some thing. And so, by means of sense we pass from the expressible or the expressed of the proposition to the attribute of a state of affairs—"two sides without thickness," writes Deleuze in a locution reminiscent of Merleau-Ponty, though these sides cannot be reduced to the thesis of reversibility. Sense has one "side" turned toward things and one "side" turned toward propositions, and we pass from one side to the other only by following their "length."[41] This is more like the image of the figure "8" that Deleuze invoked to diagram the movement of active and passive syntheses of the pure form of time. Merging with neither bodies nor propositions, sense is the boundary, the event at the surface of states of affairs and things that *belongs to language,* which is *said of things.* But this still does not tell us enough about the relation between states of affairs or things and sense, or between sense and language. Insofar as events/sense are the effect of corporeal things and do not exist outside of the propositions that express them, we find ourselves positing a rather unusual set of dichotomies, that of things and propositions or of bodies and language. Let us look briefly at what makes the dichotomy so necessary and then finally at how language, too, becomes creative.

Does the Linguistic Signifier Rule?

At the beginning of the last section I wrote that I am not asking about the origin of language any more than I asked about the origin of works of art or photography (for which precursors can always be found). There is no beginning with respect to language, the manifestor (who is a someone) begins to speak; that someone speaks about the *denotatum,* and what she says are significations, yet it is the event that makes all this work.[42] We have seen that according to Hume, Bergson, and Deleuze, all life begins with affectivity, the contraction of earth, air, fire, and water, the folding over of the outside onto the inside until the figure "8" emerges as the diagram of life and creation. But how does life create language and how can language be put into motion? Deleuze provides some preliminary requirements: "To render language possible thus signifies assuring that sounds are not confused with the sonorous qualities of things, and with the sound effects of bodies, or with their actions and passions. What renders language possible is that which separates sounds from bodies and organizes them into propositions, freeing them for the expressive function."[43] If sounds remain attached to bodies as qualities, then the sound is that of a body eating or of a body sleeping, yawning, chewing, slobbering, sputtering, choking. This is the depth where Artaud experimented continuously and painfully, testing the boundaries between sound and language; but this is not language. Language requires a new relation between sounds and bodies. It requires denotation, a designation, a mark, and it requires that sounds express the power, the force of speaking and being spoken.[44] To say that events are attributed to bodies or states of affairs does not mean that they are attributed as physical qualities. They are dialectical in the Stoic sense, that is, they consist of two parts: one the *lekta,* literally "things said"; the other how the human voice is articulated to say things.[45] Or, Deleuze argues, they are "noematic" in Husserl's sense, as when Husserl distinguishes the sense of perception from the physical and psychological, as well as from mental representations and logical concepts: the pure appearance not existing outside the proposition that expresses it, though it is not the same as that expression.[46] From the point of view of the event or sense, two series are organized: that of the event referring to bodies noematically, and that of sense expressed in the proposition it makes possible. It is the organization of these two series that differentiates the event/sense from bodies and from propositions, and that separates the sounds that are language from the sounds that are those of the body. In the creation of these series, the event or sense *is* the slash mark "/" between bodies and expressions or, as Deleuze writes, between "to eat/to speak," even as it "makes possible" propositions and so differentiates denotations (referring to bodies) and expressions (expressible meanings).[47] The slash mark, the separation, is created in the articulation of the two series. Deleuze traces the genesis of such series to the paradox of indefinite regress such as that which occurs in the proposition when affirming the conclusion is possible only insofar as the truth of the premises is affirmed, but this requires another proposition ("the conclusion is true only if its premises are true"), which in turn relies on an additional proposition that affirms this newest proposition that "the conclusion is true only if its premises are true," and so on to infinity (see above). How we conceptualize such a series is a question of point of view. From the point of view of representation or homogeneity, each proposition denotes the one preceding it, and they form a homogeneous synthesis of propositions. Although this point of view, that of representation, can always be assumed and seems, in fact, to take precedence where static and hierarchical order is demanded, it has *no necessity*. For there is also a heterogeneous point of view, according to which the proposition is taken first in terms of its denotation and second in terms of its sense, for each proposition denotes the *sense* of the preceding proposition and is also taken to be superior in "degree" to that proposition (thus regress is symbolized as "n(1), n(2), n(3), and so on").[48]

The heterogeneous point of view differentiates according to differences in "kind" or in "nature," and not merely by degree, thereby introducing Bergson's definition of real difference into series. Insofar as what each successive proposition denotes is the sense of the preceding one, the homogenous series actually includes two series that are heterogeneous: one consisting of terms of the same type or degree and one whose terms differ in kind or nature from those of the other. So, for example, given the problematic of "to eat/to speak," as "event/sense," two heterogeneous series are there, one consisting of terms of the same type or degree and one whose terms differ in kind or nature from those of the other, that is, denotations (referring to bodies) and expressions (expressible meanings). Series are always "multi-serial."[49] Another way to approach this is to repeat the discussion introduced by Deleuze's critique of Lacan and to say that the series consists of a signifier (any sign that presents itself as an aspect of sense) and a signified (what is defined as correlative to sense, principally the state of affairs with its qualities and real relations).[50] We saw in chapter 6 that Lacan discovers series in his account of Edgar Allen Poe's "The Purloined Letter." Deleuze's remarks that the first series consists of the King, who does not see the letter; the Queen, who is relieved to have hidden it by not hiding it; and the Minister, who sees all and takes the letter. The second series consists of the police, who find nothing; the Minister, who hides the letter by leaving it in plain sight; and Dupin, who retrieves the letter. What is intriguing about this is that in spite of the signifier-signified relationship and the multi-serial complexity of series,

> [i]t is obvious that series relations—that which relates the signifying series to the signified and the signified to the signifying—may be assured in the simplest fashion by the continuation of a story, the resemblance, or the

> identity of characters. But *nothing in all this is essential.* On the contrary, the essential appears when small *or* great differences predominate over resemblances and become primary; in other words, when two quite distinct stories are developed simultaneously, or when the characters have a vacillating and ill-determined identity.[51]

In the end, it is essential that the terms of one series are in "perpetual displacement" in relation to those of the other (for example, the displacement of the Minister); it is this that produces the doubling and the double reference, one series sliding over the other in perpetual disequilibrium. But this is not all, for the displacement must be oriented in terms of an excess of signifier (the aspect of sense) and this, along with displacement, is guaranteed only by the figure "8," the uneven but two-sided entity that is at once word and thing, name and object, sense and *denotatum,* expression and designation; in short, the upsurge of time, "an *occupant without a place.*"[52] The empty form of time is the essential condition of displacement and disguise with respect to the event.

In relation to the upsurge of the empty form of time, the infinitive form of the verb is this empty form; but it is infinitely divided into past and future, and thus it is without person and without a present. In articulating the time internal to language, the infinitive also makes possible the expression in a proposition of the sense. So we also see that if the infinitive is the empty form of time internal to language and it splits into past and future, it can never express action. To do so, it would have to be the sound of the second synthesis, the synthesis of action rather than the surface that separates bodies from propositions, even while, as the expression of sense in the proposition, the event also connects the sound that is the infinitive form of the verb to the exteriority of Being, to the outside.[53]

Yet why does sense get passed over in the language system? Sense gets passed over because sense arises out of bodies with their actions and passions. Instead of giving voice to sense as it emerges out of the actions and passions of bodies, the sounds of the body becoming language, the child is presented with a finished product, language as the voice of God.[54] Melanie Klein's theater of terror sets the stage for this process in this account. I have already visited this theater in chapter 6 and have laid out how, for Klein, the child attempts and must attempt to reconstitute the partial (and bad) introjected object (Deleuze's simulacrum) into a complete and whole object, thereby a good object, and then to identify with this object. This good object always belongs to the dimension of "heights" bypassing the surface; it is the superego, the Platonic Ideas. As belonging to the heights, the good object is never really introjected; rather, Deleuze argues, it seeks to extract the force of the partial objects in a violent confrontation representative of the various psychopathological positions that Klein attributes to the infant: "The body of the infant is like a den full of introjected savage beasts which endeavor to snap up the good object; the good object in turn, behaves in their presence like a pitiless bird of prey. Under these circumstances, the ego [*le moi*] identifies with the good object, patterning itself after it in a model of love and partaking of its power and hatred toward the internal objects. But it also partakes of its wounds and its suffering under the blows of these bad objects."[55] So the ego suffers and is wounded under the blows of the so-called bad objects, the partial or virtual objects that the ego has introjected. But the good object is always only reached as the object of reminiscence, what is already there, that which preexists every child and comes to her through the voice.[56] Presumably this is the voice of the parent, but in the equivocity of its denotations, the analogy of its significations, and the ambivalence of its manifestations, it is the voice of the superego, the voice of God. The problem is that this voice has stolen the living being's own sonorous prevocal system from her/him. It presents the dimensions of an organized language to the child without grasping the organizing principle, that of *sense,* according to which the voice itself (that of the living being) would be a language.

The voice of God, the Platonic Idea, appears to have all it needs for organized language. After all, it reaches the good object by means of denotation; likewise it denotes the introjected objects, and it signifies concepts and classes structuring the Ideal domain. Manifestation, too, is present in the full range of the person's emotional variations, complaining about its wounds or simply withdrawing from the authority of the Idea. But there is no dimension of sense because everything is given and obedience (that due to a superego) is demanded. As Deleuze proclaims rather dramatically, since the voice comes from the heights as reminiscence we never really know the lost object it denotes; since it signifies an order that already exists, we never really know what it signifies; nor do we know what it manifests, since the manifester either gives way to its authority or withdraws: "It is at once the object, the law of the loss, and the loss itself."[57] Thus we again confront the Lacanian schema, the words that will make us faithful or renegade. The question is: How does language add the fourth dimension of sense so as to become creative and not merely to be representational?

Conclusion: Making Language Stutter

Against the linguists who maintain that language is informational and communicational Deleuze and Guattari demur; the elementary unit of language, the statement (*l'énoncé*), is the order-word, both a command

and a word creating order.[58] Information and communication, we have seen, are the work of common sense, the common language Bergson objects to because it omits the singular coloring and personality, thus the heterogeneity and becoming characteristic of duration. Rules of grammar, then, are not so much syntactic markers as power markers of the dual foundations of grammar: masculine and feminine, singular and plural, noun and verb, subject of statement and subject of enunciation, which we impose upon children in teaching them languages.[59] What is amazing is that society does not really even attempt to hide the fact that language is there to be obeyed and not to be believed, as if everyone knew already what Deleuze's analysis of the infinite regress of the proposition revealed: that without the stability of concepts that give desires and beliefs signification, manifestation is reduced to need or opinion, desires amount to demands and duties, and beliefs become the product of inferences. As Deleuze and Guattari write, the teacher "insigns," giving orders or commands, and whatever "information" her orders contain is only the minimum necessary to transmit order-words, that is, their semantic content: the student must be informed of no more than the fact that *red* and *read* differ semantically.[60]

Thus language is neither informational nor communicational; rather, it participates in a relay between forms of *expression* (the pure event that inheres or subsists in the proposition) and the actions and passions of bodies in concrete social formations. That is, language (expression/enunciation) intervenes in circumstances and those circumstances of life are reflected again in language. Every word is inhabited by a crowd; the organization of various social bodies has a great impact on what is expressed/enunciated since words are passed from one body to another intervening in bodies and transforming them. The British philosopher of language J. L. Austin provides the alternative, for Deleuze and Guattari, to a theory of language as information and communication by recognizing the importance of intrinsic or immanent relations between speech and action. In addition to the obviously extrinsic relations between speech and action, such as "look!" (an indicative) or "go now" (an imperative), Austin makes a claim for two standard forms of immanent relations. In one, "I promise," we commit ourselves by saying something, and in the other, "passengers are permitted to cross the tracks by the bridge only," we exercise certain rights or powers.[61] In this way Austin breaks down all distinctions between speech and action in language to *performatives,* which do something, and *statements,* which are said to be true or false. However, "[w]hen we state something or report something, we do perform an act which is every bit as much an act as an act of ordering or warning. . . . What we need to do for the case of stating and by the same token describing and reporting, is to take them a bit off their pedestal, to realize that they are speech-acts no less than all these other speech-acts that we have been mentioning and talking about as performatives."[62] The effect of Austin's argument is to expand the realm of speech-acts not only to performatives but also beyond this to so-called true and false statements.

The importance of this move for Deleuze and Guattari lies in their conclusions that the immanence of speech to action in speech-acts (otherwise called pragmatics) "effectuate[s] these specific, immanent, and implicit acts," that pragmatics is presupposed by semantics, syntactics, and phonematics, and finally, that signification and syntax are not prior to and independent of speech.[63] We can see that we have once and for all abandoned what Austin calls the "old doctrine about meaning" in favor of a new doctrine about "all the possible forces of utterances," the positioning of bodies in a field of forces.[64] In *The Logic of Sense,* Deleuze proposes that only verbs articulate the event or sense; this makes it especially fascinating to discover that Austin proposes a list of explicitly performative *verbs,* not for the purpose of determining what they mean, their signification, but rather in order to experiment with their "force," that is, whether the verb functions in a particular usage as an order, entreaty, or something else. And though illocutionaries (doing in speaking, as for example, "It's time for everyone to do it.") are the implicit presupposition of all performatives ("Here I go!"), illocutionaries themselves arise only in terms of the social collective of statements or enunciations. This leads Deleuze and Guattari to the conclusion that "the only possible definition of language is that it is the set of order-words, implicit propositions, or speech-acts current in a language at a given moment"[65]

The implication of this is that language is always transformative. Between the implicit presupposition ("It's time!") and the performative ("I'm going!") an incorporeal transformation takes place, evidence that signs are at work in things. Incorporeal transformations can be more or less complicated, reversible, serious. "It's time!" can perform a range of transformations, from jumping into a pool, to starting a class, to engaging in political action. The words never represent bodies; they form, instead, a kind of relay from the order-words to the ordering of bodies. The dates of events, to which both Bergson and Deleuze refer (see chapter 4), provide a precise account of the moment of transformation: the date of learning to swim, the date of graduating, the date of a major social upheaval. "It's time!" or "I'm going!" are, in this way, entirely dependent on circumstances. "A statement can be evaluated only as a function of pragmatic implications."[66] And most important, these circumstances are part of the immanent relation. Circumstances are not external to the immanence of speech and action; "I'm going!" is not the same at the poolside, at the graduation ceremony, in the midst of social upheaval. As

Deleuze and Guattari insist, "it is not the same bodily situation, and neither is it the same incorporeal transformation."[67] Everything depends upon which semiotic regime of signs dominates.

We have seen that under the rule of representation designated by Lacan or Freud, all signs are signs of signs. The formal relation of sign to sign constitutes a signifying chain in which a limitless *signifiance* (the effects of the signifier when there is no external referent) replaces the sign so that it becomes a symbol in constant movement from one sign to the next. This signifying regime produces nothing but an interpreter, the psychoanalyst, to unravel the endless chain of signifiers. The futility of this move is obvious; every step in this circle of signs is already an interpretation. In effect, as Deleuze notes, with this type of semiotic system any social disturbance or even domestic incident must and does call into question the entire system of the universe, producing a sort of cosmic paranoia. Deleuze and Guattari characterize this as a paranoid despotic regime because, given the limitless *signifiance* of the signifying chain, the world begins to signify before anyone knows what it signifies.[68] But psychoanalysis is more than this; it is a mixed semiotic (as they all are), and in addition to the despotic regime of *signifiance* and interpretation, it takes on the characteristics of an authoritarian regime of subjectification and prophesy such as those indicated by the Lacanian pronouncement that the signifier represents the subject for another signifier, that is, no subject communicates or represents an idea by means of the signifier; instead, the signifier subjects the subject (subjectifies), makes it passive, feeds it the message, makes it a subject who then carries the message it is given (prophesies), and thereby grows increasingly submissive to the normalization of a dominant reality.[69]

The paranoid despotic regime mixed with the authoritarian prophetic regime is the world that Mary Kelly encounters when she examines the representation of women's roles in society. It is a world governed by Freud's account of female narcissism, according to which the mother fetishizes the child by dressing and feeding her/him even when s/he grows too old for such attentions, or she has another child and restarts the cycle. It is a world that has determined in advance that when the child no longer needs the mother, society no longer needs her either. And all along the way the mother's role is predetermined, that is, represented, but Kelly creates her way out of this, causing a scandal in the art world as well as in the social and political world that tacitly accepts the psychoanalytic dogma even if it does not thematize this acceptance. After all, Deleuze and Guattari argue that all hierarchical, centered groups operate so as to normalize their regime, whether they are political parties, literary and artistic movements, families, or psychoanalytic movements; they scapegoat and judge as bad anything or anyone who resists the referral from sign to sign.[70] Kelly is obviously unwilling to accept the psychoanalytic interpretation and representation of her role, but she is no more willing to endorse and fall into line with the dominant reading of her work as "feminist art." She makes works of art that question the attribution of fetishism by taking it to its extreme in highly crafted, detailed, and precise works of art documenting specific moments of the process of the child's growth and her own responses to it. She creates works that redefine the role of mother, woman, artist, thinker, and member of society in terms of a new artistic sensibility that she creates by mixing the wound effected by the Lacanian schemas and the predefined placement of the woman's body in social hierarchy with her own deepening passive synthesis—that is, with the assiduous detail, the scientific mindset, the beautiful surfaces and constructions, the assemblage of words and images that make up her work, that form a mixture of bodies in tension with language—producing a continuous series of incorporeal transformations, the event of the new.

But the problem of language remains to be examined in the creative context. Is there a creative regime of linguistic signs? Is there a way in which the upsurge of the empty form of time operates to displace and disguise in language? Deleuze's response to this problem is, I think, singular:

> Make the language system stutter—is it possible without confusing it with speech? Everything depends on the way in which language is thought: if we extract it like a homogeneous system in equilibrium, or near equilibrium, and we define it by means of constant terms and relations, it is evident that the disequilibriums and variations can only affect speech (nonpertinent variations of the intonation type). But if the system appears to be in perpetual disequilibrium, if the system bifurcates—and has terms each one of which traverses a zone of continuous variation—language itself will begin to vibrate and stutter.[71]

The performative must be the motion that inaugurates any such variation in language, for the performative is both language and body. The performative is language, in that it expresses sense in a proposition; it is simultaneously corporeal insofar as it actualizes something in bodies, it involves the actions and passions of bodies; it is doing by saying.

What matters is that stuttering is a power of bodies and it gets expressed in the language system, so it does not and cannot start with words that already exist embedded in the language system. That is, stuttering, setting a language system in motion, is not merely a matter of inserting modulations, what Deleuze refers to as dialogic markers, from among the following types: she murmured, stumbled, coughed, faltered, quavered, and so forth; nor is it making characters stutter, murmur, stumble, cough, falter, or quaver in a literary text; nor is it making the reader actualize stuttering out of textual indications. Stuttering is not something restricted to individual characters in a novel; stuttering is the performative at work in the language system, the writer causing language as such to stutter.[72]

Deleuze's principle example of stuttering on the formal level comes from the work of Gustave Guillaume. For example, Guillaume maintains that "the indefinite article 'a' [rather than responding to a rule in a rigid and consistent manner] covers the entire zone of variation generated by the movement of particularization," while any movement of the language toward generalization is covered by the definite article *the.*[73] The effect of these movements is to make language vibrate, and in using language the writer becomes a foreigner, struggling to put words together even, or especially, in her/his own language. Such a language is evident even in pure science, for discovery, innovation, and creation are never a matter of simply making use of the constant terms supplied by a homogeneous system of reference. They are, rather, the "boom" of disequilibrium that lets language flee so as to vary constantly in every one of its terms.[74] Such a "boom" is evident, I would argue, in Mary Kelly's *Post-Partum Document,* since she appears to write it entirely in the language-system of Lacanian and Freudian psychoanalyses. But in her writing she creates the "boom" when the images free the language from its schematic determinacy. By filling in Lacan's schemas with images, assemblages, and constructions, with her child's acts and words, and with her own responses to the child and to the schema, she radically transforms and thereby cracks open the dominant system, disguising and displacing its order with her own creations. In creating the work of art, Kelly literally destroys the mother language by putting the syntax into motion, making what Ronald Bogue refers to as creative syntax.[75] And even Roland Barthes, whose *Camera Lucida* has been so fully and completely accounted for as "anything but an affirmation of life,"[76] nonetheless undermines the order and arrangement of the language systems of phenomenology, existentialism, linguistics, and psychoanalysis, not to mention aesthetics in any form, to produce precisely that, a celebration of the creation of selves (his own selves and those of his mother) in the upsurge of Death.

Kelly and Barthes succeed in creating because even though they are confronted with the dominant system of language and representation, they set it in motion, they transform the order and organization of the social, political, cultural, scientific, epistemological, and artistic schemas that knowledge seekers, experts, ideologues, anyone who has abandoned intuition, confines them to the ordinary, common, homogeneous, and mundane language of dominant orders. But as Bogue affirms, philosophy, theories of all kinds, can also transform the language system; the example of political theorists like Michael Katz and political philosophers like Iris M. Young should be instructive here. To make philosophy stutter we can recall Bergson's recommendation that we practice "philosophical intuition," by which means we look for differences in kind and the articulations of the real. As I have noted, Bergson argued that the more clear and precise the concepts are, the farther away they are from philosophical intuitions and images, and the more "superlatively insipid and uninteresting . . . banal in the extreme" the intuitions/images become.[77] Thus even the most creative philosophy, even Deleuze and Deleuze-Guattari, can be reduced to banal, common language, and those philosophies that are not creative, that do not seek differences in kind and articulations of the real, are nothing but banalities; they are representations. Yet even insofar as each thinker operates with the preexisting ideas philosophy and society impose upon her/him, the mere attempt to revise these ideas, to produce some slight variation, can have unexpected results, a radical new thought and creative language. When philosophy begins with intuition, with the force of creativity and innovation, it makes use of the "disorder of all the senses," the "unregulated exercise of all the faculties."[78] For it is with such disorder that philosophy can become misosophy, an original violence, a strangeness or enmity, inflicted on thought, a contingency that forces us to think and generates "the act of thinking in thought itself."[79] What forces us to think is a particular encounter that deranges our ordered schemas and produces a profound affectivity: terror, rage, wonder, hatred, suffering, awe. This is why Deleuze argues that even in a philosophy of the "enemy," like that of Kant, there is evidence of a significant derangement, a thought-provoking encounter, one that is ultimately central to the project of this book.

Kant's philosophical intuition of the sublime gives us a direct subjective relationship between imagination and reason. This relationship is one of dissension, *discord,* and contradiction between the demands of reason and the power of imagination, though the pain of this discord makes possible a pleasure, that of imagination exceeding its own limits, representing to itself the unattainable rational idea.[80] This occurs because the sublime is not conditioned by the logic of concepts: the sublime includes no objects of nature as mechanism, only "nature in its chaos or in its wildest and most irregular disorder and desolation."[81] Thus the sublime appears through the condition of nature regarded not as mechanism but as "art," that is, art free from all constraints or agreement of rules. In an intuition of the sublime, the imagination fails to apprehend the absolutely great, so the sublime produces pain with regard to imagination's inadequacy. It is also violent with regard to inner sense, the flow of elements successively apprehended. For the effort to intuit all at once a magnitude requiring an "unimaginable" time *annihilates* the time sequence and violates inner sense as a unity. What should be given in a temporal series is given all at once, eliminating time.[82] An intuition of the sublime would mean the end of time and space understood as mathematical or dynamic succession, the end of representation as the play of the time series, and the impossibility of bringing anything to presentation by means of representation. It leaves us confused because of the sudden powerlessness of representation, but we celebrate what emerges out of this: the power to conceive.[83]

For Kant, Ideas of Reason generate "respect" for the Idea, which is a "law" to us, a law that prescribes the comprehension of every intuition as an absolute whole, as a totality, and not even the infinite is exempt from this.[84] For Deleuze, the Idea is taken to be neither an absolute whole nor a totality; it is always differential and genetic.[85] Thus, another way to think of Ideas, for Deleuze, is as virtual multiplicities.[86] A fuller account of this, which will bring us back to Bergson, appears in the final chapter of *Bergsonism.* The virtual, I have noted, is real, so it does not have to be realized, but actualized. Actualization of the virtual can never be a matter of resemblance, since there is no longer any conception of time as unfolding recollection that represents the mythical Platonic Idea with the greatest possible degree of resemblance. Thus, actualization of the virtual is a matter of difference, divergence, or creation. As Deleuze reads Bergson, the virtual creates its own lines of actualization in positive acts and its actualizations do not resemble the virtuality they embody.[87] Since, for Bergson, concrete perception is the perception of heterogeneous qualities that are discontinuous and cannot be deduced from one another but are contracted in memory, perception is the perception of difference according to which matter is the same concrete perceptions emanating from memory.[88] And as I have noted, there is a multitude of "virtualities," memories capable of squaring with the same actual situation, but the intelligence chooses the "useful memory," that which "completes and illuminates the present situation with a view to ultimate action."[89] To actualize the virtual is to differentiate it; it develops according to divergent lines. There is no existing whole or totality as in the Kantian Idea of Reason; there are only successive and simultaneous lines of actualization, each one actualizing the whole in one direction and so not combining with other lines or directions, that is, each actualizing its level.[90] No longer do the different levels of virtuality coexist; instead, they divide into matter and life, and then each of those divide further, always differentiating and always creative, always continuing to differentiate, thus belonging to an open whole.

So, unlike Kant's totality or absolute whole, the whole for Deleuze, following Bergson, is virtual: real but not actualized, differentiated and open. And actualizations never resemble the lines of virtuality they embody, so actualization is genuine creation and differentiation according to directions created in the act of interest and usefulness that completes and illuminates the situation. If we bring back the issue of philosophy, creation takes on another dimension. For it is my claim that Deleuze's work exists as the open form of philosophy: it is the crack in time and not a representational model in terms of which philosophical inquiries can be answered with mastery. "What is philosophy?" is too often a false problem, either a nonexistent problem such as the "problem" of the nonbeing of a being, or a badly analyzed composite, arbitrarily grouping together things that differ in kind. So when we ask, "What is philosophy?" we expect certain representations to provide us with a rule from which we may deduce all "answers" to the problems we have determined, or we determine what possibilities that rule entails. On the other hand, when we look for representations, we assume those representations provide us with an account of a single thing; we muddle together what should remain a multiplicity of divergent and discontinuous lines. Either way we have created an obstacle.[91] Everything depends on how we ask the question, what we take the problem to be, the pragmatics of our situation that brings into the performative this or that particular sense.

Bergson's method of intuition recognizes that stating the problem is the first creative act, so it demands that we first of all look for differences in kind and articulations of the real.[92] Thus, the question "What is philosophy?" demands a separation in *kind* from other fields. Philosophy, unlike other fields of thought and action, creates "concepts." But as we have seen, such creation is never a matter of realizing a possible, but of actualizing through differentiation of the virtual multiplicity. According to Deleuze, such a moment arises in Bergson's "interval" between a received stimulus and an executed movement; that is, concepts are created in an intuition specific to them, and this is what constitutes their singularity.[93] In the interval between excitation and reaction, the whole of freedom, a whole level of virtual ontological memory is actualized insofar as it is a useful memory. As such, perception, memory, and intelligence itself, which comprehends needs and organizes activities rationally, still function together in a "deranged"—that is, creative—manner.

The "interval" between perception and memory, intelligence and social life, is decisive for humans. And what appears in the interval is creative emotion. At the end of *Bergsonism* Deleuze writes: "It is the genesis of intuition in intelligence. If man accedes to the open creative totality, it is therefore by acting, by creating rather than contemplating. In philosophy itself, there is still too much *alleged* contemplation: Everything happens as if intelligence were already imbued with emotion, thus with intuition, but not sufficiently so for creating in conformity to this emotion."[94] So for Deleuze creative action requires two things: acceding to the "open creative totality" and emotion. Bergson at first says little about the source of such emotion, but if we recall Hume, the connection between emotion and creation becomes clearer. Ideas are always derived from impressions, and when these impressions fade, what is left is an idea that "returns upon the soul." The idea produces "impressions of reflection," which are again copied or repeated. Thus, emotions are for Hume an effect of reflection and contemplation.[95] But the original impressions from which reflections arise always and only come from "natural and physical causes," from the outside, from the contraction, the folding of what is outside to the inside, from impressions such as hunger, cold, thirst, and heat.[96] When impressions of reflection that resemble one another are connected they generate an even more violent "double impulse" of the passions.[97] Regarding the definition of emotion, perhaps Bergson simplifies Hume's more complex definition; but in determining that "an emotion is an affective stirring of the soul," Bergson is fundamentally in agreement with Hume, especially when Bergson recognizes that an emotion of great force unifies the living being in the sense that it "intensifies" that individual so that the emotion unfolds into a creative act.[98] When emotion is produced by a "representation" (in Bergson's sense), a mental picture, then it has little impact. But when emotion itself produces and drives intelligence from its affective stirrings, from the passive synthesis of the creative whole, from ontological memory, then its impact is profound. This may well be why Deleuze connects emotion with intuition, the method of philosophy that sets into motion divisions in nature or kind rather than distinctions of degree. Thus, philosophy, art, and human beings' creative evolution, when they are truly creative, are not the work of an agent-signator, nor do they proceed according to a set of formulas, laws, or dogmas. Rather, like Bergson's ontological memory, creation begins again, eternally recurs, each time we are open to the creative whole and the open totality, each time affectivity propels thought.

Notes

Throughout the notes, page references that include a slash refer to the English translation (to the left of the slash) and the original (to the right of the slash).

Chapter 1

1. I have in mind much of the provocative but frustrating work of feminist film theorists including Laura Mulvey, "Visual Pleasure and Narrative Cinema," in *Film Theory and Criticism,* ed. Gerald Mast and Marshall Cohen (Oxford: Oxford University Press, 1985): Joan Copjec, "The Orthopsychic Subject: Film Theory and the Reception of Lacan," *October* 49 (spring 1989): 53–71; and one of the most interesting analyses, Constance Penley, *The Future of an Illusion* (Minneapolis: University of Minnesota Press, 1989). It appears that at a certain point in the history of feminist theory and practice this approach was largely abandoned for more empirical studies, which I do not find much more useful.

2. See my essay "The Postmodern Dead End: Minor Consensus on Race and Sexuality," *Topoi* 12 (1993): 161–166, where I discuss MacKinnon's concept of "heterosexual" society, which institutionalizes male dominance and female sexual submission in the name of white, male standards of equality.

3. See, for example, my "Heidegger and the Limits of Representation," in *Postmodernism and Continental Philosophy,* ed. Hugh J. Silverman and Donn Welton (Albany: State University of New York Press, 1988), pp. 96–109; and my "Space, Time, and the Sublime," in *The Question of the Other: Essays in Contemporary Continental Philosophy,* ed. Arleen B. Dallery and Charles E. Scott (Albany: State University of New York Press, 1989), pp. 175–185.

4. MacKinnon's alliance with the religious right in order to establish an antipornography ordinance in Minneapolis strikes me as a typical instance of MacKinnon's failure to see the larger implications of *her* own actions. My thanks to Gary Dowsett for drawing my attention to the antisex implications of some of MacKinnon's polemic.

5. For the standard approach see, for example, Zillah R. Eisenstein, *The Female Body and the Law* (Berkeley and Los Angeles: University of California Press, 1988); and Kathleen B. Jones, *Compassionate Authority: Democracy and the Representation of Women* (New York: Routledge Press, 1993). In *Beyond Accommodation* (New York: Routledge Press, 1991), Drucilla Cornell objects to MacKinnon on the grounds that for MacKinnon, "femaleness . . . has the 'being' that has been given to it within our social reality. More specifically, femaleness is *literally* what men see it 'to be.' We are constructed, and completely so, by their gaze. What they see is then given 'being' as *social reality*. . . . Because the gaze is reinforced and legitimated through male power. What they 'see' is taken to be objective." (p. 120) Setting aside for the moment the difference between Cornell's and MacKinnon's assumptions and approaches (and there are great differences), it seems appropriate to note that both are legal theorists and both are concerned with questions of social justice and the representation of women. Cornell approaches these questions through the avenues provided by postmodern critique and Lacanian psychoanalysis whereas MacKinnon takes an apparently opposed approach that combines Marxist-inspired critiques of liberal theory with a feminist epistemology. In short, one approach seems to privilege theoretical linguistics, the other pragmatic or material realities. Neither can fully respond to the need for abstract-particulars but both may contribute to the endeavor. There is an extensive language-based critique of MacKinnon in Judith Butler's book *Excitable Speech: A Politics of the Performative* (New York: Routledge Press, 1997). Butler repeatedly states that MacKinnon opposes pornography as representation because this is all it can be for Butler. MacKinnon explicitly denies that pornography is representation or imaginary, instead claiming that it is real.

6. Catharine MacKinnon, *Toward a Feminist Theory of the State* (Cambridge, Mass.: Harvard University Press, 1989).

7. Ibid., p. 40.

8. In July 1993 the Colorado state supreme court voted six to one against Amendment 2, having determined that it unconstitutionally limited the civil rights of those it was aimed against. In 1996 the U.S. supreme court struck down Amendment 2 as unconstitutional for attempting to exclude certain groups from sharing in the rights granted to all citizens.

9. John Stuart Mill and Harriet Taylor, *The Subjection of Women* (Indianapolis: Hackett Books, 1988).

10. Paraphrased in MacKinnon, *Toward a Feminist Theory*, p. 42.

11. Mill and Taylor, *Subjection of Women*, p. 136. Cited in MacKinnon, *Toward a Feminist Theory*, p. 44.

12. Compare Immanuel Kant, *The Critique of Judgement*, trans. James Creed Meredith (Oxford: Clarendon Press, 1952).

13. MacKinnon, *Toward a Feminist Theory*, p. 45.

14. Ibid., p. 46.

15. Ibid.

16. Mill and Taylor, *Subjection of Women,* p. 125. Cited in MacKinnon, *Toward a Feminist Theory,* p. 46.

17. MacKinnon, *Toward a Feminist Theory,* p. 46.

18. Merle Thornton, "Sex Equality Is Not Enough for Feminism," in *Feminist Challenges,* ed. Carole Pateman and Elizabeth Gross (Boston: Northeastern University Press, 1986), pp. 77–98, quotation on p. 91.

19. Ibid. p. 92.

20. Ibid.

21. Ibid., p. 98.

22. These principles have been well established by John Rawls in *A Theory of Justice* (Cambridge, Mass.: Harvard University Press, 1971) and *Political Liberalism* (New York: Columbia University Press, 1993). Whereas the first volume lays out the principle of justice as fairness and articulates the importance of the "original position" as a model, the second volume spends a great deal of energy discussing "overlapping consensus." In both, the basic unit of political systems is the individual and Rawls's only mention of minorities comes in the second volume, when he states briefly that any claims for individuals have merely to be extended to apply to groups. We shall see shortly that this is not feasible.

23. MacKinnon, *Toward a Feminist Theory,* p. 51.

24. Thornton, "Sex Equality Is Not Enough," p. 95.

25. MacKinnon criticizes Susan Brownmiller, for example, for tying rape to physiology, to women's "structural vulnerability." To MacKinnon this reveals an inability to distinguish intercourse from rape (an inability, it must be pointed out, that MacKinnon also seems to share, at least polemically if not theoretically): they are taken to be biologically the same. Although it is quite true that according to the *law* sexual intercourse and rape may be difficult to distinguish (especially in states and nations where marriage remains tantamount to ownership of the woman's body), this does not mean that this is due to some biological necessity of women. See Susan Brownmiller, *Against Our Will* (New York: Simon and Schuster, 1975).

26. See ibid., pp. 5, 73. Cited in MacKinnon, *Toward a Feminist Theory,* p. 56.

27. See Adrienne Rich, "Compulsory Heterosexism and Lesbian Existence," *Signs* 5, no. 4 (1980): 631–660.

28. MacKinnon, *Toward a Feminist Theory,* p. 61.

29. Ibid., pp. 84, 95. For MacKinnon feminism, as a practice, operates by becoming visible to itself, by attaining a lived knowledge of women's situation out of which women can create themselves and not merely live in terms of the system of oppressor and oppressed.

30. Ibid., pp. 93, 94.

31. Ibid., pp. 98, 99.

32. Catharine MacKinnon, *Feminism Unmodified* (Cambridge, Mass.: Harvard University Press, 1987), p. 32. This point is made by Timothy Kovac in "The Epistemology of Gender Relations" (Honors thesis, University of Colorado, Colorado Springs, 1995). Kovac argues that Sally Haslanger's critique of MacKinnon arises out of a misreading, that MacKinnon does not argue that reason is

necessarily linked to objectivity (quite the contrary) but that only *male-dominated society* holds the view that reason is necessarily linked to objectivity. See Sally Haslanger, "On Being Objective, and Being Objectified," in *A Mind of One's Own,* ed. Louise M. Antony and Charlotte Witt (Boulder, Colo.: Westview Press, 1993), pp. 85–126.

33. MacKinnon, *Toward a Feminist Theory,* pp. 96, 97. Here also MacKinnon clearly differentiates "rationality" (adherence to methodology) from objectivity (distance and aperspectivity).

34. Ibid., p. 98.

35. Ibid., p. xiv.

36. Ibid., p. 37.

37. Michele Montrelay, "Inquiry into Femininity," trans. Parveen Adams, *m/f* 1 (1978): 83–101.

38. *Form of expression* and *form of content* are terms of analysis brought into play by Gilles Deleuze and Félix Guattari. The first refers to the organization of functions in order to carry out an action, a methodology, or a manner of proceeding, whether it is in writing or in organizing governments. The second refers to so-called raw materials and their qualities, which are always organized in some manner and never just brute material.

39. The work of Sandra Harding is of great importance in questioning the "objectivity" of science and scientific practices. I find her analysis of the inequality of the social structure supporting scientific practice to be of tremendous value. See Sandra Harding, *The Science Question in Feminism* (Ithaca, N.Y.: Cornell University Press, 1986). Her more recent work on standpoint epistemology and strong objectivity likewise deserves careful consideration. See Sandra Harding, *Whose Science? Whose Knowledge? Thinking from Women's Lives* (Ithaca, N.Y.: Cornell University Press, 1991). I hope to be able to address both books in a future work.

40. Iris Marion Young, "Together in Difference: Transforming the Logic of Group Political Conflict," in *The Rights of Minority Cultures,* ed. Will Kymlicka (Oxford: Oxford University Press, 1995), pp. 155–176.

41. Ibid., p. 157.

42. Ibid., p. 158. Young develops the thesis of the relation between difference as otherness and disgust in chapter 5 of her book *Justice and the Politics of Difference* (Princeton, N.J.: Princeton University Press, 1990).

43. See, for example, Nancy Tuana's excellent essay "The Weaker Seed: The Sexist Bias of Reproductive Theory," *Hypatia* 3, no. 1 (spring 1988): 35–59. Tuana gives an account of reproductive theories from Aristotle through the early twentieth century. She argues that the belief in the inferiority of the female creative principle biased scientific perception of and research into the contribution of the female to reproduction.

44. Young, "Together in Difference," p. 160. The authority of the system of capital is one of the main themes of Gilles Deleuze and Felix Guattari's *Anti-Oedipus,* trans. Robert Hurley, Mark Seem, and Helen R. Lane, vol. 1 of *Capitalism and Schizophrenia* (Minneapolis: University of Minnesota Press, 1983); originally published in French as *L'anti-Oedipe: Capitalisme et schizophrénie* (Paris:

Minuit, 1972). Like Young, I will treat the system of capital only briefly in this book although I recognize its power and authority to determine social structure.

45. Young, "Together in Difference," pp. 161, 165.

46. Ibid., p. 165. Young's examples in this essay—the ethnic conflicts in Eastern Europe and the Maori movement in New Zealand—make it clear that the liberal individualist conception of politics does not provide a workable framework for either of these specific problems. As she notes, political liberalism presumes an abstract and voluntarist conception of the self that denies group differences. The real attachments of people to their group differences make this approach utopian and, as history has shown again and again, no solution at all (p. 170).

47. Ibid., p. 165.

48. Paul Patton has taken up a related political cause, the Australian High Court "Mabo" judgment, in the context of Gilles Deleuze's philosophy of freedom. The Mabo decision grants "native title" of land to Aboriginal people in Australia and so extends legal protection to those rights. While operating within the "power of the Crown" and its authority, Mabo nonetheless breaks with the past and creates a new field of legal and political options that did not previously exist. See Paul Patton, "Mabo: Freedom and the Politics of Difference," *Australian Journal of Political Science* 30 (1995): 108–119.

49. Gilles Deleuze, "He Stuttered," trans. Constantin V. Boundas, in *Gilles Deleuze and the Theater of Philosophy,* ed. Constantin V. Boundas and Dorothea E. Olkowski (New York: Routledge Press, 1994), pp. 23–29; especially pp. 24, 28.

50. Gilles Deleuze, *Difference and Repetition,* trans. Paul Patton (New York: Columbia University Press, 1994); originally published in French as *Différence et répétition* (Paris: Presses Universitaires de France, 1968).

51. See, for example, Gilles Deleuze, *Francis Bacon: Logique de la sensation* (Paris: La Différence, 1984); also Deleuze, *Cinema I: The Movement-Image,* trans. Hugh Tomlinson and Barbara Habberjam (Minneapolis: University of Minnesota Press, 1986), and Deleuze, *Cinema II: The Time-Image,* trans. Hugh Tomlinson and Robert Galeta (Minneapolis: University of Minnesota Press, 1989).

52. Deleuze, *Difference and Repetition,* p. 28, translation altered; *Différence et répétition,* p. 43.

53. See Svetlana Alpers, *The Art of Describing: Dutch Painting in the Seventeenth Century* (Chicago: University of Chicago Press, 1983), p. 41. Alpers distinguishes between single-point perspective and what she calls eye-point perspective—which she thinks thrived in seventeenth-century Dutch painting—through a series of differences: a concern for objects in space versus surfaces, for form versus texture, for a few large objects versus many large ones, for objects modeled by light and shadow versus light reflected off objects, for framed versus unframed images, for a clearly situated viewer versus none, for the picture as an object in the world like a framed window versus the picture taking the place of the eye (pp. 44–45).

54. David Summers, *Michelangelo and the Language of Art* (Princeton, N.J.: Princeton University Press, 1981), pp. 73, 478–479.

55. Ibid., p. 479.

56. H. W. Janson, *History of Art* (New York: Harry N. Abrams, 1971), p. 471.

57. Julia Kristeva, *Desire in Language: A Semiotic Approach to Literature and Art,* trans. Thomas Gora, Alice Jardine, and Leon S. Roudier, ed. Leon S. Roudier (New York: Columbia University Press, 1980), p. 214.

58. Deleuze, *Difference and Repetition,* p. 29, translation altered; *Différence et répétition,* p. 44.

59. Aristotle, *Metaphysics,* trans. W. D. Ross, in *The Basic Works of Aristotle,* ed. Richard McKeon (New York: Random House, 1970), X, 4, 1055a5.

60. Deleuze, *Difference and Repetition,* pp. 30–31; *Différence et répétition,* p. 46.

61. Ibid., p. 32/p. 47.

62. Aristotle, *Metaphysics,* X, 5, 1054b25; emphasis added.

63. Deleuze, *Difference and Repetition,* p. 32, translation altered; *Différence et répétition,* p. 48.

64. Aristotle, *Metaphysics,* III, 3, 998b20; emphasis added.

65. Deleuze, *Difference and Repetition,* p. 33; *Différence et répétition,* p. 49.

66. Franz Brentano, *On the Several Senses of Being in Aristotle,* trans. Rolf George (Berkeley and Los Angeles: University of California Press, 1975), p. 58.

67. Ibid., pp. 59–60.

68. Aristotle, *Metaphysics,* VIII, 6, 1045a36.

69. Brentano, *On the Several Senses of Being,* p. 60.

70. Aristotle, *Metaphysics,* IV, 2, 1003b; emphasis added.

71. Ibid., IV, 1, 1003b15.

72. Deleuze, *Difference and Repetition,* p. 33; *Différence et répétition,* pp. 49, 50.

73. Ibid., p. 34/p. 51.

74. Ibid., pp. 34–35, translation altered/p. 52.

75. The original impetus for looking at Aristotle's conception of time in this way came to me by way of Jacques Derrida in "*Ousia* and *Grammé:* A Note to a Footnote in *Being and Time,*" trans. Edward S. Casey, in *Phenomenology in Perception,* ed. F. J. Smith (The Hague: Nijhoff, 1970), pp. 54–93; originally published in French as *L'endurance de la pensée* (Paris, 1968). Derrida has provided this extraordinary and insightful reading of time in order to show how traditional ontology can be destroyed through the interrogation and repetition of its relation to the problem of time. I am deliberately avoiding restating Derrida's argument in the terms he has used—that is, in terms of the metaphysics of presence—in order to avoid confusing Derrida's argument with mine. My own concern here is with the power and authority of representation to defeat motion and change, not with the metaphysics of presence. Derrida also makes certain moves that totalize this history of philosophical conceptions of time in relation to the metaphysics of presence and the conception of space; these I reject insofar as, for me, they belong to a substantive account of being and thought, not an ontology of becoming.

76. Aristotle, *Physics,* trans. R. P. Hardie and R. K. Gaye, in *The Basic Works of Aristotle,* ed. Richard McKeon (New York: Random House, 1970), IV, 11, 219a10.

77. Derrida, "*Ousia* and *Grammé,*" p. 83. Derrida claims that the correspondences cited here are analogy; but if they are experienced, not thought, it would seem that they are resemblance.

78. Aristotle, *Physics*, IV, 11, 219a10–20.
79. Ibid., IV, 10, 218a5–10.
80. Derrida, in particular, stresses the togetherness of motion and time (*ama*) and the incipient self-criticism of Aristotle's concept of time. Derrida, "*Ousia* and *Grammé*," pp. 72, 73.
81. Aristotle, *Physics*, IV, 11, 218a.
82. Ibid., IV, 11, 219b15.
83. Ibid., IV, 11, 219b20–30.
84. Ibid., IV, 11, 219b30.
85. Michel Foucault, "Theatrum Philosophicum," in *Language, Counter-memory, Practice,* trans. Donald F. Bouchard and Sherry Simon (Ithaca, N.Y.: Cornell University Press, 1977), p. 183. Given that Foucault's analysis occurs in the context of an essay that remarks that "perhaps one day, this century will be known as Deleuzian" (p. 165), he tends to characterize "freeing difference" (p. 185) in euphoric terms that I take to be too closely associated with those who see in Deleuze a turn to some romanticized anarchism. It is my intent to show that a form of reason operates in Deleuze's philosophy of difference but that it is simply not the hierarchized, conceptualized reason of equivocal being.
86. Gilles Deleuze and Félix Guattari, *A Thousand Plateaus,* trans. Brian Massumi, vol. 2 of *Capitalism and Schizophrenia* (Minneapolis: University of Minnesota Press, 1987), p. 43; originally published in French as *Mille plateaux: Capitalisme et schizophrénie* (Paris: Minuit, 1980), p. 57. Deleuze and Guattari insist that there are always two kinds of articulation and two kinds of multiplicity. The proposition, therefore, is no more than an expression of the other articulation and the other multiplicity that have mostly been submitted to the domination of the model of judgment.
87. Deleuze, *Difference and Repetition,* p. 35, translation altered; *Différence et répétition,* pp. 52–53.
88. Ibid., p. 35/p. 53.
89. Ibid, p. 37, translation altered/p. 55.
90. Ibid., p. 36, translation altered/p. 54. Final emphasis added.
91. Summers, *Michelangelo and the Language of Art,* p. 73.
92. Deleuze, *Difference and Repetition,* p. 55–56, translation altered; *Différence et répétition,* p. 78.
93. Ibid., p. 56, translation altered/p. 79.
94. Ibid., p. 56/p. 79.
95. Ibid., p. 56/pp. 78–79.
96. Alpers, *Art of Describing,* pp. 77, 78.
97. Ibid., p. 58.
98. Deleuze, *Difference and Repetition,* p. 56, translation altered; *Différence et répétition,* p. 79.
99. See Brian Massumi, *A User's Guide to Capitalism and Schizophrenia: Deviations from Deleuze and Guattari* (Cambridge, Mass.: MIT Press, 1992), pp. 120–121, 194–195n53. Massumi characterizes nomadism politically in terms of anarchy. I specifically avoid this insofar as anarchy is posited in opposition to statism and as one pole in a continuum. It seems to me that such a characterization obscures the hard-won ground of difference as what is, and thus of differ-

ences each having their own essence, their own meaning. I am loath to take this risk and I am also unwilling to place Deleuze and Guattari back into the context of choosing between extremes. Any particular group of "anarchists" may or may not practice nomadism; it depends largely on how they position themselves with regard to difference.

100. See Jean-Clet Martin, *Variations: La philosophie de Gilles Deleuze* (Paris: Payot, 1993). Martin develops the notion of difference and multiplicities in the context of Deleuze's aesthetic and ethical formulations as a poetic organization of thought. I hope that my own approach approximates Martin's simultaneously logical and poetic analysis.

101. Deleuze and Guattari, *Thousand Plateaus,* p. 41; *Mille plateaux,* p. 55.

102. Ibid., p. 41/p. 55.

103. Ibid., pp. 3–4/pp. 9–10.

104. Ibid., p. 4/p. 10.

105. Ibid., p. 503/p. 628.

106. Ibid., p. 41/p. 55.

107. Ibid., p. 366/p. 453.

108. Ibid., p. 352/p. 436.

109. Ibid., p. 353/p. 436.

110. Alphonso Lingis, "The Society of Dismembered Body Parts," in *Gilles Deleuze and the Theater of Philosophy,* ed. Constantin V. Boundas and Dorothea Olkowski (New York: Routledge, 1994), pp. 228–229.

111. Ibid., p. 228.

112. Ibid., p. 229.

113. Deleuze and Guattari, *Thousand Plateaus,* p. 352; *Mille plateaux,* p. 435.

114. Ibid., p. 119/p. 149. Deleuze and Guattari name four such assemblages: the despotic signifying regime of signs (the state apparatus discussed above); the "so-called primitive *presignifying semiotic,* which is much closer to the 'natural' codings operating without signs" (exemplified by societies of hunter-nomads) (p. 117/p. 147); a "countersignifying semiotic" ("fearsome, warlike, animal-raising nomads" who remain exterior to the state apparatus) (p. 118/p. 148); and the "postsignifying regime," effecting a "finite legislator-subject" who replaces the absolute signifying despot (p. 130/p. 162).

115. Ibid., p. 121/p. 152.

Chapter 2

1. Alice Jardine, "Woman in Limbo: Deleuze and His Br(others)," *Sub-Stance* 44/45 (1984): 46–59.

2. Ibid., p. 47.

3. According to Jardine, this was Rosi Braidotti, then a doctoral candidate in philosophy. See Alice Jardine, *Gynesis: Configurations of Woman and Modernity* (Ithaca, N.Y.: Cornell University Press, 1985), p. 59n4. Still somewhat ambivalent in her support of Deleuze and Guattari, Braidotti will be discussed below.

4. In 1988, *Magazine litteraire* published an issue whose "*dossier*" was entirely devoted to Deleuze. Among the contributors, the American academic

Dana Polan comments that from the 1980s on there was a veritable explosion of commentaries on and translations of Deleuze's work in the United States. See *Magazine litteraire* 257 (September 1988): 14–65, especially p. 63.

5. At an American academic conference in 1995 attended by philosophers and theorists in languages, literature, and cultural studies, a session of papers on Deleuze drew an audience that included only four women out of thirty or so participants, despite the obviously feminist title of one of the papers.

6. Jardine is clear that since the mid 1970s in France, few female academics have accepted the label "feminist." This has to do principally with the political and philosophical splits within the French *Movement de libération des femmes.* Jardine, *Gynesis,* p. 19. See also Alice A. Jardine and Anne M. Menke, eds., *Shifting Scenes: Interviews on Women, Writing, and Politics in Post-68 France* (New York: Columbia University Press, 1991), for interviews with fifteen French women philosophers, writers, and literary theorists who mostly refuse to identify themselves as feminists.

7. Jardine, "Woman in Limbo," p. 48.

8. Jardine, *Gynesis,* p. 25.

9. Ibid., p. 209.

10. Ibid., p. 211, emphasis added. In one sense this is the case, for I continue to maintain that "body" is too general a concept for Deleuze and Guattari. It is, as we shall see, in Deleuze's historical and aesthetic philosophies that the concept of body is again and again articulated and revealed in all its complexity.

11. Jardine, "Woman in Limbo," p. 49. See Deleuze and Guattari, *Anti-Oedipus.*

12. Luce Irigaray, *This Sex Which Is Not One,* trans. Catherine Porter (Ithaca, N.Y.: Cornell University Press, 1985), pp. 140–141. Cited in Jardine, *Gynesis,* pp. 212–213. Originally published in French as *Ce sexe qui n'en est pas un* (Paris: Minuit, 1977), pp. 138–139.

13. Jardine, "Woman in Limbo," p. 47.

14. See " Desiring-Production," in Deleuze and Guattari, *Anti-Oedipus,* pp. 1–8; *L'anti-Oedipe* pp. 7–15; as well as Gilles Deleuze and Claire Parnet, *Dialogues,* trans. Hugh Tomlinson and Barbara Habberjam (New York: Columbia University Press, 1987), originally published in French as *Dialogues* (Paris: Flammarion, 1977). In *Dialogues,* mechanics is defined as a system of closer and closer connections between dependent terms, but the machine is a proximity grouping between independent and heterogeneous terms and may or may not include humans among its parts (p. 125/p. 104). Given the misinterpretations of the term *desiring-machine*—that is, a persistent will to subjectivize—Deleuze and Guattari ceased to employ it and instead took up the term *assemblage.* Deleuze and Guattari, *Thousand Plateaus; Mille plateaux.* See, for example, the book-assemblage (pp. 9–10/pp. 3–4). See also Dorothea Olkowski, "Semiotics and Gilles Deleuze," in *The Semiotic Web, 1990: Recent Developments in Theory and History,* ed. Thomas A. Sebeok and Jean Umiker-Sebeok (Berlin: Mouton de Gruyter, 1991), pp. 285–306.

15. Jardine, *Gynesis,* p. 211.

16. Ibid., p. 215.

17. Deleuze and Parnet, *Dialogues,* p. 13.

18. Deleuze and Guattari, *Thousand Plateaus,* p. 277; *Mille plateaux,* p. 340.

19. Jardine, *Gynesis,* p. 216.

20. *Webster's New Universal Unabridged Dictionary,* second edition.

21. Jardine, *Gynesis,* p. 217.

22. Ibid.

23. Deleuze and Guattari, *Thousand Plateaus,* pp. 275–276; *Mille plateaux,* p. 338. First emphasis added.

24. Ibid., p. 276/p. 339.

25. Jardine, "Woman in Limbo," p. 59.

26. Michel Tournier, *Vendredi ou les limbes du Pacifique* (Paris: Gallimard, 1972). Interestingly, Tournier also wrote a children's version that has been translated into English. Deleuze's commentary on the original book appears as an appendix to *The Logic of Sense,* trans. Mark Lester and Charles Stivale, ed. Constantin V. Boundas (New York: Columbia University Press, 1990); originally published in French as *Logique du sens* (Paris: Minuit, 1969).

27. Jardine, *Gynesis,* p. 223.

28. Elizabeth Grosz, "A Thousand Tiny Sexes: Feminism and Rhizomatics," in *Gilles Deleuze and the Theater of Philosophy,* ed. Constantin V. Boundas and Dorothea Olkowski (New York: Routledge Press, 1994), pp. 187–210, quotation on p. 206.

29. See Constantin V. Boundas, "Deleuze: Serialization and Subject-Formation," in *Gilles Deleuze and the Theater of Philosophy,* ed. Constantin V. Boundas and Dorothea Olkowski (New York: Routledge Press, 1994), pp. 99–116. See especially p. 101.

30. Ibid., p. 100. Boundas cites David Carr, *Time, Narrative, and History* (Bloomington: Indiana University Press, 1986), and Carr, "Narrative and the Real World," *Theory* 15 (1986): 118–131, for accounts of the role of narrative structure in subject-formation.

31. Boundas, "Deleuze: Serialization and Subject-Formation," pp. 100–101.

32. Deleuze derives his account of series from his readings of logician Lewis Carroll's *Alice in Wonderland* and *Through the Looking-Glass, and What Alice Found There* (London: Octopus Books, 1978), both of which, along with Carroll's poems, exhibit fully the paradoxes of logic. See chapter 8.

33. Deleuze, *Logic of Sense,* p. 303; *Logique du sens,* p. 352. Defoe's Crusoe constitutes himself by salvaging all he can (including a bible) from the wreck of the ship that brought him to his deserted island. He then proceeds to build a fortress as well as a summer bower, capture and raise goats, plant grain to make bread, harvest grapes and dry them into raisins, and in moments of despair, study the bible. See Daniel Defoe, *Robinson Crusoe* (New York: Random House, 1990).

34. Ibid., p. 307/p. 357.

35. Ibid., p. 366n12/p. 360n11. See also Jean-Paul Sartre, *Being and Nothingness,* trans. Hazel Barnes (New York: Washington Square Press, 1971), p. 340–400, for an account of the look.

36. Deleuze, *Logic of Sense,* p. 310; *Logique du sens,* p. 360.

37. Jardine, "Woman in Limbo," p. 58. See also Rem Koolhaas and Bruce Mau, *S, M, L, XL* (New York: Monacelli Press, 1995), pp. 182, 188. Koolhaas

provides two entries in his recent volume, one for the word *collapse* and a second for the word *collapsed.* Both are overlaid by architectural drawings of the Villa Dal'Ava, a modernist residence Koolhaas and his associates at OMA (Office of Metropolitan Architecture) designed and constructed in the St. Cloud neighborhood of Paris. The first entry defines collapse in terms of the triumphant atmosphere, the attention and celebrity surrounding contemporary architecture countered by the lack of "things of real quality," producing a contradiction about to collapse under its own weight. The collapse, Koolhaas argues, is healthy because it allows architects and planners to regain their *anonymity.* Following this entry is a quotation from Defoe's *Robinson Crusoe* describing the collapse of Crusoe's cave during an earthquake, which nearly buried him. He simply rebuilds, never again mentioning earthquakes in twenty-eight years.

38. Deleuze, *Logic of Sense,* p. 312; *Logique du sens,* p. 362.

39. Ibid., p. 312/pp. 362–363.

40. Ibid., p. 311/p. 362.

41. For a full account of the "paradox" see "Twelfth Series of the Paradox," in ibid., pp. 92–100/pp. 74–81.

42. Judith Butler, "The Life and Death Struggle of Desire: Hegel and Contemporary Theory," in *Subjects of Desire: Hegelian Reflections in Twentieth-Century France* (New York: Columbia University Press, 1987), pp. 175–238.

43. Ibid., p. 175.

44. Butler, *Subjects of Desire,* p. 9.

45. Ibid.

46. Ibid., pp. 10, 23. An interesting alternative view can be found in Rosalyn Diprose, "In Excess: The Body and the Habit of Sexual Difference," *Hypatia* 6, no. 3 (fall 1991): 156–171.

47. Butler, *Subjects of Desire,* p. 30.

48. Ibid., p. 31. Throughout all her work, Butler never gives up this position that "consciousness reveals itself as *an articulated phenomenon,* that which only becomes itself *as articulation*" (p. 31), though this position remains, perhaps, the source of the greatest misunderstandings and questions about her work. What is the ontological status of a rhetorical movement? Does a change of perspective produce a change of interpretation, or, beyond this, a change in ontological status, or both? The last seems to present the greatest problem to feminists, in particular, insofar as they tend to take the ontological status of women's materiality to be one of the principle problems of feminist philosophy.

49. Ibid., p. 93.

50. Ibid., p. 33.

51. Ibid., p. 35.

52. Judith Butler, "Sexual Ideology and Phenomenological Description: A Feminist Critique of Merleau-Ponty's *Phenomenology of Perception,*" in *The Thinking Muse,* ed. Jeffner Allen and Iris Marion Young (Bloomington: Indiana University Press, 1989), pp. 85–100.

53. Ibid., p. 98.

54. Ibid., pp. 98–99.

55. Butler, *Subjects of Desire,* p. 24.

56. Ibid., p. 25.

57. Ibid., p. 45.
58. Ibid., p. 206.
59. Ibid., pp. 213, 214, 215.
60. See Dominique Grisoni, "Onomatopoeia of Desire," trans. Paul Foss, in *Theoretical Strategies,* ed. Peter Botsman (Sydney: Local Consumption Publications, 1989), pp. 169–182; originally published in French as "Les onomatopées du désir," in *Les dieux dans la cuisine* (Paris: Éditions Aubier, 1976).
61. Butler, *Subjects of Desire,* p. 212. See Gilles Deleuze, *Nietzsche and Philosophy,* trans. Hugh Tomlinson (New York: Columbia University Press, 1983); originally published in French as *Nietzsche et la philosophie* (Paris: Presses Universitaires de France, 1962).
62. Butler, *Subjects of Desire,* p. 212.
63. Ibid.
64. Ibid., p. 11.
65. Ibid., pp. 12–13.
66. Deleuze and Guattari, *Thousand Plateaus,* p. 121; *Mille plateaux,* p. 152.
67. Deleuze, *Nietzsche and Philosophy,* p. 39; *Nietzsche et la philosophie,* p. 45.
68. Although the appearance of the term *regime* in *Nietzsche and Philosophy* is interesting, the use of the term becomes central in volume 2 of *Capitalism and Schizophrenia,* where the notion of "regimes of signs" takes precedence as the means by which desiring- and social-machines organize themselves in various arrangements of power. At this point, the word seems to maintain a more conventional French meaning than the specific semiotic use in volume 2; it indicates not only a set of rules or laws, but also a rate of flow or a rate of speed—not only do different regimes have different laws or rules, they occur at different speeds.
69. Deleuze, *Nietzsche and Philosophy,* p. 44; *Nietzsche et la philosophie,* pp. 49–50.
70. Ibid.
71. Plato, *Gorgias,* trans. W. D. Woodhead, in *Plato: The Collected Dialogues,* ed. Edith Hamilton and Huntington Cairns (Princeton, N.J.: Princeton University Press, 1961), pp. 229–307. See especially pp. 481–527.
72. Deleuze, *Nietzsche and Philosophy,* p. 59; *Nietzsche et la philosophie,* pp. 66–67. Emphasis added.
73. See Dorothea Olkowski, "Nietzsche-Deleuze: The Aesthetics and Ethics of Chance," *Journal of the British Society for Phenomenology* 26, no. 1 (January 1995): 27–42.
74. Friedrich Nietzsche, *The Will to Power,* trans. Walter Kaufmann and R. J. Hollingdale (New York: Vintage Books, 1968), p. 634; cited in Deleuze, *Nietzsche and Philosophy,* p. 206n17; *Nietzsche et la philosophie,* p. 66n3. Deleuze, *Difference and Repetition,* p. 32, translation altered; *Différence et répétition,* p. 55.
75. Deleuze and Parnet, *Dialogues,* pp. 91, 95.
76. Butler, *Subjects of Desire,* p. 213.
77. Ibid., p. 214.
78. Friedrich Nietzsche, *On the Genealogy of Morals,* trans. Walter Kaufmann (New York: Vintage Books, 1969), part I, sect. 2, p. 36.
79. Deleuze, *Nietzsche and Philosophy,* p. 1; *Nietzsche et la philosophie,* p. 2.
80. Ibid., p. 93/p. 107.

81. Ibid., p. 92/p. 106.

82. Rosi Braidotti, *Patterns of Dissonance,* trans. Elizabeth Guild (New York: Routledge Press, 1991); originally written in French as *Itinéraires dans la dissonance.*

83. Ibid., p. 13.

84. Ibid., p. 14.

85. Ibid., p. 23.

86. Ibid., p. 24.

87. Ibid., p. 25.

88. Ibid., p. 27.

89. Ibid., p. 28. Taken literally, this would be an astounding claim, for it would mean that theoretical constructs and concepts have the same kind of existence, ontological and epistemological status, as dreams and fantasies. As it stands, much depends on what Braidotti means by "no separation between" thought and fantasy.

90. Ibid. This is a claim frequently voiced by feminists who make use of Freudian insights or who embrace Freud as friendly and useful to feminism. Teresa Brennan, for example, takes this approach in her book *The Interpretation of the Flesh: Freud and Femininity.* It is a position concerning which I remain skeptical precisely to the extent that one encounters descriptions of such intertwining of body and thought, but no theory to account for it. See my review of Brennan's book, "Teresa Brennan's *The Interpretation of the Flesh: Freud and Femininity,*" *Journal of the History of Sexuality* 4, no. 4 (April 1994): 648–650.

91. Freud developed both psychical and physiological models of how unconscious drives are translated into conscious thought and action as well as unconscious thought and action.

92. Michel Foucault, *The Order of Things: An Archaeology of the Human Sciences* (New York: Vintage Books, 1973), p. 325; originally published in French as *Les mots et les choses* (Paris: Gallimard, 1963).

93. Braidotti, *Patterns of Dissonance,* p. 37.

94. Ibid., p. 40.

95. See Michel Foucault, "Truth and Power," in *Power/Knowledge,* trans. Colin Gordon, Leo Marshall, John Mepham, Kate Soper, ed. Colin Gordon (New York: Pantheon Books, 1980), pp. 109–133. Braidotti, *Patterns of Dissonance,* p. 39.

96. Braidotti, *Patterns of Dissonance,* pp. 45, 30.

97. Rosi Braidotti, "Toward a New Nomadism: Feminist Deleuzian Tracks, or Metaphysics and Metabolism," in *Gilles Deleuze and the Theater of Philosophy,* ed. Constantin V. Boundas and Dorothea Olkowski (New York: Routledge Press, 1994), pp. 157–186, quotation on p. 160.

98. Ibid.

99. Ibid.

100. Ibid., p. 163.

101. Ibid., p. 176.

102. Rosi Braidotti, *Nomadic Subjects: Embodiment and Sexual Difference in Contemporary Feminist Theory* (New York: Columbia University Press, 1994), p. 204.

103. Ibid., p. 114.
104. Ibid.
105. Ibid., p. 115.
106. Ibid.
107. Ibid., p. 116. It is interesting that Braidotti reads the concept of "machine" not as Deleuze and Guattari do—as an *agencement,* an arrangement of forces—but as the "scientific, political, and discursive field of technology in the broadest sense of the term" (p. 77). Ultimately, such conceptual differences will produce entirely different ontologies.
108. Ibid., p. 101.
109. Ibid., p. 211.
110. This is why Braidotti cites approvingly such disparate feminist thinkers as Teresa de Lauretis, Luce Irigaray, Antoinette Fouque, Simone de Beauvoir, and Donna Haraway.
111. Grosz, "A Thousand Tiny Sexes," p. 187.
112. Ibid., p. 191. Grosz recognizes that much feminist criticism was directed specifically toward *Anti-Oedipus.*
113. Ibid., p. 201.
114. Ibid., p. 190.
115. Ibid., p. 192.
116. Ibid.
117. Ibid., p. 196.
118. Ibid.
119. Elizabeth Grosz, *Volatile Bodies: Towards a Corporeal Feminism* (Bloomington: Indiana University Press, 1994), p. 169. See also Grosz, *Space, Time, and Perversion* (New York: Routledge Press, 1995), where she addresses a variety of issues related to bodies, space and time, and desire and makes frequent though not exhaustive use of the work of Deleuze and Guattari.
120. See Moira Gatens, *Imaginary Bodies, Ethics, Power and Corporeality* (New York: Routledge Press, 1996), and Gatens, "Through a Spinozist Lens: Ethology, Difference, Power," in *Deleuze: A Critical Reader,* ed. Paul Patton (London: Blackwell, 1996), pp. 162–187.

Chapter 3

1. For Grosz's account of Merleau-Ponty's phenomenology see Elizabeth Grosz, "Merleau-Ponty and Irigaray in the Flesh," *Thesis Eleven* 36 (1993): 37–60, as well as her chapter "Lived Bodies: Phenomenology and the Flesh," in *Volatile Bodies,* pp. 86–114. Grosz has also written extensively on psychoanalysis. See Elizabeth Grosz, *Jacques Lacan: A Feminist Introduction* (London: Routledge, 1990); Grosz, "Psychoanalysis and Psychical Topographies," in *Volatile Bodies,* pp. 27–61; and her accounts of Julia Kristeva and Luce Irigaray in Grosz, *Sexual Subversions: Three French Feminists* (St. Leonards: Allen and Unwin, 1989).
2. Simone de Beauvoir, "La *Phénoménologie de la perception* de Maurice Merleau-Ponty," *Les temps modernes* 1, no. 2 (November 1945): 363–367.

3. Simone de Beauvoir, *The Second Sex,* trans. H. M. Parshley (New York: Knopf, 1952; rpt., New York: Vintage, 1972); originally published in French as *Le deuxième sexe* (Paris: Gallimard, 1949). For a fine account of the errors of translation that obliterate Beauvoir's classic book, see Anna Alexander, "The Eclipse of Gender: Simone de Beauvoir and the *Différence* of Translation," *Philosophy Today* 41, no. 1/4 (spring 1997): 112–122.

4. Simone de Beauvoir, *The Ethics of Ambiguity,* trans. B. Frechtman (New York: Philosophical Library, 1948); originally published in French as *Pour une morale de l'ambiguité* (Paris: Gallimard, 1947).

5. Iris Marion Young, "Throwing Like a Girl: A Phenomenology of Feminine Body Comportment, Motility, and Spatiality," in *The Thinking Muse: Feminism and Modern French Philosophy,* ed. Jeffner Allen and Iris Marion Young (Bloomington: Indiana University Press, 1989), pp. 51–70.

6. Butler, "Sexual Ideology and Phenomenological Description."

7. Grosz, *Volatile Bodies,* p. 104.

8. See Grosz, "Merleau-Ponty and Irigaray in the Flesh." This is also what I take Butler to be implying when she writes, "Theorizing from the ruins of the Logos invites the following question. . . . 'What about the materiality of the body, *Judy?*' I took it that the addition of 'Judy' was an effort to dislodge me from the more formal 'Judith' and to recall me to a bodily life that could not be theorized away." Judith Butler, *Bodies That Matter: On the Discursive Limits of "Sex"* (New York: Routledge Press, 1993), p. ix.

9. See Maurice Merleau-Ponty, *The Visible and the Invisible,* trans. Alphonso Lingis (Evanston, Ill.: Northwestern University Press, 1968); originally published in French as *Le visible et l'invisible* (Paris: Gallimard, 1964).

10. Luce Irigaray, "The Invisible of the Flesh: A Reading of Merleau-Ponty, *The Visible and the Invisible,* 'The Intertwining—The Chiasm,'" in *An Ethics of Sexual Difference,* trans. Carolyn Burke and Gillian C. Gill (Ithaca, N.Y.: Cornell University Press, 1993), p. 151; originally published in French as *Éthique de la différence sexuelle* (Paris: Minuit, 1984), p. 143.

11. Maurice Merleau-Ponty, *The Prose of the World,* trans. John O'Neill (Evanston, Ill.: Northwestern University Press, 1973), p. 10; originally published in French as *La prose du monde* (Paris: Gallimard, 1969).

12. Merleau-Ponty, *Prose of the World,* p. 13.

13. Ibid., p. 14.

14. Merleau-Ponty, *Visible and the Invisible,* p. 155; *Le visible et l'invisible,* p. 203. Cited in Irigaray, *An Ethics of Sexual Difference,* p. 179; *Éthique de la différence sexuelle,* p. 167.

15. Merleau-Ponty, *Prose of the World,* p. 19. See my essay "Merleau-Ponty: The Demand for Mystery in Language," *Philosophy Today* 31, no. 4/4 (winter 1987): 252–258.

16. Merleau-Ponty, *Visible and the Invisible,* p. 155; *Le visible et l'invisible,* p. 203.

17. Irigaray, *An Ethics of Sexual Difference,* p. 182; *Éthique de la différence sexuelle,* p. 169.

18. Ibid., p. 183/p. 170.

19. Ibid., p. 176/p. 164.

20. Luce Irigaray, "When Our Lips Speak Together," in *This Sex Which Is Not One,* p. 212.

21. Luce Irigaray, "The 'Mechanics' of Fluids," in *This Sex Which Is Not One,* pp. 107, 109.

22. For the discussion of Aristotle's *Metaphysics* see Deleuze, *Difference and Repetition,* p. 30; *Différence et répétition,* p. 46. See also Aristotle, *Metaphysics,* X, 4, 1055a5.

23. Aristotle, *Metaphysics,* X, 5, 1054b25 (emphasis added).

24. See Ferdinand de Saussure, *Course in General Linguistics,* trans. Wade Baskin, ed. Charles Bally and Albert Sehehaye (New York: McGraw-Hill, 1966), pp. 71–72.

25. Ibid., pp. 73, 74.

26. See especially Judith Butler in *Bodies That Matter,* where she claims that the Aristotelian notion of "schema" is the grammatical form under which matter appears, yet for Aristotle "schema" does not entail any distinction between form and matter. See also my essay "Materiality and Language: Butler's Interrogation of the History of Philosophy," *Philosophy and Social Criticism* 23, no. 3 (spring 1997): 37–53, for a discussion of Butler's approach.

27. See, for example, Judith Butler, *Gender Trouble* (New York: Routledge Press, 1990), p. 10; Butler, *Bodies That Matter,* pp. 47–48. For a more explicit account of this view see Cornell, *Beyond Accommodation,* pp. 147–152. See Jacques Derrida, *Of Grammatology,* trans. Gayatri Chakravorty Spivak (Baltimore: Johns Hopkins University Press, 1976), p. 304; originally published in French as *De la grammatologie* (Paris: Minuit, 1967).

28. Grosz, *Sexual Subversions,* pp. 129–130.

29. Butler, *Gender Trouble,* pp. 9–10.

30. Tina Chanter, *The Ethics of Eros: Irigaray's Rewriting of the Philosophers* (New York: Routledge Press, 1995), p. 241. The literature addressing itself to this issue and to whether or not such a reading averts Irigaray's supposed essentialism is vast and includes the influential essay by Naomi Schor, "This Essentialism Which Is Not One: Coming to Grips with Irigaray," *Differences* 1, no. 2 (summer 1989): 38–58; as well as Margaret Whitford, *Luce Irigaray: Philosophy in the Feminine* (New York: Routledge Press, 1991). Whitford criticizes the narrow literalist reading of Irigaray as an essentialist and links Irigaray's morphology to "the aim of transforming the social contract" (p. 173). Also see Seyla Benhabib, "Feminism and Postmodernism: An Uneasy Alliance," in *Feminist Contentions: A Philosophical Exchange,* ed. Linda Nicholson (New York: Routledge Press, 1995), pp. 17–34; Toril Moi, *Sexual/Textual Politics: Feminist Literary Theory* (New York: Methuen, 1985); and Diana Fuss, *Essentially Speaking* (New York: Routledge Press, 1989).

31. Derrida, *Of Grammatology,* p. 285.

32. Ibid., pp. 285–286.

33. Ibid., p. 315.

34. Ibid., p. 286.

35. Ibid., p. 312.

36. Irigaray, "When Our Lips Speak Together," p. 107. Irigaray is referring to some hope she has for Fregean logic, a hope she soon gives up because Frege maintains a Platonist conception of objects of thought that leaves language ex-

ternally related to the thoughts it expresses. Thus natural languages fall short because they are unstable: they are rooted in the necessity of versatility and potential for change. Frege's logic, on the other hand, is concerned only with ideal language. See G. P. Baker and P. M. S. Hacker, *Frege: Logical Excavations* (Oxford: Basil Blackwell, 1984), p. 66.

37. Baker and Hacker, *Frege,* p. 139.

38. Andrea Nye, *Words of Power: A Feminist Reading of the History of Logic* (New York: Routledge Press, 1990), p. 131. I do not mean to endorse Nye's vision of western logic, for it appears to me to be deeply flawed, particularly the notion that ethics should be derivable from logic. However, she does open the discussion and critique the exclusion of women from that field.

39. Marjorie Hass, personal communication, June 20, 1997. Hass has pointed out that Nye's work on Frege "doesn't reflect the distinction between syntax and semantics." Nye fails to state that "Fregean first-order logic allows, but does not require [Socrates is mortal] to be represented as [If anything is Socrates, then it is mortal]." Nye (and I do follow her in this) seems to be talking only about semantic validity and not syntactic validity, which, as Hass points out, is principally a matter of deriving validity using proof rules.

40. I am thinking here of Derrida's attempted incursions into the feminine structural position, which I have discussed in my essay "*Kolossos:* The Measure of a Man's Cize," in *Feminist Interpretations of Jacques Derrida,* ed. Nancy Holland (State College, Penn.: Pennsylvania State University Press, 1997), pp. 215–230. Hass reinforces this point in her groundbreaking essay "Thinking Fluids/Fluid Thinking: Irigaray's Critique of Formal Logic," in *Feminist Interpretations of Logic,* ed. Marjorie Hass and Rachel Joffe Falmagne (forthcoming). There, Hass argues that in modern symbolic logic, "P can represent either 'the cat is on the mat' or 'the cat is not on the mat' and in either case −P will represent its negation. But in Irigaray's model, reversibility is not possible in that the two poles of difference are not interchangeable." This argument also must have profound implications for Merleau-Ponty's reversibility thesis. Following Hass's argument, reversibility would be part of a masculinist Imaginary.

41. Irigaray, "The 'Mechanics' of Fluids," p. 107.

42. Ibid., p. 109.

43. Ibid., pp. 109, 111.

44. Irigaray, "When Our Lips Speak Together," p. 212.

45. Luce Irigaray, *Je, Tu, Nous: Toward a Culture of Difference,* trans. Alison Martin (New York: Routledge Press, 1993), p. 59; originally published in French as *Je, tu, nous* (Paris: Grasset et Fasquelle, 1990).

46. Irigaray, "The 'Mechanics' of Fluids," p. 110.

47. Irigaray, "When Our Lips Speak Together," pp. 211–212.

48. Irigaray, "Sexual Difference," in *An Ethics of Sexual Difference,* p. 10; *Éthique de la différence sexuelle,* p. 17.

49. Irigaray, "When Our Lips Speak Together," p. 213.

50. Ibid., pp. 210, 211.

51. Ibid., p. 211.

52. Joanna Isaak "Women: The Ruin of Representation," *AFTERIMAGE* (April 1985): 6. It is with this kind of creative work in mind that I have titled this book.

53. Montrelay, "Inquiry into Femininity," pp. 232–233.

54. Mary Kelly, *Interim* (Edinburgh: Fruitmarket Gallery; Cambridge, Eng.: Kettle's Yard Gallery; London: Riverside Studios, 1986).

55. Mary Kelly, "Re-Presenting the Body: On *Interim,* Part I," in *Psychoanalysis and Cultural Theory: Thresholds* (New York: St. Martin's Press 1986), p. 60. This theme is reminiscent of that proposed by Martin Jay in *Downcast Eyes: The Denigration of Vision in Twentieth-Century French Thought* (Berkeley and Los Angeles: University of California Press, 1993). Jay takes Freud to be somewhat more sympathetic to the visual than Kelly, the artist, does; however, both appear to agree that Freud placed more emphasis on listening than seeing (p. 334). Although I have some sympathy with Jay's thesis on the denigration of vision, I do not take the critique of representation to be a denigration of vision; rather, it is an attempt to question the eye-mind dichotomy and to replace this dualism with something multiple that cannot be broken down into dualisms.

56. Sigmund Freud, "Charcot," in *The Standard Edition of the Complete Psychological Works of Sigmund Freud* (London: Hogarth Press, 1962), 3:12.

57. Kelly, "Re-Presenting the Body," p. 60.

58. Ibid., pp. 60–61.

59. Georges Guillain, *J.-M. Charcot, 1825–1893: His Life—His Work,* trans. Pearce Bailey (New York: Paul B. Hoeber, 1959), p. 136. Mimicry is a powerful symptom of hysteria.

60. Ibid., p. 138. Charcot wrote of the importance of speaking to the patients suffering from hysteria to impress upon them that their paralysis was curable. Physical therapy was designed to stimulate motor centers in the brain connected to voluntary movement. Massage and the application of electric current to muscles were parts of the treatment as well (p. 141). See J.-M. Charcot, "De l'ischurie hystérique," 9e leçon, in *Oeuvres complètes* ([Paris]: AMS Press, n.d.), 1:275–299. Cited in Guillain, *J.-M. Charcot.*

61. Guillain, *J.-M. Charcot,* p. 139. See J.-M. Charcot, "Leçon d'ouverture: Hystérique," in *Oeuvres complètes,* 3:1–22. Cited in Guillain, *J.-M. Charcot.*

62. Kelly, "Re-Presenting the Body," p. 61.

63. Ibid. See also Parveen Adams, "Symptoms and Hysteria," *Oxford Literary Review* 8, nos. 1–2 (1986), cited in Kelly, "Re-Presenting the Body," p. 67. Also see Luce Irigaray, "Plato's Hystera," in *Speculum of the Other Woman,* trans. Gillian C. Gill (Ithaca, N.Y.: Cornell University Press, 1985), pp. 243–364.

64. Kelly, "Re-Presenting the Body," p. 61.

65. I am referring here to Luce Irigaray.

66. Kelly, *Interim,* p. 53.

67. Joan Copjec, "Flavit et Disipati Sunt," *October* 18 (fall 1981): 39. Quoted in Isaak, "Women: The Ruin of Representation," p. 7.

68. Isaak, "Women: The Ruin of Representation," p. 8.

69. Maureen Turim, "What Is Sexual Difference?" *AFTERIMAGE* (April 1985): 4.

70. Victor Burgin, "Geometry and Abjection," in *Psychoanalysis and Cultural Theory: Thresholds* (New York: St. Martin's Press 1986), p. 12.

71. Ibid.

72. Ibid., p. 13.
73. Ibid., p. 15.
74. Ibid., p. 16.
75. See Gatens, *Imaginary Bodies,* p. 17.
76. Irigaray, *An Ethics of Sexual Difference,* p. 6; *Éthique de la différence sexuelle,* p. 14.
77. Ibid., p. 7/p. 15.
78. Ibid.
79. In particular, I am thinking of the second of Foucault's two lectures in the essay "Two Lectures," in *Power/Knowledge,* trans. Colin Gordon, Leo Marshall, John Mepham, and Kate Soper, ed. Colin Gordon (New York: Pantheon Books, 1980), pp. 78–108. In this lecture Foucault declares that in contemporary western societies, "Power never ceases its interrogation, its inquisition, its registration of truth: it institutionalizes, professionalizes and rewards its pursuit. . . . In another way, we are also subjected to truth in the sense in which it is truth that makes the laws, that produces the true discourse which, at least partially, decides, transmits and itself extends upon the effects of power. In the end, we are judged, condemned, classified, determined in our undertakings, destined to a certain mode of living or dying, as a function of the true discourses which are the bearers of the specific effects of power" (p. 94).
80. Maurice Merleau-Ponty, *Phenomenology of Perception,* trans. Colin Smith, ed. Forrest Williams (New York: Routledge Press, 1962), p. 243; originally published in French as *Phénoménologie de la perception* (Paris: Gallimard, 1945), p. 281.
81. Ibid., p. 244/p. 282.
82. Ibid.
83. Ibid., pp. 248, 250/pp. 286, 289.
84. Ibid., p. 253/p. 292.
85. Ibid., p. 252/p. 292.
86. Ibid., p. 253/p. 292. In his essay "The Element of Voluptuousness: Depth and Place Reexamined," Edward Casey addresses precisely these kinds of issues in terms of the concept and experience of depth and its relation to place. See Edward S. Casey, "The Element of Voluptuousness: Depth and Place Reexamined," in *Merleau-Ponty Vivant,* ed. M. C. Dillon (Albany: State University of New York Press), pp. 1–29. Casey concludes that Merleau-Ponty does not give depth, which seems to be related to the "determining of up and down and in general of place," the kind of attention it merits (p. 14). Casey suggests that the body is a kind of place that orients two kinds of depth: a depth in relation to the body, which complements a second depth in relation to the horizon (p. 17). Perhaps this more complex space could begin to provide a less static spatiality than Merleau-Ponty's. Casey also cites William James, *The Principles of Psychology* (New York: Dover Books, 1950), vol. 2; J. J. Gibson, *The Senses Considered as Perceptual Systems* (Boston: Houghton Mifflin, 1966); Gibson, *Eye and Brain: The Psychology of Seeing* (New York: World University Library, 1976); and Gibson, *The Ecological Approach to Visual Perception* (Ithaca, N.Y.: Cornell University Press, 1976), as important contributions to a theory of depth.

87. Henri Bergson, *Matter and Memory,* trans. N. M. Paul and W. S. Palmer (New York: Zone Books, 1988), pp. 35–37; published in French in *Bergson oeuvres* (Paris: Presses Universitaires de France, 1959), pp. 185–187.

88. Henri Bergson, *Creative Evolution,* trans. Arthur Mitchell (New York: Modern Library, 1944), pp. 207, 208; *Bergson oeuvres,* pp. 670, 671.

89. Bergson, *Matter and Memory,* p. 245; *Bergson oeuvres,* p. 374.

90. Young, "Throwing Like a Girl," p. 61.

91. See Michael B. Katz, "The Underclass?" in *The Undeserving Poor: From the War on Poverty to the War on Welfare* (New York: Pantheon, 1989), pp. 185–235. Katz concludes that available data prove that black youths are very willing to work but since their experience and rejection of low-paying, dead-end jobs has been determined an invalid reason for their unemployment, the employment market shows no interest in them and they become increasingly trapped.

92. Katz, *Undeserving Poor,* pp. 190–191.

93. Irigaray, *An Ethics of Sexual Difference,* p. 8; *Éthique de la différence sexuelle,* pp. 15–16.

94. Henri Bergson, *The Creative Mind,* trans. Mabelle L. Andison (New York: Philosophical Library, 1946), p. 117; in French, *Bergson oeuvres,* p. 1339.

95. Ibid., pp. 118–119/pp. 1339–1340.

96. Bergson, *Matter and Memory,* chapter 1; *Bergson oeuvres,* pp. 169–222.

97. Merleau-Ponty, *Phenomenology of Perception,* p. 158; *Phénoménologie de la perception,* p. 184.

98. Irigaray, *An Ethics of Sexual Difference,* p. 9; *Éthique de la différence sexuelle,* p. 16.

99. Merleau-Ponty, *Phenomenology of Perception,* p. 158; *Phénoménologie de la perception,* p. 184.

100. Butler, "Sexual Ideology and Phenomenological Description."

101. Merleau-Ponty, *Phenomenology of Perception,* p. 160; *Phénoménologie de la perception,* p. 187.

102. Ibid., p. 162/p. 190.

103. Ibid., p. 163/p. 190.

104. Ibid., p. 164/p. 191.

105. Luce Irigaray, "How to Conceive (of) a Girl," in *Speculum of the Other Woman,* p. 160.

106. Ibid., p. 161.

107. Ibid. See also Luce Irigaray, "Place, Interval: A Reading of Aristotle, *Physics* IV," in *An Ethics of Sexual Difference,* pp. 34–55; in French, "Le lieu, l'intervalle: Lecture d'Aristote, *Physique* IV, 2, 3, 4, 5," in *Éthique de la différence sexuelle,* pp. 41–59, where Irigaray makes a related point. She challenges Aristotle regarding the apparent nonexistence of what does not have a place, insofar as this would appear to include women. This is because women are characterized by philosophy as place (p. 35/p. 41) but not as having a place of their own. Aristotle particularly affirms that the interval is not place, whereas Irigaray, as we have seen, maintains that "the interval would produce place" (p. 48/p. 53). Chanter (*The Ethics of Eros,* pp. 151–158) also comments on the suppression, in

the history of metaphysics, of the space between women's place as first place, the place of birth, and her place as last place, her relation to the infinity of God. That is, that woman is the fluid place for man and child disqualifies her from any more spiritual role, that of accompanying cosmic time. Irigaray, "Place, Interval," p. 53; "Le lieu, l'intervalle," p. 57.

108. Irigaray, "How to Conceive (of) a Girl," p. 164.

109. Ibid., p. 166.

110. Ibid.

111. Irigaray, "Sexual Difference," in *An Ethics of Sexual Difference,* p. 10; *Éthique de la différence sexuelle,* p. 17.

112. Ibid., p. 9/p. 16.

113. I do not mean to overlook Irigaray's critique of Merleau-Ponty for privileging the visual over the tactile; however, because it is not my main point, I am not discussing it here. See my article "Phenomenology and Feminism," in *Edinburgh Encyclopedia of Continental Philosophy* (Edinburgh: Edinburgh University Press, 1999).

114. Merleau-Ponty, *Visible and the Invisible,* p. 134; *Le visible et l'invisible,* p. 177.

115. Ibid., p. 135/p. 178.

116. Ibid., p. 138/p. 182. In *The Origin of Perspective,* trans. John Goodman (Cambridge, Mass.: MIT Press, 1995), Hubert Damisch maintains—following Filarete, who comments on Alberti that two mirrors are the best way to produce a representation—"But the essential thing remains the place, the function that Filarete assigns to the mirror in the circuit of representation: the mirror . . . by means of which one can judge not only the diminution of figures, but the distribution of light and shadow, but the mirror, more important, whose image of the reality it faces will be implicitly understood as analogous to the one the painter has constructed on a plane, *con ragione.* Save for the fact that a single mirror is insufficient, since its image of the things in front of it is reversed, or turned around, and can only be set right if one repeats the transformation—nullifies it—by means of a *di-montratio,* a double showing. In the matter of representation, the reflection will always be one mirror behind, and vice versa: 'If you dispose of two mirrors facing one another, it will be easier to draw whatever you want to do'" (pp. 65–66). See Filarete, *Treatise on Architecture,* trans. John R. Spencer (New Haven: Yale University Press, 1965), cited in Damisch. The double mirror thus guarantees representational perspective; it is not clear that decentering it would do much to produce a more fluid space.

117. Irigaray, "Sexual Difference," in *An Ethics of Sexual Difference,* pp. 17–18; *Éthique de la différence sexuelle,* p. 24.

Chapter 4

1. Gilles Deleuze, *Bergsonism,* trans. Hugh Tomlinson and Barbara Habberjam (New York: Zone Books, 1988), p. 15; originally published in French as *Le Bergsonisme* (Paris: Presses Universitaires de France, 1966), p. 3. It is of some interest that Deleuze titles his book *Bergsonism.* In his essay "Bergson in the

Making," Merleau-Ponty rejects what he refers to as "Bergsonism," claiming that "[e]stablished Bergsonism distorts Bergson. Bergson disturbed; it reassures. Bergson was a conquest; Bergsonism defends and justifies Bergson. Bergson was a contact with things; Bergsonism is a collection of accepted opinions." Maurice Merleau-Ponty, *Signs,* trans. Richard McCleary (Evanston, Ill.: Northwestern University Press, 1964), p. 183. In naming his book *Bergsonism* Deleuze appears to reject both the accepted opinions of Bergson and Merleau-Ponty's recuperation of him.

2. Although little has been written on Deleuze and semiotics, there are several accounts. See Massumi, *A User's Guide,* pp. 10–46; Ronald Bogue, "Word, Image and Sound: The Non-Representational Semiotics of Gilles Deleuze," in *Mimesis in Contemporary Theory: An Interdisciplinary Approach,* ed. Ronald Bogue (Philadelphia: John Benjamins, 1991), 2:77–97; and Olkowski, "Semiotics and Gilles Deleuze."

3. Deleuze and Guattari, *Thousand Plateaus,* p. 77; *Mille plateaux,* p. 97.

4. Ibid., p. 75/p. 95.

5. Deleuze and Guattari, *Thousand Plateaus,* p. 79; *Mille plateaux,* p. 99. See J. L. Austin, *Philosophical Papers* (Oxford: Clarendon Press, 1961); and Émile Benveniste, "Man and Language," in *Problems in General Linguistics,* trans. Mary Elizabeth Meek (Coral Gables, Fla.: University of Miami Press, 1971), pp. 195–248.

6. Henri Bergson, *Time and Free Will: An Essay on the Immediate Data of Consciousness,* trans. F. L. Pogson (New York: Macmillan, 1959), p. 138; *Bergson oeuvres,* p. 91.

7. Henri Bergson, *The Two Sources of Morality and Religion,* trans. R. Ashley Audra and Cloudesley Brereton (Garden City, N.Y.: Doubleday, 1935), pp. 14–15; *Bergson oeuvres,* p. 986. According to Bergson, only by delving "down" into the more original personality can citizens produce a dynamic and creative open society (p. 267/p. 1202).

8. Bergson, *Creative Mind,* pp. 58–59; *Bergson oeuvres,* pp. 1292–1293.

9. Deleuze points out that in Bergson there are two kinds of false problems: (1) the nonexistent problems, whose terms confuse "more" and "less," for example, the false problem of nonbeing, in which there is being, then a logical operation negating that being, plus the psychological motivation for it; and (2) badly stated questions, whose terms represent badly analyzed composites, which arbitrarily group things that differ in kind, for example in the case of "intensity," in which a quality of a sensation of an affective temporality is confused with the muscular space that merely corresponds to it—that is, a quality is transformed into a quantity. See Deleuze, *Bergsonism,* pp. 17–19; *Le Bergsonisme,* pp. 6–9.

10. Deleuze, *Bergsonism,* p. 20; *Le Bergsonisme,* p. 10. See also Bergson, *Creative Mind,* pp. 130–132; *Bergson oeuvres,* pp. 1348–1350.

11. Bergson, *Creative Mind,* pp. 140–141; *Bergson oeuvres,* p. 1356. Bergson's clues for discovering the "mediating image," which is itself an interval, both almost matter (seeable) and almost mind (not touchable), seem to be textual but require an extraordinary attunement to the descriptions Berkeley or any other philosopher provides. So Bergson argues that Berkeley perceives matter as a "thin transparent film" between man and God through which God reveals himself until philosophers meddle with it and common sense obscures it. The

image comes from Berkeley, who wrote that "we first raise a dust and then complain that we cannot see." Bergson, *Creative Mind,* pp. 140–141; *Bergson oeuvres,* p. 1356.

12. Ibid., pp. 140–141/pp. 1356–1357.

13. Ibid., p. 141/p. 1357.

14. Deleuze, *Bergsonism,* pp. 21–22; *Le Bergsonisme,* pp. 11–12.

15. Gilles Deleuze, "La conception de la différence chez Bergson," *Les études bergsoniennes* 4 (1956): 77–112, especially pp. 83, 85.

16. See Michael Hardt, *Gilles Deleuze: An Apprenticeship in Philosophy* (Minneapolis: University of Minnesota Press, 1993), pp. 6–7. Hardt shows how Deleuze makes use of Bergson to launch an attack on causality conceived of as external to its effect, showing that in Bergson, vital difference is always internal difference. In this way Deleuze obtains a conception of actualization out of the virtual that is not a degradation of being but a positive process. Perhaps, however, this limits Bergson's importance for Deleuze to too small an area of concerns and it overlooks the relation to the outside as well, a relation that creative evolution calls for.

17. Deleuze, "La conception de la différence chez Bergson," p. 96.

18. Bergson, *Creative Mind,* p. 13; *Bergson oeuvres,* p. 1256.

19. Bergson, *Time and Free Will,* p. 232; *Bergson oeuvres,* p. 151.

20. Bergson, *Matter and Memory,* p. 17; *Bergson oeuvres,* p. 169.

21. Ibid., p. 18/p. 170.

22. Nietzsche, *On the Genealogy of Morals,* book 2, chap. 12, p. 77. Also see Deleuze, *Nietzsche and Philosophy,* p.3; *Nietzsche et la philosophie,* p. 3. For a fuller account of Deleuze's reading of Nietzsche's critique see my essay "Nietzsche's Dice Throw: Tragedy, Nihilism, and the Body without Organs," in *Gilles Deleuze and the Theater of Philosophy,* ed. Constantin V. Boundas and Dorothea Olkowski (New York: Routledge Press, 1994), pp. 119–140.

23. Nietzsche, *On the Genealogy of Morals,* p. 78.

24. See Todd May, "Gilles Deleuze and the Politics of Time," *Man and World* 28, no. 3 (July 1996): 293–304. See also Todd May, "Difference and Unity in the Thought of Gilles Deleuze," in *Gilles Deleuze and the Theater of Philosophy,* ed. Constantin V. Boundas and Dorothea Olkowski (New York: Routledge Press, 1994), pp. 33–50.

25. I have written about the "modeling" of Deleuze and Guattari at length in "Beside Us, in Memory," *Man and World* 28, no. 3 (July 1996): 283–292. Deleuze and Guattari's provocative comments on the marketing of concepts appear in *What Is Philosophy?,* trans. Hugh Tomlinson and Graham Burchell (New York: Columbia University Press, 1994), p. 10; published originally in French as *Qu'est-ce que la philosophie?* (Paris: Minuit, 1991).

26. Deleuze, *Bergsonism,* p. 28; *Le Bergsonisme,* p. 19.

27. Ibid. Roland Barthes argues for precisely this approach to understanding photography. He calls the concept that only suits a particular thing the science of the singular. This will be the basis of my reformulation of psychology along ontological lines in chapters 5 and 7.

28. Bergson, *Matter and Memory,* pp. 18–19; *Bergson oeuvres,* pp. 170–171. For a typical contemporary internalist or idealist view see Antonio D'Amasio,

Descartes' Error: Emotion, Reason and the Human Brain (New York: Avon Books, 1994).

29. Bergson, *Matter and Memory,* pp. xi–xii; *Bergson oeuvres.* Cited in Paul Douglass, "Deleuze's Bergson," in *The Crisis in Modernism: Bergson and the Vitalist Controversy,* ed. Frederick Burwick and Paul Douglass (Cambridge, Eng.: Cambridge University Press, 1992), p. 373.

30. Bergson, *Matter and Memory,* p. 22; *Bergson oeuvres,* pp. 173–174.

31. Ibid., pp. 27–28/pp. 178–179.

32. Ibid., p. 25/p. 175.

33. See Shaun Gallagher, "On the Pre-Noetic Reality of Time," in *Écart et Différence: Merleau-Ponty on Seeing and Writing,* ed. Martin Dillon (Atlantic Highlands, N.J.: Humanities Press, 1997), pp. 134–148, for an interesting account of the reality of time. Gallagher maintains that Husserl and Derrida do not make time real, but Merleau-Ponty's embodied subjectivity does. However, this does not prevent Merleau-Ponty from conceiving time on the model of space, even if it is embodied space.

34. Bergson, *Matter and Memory,* p. 36; *Bergson oeuvres,* p. 186.

35. Ibid., pp. 48–49/p. 197.

36. Ibid., p. 38/pp. 187–188. Compare this to Merleau-Ponty, who insists that in human acts the psychological and physiological are integrated, though ambiguously, since every intention is multidimensional. Either this eliminates choice (because the zone of indetermination would be narrowed and integrated) or it conceives of the totality of images as already spatial, thus eliminating duration and, thereby, the actualization of multiple virtual acts.

37. Ibid., p. 45/p. 194.

38. Ibid., p. 56/p. 204.

39. Ibid., p. 60/p. 208.

40. Ibid., p. 58/p. 206.

41. Ibid., p. 28/p. 179.

42. Deleuze, *Difference and Repetition,* p. 73, translation altered; *Différence et répétition,* pp. 99–100.

43. Deleuze and Guattari, *Thousand Plateaus,* p. 320; *Mille plateaux,* p. 394.

44. Ibid., p. 40/p. 54.

45. Ibid. See also Arthur Conan Doyle, *When the World Screamed and Other Stories,* Professor Challenger Adventures, vol. 2 (San Francisco: Chronicle Books, 1990). In Doyle's version, Professor George Edward Challenger, an eccentric and unorthodox scientist, carries out his plan to sink a shaft through the earth's crust. Following Challenger's plan, "'The exposed and sensitive substance will be pricked, and how it will react is a matter for conjecture'" (p. 25). The comments of the narrator, Mr. Edward Malone, a newswriter, upon the appearance of the earth eight miles down, are instructive: "It was an amazing sight which lay before us. By some strange cosmic telepathy, the old planet seemed to know that an unheard-of liberty was about to be attempted. The exposed surface was like a boiling pot. Great grey bubbles rose and burst with a crackling report. The air surfaces and vacuoles below the skin separated and coalesced in an agitated activity. The transverse ripples were stronger and faster in their rhythm

than before. A dark purple fluid appeared to pulse in the tortuous anastomoses of channels which lay under the surface. The throb of life was in it all" (pp. 24–25).

46. Deleuze and Guattari, *Thousand Plateaus,* p. 43; *Mille plateaux,* p. 58.

47. See Massumi, *A User's Guide,* p. 48.

48. Deleuze, *Bergsonism,* p. 25; *Le Bergsonisme,* pp. 15–16.

49. Deleuze and Guattari, *Thousand Plateaus,* p. 40; *Mille plateaux,* p. 55.

50. Ibid., p. 43/pp. 56–57.

51. Bergson, *Matter and Memory,* p. 30; *Bergson oeuvres,* p. 181.

52. Maria de Issekutz Wolsky and Alexander A. Wolsky, "Bergson's Vitalism and Modern Biology," in *The Crisis in Modernism: Bergson and the Vitalist Controversy,* ed. Frederick Burwick and Paul Douglass (Cambridge, Eng.: Cambridge University Press, 1992), p. 168.

53. Bergson, *Creative Evolution,* p. 99; *Bergson oeuvres,* p. 579.

54. At times, some feminist theorists come precariously close to this position, for example, Teresa Brennan in *The Interpretation of the Flesh.* She provides numerous examples of material bodies and thoughts that implicate one another, and her text is full of descriptions of such actions, but a theory that spells out how this occurs is nowhere offered and the text leaves the uneasy sense that conscious and unconscious "thoughts" are somehow produced out of crass materiality.

55. Bergson, *Matter and Memory,* pp. 71–72; *Bergson oeuvres,* pp. 218–219.

56. Deleuze, *Bergsonism,* p. 18; *Le Bergsonisme,* pp. 7–8. For example, the quality of sensation called intensity, the subject of chapter 1 of Bergson's *Time and Free Will,* is confused with the muscular space that corresponds to it or with the quality of the physical cause producing it.

57. Bergson, *Creative Evolution,* pp. 102–103; *Bergson oeuvres,* pp. 581–582.

58. Bergson, *Creative Evolution,* p. 98; *Bergson oeuvres,* p . 578.

59. Wolsky and Wolsky argue that Bergson rejected neo-Darwinian gradualism (which postulates that evolution progresses smoothly by small changes) and radical-finalism (which postulates a vital force within the organism that regulates its development; see chapter 1 of *Creative Evolution*). This seems to have left him with a position that is today called "punctuated equilibria," meaning that evolution proceeds unevenly, by occasional major steps, but between them there is gradual adaptation through natural selection by micromutations. See Wolsky and Wolsky, "Bergson's Vitalism and Modern Biology," pp. 156–160. See also Stephen Jay Gould, *Dinosaur in a Haystack: Reflections in Natural History* (New York: Free Press, 1995).

60. Bergson, *Matter and Memory,* p. 71; *Bergson oeuvres,* p. 218. Thus, Bergson concludes there is something more in perception than is actually given or, as he also states it, between pure perception (separated from memory for purposes of analysis) and matter there is only a difference of degree, not of kind. Yet in the real, perception and recollection always interpenetrate one another.

61. Bergson, *Time and Free Will,* p. 104; *Bergson oeuvres,* p. 70.

62. Deleuze, *Difference and Repetition,* p. 86; *Différence et répétition,* p. 116. See also Gilles Deleuze, *Kant's Critical Philosophy: The Doctrine of the Faculties,*

trans. Hugh Tomlinson and Barbara Habberjam (Minneapolis: University of Minnesota Press, 1984), introduction; originally published in French as *La philosophie critique de Kant* (Paris: Presses Universitaires de France, 1963); and see my essay "Beside Us, in Memory."

63. Bergson, *Time and Free Will,* pp. 104–105; *Bergson oeuvres,* p. 70.

64. Deleuze, *Difference and Repetition* p. 70, translation altered; *Différence et répétition,* p. 96. See David Hume, *A Treatise of Human Nature* (Oxford: Clarendon Press, 1968), book I, part 3, sect. 14, pp. 164–165: "Tho' the several resembling instances, which give rise to the idea of power have no influence on each other, and can never produce any new quality *in the object,* which can be the model of that idea, yet the *observation* of this resemblance produces a new impression *in the mind,* which is its real model."

65. Hume, *Treatise,* p. 11.

66. Deleuze, *Difference and Repetition,* pp. 70–71, translation altered; *Différence et répétition,* p. 97.

67. Ibid., p. 73/p. 100.

68. Deleuze, *Bergsonism,* pp. 32–34; *Le Bergsonisme,* pp. 24–25.

69. Deleuze, *Kant's Critical Philosophy,* p. vii.

70. Hume, *Treatise,* pp. 5, 8.

71. Ibid., p. 275.

72. Ibid., pp. 8, 283–284.

73. Ibid., p. 179; cited in Gilles Deleuze, *Empiricism and Subjectivity: An Essay on Hume's Theory of Human Nature,* trans. Constantin V. Boundas (New York: Columbia University Press, 1991), p. 30; originally published in French as *Empirisme et subjectivité: Essai sur la nature humaine selon Hume* (Paris: Presses Universitaires de France, 1953), p. 13.

74. Hume, *Treatise,* p. 283.

75. Ibid.

76. Ibid., p. 165.

77. Ibid., p. 265, emphases added.

78. Deleuze, *Empiricism and Subjectivity,* pp. 26, 30; *Empirisme et subjectivité,* pp. 7–8, 13.

79. Ibid., p. 31/p. 15.

80. Hume, *Treatise,* pp. 251–252.

81. Ibid., p. 253.

82. Ibid., p. 254.

83. In fact, more important than the constitution of a government to Hume is the observation of justice, without which no society can be maintained. Justice requires the fulfillment of promises that carry with them moral obligations. See Hume, *Treatise,* p. 541.

84. Deleuze, *Difference and Repetition,* p. 80, translation altered; *Différence et répétition,* p. 109.

85. Bergson, *Matter and Memory,* pp. 65–66; *Bergson oeuvres,* p. 213.

86. Deleuze, *Difference and Repetition,* p. 80, translation altered; *Différence et répétition,* pp. 109–110.

87. Ibid., pp. 81–82, translation altered/p. 111.

88. Bergson, *Matter and Memory,* pp. 127–129; *Bergson oeuvres,* pp. 271–274.
89. Ibid., p. 162/p. 293.
90. Ibid., p. 138/p. 281.
91. Ibid., pp. 139–141/pp. 281–283.
92. Ibid., pp. 73–76/pp. 220–223.
93. Hilda Doolittle (H.D.) "Heat" (1916), in *Chief Modern Poets of Britain and America,* ed. Gerald DeWitt Sanders, John Herbert Nelson, and M. L. Rosenthal (New York: Macmillan, 1970), 2:211–212.
94. Bergson, *Matter and Memory,* p. 82; *Bergson oeuvres,* p. 227.
95. Ibid., p. 80/p. 226.
96. Ibid., p. 95/p. 241.
97. Ibid., p. 102/p. 248.
98. Ibid., pp. 104–106/pp. 250–251. Emphasis added.
99. Deleuze, *Bergsonism,* pp. 56–57; *Le Bergsonisme,* pp. 51–52.
100. Bergson, *Matter and Memory,* p. 102; *Bergson oeuvres,* p. 248. Bergson sometimes says that the image is similar to or even that it imitates the perceived object, but I avoid this language insofar as similarity and resemblance are categories of thought and organic representation in Aristotle. Bergson, however, is analyzing spontaneous perception and the reflection of *images,* not the thought of substances. Thus he speaks of the "afterimage," the image returned from the central nervous system to the periphery so as to "echo" the object, the image "photographed" onto the object (p. 103/p. 248).
101. Ibid., p. 168/p. 307. See, for example, Jacques Derrida, "*Différence,*" in *Margins of Philosophy,* trans. Alan Bass (Chicago: University of Chicago Press, 1982), pp. 1–27. Derrida refers to *différence* as the middle voice, neither passive nor active, the unity of chance and necessity in the notion of play in calculations without end, and as that which produces the play of differences.
102. Bergson, *Matter and Memory,* pp. 152–153; *Bergson oeuvres,* p. 293.
103. Ibid., p. 139/p. 281.
104. Hume, *Treatise,* p. 20.
105. Kazuo Ishiguro, *The Unconsoled* (New York: Knopf, 1995).
106. Bergson, *Matter and Memory,* pp. 168–169; *Bergson oeuvres,* pp. 307–308.
107. Deleuze, *Bergsonism,* pp. 71–72; *Le Bergsonisme,* pp. 70–71.

Chapter 5

1. Bergson, *Matter and Memory,* pp. 168–169; *Bergson oeuvres,* pp. 307–308.
2. Deleuze, *Bergsonism,* p. 74; *Le Bergsonisme,* pp. 72–73.
3. Bergson, *Matter and Memory,* pp. 165–166; *Bergson oeuvres,* p. 304. See also Bergson, *Creative Evolution,* p. 117; *Bergson oeuvres,* pp. 594–595.
4. Bergson, *Matter and Memory,* pp. 170–171; *Bergson oeuvres,* p. 310.
5. Contemporary physics in some respects does affirm this Bergsonian thesis. See Milič Čapek, "Microphysical Indeterminacy and Freedom: Bergson and Peirce," in *The Crisis in Modernism: Bergson and the Vitalist Controversy,* ed. Frederick Burwick and Paul Douglass (Cambridge, Eng.: Cambridge University Press, 1992), pp. 171–189. Čapek argues that Bergson's conception

of expansion agrees with the concept of a "genuinely growing world" advocated by Whitehead, Reichenbach, Heisenberg, Bondi, and Whiterow (p. 175). Čapek also refers to the tendency of memory to expand in the direction of life and action, as a "'one-to-many-correlation' between the mental and the physical" (p. 183). This term is much more difficult to work with than Bergson's conceptualization, as it does not really reflect the virtual complexity of the levels of memory.

6. Deleuze, "La conception de différence chez Bergson," p. 88.

7. Bergson, *Time and Free Will,* p. 100, translation altered; *Bergson oeuvres,* p. 67.

8. Maurice Merleau-Ponty, *The Structure of Behavior,* trans. Alden L. Fisher (Boston: Beacon Press, 1967), pp. 120–122; Merleau-Ponty, *Phenomenology of Perception,* p. 84.

9. Bergson, *Creative Evolution,* pp. 135–136; *Bergson oeuvres,* pp. 609–610. See also Deleuze, "La conception de différence chez Bergson," p. 93, where Deleuze argues that difference in Bergson is the force of differenciation that life carries in itself.

10. See Beauvoir, *Second Sex,* chap. 1, "The Data of Biology."

11. Deleuze, *Bergsonism,* p. 95; *Le Bergsonisme,* pp. 96–97. This means that unity is always a virtual totality that gets actualized according to divergent lines that differ in kind, developing or explaining what had been kept enclosed in a virtual manner.

12. Ibid., p. 97/pp. 99–100.

13. Bergson, *Creative Evolution,* p. 140; *Bergson oeuvres,* pp. 613–614.

14. Deleuze and Parnet, *Dialogues,* p. 104.

15. Deleuze and Guattari, *Anti-Oedipus,* p. 63; *L'anti-Oedipe,* p. 54. The notion of "partial objects" is borrowed from Melanie Klein's analysis of the infantile basis of schizophrenia. Klein writes, "In this very early phase . . . the ego's power of identifying itself with its objects is as yet small, partly because it is itself still uncoordinated and partly because the introjected objects are still mainly partial objects." See Melanie Klein, "A Contribution to the Psychogenesis of Manic-Depressive States" (1935), in *Love, Guilt and Reparation* (New York: Delacorte Press, 1975), p. 363. Presumably this is of use to Deleuze and Guattari because it allows them to talk about bodies or body connections in terms of flows as opposed to complete egos and complete objects that are already totalized and structured in accordance with the Oedipal signifier.

16. Deleuze and Guattari, *Anti-Oedipus,* pp. 63, 64; *L'anti-Oedipe,* pp. 54, 55.

17. Bergson, *Creative Evolution,* p. 147; *Bergson oeuvres,* p. 620.

18. Ibid., pp. 140–141/pp. 614–615.

19. Bergson, *Time and Free Will,* p. 128; *Bergson oeuvres,* p. 85. See also *The Creative Mind,* where Bergson comments that intellectualized time is space and that the elimination of time is the habitual, normal, commonplace act of our understanding. Bergson, *Creative Mind,* p. 34; *Bergson oeuvres,* pp. 1271–1272.

20. Bergson, *Matter and Memory,* p. 187; *Bergson oeuvres,* p. 323.

21. Irigaray, "When Our Lips Speak Together," p. 212.

22. Bergson, *Time and Free Will,* p. 8; *Bergson oeuvres,* p. 9.

23. Ibid., p. 13/p. 13.

24. Ibid., pp. 24–26/pp. 19–21.

25. Ibid., p. 47/p. 34. The problem, once again, is that because heat and cold provoke us so quickly to action (or really reaction), we assume that changes in kind are merely escalations of degree, a matter of being spatially nearer to or further away from the source of heat or cold.

26. Ibid., pp. 46–48/pp. 33–35.

27. Ibid., pp. 50–51/pp. 36–37.

28. Irigaray, *Speculum,* p. 30. Elsewhere Irigaray specifically names the sexual aspects of the woman's body, the two (sets of) lips, the clitoris, and the vagina, as well as the layering of her body. She argues that because the male is taken to be the standard (the spatialized and homogeneous standard), from this point of view "*there never is (or will be) a little girl.*" Irigaray, "When Our Lips Speak Together," p. 48.

29. Bergson, *Time and Free Will,* p. 84; *Bergson oeuvres,* p. 57.

30. Ibid., pp. 75–81/pp. 51–56.

31. Ibid., p. 84/p. 57.

32. Ibid., p. 87/p. 59.

33. Ibid., pp. 98–99/pp. 66–67.

34. Bergson, *Matter and Memory,* pp. 181–182; *Bergson oeuvres,* pp. 317–318.

35. Ibid., pp. 183–184/pp. 319–320.

36. Ibid., p. 185/pp. 321–322.

37. Bergson, *Time and Free Will,* pp. 129–130, 132; *Bergson oeuvres,* pp. 86–88.

38. Bergson, *Creative Evolution,* pp. 156–157; *Bergson oeuvres,* p. 628.

39. Ibid., pp. 158–161/pp. 629–931. Bergson's theory of language resembles, to some extent, that of Ferdinand de Saussure, for whom language is organized diacritically, whereas Bergson proposes that the sign is freely mobile. Bergson notes that the existing language system keeps the signifier relatively stable. Ultimately, for Saussure the stability of language overrides its mobility and "[l]anguage is speech less speaking"; it is tied to social fact. See Saussure, *Course in General Linguistics,* p. 77.

40. Bergson, *Creative Evolution,* pp. 211, 213; *Bergson oeuvres,* pp. 674, 676.

41. Ibid., pp. 214–216; *Bergson oeuvres,* pp. 676–678.

42. Gilles Deleuze and Félix Guattari, *Kafka: Toward a Minor Literature,* trans. Dana Polan (Minneapolis: University of Minnesota Press, 1986), p. 19; originally published in French as *Kafka: Pour une littérature mineur* (Paris: Minuit, 1975).

43. Bergson, *Creative Evolution,* pp. 217–218; *Bergson oeuvres,* pp. 679–680.

44. Deleuze, *Bergsonism,* pp. 92–94; *Le Bergsonisme,* p. 93–95.

45. Bergson, *Matter and Memory,* pp. 188–189; *Bergson oeuvres,* pp. 324–325.

46. Ibid., p. 193/p. 329. Bergson argues that in physics, at least, the internal configuration of every system varies and movement becomes a reality. Only in geometry is movement relative. To persist in this belief requires positing absolute positions in space, a distinction that demands a difference either in quality or relation to a totality. This would make space either heterogeneous or finite. The former would require the positing of a homogeneous space under it; the latter would

require a boundary consisting of another space. That is, both hypotheses require a homogeneous and indefinite space. Ibid., p. 194/p. 330.

47. Ibid., p. 198/p. 334.

48. Ibid., p. 197/p. 333.

49. Ibid., pp. 203, 201/pp. 338, 337.

50. Constantin V. Boundas, "Deleuze, Empiricism, and the Struggle for Subjectivity," in Deleuze, *Empiricism and Subjectivity,* pp. 15, 17. Boundas goes on to discuss how the constitution of the subject is also the synthesis of time, much in the manner I have tried to develop in this book. See also Patrick Hayden, "From Relations to Practice in the Empiricism of Gilles Deleuze," *Man and World* 4 (July 1995): 1–20. Like Boundas, Hayden emphasizes that principles of association alone cannot account for the difference between terms but concrete practical circumstances—that is, the world as a dynamic continuum of social practices—are what guarantee difference.

51. Bergson, *Creative Evolution,* p. 212; *Bergson oeuvres,* p. 675.

52. Ibid., p. 2/p. 496.

53. Deleuze, *Difference and Repetition,* p. 83; *Différence et répétition,* p. 113.

54. Bergson, *Creative Evolution,* pp. 9–11; *Bergson oeuvres,* pp. 501–503.

55. This makes apparent the insufficiency of explanations of Deleuze that do not take into account immanence and depth. In *The Logic of Sense* Deleuze sums up the difference between Antonin Artaud and Lewis Carroll from Artaud's point of view, stating that for Artaud, Carroll is a pervert who holds on to surface language and has not felt its depths in the schizophrenic problem of suffering, death, and life. The effect of this is that Carroll's logical games are puerile, hypocritical, and too well bred. One might say the same of Bergson's view of Einstein. Finally, Deleuze himself proclaims, "We would not give a page of Artaud for all of Carroll. Artaud is alone in having been an absolute depth in literature, and in having discovered a vital body and the prodigious language of this body" (pp. 93, 84; *Logique du sens,* pp. 113–114, 103–104).

56. Deleuze, *Difference and Repetition,* pp. 83–84, translation altered; *Différence et répétition,* pp. 113–114.

57. Deleuze and Guattari, *Kafka,* p. 17.

58. Deleuze, *Difference and Repetition,* p. 85; *Différence et répétition,* p. 115.

59. Ibid.

60. Ibid., p. 83/p. 113.

61. Bergson, *Creative Evolution,* p. 201; *Bergson oeuvres,* p. 666.

62. Deleuze, *Difference and Repetition,* p. 85; *Différence et répétition,* p. 115.

63. Deleuze, *Kant's Critical Philosophy,* pp. 14, 12; *La philosophie critique de Kant,* pp. 23, 21.

64. Ibid., p. vii (English edition only).

65. Deleuze, *Difference and Repetition,* p. 86; *Différence et répétition,* p. 116.

66. Deleuze, *Kant's Critical Philosophy,* pp. viii–ix (English edition only).

67. Deleuze, *Difference and Repetition,* p. 86, translation altered; *Différence et répétition,* p. 116.

68. Ibid., p. 87/p. 117.

69. Ibid., p. 88/p. 118.

70. Ibid., p. 35, translation altered/p. 52.

71. Deleuze, *Nietzsche and Philosophy,* p. 40.

72. Friedrich Nietzsche, *Thus Spoke Zarathustra,* trans R. J. Hollingdale (New York: Penguin Books, 1961), p. 245.

73. Ibid., p. 186.

74. See Robert Graves, *The Greek Myths* (New York: Penguin Books, 1980), 2:9.

75. William Shakespeare, *Hamlet,* in *The Complete Works,* ed. Stanley Wells and Gary Taylor (Oxford: Clarendon Press, 1991), III, i, p. 669.

76. Deleuze, *Difference and Repetition,* pp. 89–90, translation altered; *Différence et répétition,* p. 121. This statement resonates greatly with Bergson's description of life itself as proceeding like a shell that bursts into fragments, which in turn burst into fragments, which burst again. Bergson, *Creative Evolution,* p. 98; *Bergson oeuvres,* p. 579. Both Bergson and Deleuze use the word *éclat* to characterize the bursting into fragments, the shattering.

77. For a fuller account of this in terms of Freud and Plato and the critique offered by both Luce Irigaray and Deleuze, see my "Body, Knowledge, and Becoming-Woman: Morpho-logic in Deleuze and Irigaray," in *Feminism and Gilles Deleuze,* ed. Ian Buchanan and Claire Calebrook (London: Blackwell Press, forthcoming). See especially Irigaray, "Plato's Hystera"; and Gilles Deleuze, "Plato and the Simulacra," in *The Logic of Sense,* pp. 253–266; *Logique du sens,* pp. 292–307.

78. Kelly, *Interim,* p. 39.

79. Deleuze, *Difference and Repetition,* p. 90, translation altered; *Différence et répétition,* p. 121.

80. Kelly, *Interim,* p. 39.

81. Ibid., p. 37.

82. Deleuze, *Difference and Repetition,* p. 90, translation altered; *Différence et répétition,* p. 121.

83. See Lawrence Mead, *Beyond Entitlement: The Social Obligation of Citizenship* (New York: Free Press, 1986).

84. See Katz, *Undeserving Poor,* pp. 157, 160, 161. I have altered Katz's argument slightly to emphasize the role of the workers in promoting their own interests. He says: "These gains, however, remain fragile. Only vigorous federal action can prevent their erosion" (p. 161).

Chapter 6

1. See Sigmund Freud, *Beyond the Pleasure Principle,* trans. James Strachey (New York: Bantam Books, 1972), p. 21.

2. Deleuze, *Difference and Repetition,* p. 96; *Différence et répétition,* p. 128; and Freud, *Beyond the Pleasure Principle,* pp. 22–24, 27.

3. Deleuze, *Difference and Repetition,* p. 96, translation altered; *Différence et répétition,* p. 128.

4. Deleuze, *Empiricism and Subjectivity,* pp. 25, 26, 30; *Empirisme et subjectivité,* pp. 7–8, 13.

5. Ibid., p. 31/p. 15.

6. Hume, *Treatise,* pp. 251–252.

7. Ibid., p. 254.

8. Sigmund Freud, *The Ego and the Id,* trans. Joan Riviere, revised and ed. James Strachey (New York: W. W. Norton, 1960), pp. 11, 12, 5.

9. Deleuze, *Difference and Repetition,* p. 97, translation altered; *Différence et répétition,* p. 129.

10. Whereas Jean-François Lyotard is willing to associate even this habitual level with the sublime, I would not be so easily satisfied. See Jean-François Lyotard, "What Is Postmodernism?" in *The Postmodern Condition: A Report on Knowledge,* trans. Geoff Bennington and Brian Massumi (Minneapolis: University of Minnesota Press, 1984), p. 40. I have objected that negative delight in not being subject to privation is not enough to produce the derangement of the senses that unseats the power and authority of representation. See my "Space, Time, and the Sublime."

11. Freud, *Beyond the Pleasure Principle,* p. 35.

12. Ibid., p. 42. Freud provides the example of infantile sexual life, when wishes are incompatible with reality as well as with the child's own immature development and so result in the child's disappointment with her abilities and chances of success in the rest of life.

13. Deleuze, *Difference and Repetition,* p. 98, translation altered; *Différence et répétition,* p. 130. Emphasis added.

14. See Freud, *Beyond the Pleasure Principle,* pp. 37–38, where Freud discusses various situations in which something disagreeable, like tragedy in the theater, can be worked over by the mind to produce pleasure after all. Such cases are of no interest to him because they do not provide evidence of tendencies beyond the pleasure principle, that is, evidence of more primitive tendencies.

15. See ibid., p. 24; and Freud, *Ego and the Id,* p. 45.

16. Deleuze, *Difference and Repetition,* p. 98; *Différence et répétition,* p. 131.

17. Ibid., p. 99/p. 131. Deleuze provides several examples of the child's constitution of the virtual object. Most telling, perhaps, is his revision of Melanie Klein's own formulation of the child whose envy interferes with the ability to accept the good food and the primal good object. The child's response is to suck his (*sic*) own fingers because he has a "grievance" that the milk comes too quickly or too slowly, or that he was not given the breast when he craved it. Some infants, she writes, have great difficulty overcoming these grievances. The child seeks to be free of these feelings of persecutory anxiety and destructive impulses and it is the mother who is thought to be able to accomplish this. See Melanie Klein, *Envy and Gratitude and Other Works* (New York: Free Press, 1975), p. 185.

18. Deleuze, *Difference and Repetition,* p. 99; *Différence et répétition,* p. 131. In *Beyond the Pleasure Principle,* for example, Freud argues that everything living dies for internal reasons, so that self-preservation, self-assertion, and mastery are merely components of the drive toward death warding off all interference so that the organism can die in its own manner. Even the sexual instincts are simply a more extreme version of the other instincts against which they play, that is, which they apparently oppose (pp. 73–75).

19. Deleuze, *Difference and Repetition,* p. 85; *Différence et répétition,* p. 115.

20. Ibid., pp. 75, 75, translation altered/pp. 102, 101.

21. See, for example, Sigmund Freud, "On Narcissism: An Introduction," in *General Psychological Theory,* ed. Philip Rieff (New York: Collier Books, 1972), p. 58.

22. Deleuze, *Difference and Repetition,* p. 100; *Différence et répétition,* p. 133.

23. Freud, *Beyond the Pleasure Principle,* p. 26.

24. Plato, *The Symposium,* trans. Michael Joyce, in *Plato: The Collected Dialogues,* ed. Edith Hamilton and Huntington Cairns (Princeton, N.J.: Princeton University Press, 1969), pp. 526–574. Aristophanes claims that the original globes were half male–half female, but also male-male and female-female, a claim that Plato does not challenge.

25. Freud, *Beyond the Pleasure Principle,* pp. 102, 108–109.

26. See Grisoni, "Onomatopoeia of Desire," p. 170. My thanks to Elizabeth Grosz for pointing out Grisoni's work to me.

27. Ibid., p. 172. Emphasis added.

28. Ibid., p. 177.

29. Deleuze, *Difference and Repetition,* p. 100; *Différence et répétition,* p. 133.

30. Freud, "Instincts and Their Vicissitudes," in *General Psychological Theory,* p. 90.

31. Freud, "On Narcissism: An Introduction," in *General Psychological Theory,* pp. 68–69.

32. Deleuze and Parnet, *Dialogues,* p. 104.

33. Deleuze and Guattari, *Anti-Oedipus,* p. 63; *L'anti-Oedipe,* p. 54.

34. Ibid., pp. 63, 64/pp. 54, 55.

35. Bergson, *Creative Evolution,* p. 147; *Bergson oeuvres,* p. 620.

36. Sigmund Freud, *Three Contributions to the Theory of Sex,* trans. A. A. Brill (New York: E. P. Dutton, 1962), p. 44. At this stage, Freud argues, none of these connections are related to knowledge of a sexual object; they are life-preserving but also autoerotic.

37. See, in particular, Sigmund Freud, "The Development of the Libido and Sexual Organization," in *Introductory Lectures on Psychoanalysis,* trans. James Strachey (New York: W. W. Norton, 1966), pp. 327–329; and Freud, *Three Contributions,* pp. 52, 57.

38. Deleuze, *Difference and Repetition,* p. 101; *Différence et répétition,* p. 134.

39. Freud, "Development of the Libido," p. 329. For an account of "narcissistic identification," see Sigmund Freud, "Mourning and Melancholia," in *The Complete Psychological Works of Sigmund Freud,* ed. James Strachey (London: Hogarth Press, 1974), 4:239–258.

40. Deleuze, *Difference and Repetition,* p. 101, translation altered; *Différence et répétition,* p. 134.

41. Klein, *Envy and Gratitude,* pp. 31–32, 34. Klein also specifies the part-object, the "bad penis," as contributing to the infant's persecutory anxiety, which is ultimately motivated by fear of ego annihilation (an ego built up out of these external and internal part-objects, external bodily parts representing drives and internal drives), which would be executed by the death drive.

42. Deleuze, *Difference and Repetition,* p. 101; *Différence et répétition,* p. 134.

43. Bergson, *Matter and Memory,* pp. 127–129. *Bergson oeuvres,* pp. 271–274.

44. See Edgar Allen Poe, "The Purloined Letter," in *Collected Works of Edgar Allen Poe,* ed. Thomas O. Mabbot (Cambridge, Mass.: Belknap Press, 1978), 3:972–997.

45. See Jacques Lacan, *Écrits,* trans. Alan Sheridan (London: Tavistock Publications, 1977), p. 68. This passage is quoted by Bice Benvenuto and Roger Kennedy in *The Works of Jacques Lacan: An Introduction* (New York: St. Martin's Press, 1986), p. 88. Along with Jane Gallop, Benvenuto and Kennedy manage to retain the disappearing or sliding character of Lacan's pronouncements—Gallop because she reads Lacan on the basis of linguistic theory, and Benvenuto and Kennedy because they recognize the embedded structures of Levi-Strauss. See Jane Gallop, *Reading Lacan* (Ithaca, N.Y.: Cornell University Press, 1985).

46. Deleuze, *Difference and Repetition,* p. 102; *Différence et répétition,* pp. 135–136.

47. Ibid., pp. 85, 102/pp. 115, 136.

48. Ibid., p. 85/p. 115.

49. Ibid., p. 103, translation altered/p. 136. Deleuze is playing here with the chief characteristic of the signifier, that it signifies only in relation to another signifier. So the subject who speaks is but another signifier and disappears as subject. But this greatly contrasts with the virtual past, which has never been a present, which does not even exist but subsists as real but virtual memory, and which therefore cannot be absent, as it has never been present.

50. What fascinates in this scenario are the many layers of repetitions involved, including the past relation between Dupin and the Minister, the exchange of the man's letter for the woman's, the effeminacy of the victim's position shared by the Queen and the Minister, and the invisibility of the letter first to the King, then to the police. See Benvenuto and Kennedy, *Works of Jacques Lacan,* pp. 96–97. See also Jacques Lacan, "Seminar on 'The Purloined Letter,'" trans. Jeffrey Mehlman, in *The Purloined Poe: Lacan, Derrida, and Psychoanalytic Reading,* ed. John P. Muller and William J. Richardson (Baltimore: Johns Hopkins University Press, 1988), pp. 28–54, for example, "what is illustrated here is more gripping still; it is not only the subject, but the subjects, grasped in their intersubjectivity, who line up, in other words, our ostriches, to whom we here return, and who, more docile than sheep, model their very being on the moment of the signifying chain which traverses them" (p. 43).

51. Deleuze, *Difference and Repetition,* p. 103, translation altered; *Différence et répétition,* p. 137.

52. Lacan, "Seminar on 'The Purloined Letter,'" pp. 43–44.

53. Freud, *Beyond the Pleasure Principle,* pp. 69–71, 59, 77.

54. Ibid., pp. 42–43.

55. See Benvenuto and Kennedy, *Works of Jacques Lacan,* p. 167; and Jacques Lacan, "Agency of the Letter in the Unconscious," in *Écrits,* especially pp. 160–161.

56. Deleuze, *Difference and Repetition,* p. 104, translation altered; *Différence et répétition,* p. 137.

57. Lacan, "Seminar on 'The Purloined Letter,'" p. 30.

58. Deleuze, *Difference and Repetition,* pp. 104–105; *Différence et répétition,* p. 138. See also Freud, *Ego and the Id,* pp. 34–35, for an account of primary processes.

59. Deleuze and Guattari, *Anti-Oedipus,* p. 31; *L'anti-Oedipe,* p. 24.

60. See especially "Epilogue: 'Them' or 'Us,'" in Katz, *Undeserving Poor,* pp. 236–244. Katz cites in particular Michael Harrington, who is among the few to point to massive economic and social *transformations* unlike those of the past as chiefly responsible for poverty. See Michael Harrington, *The New American Poverty* (New York: Holt, Rinehart and Winston, 1984).

61. Deleuze, *Difference and Repetition,* p. 106, translation altered; *Différence et répétition,* p. 139.

62. Bergson, *Creative Evolution,* p. 212; *Bergson oeuvres,* p. 675.

63. Deleuze, *Bergsonism,* p. 20. See also Bergson, *Creative Mind,* pp. 130–132; *Bergson oeuvres,* pp. 1348–1350.

64. See my essay "Flows of Desire and the Body," in *Continental Philosophy VII,* ed. Hugh J. Silverman (New York: Routledge Press, forthcoming); reprinted in *Becomings,* ed. Elizabeth Grosz (Ithaca, N.Y.: Cornell University Press, forthcoming).

65. Deleuze, *Nietzsche and Philosophy,* p. 42; *Nietzsche et la philosophie,* p. 49.

66. Ibid., pp. 43–44/pp. 49–50.

67. Ibid., p. 46/p. 51. What is useful here is that this theory opposes both mechanist ideas that differences in quantity balance or cancel out one another between the beginning and final states of a fully reversible system, as if nothing of any import could alter the system along the way. It also opposes thermodynamic ideas that insist that differences in quantity cancel out one another in a system's final state. Both, Deleuze argues, insist upon a final becoming, a final state in which being and nonbeing are equally undifferentiated.

68. Deleuze, *Nietzsche and Philosophy,* pp. 59, 62; *Nietzsche et la philosophie,* pp. 66–67, 70.

69. Deleuze, *Difference and Repetition,* p. 37, translation altered; *Différence et répétition,* p. 55.

70. Ibid., p. 106/p. 141.

71. Ibid., p. 107/p. 141.

72. Foucault, "Theatrum Philosophicum."

73. Deleuze, *Difference and Repetition,* pp. 108–109; *Différence et répétition,* pp. 143–144.

74. Freud argues that although there is no dominance of the pleasure principle in the course of mental processes, there is nonetheless a strong tendency, which is only stopped by other forces or circumstances. In the end, the reality principle only delays the effects of the pleasure principle. See Freud, *Beyond the Pleasure Principle,* pp. 25–26.

75. Ibid., pp. 105–106n, 106–109.

76. Deleuze, *Difference and Repetition,* pp. 109–110; *Différence et répétition,* p. 145. Elsewhere ("Flows of Desire and the Body") I have argued that Deleuze and Guattari believe that the Freudian conception is part of a social and political process that uses it to produce capitalist society. See also the enormously interesting

work of Eugene Holland, "Schizoanalysis: The Postmodern Contextualization of Psychoanalysis," in *Marxism and the Interpretation of Culture,* ed. Cary Nelson and Lawrence Grossberg (Urbana: University of Illinois Press, 1988), pp. 405–416.

77. See Freud, "Narcissism: An Introduction," in *General Psychological Theory,* pp. 57–59.

78. Ibid., p. 61.

79. Deleuze, *Difference and Repetition,* p. 110; *Différence et répétition,* p. 145.

80. Ibid., p. 110, translation altered/pp. 145–146.

81. Freud, *Ego and the Id,* p. 35; see also pp. 30–35 for the account of the previous two paragraphs.

82. Ibid., p. 36.

83. Deleuze, *Difference and Repetition,* p. 111; *Différence et répétition,* p. 147.

84. Freud, *Ego and the Id,* pp. 14–15.

85. Freud, "Narcissism: An Introduction," in *General Psychological Theory,* p. 74.

86. Freud, *Ego and the Id,* p. 20.

87. Ibid., p. 24. Emphasis added.

88. Deleuze, *Difference and Repetition,* p. 111, translation altered; *Différence et répétition,* p. 146.

89. Bergson, *Introduction to Metaphysics,* p. 31; *Bergson oeuvres,* p. 1403.

90. Ibid., p. 32/p. 1404.

91. Ibid., pp. 35–36/pp. 1406–1407.

92. Ibid., p. 36/pp. 1407–1408.

93. Ibid., p. 37/p. 1408.

94. Freud, *Beyond the Pleasure Principle,* pp. 106n, 109.

95. Deleuze, *Difference and Repetition,* p. 111, translation altered; *Différence et répétition,* p. 147.

96. Ibid.

Chapter 7

1. Freud, *Beyond the Pleasure Principle,* p. 37.

2. Bergson, *Creative Mind,* pp. 58–59; *Bergson oeuvres,* pp. 1292–1293.

3. Deleuze, *Difference and Repetition,* p. 112, translation altered; *Différence et répétition,* p. 148.

4. Ibid., p. 114/p. 151. See also Deleuze, *Empiricism and Subjectivity,* p. 92; *Empirisme et subjectivité,* p. 103.

5. Deleuze, *Difference and Repetition,* p. 96; *Différence et répétition,* p. 128; and Freud, *Beyond the Pleasure Principle,* pp. 22–24, 27.

6. Deleuze, *Difference and Repetition,* p. 97; *Différence et répétition,* p. 129.

7. Ibid., p. 113, translation altered/p. 150.

8. First published as the preface to the English translation in Deleuze, *Kant's Critical Philosophy,* pp. vii–xiii. Published in French as "Sur quatre formules poétique qui pourraient résumer la philosophie kantienne," *Philosophie 9* (1986): 29–34. Revised and expanded in *Critique et clinique* (Paris: Minuit, 1993), p. xi.

9. Arthur Rimbaud, "Letter to Paul Demeny, 15 May 1871," in *Rimbaud: Complete Works, Selected Letters,* trans. Wallace Fowlie (Chicago: University of Chicago Press, 1966), p. 304.

10. Kant, *Critique of Judgement,* sect. 23.

11. Ibid., sect. 27. Nonetheless, my impression of Deleuze's reading of Kant in *Kant's Critical Philosophy* is that even the introduction of the Idea of Reason cannot override the "discordant-accord" of free and ultimately unregulated faculties; thus no single faculty dominates. Kant's success in this matter may still be subject to scrutiny.

12. Deleuze, *Difference and Repetition,* p. 115; *Différence et répétition,* pp. 151–152.

13. Nietzsche, *Will to Power,* p. 1062.

14. Deleuze, *Nietzsche and Philosophy,* p. 68; *Nietzsche et la philosophie,* p. 77.

15. Antonin Artaud, "Here Lies," in *Anthology,* ed. Jack Hirschman (San Francisco: City Lights Books, 1965), pp. 238–248.

16. Deleuze, *Difference and Repetition,* p. 113; *Différence et répétition,* p. 148.

17. Artaud, *Anthology,* p. 56.

18. Deleuze, *Logic of Sense,* p. 187; *Logique du sens,* p. 218. In the context of depths and surfaces, bodies and events, or bodies and language, Klein's partial objects come off as "simulacra," entities that have fallen below the level of the idea. It is important to keep in mind that for Klein these partial objects seek integration into the "good" whole, but for Deleuze the simulacrum is exactly what is necessary for the production of becoming or the unconscious because simulacra do not totalize, make laws, or proscribe Ideas. See, especially, the "Twenty-seventh Series: Of Orality," and the "Twenty-eighth Series: Of Sexuality," and—my favorite—the "Twenty-ninth Series: Good Intentions Are Inevitably Punished," all in ibid., pp. 186–209/pp. 217–244.

19. See Melanie Klein, *The Psycho-Analysis of Children,* trans. Alix Strachey (New York: Delacourt Press, 1975). The first quotation is on pp. 125–126, the second on pp. 128–129, and the third on p. 129.

20. Deleuze, *Logic of Sense,* p. 187; *Logique du sens,* p. 218.

21. Ibid., p. 136/p. 161. This is cited more broadly by Philip Goodchild in *Deleuze and Guattari: An Introduction to the Politics of Desire* (London: Sage Publications, 1996), p. 81.

22. Graves, *Greek Myths,* especially sections 118–146. The murder of Linus with a lyre; the murder of Minyan messengers; the sacrifice (or murder) of his own children and his nephew; the murder of Titias in a boxing match; the murder of Sarpdon, a son of Poseidon, for insolence; and the killing of Polygonus and Telegonus, sons of Proteus, in a wrestling match are just of few of Heracles' many familial and social transgressions, most serious enough to require purification.

23. Goodchild, *Deleuze and Guattari,* p. 76.

24. Deleuze, *Difference and Repetition,* p. 33; *Différence et répétition,* pp. 49, 50.

25. Ibid., p. 34/p. 51.

26. Deleuze, *Logic of Sense,* p. 259; *Logique du sens,* pp. 298–299.

27. Ibid., p. 263/p. 304.

28. Deleuze, *Difference and Repetition,* p. 116; *Différence et répétition,* p. 154.

29. Ibid., p. 117/p. 154. See also Constantin V. Boundas, "Deleuze-Bergsonian Ontology of the Virtual," in *Deleuze: A Critical Reader,* ed. Paul Patton (London: Basil Blackwell, 1996), pp. 81–106. According to Boundas, "Deleuze calls 'differen*t*iation' the totality of the diacritical relations which occur 'inside' an Idea-structure [virtual multileveled memory] and their actualizations. 'Differen*c*iation,' therefore, designates the actualization of a virtuality, and it is only one-half the notion of difference. It is the half that cannot account for itself without prior appeal to the process of differen*t*iation" (p. 91).

30. Deleuze, *Difference and Repetition,* p. 117; *Différence et répétition,* p. 154.

31. Ibid., pp. 117–118/p. 155.

32. Antonin Artaud, *Selected Writings,* trans. Helen Weaver, ed. Susan Sontag (New York: Farrar, Straus and Giroux, 1976), p. 243.

33. Ibid., especially pp. 244–267.

34. Ibid., pp. 252–253. It is amusing that the example Artaud uses here is Sophocles' *Oedipus Rex,* which, he maintains, was written to exclude exactly the most powerful forces of destiny or fate in favor of a language that has lost contact with nature's cruelty.

35. Deleuze, *Difference and Repetition,* p. 118, translation altered; *Différence et répétition,* pp. 155–156.

36. *Webster's New Universal Unabridged Dictionary.*

37. Deleuze, *Difference and Repetition,* p. 118; *Différence et répétition,* p. 156.

38. Ibid., p. 120/p. 157. Massumi prefers to call the differenciating of difference "hyperdifferentiation"—that would be, having a differenciation in excess of difference itself. See Massumi, *User's Guide,* p. 91.

39. Deleuze, *Difference and Repetition,* p. 121; *Différence et répétition,* p. 158.

40. Bergson, *Introduction to Metaphysics,* pp. 41–42; *Bergson oeuvres,* pp. 1412–1413.

41. Ibid., p. 31/p. 1403.

42. Ibid., p. 37/p. 1408.

43. Roland Barthes, *Camera Lucida: Reflections on Photography,* trans. Richard Howard (New York: Hill and Wang, 1981); originally published in French as *La chambre claire: Note sur la photographie* (Paris: Cahiers du cinéma, Gallimard, Le Seuil, 1980).

44. See especially Jay, *Downcast Eyes.* Jay's claim that Barthes can be read in terms of Lacan's "Imaginary" and "Symbolic" is supported by other leading critics. Jay cites Gregory L. Ulmer, "The Discourse of the Imaginary," *Diacritics* 10 (March 1980): 61–76; and Lynn A. Higgins, "Barthes's Imaginary Voyages," *Studies in Twentieth Century Literature* 5, no. 2 (spring 1981): 157–174.

45. Roland Barthes, "From Work to Text," in *Textual Strategies,* ed. Josue V. Harari (Ithaca, N.Y.: Cornell University Press, 1979), pp. 76–77.

46. Tom Conley, "A Message without a Code?" *Studies in Twentieth Century Literature* 5, no. 2 (spring 1981): 147–156, cited in Jay, *Downcast Eyes,* p. 450; Jay, *Downcast Eyes,* p. 451.

47. Barthes, *Camera Lucida,* p. 3; *La chambre claire,* p. 13. An obvious issue that has arisen in the years since Barthes wrote this book is the use of computers to alter and even create "photographic" images. Although digital imagery and its manipulation is an important issue, I am going to approach Barthes's texts as he

wrote them, on the basis of the mechanical camera—that is, a camera that relies on what actually has been. I am not sure that his analysis would apply to digital images; however, there is nothing intrinsic to digital images that prevents them from being singular and unique.

48. Ibid., pp. 4, 8/p. 21.

49. Mary Kelly, *Post-Partum Document* (London: Routledge & Keegan Paul, 1985). Kelly's work has finally begun to be given widespread acknowledgment. See, for example, Margaret Iverson, Douglas Crimp, and Homi K. Baba, *Mary Kelly* (London: Phaidon, 1997).

50. Lucy Lippard, "Foreword," in Kelly, *Post-Partum Document,* p. ix.

51. Ibid., p. x.

52. Ibid., p. xiii.

53. Goodchild, *Deleuze and Guattari,* p. 104.

54. Kelly, *Post-Partum Document,* p. xvi.

55. Barthes, *Camera Lucida,* p. 9; *La chambre claire,* pp. 22–23.

56. Ibid., pp. 13–16/pp. 29–31.

57. Kelly, *Post-Partum Document,* p. xvii.

58. Ibid., p. 1.

59. Deleuze, *Logic of Sense,* p. 309; *Logique du sens,* p. 359.

60. Ibid., pp. 304–305/p. 354.

61. Ibid., p. 305, translation altered/p. 354. Tournier's Robinson discovers that the other is a "powerful factor of distraction," precisely because its possibility for showing up casts a dim glimmer of light on objects that are marginal to our attention but could suddenly become the center of our attention because of the presence of the other. See Tournier, *Vendredi,* p. 36.

62. Gatens, "Through a Spinozist Lens," p. 173.

63. Cited in ibid. See Tournier, *Vendredi,* p. 229–230, translation altered.

64. Bergson, *Two Sources of Morality and Religion,* p. 16; *Bergson oeuvres,* p. 987.

65. Deleuze, *Logic of Sense,* p. 309; *Logique du sens,* pp. 358–359. Nothing frightens Defoe's Robinson Crusoe as much as the anticipation of the native cannibals; his elaborate fortifications are constructed principally out of this fear.

66. Ibid., p. 306/p. 355.

67. The photograph Barthes is referring to is by Koen Wessing and was taken in 1979. Wessing seems to have many photographs with this heterogeneous element. See Barthes, *Camera Lucida,* pp. 22, 23; *La chambre claire,* pp. 42, 43, 44.

68. Ibid., p. 20/p. 39.

69. Ibid., pp. 26, 28/pp. 50–51.

70. Deleuze and Guattari, *Anti-Oedipus,* pp. 125, 101; *L'anti-Oedipe,* pp. 105, 85.

71. Barthes, *Camera Lucida,* pp. 26–27; *La chambre claire,* pp. 48–49.

72. Ibid., p. 31/p. 56. Emphasis added.

73. Ibid., pp. 31–32/p. 56.

74. Ibid., pp. 34, 36/p. 61.

75. Kelly, *Post-Partum Document,* pp. 9, 37.

76. Ibid., p. 41.

77. Ibid., p. 72.

78. Bergson, *Creative Evolution,* p. 212; *Bergson oeuvres,* p. 675.
79. Kelly, *Post-Partum Document,* p. 72.
80. Ibid., p. 78.
81. Ibid., p. 92.
82. See Lacan, *Écrits,* p. 68.
83. Kelly, *Post-Partum Document,* p. 100.
84. Ibid., p. 114.
85. Paul Smith, "Mother as Site of Her Proceedings: Mary Kelly's *Post-Partum Document,*" in Kelly, *Post-Partum Document,* pp. 211–212. Originally published in *Parachute* 26 (1982).
86. Deleuze, *Difference and Repetition,* p. 85; *Différence et répétition,* p. 115.
87. Margaret Iverson, "The Bride Stripped Bare by Her Own Desire: Reading Mary Kelly's *Post-Partum Document,*" in Kelly, *Post-Partum Document,* p. 206. Originally published in *Discourse* 4 (1981).
88. Ibid., p. 207.
89. Ibid.
90. Artaud "passed through" the Henri-Rousselle asylum at Sainte-Anne in Paris, whose director, Jacques Lacan, declared that Artaud's psychological state was "fixed" and that he would neither change nor write another line. When, after World War II, Artaud's friends finally got him released from Roudez, where he had undergone some fifty electroshocks, Artaud began to write ceaselessly after many years of near silence. See Stephen Barber, "A Foundry of the Figure: Antonin Artaud," *Artforum* (September 1987): 88–95.
91. Barthes, *Camera Lucida,* p. 43; *La chambre claire,* p. 73.
92. Ibid., p. 45/p. 74.
93. Ibid., sect. 32, 34/sect. 32, 34.
94. An obvious and remarkable case of such a science of the singular is Gilles Deleuze's *Francis Bacon,* which claims to consider the paintings of Francis Bacon from a single aspect, which orders them from the simplest to the most complex from the point of view of a general logic of sensation. Yet there are other aspects to these works as well, aspects that converge in a sensation of color. Each of these two aspects can, as well, thematize a particular series in the history of painting.

Chapter 8

1. Barthes, *Camera Lucida,* pp. 85, 90; *La chambre claire,* pp. 133, 140.
2. Ibid., pp. 92, 96/pp. 144–145, 150.
3. Ibid., pp. 102–105/pp. 157–160.
4. Ibid., p. 87/p. 135.
5. See Félix Guattari, "The Postmodern Dead End," *Flashart* 128 (May/June 1968): 40–41, especially p. 40. See also my essay on the question of the domination of language over other semiotic systems, "The Postmodern Dead End."
6. Deleuze, *Logic of Sense,* p. 1; *Logique du sens,* p. 9.
7. Ibid., p. 2/p. 9.
8. Ibid., p. 2/p. 10.

9. See Plato, *Cratylus,* trans. Benjamin Jowett, in *Plato: The Collected Dialogues,* ed. Edith Hamilton and Huntington Cairns (Princeton, N.J.: Princeton University Press, 1964), pp. 437ff.

10. Deleuze, *Logic of Sense,* pp. 4–5; *Logique du sens,* p. 13.

11. Ibid., p. 5/p. 13.

12. Émile Bréhier, *La théorie des incorporels dans l'ancien stoïcisme* (Paris: Vrin, 1928), pp. 11—13; cited in Deleuze, *Logic of Sense,* p. 5; *Logique du sens,* p. 14.

13. What these forces are and how they act are the subjects of Deleuze and Guattari's study of semiotic systems. A particularly clear account of the material and formal relations involved in the account of forces is given by Brian Massumi in *A User's Guide to Capitalism and Schizophrenia.*

14. Deleuze, *Logic of Sense,* p. 5; *Logique du sens,* p. 14.

15. Ibid., p. 7/pp. 16–17.

16. Ibid., p. 7/p. 17.

17. Ibid.

18. Deleuze sometimes characterizes events as "dialectical" attributes, by which he does not mean to imply that the past and future are synthesized in the infinitive. Rather, past and future inhere in time and divide each present *infinitely;* they are mutually exclusive. The Stoics used the notion of "dialectic" to refer to one of the two parts of logic, the other being rhetoric. Dialectic, in turn, consisted of two parts: the *lekta,* literally "things said," and how the human voice is articulated to say things. See Michael Frede, "Principles of Stoic Grammar," in *Essays in Ancient Philosophy* (Minneapolis: University of Minnesota Press, 1987), p. 303.

19. Deleuze, *Logic of Sense,* p. 6; *Logique du sens,* p. 15. See also Deleuze and Guattari, *Thousand Plateaus,* p. 86; *Mille plateaux,* p. 109.

20. Deleuze, *Logic of Sense,* p. 6; *Logique du sens,* p. 15.

21. Ibid., p. 12/p. 22.

22. Bertrand Russell argues that language serves three purposes: to indicate facts, to express the state of the speaker, and to alter the state of the hearer, though all three are not always present. See Bertrand Russell, *An Inquiry into Meaning and Truth* (London: Allen and Unwin, 1940), p. 204. However, when dealing with the question of what makes a sentence significant, Russell argues that every assertion has a subjective and an objective side. Subjectively the sentence expresses the speaker's beliefs, whereas objectively it indicates or at least intends to indicate a fact (the former if it is true, the latter if it is false). Russell claims that the significance of a sentence is what it expresses, so that true and false sentences are equally significant, but any string of words that cannot express a state of the speaker (beliefs) is nonsense and cannot have any effect on any hearer (p. 171). Most interesting are Russell's conclusions that propositions are psychological occurrences such as images and expectations, and that they are expressed by sentences that assert something else. Thus two sentences with the same meaning express the same proposition (p. 189).

23. Deleuze, *Logic of Sense,* p. 13; *Logique du sens,* p. 23.

24. Ibid.

25. Ibid., pp. 13–14/p. 24.
26. Ibid., pp. 12–13/pp. 22–23.
27. Ibid., p. 14/p. 24.
28. Ibid.
29. Ibid., p. 14/pp. 24–25.
30. Ibid., p. 15/p. 25. Deleuze follows up the implications of this conclusion regarding the absurd in the fifth chapter or series of *The Logic of Sense,* where he develops the series of the absurd in signification as one of four paradoxes that prove the priority of sense over signification.
31. Ibid., p. 15/p. 26.
32. Ibid., p. 16/p. 26.
33. Ibid., p. 16/pp. 26–27.
34. Ibid., p. 16/p. 27.
35. Ibid.
36. Ibid., pp. 17–18/pp. 28–29.
37. Ibid., p. 18/p. 29.
38. Ibid., p. 19/p. 30.
39. Ibid., p. 20/pp. 31–32.
40. Ibid., p. 21/p. 33.
41. Ibid., p. 23/p. 34.
42. Ibid., p. 181/p. 212.
43. Ibid.
44. Ibid., p. 182/p. 212.
45. See note 18, above.
46. Deleuze, *Logic of Sense,* pp. 20–21; *Logique du sens,* p. 32. See also Husserl's account of the noema and noematic expression in Edmund Husserl, *Ideas,* trans. W. R. Boyce Gibson (New York: Collier, 1962), sect. 124.
47. Deleuze, *Logic of Sense,* pp. 182–183; *Logique du sens,* p. 213.
48. Ibid., p. 36/p. 50.
49. Ibid., p. 37/pp. 50–51.
50. Ibid., pp. 37–38/p. 51.
51. Ibid., p. 38/pp. 52–53.
52. Ibid., pp. 40–41/pp. 55–56.
53. Ibid., pp. 184–185/pp. 214–216.
54. The process by which propositional language without a fourth dimension of sense is disengaged from the body begins with the question of how speaking is disengaged from eating and is the subject of the "Twenty-seventh Series: Of Orality," in ibid., pp. 186–195/pp. 217–227.
55. Ibid., p. 190/p. 222. Deleuze points out that this conflict occurs in what Klein characterizes as the infant's "manic-depressive" position of cruelty, whereas the final identification of the ego with the good object comes about in the "paranoid-schizoid" position of aggressiveness, where it *interferes with the depth*—that is, with the body—and so with the sense that it otherwise might produce.
56. So the infant first undergoes a schizophrenic split between the explosive, introjected, and projected internal objects—meaning the body that is fragmented by these objects—and another body named, following Antonin Artaud, the body

without organs. The latter is a body that renounces projection and introjection, a kind of complete body, not unified, not integrated, but the body of heterogeneous affects, of the flow of duration, the first and second passive synthesis, complete in the sense that "everything is action and passion, everything is communication of bodies in depth." Then the infant undergoes a manic-depressive split in which the good object, the idol on high, demands fealty. Ibid., p. 192/p. 224.

57. Ibid., p. 194/pp. 225–226.

58. Deleuze and Guattari, *Thousand Plateaus,* p. 76; *Mille plateaux,* p. 95. See also note 1 in the English translation, where Massumi connects this word to commanding and creating order (p. 523).

59. Ibid., pp. 75–76/pp. 95–96.

60. Ibid., pp. 75–76/pp. 95–96.

61. See Austin, *Philosophical Papers,* pp. 229, 231.

62. Ibid., p. 237.

63. Deleuze and Guattari, *Thousand Plateaus,* pp. 77, 78; *Mille plateaux,* p. 98.

64. Austin, *Philosophical Papers,* p. 238. See also Massumi, *User's Guide,* p. 31. Massumi argues that Austin comes close to asserting a theory of incorporeal transformation (p. 153n42). Treating verbs as forces certainly contributes to this.

65. Deleuze and Guattari, *Thousand Plateaus,* p. 79; *Mille plateaux,* p. 99.

66. Ibid., p. 82/p. 104.

67. Ibid.

68. Ibid., pp. 112, 114, 115/pp. 141, 143, 144.

69. Ibid., pp. 125, 131/pp. 157, 163. See Jacques Lacan, *The Four Fundamental Concepts of Psychoanalysis* (London: Hogarth Press, 1977), pp. 198–199.

70. Deleuze and Guattari, *Thousand Plateaus,* p. 116; *Mille plateaux,* p. 146.

71. Deleuze, "He Stuttered," p. 24.

72. Ibid., p. 23.

73. Ibid., p. 24. See Gustave Guillaume, *Foundations for a Science of Language,* trans. W. Hirtle and J. Hewson (Philadelphia: Benjamins, 1984).

74. Deleuze, "He Stuttered," p. 25.

75. Ronald Bogue, "Deleuze's Style," *Man and World* 29, no. 3 (July 1996, special issue: Gilles Deleuze [1925–1995]): 251–268, especially p. 262.

76. Jay, *Downcast Eyes,* p. 450.

77. Bergson, *Creative Mind,* p. 141; *Bergson oeuvres,* p. 1357. Brian Massumi recounts an interesting experiment that affirms this point. German scientists discovered that when a factual, objective, and everyday account was provided as an explanation of a short story depicted on television, the factual language dampened the story's affective intensity and the story was much more likely to be forgotten by children and adults than when it was presented alone or without this objective language. See Brian Massumi, "The Autonomy of Affect," in *Deleuze: A Critical Reader,* ed. Paul Patton (London: Basil Blackwell, 1996), p. 219.

78. Deleuze, *Kant's Critical Philosophy,* p. xi.

79. Deleuze, *Difference and Repetition,* p. 139; *Différence et répétition,* pp. 181–182.

80. Deleuze, *Kant's Critical Philosophy,* p. 51.

81. Kant, *Critique of Judgment,* sect. 23.

82. Ibid.

83. For a more detailed account of the relation between art and the sublime, see my "Space, Time, and the Sublime."

84. Kant, *Critique of Judgement,* sect. 27, sect. 26.

85. My thanks to Daniel Smith for an account of this in "Deleuze's Concept of the Virtual and the Critique of the Possible," read at the International Association for Philosophy and Literature conference, Villanova University, May 1995.

86. For a fuller treatment of "Ideas as virtual multiplicities" see Paul Patton, "Society as Virtual Idea and Event," read at the International Association for Philosophy and Literature conference, Villanova University, May 1995.

87. Deleuze, *Bergsonism,* p. 97; *Le Bergsonisme,* pp. 99–100.

88. Bergson, *Matter and Memory,* pp. 237–238/p. 367.

89. Ibid., pp. 233–234/pp. 363–364.

90. Deleuze, *Bergsonism,* p. 99; *Le Bergsonisme,* p. 102.

91. See ibid., pp. 17–21/pp. 6–11, for an account of the false problem.

92. A full account of intuition as a method appears in ibid., chap. 1/chap. 1.

93. Deleuze and Guattari, *What Is Philosophy?,* p. 7.

94. Deleuze, *Bergsonism,* pp. 112–113, emphasis added; *Le Bergsonisme,* pp. 118–119.

95. Hume, *Treatise,* pp. 5, 8.

96. Ibid., p. 275.

97. Ibid., pp. 8, 283–284.

98. Bergson, *Two Sources of Morality and Religion,* pp. 43, 252–253; *Bergson Oeuvres,* pp. 1011, 1189–1190. It is somewhat sad that in this text Bergson defends women against the charge of having a lesser intellect than men only to accuse them of being less capable of emotion, although "[w]e need hardly say that there are many exceptions" (p. 44n2/p. 1012n1).

Bibliography

Adams, Parveen. "Symptoms and Hysteria." *Oxford Literary Review* 8, nos. 1–2 (1986).

Alexander, Anna. "The Eclipse of Gender: Simone de Beauvoir and the *Différence* of Translation." *Philosophy Today* 41, no. 1/4 (spring 1997): 112–122.

Alpers, Svetlana. *The Art of Describing: Dutch Painting in the Seventeenth Century.* Chicago: University of Chicago Press, 1983.

Aristotle. *Metaphysics.* Trans. W. D. Ross. In *The Basic Works of Aristotle,* ed. Richard McKeon, pp. 689–926. New York: Random House, 1970.

———. *Physics.* Trans. R. P. Hardie and R. K. Gaye. In *The Basic Works of Aristotle,* ed. Richard McKeon, pp. 218–394. New York: Random House, 1970.

Artaud, Antonin. "Here Lies." In *Anthology,* ed. Jack Hirschmann, pp. 238–248. San Francisco: City Lights Books, 1965.

———. *Selected Writings.* Trans. Helen Weaver, ed. Susan Sontag. New York: Farrar, Straus and Giroux, 1976.

Austin, J. L. *Philosophical Papers.* Oxford: Clarendon Press, 1961.

Baker, G. P., and P. M. S. Hacker. *Frege: Philosophical Excavations.* Oxford: Basil Blackwell, 1984.

Barber, Stephen. "A Foundry of the Figure: Antonin Artaud." *Artforum* (September 1987): 88–95.

Barthes, Roland. *Camera Lucida: Reflections on Photography.* Trans. Richard Howard. New York: Hill and Wang, 1981. Originally published as *La chambre claire: Note sur la photographie.* Paris: Cahiers du cinéma, Gallimard, Le Seuil, 1980.

———. "From Work to Text." In *Textual Strategies,* ed. Josue V. Harari, pp. 76–77. Ithaca, N.Y.: Cornell University Press, 1979.

———. *The Pleasure of the Text.* Trans. R. Miller. New York: Hill and Wang, 1975.
Beauvoir, Simone de. *The Ethics of Ambiguity.* Trans. B. Frechtman. New York: Philosophical Library, 1948. Originally published as *Pour une morale de l'ambiguité.* Paris: Gallimard, 1947.
———. "La *Phénoménologie de la perception* de Maurice Merleau-Ponty." *Les temps modernes* 1, no. 2 (November 1945): 363–367.
———. *The Second Sex.* Trans. H. M. Parshley. New York: Knopf, 1952; rpt., New York: Vintage, 1972. Originally published as *Le deuxième sexe.* Paris: Gallimard, 1949.
Benhabib, Seyla. "Feminism and Postmodernism: An Uneasy Alliance." In *Feminist Contentions: A Philosophical Exchange,* ed. Linda Nicholson, pp. 17–34. New York: Routledge Press, 1995.
Benveniste, Émile. "Man and Language." In *Problems in General Linguistics,* trans. Mary Elizabeth Meek, pp. 195–248. Coral Gables, Fla.: University of Miami Press, 1971.
Benvenuto, Bice, and Roger Kennedy. *The Works of Jacques Lacan: An Introduction.* New York: St. Martin's Press, 1986.
Bergson, Henri. *Bergson oeuvres.* Paris: Presses Universitaires de France, 1959.
———. *Creative Evolution.* Trans. Arthur Mitchell. New York: Modern Library, 1944.
———. *The Creative Mind.* Trans. Mabelle L. Andison. New York: Philosophical Library, 1946.
———. *Introduction to Metaphysics.* Trans. T. E. Hulme. Indianapolis: Bobbs-Merrill, 1955.
———. *Matter and Memory.* Trans. N. M. Paul and W. S. Palmer. New York: Zone Books, 1988.
———. *Time and Free Will: An Essay on the Immediate Data of Consciousness.* Trans. F. L. Pogson. New York: Macmillan, 1959.
———. *The Two Sources of Morality and Religion.* Trans. R. Ashley Audra and Cloudesley Brereton. Garden City, N.Y.: Doubleday, 1935.
Bogue, Ronald. "Deleuze's Style." *Man and World* 29, no. 3 (July 1996, special issue: Gilles Deleuze [1925–1995]): 251–268.
———. "Word, Image and Sound: The Non-Representational Semiotics of Gilles Deleuze." In *Mimesis in Contemporary Theory: An Interdisciplinary Approach,* ed. Ronald Bogue, 2:77–97. Philadelphia: John Benjamins, 1991.
Boundas, Constantin V. "Deleuze-Bergsonian Ontology of the Virtual." In *Deleuze: A Critical Reader,* ed. Paul Patton, pp. 81–106. London: Basil Blackwell, 1996.
———. "Deleuze, Empiricism, and the Struggle for Subjectivity." In *Empiricism and Subjectivity: An Essay on Hume's Theory of Human Nature,* by Gilles Deleuze, trans. Constantin V. Boundas, pp. 1–19. New York: Columbia University Press, 1991.
———. "Deleuze: Serialization and Subject-Formation." In *Gilles Deleuze and the Theater of Philosophy,* ed. Constantin V. Boundas and Dorothea Olkowski, pp. 99–116. New York: Routledge Press, 1994.
———. "The Foreclosure of the Other: From Sartre to Deleuze." *Journal of the British Society for Phenomenology* 24, no. 1 (January 1993): 32–43.

———. "Remember to Forget." Read at the American Philosophical Association, Pacific Division Conference, March 1996.
Braidotti, Rosi. *Nomadic Subjects: Embodiment and Sexual Difference in Contemporary Feminist Theory.* New York: Columbia University Press, 1994.
———. *Patterns of Dissonance.* Trans. Elizabeth Guild. New York: Routledge Press, 1991.
———. "Toward a New Nomadism: Feminist Deleuzian Tracks; or Metaphysics and Metabolism." In *Gilles Deleuze and the Theater of Philosophy,* ed. Constantin V. Boundas and Dorothea Olkowski, pp. 157–186. New York: Routledge Press, 1994.
Bréhier, Émile. *La théorie des incorporels dans l'ancien stoïcisme.* Paris: Vrin, 1928.
Brennan, Teresa. *The Interpretation of the Flesh: Freud and Femininity.* New York: Routledge Press, 1992.
Brentano, Franz. *On the Several Senses of Being in Aristotle.* Trans. Rolf George. Berkeley and Los Angeles: University of California Press, 1975.
Brownmiller, Susan. *Against Our Will.* New York: Simon and Schuster, 1975.
Burgin, Victor. "Geometry and Abjection." In *Psychoanalysis and Cultural Theory: Thresholds,* pp. 11–26. New York: St. Martin's Press, 1986.
Butler, Judith. *Bodies That Matter: On the Discursive Limits of "Sex."* New York: Routledge Press, 1993.
———. *Excitable Speech: A Politics of the Performative.* New York: Routledge Press, 1997.
———. *Gender Trouble.* New York: Routledge Press, 1990.
———. "The Life and Death Struggle of Desire: Hegel and Contemporary Theory." In *Subjects of Desire: Hegelian Reflections in Twentieth-Century France,* pp. 175–238. New York: Columbia University Press, 1987.
———. "Sexual Ideology and Phenomenological Description: A Feminist Critique of Merleau-Ponty's *Phenomenology of Perception.*" In *The Thinking Muse,* ed. Jeffner Allen and Iris Marion Young, pp. 85–100. Bloomington: Indiana University Press, 1989.
———. *Subjects of Desire: Hegelian Reflections in Twentieth-Century France.* New York: Columbia University Press, 1987.
Čapek, Milič. "Microphysical Indeterminacy and Freedom: Bergson and Peirce." In *The Crisis in Modernism: Bergson and the Vitalist Controversy,* ed. Frederick Burwick and Paul Douglass, pp. 171–189. Cambridge, Eng.: Cambridge University Press, 1992.
Carr, David. "Narrative and the Real World." *Theory* 15 (1986): 118–131.
———. *Time, Narrative, and History.* Bloomington: Indiana University Press, 1986.
Carroll, Lewis. *Alice's Adventures in Wonderland* and *Through the Looking-Glass, and What Alice Found There.* London: Octopus Books, 1978.
Casey, Edward S. "The Element of Voluptuousness: Depth and Place Reexamined." In *Merleau-Ponty Vivant,* ed. M. C. Dillon, pp. 1–29. Albany: State University of New York Press, 1995.
Chanter, Tina. *The Ethics of Eros: Irigaray's Rewriting of the Philosophers.* New York: Routledge Press, 1995.
Charcot, J. M. *Oeuvres complètes.* [Paris]: AMS Press, n.d.

Conley, Tom. "A Message without a Code?" *Studies in Twentieth-Century Literature* 5, no. 2 (spring 1981): 147–156.

Copjec, Joan. "Flavit et Disipati Sunt." *October* 18 (fall 1981): 20–40.

———. "The Orthopsychic Subject: Film Theory and the Reception of Lacan." *October* 49 (spring 1989): 53–71.

Cornell, Drucilla. *Beyond Accommodation.* New York: Routledge Press, 1991.

D'Amasio, Antonio. *Descartes' Error: Emotion, Reason and the Human Brain.* New York: Avon Books, 1994.

Damisch, Hubert. *The Origin of Perspective.* Trans. John Goodman. Cambridge, Mass.: MIT Press, 1995.

Defoe, Daniel. *Robinson Crusoe.* New York: Random House, 1990.

Deleuze, Gilles. *Bergsonism.* Trans. Hugh Tomlinson and Barbara Habberjam. New York: Zone Books, 1988. Originally published as *Le Bergsonisme.* Paris: Presses Universitaires de France, 1966.

———. *Cinema I: The Movement-Image.* Trans. Hugh Tomlinson and Barbara Habberjam. Minneapolis: University of Minnesota Press, 1986. Originally published as *Cinéma 1: L'image-mouvement.* Paris: Minuit, 1983.

———. *Cinema II: The Time-Image.* Trans. Hugh Tomlinson and Robert Galeta. Minneapolis: University of Minnesota Press, 1989. Originally published as *Cinéma 2: L'image-temps.* Paris: Minuit, 1985.

———. *Difference and Repetition.* Trans. Paul Patton. New York: Columbia University Press, 1994. Originally published as *Différence et répétition.* Paris: Presses Universitaires de France, 1968.

———. *Empiricism and Subjectivity: An Essay on Hume's Theory of Human Nature.* Trans. Constantin V. Boundas. New York: Columbia University Press, 1991. Originally published as *Empirisme et subjectivité: Essai sur la nature humaine selon Hume.* Paris: Presses Universitaires de France, 1953.

———. *Francis Bacon: Logique de la sensation.* Paris: La Différence, 1984.

———. "He Stuttered." Trans. Constantin V. Boundas. In *Gilles Deleuze and the Theater of Philosophy,* ed. Constantin V. Boundas and Dorothea Olkowski, pp. 23–29. New York: Routledge Press, 1994. Originally published as "Begaya-t-il" in *Critique et clinique* (Paris: Minuit, 1993).

———. *Kant's Critical Philosophy: The Doctrine of the Faculties.* Trans. Hugh Tomlinson and Barbara Habberjam. Minneapolis: University of Minnesota Press, 1984. Originally published as *La philosophie critique de Kant.* Paris: Presses Universitaires de France, 1963.

———. "La conception de la différence chez Bergson." *Les études bergsoniennes* 4 (1956): 77–112.

———. *The Logic of Sense.* Trans. Mark Lester and Charles Stivale, ed. Constantin V. Boundas. New York: Columbia University Press, 1990. Originally published as *Logique du sens.* Paris: Minuit, 1969.

———. *Nietzsche and Philosophy.* Trans. Hugh Tomlinson. New York: Columbia University Press, 1983. Originally published as *Nietzsche et la philosophie.* Paris: Presses Universitaires de France, 1962.

———. "Sur quatre formules poétique qui pourraient résumer la philosophie kantienne." *Philosophie* 9 (1986): 29–34. Revised and expanded in *Critique et clinique.* Paris: Minuit, 1993.

Deleuze, Gilles, and Félix Guattari. *Anti-Oedipus.* Trans. Robert Hurley, Mark Seem, and Helen R. Lane. Vol. 1 of *Capitalism and Schizophrenia.* Minneapolis: University of Minnesota Press, 1983. Originally published as *L'anti-Oedipe: Capitalisme et schizophrénie.* Paris: Minuit, 1972.

———. *Kafka: Toward a Minor Literature.* Trans. Dana Polan. Minneapolis: University of Minnesota Press, 1986. Originally published as *Kafka: Pour une littérature mineur.* Paris: Minuit, 1975.

———. *A Thousand Plateaus.* Trans. Brian Massumi. Vol. 2 of *Capitalism and Schizophrenia.* Minneapolis: University of Minnesota Press, 1987. Originally published as *Mille plateaux: Capitalisme et schizophrénie.* Paris: Minuit, 1980.

———. *What Is Philosophy?* Trans. Hugh Tomlinson and Graham Burchell. New York: Columbia University Press, 1994. Originally published as *Qu'est-ce que la philosophie?* Paris: Minuit, 1991.

Deleuze, Gilles, and Claire Parnet. *Dialogues.* Trans. Hugh Tomlinson and Barbara Habberjam. New York: Columbia University Press, 1987. Originally published as *Dialogues.* Paris: Flammarion, 1977.

Derrida, Jacques. "*Différence.*" In *Margins of Philosophy,* trans. Alan Bass, pp. 1–27. Chicago: University of Chicago Press, 1982.

———. *Of Grammatology.* Trans. Gayatri Chakravorty Spivak. Baltimore: Johns Hopkins University Press, 1976. Originally published as *De la grammatologie.* Paris: Minuit, 1967.

———. "*Ousia* and *Grammé:* A Note to a Footnote in *Being and Time.*" Trans. Edward S. Casey. In *Phenomenology in Perception,* ed. F. J. Smith. The Hague: Nijhoff, 1970, pp. 54–93. Originally published in *L'endurance de la pensée,* pp. 219–266. Paris, 1968.

Diprose, Rosalyn. "In Excess: The Body and the Habit of Sexual Difference." *Hypatia* 6, no. 3 (fall 1991): 156–171.

Doolittle, Hilda (H.D.). "Heat" (1916). In *Chief Modern Poets of Britain and America,* ed. Gerald DeWitt Sanders, John Herbert Nelson, and M. L. Rosenthal, 2:211–212. New York: Macmillan, 1970.

Douglass, Paul. "Deleuze's Bergson." In *The Crisis in Modernism: Bergson and the Vitalist Controversy,* ed. Frederick Burwick and Paul Douglass, pp. 368–388. Cambridge, Eng.: Cambridge University Press, 1992.

Doyle, Arthur Conan. *When the World Screamed and Other Stories.* Professor Challenger Adventures, vol. 2. San Francisco: Chronicle Books, 1990.

Eisenstein, Zillah R. *The Female Body and the Law.* Berkeley and Los Angeles: University of California Press, 1988.

Filarete. *Treatise on Architecture.* Trans. John R. Spencer. New Haven: Yale University Press, 1965.

Foucault, Michel. *The Order of Things: An Archaeology of the Human Sciences.* New York: Vintage Books, 1973. Originally published as *Les mots et les choses.* Paris: Gallimard, 1963.

———. "Theatrum Philosophicum." In *Language, Counter-memory, Practice,* trans. Donald F. Bouchard and Sherry Simon, pp. 165–196. Ithaca, N.Y.: Cornell University Press, 1977.

———. "Truth and Power." In *Power/Knowledge,* trans. Colin Gordon, Leo Marshall, John Mepham, and Kate Soper, ed. Colin Gordon, pp. 109–133. New York: Pantheon Books, 1980.

———. "Two Lectures." In *Power/Knowledge,* trans. Colin Gordon, Leo Marshall, John Mepham, and Kate Soper, ed. Colin Gordon, pp. 78–108. New York: Pantheon Books, 1980.

Frede, Michael. "Principles of Stoic Grammar." In *Essays in Ancient Philosophy,* pp. 301–337. Minneapolis: University of Minnesota Press, 1987.

Freud, Sigmund. *Beyond the Pleasure Principle.* Trans. James Strachey. New York: Bantam Books, 1972.

———. "The Development of the Libido and Sexual Organization." In *Introductory Lectures on Psychoanalysis,* trans. James Strachey, pp. 327–329. New York: W. W. Norton, 1966.

———. *The Ego and the Id.* Trans. Joan Riviere, ed. James Strachey. New York: W. W. Norton, 1960.

———. *General Psychological Theory.* Ed. Philip Rieff. New York: Collier Books, 1972.

———. "Mourning and Melancholia." In *The Complete Psychological Works of Sigmund Freud,* ed. James Strachey, 4:239–258. London: Hogarth Press, 1974.

———. *The Standard Edition of the Complete Psychological Works of Sigmund Freud.* London: Hogarth Press, 1962.

———. *Three Contributions to the Theory of Sex.* Trans. A. A. Brill. New York: E. P. Dutton, 1962.

Fuss, Diana. *Essentially Speaking.* New York: Routledge Press, 1989.

Gallagher, Shaun. "On the Pre-Noetic Reality of Time." In *Écart et Différence: Merleau-Ponty on Seeing and Writing,* ed. Martin Dillon, pp. 134–149. Atlantic Highlands, N.J.: Humanities Press, 1997.

Gallop, Jane. *Reading Lacan.* Ithaca, N.Y.: Cornell University Press, 1985.

Gatens, Moira. *Imaginary Bodies: Ethics, Power and Corporeality.* New York: Routledge Press, 1996.

———. "Through a Spinozist Lens: Ethology, Difference, Power." In *Deleuze: A Critical Reader,* ed. Paul Patton, pp. 162–187. London: Basil Blackwell, 1996.

Gibson, J. J. *The Ecological Approach to Visual Perception.* Ithaca, N.Y.: Cornell University Press, 1976.

———. *Eye and Brain: The Psychology of Seeing.* New York: World University Library, 1976.

———. *The Senses Considered as Perceptual Systems.* Boston: Houghton Mifflin, 1966.

Goodchild, Philip. *Deleuze and Guattari: An Introduction to the Politics of Desire.* London: Sage Publications, 1996.

Gould, Stephen Jay. *Dinosaur in a Haystack: Reflections in Natural History.* New York: Free Press, 1986.

Graves, Robert. *The Greek Myths.* 2 vols. New York: Penguin, 1960.

Grisoni, Dominique. "Onomatopoeia of Desire." Trans. Paul Foss. In *Theoretical Strategies,* ed. Peter Botsman, pp. 169–182. Sydney: Local Consumption

Publications, 1989. Originally published as "Les onomatopées du désir." In *Les dieux dans la cuisine.* Paris: Aubier, 1976.

Grosz, Elizabeth. *Jacques Lacan: A Feminist Introduction.* London: Routledge Press, 1990.

———. "Merleau-Ponty and Irigaray in the Flesh." *Thesis Eleven* 36 (1993): 37–60. Reprinted in *Merleau-Ponty: Interiority and Exteriority,* ed. Dorothea Olkowski and James Morley. Albany: State University of New York Press,1999.

———. *Sexual Subversions: Three French Feminists.* St. Leonards: Allen and Unwin, 1989.

———. *Space, Time, and Perversion.* New York: Routledge Press, 1995.

———. "A Thousand Tiny Sexes: Feminism and Rhizomatics." In *Gilles Deleuze and the Theater of Philosophy,* ed. Constantin V. Boundas and Dorothea Olkowski, pp. 187–210. New York: Routledge Press, 1994.

———. *Volatile Bodies: Towards a Corporeal Feminism.* Bloomington: Indiana University Press, 1994.

Guattari, Félix. "The Postmodern Dead End." *Flashart* 128 (May/June 1968): 40–41.

Guillain, Georges. *J.-M. Charcot, 1825–1893: His Life—His Work.* Trans. Pearce Bailey. New York: Paul B. Hoeber, 1959.

Guillaume, Gustave. *Foundations for a Science of Language.* Trans. W. Hirtle and J. Hewson. Philadelphia: Benjamins, 1984.

Harding, Sandra. *The Science Question in Feminism.* Ithaca, N.Y.: Cornell University Press, 1986.

———. *Whose Science? Whose Knowledge? Thinking from Women's Lives.* Ithaca, N.Y.: Cornell University Press, 1991.

Hardt, Michael. *Gilles Deleuze: An Apprenticeship in Philosophy.* Minneapolis: University of Minnesota Press, 1993.

Harrington, Michael. *The New American Poverty.* New York: Holt, Rinehart and Winston, 1984.

Haslanger, Sally. "On Being Objective, and Being Objectified." In *A Mind of One's Own,* ed. Louise M. Antony and Charlotte Witt, pp. 85–126. Boulder, Colo.: Westview Press, 1993.

Hass, Marjorie. "Thinking Fluids/Fluid Thinking: Irigaray's Critique of Formal Logic." In *Feminist Interpretations of Logic,* ed. Marjorie Hass and Rachel Joffe Falmagne. Forthcoming.

Hayden, Patrick. "From Relations to Practice in the Empiricism of Gilles Deleuze." *Man and World* 4 (July 1995): 1–20.

Higgins, Lynn A. "Barthes's Imaginary Voyages." *Studies in Twentieth Century Literature* 5, no. 2 (spring 1981): 157–174.

Holland, Eugene. "Schizoanalysis: The Postmodern Contextualization of Psychoanalysis." In *Marxism and the Interpretation of Culture,* ed. Cary Nelson and Lawrence Grossberg, pp. 405–416. Urbana: University of Illinois Press, 1988.

Hume, David. *A Treatise of Human Nature.* Oxford: Clarendon Press, 1968.

Husserl, Edmund. *Ideas.* Trans. W. R. Boyce Gibson. New York: Collier, 1962.

Irigaray, Luce. *An Ethics of Sexual Difference.* Trans. Carolyn Burke and Gillian C. Gill. Ithaca, N.Y.: Cornell University Press, 1993. Originally published as *Éthique de la différence sexuelle.* Paris: Minuit, 1984.

———. *Je, Tu, Nous: Toward a Culture of Difference.* Trans. Alison Martin. New York: Routledge Press, 1993. Originally published as *Je, tu, nous.* Paris: Grasset et Fasquelle, 1990.

———. *This Sex Which Is Not One.* Trans. Catherine Porter. Ithaca, N.Y.: Cornell University Press, 1985. Originally published as *Ce sexe qui n'en est pas un.* Paris: Minuit, 1977.

———. *Speculum of the Other Woman.* Trans. Gillian C. Gill. Ithaca, N.Y.: Cornell University Press, 1985. Originally published as *Speculum de l'autre femme.* Paris: Minuit, 1974.

Isaak, Joanna. "Women: The Ruin of Representation." *AFTERIMAGE* (April 1985): 6–8.

Ishiguro, Kazuo. *The Unconsoled.* New York: Knopf, 1995.

Iverson, Margaret, Douglas Crimp, and Homi K. Bhabha. *Mary Kelly.* London: Phaidon, 1997.

James, William. *The Principles of Psychology.* New York: Dover Books, 1950.

Janson, H. W. *History of Art.* New York: Harry N. Abrams, 1971.

Jardine, Alice. *Gynesis: Configurations of Woman and Modernity.* Ithaca, N.Y.: Cornell University Press, 1985.

———. "Woman in Limbo: Deleuze and His Br(others)." *SubStance* 44/45 (1984): 46–59.

Jardine, Alice, and Anne M. Menke, eds. *Shifting Scenes: Interviews on Women, Writing, and Politics in Post-68 France.* New York: Columbia University Press, 1991.

Jay, Martin. *Downcast Eyes: The Denigration of Vision in Twentieth-Century French Thought.* Berkeley and Los Angeles: University of California Press, 1993.

Jones, Kathleen B. *Compassionate Authority: Democracy and the Representation of Women.* New York: Routledge Press, 1993.

Kant, Immanuel. *The Critique of Judgement.* Trans. James Creed Meredith. Oxford: Clarendon Press, 1952.

Katz, Michael B. *The Undeserving Poor: From the War on Poverty to the War on Welfare.* New York: Pantheon, 1989.

Kelly, Mary. *Imagining Desire: Mary Kelly, Selected Writings.* Cambridge, Mass.: MIT Press, 1997.

———. *Interim.* Edinburgh: Fruitmarket Gallery; Cambridge, Eng.: Kettle's Yard Gallery; London: Riverside Studios, 1986.

———. *Post-Partum Document.* London: Routledge & Keegan Paul, 1985.

———. "Re-Presenting the Body: On *Interim,* Part I." In *Psychoanalysis and Cultural Theory: Thresholds,* pp. 51–67. New York: St. Martin's Press, 1986.

Klein, Melanie. "A Contribution to the Psychogenesis of Manic-Depressive States" (1935). In *Love, Guilt and Reparation.* New York: Delacorte Press, 1975.

———. *Envy and Gratitude and Other Works.* New York: Free Press, 1975.

———. *The Psycho-Analysis of Children.* Trans. Alix Strachey. New York: Delacourt Press, 1975.

Koolhaas, Rem, and Bruce Mau. *S, M, L, XL.* New York: Monacelli Press, 1995.

Kovac, Timothy. "The Epistemology of Gender Relations." Senior thesis, University of Colorado, Colorado Springs, 1995.

Kristeva, Julia. *Desire in Language: A Semiotic Approach to Literature and Art.* Trans. Thomas Gora, Alice Jardine, and Leon S. Roudier, ed. Leon S. Roudier. New York: Columbia University Press, 1980.

Lacan, Jacques. *Écrits.* Trans. Alan Sheridan. London: Tavistock Publications, 1977.

———. *The Four Fundamental Concepts of Psychoanalysis.* London: Hogarth Press, 1977.

———. "Seminar on 'The Purloined Letter.'" Trans. Jeffrey Mehlman. In *The Purloined Poe: Lacan, Derrida, and Psychoanalytic Reading,* ed. John P. Muller and William J. Richardson, pp. 28–54. Baltimore: Johns Hopkins University Press, 1988.

Lingis, Alphonso. "The Society of Dismembered Body Parts." In *Gilles Deleuze and the Theater of Philosophy,* ed. Constantin V. Boundas and Dorothea Olkowski, pp. 289–303. New York: Routledge, 1994.

Lippard, Lucy. "Foreword." In *Post-Partum Document,* by Mary Kelly, pp. ix–xiv. London: Routledge & Keegan Paul. 1985.

Lyotard, Jean-François. "What Is Postmodernism?" In *The Postmodern Condition: A Report on Knowledge,* trans. Geoff Bennington and Brian Massumi, pp. 71–82. Minneapolis: University of Minnesota Press, 1984.

MacKinnon, Catharine. *Feminism Unmodified.* Cambridge, Mass.: Harvard University Press, 1987.

———. *Toward a Feminist Theory of the State.* Cambridge, Mass.: Harvard University Press, 1989.

Magazine litteraire 257 (September 1988): 14–65.

Martin, Jean-Clet. *Variations: La philosophie de Gilles Deleuze.* Paris: Payot, 1993.

Massumi, Brian. "The Autonomy of Affect." In *Deleuze: A Critical Reader,* ed. Paul Patton, pp. 217–239. London: Basil Blackwell, 1996.

———. *A User's Guide to Capitalism and Schizophrenia: Deviations from Deleuze and Guattari.* Cambridge, Mass.: MIT Press, 1992.

May, Todd. "Difference and Unity in the Thought of Gilles Deleuze." In *Gilles Deleuze and the Theater of Philosophy,* ed. Constantin V. Boundas and Dorothea Olkowski, pp. 33–50. New York: Routledge Press, 1994.

———. "Gilles Deleuze and the Politics of Time." *Man and World* 28, no. 3 (July 1996): 293–304.

Mead, Lawrence. *Beyond Entitlement: The Social Obligation of Citizenship.* New York: Free Press, 1986.

Merleau-Ponty, Maurice. *La nature: Notes, cours du Collège de France.* Ed. Dominique Séglard. Paris: Seuil, 1995.

———. *Phenomenology of Perception.* Trans. Colin Smith, ed. Forrest Williams. New York: Routledge Press, 1962. Originally published as *Phénoménologie de la perception.* Paris: Gallimard, 1945.

———. *The Prose of the World.* Trans. John O'Neill. Evanston, Ill.: Northwestern University Press, 1973. Originally published as *La prose du monde.* Paris: Gallimard, 1969.

———. *Signs.* Trans. Richard McCleary. Evanston, Ill.: Northwestern University Press, 1964. Originally published as *Signes.* Paris: Gallimard, 1960.

———. *The Structure of Behavior.* Trans. Alden L. Fisher. Boston: Beacon Press, 1967. Originally published as *La structure du comportement.* Paris: Presses Universitaires de France, 1942.

———. *The Visible and the Invisible.* Trans. Alphonso Lingis. Evanston, Ill.: Northwestern University Press, 1968. Originally published as *Le visible et l'invisible.* Paris: Gallimard, 1964.

Mill, John Stuart, and Harriet Taylor. *The Subjection of Women.* Indianapolis: Hackett Books, 1988.

Moi, Toril. *Sexual/Textual Politics: Feminist Literary Theory.* New York: Methuen, 1985.

Montrelay, Michele. "Inquiry into Femininity." Trans. Parveen Adams. *m/f* 1 (1978): 83–101. Reprinted in *French Feminist Thought,* ed. Toril Moi, pp. 227–249. Oxford: Basil Blackwell, 1987.

Mulvey, Laura. "Visual Pleasure and Narrative Cinema." In *Film Theory and Criticism,* ed. Gerald Mast and Marshall Cohen, pp. 57–69. Oxford: Oxford University Press, 1985.

Nietzsche, Friedrich. *On the Genealogy of Morals.* Trans. Walter Kaufmann. New York: Vintage Books, 1969.

———. *Thus Spoke Zarathustra.* Trans. R. J. Hollingdale. New York: Penguin, 1961.

———. *The Will to Power.* Trans. Walter Kaufmann and R. J. Hollingdale. New York: Vintage Books, 1968.

Nye, Andrea. *Words of Power: A Feminist Reading of the History of Logic.* New York: Routledge Press, 1990.

Olkowski, Dorothea. "Beside Us, in Memory." *Man and World* 28, no. 3 (July 1996): 283–292.

———. "Body, Knowledge, and Becoming-Woman: Morpho-logic in Deleuze and Irigaray." In *Feminism and Gilles Deleuze,* ed. Ian Buchanan and Claire Calebrook. London: Blackwell Press, forthcoming.

———. "Flows of Desire and the Body." In *Continental Philosophy VII,* ed. Hugh J. Silverman. New York: Routledge Press, forthcoming. Reprinted in *Making Futures: Explorations in Time, Memory, and Becoming,* ed. Elizabeth Grosz. Ithaca, N.Y.: Cornell University Press, forthcoming.

———. "Gilles Deleuze." In *Routledge Encyclopedia of Philosophy,* pp. 856–861. London: Routledge Press, 1998.

———. "Heidegger and the Limits of Representation." In *Postmodernism and Continental Philosophy,* ed. Hugh J. Silverman and Donn Welton, pp. 96–109. Albany: State University of New York Press, 1988.

———. "*Kolossos:* The Measure of a Man's Cize." In *Feminist Interpretations of Jacques Derrida,* ed. Nancy Holland, pp. 215–230. State College: Pennsylvania State University Press, 1997.

———. "Materiality and Language: Butler's Interrogation of the History of Philosophy." *Philosophy and Social Criticism* 23, no. 3 (spring 1997): 37–53.

———. "Merleau-Ponty: The Demand for Mystery in Language." *Philosophy Today* 31, no. 4/4 (winter 1987): 252–258.

———. "Nietzsche-Deleuze: The Aesthetics and Ethics of Chance." *Journal of the British Society for Phenomenology* 26, no. 1 (January 1995): 27–42.

———. "Nietzsche's Dice Throw: Tragedy, Nihilism, and the Body without Organs." In *Gilles Deleuze and the Theater of Philosophy,* ed. Constantin V. Boundas and Dorothea Olkowski, pp. 119–140. New York: Routledge Press, 1994.

———. "Phenomenology and Feminism." In *Edinburgh Encyclopedia of Continental Philosophy.* Edinburgh: Edinburgh University Press, 1999.

———. "The Postmodern Dead End: Minor Consensus on Race and Sexuality." *Topoi* 12 (1993): 161–166.

———. "Semiotics and Gilles Deleuze." In *The Semiotic Web, 1990: Recent Developments in Theory and History,* ed. Thomas A. Sebeok and Jean Umiker-Sebeok, pp. 285–306. Berlin: Mouton de Gruyter, 1990.

———. "Space, Time, and the Sublime." In *The Question of the Other: Essays in Contemporary Continental Philosophy,* ed. Arleen B. Dallery and Charles E. Scott, pp. 175–185. Albany: State University of New York Press, 1989.

———. "Teresa Brennan's *The Interpretation of the Flesh: Freud and Femininity.*" *Journal of the History of Sexuality* 4, no. 4 (April 1994): 648–650.

Patton, Paul. "Mabo: Freedom and the Politics of Difference." *Australian Journal of Political Science* 30 (1995): 108–119.

———. "Society as Virtual Idea and Event." Read at the International Association for Philosophy and Literature conference, Villanova University, May 1995.

Penley, Constance. *The Future of an Illusion.* Minneapolis: University of Minnesota Press, 1989.

Plato. *Cratylus.* Trans. Benjamin Jowett. In *Plato: The Collected Dialogues,* ed. Edith Hamilton and Huntington Cairns, pp. 421–525. Princeton, N.J.: Princeton University Press, 1961.

———. *Gorgias.* Trans. W. D. Woodhead. In *Plato: The Collected Dialogues,* ed. Edith Hamilton and Huntington Cairns, pp. 229–307. Princeton, N.J.: Princeton University Press, 1961.

———. *The Symposium.* Trans. Michael Joyce. In *Plato: The Collected Dialogues,* ed. Edith Hamilton and Huntington Cairns, pp. 526–574. Princeton, N.J.: Princeton University Press, 1969.

Poe, Edgar Allen. "The Purloined Letter." In *Collected Works of Edgar Allen Poe,* ed. Thomas O. Mabbot, 3:972–997. Cambridge, Mass.: Belknap Press, 1978.

Rawls, John. *Political Liberalism.* New York: Columbia University Press, 1993.

———. *A Theory of Justice.* Cambridge, Mass.: Harvard University Press, 1971.

Rich, Adrienne. "Compulsory Heterosexism and Lesbian Existence." *Signs* 5, no. 4 (1980): 631–660.

Rimbaud, Arthur. *Rimbaud: Complete Works, Selected Letters.* Trans. Wallace Fowlie. Chicago: University of Chicago Press, 1966.

Russell, Bertrand. *An Inquiry into Meaning and Truth.* London: Allen and Unwin, 1940.

Sartre, Jean-Paul. *Being and Nothingness.* Trans. Hazel Barnes. New York: Washington Square Press, 1971.

Saussure, Ferdinand de. *Course in General Linguistics.* Trans. Wade Baskin, ed. Charles Bally and Albert Sehehaye. New York: McGraw-Hill, 1966.

Schor, Naomi. "This Essentialism Which Is Not One: Coming to Grips with Irigaray." *Differences* 1, no. 2 (summer 1989): 38–58.

Shakespeare, William. *Hamlet.* In *The Complete Works,* ed. Stanley Wells and Gary Taylor, pp. 653–690. Oxford: Clarendon Press, 1991.

Smith, Daniel. "Deleuze's Concept of the Virtual and the Critique of the Possible." Read at the International Association for Philosophy and Literature conference, Villanova University, May 1995.

Summers, David. *Michelangelo and the Language of Art.* Princeton, N.J.: Princeton University Press, 1981.

Thornton, Merle. "Sex Equality Is Not Enough for Feminism." In *Feminist Challenges,* ed. Carole Pateman and Elizabeth Gross, pp. 77–98. Boston: Northeastern University Press, 1986.

Tournier, Michel. *Vendredi ou les limbes du Pacifique.* Paris: Gallimard, 1972.

Tuana, Nancy. "The Weaker Seed: The Sexist Bias of Reproductive Theory." *Hypatia* 3, no. 1 (spring 1988): 35–59.

Turim, Maureen. "What Is Sexual Difference?" *AFTERIMAGE* (April 1985): 4–5.

Ulmer, Gregory L. "The Discourse of the Imaginary." *Diacritics* 10 (March 1980): 61–76.

Whitford, Margaret. *Luce Irigaray: Philosophy in the Feminine.* New York: Routledge Press, 1991.

Wolsky, Maria de Issekutz, and Alexander A. Wolsky. "Bergson's Vitalism in the Light of Modern Biology." In *The Crisis in Modernism: Bergson and the Vitalist Controversy,* ed. Frederick Burwick and Paul Douglass, pp. 153–170. Cambridge, Eng.: Cambridge University Press, 1992.

Young, Iris Marion. *Justice and the Politics of Difference.* Princeton, N.J.: Princeton University Press, 1990.

———. "Throwing Like a Girl: A Phenomenology of Feminine Body Comportment, Motility, and Spatiality." In *The Thinking Muse: Feminism and Modern French Philosophy,* ed. Jeffner Allen and Iris Marion Young, pp. 51–70. Bloomington: Indiana University Press, 1989.

———. "Together in Difference: Transforming the Logic of Group Political Conflict." In *The Rights of Minority Cultures,* ed. Will Kymlicka, pp. 155–176. Oxford: Oxford University Press, 1995.

Index

Compositor:	Impressions Book and Journal Services, Inc.
Text:	10/12 Times Roman
Display:	Helvetica
Printer:	Edwards Bros.
Binder:	Edwards Bros.

Al-

ace

Book 3: Shadow Soul

What Follows

SHADOW SOUL

A DI TUDOR MANX MYSTERY

DYLAN H. JONES

LUME BOOKS
A JOFFE BOOKS COMPANY

LUME BOOKS
A JOFFE BOOKS COMPANY

Revised edition 2023
Lume Books, London
A Joffe Books Company
www.lumebooks.co.uk

First published by Bloodhound Books in Great Britain in 2020

Cover art by Imogen Buchanan

ISBN: 978-1-83901-538-0

First to read. First to comment. First to say he was proud.
This book is dedicated to Hugh John Jones; avid crime thriller reader, ex-RAF serviceman, devoted father. 1936–2018

How can I be substantial if I do not cast a shadow? I must have a dark side also if I am to be whole.—Carl Jung

PART I

KILL STRIKE

Prologue

RAF Waddington, Lincolnshire, UK

Flight Lieutenant Bobbie Matthews wasn't the kind of woman who scared easily. But that morning, as she walked across the parade ground, she was hit by a sensation of impending dread that shook her to the bone. To her west, the ground control station appeared to take the shape of an oversized metallic coffin, the flat light of dawn falling across its brutal angular shape like a shroud. The image struck her with such force she imagined the earth would swallow the structure whole; ashes to ashes, dust to dust.

The Box, as it had become known to the Royal Air Force's Thirteen Squadron, was a former shipping container. Stripped to the bones, it now housed four banks of high definition monitors, several rows of back-lit switches, and a pair of joysticks that sometimes in her sleep Bobbie would imagine her fingers were still coiled around, as if for those eight hours she missed their satisfying feel in her hand.

The Box, however, required no sleep. All it required was a constant feed of electricity and the low hum of air conditioning to cool the racks of hard drives and communication systems. It was staffed 24/7 to accommodate the demands of the United States Joint Special Operations Command at Creech Air Force Base, located in the Nevada desert. RAF Waddington was eight hours ahead and served as an extension of the US Air Force, helping to facilitate round-the-clock surveillance with handovers between Creech and Waddington every twelve hours.

The demands of the war on terror, Bobbie had come to learn, were as ceaseless as the war itself.

The day had cast its typical soupiness over Lincolnshire, the sky undecided as to its true intentions, shifting from peaks of blue to murky greyness depending on the wind. To Bobbie's left, the Air Seeker Annex jutted out sharply from the ground, as if the building were constructed in italic to make some kind of point. To her right, the hangars housing the Sentry, Sentinel and Shadow aircraft loomed wide, and beyond the hangars, the wide expanse of the airfield butted against the outskirts of the RAF families' accommodation from where Bobbie had just driven.

She drew her jacket tight over her flying suit as a regiment of cadets jogged past. 'Squintos' – a new batch of intelligence officers in basic training. *They'll need the exercise*, Bobbie thought, as the dull march of their boots faded to silence. Squintos were expected to stare into computer screens for hours, analysing the constant data flow streaming into the command centre. Bobbie herself had spent twelve months as a squinto. She'd left after a year and enrolled in the RAF's unmanned aircraft training programme, which had just opened its doors to non-commissioned pilots. She completed her officer training at RAF Cranwell, then was posted to USAF Creech to complete her formal drone training, graduating with the clunky title of remote piloted aircraft systems (pilot). Six months later she found herself in command of a MQ-9 Reaper Drone as a flight lieutenant. She may still have been sitting behind a desk, but that desk connected her to £20 million of weaponry, which was capable of striking a target with surgical accuracy from fifty thousand feet. Bobbie had never felt more alive than when she took control of the drone, seven hundred pounds of explosive racked in the rails, her finger poised to rain a Hellfire missile on a convoy of insurgents.

As she pulled open the station door, a blast of cold air brushed over her face. Typically, she would have begun visualising the day's mission – slipping herself into the zone – but the feeling of dread she'd had minutes before arced through her. She shrugged it off as pre-mission jitters.

'You're late,' Officer Cadet Cole Dawson said, smiling.

Bobbie stood by the doorway and took a deep, meditative breath.

The sense of something not being quite right lay heavy on her chest. Settling herself into her chair, she glanced at her watch. 'Twenty-three seconds late, Dawson. Seriously?'

'Nah,' he said, adjusting his neck. 'Just pulling your leg, blame it on the boredom.'

Bobbie checked her monitors. 'If I'd known I was here for your entertainment, I'd have prepared some suitable material.'

Dawson chuckled. Thirty-one years old, and with a sickly complexion in need of a long holiday somewhere sun-drenched, Dawson was a sensor operator in command of the Reaper's high definition camera and tasked with ensuring they had constant eyes on the high value target (HVT). He also controlled the Reaper's laser, which was required to be pinpoint accurate before Bobbie pulled the trigger. If the laser was one degree off azimuth when the missile left the rails, it could mean the difference between striking an HVT right between the eyes or obliterating the convoy of families travelling with him – a mistake Dawson wasn't keen to repeat.

'Don't you know the party doesn't start until I get here?' Bobbie said, adjusting the chair to accommodate her slender five-feet-nine-inch frame, though in her flying suit she looked shorter, and more vulnerable than she wanted to appear.

'They didn't mention that in the mission briefing.'

'You don't have it tattooed on your arse by now?'

He smiled and tilted the camera, revealing miles of dirt-brown desert fifty thousand feet below. 'Bobbie's way, or the highway?'

'I respect a man who knows his place.' Bobbie secured her headset and adjusted her comms. The voice of the 89th Attack Squadron Reaper pilot broke through the static – Lieutenant Colonel Benton Lowell. She'd trained with Benton back at Creech.

'All's good in the free world, Dazzle's in the Box,' Benton said, his voice oozing an easy American confidence. Bobbie had earned the moniker Dazzle when she began customising her headset with imitation gems she bought at a cheap craft store off the Las Vegas strip. At the time, she imagined the gems were some nod to her femininity, but later she began to wonder if she had just been trying to infuse a jolt of colour into the drab sandy beige of war.

'Are we clear to match eyes?' Bobbie said, studying the barren desert topography.

'Straight down to it, huh?' Benton said. 'You see what I'm seeing?'

Dawson gave Bobbie the thumbs up and rotated the camera. 'Brown terrain. Lots of it.'

'Yeah, different day, same shit.'

'Recon details?'

Dawson slid her a document. 'Red card holder approved,' he confirmed, pointing at the base commander's signature – the final word in authorising kill strikes.

Benton spoke. 'We've been tracking a convoy of technicals, driving south from Mosul, since zero hundred hours, but we've had bugs on the windshield for the past ninety minutes.'

'Sandstorm?'

'The goddamn mother of. Visibility's returning to situation normal, but the weather geeks predict an encore by sundown.'

'Roger that,' Bobbie said, scribbling on her notepad. 'Any additional intel you lot need to brief us on?'

'You lot?' Benton laughed. 'You mean the guys who trained your sorry asses?'

'Correct.' If Bobbie had eyes on Benton, he'd no doubt be making a gesture that included lifting one, or both, of his middle fingers to the screen.

'Yeah, we got your intel. Technicals are axle-heavy with metal. Check out the trailer we made earlier.' Benton chuckled as he replayed the footage of a convoy of trucks reversing into a narrow entrance to the right of a high-walled compound. 'That's some real Mister Bean parking shit, right there,' he said, as the trucks took several attempts to reverse into position. 'Now, watch this,' he added, as a group of men jumped from the trucks and stood in a chain formation at the entrance.

'Anti-aircraft?' Bobbie asked, as the men passed large items of weaponry to each other and onto the truck's flatbeds.

'Fifty-millimetre, standard Russian Army issue, captured from their shitshow in Afghanistan. We counted six weapons stacked like they were heading to holy freakin' war.'

'Why didn't you strike before they left the compound?'

'CIVACS,' Benton confirmed. 'Women and children in the vicinity. We began tracking as soon as they stepped on the gas.'

'Copy that,' Bobbie said.

'FYI, we're keeping safety eyes on another convoy travelling three kilometres behind,' Benton said.

'Friendlies?'

'Unconfirmed, but we scrambled an F15 to keep eyes on them.'

'Can you patch me into their comms?'

'Negative. We've got signal blockers along the route. If they're friendlies, let's hope they've got enough smarts to keep their distance when you rain down the shit parade. If they're with the HVT, then send the other Hellfire their way, compliments of the US of A.'

'Roger that. Assuming control of Reaper in fifteen,' she said, folding her fingers gently around the joystick.

'You ready to save the world?'

'Always. Assuming control in ten.'

'Don't fuck up our good work now, ya hear?'

'Good pep talk, Benton.'

Dawson nodded at Bobbie. 'It's all yours.'

'Confirm. I have control of Reaper craft.'

'Have a nice day blowing shit up, Dazzle. Out.'

With the Reaper under her command, Bobbie rested the joystick in her palm, her muscle memory kicking in. She sensed herself falling into the zone – the critical mindspace where her mind bonded with the pitch and roll of the Reaper as it cleaved through the atmosphere 3,000 miles away. Lost in the motion, she barely heard her overseer, Flight Commander James Flynt, step in and take position at the rear of the Box. Flynt had a reputation for making swift decisions concerning kill strikes – 'the more the merrier' seemed to be his default setting.

‘Ready to show those Johnny Jihadis some of our Yorkshire mettle, Flight Lieutenant Matthews?’

‘I’m from Wales sir, but yes, I’m briefed and strike-prepared.’

‘Christ, not the sentimental Welsh type, are you? Cry at the sight of a leek or a bloody daffodil?’

‘No, no sentiment at all, sir, just here to do my job,’ she confirmed, keeping her focus steely-eyed and unblinking.

Flynt swiped the nine-line approval document from the desk. ‘Estimated strike time?’

Bobbie confirmed the convoy’s co-ordinates. ‘Two miles south there’s an open stretch of road, should be a safe strike zone.’

‘Visibility?’

Dawson checked his instruments. ‘Significant cloud cover, I could lose altitude, but the HVT might spot the craft.’

‘Drop thirty angels,’ Flynt said, as the convoy throttled fast over the dust-ridden road. ‘At this speed, they’ve got one eye on the road and the other on those seventy-two virgin maidens they’ve been promised.’

Bobbie pushed forward on the joystick, felt herself sinking into the chair as the drone dropped 22,000 feet in seconds.

Flynt jabbed Dawson in the shoulder. ‘Keep that laser clear of the windows. If they see that little red dot, they’re squirting out of there faster than ten pints and a vindaloo.’

‘Nice image, sir,’ Dawson said, tracking the laser as it traced past the trucks and to the roadside to avoid any reflections.

‘What’s our strike azimuth?’ Bobbie asked, rolling the joystick left and right so Dawson could match the roll of the gyroscopic camera ball with the Reaper’s pitch.

‘Two degrees. Once they hear the sonic boom, it’s bye-bye time.’

‘Like shooting shopping trolleys in the Manchester Ship Canal,’ Flynt said, stretching out his back.

Bobbie focused on the laser as it swept ahead of the convoy. ‘Releasing Hellfire in twenty,’ she said, bracing herself. A hush fell over the station. ‘Releasing in ten. Standby.’

As he ran his index finger along the rib of the tracker, Dawson turned. 'What the...?' he asked, rotating the camera and directing the lens towards a large mass on a collision course with the convoy.

'Shit!' Bobbie said, her eyes scanning across the monitors. 'Creech alerted us of sandstorms in the vicinity.'

Flynt huffed. 'Not going to let a bit of sand fuck up our mission are we, Matthews?'

'No, sir. I'll drop angels, pull down past the cloud cover.'

Dawson swung the camera around. 'I'm losing eyes on the laser track,' he said. 'We're fighting a forty-five-knot crosswind from the sandstorm, and it's increasing.'

'No time like the present, then, Matthews. You're red card holder approved, make the strike.'

Bobbie hesitated. 'Sir, I don't think–'

'Right,' Flynt interrupted. 'You don't think. You carry out the orders as presented. Flight Lieutenant, take the strike.'

'Shit!' Dawson said, his voice a pitch higher. He swivelled the camera. 'There's another convoy following behind.'

'Identification?'

'Visibility's gone to shit.'

'More Johnny bloody Jihadis. One stone, two birds, I'd count that as a good day in the Box. Now take the strike,' Flynt said.

Bobbie wiped the sweat from her brow. 'You don't have all the intel. Creech thinks we have friendlies tailing the convoy.'

'Christ!' Flynt said, flinging the document onto the desk. 'Make comms contact, find out who they are and what the fucking high hell they're doing in our strike zone.'

'Negative. US Forces planted signal blockers along the route.'

'Oh, it just gets better and better,' Flynt said, leaning over Bobbie's shoulder. 'Dawson, how close are they?'

He surveyed the bank of monitors. 'Less than two kilometres, but the HVT's decreasing speed because of the storm.'

'What's the blast radius of the Hellfire, Dawson?'

'Fifteen-metre kill radius. Wounding radius twenty metres.'

Flynt slapped the back of Dawson's chair. 'Then we strike. They'll see the fireworks but they're clear of the kill radius. If they're friendlies they can assist with the battle damage assessment, if not, we'll send them the other Hellfire with our compliments.'

Sweat oozed from Bobbie's palms as she tightened her grip and dragged her index finger hesitantly along the trigger.

'Matthews, do I have to jump in that seat myself?'

'No, sir!' she said, shaking her head as if she were dislodging the fragments of doubts lodged in there.

Flynt leaned close, his mouth inches from Bobbie's ear. 'You said you weren't the sentimental type,' he said. 'Prove it.'

Rebelling against everything her body and mind seemed to be telegraphing, she drew back the trigger.

'Three… two… one.'

Bobbie's eyes were focused tight on the monitors as the missile sliced effortlessly through the clouds towards its target.

'Rifle, rifle. Hellfire has left the rails,' she confirmed.

Silence fell over the Box, all eyes focused on the central monitor as the ground approached at supersonic speed.

'Contact in ten,' Dawson said. 'Nine, eight, seven.'

Fine. It's all going to be fine. Just another day in the Box, Bobbie mouthed silently.

'Three, two, one…'

The missile ploughed into the heart of the convoy just as the rolling dirt cloud of the sandstorm did the same. A momentary flash of bright white saturated the screens. Bobbie sighed with relief as the trailing convoy came to a stop. Whoever they were, they were safe.

She was about to drop the Reaper to conduct a routine battle damage assessment when the screen seemed to implode in a bleach-white flash. The staff reeled back, as if they could feel the blast from the secondary explosion sear their faces.

It seemed to take an eternity for the screen to clear. When it finally did, Bobbie blinked several times to allow the scene to sink in. Below them, a tangle of metal was strewn across the ground. Smoke drifted in thick, black billows, the desert black and scorched as if a huge blow torch had been taken to the earth.

'BDA, now!' Flynt barked.

As the camera swooped over the wreckage the collateral damage was undeniable. Spirals of metal tossed in every direction; human limbs scattered across the road like discarded doll parts. Battle damage assessment: it was the worst part of the job for a Reaper pilot. Maybe the Reaper drone was named for that very reason; you were required to reap what you sowed.

'What the bloody hell just happened?' Flynt said. 'There's no way our missile caused that cluster fuck.'

A solemn shaking of heads was followed by silence as the camera conducted a secondary recon over the devastation.

'We must have hit the second convoy,' Dawson said.

'No. Can't have, we didn't have the fire power,' Flynt said.

Dawson directed the cameras high to scour the scene; an apocalypse broadcast in 1080p high definition.

Bobbie sat bolt upright. 'Zoom in, there,' she said, gesturing to the lower third of the screen.

Dawson focused on a truck door flung several metres from the road, smoke rising from the steel. The camera lingered over a dust-baked cartoon image painted on the side of the door. 'Road Runner? Someone's got a sick sense of humour,' he said.

A cold slab of stone settled in Bobbie's stomach – the aftershock of the feeling of dread that had overcome her an hour earlier.

'Matthews?' Dawson said, noticing her thousand-yard stare.

Bobbie's words scraped dry over her throat. 'It's Danvir–' she said, her voice barely a cracked whisper. 'Danvir's regiment.'

Dawson glanced at the six by four inch photograph taped to the hard drive closest to Bobbie. 'Shit,' he said, looking over the snapshot: Six uniformed officers assigned to the RAF Medical Services Branch kneeling by a truck with a Road Runner cartoon painted onto the door.

'You don't even know—'

'A wife knows,' she interrupted. She stared down at the joystick – it was slick with sweat. She wanted to wrench it from its foundations, crush it until it was nothing but dust.

'Was he even–' Dawson began.

'Trust me,' she said, standing, though her legs felt as if they might betray her at any moment. She pushed away her chair and walked towards the station door.

'Matthews!' Flynt said. 'You require your commanding officer's permission to leave this station.'

Bobbie wasn't listening. His voice was background noise as she shut the steel door behind her.

She walked to her car, steadied herself, then bent over, hands on knees, and retched. Raising her head, she looked over to the ground control station and wondered if maybe it had all been a bad dream, a nightmare she would soon wake from.

The tears pooling in her eyes and the blackness gathering deep inside her told her otherwise. A wife knew. A wife always knew.

ISLE OF ANGLESEY, WALES

TWELVE MONTHS LATER

Chapter 1

Detective Inspector Tudor Manx had, by the age of forty-nine, come to accept his father's failings; they were all too human, just like his own. He'd forgiven his father for running out on his family when he did. He'd also forgiven him for the missed birthday parties and the Christmas mornings spent waiting for Tommy to recover from another hangover. He'd even absolved him of guilt for the paltry child support that had arrived every few months, stuffed into thin, dirty envelopes with no return address. Manx suspected his mother had burned them soon after they were dropped through the letterbox. She didn't need the money. The kind of support Alice Manx-Williams required didn't come stuffed in envelopes with *sorry* scribbled hurriedly across them in thick marker pen.

However, one thing Manx found harder to forgive Tommy for was his parting gift of his midnight blue, 1971 Mark III Jensen Interceptor. Not because it was a hulking, petrol-guzzling steel tank that was as impractical as it was unreliable, but because, try as he might, Manx couldn't bring himself to sell the damn car. It was the gift that kept on taking.

Manx had spent the last hour at Lloyd Lugnut's workshop. The curmudgeonly old mechanic had lectured Manx on how he should take better care of the 'old girl', and said he could guarantee the car would pass its MOT if Manx paid him £2,000 for a set of new tyres and a refurbished exhaust system from a company in Birmingham specialising in manufacturing old Jensen parts. It was at that point, as Manx scraped his jaw up from the floor, that Lloyd had suggested maybe he should consider selling.

'Classic this is. Collectors pay good money for one of these in original condition. Unless you're sentimental about the old girl; attached, like?'

Sentimental? Attached? Manx considered Lloyd's words as he glanced over the cracked leather interior and the bank of gauges – some of which, he assumed, still worked – set deep into the walnut dashboard. 'Sentimental' wouldn't be the first adjective he'd use to describe himself. Manx was practical, that was all. Why throw money away on a new car when the Jensen transported him to wherever he needed to be? At least, on most days. No, the 'old girl' would suit him fine. He'd drive it until one of them gave up the ghost. Most days Manx had the unnerving feeling it would be a close call, with the Jensen having a slim margin of advantage.

This day, however, Manx's state of mind was bordering on the optimistic. The morning was collar-stiff fresh, the sky deep blue with the faintest brush of high clouds. Manx, though, was taking none of this in as he drove, with Lucinda Williams's 'Righteously' turned up to full volume. He did take some pleasure in noticing the great ball of yellow kicking back over the Snowdonia mountain range – it was a welcome change from the persistent rain and cold of the past few weeks. It was late July, when blue skies and warm fronts were to be expected, but this, after all, was Anglesey where the weather thumbed its nose at such conventions – summers could be as balmy as the French Riviera or as rain-soaked as a Prague winter; sometimes both in the same day.

The message he'd received an hour earlier from the desk sergeant at Llangefni station had been cryptic. Someone named Walter Edwards had called with a report of multiple deaths on a minor road off the A55. The desk sergeant had hinted the caller sounded, in his words, 'two digestives short of a full pack, boss'. Typically, Manx would have left this to one of the young PCs, but the location was on his way back from Lloyd's workshop and there was little else on his docket to take care of this morning, other than paperwork and a meeting with DCI Ellis Canton.

* * *

'Well, it's hardly a crime scene, is it?' Manx said, as he studied the narrow, hedge-hemmed road and what looked like hundreds of freshly-dug molehills scattered across the surface. 'Multiple bodies? I could book you for wasting police time.'

'Thought it was your speciality,' Walter said, cocking his thumbs in the pockets of his dungarees. 'Dead bodies.' Walter was in his mid-seventies, and farmed twenty hectares close to the town of Valley.

'Dead bodies, not dead birds,' Manx said, studying the gruesome scene of a hundred or so dead starlings, scattered on the ground as if they'd been thrown from the back of a lorry.

He shook his head – how the mighty had fallen. Ten months ago, Manx was the strategic lead on a high-profile human trafficking case at the Met. Now, here he was trying to establish cause of death on a flock of dead starlings. Not that he'd been given much choice in the transfer; it was either a DI position on Anglesey or a swift demotion and a career spent logging evidence until he was pensioned off. It didn't make his situation any easier to swallow, but he hadn't yet given up on hope that he'd soon be back in London, with the city fumes in his lungs and the whole concrete and brick, rotten underbelly, razor's edge splendour of it all under his fingernails. London didn't care who you were, or where you came from, and Manx loved the city for that. Walking the streets, he was anonymous – nobody's son, nobody's brother – just a copper doing his job and going about his business. He missed that; missed it like he missed the Capital Kebab House at 2.00 am when he was famished and nothing else was open; missed it like he missed the crowds piling out from the pubs onto Camden High Street on a Friday night, and the rush of a well-executed raid and arrest in some murky Soho underground gambling den. There was plenty more he missed about the city, but mentally ticking off that laundry list was a hiding to nothing – he'd been down that road too many times over the past ten months. And anyway, he had the mysterious demise of a hundred starlings to attend to.

'Saw 'em last night,' Walter explained, gesturing at the litter of cadavers. 'I was driving back from the shops, hundreds of them in the sky doing that murmuration; beautiful it was. Drove past this morning, they're all dead. Never seen anything like it.'

Manx nodded. 'It's a mystery no doubt, but this kind of thing's handled by the RSPB and the Animal and Plant Health Agency.'

'But if someone shot them, then it'd be a crime, yeah?'

Manx squatted, found a twig and turned over three of the birds. 'No gunshot wounds.'

Walter craned his neck up to the cloudless blue sky. 'It's like they all committed suicide or something.'

'A mass starling suicide? That'd be a first.'

Walter beckoned Manx to come closer. 'Either that, or it's the bloody RAF. You've got to wonder what goes on over at that base, yeah?' he said, lowering his voice. 'Probably some top secret project they don't want us knowing about killed them.'

'Come down to the station and one of our PCs will take your statement,' Manx said, getting ready to leave.

'Unsettled me good and proper, this has.'

'There's probably a rational explanation. Always is,' Manx assured him.

Walter folded his arms tight across his belly. 'It's a bad omen, I can feel it in my bones.'

Manx wasn't the superstitious type but looking over the carrion carpeting the road, he had to agree with the old farmer – it was enough to send a cold shudder through anyone's bones.

Chapter 2

'I don't regret killing any of them, if that's what you're asking.' As Bobbie Matthews spoke, a fast jet rattled the windows of the base commander's office, belly-rolling low over the RAF Valley airstrip before thundering across the deep green countryside towards the grey outline of the Snowdonia mountains. For the past three days a rare heatwave had settled itself over Anglesey; the sun was warm but not searing; the breeze off the Irish Sea cooling but not bracing; and the nights balmy but not stifling. Above the commander's desk, the draught from air conditioning wafted down in a steady stream, ruffling the loose papers in his inbox.

Bobbie studied the two men sitting across from her – her former overseer at Waddington, Base Commander James Flynt, who'd been transferred to RAF Valley ten months previously, and Doctor Andrew 'Call Me Andy' Pierce.

Pierce was in his late thirties, with a studious, pinched face. He and Bobbie had trained together at RAF Cranwell, but their careers had taken different forks from the same road. Bobbie had found her calling sitting in the pilot's seat with seven hundred pounds of state-of-the-art weaponry under her command. Call Me Andy had become an RAF clinical psychologist and a chaplain, finding his calling sitting behind a desk and dispensing words of comfort at the pulpit. He was the dual-doctorate type that the RAF preferred to assign to cases like hers, versed in both theology and psychology – if God couldn't provide the answers, then maybe medical science could.

She'd spent three afternoons a week for the past ten months sitting across from Call Me Andy as he conducted his trauma risk management (TRiM) assessment: required counselling for any drone pilot suspected of suffering from post-traumatic stress disorder. Maybe Flynt had thought she was more likely to bare her soul to someone she knew; a friend.

Bobbie had found the opposite to be true.

Call Me Andy had always made her feel uncomfortable, as if he were constantly studying her, looking for an opening to access her secret doors and passageways. She'd suspected back at Cranwell he had a crush on her, but he had never made his feelings known. During their counselling sessions, she'd often catch his eyes roaming the hem of her skirt or casting their gaze over her legs when he suspected her attention was diverted. If he'd been doing his job, he'd have known Bobbie's attention was never diverted.

Bobbie ran a finger over the plastic gems glued to her headset, which was resting in her lap, rubbing them like a talisman – today, she needed all the luck she could get and then some. Call Me Andy had insisted the meeting was just a formality and that Flynt was more than likely to keep her combat-ready status as temporarily suspended rather than permanently revoked. Despite his assurances, Bobbie couldn't recall a time she'd felt more anxious, or more powerless.

Flynt peered through his glasses, his ruddy, lean face scrunched in concentration as he studied the report, each flick of the page like the loud pop of a gunshot behind Bobbie's eyes. As he read, she glanced at the photograph on Flynt's desk. The wife, she imagined. A pleasant-looking woman, with a kind smile set across a soft face.

Bobbie had never been soft. She had a brittle presence that seemed engineered to poke the world in the eye, rather than fold unquestioningly to its order. Above her right eyebrow, a small purple birthmark bloomed like an ink blot. People would tell her she had a pretty face, but she'd argue it was more capable than pretty: wide cheekbones, firm chin and deep, chestnut-coloured eyes. People had also told Bobbie she was too serious, that she should smile more. Those were mostly men, of course. It was pointless insisting that from where she sat the world was a serious place – more serious than they could ever imagine. But men liked to imagine they could fix things, especially her.

A few minutes passed before Flynt set the report back on the table. 'I'm not one to mince my words, Matthews. I'll take Andrew's recommendations on board, but as your commanding officer, I'm charged with making the final decision.'

Bobbie pushed her palms deeper into the crust of gems as Flynt read aloud from the report.

'Flashbacks, insomnia, severe irritation, often developing into anger when questioned about her actions on the day in question, feelings of guilt.' He turned to Pierce. 'I'm not a doctor, but these are the key indicators of PTSD, correct?'

'Em… it's more complicated. Maybe with more time, myself and Flight Lieutenant Matthews could address the issues more fully,' Pierce offered. 'I'd highly recommend keeping the temporary suspension in place for now.'

'No, I don't think so,' Flynt said, shaking his head.

'Don't do this,' Bobbie said, her voice barely a whisper.

'And what about all this correspondence?' Flynt stabbed his finger at a thick wedge of papers on the desk. 'Twenty-four letters, including transcripts of multiple phone calls to senior officers at Air Command Headquarters demanding what you call "the truth about Operation Vanguard". What the bloody hell were you playing at?'

'The report is flawed, sir.'

Flynt sat back, and for a moment Bobbie imagined she saw a flicker of hesitation in Flynt's eyes; a deliberate pause to ensure his words came out exactly as he intended. 'No, Matthews, it is not flawed.' He regained his poise and pointed at Bobbie. 'I was there. The only thing flawed in that report was omitting the fact that the bloody Yanks failed to inform us that there were more insurgents in the area. Those bad actors detonated an IED, killed our lads. That, Matthews, is the truth of it.'

'With all due respect, sir, you're incorrect. Neither Waddington nor Creech reported sightings of additional insurgents. My husband did not die at the hands of enemy combatants. I will not stop asking RAF Command for the truth of what happened. I owe that to Danvir.'

Flynt shook his head. 'You do realise you're making this decision a hell of a lot easier for me.'

'No!' Bobbie said, her fists bunching. 'Please, don't do this.'

'Come on, Matthews, this can't be news to you. Any other active combat officer exhibiting these symptoms and I'd have had them marched off base and into a psychiatric facility months ago.'

'I think we should talk about this, sir,' Pierce said, turning to face Flynt. 'Bobbie's case is complex, she's making great breakthroughs under my continued counselling–'

Flynt interrupted. 'I've given her the benefit of the doubt, that grace period is now over, Pierce.'

Bobbie's skin snapped tight around her bones. 'You were there that day, sir. You ordered me to pull the trigger.'

Flynt's eyes hardened. 'And I stand by that order.'

'And you were given a base commander position while I get sent off to a psychiatric ward and then administrative duties. It's not what I signed up for, sir.'

Flynt laid his forearms across the desk. 'Flight Lieutenant Matthews, you are permanently relieved of your combat-ready status.'

Bobbie's eyes were moist as she turned to Pierce. 'Andrew?'

'Sir, this is a mistake,' Pierce said, sitting forward. 'Flight Lieutenant Matthews has served with distinction. She was one of the few drone pilots to receive a medal in Operation Shader. She's a valuable asset in our war on terror.'

'So are the five other drone pilots graduating this month. The RAF thanks you for your dedication and service, but your days flying combat missions are over. I've made arrangements for you to attend a residential veterans psychiatric facility in Liverpool, they're expecting you in two weeks. Maybe they'll succeed where Pierce failed. In the meantime, take some time off.'

Bobbie composed herself, kept the tears from flowing. 'If it's all the same to you, sir, I'd rather be busy.'

'Suit yourself, Matthews, I can't force you to take a holiday, but I will insist you continue your therapy with Pierce. That, as they say, is non-negotiable.'

Bobbie stood. 'If that's all, sir, I'd like to be excused.'

Flynt nodded and dismissed her with a casual wave of his arm.

Outside, the morning held the ominous promise of a bright, warm day – a heavy sky brimming with grey clouds would have suited Bobbie's mood far better. She watched a clutch of fast jet pilots fresh from their flight simulator training walk past laughing and wondered if she'd ever feel anything close to that sense of elation and optimism again. For the past year all she'd felt was a growing darkness, like a shadow casting itself inside her. She heard Call Me Andy shouting her name.

'Bobbie, I just wanted to say–'

'Say what, Andrew?' she said, turning sharply.

Pierce ran a hand through his hair. 'I wanted to apologise. Flynt made the wrong decision. I can appeal, write another report.'

'Why? Why would you do that, Andrew?'

'Well, I consider us friends, not just colleagues.' He paused and gestured to the flag fluttering above the base welfare hub. 'Remember the motto they drilled into us in basic training?'

'Of course,' she said, her hands tapping impatiently on her headset. '*Per ardua ad astra*. Why is that relevant?'

'Through adversity to the stars,' Pierce said, placing his hands across her shoulders. 'You'll come through this, Bobbie, you're one of the strongest women I know. Have faith… in yourself.'

Bobbie winced at the clumsy attempt to bring his god into the conversation. Where faith was concerned, Bobbie's coffers were as good as spent, had been for some time now. When she joined the RAF, she'd been young and idealistic with a vague hope of making some kind of difference in the world. That Bobbie Matthews had died twelve months ago on a dust-ridden road south of Mosul and wouldn't be resurrected anytime soon.

'Here, take this,' she said, handing Pierce her headset. 'I won't be needing it anymore.'

Chapter 3

Stripes, yellow ball nine, gave a satisfying clank as it barrelled into the middle pocket of the pool table. The ancient transistor radio perched on the windowsill played a rousing Welsh folk song. Next to the radio a half-smoked joint fizzled lazily, the ash flaking onto the cracked green enamel of the radiator below.

Melvin Powell set himself up for his next shot. He was in his early sixties, chest thick like a Rottweiler and a solid beer paunch spilling over his red dragon belt buckle. Back in the day, Melvin was lean and muscular with a hard, chiselled face that seemed sculpted to absorb the force of a well-driven punch. At the age of twenty-one, Melvin had been a fast and wiry welterweight with enough promise to earn himself the moniker of 'the Great Welsh Hope'. But those days were long gone, ancient history in Melvin's book, as was the motorcycle accident which had crushed the bones of his right hand and taken him out of the ring for good. Forty years later, he still held himself like the contender he could have been; eyes hard, posture hunched and closed as if he were bracing himself for the next punch to land.

He looked through the window. The pub sign forthe Lantern Arms, swung in the soft breeze. He'd been renting the back room of the pub for two years now. It was a former stable, but Melvin just referred to it as the 'shit-hole', and that suited him just fine; people didn't poke their noses around shit-holes. The rent was cheap, and the landlady didn't ask too many questions. He suspected she was sympathetic to the cause, but they'd never talked about it. They'd screwed though, plenty of times, but the subject never came up – some people preferred to turn their backs on shit they would rather not know about. Lydia enjoyed the smokes, though, bought at least five joints a week. Maybe she wasn't sympathetic and just liked keeping her dealer close to hand. No matter. So long as he was screwing her, keeping Lydia happy, he was guaranteed free pints and pub lunches most days; a win-win situation in his book.

Lydia was ten years younger than Mel and could still carry off a tight T-shirt and jeans without looking like mutton dressed as lamb. He'd moved in with her to the flat above the pub six months ago, with a promise to add his name on the lease. He was still thinking on it. If he agreed, he wouldn't start pandering to tourists looking for sustainably raised chickens, gin cocktails and fresh fucking fish platters. He'd keep it real: a pub run by the Welsh, for the Welsh.

Melvin re-chalked and leaned low over the table, catching a whiff of the stale ash and beer soaked into the baize. He was set to hammer the cue ball when he felt a sharp tug at the back of his head. He spun around.

Ronnie Powell took a step back, held his belly and laughed. 'You should see your face, bloody picture it is. By the way, got a call for you.' Ronnie raised his mobile as Melvin checked out his reflection in the mirror on the far wall.

'Yeah? Who?'

'1983,' Ronnie chuckled. 'Says it wants its haircut back.'

Melvin smoothed his palms over his hair and tugged on the elastic wrapped around the grey ponytail that hung six inches below his neckline. He adjusted his shirt collar and brushed a dusting of chalk from his dark-rinse Levi jeans. 'You're a fuckin' moron. What if you'd been the cops? I could have beat the shit out of you.'

Ronnie backed away; his hands held high in mock surrender. 'Pigs don't come here, do they? Way off their patch.'

'What do you want? You look like a tramp, as bloody usual. You should smarten up, get some bloody decent clothes for a start, show some respect for yourself.'

Ronnie shrugged. 'I don't feed the corporate fashion machine. Buy all my clothes from the Oxfam shop. Recycling, it is.'

Melvin shook his head. His nephew was twenty-three, wiry and hard like Melvin used to be, with a beard he was still growing into. 'Make yourself useful and brew us a fresh one,' he said, gesturing at the sorry collection of stained and chipped mugs on the table.

Ronnie pulled on the joint. 'I'm not your errand boy.'

Melvin ran the cue tip along Ronnie's chest, applying a small amount of pressure. 'Got yourself a better offer? A job?'

Ronnie shrugged, looked to the floor.

'Didn't think so. Kettle, teabags, mug. Even you can't fuck that up. And don't forget to use the right bloody socket,' Melvin said, snapping the joint from the lad's lips.

Ronnie parried away the cue. 'All right, but only because you're an old fart and I feel sorry for you.' He unplugged the radio and connected the kettle plug to the only working socket in the room. Mel's mobile chirped to life.

'That her?' Ronnie said. 'Thought you were done doing favours, it's not like she's family.'

'Tea. Now,' Melvin said, brushing off a flurry of cue chalk from his shirt and stepping outside.

As Ronnie threw the teabags into the mugs, a twist of anger cast itself in his gut. Or was it envy? Sometimes it was hard to tell them apart. All he knew for certain was that he'd been loyal to Mel for years, been like a son to him, and this was how he repaid him.

It had been weeks since he and his uncle had gone out lamping together. He missed it; missed the camaraderie of two men against nature, driving into the dead of night on the Arctic Wildcat quad bike Mel had bought; though he rarely drove these days, preferring to let Ronnie take the driving seat. Ronnie hardly cared if they shot anything – he lived for the thrill of the hunt. If he was lucky and skewered a perfectly-aimed bolt in the warm belly of a rabbit or a fox, so much the better, it was something to brag about later over a few beers. Those were the moments he hunted for; Mel and him watching the dawn breaking through the tree branches, a chorus of birdsong heralding the sunrise over the island.

Mel had first taken him lamping when Ronnie was a teenager, taught him how to tune his senses to the forest floor, trained him how to rig his crossbow in the pitch dark, showed him the importance of double-checking his range estimation before firing the bolt, insisted that the best nights for hunting were those when the dark was thick with blackness and the wind rustled in hurried, whistling gasps through the trees and hedges.

But his uncle had also taught him much more.

Mel had taken Ronnie in when he was most in need of a steady guiding hand – even if that hand would sometimes clench to a fist that found a fast trajectory to Ronnie's cheekbone. He never doubted he deserved it when Melvin snapped him with a punch he didn't see coming. His father, Dafydd Powell, was a fan of the more drawn-out approach to punishment. Most nights, Dafydd had come home full of bile and beer, itching for a fight he'd been unable to kick off in the local. Ronnie had learned not to put up a fight; it was easier that way. Melvin had taken him away from all that, raised him as near to a son as any man could, just the two of them sharing the old cottage near Church Bay. But since Yoko fuckin' Ono had come on the scene, she'd upset the dynamic. Not that she was Japanese, Ronnie just called her that behind his uncle's back; it made him feel better, like he had some control over the situation.

Mel returned a few minutes later, unlocked the cupboard and took out both Ten Point Titan crossbows, laying them on the pool table. 'Clean these. Remember to check the retention spring and lubricate the flight groove.'

Ronnie reached for an old rag. 'More fuckin' favours?'

'She's a friend, met her at the pub, she needed my help, end of,' Melvin said.

'Lydia know about her, then? This fancy woman—'

Before Ronnie could finish, Melvin stepped forward with the speed of a prize fighter, wrapped his thick fingers around his nephew's neck and pushed him up against the wall. 'You keep that big mouth of yours shut, got it?'

'All right, calm down, give yourself a heart attack,' Ronnie mumbled.

He glanced at the tattoo on the back of Melvin's hand: *Cymru am Byth* – Wales Forever; it pulsed with the throb of his thick veins. Ronnie would often forget how strong his uncle was – like a prize bull, all muscle and coiled-up energy.

Melvin leaned in close. 'You want to keep working for me? Earn your beer money? Keep it shut,' he said, cupping his fingers into a tight grip around his nephew's chin.

'Yeah, yeah, keep your hair on.'

He released his grip. 'The lads all set for tomorrow night?'

'Yeah, told them to be here by seven.'

Melvin leaned against the pool table. 'It's a fucking plan this is. A real plan.'

'The brotherhood know about this plan of yours, then?'

'They'll know when they need to know.'

'If you ask me, they won't want to take things this far.'

'Good job nobody's asking you, then,' Melvin said. 'You got that tea brewed yet?'

Tea? Errand Boy? Ronnie's blood peaked to boiling for the second time that morning. Only this time he kept his mouth shut, kept it locked down.

'Three sugars, yeah?' he said, grabbing the cue ball and shooting it down the green baize. It rattled against one of the corner pockets before dropping into the net.

He'd bide his time, just like his uncle had taught him back in the woods, waiting for rabbits to bolt from their warrens and into the blinding glare of the spotlight. Yeah, there was plenty of time to prove Melvin Powell wrong, and surprise the old bastard with a plan of his own one day.

Chapter 4

The road's narrow gulley came fast as Bobbie throttled over the rough country lanes. Nine fifteen at night, the final remnants of dusk vanishing into the darkness. Sleep had been hard to come by lately, and tearing her Golf GTI through the roads Bobbie had known growing up was as therapeutic as any medication or empty words Call Me Andy had proffered.

Ahead, a tight right-hand corner. She slipped into second, powering down on the accelerator as she exited the apex of the curve. The back end of the Golf twitched, before snapping back into line for the upcoming straight. The needle nudging seventy-five, the headlights caught something blocking the road some twenty metres ahead. Bobbie braced herself and slammed the brake pedal. The tyres skidded on the muddy surface as if it were made of ice. Nineteen metres later, the car came to a sharp stop. She looked up. Staring back at her, two soulful eyes of a huge black bull that had wandered into the road. Bobbie and the creature locked eyes for a few short heartbeats before the beast seemed to shrug its powerful shoulders and saunter back into the field. She let out the breath she'd been holding on to and slipped back into first gear.

Thirty minutes later, Bobbie found herself in the town of Trearddur Bay. She'd parked across from a large detached house with floor-to-ceiling windows and a distinctive 1970s box-like design. She knew the occupants. She'd been invited here by Flynt and his wife for a housewarming party a year ago. Bobbie had attended with the hope of catching Flynt off-guard, to press him on the truth about Operation Vanguard, but the sight of Flynt relishing all the attention had turned her stomach.

She'd slunk out through the back door after thirty minutes, figuring – correctly – that she wouldn't be missed.

Why the hell was she parked outside his house? No doubt Call Me Andy would have a few theories, but she had one of her own. Bobbie had always believed peace was only ever achieved through balance. Bad actors needed to be neutralised – it was what kept that balance in check. That's why she'd never hesitated in pulling the trigger, not once, other than her last day in the Ground Control Centre. 'I stop the bad guys before they kill the good guys.' It was a phrase one of the drone pilots at Creech had said to her one night over beers; it had stuck with her ever since. Since Danvir's death, Bobbie's world was seriously off-kilter, and she was sure Flynt held the key to restoring that balance. She'd never bought into the RAF's report on Operation Vanguard and suspected Flynt felt the same, but he'd probably followed the party line in exchange for a fat promotion. He'd also requested that Bobbie be transferred to Valley at the same time; far easier to keep an eye on her when she was under his jurisdiction, she imagined.

She made up her mind to knock on his door, demand to speak with Flynt, try to persuade him to reverse his decision, keep her suspension temporary, and allow her to stay at Valley. As much as Call Me Andy irritated her, he was familiar, and he was manageable. She wasn't sick, not in the way Flynt and Pierce insisted she was. It was grief and in time she'd get over it, but for that to happen she needed to find the truth; armed with the truth she could move on with her life, whatever the hell that looked like. But maybe there was never any such thing as closure and death itself always had the last laugh; death, the ultimate closure.

Her hand was on the door handle, her foot ready to step out, when Flynt, wearing his service dress, left the house, walked to his car and pulled out from the driveway. A light flicked on in the upstairs bedroom. Bobbie looked up as someone pulled back a slip of curtain. The soft outline of a face appeared behind the glass and stayed there for a minute before stepping back into the shadows. By the time Bobbie looked back to the road, the red blur of Flynt's tail lights had already disappeared into the descending darkness.

Chapter 5

As Manx entered Benllech town centre, the squeal of worn brake pads against rough steel cut through the morning air. He'd narrowly avoided driving into a family lugging sand buckets, spades, beach blankets, ice coolers, umbrellas and two large, multi-coloured windbreaks across the road. *Obviously professionals*, he thought, *prepared for whatever the day will bring*. The mother – harried and scowl-faced – threw him a dirty look, grabbed her kids and yanked them towards the hill leading down to the beach.

Manx had forgotten it was the school holidays: with no children of his own, those seasonal measures of time typically passed him by. His sister, Sara, had reminded him of this fact just yesterday, though her statement was more of a complaint than it was information. Her grievance concerned the length of the summer holidays and what she was expected to do with her seven-year-old son, Dewi, for six weeks, and if Manx had an ounce of paternal instinct he would offer to help. Manx agreed; he possessed no paternal instinct. Sara had told him to 'grow the hell up' before hanging up. It was the typical ebb and flow of their relationship; his sister expecting more, Manx failing to deliver. One day, maybe the tide would turn – but he wasn't holding his breath.

A few minutes later, the Jensen parked at the beach, he inched up the windows. At 8.15 am, it was already too warm for his regular wardrobe of a black sports jacket, black trousers, white cotton shirt and a thin, black tie knotted loosely so it hung an inch or so below his undone top button.

It was low tide, the sea drawn back to reveal a six-pack torso of sand. Across the sand, a scattering of seagulls and cormorants picked at whatever bounty the ocean had left in its wake. At the entrance, PC Kevin Priddle, arms stretched wide like a scarecrow costumed in a high visibility jacket, tried to appease a pack of dog-walkers complaining about the interruption to their routine.

'Nothing to see here, please move away.' Priddle's long, pale face was pulled into a grimace as he sized up the gang, who looked as if they might make a run for the beach at any moment.

A gruff man, with a hyperactive border collie at his ankles, spoke. 'Why you lot here then, if there's nothing to see?' He craned his neck, trying to peer past Priddle.

'Nothing for the public to see, sir,' Priddle said, emphatically. 'Police business. I'm asking you nicely to move away, please. Now.'

The man searched for a fresh angle. 'We'll just walk on the other side,' he said, gesturing at a patch of sand under the cliffs. 'No one's minding over there.'

'You could,' Manx said, stepping into the man's personal space. 'Then we'd have to arrest you.'

The man pulled his dog to heel. At six foot three, Manx had perfected the art of intimidation without needing to lift a finger. 'Your choice. Find another beach or I'll have you escorted to the station. We're short-staffed, what with all this activity, so it'll take a few hours to get you processed. But if you're game, I'm game.'

The man tugged at his cap and spat on the pavement. 'Be on the news anyway.' He yanked on the dog's lead, taking his time walking back to his van, glimpsing over the beach in the hope of a sneak peek of that evening's headline story.

A flush of red bloomed across Priddle's cheeks. 'Cheers, like, but there was no need. I was about to read him the riot act myself.'

'Balls,' Manx said, resting a hand on the PC's shoulder. 'About time you grew a pair. Do your job and keep the looky-loos in the car park until we give the all clear.'

Manx turned towards the activity further down the beach.

Detective Sergeant Malcolm Nader marched towards him. 'Bread of Bevan's just got here,' he said, gesturing to Ashton Bevan, lead CSI, and his team stepping into their oversuits.

'That's going to put a dent in the day's deckchair rentals,' Manx said, ducking nimbly under the police cordon. 'Details?'

Nader wiped a sop of sweat from his brow. 'Dog walker called it in. In a right state she was, took forever to calm her down. She's with Minor getting the full-on victim support.'

PC Delyth Morris was on a nearby bench, wrapping a blanket around an elderly woman petting a terrier on her lap.

'Any positive ID on the body?'

'Not yet, but shouldn't take too long, you'll see for yourself.'

As Manx stepped over the metal plates the CSI team had set out several metres across the sand, Bevan shot out his arm. 'Any closer and I'll have to insist you don one of our oversuits, Manx,' he said, barely looking at the inspector.

'Good morning to you, too, Bevan.'

Manx looked at the body laid on the sand. Male, the right leg contorted as if it had come loose from the knee socket, his left arm at a right angle to his shoulder, also probably dislocated. From several metres away he could see the man's right temple was bloodied, the skin split open, tendrils of what he imagined was brain matter leaking from the wound. Nader was right: securing a positive ID on the man shouldn't take more than a couple of phone calls. He was wearing a dark blue suit with three stripes on the arms. On the cuffs, a dark band with white stitching. Tracking down the front of his jacket, three brass buttons that ended at the stable belt, which was unclipped. His shirt was a lighter blue, fastened to the top button with a black tie in a classic Windsor knot. Above his left jacket pocket, a finely stitched gold emblem of wings and crown surrounded by a blue laurel wreath. Manx recognised it immediately. Royal Air Force service dress.

'The beach is off limits until we give the all clear,' Manx said.

'That'll go down like shit on a doorstep,' Nader huffed. 'Council will be on the blower to El Vera before morning's done.'

Manx took in a deep inhale of salt-tinged air. Detective Chief Superintendent Vera Troup was top of the food chain at the North Wales Constabulary. Her pale, vampire-like complexion and raven-black hair had earned her the nickname of El Vera amongst the local coppers. She was well connected; a modern breed of DCSIs who liked to cosy up to the local power players – players that included the county council and the more influential business owners and politicians on the island. It was her take on community policing: the closer you were to those wielding power the easier it was to keep tabs on them.

'Put these on, I've got one for each of you,' Bevan said, snatching a pair of oversuits from one of his techs. 'Unless you clumsy lot have already contaminated the scene, which is highly likely,' he added, with an ugly smirk that Manx had, on more than one occasion, wanted to smack off Bevan's smug face.

'I think the tide probably beat us to it,' Manx said. 'Unless you can hold back the sea for a few more hours.'

'Aye, or walk across the bloody thing,' Nader muttered, just loud enough for Bevan to hear.

Bevan ignored the barbs – they were just noise to him by now. 'We'll find something,' he said, directing his techs to get to work. 'Tide or no tide, if there's human remains chances are some other human's left something of interest.'

After Manx had instructed Nader and Morris to begin the necessary drudgery of door-to-doors, he noticed a car parked across from the beach. It was the only vehicle in the car park. He crossed the road, walked around the silver Audi A7, and peered through the windows. The keys were still on the centre console, the doors unlocked. On the passenger seat was what Manx recognised as a blue RAF officer's cap.

Chapter 6

Detective Chief Inspector Ellis Canton's desk was typically a cluttered affair. Today, however, DI Manx was struck by its neatness. No scattering of papers, half-eaten packs of mints or illegible notes littering the desk, just a large white gift box wrapped with a thick black ribbon, which Canton was in the process of snipping with a pair of pruning shears.

'If you're feeling inspired,' Manx said, settling into the chair. 'Mine could do with a bit of a clear-out.'

Canton smiled as if he were in the midst of some meaningful meditation from which Manx had just disturbed him. 'Happiness, Manx, is a place between too little and too much,' he said, reading a quote from a card he'd slipped from inside the box, before tucking it carefully under the fold of ribbon.

'Is it your birthday? I don't remember signing a card.'

Canton shook his large, bald head, which in the heat seemed to have garnered an extra patina of shine. 'Study material,' he said, dragging the box closer. 'Arrived this morning.'

'Looks a bit fancy for the force, or are they upping their game in the continuing education department?'

Canton brought his palms together. 'Do you know it takes six years of training to become a Bonsai Master, Manx?'

'Better get on it then, Ellis, you're not getting any younger.'

'None of us are.' Canton tapped a finger on the box. 'Bonsai Master in six months or my money back.'

'Do you get a certificate or something?'

'Several,' Canton confirmed. 'I've already made space.' He gestured to a blank space on his wall. 'Positive thinking. Make space for the things you desire, and they will appear.'

'Oh, right. So, if I leave out an empty glass it'll get filled with single malt scotch? That kind of positive thinking?'

'You've never felt the urge for enlightenment, Manx?'

'Can't say I have, Ellis.'

'Hm,' he said, looking at the inspector as if he were searching for something of value but had come up empty-handed. He pushed back his chair. 'Vera's already been chewing my ear off about this business down at Benllech.'

'To be expected.'

Canton pulled himself up in a series of groans. 'Closing down the beach? I told her you must have had a bloody good reason. Convince me I was right.'

'Dead body. Bevan's on the fence on the COD. We'll get a clearer picture once Hardacre's completed the autopsy.'

Canton brushed the leaves of an azalea bonsai tree. 'ID?'

'The victim was wearing RAF service dress. Nader's following up with Valley to see if they're missing an officer. If not, we'll contact the administrative base at High Wycombe.'

'Good man,' Canton said. 'Now, take a look at this,' he added, sliding a slip of paper from his inbox. 'Preliminary fire investigation origin and cause reports came in this morning.'

Manx glanced at the document. 'The holiday homes?'

'None of them were occupied at the time, though I'd put that down to good fortune rather than good planning.'

'So, what are we looking at, arson?'

'Appears so,' Canton agreed. 'The fire inspector's at the location of the latest one this afternoon. Might be a good time for you to introduce yourself.'

Manx laid the document back on the table. 'Any link between the homes? Same owners? Management company?'

'Nothing conclusive, other than they were all available on those holiday home listing sites. None of them were owned by anyone living on the island, except the latest one, which was owned and managed by Logan Collins.'

'Should I know him?'

'Local politician, running for election. Conservative.'

'Well, there's your motive right there,' Manx said, smiling.

Canton narrowed his eyes. 'Best keep an open mind, eh? And give the investigators any help they need.'

'Anything else?'

Canton slid open a drawer and took out an A4 poster which he flattened across his desk. 'Since you ask.'

Manx checked out the lettering, which was colourful and in a bold, upper case font. 'What in God's name is a "food slam"?' he asked, turning over the paper and hoping for some further clarity on the flip side. There was none, just a roll call of names and logos of a handful of local businesses sponsoring the event.

'Somewhere you need to be this Thursday evening. Vera requested you, specifically.'

Manx sensed another Canton ambush. 'To do what, exactly?'

'Be the friendly face of the North Wales Constabulary. Bring Morris along, add a female touch to the proceedings.'

'I'm a bit busy, Ellis, what with all this—'

'Three hours at most. Hand out a few leaflets, play nice with the locals and tourists. It's Vera's big summer initiative, she's even got a catchphrase for the whole shebang.'

'A catchphrase? Do I want to know?'

'Just Ask a Copper,' Canton said, grimacing.

'That's original. Can't you–'

Canton's cheeks quivered as he shook his head. 'I'd hate to disappoint my boss. She doesn't respond well to the word no.'

'I know the feeling,' Manx said, folding the poster and slipping it in his pocket.

Canton rubbed his hands together. 'That's the spirit.'

'You owe me, Ellis.'

‘Put it on the tab. And close the door on your way out, my trees require a constant temperature.’

‘Yes… master,’ Manx replied, drawing the door closed with a reverent and graceful pull.

Chapter 7

'Busy afternoon ahead,' Manx said, sitting on the edge of his desk. 'Any uplifting news to share from the door-to-doors?'

DS Nader shrugged. 'Dead end. We interviewed seventy-two people; nobody saw a bloody thing.'

'Load of tourists. not too happy being woken up first thing,' Morris said. 'Same with the locals. Nobody noticed anything suspicious, except for this one pensioner who reckoned he saw something unusual in the sky that morning.'

'And?' Manx prompted.

'Told me it was big, yellow and shiny – until I realised he meant the sun.'

Nader chuckled. 'Good one, that.'

'There's a couple in every pack,' Manx said. 'Now, Bevan's estimate puts our victim in the water for at least twelve hours. Hardacre should give us a more definitive cause of death, but in the meantime take another shot at the door-to-doors. Ask if anyone saw anything suspicious on Sunday night, not just this morning. Someone must have seen or heard something. We have no CCTV of the beach, and until we get a positive ID on the victim, very little to go on.'

'So a dead end, boss,' Nader said. 'Now what?'

'We keep looking until we find something that isn't a dead end. We need to find out who the hell this is,' he said, pinning a photo of the body to the board. 'Morris, pull up any missing person's reports in the past week. Nader, keep on RAF Valley's arse, they must know if they're missing an officer or two by now.'

A rumbling of 'yes boss' echoed through the room.

'By the way, boss,' Nader said, pushing back his chair. 'Anything you want me to follow up on those dead starlings over by Valley? Everyone's asking about them.'

'Do they have a next of kin we need to inform? IDs we need to verify?'

'Erm… no,' Nader said.

'Then we let the RSPB and the Animal and Plant Health lads handle it.'

'It's all over the papers,' Nader said, showing him the front page of that day's*Daily Post*. 'All kinds of theories, the wife's Facebook feed's full of it.'

Manx grabbed his jacket from behind the chair. 'The press are magpies, Nader, something new and shiny will have caught their attention by tomorrow, so let's get an ID on this victim. Priorities, let's stick to them, eh?'

Chapter 8

Manx pulled up next to the charred remains of the cottage and glanced over at the camera crew gathered at the front gate. As he exited the Jensen, the crew briefly looked him over, then turned their attention back to their phones.

He checked out the naked shell of the building, which was covered in a layer of black soot. The roof had disintegrated, as had the windows, leaving holes that reminded him of dead men's eyes; empty and cold. The iron beams remained and ran the length of the cottage to meet at the chimney stack which was leaning dangerously sideways.

'Unless you're looking to find out what it's like to be buried under a few hundred pounds of bricks, I'd move back if I were you.'

Manx turned, as a man with a clipboard approached. He was under five feet tall, wearing a hard hat and possessed an officious manner. 'The fire's drawn the moisture from the mortar, so there's no glue holding the structure together. One wrong move and the stack's likely to collapse, right about where you're standing.'

Manx complied, stepped back. 'Long shot,' he said, 'but you wouldn't happen to be the fire inspector?'

'And you'd be the copper Canton said he was sending over?'

'Detective Inspector Tudor Manx.'

'Rhys Hopkins, chief fire investigator,' he said, flipping up the badge attached to his vest.

'Your report concluded arson?'

'Aye, just like the other four. They used the same accelerant: paint thinner. Just splashed the stuff everywhere and hoped it would catch. Definitely arsonist amateur hour.'

'Any security cameras on the property?'

'They'd be ashes by now, if there were.'

'You think it was kids maybe? A prank?'

Rhys tapped the clipboard with his pen. 'Kids? Not likely.'

'But you're convinced the attacks are connected?'

'No doubt.'

'And they were all holiday homes?'

'They were all listed on those online sites, we checked.'

'You've lived on the island all your life?' Manx asked.

'Why's that important?'

'Wasn't there something similar back in the eighties? Welsh nationalists burning down holiday homes? They set the Britannia Bridge on fire too, if I recall?'

'I'd just signed up for the service,' Rhys said. 'Huge bloody fire, the Britannia Bridge, but it wasn't Welsh nationalists, just a bunch of kids playing silly buggers with matches. The flames caught on the bridge, then when the tar started to melt onto the trees, that's when the real fireworks kicked off. Nine hours it took us to get it under control. Never seen anything like it before or since.'

'But the holiday home fires, they weren't kids?'

Rhys shook his head. 'Welsh freedom fighters, if I recall. Nasty buggers too, made bombs too, shoved them through English MPs' letterboxes, miracle nobody died.'

'Do you think these new fires could be connected?'

'No idea, but I'll tell you this,' he said, rocking back on the heels of his boots. 'A fire needs three things to ignite; heat, fuel and oxygen. Take one of those things away, and there's no fire.'

'I'm not sure what you're getting at.'

Rhys placed his clipboard in the crook of his arm. 'If someone's taking up the cause forty years later, you can be sure something ignited that spark, gave it oxygen. People don't usually set fire to houses without a bloody good reason.'

The news crew suddenly jumped to action as a car pulled up. A tall, well-put-together man exited a grey BMW 5 series, fastened the middle button of his jacket and stood, camera ready, in front of the house.

'The owner,' Rhys explained 'Logan Collins, Conservative, running for election later this year.'

'So I heard.'

Manx stepped closer as Collins addressed the camera and spoke with the practised ease of a politician. 'I've said this before, but it bears repeating. This kind of criminal activity will not be tolerated. Behind me is what remains of the home my wife and I spent two years of our lives restoring. There are no words to convey our sense of loss, but I assure you, if I'm elected as Anglesey's next Member of Parliament I will make it my priority to work closely with the police to make sure nobody else's hard work and sacrifice ends up in ruins.'

'And any messages to whoever did this?' a reporter asked.

Collins turned his face to the cottage, composed himself, and turned to face the camera. 'Progress is inevitable. Anglesey is a vibrant community. Don't think you can stop progress, don't think you can roll back the tide, and don't for one second think you'll get away with this. You break the law; you pay the price. It's that simple. Thank you.'

Manx watched Collins scuttle back to his car and drive away.

'If he was Welsh, he'd have half a chance of getting elected,' Rhys said.

'And because he's not?'

'May as well piss on a bonfire for all the good it'll do him. Right, best be getting off.'

As Manx made a final circle of the property, the stench of burned wood still pungent, he thought on Collins' words. Manx had a deep mistrust of any politician, no matter the party affiliation, but he found himself agreeing with Collins. Wanton property destruction and risking lives in the name of nationalism made him sick to his stomach. He'd always fallen on the side of George Bernard Shaw when it came to that sort of thing: 'patriotism is your conviction that this country is superior to all other countries because you were born in it.' If that made him less of a Welshman and more of a human being, then so be it. Of his many character flaws, it was one he could comfortably live with.

Manx had left Wales over thirty years ago, hightailed it down to London with a small dream and an Adidas bag packed with clothes and his favourite mix tapes. It had become clear to Manx early in his police career that killers, hardened criminals or just your average arsehole with a chip on his shoulder and a taste for violence were, at their core, the same no matter where they came from.

The Glaswegian 'hard bastards' always ready with a Doc Marten to the bollocks and a knuckle duster to the nose when the chance came and the price was right; the Belfast drug cartels, all soft brogue and 'what's the craic?' until it came time to stab you in the back; the West Indian gangs from Ladbroke Grove housing estates, all patois and laid-back menace as they trained their young roadmen on the finer points of distributing their latest imports; the Ukrainian mobsters trafficking underaged girls for greasy-fingered men with sick appetites. They all had one thing in common; they were born somewhere; and that somewhere hadn't made them who they were. That was a choice they'd made, plain and simple. Manx had never been convinced by the argument that circumstances drove people to crime. He'd met enough people who'd suffered unimaginable tragedy and hardships and had come through a damn sight more sane and empathic than he could ever hope to be. There was always a choice; a bad choice road or a good choice road. Whichever road you travelled wasn't dictated by where you came from: it was dictated by the kind of person you were or wanted to become. Crime, Manx has always believed, was a personal choice; the most personal choice of all.

As Manx finished circling what remained of the downstairs bedroom of the cottage, he noticed the charred ruins of a wrought iron bed frame, the mattress shredded and black. Canton was right. So far, it had just been good luck that the houses were unoccupied when the fire took hold.

How long that luck would last was anyone's guess.

Chapter 9

Manx stood in the chill of the mortuary waiting for the coroner and listening to the rousing drama of an aria he couldn't name but had heard enough times he felt he should know its origins by this time in his life.

'La Traviata,' Doctor Richard Hardacre said, shouldering the door open and tying his apron strings around his rotund belly.

'Sorry?' Manx said.

'That look on your face? It's the same one I get when I'm trying to remember where I put my car keys. "Sempre libera", Act One. Renée Fleming sang it best. I've got the original recording at home. If I could remember where I stored it, I'd lend it to you.'

'My loss, then,' Manx said, figuring he'd dodged a small bullet. He gestured to the body. 'What's the prognosis?'

'Well, death, that's for sure.'

'Whatever they're paying you, it's not enough.'

'You're not going to like this.' Hardacre drew down the sheet, revealing the man's head and upper chest. 'Time of death, early hours of Monday morning. Cause of death, undetermined.' He ran the tip of his scalpel just above the man's right temple. 'Multiple bruises and lacerations consistent with a fall. Minimal seawater in the lungs, coup damage to the right side of the temple, contrecoup damage to the left.'

'In English,' Manx said.

'Whatever caused the head trauma was powerful enough to slap the brain against the opposite side of the skull, causing what we call a contrecoup injury. The cliffs around Benllech aren't particularly high, but mind you, stumble the wrong way off a kerb and you could end up under this,' he said, waving his scalpel.

'Our victim might have been out walking, slipped, bashed his head on the rocks as he fell. He could also have been lying there for quite some time before the tide claimed him. And of course, we have no DNA to speak of, the Irish Sea took care of that.'

'Fall or pushed?' Manx asked.

'No way to confirm at this point, however,' Hardacre said, slipping the scalpel into the cavity and pulling back the tissue, 'I did excavate some rock fragments deep in the wound.'

'Excavate?'

'To dig out, Manx, from the Latin, *cavare*, to hollow out.'

'Unusual choice of word, that's all.'

'Seemed perfectly apt to me. Anyway, I sent the samples to a geologist friend of mine working on a dig site near Llanfair PG. She promised to get me an analysis back in the next couple of days.'

'And that would prove?'

'Prove? Probably nothing, but it should confirm if the fragments found in said cavity were from the cliffs around where the body was discovered.'

'Got it,' Manx said. He scratched the back of his neck. 'Benllech is a thirty-minute drive from RAF Valley. Why go out hiking in RAF dress uniform late on a Sunday night?'

'Autopsies don't generally provide those kinds of answers. But if you were contemplating suicide, you might want to wear what's important to you as your last dress change, human vanity being what it is.'

'Dress in your Sunday best to meet your maker?'

'It's an important meeting, you'd want to make a good impression. Wouldn't you, Manx?'

Manx was about to reply when the raucous opening chords to Jack White's 'I'm Shakin'' echoed through the mortuary. Hardacre's eyebrows arched as Manx checked his mobile. He raised his index finger and took the call outside. He returned less than a minute later as Hardacre was tidying his tray of implements.

'Well, one mystery solved,' he said, slipping the phone back into his pocket.

'I'm all ears,' Hardacre said, dragging the sheet back over the victim's face.

'Seems RAF Valley's missing a base commander.'

Chapter 10

The back room of the Lantern Arms held on to the constant stench of damp and mould like a bad grudge. Melvin could have fixed the damp and replastered the walls, but he'd already done enough for Lydia. His lads had painted the flat above the pub for her last winter for free. He figured doing favours for Lydia was an investment in his future, God knows he had little to show for his life so far. A cottage in Church Bay he'd been renting for ten years, a 1997 Volvo estate where he kept his supplies, and an old boat with a dodgy outboard motor purchased cheap from a friend with a chronic gambling habit. Whatever government pension he was owed, it wasn't going to pay for a bellyful of beer every night and a summer holiday in a static caravan down in St David's, that was for sure.

He slipped a CD into the stereo – one of his favourite Dafydd Iwan tracks. As the song, 'Rwy'n Gweld Y Dydd' (I See the Day) hummed through the speakers, he glanced at the flag draped across the opposite wall and felt a thick wedge of pride swell in his chest.

The banner was divided into four equal quarters, each in an alternating yellow and gold colour, an outline of a lion stitched into the individual squares. It was the battle banner of Meibion Glyndŵr – Sons of Glyndŵr – one of four Welsh nationalist rebel factions formed in the late seventies. Melvin had kept the flag for years, never imagined he'd be inspired to hang it again, imagined even less that when he unfurled the banner and brushed away the cobwebs, he'd feel the same surge of patriotism, as deep and urgent as it had grabbed him back then.

Melvin had been an active member of the Anglesey division of Meibion Glyndŵr for five years. He'd signed up when his older brother, Dafydd, had joined the organisation the year before. They were fighting for Welsh independence, saving the Welsh language from becoming a footnote in history. It was a time when protest singers like Dafydd Iwan were lauded as folk heroes, rallying against the destruction of Welsh culture. But protest songs and passionate rhetoric only went so far. Any Welshman with a true and unwavering dedication to the cause knew that by the early eighties it was time to lay down guitars and tambourines and ratchet up the pressure. Burning holiday homes owned by the English was the beginning, followed by a campaign of targeting local MPs with letter bombs and calling in bomb threats to government buildings. By the late 1980s, Meibion Glyndŵr was responsible for fire-bombing two hundred and twenty English-owned holiday homes in Wales. Melvin himself took credit for eight of those.

Over the decades, he'd let his fealty wane; most of his compatriots had. He didn't feel any less patriotic, it was just that the practicalities of life had got in the way: marriage, divorce, earning money. And besides, political tides had turned in Wales's favour. Come the mid-1990s, Meibion Glyndŵr had all but disbanded. In 1981, Wales was granted its own TV station, and by 2007, the Welsh Government had implemented a strategy that ensured all children attending schools in Wales learned the Welsh language. No doubt it was progress, but in the past few years he'd felt the old fires of patriotism stir once more. For Melvin, it was unfinished business – the kind of business a man needed to attend to when facing death.

Checking his reflection, he carefully studied the contours of his face for any change. It looked the same to him. A shade more flushed than usual maybe, but he'd been outside yesterday supervising a paint job.

The doctor had cautioned him to take better care of himself now the disease was stepping up its assault. 'Small cell lung cancer is extremely aggressive, Mr Powell, and yours is very advanced. We can help alleviate some of the pain, but that's about it.'

'How long?'

'A few months, maybe more with intense chemotherapy.'

'Fuck cancer,' he'd told the doctor. 'Fuck the chemo, too.' That was weakness, staying on the back foot, throwing in the towel for an extra few months drooling into a cup and shitting his bed.

That was no way to exit the world, not for Melvin Powell.

He pulled the elastic around his ponytail – the chemotherapy wasn't going to take his hair, either; a man had to hold on to some dignity. He hadn't told Lydia and wouldn't until it was too late for her to make a fuss. It wasn't the way he'd imagined it would all end, but death didn't play by the Queensberry rules; it fought dirty, scrappy; without mercy.

'All right! You look fuckin' gorgeous. Who's the lucky man?' Melvin turned. Stan Thomas's bulky frame was filling the door frame like a human mechanical digger.

'You smell like you've come right off the building site,' he said, looking over Stan's white T-shirt with the faded red dragon flag on the front. He reeked of body odour and dried cement.

'Didn't have time to go home and get myself all dolled up for the likes of you, did I? We havin' a drink or not?'

'I'll put the kettle on.'

'Tea? Bugger that.'

Stan pulled a bottle from his Lidl shopping bag. 'Penderyn Legend, Welsh single malt.' He slapped the bottle on the table. 'Bet our brothers wish they had this back in the day,' he said, gesturing at the photograph next to the flag; seven men standing in front of a stone wall with 'Wales Rising' spray painted across its surface.

'Might not have got much done, mind,' Melvin said, pouring the whisky into two mugs and handing one to Stan.

'To the cause,' Stan said, clinking mugs.

'Land of our fucking fathers,' Melvin said. 'Time to take back what's ours, no mistake.'

Chapter 11

Bobbie's pace was brisk and determined as she passed the RAF service housing, heading towards Valley town centre. If she walked fast enough the other wives would be less likely to approach her, ply her with questions she had no interest in answering.

The evening was warm, the sky cloudless – what the weather jockeys back at the base would have called 'Ginners all the way, Bobbie.' She stopped at the small church on the outskirts of town and ran her palm along the rough stone wall. The church had always reminded her of a Hansel and Gretel cottage; rugged walls with a patchwork of stones and a chimney-like steeple shaded by the branches of an old oak tree standing guard over its dominion. All that was missing was a path of breadcrumbs leading to the doorway.

For a moment she lost herself in a memory that was as crisp and fresh as the wedding dress she had worn the day she was last here. That was nine years ago. She and her husband of seven minutes, Danvir, had posed for photographs under the ancient oak. If she closed her eyes, she could almost catch the breath of the day, the smell of it; gardenias and trumpet lilies, summer-trimmed grass and the bark from the oak tree still damp from the rain the previous night. She hadn't imagined happiness like that existed before she met Danvir, or if it did, it was meant for other people, not for her.

She missed Danvir more than she was prepared to confess to anyone. She missed his reassuring presence when she sensed the world was slipping from her grasp. When he was away on active duty – sometimes months at a time in some warzone, unable to reveal his location – she'd begin to feel untethered, the ebb of his influence gradually unmooring her from everything that made the world right. People had always said Danvir was her rock. They were wrong. Danvir had always insisted she was the moon and he was her gravity, the force that kept her from spinning out from her orbit. She hadn't doubted it for a second.

In certain ways, living back on Anglesey was harder; too many reminders of Danvir. If she were still alive, her mother would have told her: 'Have yourself a good cry, then get over it.' It was Maggie Matthews' advice for everything from a broken heart to a broken fingernail. Bobbie sometimes saw more of herself in her mother than she cared to admit, but her father? He'd been absent most of Bobbie's life. Maggie had told her she'd met Bobbie's father when he worked as a contractor at the local Wylfa Nuclear Power Station. She'd refused to tell Bobbie his name, 'It was a stupid one-night stand, Bobbie. Leave it be, eh?' After a while, Bobbie had stopped asking.

Her mother had never married, though she had lived with another man for several years. They'd had a daughter together; Bobbie's half-sister, Tammy. That man eventually left, moved to Dubai promising to bring Maggie and the kids over; he never did. Bobbie often wondered if the stability she found in the predictable routine of the RAF stemmed from her mother's casual approach to child-rearing. Maggie would move her and her sister every few months, depending on where her romantic attentions were drawn to at the time. *No doubt Call Me Andy would have something to say about that*, Bobbie thought. After Maggie had died, four years ago, Bobbie found a bundle of tenderly wrapped, yellowing love letters while clearing out her mother's attic.

Maggie had been lying to Bobbie for decades.

Her father wasn't a one-night stand. It was a full-blown love affair, one that continued for several years after Bobbie was born. After her transfer back to Valley twelve months ago, Bobbie had made contact with her biological father; it seemed the right thing to do. Excluding Tammy, he was the only family she had left now. She'd never found the right moment to tell her sister. Maybe tonight she'd sow the seeds. But

Tammy was more like her mother, and Bobbie could already predict her reaction: 'Leave it be, eh, Bobbie.' Problem was, Bobbie wasn't very good at letting things be.

As she walked into the pub, the landlady, Lydia Clarke – a bottle-blonde who wore her T-shirts too tight and her lipstick a shade too red – was polishing the hallway mirror. She greeted her with a smile. Bobbie heard her sister's infectious laugh echo off the pub walls as she passed. Tammy was two gin and tonics into her evening and chatting to the young barman as if they were long-lost friends.

She dragged up a stool and sat. 'Hiya.'

They kissed on the cheek. Tammy wore another one of her expensive perfumes and was dressed as if she were expecting her evening to end up someplace better than here; in spotless cream-coloured capri pants, a red summer-weight blouse with a white cardigan thrown across her shoulders, her make-up perfectly applied to highlight the cornflower blue of her eyes.

'She'll have the same as me.' Tammy turned to face Bobbie. 'You made it then? Expected you to stand me up again.'

'Can't make it an all-nighter, Tam. Got to be up early tomorrow, you know how it goes.'

'Not really,' Tammy said, leaning into her sister in a conspiratorial fashion. 'All top secret, yeah? Bobbie Matthews saves the world,' she added, raising her glass and taking a sip.

A year younger than Bobbie, Tammy had married at twenty-three, was divorced by twenty-six, but had kept her husband's surname of Povey. Her features were the opposite of Bobbie's; fleshier around the face, blue eyes that caught the light with a playful glint. Bobbie was leaner, pricklier: 'You're all bones and right angles, like me,' her mother would say. People would never have guessed they were half-sisters; Tammy was 'the social one,' which by default made Bobbie the 'anti-social one'. They were roles they both had slipped into, each by now expecting the same of the other.

'Like it?' Tammy asked, noticing Bobbie looking at her hair.

'I do. I do like it.'

'New stylist over in Beaumaris,' she said, flipping a hand under her hair. 'Not cheap mind you, but worth it, yeah?'

Bobbie had no idea if it was worth it or not. She always had her hair cut at the base salon; a trim every four weeks and the extravagance of a deep conditioning treatment every few months.

Tammy looked around the pub, her lips puckering as if they'd been brushed with something unpleasant. Loose scabs of paint peeled from the walls and the ceiling was yellowed with old cigarette smoke. There was an attempt to appeal to the RAF personnel with photographs of the base taken back in the 1940s when it was first built, and several faded watercolours of the RAF's most iconic planes; Spitfires, Wellington Bombers, Hurricanes. Over the sound system, Heart FM was playing a cheesy eighties pop song by a long-forgotten one-hit-wonder. At the entrance, the irritating cha-ching of someone staking their luck on the electronic trivia machine spilled through into the main bar.

'Why didn't you invite me over to the bar on the base? It's like an old people's home in here,' Tammy said, pointing at three old men brooding into their pints.

'I'm on the base all day, why would I stay?'

Tammy softened her tone. 'Thought you might introduce me to his royal highness, or are you keeping him all to yourself?'

'I'm not affiliated with Air Mountain Rescue,' Bobbie said, having maybe caught a glimpse of the Duke and Duchess of Cambridge stepping into their Range Rover one rainy afternoon.

Tammy took another sip. 'So, I read about all those dead starlings. Nothing to do with you lot over at the base, was it?'

'Don't believe everything you read in the papers, Tam.'

Tammy shrugged and tapped her glossed fingernails on the bar. 'We should have gone to Menai Bridge, Bangor even, strike out of your comfort zone.'

'I didn't want to go too far, I was sorting Danvir's stuff—'

'Bobbie, love,' Tammy interrupted, placing her hand over Bobbie's. 'You can't keep doing this to yourself, it's not healthy.'

Bobbie snapped her hand away.

'I'm worried about you, that's all. Since you've come back you've been different, like you're not yourself.'

'And what is myself, Tammy?'

'I don't know, do I? You just seem more off than usual. And then there's that whole business with Dani.'

'I don't want to talk about it.'

'Fine.' Tammy leaned back. 'What do you want to talk about, since you invited me to this shit-hole in the first place?'

Bobbie ran a finger across the rim of her glass. 'Forget it, this was a mistake,' she said, looking at the threadbare carpet, peppered with remnants of pork scratchings and crisps. Tammy was right; the place was a shit-hole – the kind of pub only a local could love. They both turned as a group of four young men – auggies, auxiliary RAF personnel – walked towards the bar.

Tammy nudged her sister gently in the ribs. 'This should liven the place up a bit.' She caught the attention of the taller of the men. 'Couple of ladies here in need of a refill,' she said, rattling the ice cubes around her empty glass. 'If you're interested.'

The man looked Tammy up and down. 'Bit forward, int ya?' he said, leaning back. 'All you Welsh girls like that?'

'No, I'm one of the special ones.'

'Bet you are, love,' he said, leaning closer. 'Tell me your names, I might buy you a drink.'

'We can buy our own drinks,' Bobbie snapped.

Tammy ignored her sister. 'I'm Tammy, this is Bobbie.'

'Tammy and Bobbie? You two country and western singers?'

'I can see why the RAF snapped up a smart one like you,' Tammy said, dazzling him with one of her trademark smiles. 'I'm named after Tammy Wynette, she's named after Bobbie Gentry.'

'You doing a duet later?' he asked. 'Karaoke?'

'Not likely, but I'll take a double. She'll have the same.'

'I already said, I can buy my own drinks,' Bobbie said, setting her glass on the bar.

'Come on, love, cheer up, might never happen.'

Bobbie felt the blood thundering in her ears. 'You know nothing about me,' she snapped.

'Wouldn't mind getting to know you better. Both of you,' the man said, smiling. He placed his hand on Bobbie's knee.

His touch was like a shock sparking through Bobbie's veins, and her reaction pure instinct. She span around, grabbed the man's arm and wrenched it midway up his spine.

'Bobbie! What the bloody hell are you doing?' Tammy jumped from her stool, toppling over the glasses.

'Hey!' the barman called out. 'Everything okay over there?'

'We're fine,' Bobbie said. 'This young man was just about to apologise, weren't you?'

The man took stock of the situation and realised there was no way to come out of this well. He apologised through gritted teeth.

'Good,' Bobbie said. 'Apology accepted.'

The man rubbed his arm. 'Jesus, what's your problem?'

'Trust me, you really don't want to know,' Bobbie said, slapping a fiver on the bar. 'I'll call you, later, Tam.'

Chapter 12

Bobbie circled the car park, blood thumping, fists clenched; skin drawing taut over knuckles, the storm clouds in her head gathering fast. Everything was a sign, it had to be, she thought as she walked in circles, muttering to herself. First there were the starlings: she remembered Maggie – always one for believing in superstition and old wives' tales – once telling her that dead birds were a sign of a new beginning, a rebirth. The bull she'd almost ploughed into must have been another sign; something powerful and masculine blocking her path? The significance was too obvious, but the contained rage and fury of the animal? That was something she could relate to. And the bloke in the pub? Had he been sent to test her? And if so, had she passed or failed?

These thoughts rattling around her mind, Bobbie crossed the courtyard towards the back room. A swatch of yellow light spilled through the window onto the cobblestones. She heard a low murmur of voices from inside. Pushing gently on the door, she walked in and stood off to the side where no one could see her.

Seven men sat in a semi-circle, the smell of weed and whisky heavy in the air. Melvin Powell stood and cleared his throat. Bobbie could tell he was nervous; he kept hiking up his trousers and smoothing down his hair as he spoke, softly at first, speaking louder as his confidence grew. 'Right, how many of you are still renting your homes or living in the same council house you were thirty years ago?'

Six out of the seven hands shot up.

'And we all know why, right?' he said, his bile steadily rising.

‘Too fuckin’ right,’ one of the men barked. ‘Bloody English buying up our houses for holiday homes. Travesty, it is.’

‘It’s not like our wages have gone up,’ said another. ‘My youngest’s just married, can’t afford to buy a house on the island he was born on. Had to move away, Conwy Valley of all places.’

A man stood, his face red and etched with anger. ‘They closed down Wylfa power because they reckon nuclear’s not clean enough, but they don’t give us any new jobs. When the site’s decommissioned the place will just about run itself. Even if that Chinese company buys it and starts generating, we’ll still have to apply for the same jobs we’ve been doing for twenty years.’

Another voice. ‘They’ll probably put us all on zero-hour contracts, like they own the bones of us.’

A muttering of agreement hummed through the room.

‘That’s why we can’t sit on our arses anymore,’ Melvin urged. ‘If Plaid Cymru and the local council won’t do nothing, then it’s up to us, yeah? We take the fight to them, get them to take notice, make some bloody changes of our own.’

‘God helps him who helps himself,’ another man offered.

Melvin paused. He doubted the existence of any god, benevolent or otherwise, but decided against engaging in theological discussion. He had their attention and wasn’t about to risk losing it. He continued. ‘The more holiday homes get sold, the higher the prices for us locals. There’ll come a time none of our kids or grandkids will be able to afford to buy a house on the island.’

Another voice. ‘It’s not fucking right, Mel. Not right at all.’

Ronnie raised his hand as if he were back in school. ‘I heard they’re trying to pass some new law. The owners have to prove the house is their permanent residence, or something.’

‘I heard,’ another man said. ‘Too little too fucking late, if you ask me. Damage is already done.’

‘If that Logan Collins gets elected, he’s not going to let that happen; bastard owns at least seven holiday homes on the island.’

‘One less, now,’ Ronnie said, with a wide smile.

The room erupted with a crack of laughter – a release of tension Melvin wasn't sure he liked or wanted, but rolled with anyway.

Another man spoke up. 'He's doing all right in the polls,' he said. 'The more English living on the island, better chance he's got of winning. They vote like for like, that lot. The election's only four months away. He could get even more votes by then, win the whole bloody thing.'

'Then it's up to us to make sure he doesn't get anywhere close to fuckin' winning,' Melvin urged.

'Oh yeah, and how you going to do that?' Ronnie said. 'Use your painting and decorating skills to mess up his election posters?'

Another ripple of laughter. This time Melvin didn't roll with it. Instead, he clenched his fists and stepped into his old boxer stance; right foot slightly back, his posture low and aggressive. 'Shut it, Ronnie,' he said, his lips curling back over his teeth.

'Hey, calm down there, raging bull, you'll give yourself an aneurysm,' Ronnie said.

Melvin composed himself. 'There's a new plan,' he said, gesturing to his nephew.

Ronnie ambled to the front and turned to face the men. 'Uncle Mel's right,' he said. 'New plan.'

'What's involved?' one of the men asked.

'Best you don't know. Just me and Ronnie on this one.'

'Yeah,' Ronnie confirmed. 'It's a stealth mission, like.'

'But we'll all share in the glory,' Melvin said, quickly.

'When's it happening, so we know?' one of the men asked.

'Next Thursday night,' Ronnie blurted.

Melvin scowled. 'Yeah, maybe, we still got some details to work out,' he said. 'Oh, and by the way, if anyone knows of an old van we can nick from somewhere, let Ronnie here know, eh?'

Bobbie waited for the men to drift off into the car park before entering the room.

'Jesus Christ!' Melvin said, tugging at the cuffs of his Ben Sherman button-down, his eyes darting around the room nervously. 'What the bloody hell are you doing here?' He pulled her to the far end of the room, close to the pool table. 'What did you hear?'

'All of it,' Bobbie said, checking out the gleaming black crossbow laid out across the baize.

Melvin wiped a hand over his lips. 'It's not what—'

'Meibion Glyndŵr,' she said, gesturing at the flag. 'Were you part of it, back then?'

Melvin shook his head. 'Another bloody lifetime.'

Bobbie leaned on the side of the table and ran her hand down the crossbow's tiller. 'And those men?'

'Most of them fought for the cause, apart from Ronnie, he wasn't born then. But he's family and he's committed.'

Melvin reached for his glass of Penderyn and took a large slug. 'You going to tell the police then? Shop us all?'

Bobbie thought on his question. A few months ago, she probably would have, but now things weren't as black and white as they once were. 'Why? Why now?' she asked.

'You just heard why,' Melvin said.

'No. Why is this so important to you?'

Melvin shrugged. 'A man's got to go out fighting, or else what's the point of it all?'

Bobbie nodded, satisfied with his answer, and lifted the crossbow, letting it rest in her palms. 'Heavier than I thought.'

'Kill a fox from twenty metres,' Melvin said, taking the crossbow from Bobbie and laying it back on the table. 'You want to be careful handling that.'

Pinned to the wall next to the banner, Bobbie noticed a brightly coloured pamphlet with the date circled with a thick marker pen. She walked over, unpinned it and held it to the light. 'Is this the plan you were talking about?'

Melvin snatched the Menai Bridge Food Slam flyer from her hands and rolled it up. 'No offence, but maybe it's best you get going now, eh, it's getting late.'

'Late? I don't sleep much, anyway. So, are you going to tell me or not? Maybe I can help.'

'Look, love,' Mel said, his voice suddenly edgier. 'You hardly know me. I can't let you get involved with all this; you've got your career—'

'Had,' Bobbie interrupted, drawing a strand of hair from her face. 'I *had* a career. Now I'm just another problem they think they can brush under the carpet. I'm done following orders.'

Melvin's eyes narrowed. 'This isn't your fight. I'd go back home if I were you. Go on, on your way, I've got the pub to close up,' he said, coughing loudly into his fist.

'Didn't you hear what I just said? I'm done with orders. Anyway, seems to me you could do with all the help you can get.'

Melvin composed himself, ran a tissue across his mouth. 'I don't need your help, don't need anyone's help.'

Bobbie shook her head. 'Well, you know how to contact me.' As she left, Bobbie was sure what she'd just witnessed was another sign. She wasn't sure of its significance yet, but that's how signs worked, they took their time to reveal their intended meaning. She just needed to be wide-awake and responsive when the final reveal made itself known.

Chapter 13

The temperature reader attached to the air conditioning unit in the incident room signalled fifteen degrees Celsius. That was a lie. It was closer to twenty-two degrees, the air stagnant and dry.

'Should have worn my shorts,' DS Nader said, walking in.

'Yeah, air con's on the blink,' Priddle said. 'Don't understand it, the station was just built a few months ago.'

'Just in time for summer, perfect that is,' Nader said, drawing up a chair. 'Boss here yet?'

'Yes, I am, sergeant,' Manx said, entering with an armful of files, which he stacked on the desk.

Nader watched PC Delyth Morris enter the room. 'Girlfriend playing rough again, Minor?' he said, gesturing at the bruise around her left eye.

'Got it playing five-aside. Not that it's any of your business,' she said, turning to face the sergeant. 'Anyway, I told you, my name's Morris, not Minor.'

'Until the day I'm obliged to call you ma'am, you'll always be Minor to me, love.'

PC Morris, a shade under five feet three with the build of a gymnast, slouched into the chair. Normally, she would have fired a sharp retort Nader's way, but this morning she couldn't muster up the enthusiasm. Her typically bright, intelligent eyes were bloodshot and bleary, but still sharp enough to throw Nader a pointed scowl. 'Sorry I'm late, sir.'

'We have a positive ID on our victim,' Manx said, arranging the scene-of-crime photographs on the incident board. 'Base Commander James Brian Flynt. Fifty-eight. Flynt was reported missing on Monday morning when he was a no-show for a scheduled meeting.'

'He wasn't on any missing persons reports,' Morris said.

'Makes sense,' Nader said. 'Military like to keep that kind of thing to themselves until they confirm if one of their lads is really missing and not on some weekend bender in Amsterdam.'

'Flynt's wife will identify the body this afternoon, after that we'll release the name to the press. Morris, accompany Mrs Flynt and if she's up to it, have her come into the station to answer a few additional questions. Tell her it's just routine, but gently does it.'

'Got it, sir,' Morris confirmed.

Priddle raised his hand. 'Do we know the cause of death?'

Manx attached a slip of paper to the board. 'According to Hardacre, COD is still inconclusive. We can confirm the Audi A7 belonged to James Flynt.'

'Maybe he was meeting someone,' Priddle offered.

'Bevan should get back to us soon on the tyre prints he found next to Flynt's car,' Manx said. 'But I'm not holding my breath.'

'If Flynt left a nice car like that unlocked, with the keys inside, I reckon he wasn't intending on wandering off far.'

'Or,' Manx said, writing the word *suicide?* on the incident board, 'he wasn't intending on coming back.' Manx was about to continue when the incident room door swung wide open.

'Nothing like the sound of a well-oiled crime-solving machine in action,' Canton bellowed, settling himself on the edge of one of the desks. 'Troup's just been on the blower.'

'That's the kind of news guaranteed to cheer me up.'

'That aside, Manx, she's already spoken with the RAF Valley new acting base commander. He's expecting you this morning and has requested our discretion around this matter.'

'By which he means keeping our noses out of RAF business?'

Nader stretched out his legs. 'If they're anything like the army, they'll close ranks quicker than a tart pulling down her knickers.'

'You can't call them tarts,' Morris snapped. 'It's not the nineteen bloody fifties.'

'Oh, yeah,' Nader said. 'Must have meant sex worker. Quicker than a sex worker pulling down her knickers, boss.'

'Nader has a point,' Manx said. 'Our jurisdiction will be limited on an RAF base.'

Canton brushed the errant crumbs from an early morning pastry off his shirt. 'With your well-honed diplomatic skills, he'll be eating out of your hand in no time, Manx.'

As Canton walked out, Manx turned to face the team. 'Right, as our fearless leader says, apparently we're a well-oiled crime-solving machine, whatever the hell that means.' He added the final few photographs to the board. 'Any luck with the additional door-to-doors yesterday, Priddle?'

'Nah, but we're going to knock on a few more this morning.'

Manx nodded. 'Canton's approved a floater for the collating and entering of evidence, which leaves you, Morris, free to scour Flynt's bank accounts for any unusual transactions, money problems, gambling addictions. Gently does it with the wife, but probe her about Flynt's work; anyone with a grudge, jealous colleagues, the usual drill.'

'Got it, sir,' Morris confirmed.

'Nader, as you seem to have some background in these military matters, you can accompany me to the base.'

'Happy to,' he said, scooting back his chair.

Manx addressed the team. 'This is the first full day of what could be a murder or a tragic accident. I don't need to remind you, but I will; we'll all conduct this investigation with professionalism, all our Is dotted, our Ts crossed. Anyone got a problem with that?'

A communal shaking of heads and a series of *no bosses* echoed around the incident room.

Chapter 14

The roar of a fast jet rattled the Jensen's old bones as it passed overhead. Manx and Nader were waiting at the RAF Valley sentry gate while a young corporal checked over their paperwork.

'Bloody impressive, eh?' Nader said, craning his neck as the BAE HawkT2 training jet thundered across the airstrip.

'Bloody noisy,' Manx said, squirming the tip of his little finger in his right ear.

The corporal handed back the paperwork. 'Park at the red and white checks by the squadron building. Nowhere else.'

As they pulled up a few hundred metres away from the checkpoint, another serviceman was already waiting.

'Don't want us wandering off on our own, looks like,' Manx said, looking up at the vast, L-shaped glass building.

'Probably like this on all the bases these days, anti-terrorist precautions and all that.'

'Papers,' the sergeant demanded. He double-checked their IDs, clicked his heels sharply and turned. 'Follow me.'

Inside, the building was cavernous, the ceiling at least thirty feet high and supported by several iron girders. The morning sun streamed through the glass, casting geometrical shapes along the gleaming tiled floor. A wide sliding door fitted with a high-tech security entry system led from the main reception area. The sign above read *Training School, Advanced Flight Simulator #3.*

The sergeant stopped at the reception desk. 'Wait here. The

commander will meet you shortly,' he said, and marched, stiff-backed, down one of the adjacent corridors.

As they waited, Nader and Manx studied the collection of photographs arranged in a perfectly regimented line along the wall.

'Saw that one in the *Daily Mirror*,' Nader said, pointing at a shot of William, Duke of Cambridge, smiling from a cockpit. He leaned in close, squinting. 'You think he's really flying that chopper?'

'He most definitely is.' The voice was efficient, clipped.

Manx and Nader both turned.

'And, by the way, choppers are typically single-rotor commercial craft, this is a Sea King 3A Helicopter. American made, but we try not to hold that against them.'

'Oh, yeah,' Nader said. 'I recognise it now.'

The man smiled. He was as tall as Manx, in his late thirties and wearing RAF service dress. His eyes alert, blond hair shorn close on the sides with a razor-sharp parting. 'Group Captain Hamish Boyd, acting base commander,' he said, extending his hand. 'Apologies for all the protocol. With his royal highness on the base, we're on a far tighter lockdown than usual.'

Manx shook his hand and introduced himself and the sergeant. Nader almost stood to attention as Manx said his name.

'Welsh Guards eighty-one to eighty-seven. Honourable discharge,' the sergeant added.

The commander nodded. 'Eighty-one? Falklands veteran?'

'Signed up the November before.'

'Oh, bad luck. But you made it back in one piece.'

'Yeah, just about,' Nader said. He paused for a moment. 'But keep calm and carry on, that's what they say, right?'

'Indeed, they do.'

'We have some questions concerning Mr Flynt,' Manx said.

'Of course, but not here,' the commander said. 'Let's use the conference room. There's someone there who I think should also be part of this conversation.'

'Lead the way,' Manx said.

The commander stopped midway down the hallway, pushed opened the door marked *Valley #1* and gestured for them to enter.

The room had floor-to-ceiling windows; the blinds pulled down to diffuse the sunlight. At the far end of the table, Jack Carlisle rested an arm on the back of a chair and smoothed down the front of his tie with his hand. His demeanour suggested he was there under protest and had better, more important places to be.

Manx had been formally introduced to Jack Carlisle ten months earlier, when he'd first been transferred to Anglesey – it was standard protocol. The Royalty Protection Group insisted they were introduced to all senior-level police officers assigned to the island. Manx had worked alongside plenty of men like Carlisle during his time at the Met; ex-military types who imagined themselves a cut above regular officers because they rubbed shoulders with some minor royals too fond of partying and having their faces slapped on the gossip pages of the tabloids. Jack Carlisle had been assigned senior royal protection officer to the Duke and Duchess of Cambridge for the duration of the Duke's tour of duty at RAF Valley. Carlisle was in his early forties, square-jawed, clean shaven and wearing a perfectly tailored black suit with a Union Jack badge pinned to the lapel. The last Manx knew, Carlisle had been promoted to a top-tier position at the MoD in Whitehall some six months ago. The fact he was here now, sitting across from Manx, cucumber cool, staring Manx down as if he were someone to be evaluated and if necessary neutralised, didn't bode well.

Carlisle rose to shake Manx and Nader's hands. 'Good to see you again, Manx,' he said.

'I thought your tour of duty here was over months ago.'

'Whitehall insisted. Just treat me like a fly on the wall, I'm here only as a passive observer.'

Manx doubted the veracity of that statement and slipped into the nearest chair.

The commander sat opposite, rested his hands on the perfect crease of his trousers and spoke. 'I'm only a few hours into this job, flew in this morning from Brize Norton. I never had the pleasure of meeting Commander Flynt, but I heard he was an exemplary officer and a mentor to the young officers. He'll be sorely missed.'

Manx listened to his words with a creeping sense they'd been finely honed, obituary-ready. 'Anything more substantial you could add?' he asked, drawing out his notebook.

The commander brought his hands together. 'Before transferring, he was stationed at RAF Waddington in Lincolnshire. It was a significant promotion for Commander Flynt.'

'What was his previous role?'

'Ah, I'm afraid I'm not at liberty to disclose.'

'Why Anglesey?' Manx asked.

The commander tugged at the fringe of his jacket. 'RAF Valley is one of our most critical fast jet training bases, we'll take all the seasoned officers we can. The gene pool's not that deep for the kind of expertise Flynt had.'

'What about grudges, any enemies on the base?'

'I was under the impression he was well-liked. Believe me, we keep a close eye on any kind of abuse of power these days.'

'Changed a bit since my time,' Nader said. 'Put up and shut up or end up on shit-shovelling duty for the duration.'

'We've been fashioned into a military operation fit for the twenty-first century,' the commander insisted. 'What with Home Office oversight and pressure from counter terrorism we can't escape the glaring light of culpability, much like the police force.'

Manx pointed his pen at the commander. 'Except the police force is directly answerable to the public,' he said. 'We don't work under the protection of the Official Secrets Act.'

Nader bristled. 'The commander's only saying.'

'No, no,' the commander said, raising his palm. 'Your inspector is correct. The police force has been subject to more than its fair share of negative publicity, but I like to think we're two sides of the same coin. You protect the public from imminent dangers, we protect them from the dangers no one sees coming.'

Nader leaned forward, stabbing the air between them with his index finger. 'Most people don't know the half of it. It's because of people like us they can sleep in their beds at night.'

'Couldn't agree more, sergeant,' said the commander.

Manx sat back. 'Did Flynt have money problems?'

'None that were brought to my attention.'

At the far end of the room, Jack Carlisle stirred as if he'd been poked with a stick. 'Listen, Manx,' he said, leaning across the table. 'We're as keen to solve this case as you are, maybe even more so.'

'How so, Carlisle?' Manx asked.

'Let's just underline it as a matter of national security. If you find all this was a tragic accident, then all well and good, I'll sleep better at night. We all will.'

Manx gave a tight smile. 'I'll be sure to let the widow know.'

Carlisle continued. 'If, during your investigation, you discover that Flynt's death was something more ominous, then that would give us cause for concern. The commander of the base where second in line to the throne is currently stationed is killed—'

'I don't remember mentioning anything about anyone being killed, do you, Nader?' Manx interrupted.

'Em, I expect Mr Carlisle – Jack – is just saying—'

'What was Flynt's state of mind?' Manx asked, quickly cutting off Nader mid-sentence.

'Ah,' Carlisle said, sitting back and wagging a finger. 'You're reaching now, Manx. Investigating outside the box.'

'Commander?' Manx said, steering the conversation back on track.

'You'd have to ask the personnel he worked with.'

'And you'll give us access?'

The commander shuffled. 'Within reason, yes.'

'Within reason? Right you are,' Manx said. 'And when can I expect a list of these personnel?'

'Would end of day work?'

'The sooner we get those names, the sooner we can clear this up and be out of your hair.'

The commander smiled: the kind of smile that hid something less friendly, coarser, beneath its smooth veneer.

Manx closed his notebook. 'We'll be interviewing Mrs Flynt later. Maybe she can help us paint a more rounded picture.'

'I really need to get on,' the commander said, standing and stretching out his hand. 'It's been a pleasure, although I wish it were under better circumstances.'

'Appreciate you taking the time, sir,' Nader said, barely stopping himself from saluting the commander.

'You on the island for a while, Carlisle?' Manx asked.

'As long as my country needs me,' he said. 'Good luck with all this unsavoury business. The copper's lot, eh, Manx?'

* * *As they drove past the checkpoint, Manx, still irritated at Carlisle's presence, turned to Nader. 'What the hell was all that about?'

'Closing ranks, you mean, boss? Always happens.'

'No, Nader, you, brown-nosing the base commander like you were hoping for a bloody officer commission.'

'Nah, weren't like that, boss, just looking for common ground, get him to open up.'

'And how did that work out for you?'

'Em—'

'Don't bother. It was fucking rhetorical.'

Chapter 15

The late-afternoon air felt good against Bobbie's face as she ran the narrow track that circled the lake across from the base. Her back was slick with sweat, her breathing measured as she crossed the road and passed the sentry gate. She headed towards the gym, where she could shower and change before starting her shift. She noticed a flurry of activity around the squadron building. Several Range Rovers with thick privacy glass were parked outside, with two RAF police vehicles next to them.

'Hell of a morning.'

Bobbie turned. Call Me Andy was standing next to her, dressed in sweatpants and a grey hoodie.

'What's going on?'

'You haven't heard?'

'I wouldn't be asking otherwise.'

'Commander Flynt. They found his body this morning.'

Bobbie's blood ran to ice. 'How? Where?' she asked.

'Other side of the island, I think. They're not releasing much information at the moment.'

'Do they know what happened? How he died?'

'They found his body on a beach, that's all I know.'

'Who's that?' Bobbie asked, gesturing at a tall man in service dress stepping out of a Range Rover.

'Acting base commander, I expect.'

'That was quick.'

'Time and tide and all that.'

Bobbie took a deep breath. She suddenly felt light-headed and bent over, securing her hands on her knees.

'You okay?' Pierce said, placing his hand on her back.

'Yeah,' she said, standing and shrugging off his touch. 'It's just a shock, that's all.'

'Unexpected, no doubt. But the pressures of running a base this size can't have been easy.'

Bobbie stepped back and shook her head. 'No, not Flynt, he wasn't the suicidal type.'

'Time will tell,' Pierce said, handing Bobbie an envelope.

'What's this?'

'Your paperwork for the VA hospital. Routine, nothing to worry about.'

Bobbie reluctantly took the envelope.

'I can drive you there, so you don't have to travel alone.'

'Or make sure I don't get lost on the way?'

Pierce blushed. 'No, it's just–'

'When you find the name of this new base commander can you come and find me?' Bobbie said, stuffing the envelope into the back pocket of her sweatpants.

'Yes, I suppose. Why?'

'There's something he needs to know.'

Chapter 16

'Bet you drank here all the time, underage too,' Gwen Schofield said, sliding Manx's pint across the bar.

Manx sat on the threadbare stool. 'Maybe, but it wasn't like this in my day,' he said, cocking his thumb behind him.

The pub was adjacent to Moelfre beach, set a few metres across from the ice cream stand and souvenir shop, and at 7.00 pm was packed with tourists. The locals tended to give the pub a wide berth during the summer, preferring to do their drinking further inland, where the only tourists were the ones hiking their way through Anglesey's ancient druid burial sites, or the kind who had taken a wrong turn on a narrow country back road. For Manx, the Pilot Arms was less than a ten-minute walk from his house; reason enough to call the place his local, no matter the season.

He turned as two young boys on a sugar high screamed and swung on the fishing nets draped across the window. Their mother, fast on her feet, grabbed them around the waist, dragged them back to the table and ordered them to sit.

Gwen shook her head. 'I keep reminding his landlordship they'll be gone in six weeks, then we'll be left with the old boys nursing their pints all night and complaining about the prices.'

Manx looked over the rim of his glass as he sipped.

'Present company excepted, of course. Never seen you nurse a pint, probably wouldn't know how.'

'I'll take that as a compliment.'

'Take it any way you want,' Gwen said, leaning over the bar to serve a young man with a strong scouse accent. 'So, did you drink down here when you were younger?' she asked, gathering a stack of damp beer mats.

'Might have snuck a pint or two.'

Gwen tossed the mats into the bin. 'And the rest.'

'Why are you asking? Got someone matching my description wanted for underage drinking thirty-five years ago?'

Gwen wiped the inside of a pint glass. 'Just been wondering lately about all this change on the island. It's not like it used to be.'

'Nothing is, Gwen.'

'I reckon there's more holidaymakers here every summer. And all those new flats they're building? They're not for the likes of us locals at those prices, are they?'

'First sign of old age, nostalgia, Gwen.'

'But you came back, you must have missed the place?'

'Oh, this is just temporary until I figure things out, then I'm back down to London, get the grit of the city back in my blood.'

Gwen pulled Manx a fresh pint. 'Yeah, I suppose we have to tell ourselves stuff like that so we don't go bloody mad. Always somewhere better to move on to, greener grass, yeah?'

As she turned to serve an older couple who'd just walked in, Manx laid out the leaflet Canton had given him across the bar.

'Into food slams, now, Inspector?' Gwen asked.

'If I knew what the hell that was, maybe I could answer.'

'A food slam? A load of restaurants from the island come together to cook in one place. That politician, Logan Collins, is meant to be opening it this year.'

'That name keeps cropping up.'

'Yeah, wants to be Anglesey's next MP. He's delusional, no bloody clue.'

'So, he's more than qualified for the job, then.'

'He's English, but thinks he's learned to speak Welsh. He sounds like that Prince Charles after a few too many pints, nobody can understand a bloody word he says—' Gwen stopped mid-sentence. 'Oh, and talking about the English,' she said, nodding towards the man ambling towards the bar: lead CSI, Ashton Bevan.

'They say the old lion never strays far from its watering hole,' Bevan said. 'Or are you the antelope, Manx? The quarry?'

From behind his left shoulder, Manx heard a familiar voice. 'It's not going to be a work evening is it, Ash?' Bevan's wife, Sherry, moaned and set her purse on the bar. 'You promised.'

'Just five minutes, love. Quick bit of business with the inspector here.'

Sherry draped her arm elegantly across the bar, dipping her hand at the wrist as if expecting Manx to kiss it. 'How are you, Inspector Manx? Enjoying the warm weather?'

'Not particularly,' Manx said, shaking her hand.

Sherry smiled. 'Yes, you don't look like the summer-loving type,' she said, flipping her blonde hair and checking herself out in the mirror behind the optics. The gesture wasn't required. Sherry always looked as if she'd stepped out of a fashion shoot and tonight was no exception. She wore a tight blue T-shirt tucked into white jeans which accented her taut waistline. She'd pushed her oversized sunglasses over her forehead so they rested on her hair, giving an air of casual elegance; more Euro chic than Anglesey food slam.

And then there was Bevan. Several inches shorter than his wife and with a fast-thinning comb-over. The middle buttons of his short-sleeved shirt strained as he leaned on the bar – more than likely hadn't worn it since last summer when he was a few pounds lighter around the belly. Bevan and his wife were like a puzzle Manx could never figure out; a mismatch made in heaven.

Bevan tapped his wife's arm. 'Why don't you grab a table outside, I'll bring the drinks over.'

Sherry pulled down her sunglasses and pointed at Bevan. 'Five minutes, Ash, or you'll be drinking by yourself. Nice to see you, Inspector. Keep in the shade, too much sun can't be good for a complexion like yours.'

Bevan ordered. 'Two gin and tonics, Bombay Sapphire, not that cheap rubbish. And limes, not lemons, if you've got them.'

Gwen smiled, gave him a two-fingered salute under the bar.

'So, Bevan, is this social or professional?'

'One and the same in my book, Manx.' Bevan slid a tenner across the bar. 'Treat the social like the professional, and vice versa, you learn a lot more.'

'You should hurry up with whatever it is you need to get off your chest before your wife ditches you for a younger man,' Manx said, cocking his head in the direction of the window.

Bevan glanced towards the patio. Sherry was being chatted up by two young lads and didn't seem in any hurry to send them packing. He turned to Gwen. 'Get a rush on with those drinks, eh?' Bevan's brow glistened with a mist of perspiration. 'That matter down at Benllech beach. As we all know, our victim was found in RAF service dress.'

'Flynt was the base commander at Valley. We spoke to the new bloke over there this morning.'

'And did he enlighten you as to Flynt's previous role?'

'Flight training, apparently.'

Bevan reached into his pocket and showed Manx a print-out of the insignia on Flynt's jacket. 'Here's the thing,' he said. 'RAF wings are typically surrounded by a gold laurel wreath; this one, however, is surrounded with a blue laurel.'

'Significance?'

Bevan became increasingly flustered as Sherry's familiar laughter wafted through the open window. 'Right,' he said, pouring the tonic sloppily over the ice. 'Blue laurel leaves are assigned to only one division in the RAF, Thirteen Squadron.'

'Which is?'

'Flynt was assigned to the RAF's unmanned aircraft programme.'

'Drones? The commander forgot to mention that.'

Bevan grabbed his drinks. 'And guess where the only active British RAF drone programme operates from?'

Manx paused, recalling his meeting with the Base Commander. 'Wild guess. Waddington, Lincolnshire?'

'Bingo,' Bevan said. 'Which makes me wonder.'

'Wonder what?'

'What else this base commander has been keeping from you,' Bevan said, with a thin press of his lips that he could have trademarked as his own personal smirk. 'Enjoy your night.'

Chapter 17

The following morning, Bobbie stood in front of the base commander, field service cap tucked under the crook of her arm.

'Flight Lieutenant Bobbie Matthews, correct?' Commander Boyd said, looking up from his computer screen.

Bobbie stood to attention. 'Sir.'

He sat back. 'Your reputation, as they say, precedes you.'

'I'm not sure I understand–'

'If this is why you're here,' he said, gesturing at the same thick pile of letters and correspondence Flynt had as near as spat on three days ago. 'I'm afraid I don't have the time to deal with your Enid bloody Blyton *Boys' Own* conspiracies. I have a base to run.'

'It's not that, sir,' Bobbie said, flinching inwardly.

The commander sighed. 'Right. Sit. Make it brief.'

'I saw Commander Flynt the night before he died,' Bobbie explained, settling into the chair.

The commander arched his eyebrows. 'You met with Flynt?'

The moment the words left her mouth Bobbie regretted speaking. She could already tell Boyd was a different breed of commander to Flynt. At least twenty years younger, his accent polished, his mannerisms controlled. Privately educated, Bobbie guessed, top-tier university, followed by officer training and a fast-track to base commander. Flynt had his faults, but at least she always knew where she stood with the man. Bobbie sensed a brittle iciness from Boyd; ambitious, but with an edge that suggested he didn't care who he stepped over to get there. At that moment, Bobbie was in no doubt Flynt had been given the base commander position in exchange for toeing the line on the Operation Vanguard findings. Men of Flynt's background – recruited directly from school, working-class upbringing, fought his way up the ranks – rarely made base commander. Bobbie chose her words carefully as she answered. 'I didn't meet with Commander Flynt, specifically.'

'Then what – specifically – are you not telling me, Matthews?'

She took a breath. 'I was out driving, I found myself outside Commander Flynt's house—'

'What time was this?'

'Just after twenty-one hundred hours—'

'What the hell were you doing outside your commanding officer's home at that time of night?'

'I wanted to speak to Commander Flynt. Off base.'

'About these?' He stabbed the papers. 'Did you and Flynt share the same disdain for official reports? I understand you were both in the ground control station during Operation Vanguard.'

'I believe Commander Flynt accepted the findings.'

'So, you were outside his house to persuade him otherwise?'

Bobbie ignored the question. 'I saw Commander Flynt leave the house before I had the opportunity to speak with him.'

'Was he with someone?'

'No. Drove off by himself, sir.'

Commander Boyd thought for a moment and shuffled forward on his chair. 'Have you informed anyone else about this?'

Bobbie shook her head.

'Then let's keep it that way. This stays between us, loose lips and all that.'

'What about the police, sir? Shouldn't—'

'Let me worry about that,' he snapped. 'I don't want the local coppers stomping their size-eleven boots all over my base. If it's relevant, I'll pass on the information. Was there anything else?'

'No, I don't think so, sir,' Bobbie said, standing.

Commander Boyd reached for a slip of paper and quickly scanned its contents. 'I understand you're leaving us at the end of the month. I'd recommend keeping yourself out of trouble and out of my hair. No more searching for this damned truth you're so obsessed with. Do not provide me a reason to sully your exemplary record. Are we clear?'

Bobbie's fists clenched. The implication was clear enough. As base commander, Boyd had the power to write her service record as he saw fit, ensured she was demoted to a less senior position with less pay and a reduced pension when she was finally discharged.

'We're clear,' she said. 'But if I don't find the truth of what happened, I can't guarantee someone else won't. Sir.'

Chapter 18

Manx walked past the oak doors at the entrance to St Gerard's and followed the cheers coming from the sports field. Back in the eighties, the school was operated by the Congregation of the Sisters of Mercy as a girls' day and boarding school. Manx knew this because, as a teenager, he'd ride the Friday bus into Bangor with his friends in the hope of catching a slow dance with one of the girls at the local disco. Convent girls, they'd been told by the older lads, were 'boy-crazy'; easy pickings under the lights of a mirror ball and went weak-kneed at the smell of Brut aftershave. Like most tales concerning girls, it was false. They were neither boy-crazy nor easy. They were no different to the girls at his school, just richer and more aware of their value when it came to dating boys from the local comprehensive. St Gerard's was now co-ed, but the girls still possessed an innate understanding of their value in the world, Manx guessed, as he passed a huddle of them striking Instagram-worthy poses under the shade of a stoic oak tree.

DCSI Vera Troup had summoned him to the school. It was the last day of the summer term; St Gerard's Sports Day. Her daughter, Angharad, was running in the four hundred-metre relay. Manx had never given much thought to Vera as a wife, let alone a mother. Her posture and icy demeanour did little to encourage small talk or the exchange of pleasantries beyond anything concerning the North Wales Constabulary, recent arrest rates, and improving public relations – Vera's hot button topic at most meetings.

Manx spotted Vera at the finish line wearing a black T-shirt, jeans and trainers. A girl, who he guessed was Angharad, crossed the finish line in third place. Vera cheered and hugged her daughter. Spotting Manx lingering on the side lines she whispered to Angharad, who sprinted off to join her friends.

'I thought the schools were all done for the summer.'

Vera gestured he should follow her to a quiet spot behind the PA system. 'St Gerard's is one of the highest rated schools in North Wales,' she explained. 'If the pupils sacrifice an extra week of doing bugger all and staring at their phones all day, then so be it. It's a competitive world these days, especially for a young woman.'

'No doubt,' Manx agreed. 'So, I suspect you didn't ask me here to sell me on the benefits of a private education?'

'No. That business at Benllech beach—'

'Ah. I had no choice but to close it down, ma'am. God knows what else we might have found there, or if a young kiddie found something before we did.'

'And did you find anything?' she asked, folding her arms.

'Only the body, but—'

'I'm not questioning your decision, Manx, I asked you here to talk about Base Commander Boyd.'

Manx stepped into the shade. 'Played his cards close to his chest. Not surprising. I've got three officers on the base taking statements from anyone who worked with Flynt.'

Vera stood for a moment. 'You're a good officer, Manx, but you don't strike me as a patient one. If we have any hope of solving this case, we need the RAF on our side and that's going to take diplomacy. No rubbing them up the wrong way with references to police oversight and the bloody Official Secrets Act.'

Manx winced. 'He's already spoken to you?'

'Beside the point. Get the job done, Manx, but don't jeopardise the investigation before we're out of the starting gate.'

'Understood, ma'am,' he confirmed.

Following the dead air of an awkward pause, Manx noticed a tall man wearing a pink polo shirt and a powder-blue sweater looped around his shoulders striding towards them – Logan Collins. His hair was gelled back in what Manx guessed was the current politician style. His smile was equally slick, and forced. 'Found those thugs who destroyed my holiday home yet, Vera?'

Troup straightened, visibly irritated. 'You'll be the first to know when we do, Logan.'

Collins huffed like a petulant horse and looked over at Manx.

'This is DI Tudor Manx. Logan's two sons also attend the school,' Vera said.

'Two, huh?' Manx said. 'That can't be cheap.'

Collins ignored the remark, studying Manx closely as he shook his hand. 'You look familiar.'

'I was outside your house when you gave that impromptu press conference a couple of days ago.'

'So, you're working on the case?'

'Amongst others.'

'Do you know what I think, DI Manx?' Collins said, pulling back his shoulders as if he were about to deliver a speech. 'I think it's just the start. These things have a tendency to escalate. Four holiday homes burned to the ground. What's next? Setting fire to someone's property when they're home, with kids sleeping?'

'Can't argue with that, Mr Collins. That's the kind of tragedy the North Wales Constabulary is keen to avoid.'

Collins was about to reply when a young boy ran up and dragged at his trouser leg. 'All right, Marcus, Daddy will be right there,' he said, with an impatient snap. 'Vera, DI Manx. I hope the next time we meet you'll have some encouraging news to share.'

'Again, you'll be the first to know,' Vera said, as Collins walked away. 'That wasn't so hard was it, Manx?'

'Here to serve, ma'am.'

She presented Manx with as close to a smile as he'd ever seen her offer, then went back to join the other parents.

Manx walked across the freshly mown grass and found some shade under an alder tree and looked over the handsome, stoic form of St

Gerard's. As the afternoon sun beat down the thick, grey bricks seemed to absorb the light as if they were feeding from its heat. The clock tower cast a long, deep shadow over the field and across Vera Troup, who was kneeling to attend to a small grass burn on her daughter's knee. It felt like an omen of sorts. He quickly dismissed the idea as an overly suspicious copper looking for meaning, in shadows but finding only darkness.

Chapter 19

From the window of her flat above the pub, Lydia Jones watched the men spill out from the old barn and walk towards the car park. Three of them, including Ronnie Powell, hung around the courtyard laughing and smoking. She pulled hard on a smoke of her own; a tightly rolled joint, one of a handful she kept in an old jewellery box, and supplied courtesy of Melvin's Paint and Plaster.

A roar of laughter drifted up from the courtyard. Another one of Melvin's meetings. *No better than bloody kids*, she thought, as Ronnie and another man jostled with each other under the eaves of the old stable. Didn't they have homes to go to? Better things to do with their time than play at being in a bloody gang like they were ten years old?

She'd expected better of Melvin, but then again, she'd expected better of all the men she'd lived with; expected a hell of a lot better from the one she'd married. But like the rest he'd carved a deep wound in her heart, along with an even deeper one in her bank account. Money was replaceable, it came and went, but the heart? That wasn't so easily repaired. In fact, she suspected it healed a little slower and a little harder with every scar.

At the age of fifty-three, she hadn't expected to fall in love again, had resisted the feeling for as long as she could, but a portion of her heart now belonged to Melvin. Would he turn out to be any different to the others? It was something she preferred not to dwell on. When she was young and stupid, she would have done just that, filled her head with some dream of marrying the perfect man, two kids, summer holidays in Spain. These days, she accepted things for what they were, didn't question where the relationship was going. Mel was good to her, most of the time at least, when he hadn't been drinking. He'd never raised a fist to her, though his silence could be as devastating as a slap in the face; sometimes more so.

'Hand me a smoke, eh, love,' Melvin said, throwing himself into the lounge chair positioned in front of the television. By default, it had become Mel's chair: like there was Mel's mug, Mel's pint glass, Mel's side of the bed. Lydia felt she should resent this, but truth was, it was comforting: the more he felt at home, the harder it would be for him to leave. It also meant she didn't have to drive the half-hour to Mel's cottage over in Church Bay. Ronnie was living there by himself these days; God knows what kind of mess the place was in; the lad could barely bend over to tie his own shoelaces.

Lydia took a joint from the box and handed it to Melvin.

'Be a love and light it for me, eh?' he said, slipping off his loafers and laying them next to each other in a neat line.

'And what did your last slave die of?'

Melvin loosened his belt. 'She didn't die, I divorced her.'

Lydia flicked her lighter. 'Aren't I the lucky bloody woman?'

He grabbed her wrist, pulled her in for a hard kiss on the lips.

'You been on the whisky again?' she said, pulling back and wiping the back of her hand across her mouth. Lydia had been in the firing line of plenty of drunks in her time – that last whisky shot was typically the trigger pull that led to something worse. She could take the beer – gin and vodka even – but there was something about the malty residue of whisky that turned her stomach, brought back those bad memories. If she had a quid for every man who'd smacked her across the mouth with the taint of whisky on his breath, she'd be a rich woman.

Melvin took a long, deep drag. The smoke hit him like a body punch to the lungs. He coughed hard, his body trembling as if everything inside him was shaking loose.

'Christ! You all right?' Lydia said. 'Do you want something?'

Melvin waved his hand. 'Leave it alone. Don't bloody fuss.'

Outside in the car park there was another cackle of loud laughter followed by a badly off-key rendition of 'Delilah'.

Lydia walked to the window, flung it open. 'Oy! Ronnie! Time you and your mates fucked off. Can't have you lot making noise after hours.'

No response, but a few minutes later the commotion stopped, followed by the loud rattle of Ronnie's quad bike accelerating.

'I told you enough times,' she said, sitting back down. 'I can't have this after closing time. If the neighbours start mouthing off and complaining to the brewery, they could take my name off the lease.'

'Leave it be, it's just a few mates having a laugh.'

'Yeah, is that all?' she asked. 'A few mates having a laugh?'

Melvin took a shorter drag this time, sharp and quick. 'Why, you heard different?' he asked, his eyes narrowing.

'Just saying, this pub is all I've got. I can't afford any trouble.'

'Won't be no trouble.' He pushed himself back in the chair, a glassy look in his eyes. 'Only trouble comes when people start poking their noses where they don't belong,' he said, pointing at Lydia. It was a signal this was the end of the matter: no debate, no questioning. 'Could do with a sandwich,' he said, his tone a degree or two softer. 'I'm bloody famished.'

'A sandwich?' Lydia said, shaking her head. 'I could do with a bloody holiday too, but I don't see anyone offering to take me on a fortnight to Benidorm.'

'Aye, good luck with that,' he said, with a half-smile that hung around a fraction too long, as if he'd forgotten it was there.

'Might have something left over from dinner,' Lydia said, getting up. 'I'll go and check in the kitchen.'

'You do that,' he said, a lazy drawl to his voice.

When Lydia returned five minutes later, Melvin was already asleep, his head tilted towards his right shoulder. She settled the plate on the table and slipped the joint from his fingers. As she did so, she noticed a splat of red on the cuffs of his white shirt. She ran her finger along the spots. They smeared, still moist to the touch.

She brought a hand to her chest and looked at Melvin. Did he seem smaller? Filling the chair less than he did when he first moved in? His shirt looked looser across the chest; his jeans baggier around the waist. Or was it the weed over-stimulating her imagination? But the blood? That wasn't imaginary, that was as devastatingly real as life got.

She felt her chest tighten. Another scar? She could already feel its first nick someplace deep in her heart. She didn't think she had the space or willpower to take any more of them. But maybe the heart always had room to carry more pain; made room for it, prepared itself for it, even.

Chapter 20

Three hours after the sun had set and the sky had deepened to a dark, impenetrable blue, Bobbie was running the pathway around the lake across from RAF Valley. A spill of moonlight caught off her reflective vest as she ran, the beam from her LED headlight band helping navigate her way. Not that she needed the help, she could run the trail in her sleep by now; if sleep were ever to come to her again.

The air was still, the countryside rustling with nocturnal life. Invisible in the darkness, the mechanical whirring – like a distant engine – of the nightjar birds filtered through the undergrowth, while a chorus of dragonflies hummed over the grasslands. Bobbie could hear none of this. She had her headphones secured tight around her ears listening to 'Brilliant Mistake'.

She and Danvir had first bonded over Elvis Costello in the RAF Cosford mess, when they were both stationed there. She'd always said she could never date anyone who didn't love Elvis Costello, and Danvir had impressed her with his knowledge and passion for his early works. He'd enticed her back to his place with the promise of a rare bootleg from 1978, 'The Last Foxtrot, Live in Frisco'. When they discovered they'd grown up less than twenty miles from each other – Danvir in Bangor, Bobbie on Anglesey – it was like some perfect kismet. After that, they were rarely apart. The fact that Danvir was a Muslim, though not a devout one, and Bobbie had been brought up in the Methodist tradition, none of that mattered. They were married four years later. After a brief honeymoon, Bobbie was posted to Intelligence Command in

Waddington, and Danvir began a series of overseas postings. Nine years later, at the age of thirty-eight, Bobbie was a widow, the bottom having fallen so completely out of her world she could barely find her footing.

As she ran, 'Everyday I Write the Book' played in her headphones. The song resonated deeper than it ever had before. Danvir's story was done, his book closed. But Bobbie's story? That was still wide open, the pages waiting to be written. It was daunting to think of the courage it would take for her to fill those blank pages. In two weeks she'd be transferred, forced to talk about the incident and face her demons with the goal of being fixed. She doubted there was any fixing what was broken inside her.

Fifteen minutes later, the swirl of her thoughts having carried her the last mile and a half, she turned towards the narrow road that passed the east sentry gate. Her body showed no signs of tiredness; there was an energy, like a charge of electricity, pulsing through her.

With 'Pump It Up' blasting, she tackled the first few metres of the hill, her hamstrings straining. If the volume had been lower, or her senses more attuned, she might have heard the car approaching behind her. It wasn't until she saw the flash of headlights catch the wall of hedges that she felt the first troubling twinge of unease.

She looked behind. Two glaring headlights filled the narrow road. She was sure the vehicle would slow down. It didn't. If anything, it was gaining speed.

She ripped off her headphones; the ominous growl from the engine was loud and persistent, the headlights, two searchlights seeking their target. The road was barely wide enough for one car, the hedges too thick and high to provide an escape path.

She picked up her pace. The vehicle slipped down a gear, notching up the revs, edging closer and swerving from one side of the narrow road to the other.

Bobbie's heart thundered in her chest, all excess adrenaline now flowing to her legs and lungs. She looked for any breaks in the hedge; there were none, just a dense, impenetrable thicket. She had one option; to keep running.

As the car caught up with her, the side draught pushed her off balance. She stumbled into the ditch between the road and the hedge. Her feet lost traction in the gulley of the ditch.

Before she fell, the wing mirror clipped her left shoulder. The last thing she saw was the bright flint of sharp rock sticking out from the earth. She knew without question that her head would strike it.

She briefly registered the irony of 'Accidents Will Happen' spilling through her headphones before she slipped into darkness.

Chapter 21

The doctor stood at the foot of Bobbie Matthews' bed and spoke. 'She was treated for mild concussion, minor lacerations and a nasty bruise on her left shoulder,' she explained. 'No lasting damage, she'll be discharged by tomorrow morning.'

Manx looked at Bobbie, her face pale and peppered with small cuts. In his opinion, she didn't look like she'd be discharged anytime soon, but he accepted the doctor's prognosis with a slow nod of his head. 'Any idea why she asked to see me?'

The doctor clipped the paperwork to the bed frame. 'Not a clue. She was insistent we contacted the 'senior officer on the Commander James Flynt investigation',' she said, reading off a scrap of paper. 'But you can ask her yourself.' She gestured towards Bobbie, who was beginning to stir.

'Bobbie Matthews?' Manx said, stepping closer. 'You wanted to speak with me?'

She opened her eyes and shuffled against the pillows with a groan.

'I'm DI Tudor Manx. I can come back later if you'd prefer.'

'No. I'm fine,' Bobbie said, reaching for her left shoulder and wincing as she touched it.

'You don't look fine.'

'Are you leading the investigation into Commander Flynt's death?' she asked, as she made herself comfortable.

'Do you know something about that?'

Bobbie ran her tongue over her lips. 'Pass me the water.'

Manx did as he was asked and waited as Bobbie placed the straw to her lips. She seemed wary, Manx thought, as if she were weighing up whether to trust him or not.

'I'll leave you to it,' the doctor said, turning to leave. 'Don't wear out my patient, Inspector.'

Bobbie wiped the back of a hand across her mouth and spoke, taking several breaks to wet her throat. She explained she was outside Flynt's house the night he disappeared, had wanted to talk to him, how she'd seen him leave the house and her subsequent conversation with Commander Boyd.

'He didn't tell you, did he?' she said.

'Unless he called one of my other officers.'

'How likely is that?'

Manx nodded. 'Point taken. And why are you in here? I'm guessing you don't think this was an accident?'

Bobbie stiffened. 'The vehicle did not slow down. I was wearing a reflective vest and an LED headband, if they didn't see me, they were either blind or drunk.'

'Can you identify the car?'

'It was dark, and it happened so fast. But I'd estimate from where the wing mirror hit me, it had to be something with a high wheelbase, like a van or an SUV.'

'That's very observant.'

'It's my job... *was* my job, to be observant.'

'Who found you and brought you here?'

'Good Samaritan?' she said, shrugging.

'Have you spoken to anyone else about this?'

'Only Commander Boyd. I should have said something sooner, but I wasn't sure if it was important.'

'I think Bobbie should rest now, Inspector Manx,' the doctor said, stepping back into the room.

Manx gave the doctor space and slipped his notebook into his pocket. 'Hope you feel better soon.'

'Oh, she'll feel more like herself tomorrow. We'll have you all fixed up.'

'Right,' Bobbie said. 'Good as new.'

As Manx left the room, Bobbie saw Andrew Pierce walk towards him and introduce himself. She couldn't hear the conversation, but the body language seemed clear enough. His glances, the serious head nods; the inspector taking notes. Call Me Andy was sure as hell not filling in the inspector on Bobbie Matthews' stellar mental stability. She had little time to dwell on this before sleep claimed her; a deep one, the deepest she'd had in months, induced by narcotics and mercifully dreamless.

Chapter 22

'If you ask me, it's the jet fuel they're putting in the planes,' Nader said. He was holding court across one of the desks in the incident room as Priddle listened intently and Morris stifled a yawn. 'It poisoned the lot of them,' he added, pointing at the *North Wales Daily Post* headline: *Anglesey Starling Deaths. Mystery Deepens.*

'The tox report was inconclusive,' PC Morris said. 'Verdict's still out as far as I'm concerned.'

'That's what they want you to believe,' Nader said, tapping the side of his nose with his index finger. 'Birds don't just fall out of the sky, do they?'

'Sarge's got a point,' PC Priddle agreed.

'Jet fuel?' Morris said, shaking her head. 'If that's the case why aren't half the birds on the island dead?'

Priddle shuffled forward. 'I heard it's a new weapon they're testing out. Sound waves or something.'

'And it only kills starlings? That'll stop the war on terror.'

'Maybe it's both,' Nader said.

'Oh, like a double threat,' Priddle offered. 'Makes sense.'

'Christ almighty!' Morris snapped, sitting back and folding her arms. 'No, Priddle, it doesn't make sense. You two should start your own podcast; plenty of nut jobs out there, happy to listen to conspiracy theories all day long.' She leaned forward. 'We're coppers. We look at the evidence, not some conspiracy theory you heard down the pub. There's a rational explanation, you'll see.'

'All right, Minor, calm down. What's got your knickers in a twist this morning?' Nader asked. 'Girl problems?'

'No,' Morris said, dragging her chair back and moving to an empty desk. 'Ignorant arsehole problems.'

As she sat, Manx walked in and took his place in front of the board. 'Morris, how did it go with our victim's wife?'

Morris flipped through her notes. 'James Flynt arrived home at eight that night, then left again at around nine. She thinks someone called him from the base, but she wasn't sure.'

'And he was wearing his service dress when he left the house?' Manx asked.

Morris nodded. 'Didn't have time to change, apparently. Happened a lot, she said, perks of being a base commander.'

'Money problems? Gambling? Debts?'

'None. His bank accounts all check out. No large deposits in the past twelve months, no unusual transactions.'

'A paragon of bloody virtue,' Nader huffed. 'Bet you fifty quid the bloke's got a bag full of dirty secrets.'

'Other than wild speculation, Nader, do you have anything positive to add?' Manx asked.

'Priddle and me interviewed all the blokes, and girls, on the list the base commander gave us. They all said Flynt was tough but fair. No grudges, he didn't owe money to anyone, not on the base at least. Everyone seemed to like the bloke. Well, at least as much as anyone can "like" the boss.'

Manx ignored the pointed remark. 'And what about alibis for the night Flynt went missing?'

'The personnel we interviewed were on shift that night. They had a training exercise, so it was all hands on deck, everyone accounted for.'

'I checked back with the base,' Morris said. 'Flynt never signed back in, probably drove straight to Benllech.'

'He could have met someone,' Manx said. 'He left the keys in his car and the doors unlocked, which suggests he knew the person he was meeting and wasn't intending to wander far from his car.'

'Maybe,' Nader said. 'But if you're going to top yourself, you wouldn't need your car keys where you're going.'

'Why meet someone if you're going to commit suicide, Sarge?' Morris asked. 'It's not the kind of thing you want an audience for.'

'Let's keep options on the table and minds open,' Manx said, pinning two photographs on the incident board. 'The forensic analysis from the fresh tyre prints taken next to Flynt's car. Eighteen-inch Goodyear, standard on several thousand cars and SUVs and sold in just about every garage and tyre shop in the country.'

'So, a dead end,' Nader said.

'Only on the tyres,' Manx said, writing the name *Bobbie Matthews* on the board. 'This woman, currently recuperating at Gwynedd Hospital A&E, was parked outside Flynt's house at 9.30 pm the night he went missing. She witnessed him leave, insisted she didn't follow him, but several hours later he's fish food in the Irish Sea.'

'Why didn't she come forward two days ago?' Nader asked.

'Isn't the more important question what she's doing in the emergency room?' Morris asked.

'You're both right,' Manx said. 'Bobbie Matthews suffered minor cuts and abrasions after being struck by a vehicle outside the base late last night. She did tell me she'd spoken to Commander Boyd and informed him she'd seen Flynt leave his home that night. The commander neglected, or forgot, to relay that information to the North Wales Constabulary.'

'So, let me get this straight,' Nader said. 'This woman sees Flynt leaving his house and a few hours later he's dead. She tells the commander, who doesn't tell us, then she's run over two days later?'

'Someone's had their coffee this morning,' Manx said.

'Did she work with Flynt?' Priddle asked.

'She wasn't on the list the commander gave us,' Morris confirmed.

'Which begs the question, if she didn't work with Flynt what the hell was she doing outside his house?' Manx said.

'Stalking the bloke?' Nader offered. 'Maybe they were having an affair?'

'It's possible,' Manx said, checking his notebook. 'The man who found her and drove her to the hospital is a Doctor Andrew Pierce.' He wrote the name on the board. 'RAF Valley's clinical psychologist and the base chaplain. He mentioned Bobbie Matthews is his patient but wouldn't get into specifics other than he's treating her for a military-related trauma.'

'She was obsessed with Flynt,' Nader said. 'He rejected her, she killed him, made it look like an accident.'

'What evidence do you have for that, Sarge?' Morris said.

'Been doing this job long enough to trust my gut by now, Morris.'

Morris threw her arms in the air. 'Great, we can all go home, case solved.'

'Ease off the accelerator, both of you,' Manx said. 'Morris, dig into Bobbie Matthews' background without stirring up things on the base. We keep this quiet for now. If she was targeted by a hit-and-run, let's not give whoever did this an excuse for a do-over.'

'Sir,' Morris confirmed.

'Oh, and Morris, this will make your day,' Manx said, picking up the food slam flyer from under a stack of papers. 'Canton and Troup request your participation this Thursday evening.'

'Jesus,' Nader huffed. 'Is this to do with that Just Ask a Copper bollocks? Rather you than me, love.'

'Be happy to do it, sir,' Morris said, smiling. 'DCSI Troup's right. It's important we're seen working with the community.'

'Christ, the face of modern-day policing,' Nader said. 'Kiss El Vera's arse any more and you'll need to reapply your lipstick, love.'

Morris pushed back her chair. 'I know an arse you could kiss, Sarge,' she said, grabbing her notebook. 'I'll be doing research if you need me,' she added before walking out.

'Was that necessary?' Manx said, gathering his papers.

Nader shrugged. 'Just some friendly banter. No harm done.'

'Watch your step. I don't want to be sitting in HR while you get reprimanded for creating a hostile working environment. Morris is right, the force is changing, and for the better in my opinion.'

'Aye, well we're all entitled to our opinion,' Nader said, standing. 'If you excuse me, boss, I've got a couple of suspects ready to beat a confession out of in the cells.'

'You're not funny, Nader.'

'So the wife keeps telling me.' He marched out of the room.

'Priddle, last man standing,' Manx said, as the young PC gathered up his notebook and slipped his chair back under the table. 'Call all garages within fifty miles of here, ask if anyone's brought in a large vehicle, an SUV or something of that kind for a driver's side mirror repair.'

'Got it, sir,' Priddle said, and headed through the door.

Manx turned to the woefully empty incident board. He looked at Flynt's scene-of-crime photographs and Bobbie Matthews' name. Other than they both worked at Valley, there was nothing else to connect them. He picked up a pen and drew a thin line between them. A second later, he wiped his sleeve over the line, leaving only a faint smudge. He was reaching, forcing tenuous connections. That was never a good sign, especially this early in an investigation.

Chapter 23

Bobbie had been discharged two days ago. The first day she'd spent at home, 'recuperating' as the doctor had insisted; it hadn't worked. She'd spent most of the day looking out at the small parcel of the back garden, drumming her fingers on the windowsill, drinking coffee, thinking about everything until it felt as if her head would implode. She signed back onto the base the following day.

She'd been temporarily assigned to writing press releases while the press officer was on maternity leave. She'd already done similar work back in Waddington, and at least it kept her brain from kicking into overdrive at every spare second. She drafted a release detailing Commander Flynt's memorial service, which was to be held in the local chapel, and conducted by Andrew Pierce – the funeral was yet to be scheduled and would take place in Waddington when the coroner had released the body. She then drafted an update on the Duke and Duchess of Cambridge's appearance at the Anglesey Agricultural Show in two weeks, highlighting the duke's excellent progress in his flight training.

Lunch was taken in the History Room Café, where all she had the stomach for was a strong coffee and half a sandwich. Lunch done with in less than ten minutes, she headed towards the transport hangar. Outside, one of the civilian contractors, passenger carrying vehicle (PCV) driver Cadwyn Evans, leaned against the wall, smoking. Cadwyn was young, friendly, and liked to talk.

'Can I bum one?' she asked.

He slipped out a pack stuffed under his T-shirt sleeve. 'Didn't know you'd stepped over to the dark side.'

Bobbie didn't smoke; or at least she hadn't since she'd met Danvir. Before that, she'd only been an occasional smoker or, as Danvir had insisted, 'You only occasionally put yourself at risk of dying of cancer.' Point taken; she'd quit for good soon after that conversation.

'I heard about your accident. Probably bloody tourists. No clue how to drive the roads around here. You okay?'

'I'll survive,' Bobbie said, coughing as the smoke sucker punched her lungs.

Cadwyn smiled. 'Yeah, if the smokes don't kill you first.'

Bobbie dropped the cigarette and ground it with the heel of her boot. 'You're in charge of the PCVs on the base?'

'Driver, mechanic, car washer. Keep the fleet spotless, the base commanders always want it that way; buffed and polished.'

'So you'd notice if any of the cars had any damage?'

'What kind of damage?'

'Like the wing mirror. Driver's side.'

'I'd know, straight off,' Cadwyn said, then gestured with his cigarette as the penny dropped. 'Ah, you don't think—?'

'No. I don't know,' Bobbie said. 'I was just wondering.'

'Don't know who'd want to harm you, mind,' he said. 'One of the good ones, you are.'

'You really think so?'

'You're a hell of a lot better than most of those higher-ups I chauffeur around.'

'That's a pretty low bar,' Bobbie said.

Cadwyn laughed. 'Best be off, lunch break over.' He ground his cigarette into the wall, flicking the butt into a nearby drain.

With forty-five minutes to kill before she was needed back at her desk, Bobbie found some shade under the awning outside the café and sat as far as possible from her colleagues who were enjoying the afternoon sun.

Was she one of the good ones? She thought on Cadwyn's words. She certainly didn't feel that way; hadn't felt that way since that day in the ground control station when her world had shifted off its axis. It was then – the memory of that day replaying in her mind like it had a million times before – that a flash of an idea came to her. Besides Bobbie and Flynt, there was one other person in the Box that day; Officer Cadet Cole Dawson. She could have kicked herself for not thinking of him sooner. She hadn't talked to him since the incident, but she was sure he was still stationed at Waddington; it was the only base in the country that required a sensor operator like Dawson in the ranks.

Her head buzzing with some glimmer of hope, she walked back to the squadron building to make her arrangements, one nagging thought at the back of her mind. With Flynt dead and herself the victim of what she was sure was no accident, she wondered if she was visiting Dawson hoping for answers, or was she travelling to Waddington to deliver him a warning?

Chapter 24

At 11.00 am the following morning, Ali Kalpar marched into Llangefni police station, examined the décor and nodded his approval. 'You lot done all right with the new digs, yeah?' he said, bounding towards the duty sergeant, Aled Rogers. 'Could do with more colour, though. Orange or yellow, something more cheerful.'

Rogers glanced up from reading the *Daily Mirror*.

'But I suppose you don't want criminals getting too comfortable. They got a word for that, right?' Ali said, scratching his thick, dark beard. 'Oh yeah, counterproductive, innit?'

'How can the North Wales Constabulary assist you today?' Rogers asked, recalling the preferred greeting the NWC public relations team had insisted be used for 'initial client interactions'.

Ali introduced himself. He was wearing a spotless white overall and white wellington boots. A fleshy indent from years of wearing a tight-fitting hairnet ran the length of his brow. 'Don't worry, I don't bite, all peace, love and understanding, me, until…' he said, pointing at Rogers, 'some bastard steals my van. Then, it's war, yeah? Full on.'

Ali took a quick inventory as Manx opened the door and walked into the reception area. 'No uniform,' he said, pointing. 'You the boss man here, then?'

'Not by a long chalk,' Manx said, barely looking up. 'But I'm sure whatever you need, the sergeant can help you out.'

Ali stepped closer. 'Some bastard stole my van. My deliveries are all kaput. People are relying on me, paying customers.'

Manx stuffed his hands in his pocket. 'Delivering what?'

Ali rummaged in his overalls and handed Manx his business card. 'Halal Al, like it says on the card.'

'Your name's Halal Al?'

'No, don't be stupid. Real name's Ali Kalpar. Funny buggers over at health and safety started calling me that, so I said I'm taking that. Good marketing, innit, Halal Al? Put a sign on the van, too.'

'The van you say was stolen?'

Ali shook his head. 'My customers, they're not going to like this, break my bollocks if I don't deliver.'

'When was it taken?'

'I parked it outside the abattoir in Gaerwen last night, came in this morning, vanished.'

'Give Evans the details, he'll input them on the system, make sure we're on the lookout,' Manx said, turning to leave.

Ali shook his head. 'Nah, take too long. I know who took it. You can just go to his place, arrest the bastard, I get my van back and still make my deliveries. Job done.'

He handed Manx a slip of paper. 'Mohsin Sadiq. Been harassing me ever since I bought the business off him, telling everyone I ripped him off. Shit to him! I paid a fair price, and health and safety made me upgrade all the bloody equipment. If anyone could be bothered to ask, I was the one who was ripped off.'

'And you have proof he stole your vehicle?'

'If the bloody CCTV cameras were working, I would.'

'Which means you don't.'

'Home-grown terrorism, they call it, yeah?' Ali said, proudly, as if he'd delivered a particularly sharp point of observation.

'Home-grown?' Manx asked, confused. 'Like vegetables?'

'What? No, I deal with meat,' Ali explained. 'No such thing as Halal veg, is there? No point.'

'I think you meant domestic terrorism,' Manx offered.

'Yeah, that's it! The bloke's a danger to society.' He lowered his voice to just above a whisper. 'All begins with a van, then what? It's all suicide vests and jihads, innit? Don't even see him at the mosque anymore. You know what that means?'

'Enlighten me.'

'Not radical enough. Found some well-radical Iman, prays at home, in his back room so he doesn't look suspicious.'

'Again, you have evidence?' Manx asked.

Ali shrugged. 'Nah, but obvious, innit?'

Manx handed back the paper. 'Rogers will follow up.'

'And you'll arrest him?' Ali nodded like a dashboard dog, hoping Manx might accompany him in the gesture.

'If he's committed a crime, he'll be arrested.'

The answer seemed to satisfy Ali. 'Honest businessman, I am. Now, I've got to hire a van and the bloody insurance company won't pay me back, that's for bloody sure. It's a fucked-up world, innit?'

'More than you can imagine,' Manx agreed, buzzing himself back into the major incident room.

Chapter 25

Officer Cadet Cole Dawson sat at his kitchen table. It was strewn with the morning's breakfast dishes and foil takeaway containers from the night before; chicken biryani, Bobbie guessed by the smell and crusted detritus of basmati rice. She pulled up a chair and slid the boxes out of her way.

'Yeah, sorry. You should have called, I would have spruced up the place,' Dawson said, pulling the ring from a can of Boddingtons. 'Sure you don't want one?'

'It's eleven in the morning, Dawson.'

'The earlier you start, the earlier you get there,' he said, taking a slug.

'Get where?'

'Anywhere but fucking here,' he said, spreading his arms wide. His eyes were bloodshot, he hadn't shaved for several days, his hair was long and unkempt and his T-shirt crumpled and stained. He was a long way down the road from the bright-eyed joker Bobbie remembered from only twelve months ago. Gone was the goofy smile and the puppy-dog eagerness to please. Cole Dawson looked like a homeless man who, by some twist of good fortune, had stumbled into someone's kitchen.

'What the hell happened?'

'You mean, when did it all go wrong? Or when did Sophie take the kids and move back in with her mother? Or when did I find out I liked the bottle better than I did my family? Or all of the above?'

'Jesus, I had no idea.'

'Yeah, none of us ever do. So why the house call? Didn't think I'd ever see you again after Operation Vanguard went to shit. Oh, Christ!' he said, slapping his forehead. 'Danvir, your husband, I'm so fuckin' sorry, Bobbie, I tried to call, afterwards—'

'It's fine,' Bobbie assured him. 'I wasn't in a good place to talk to anyone. Actually, that's why I'm here.'

Dawson reached out for a shot glass and the Absolut vodka he kept in arm's reach. 'If we're taking a stroll along drone strike memory lane, I'm going to need something a little stronger.'

'I assumed you read the official report?'

'Yeah, of course, we all did,' he said, pouring.

'And you agreed with the findings?'

Dawson slugged a mouthful then poured another. 'Didn't know there was an option to agree or disagree.'

'But in your opinion?'

'Come on, Bobbie, you know how it goes. We're foot soldiers, we don't get to have opinions.'

'Right. But you still haven't answered my question.'

Dawson downed another vodka and leaned forward. 'After Operation Vanguard, they said I was unstable, which was hard to argue with. There were only so many dead bodies in high definition I could watch. I started seeing them everywhere. Before I went to sleep, playing with the kids, out shopping with the wife. It was relentless, Bobbie, fucking relentless. Still is, if you must know. But you know how it goes.'

Bobbie nodded, though she couldn't completely relate. Maybe she was just better at compartmentalising than Dawson.

He continued. 'I was down the King's Arms on a Friday night. I'd been on late rotation; my head was well fucked up. This bloke, all lumberjack beard and CAMRA T-shirt with a bug up his arse about the RAF gets in my face, calling us murderers and terrorists. I know we're trained to step back from all that, but the bloke was a real wanker, I mean top-shelf, self-righteous, fat fuck muppet. So, we get into it, big time. Before I know it, I've got one hand around his throat, the other about to punch the living shit out of him. Took three blokes to get me off him. Turns out one of them was one of our flight commanders. I was disciplined the following Monday, got laid into good and proper from the base commander. He put me on admin duties until they'd done a full TRiM assessment. To be honest, I was happy to get away from the line of fire, but it left more time for drinking. Always a silver lining, eh?'

'When was this?'

'Christmas last year. Tis the season to be jolly,' he said, picking up the bottle by the neck and swinging it side to side like a handbell.

'They took you off active combat duties?'

'Like I was shit on their shoes. And you?'

'Same,' Bobbie said.

'Well, if that's all you came for, that's my story, flight lieutenant. The. End.'

Bobbie slid the vodka bottle to the opposite end of the table. 'Listen, there's something not adding up about this whole thing,' she said. 'Commander Flynt. They found his body five days ago on a beach on Anglesey.'

'Flynt?' Dawson's eyes were alert and focused on Bobbie for the first time since she'd sat down. 'How? What the fuck?'

'The police haven't released any details yet, but it makes sense, right, how it's all connected.'

'How what's connected?'

'All three of us were in the ground station that day; we know there were no other insurgents in the area, Creech would have informed us. The findings are flawed, but no one's willing to come out and admit that.'

'Politics,' Dawson said, swallowing another mouthful. He paused, as if hesitating to say what was on his mind before reaching for a stack of papers on the shelf behind him. 'About a week after I nearly throttled that bloke, I tracked him down. I wanted to apologise, or maybe I wanted to check out if he was pressing charges and talk him out of it. But here's the thing, part of me thought he might be right, I wanted to hear him out.'

'And did you?'

'He told me to go fuck myself at first, but I can be very persuasive with a few in me. He knew all about Operation Vanguard, been tracking this stuff for years apparently.'

'He was accessing classified information?'

'Not exactly accessing. Plenty of dissenters amongst the ranks happy to sling some mud at the RAF. All anonymous, of course. I reckoned the bloke was on the spectrum or something, anyway, he showed me all these charts, newspaper clippings. Bottom line, he's figured out that since Operation Vanguard government-sanctioned drone strikes increased over two hundred per cent, with little if no coverage by the tabloids. Once the RAF confirmed our lads – your husband – were killed by insurgents, the narrative changed. It was like they had a free pass to bomb whoever the fuck they wanted.'

'What are you saying?'

Dawson took a large swig of vodka, wiped the back of his hand across his lips. 'This bloke's one hundred per cent convinced Operation Vanguard was a false flag operation.'

Bobbie felt the blood rush to her feet, the roof of her mouth run dry. 'He's not serious?'

'He didn't seem the joking type. If what he says is true, that RAF Air Command colluded with the US Joint Special Operations Command to blow the shit out of that convoy of medics to justify ramping up drone attacks, then what the fuck does that make us, Bobbie, other than complicit?'

Bobbie sat back; the wind taken from her. She'd had a severe lack of imagination where Operation Vanguard was concerned. If it were true, it was hardly surprising the RAF had continued to push back and deny; it had become their default position and now it was obvious to Bobbie why. If this information was leaked to the press, the fallout would be catastrophic. This was the kind of cover-up that brought down powerful people, made governments nervous; and shook people's faith in the establishments designed to protect them. Had Danvir and his regiment been sacrificed in the name of continuing the war on terror? The thought made her sick.

'I need to speak to this person.'

'Don't think so. The bloke runs on a permanent Nervous Nelly setting. But here…' He ripped an edge from the *Lincolnshire Echo* and wrote down a URL. 'It's the only way he communicates.'

Bobbie took the paper and folded it into her jacket pocket. 'Thanks. Is there anything I can do to help?' she asked.

Dawson smiled, and for a second Bobbie caught a flash of the man she remembered. 'You can pass that bottle back my way.'

A second later, the smile was gone.

Chapter 26

Come Thursday evening, Ronnie Powell was jittery and anxious, his gut tight, head crackling like fireworks on November the fifth. 'Get out fast. I'll be waiting for you at the dock,' Melvin had instructed. 'And wear gloves. You won't have time to wipe down.'

Orders. Commands. Ultimatums. By now, Ronnie was dog-tired of the way his uncle spoke to him, like he was speaking to a half-wit. But that had always been the order of things when it came to the men in the Powell family. Ronnie was all too familiar with the tired routine; the older generation passing down their 'wisdom' with tough love and clenched fists. As a Powell, you were expected to grow up fast and grow up hard. Ronnie had fallen in line with the family tradition, though he'd never been hard enough or compliant enough in his father's eyes. Dafydd Powell could barely let a day pass without raising his voice, or, more typically, his fist to his son. Ronnie understood early on you couldn't choose your family, but you could choose who in your family to pledge your allegiance to. For Ronnie, that decision had been made when he was thirteen, when his father laid his fists on him for the last time.

Melvin had walked in on the scene: Ronnie, cowering like a petrified dog in the corner of the kitchen, his father zapping his son's naked torso with an electric cattle prod until Ronnie's skin was puckered raw, the kitchen thick with the stench of scorched flesh. Melvin had knocked three colours of shit out of his brother that day. Crouched in the corner, Ronnie had forced himself to watch the whole, brutal beating, if only to make sure his father wouldn't be rising again any time soon to finish what he started.

The speed and power of Melvin's fists as they pummelled into his dad that day left him in awe. The beating was done in minutes, or was it seconds? No matter, by the time it was over Dafydd Powell was unconscious, his right eye hanging from its socket, Melvin standing over him, blood dripping from his knuckles and onto the dirty yellow linoleum.

Ronnie had left with Melvin that afternoon, and was as loyal and compliant as any grateful dog might have been. Not that his uncle was an easy man, he was just the best of a bad batch. The odd slap now and again just to keep Ronnie in line and a sharp right hook when Melvin had considered he'd stepped too far over that line. Compared to living with his father, it was as close to a normal childhood as he could have hoped for. He didn't think they'd spoken after that day, the brothers. The last Ronnie heard, Dafydd Powell was living on the foothills of Snowdonia. *Good riddance*, he thought, *best place for the bastard; out in the backend of nowhere drinking himself to an early grave*. What Melvin didn't finish, Ronnie was sure the cigarettes and the scotch would.

Scotch? That would have settled him right down, or a thick joint to calm his nerves. Ronnie had never been the patient type. He guessed he'd inherited that trait from his father; an anger that burned somewhere deep in the bones of him. His uncle had always told him, 'You fight that urge, Ronnie, push it right down. If you don't, that's when your guard comes down and you expose your weakness. And what does weakness do? Gets you hurt, that's what, or worse.'

Thinking on those words, Ronnie looked towards Menai Bridge town centre. He'd have felt better if Melvin was here with him. It was his uncle's plan after all, and he was just carrying out his orders; the loyal, grateful pack dog. When Melvin had first proposed the plan, Ronnie had attempted to talk his uncle out of it. It seemed too soon, a step too far. It wasn't like they'd be setting fire to empty holiday homes in the dead of night. If Melvin's plan worked, injuries, or worse, were a given – a necessity, even.

He tilted the mirror and checked his reflection. His forehead was glistening. He took a hand to his brow, wiped, then checked again.

Christ, he was turning into his uncle. He flipped the mirror back, catching the sun's reflection as it shone off the grey shoulders of the Menai suspension bridge behind him.

From his vantage point, half a mile uphill, he had a near perfect view. The main road running through town was closed to traffic and most of the buildings were, this evening, hidden behind several rows of tented booths and food stalls. The smell of a suckling pig roast drifting from the car park of the Victoria Arms reminded Ronnie he hadn't eaten since before lunchtime – he hadn't felt like it, his stomach was churning with a slop of apprehension and fear.

He checked his watch. Quarter to seven – another fifteen minutes. He stabbed at the radio, hoping for some music to distract him; nothing but static. He tried the CD player. The sound of a woman's voice wailing in some foreign language echoed off the van walls. What he wouldn't give for some Black Sabbath or Iron Maiden right now, to put him in the right headspace. Melvin had warned him to keep off the wacky-baccy until later, but Ronnie's nerves were already fired through with bright arcs of electricity.

Fuck Mel, he wasn't on the front line, taking all the risk.

He snapped a joint from inside his jacket pocket, struck his lighter and pulled hard until the blunt fizzled angry and red. Almost immediately he felt the soothing effects of the weed. He checked the crossbow bolt he always carried in his right sock was still there – it was. He pulled down the black full-face fleece mask he always wore when he was lamping, secured his sunglasses, and applied a light pressure to the throttle.

The van moved forward, slowly at first, then gathering momentum as it caught the slope of the hill.

Chapter 27

Manx watched PC Delyth Morris tear into the Sellotape on a small box and lay its contents across the rickety table.

'Just ask a bloody copper,' he said, flipping aimlessly through one of the leaflets the public relations team had delivered earlier that morning. 'Do people even read these things?'

Morris shrugged. 'Not sure what it even means;Just Ask a Copper? Just ask a copper for what?'

'It means,' Manx said, 'we've got to stand here listening to questions we don't have answers for and taking abuse from a bunch of drunks who've overdone it on the craft beer.'

'Won't be that bad, sir,' Morris said, laying out the leaflets. 'I wasn't doing anything tonight anyway. To be honest, I was glad to get out of the house.'

'You've got nothing better to do on a Thursday night? No five-a-side?' he asked, gesturing at Morris's right eye, which was still a little swollen and purple.

Morris brought her hand to her cheek. 'The girls can get a bit over-enthusiastic,' she said, diverting her gaze. 'The centre forward's got a sharp elbow.'

'Hope you gave as good as you got,' Manx said.

'She didn't score the rest of the match,' Morris said with a brief smile. She cleared her throat, as if she might find the right words stuck somewhere in there. 'I wanted to say, sir, sorry if I've seemed a bit off lately.'

'Hadn't noticed,' Manx said.

‘It’s just my dad,’ she explained. ‘He’s been ill, so me and my mam have been taking turns looking after him.’

‘Sorry to hear that,’ Manx said, glancing down the rows of food stalls as they fired up their grills and set out their wares. ‘Family,’ he said. ‘It’s a life sentence.’

As Morris set out the rest of the leaflets, a voice made her look up. She stiffened and stood a little taller as DCSI Vera Troup stopped in front of the booth, dressed in a white *Food Slam* T-shirt and black jeans. A sliver of red lipstick was drawn across her lips like two asymmetrical scratches.

She turned to Manx. ‘Good evening, Manx. Ellis told me you’d volunteered. Your enthusiasm won’t go unrecognised.’

Volunteered? ‘Yes, ma’am, my hand was the first one up.’

‘And PC Morris, correct?’ Vera asked.

‘Ma’am,’ she said, nodding.

Vera gestured at the pamphlets. ‘Do you like the new material?’

Morris and Manx glanced at each other.

‘Erm… top notch, good quality on the printing,’ Manx said.

‘Yeah, good photos too, ma’am,’ Morris agreed.

Vera narrowed her eyes. She was well trained in spotting an evasive reply when confronted with one as transparent as this. ‘Well, the focus groups were very encouraging,’ she said. There was an awkward pause before Vera spoke again. ‘I should head to the entrance, catch Logan Collins’ speech.’

‘Police protection? I didn’t realise he was that unpopular,’ Manx said.

Vera narrowed her eyes. ‘Keep up the good work, both of you.’ She walked away, back straight, stride purposeful.

‘Ugh, he’s so slimy,’ PC Morris said, catching a glimpse of Logan Collins emerging from a side street and shaking Vera’s hand with both of his; the palm-over-hand gesture favoured by politicians of all parties. ‘Wouldn’t trust him as far as I could throw him,’ she added with a dismissive shake of her head.

‘I hear his fan base is pretty thin.’

‘The English on the island like him all right, but the Welsh, they don’t want anyone who’s learned the language. He just moved here a few years ago, it’s not like he’s even local.’

‘God forbid the good people of Anglesey would vote for anything so radical,’ Manx said, watching Troup walk Collins towards the entrance.

Three and a half minutes away, Ronnie Powell was following orders, his boot pressed on the throttle, the van hurtling downhill and at the perfect angle to inflict maximum damage.

Chapter 28

Ronnie had heard of out-of-body experiences – maybe this was one of them. He felt disconnected, his mind floating above his body. He remembered Melvin's words: 'Keep a constant speed, not too fast.' His uncle had also warned him about collateral damage; done right, it would be minimal, Logan Collins and one of his staff at most. One of Melvin's friends, a sound technician called Owen Porth, had let it slip after one too many pints that Collins would be speaking from a podium with a five-hundred-watt sound system connected to two speakers mounted on stands. 'Overkill,' Owen Porth had spat. 'Who does he think he is? The bloody prime minister or something?'

It would be a clean strike, Melvin had insisted. Take out the podium and Collins, then 'get the fuck out of there, quick.'

The entrance to the food slam less than a hundred metres away, Ronnie took a final puff and flicked the joint through the window. The draft caught the butt, blowing it back into the van. Ronnie didn't notice, he was focused on the target dead in the centre of his windscreen, his mind trying to make sense of why the hell Logan Collins wasn't anywhere near the podium.

Chapter 29

If Logan Collins was disappointed with the number of people who'd turned out to hear him speak, he didn't show it. That was the politician's way; whatever the turnout, whatever indifference, you kept on smiling, kept on-message. And this evening his message was concise and simple, as always: 'Vote for progress. Vote Logan Collins.'

He'd learned to keep things simple, speak of things people could grasp in soundbites. Tonight would be no different. He'd speak of the progress Anglesey had made; how it was now one of the UK's most popular tourist destinations, with some of the cleanest beaches in the country; how off-island investment had attracted more visitors, providing more jobs, putting more money in the pockets of working people. He'd touch on the culinary progress; how the island had rediscovered its own rich, natural bounty; sea-to-table dining that could compete with the best of Britain's coastal restaurants.

Collins wanted to push this progress further, issue more planning permissions for holiday flats and the construction of new hotels; secure an increase in tax breaks for small businesses catering to tourists; incentives for clean energy companies setting up wind farms. He'd argue there was a national security issue too; the Ministry of Defence was looking to buy more land around RAF Valley in preparation for more fast jet training and increase the number of pilots for the Air Mountain Rescue Service. Selling that land would provide new jobs, pump more money into the community.

However, the initiative he most wanted to talk about was the negotiations he'd spearheaded with a Chinese energy company, the Gonglu Corporation, to purchase the decommissioned Wylfa Nuclear Power Station. He'd worked in the industry as an energy trader for over two decades and retired three years ago at the age of forty-six to pursue his political career. The deal was far from done, but a delegation from the port city of Tianjin, in north eastern China, was due at the end of summer for a site visit. He was preparing to roll out the red carpet with the full backing of Anglesey County Council and the UK Atomic Energy Authority. If the purchase was successful, it would mean over four thousand new jobs during the construction phase, at least eight hundred when it was operational, and would supply power to over two million homes. That kind of progress didn't just garner him good publicity, it got him votes.

These were all the points Logan Collins had wanted to address before announcing the third Annual Menai Bridge Food Slam open. The fact that this never came to pass was due to one off-message decision he made that night.

The sound engineer who'd set up his PA system was right; five hundred watts was overkill for the number of people. There was a better way to handle this; a more personal, man-of-the-people approach. He dumped the microphone on the podium shelf and walked out into the small, tight-knit crowd, his smile wide and bright, his hand grasping at every palm happy to shake his.

By the time he heard the high-pitched whine of the engine, he barely had time to turn around and register the van hurtling towards him and the fifty people gathered in a tight pack around him.

Chapter 30

The screech of rubber burning against tarmac shattered the still evening air like a siren blast.

Ronnie pulled a hard right. The van's rear end swung around and skidded to a violent stop. People were frozen to the spot, as if they were imagining the whole scene, that this couldn't really be happening here on a summer's evening on Anglesey.

Ronnie shoved open the door, slipped out the crossbow bolt from his sock, and ran towards Logan Collins, cutting the air with the weapon as he neared his target.

'Move away! Now! I've got a bomb under here,' he lied, tugging at his jacket. 'Anyone tries to be a hero, I'll blow you all to fucking pieces.'

No longer frozen, the crowd complied and gave Ronnie the space he demanded. All except Logan Collins, who stood there as if he was about to make a difference – become some kind of hero.

Not on my fucking watch, Ronnie thought as he stepped closer.

Collins lifted his arms in the hope the gesture might save him. It wouldn't. Ronnie quickly span around behind Collins, wrapped his right arm around his neck. He tightened the crook of his elbow around Collins' Adam's apple and poked the sharp apex of the bolt into his neck flesh, just deep enough to draw blood.

'Keep back! All of you! Keep the fuck back!'

The crowd didn't need the second command. Those who weren't filming the scene with their phones were already stepping back or had run to the nearest side streets.

Through the slim opening in his face mask, Ronnie saw a woman moving towards him; tall, thin, raven-dark hair. One of Collins' staff, he reckoned. She held a mobile phone to her ear. *Another fucking hero*, Ronnie thought, as he pulled tighter on Collins' throat and etched another shallow nick in the politician's flesh.

'Please, put the weapon down,' the woman said, raising her palms. 'Whatever this is about, I'm sure we can work it out.'

She was calm; way too fucking calm for his liking.

'You! You… put your fucking phone down,' he stammered, waving the bolt as if drawing invisible shapes in the air.

She nodded and lowered her phone, but kept the call open.

'My phone's down. Let Mr Collins go, and we can talk. No one needs to get hurt.'

As he looked at the woman's way-too-calm posture, like she was confronted with this sort of emergency situation on a daily basis, another thought struck him. His plan was only half-formed. He hadn't figured out his next steps. All he knew was that Mel was waiting for him to return, with his mission complete and successful.

He sensed Collins push back, his arms flexing as if he were about to make some heroic gesture; Ronnie put a stop to that with a fast, sharp knee to the kidneys. Collins groaned. His legs buckled. Ronnie let him fall to his knees, then struck Collins clean in the stomach with his boot. There was little resistance from Collins after that, but he kept the bolt pressing at his neck for good measure. Collins retched out the contents of his stomach. Ronnie had the power to end this now, or step it up a notch, make his uncle proud. He could stab Collins and make a run for it, or maybe there was a longer game to be played; what Melvin might have called a strategy.

As Ronnie was debating his next move, the woman reached into her bag. By the time Ronnie had registered the movement, she already had the canister in her hand and was about to press on the nozzle. Working on instinct, Ronnie turned his head as the mist from the pepper spray caught his face. A trickle of spray seeped under his sunglasses and into his eye. The pain was instant; like staring directly into the scorching centre of the midday sun.

Ronnie did what he knew best, did what his Powell family instincts compelled him to do. He lashed out, the bolt cleaving through the air. It found its target deep in Vera Troup's abdomen.

The contact was precise and deadly; sharp steel into soft spleen. She dropped her phone and looked down to her belly where blood was spreading in a reservoir of red across her T-shirt.

Ronnie removed the blood-smeared bolt. He dug his finger under his sunglasses and into his eye; the action only intensified the pain. His anger burned deep as he looked down at Collins recovering from the kicking to his solar plexus and trying to comprehend the river of red spreading fast across the woman's T-shirt.

'Fucking walk!' he shouted, tugging on Collins' collar. 'Or you'll get the same as her.'

Collins rose slowly, stumbled like a new-born calf before finding his footing, the same blade that had just entered the woman's skin now against his neck. The warm dampness of her blood dripped under his collar as he stood.

Ronnie heard someone shout, 'She's been stabbed, she's been stabbed!' He didn't require the reminder. He marched Collins away from the crowd towards the street leading down to the shallow cove, his face sweating under the thick fleece mask as he walked.

From the cove, it was a short few steps up a rocky incline that ended at the private boat slip where Melvin was waiting. Collins stumbled and groaned, stopping several times to empty his stomach. Ronnie hurried him along with the promise of more cold steel in his neck unless he picked up the pace.

In his wake, Vera Troup struggled to maintain consciousness, blood flooding through her fingers and pooling in thick scarlet on the warm tarmac.

Chapter 31

The pain had made another unannounced visit; the third onslaught in as many days. It was as if it were building up momentum, racing Melvin to the finish. He slowly rose from his knee-bound position and looked in disgust at the red splatters across the wooden slip. Blood. The pattern reminded him of tea leaves clinging to the side of a cup; though he didn't require a fortune teller to predict his future. Like the pain, they were there to remind him that his time was short; death was merely spitting distance away.

Ronnie's voice distracted him from pondering too long on that grim thought. He looked over and squinted. Maybe his eyesight was failing too; he was sure Ronnie was with someone. As his nephew drew closer, the reality of the situation clicked into focus.

'What the fuck have you done, Ronnie?' he said, as his nephew shoved Collins towards the boat.

'Water!' Ronnie said, tearing off his sunglasses and mask. 'Give me some fucking water. And keep an eye on him, don't want the bastard making a run for it.'

Melvin, momentarily stunned, handed his nephew a bottle. Ronnie poured the water into his eyeball. He blinked rapidly as he spoke. 'Got any of those plastic ties you use for the paint supplies?'

'In the box by the lobster pots,' Melvin said, looking at Logan Collins, blood dripping onto his shirt. He didn't look much like a politician now, looked more like a man who'd narrowly avoided death and was unsure as to when the next attack would come and if he'd be lucky enough to survive it when it arrived.

Collins let out a grunt as Ronnie jerked back his arms, wrapped a cable tie around his wrists and pulled until the plastic cut into his skin. He pushed Collins down, forcing him to sit on the centre thwart running the width of the boat.

'Here,' Melvin said, handing Ronnie an oil-stained rag. 'Unless you want him recognising the both of us.'

'Oh, yeah, forgot,' Ronnie said, securing himself on the bottom boards and pulling the rag taut behind Collins' head.

Melvin ducked into the cockpit and fired up the engine. 'What the bloody hell is going on? Don't tell me you bolloxed this up too?'

'It wasn't like you said,' Ronnie stammered, wiping the back of his hands across his face. 'I couldn't do it. Too many people, Mel. Would have been a massacre, a fuckin' massacre.'

'All right, calm down and cast us off,' Melvin said. 'This was your plan? Kidnapping? Jesus Christ!'

'I had to think quick, like. No time,' Ronnie said, reaching over to unhitch the bow line from the cleat. It took him three attempts before the rope fell free. He looped it loosely around itself and threw it under the stern-sheet.

'You couldn't just abandon the mission? Turn around?'

'Didn't want to let you down,' Ronnie said, rubbing a thumb at the corner of his eye. 'We can keep him as our prisoner until they agree to our demands. We'll set a ransom, cut off his finger or something, send it to them so they know we're fucking serious, like.'

Collins spoke, a panicked throb in his voice. 'Please, let me go. I'm no one, really. I won't tell anyone. I didn't see anything.'

Ronnie leaned across the boat and edged the sharp point of the bolt closer into Collins' neck until he felt the resistance of soft cartilage. 'You saw plenty. Now shut the fuck up.'

Collins nodded his compliance.

'Put the bolt down, you're not in some bloody film.' Melvin's mind rattled through a list of possible options he should be considering, none of which were good. 'Christ, you've really dropped us in it this time,' he said, slowly backing out of the slip.

Ronnie stood, walked unsteadily to join his uncle in the cockpit. 'It's a good plan. Leverage, like, we've got leverage now.'

Maybe the lad has a point, Melvin thought, but this wasn't the time to discuss the merits of any plan his nephew had just pulled from his arse. He spun the boat around, the bow facing the open water of the Menai Strait. 'I need some time to wrap my head around what the fuck you've just done, Ronnie.'

It wasn't the reaction Ronnie was hoping for. He finger-stabbed Melvin in the shoulder. 'Done us a favour, that's what I've done,' he said, getting deep into his uncle's personal space.

Mel caught the familiar funk of weed rising from Ronnie's jacket. 'Thought I told you, no bloody smoking until the job was done,' he said, urging the throttle as fast as the old engine would tolerate. 'See, this is what happens. Your brain gets messed up, you make bad decisions.'

'What the fuck does it matter, now? I only smoked half.'

He grabbed the neck of Ronnie's T-shirt, shoving him against the cockpit's thin walls until they rattled. 'Half?' he growled. 'And what did you do with the half you didn't smoke, genius?'

Ronnie hesitated. 'Erm. Threw it out, didn't I? What do you think I am, stupid?'

Melvin nodded and released his grip. As he directed the boat towards the town of Beaumaris, then piloted the craft around the west coast of Anglesey towards Bull Bay, the burn in Ronnie's eye finally eased to a steady smoulder.

The other half? Yeah, he was a hundred per cent sure he threw it out of the van window. At least ninety per cent sure, or maybe a little less.

Chapter 32

At the entrance, Manx's sole priority, and one which demanded his urgent attention, was bleeding out on the tarmac, her head supported on the lap of one of the St John Ambulance volunteers who had rushed to the scene.

Manx knelt next to the man. Vera was falling fast into unconsciousness, her breath shallow, her pale skin almost translucent now as the loss of blood drew the life force from her. 'What's your name?' Manx asked the volunteer.

'Hugh. Hugh Jones,' the man said. He was in his seventies, flush-faced, white hair falling in thin strands over his forehead. His hands were pressing hard on a pack of bandages he'd secured over the wound. It took all of Hugh's strength to keep on the pressure, his hands soaked with Vera's blood.

Manx didn't need to ask the question, Hugh's eyes told him everything he needed to know; if the paramedics didn't arrive soon, no number of bandages, pressure or praying to whatever god Hugh put his faith in would stop the inevitable. Vera's heart would soon stop pumping, and whether that happened in the middle of the street, or in the major trauma unit five miles away, would be the difference between life and death.

'Hugh, can you keep her with us until the paramedics arrive?'

'I'll give it my best,' Hugh said, wiping an arm across his brow. 'We're not really trained to deal with this level of injury.'

'Consider it on-the-job training,' Manx said, feeling some relief as he heard the scream of sirens. If she could hold on a few more minutes there'd be some hope Vera would make it. Badly injured, but alive.

Behind him, a breathless PC Morris spoke. 'Jesus, what happened?' she said, bringing a hand to her mouth.

'Later,' Manx said. 'Let's make sure she's stabilised, then we take witness statements.'

As the sirens neared, he urged the crowd to move back, then stepped away, giving the paramedics the space to do their job. He was surplus to requirements now.

He turned to look at the van, parked at a right angle to the entrance. The engine was still running, driver's door open, front wheels straddling the kerb. He walked over, leaned in, killed the engine. The sound of jangling sitars and a woman's mournful voice coming from the speakers triggered something in his memory.

He switched the music off and examined the van's exterior. Several strips of masking tape were stuck to the sides and door panels. The number plates had been doctored; something a patrol car wouldn't have noticed from a distance, but from a few inches away the disguise looked amateur and rushed.

Focusing his attention back to the masking tape on the driver's side door panel, he caught his fingernails under one of the strips and peeled it from the metal. He did the same with the other four strips.

The revelation was no surprise. It was just as he'd expected the moment he'd heard the music and caught the metallic tinge of dried blood in his throat.

The lettering, 'Halal Al's Meats' seemed to scream at him from the side of the van in a garish, flowery font.

More than screaming, it was taunting him.

PART II

KILL THE MESSENGER

Chapter 33

'Operation Vanguard? Give me a break,' Byron Gates snorted. He snapped his fingertips on the Batman-themed pinball, attempting to smack the malevolent grin off the Joker's face taunting him from behind the glass.

Byron, early forties, thick unkempt beard he liked to tug at when he was nervous and eyes permanently rheumy from constant exposure to all things digital, was talking through his earphones with someone who gave their identity only as Reaper. This wasn't unusual for the kind of people Byron dealt with; people with valid reasons to conceal their real identities. It had taken him a decade to cultivate this web of informers, military personnel compelled to expose the covert operations of the global military and technology complex in which they worked, but still valued their careers as well as their lives. Byron was their conduit, a safe harbour from what they'd refer to as the Triple P Threat: Persecution. Prosecution. Prison.

'Listen,' Byron said, grinding his teeth and tracking the pinball as it rolled downwards. 'This is some real *Alice in Wonderland* bollocks.' He flipped the ball, firing a series of lights and ratcheting up his score. 'I'm not going down that rabbit hole. Been there, done that, moved on.'

However, the next sentence Reaper spoke made the hairs on his neck bristle like they'd been brushed crossways. His concentration was shot. The ball slipped down the gutters with a cackle of laughter and a menacing 'Hurry up and die already, sucker,' from the Joker. But Byron wasn't listening. He barely even cared he'd just blown past his personal best score. What he'd just heard beat any pinball high. 'Are you one hundred and one per cent sure?'

No response. The air was now dead air. Not that it mattered, Byron's attention was now focused on the insistent voice in his head telling him this was the one he'd been waiting for; the mother lode.

He yanked out his earphones, hauled his backpack across his shoulder and looked over the SuperBoss Arcade. The arcade was knee-deep in curated retro nostalgia: flashing pink and blue neon stripes across the walls, eighties synth pop blasting through the speakers, and a selection of vintage video games; Space Invaders, Pac-Man, Defender, Asteroids and the like. He'd played them all when he was younger; more than played them, mastered them. Surveying the teenagers hunched over the games, killing time during the summer holiday, he guessed they were too young to have played them first time round. What was the word he'd heard recently? Snowflakes? Yeah, these kids were definitely snowflakes; playing first-person-shooter games while their government committed acts of real violence in the name of the war on terror. Yeah, those kids would disintegrate like snowflakes under the weight of that knowledge; the kind of knowledge truth seekers like Byron Gates dedicated their lives to searching out.

His website, DronewatchUK, had been tracking RAF drone strikes for several years. The site had suffered several denial-of-service attacks and been served a series of cease and desist orders, all of which he'd ignored. Over the past couple of years that kind of attention had tapered off. The authorities probably concluded an amateur-looking website with little traffic and minimal influence posed little danger to their operations.

It had also become apparent to Byron that the majority of the public felt the same. They cared little about the atrocities committed thousands of miles from home – so long as it wasn't happening on their doorstep. There was even a phrase for it: 'war fatigue'. Byron imagined it was far worse than fatigue by now, more like a numbness that compelled people to bury their faces in the nearest device to hand to blot out the bad news. It was a way to hold on to your sanity, he thought, but it came at a price; a price which Byron Gates himself had never been willing to pay.

If what Reaper had said was true, this was the breakthrough story he'd been waiting for. One of his informants had sent him the Operation Vanguard report via a triple-encrypted email server several months ago. *Missile launched. Successful kill strike on a convoy of insurgents, followed by a secondary explosion, detonated by nearby IS enemy combatants that took out a convoy of RAF medics following behind.*

As Byron's mind churned, his phone buzzed. He clicked through his triple-factor authentication to access the message. Reaper wanted to meet. He could barely type his reply fast enough.

Where and when?

Several minutes later, the reply buzzed through. Byron checked the driving time from Waddington to Anglesey; three and a half hours with no traffic, closer to four-and-a-half with. The request was a no-brainer; a meeting with someone who was in the ground control station the day Operation Vanguard was launched was too golden an opportunity to ignore.

Decision made, he walked out into the warm Lincolnshire afternoon, leaving the Joker's cackles and taunts for another day.

Chapter 34

Manx walked into the waiting room outside Gwynedd Hospital's intensive care unit. Slumped in a chair, DCI Canton was half asleep, snoring like a contented dog. He sensed someone standing over him and woke with a grunt.

'The doctors induced a medical coma to assist with the healing,' he said, stifling a yawn. 'But they had to remove her spleen, which will compromise her immune system for the rest of her life. I suppose it's preferable to the alternative.'

'Christ,' Manx said, peering through the glass at the man he guessed was Vera's husband sitting at her bedside, with the young girl he recalled from the school sports day sprawled across his chest.

'Aye, when it's one of our own, always makes it harder.'

One of our own. Four words that never failed to coat Manx's spine with ice. He'd last heard the phrase three months ago, when a colleague of his from the Met, CeeCee Cartwright, had been found dead on the tracks outside Shoreditch station. Hearing those words never got any easier, in fact, he suspected it got harder each time.

'Not your fault,' Canton said, as if reading Manx's mind. 'Vera,' he clarified. 'Nothing you could have done to prevent this.'

Manx looked through the third-floor window to the news crews gathered below. 'No ransom demands?'

Canton rose from the chair. 'Not a peep. Apart from the usual nut jobs who seem to think wasting police time is a career choice.'

'Why Collins?' Manx pondered. 'I understand he's not exactly popular, but kidnapping?'

‘Been tying myself in knots over that one too. Why kidnap if there’s no ransom demand?’

‘What if it wasn’t planned that way?’

Canton cocked his head like a curious bird.

‘By Bevan’s calculations, the length of the tyre marks on the road indicates sudden braking from approximately thirty miles per hour. If the intent was to take Collins hostage, why abandon the van, run into a crowd then lead Collins away with a blade to his throat? It’s too public, too many witnesses.’

‘Where are you going with this, Manx?’

‘How many attacks have there been when some terrorist ploughs a van, or a car, into a crowd? It’s efficient, sends a big message.’

‘A terrorist attack with the intent of killing and maiming innocent bystanders? This is Anglesey for God’s sake, Manx.’

‘Collins was meant to be speaking that night,’ Manx continued, testing the theory he’d been churning over most of last night. ‘He had a podium and speakers set up at the entrance. All the witnesses state he never used it, walked straight into the crowd. What if the original plan was to drive the van directly at Collins, but that plan changed when they saw Collins wasn’t at the podium?’

Canton thought for a moment. ‘And you think there’s a terrorist angle here?’

‘Not sure, but the van was reported stolen two days ago from outside the Halal abattoir in Gaerwen. Which could point to terrorism, or more likely someone trying to frame it that way.’

Canton sighed. ‘So, do we have any actual hard evidence?’

‘Bevan retrieved the butt of a marijuana joint from the van, but if the DNA’s not in the database we’re not much further on.’

The sudden and loud shriek of an emergency alarm bouncing off the hospital walls startled them both. Seconds later, a flurry of activity as a doctor and two nurses wheeling a complex array of medical equipment barged into Vera’s room.

Canton and Manx stepped back as the team huddled around the bed and worked as one seamless unit; efficient, practised; urgent.

'Are you a religious man?' Canton asked.

'Not particularly.'

'Faith in anything?'

Manx gestured at the team attending to Vera. 'Medical science, I suppose, at times like this,' he said, his mind replaying the dark feeling he'd had that day at St Gerard's as the clock tower cast its deep shadow across the lawn.

Canton didn't reply. But from the manner in which his lips were moving, Manx guessed he was muttering a silent prayer under his breath.

'Let's hope it's enough, eh, Manx,' Canton finally said, his fingers wrapping around each other like a set of worry beads threading into a ball of tight pink flesh.

Chapter 35

When Manx returned to the station later that morning, the mood in the incident room was sombre; he could sense the tension from out in the hallway. As he walked in, the team turned to look at him – faces expectant, eager for good news, but fearing the worst. He had no good news to give, and relayed what Canton had told him. Unsurprisingly, it did nothing to lift the mood. To steer their attention elsewhere, he stood in front of the incident board, removed his jacket and rolled up his shirt sleeves.

'Right, we still have Flynt's suspicious death, Logan Collins' kidnapping and a violent assault on Vera Troup. What, if anything, connects all of these?'

Following a brief interlude of shoe-gazing from the team, Morris spoke. 'What about the hit-and-run on Bobbie Matthews? Shouldn't we include that, too?'

'Fair enough,' Manx said, circling Bobbie's name. 'Does that help us any?'

'Matthews and Flynt were both stationed at RAF Valley, and Logan Collins is always going on about expanding the airbase, adding more jobs,' Morris said.

'It's a stretch. Tenuous.'

Manx directed his attention back to the incident board. 'Let's take a few steps back. Three weeks ago, we had a spate of holiday home fires. The last house was owned by Logan Collins. According to the fire inspector, they're all connected; same accelerant, same MO. A few days later, we find James Flynt's body. No connection to the fires, or Collins, as far as we know.'

He pointed to another photograph. 'The van we found at Menai Bridge was owned by Ali Kalpar. Whoever took it knew his security cameras weren't working, which shows premeditation. Also, Kalpar had no connection to Flynt or Collins. I'm not saying there is no connection, just that we haven't found it yet. Morris, care to fill us in on what you dug up on Bobbie Matthews?'

'Not much, sir. She didn't have much of an online profile. No Facebook account, Instagram or LinkedIn.'

'Who the hell doesn't have a Facebook page?' Nader asked. 'Can't get my gran off the bloody thing and she's eighty-seven.'

'Not everyone wants to share their life all over the internet,' Morris said.

'That why you won't accept my friend request?' Nader said. 'Afraid I'll get to know too much about you?'

'No, Sarge,' Morris said. 'I'm afraid I'll get to know too much about you.'

There was a short round of chuckling that lightened the mood for a moment before Morris continued. 'According to the electoral register, Bobbie Matthews moved to Valley eleven months ago.'

'Moved? Where from?' Manx asked.

Morris checked her notes. 'Waddington, Lincolnshire.'

Manx reached for his marker pen and redrew the faint line he'd drawn between Flynt's photograph and Bobbie Matthews' name a few days back. 'That's our connection. Flynt was stationed at RAF Waddington. He transferred to Valley twelve months ago, Bobbie Matthews follows soon after.'

'Yeah, makes sense now,' Nader said. 'He makes sure she gets transferred to Valley so they can continue the affair. They had a lover's tiff. She asks him to meet her at Benllech, they argue, she smashes the bloke in the head, he falls, ends up in the Irish Sea.'

'But why would she confess to seeing Flynt that night?' Morris pushed. 'If she killed him, she'd keep that quiet.'

'Unless she's playing us,' Priddle offered. 'Like a double bluff. Saw that on a TV show once.'

'Okay,' Manx said, sensing the conversation was heading downhill fast. 'Our number one priority is finding Logan Collins. Witness statements, CCTV videos, rumblings on social media. Canton's doing a direct appeal to the public for any information. Someone on this island knows who's holding him and where. We find him, we get Collins before it's too late, and we get justice for Vera.'

'What if it's already too late, sir?' Morris asked.

A hush fell over the room.

'It's our job to make sure that it's not too late, Morris,' Manx said. 'Now, let's do our bloody jobs and find Collins.'

Chapter 36

Something about Danica Collins' eyes caught Manx's attention – something more than the expected spider web of redness after a night spent fretting about whether her husband was still alive. As she removed the tissue from her face, he realised what had made him look twice; her eyes were slightly different colours, one blue, the other a lighter green hue. It lent her an air of coolness that reminded him of a cat wary of someone trespassing on her territory.

Danica was wearing an oversized grey hoodie; not exactly wearing it, more like lost in it. Her face, bare of make-up and with lost sleep draining it of colour, was undeniably striking; her cheekbones high and those eyes, piercing and other-worldly. Her hair, naturally blonde, was pulled back in a tight ponytail. She spoke with an accent – Slavic, Manx guessed – but her diction was perfect. She had probably been educated at an expensive British private school.

'Do you know who took my husband, Inspector?'

Manx paused. She didn't seem the kind of woman who'd appreciate weak platitudes. 'To be honest, Mrs Collins, we're no further on than we were a day ago.'

'Honesty?' she said, folding her legs under her. 'Am I meant to be grateful for that?'

Manx ignored the question, which he took as rhetorical anyway. 'Have either you or your husband received any threatening letters or emails in the past few weeks? Anything that made you concerned for your safety?'

'We would have informed the police, immediately.'

'Understood,' Manx said. 'But could Mr Collins have kept them from you, so as not to worry you?'

Danica wrapped her arms around herself and sunk back into the huge white sofa. 'Logan and I have no secrets, Inspector.'

'Right you are.' If Manx had a pound for each time he'd heard that well-worn cliché from a spouse, he'd be retired by now.

'My husband is running as a Conservative candidate; I understand that can stir negative feelings in a place with such a strong Welsh identity. But kidnapping? People are more likely to spill their venom on social media these days, don't you think?'

'Or else burn down your property.'

Danica let Manx's words hang for a moment. 'And I suppose, honestly, you are no closer to solving that crime, either?'

'I suspect they may be connected.'

'Perceptive,' Danica said, raising her perfectly plucked eyebrows in an arch of sarcasm.

Manx continued. 'We'll need access to all your husband's contacts, work and friends. And if you have a recent photo, we'll need that to circulate to the press.'

She nodded to herself several times, as if counting the beats of a music track. 'Why did they take my husband? Should there not be a ransom demand? Unless…' Danica couldn't bring herself to finish her sentence.

'Best not to jump to conclusions,' Manx said. 'It's not unusual, the kidnappers will want to make you anxious.'

'Job done,' Danica deadpanned.

'There's a task-force in place to intercept any communication. We'll station a service car outside your home at all times, but my guess is that when they do make contact it's going to be less personal. Your husband's a public figure, there's value in that, they'll want to exploit it.'

'Comforting,' she replied, with a tight feline smile.

'Mrs Collins, kidnappings often resolve with the hostages being returned, unharmed,' Manx assured her.

'So you can promise me you'll find my husband alive?'

Manx paused, navigating around the trap she was laying out. 'I can promise you I'll do everything in my power to find him.'

Danica stretched out her legs and stood. 'I suppose I will have to take you at your word. I'll get you those contacts you requested.'

Manx sat back and sighed. He'd promised no platitudes, then delivered the woman one, nonetheless. Whoever was holding Collins was taking their sweet time in deciding where to place their chess piece. It was the kind of waiting game Manx had little patience for, especially with Troup fighting for her life and Collins still missing.

'Do the names James Flynt or Bobbie Matthews mean anything to you, Mrs Collins?' he asked as she returned with a print-out and photograph.

'No. Should they?' she said, handing the papers to Manx.

'Just a long shot. Thank you for your time,' he said.

Outside, Manx took in a breath of air. Two days and still no ransom demand? Danica was right. It didn't look good. Morris's words kept coming back to him. *What if it's already too late?*

Chapter 37

The old coal shed was six feet high and four feet wide and built from stones left over from the construction of the Lantern Arms. It had been decades since any coal was shovelled in or out, but the walls and floor remained coated in a film of black soot. The air inside was thick, as if it were becoming fat off the remnants of coal dust. Not that Logan Collins could see any of this. He could smell it, though; it choked his throat with mildew and dank earth. It was what he imagined the bottom of a grave might smell like.

Collins was blindfolded, with a wide strip of duct tape secured over his mouth, his hands and feet also bound. He had to breathe through his nostrils, which were crusted with coal soot, making his nose run. He couldn't remember feeling this degree of hunger before, but more than food, he needed water; buckets of the stuff. He'd read that the human body could live for weeks without food, but water? That was as basic and life-sustaining as it came.

He shuffled along the floor, lifted his feet and kicked against the door. It refused to budge, but he could see slivers of sunlight and hear voices; the same two men that had taken him; Ronnie and Mel. He'd made a point of remembering. How long had it been since they took him? A day? Two? Time seemed immaterial to him now. Surviving this was his goal now. Whatever this was.

Collins leaned his ear against the door, catching snippets of conversation as the men spoke.

'A copper! You knifed a fucking copper?' Melvin said, brandishing a copy of this morning's *North Wales Daily Post* as if it were a weapon, stabbing his finger across the headline: 'Senior police officer fighting for her life after brutal stabbing attack.'

'I didn't fucking know, did I?' Ronnie said, cowering like a scared dog. 'Stupid bitch got in the way.'

'You've really dropped us in it this time. You couldn't just follow orders? Run into the bastard like we planned?'

'Already told you, too many people. I didn't have a choice.'

'You had a choice. You just made the wrong one, as usual.'

The sound of Collins battering against the door startled them.

'Get him out,' Melvin said. 'Before Lydia gets wind.'

Ronnie complied, dragging Collins from the shed and forcing him to stand. Collins shook his head, tried to speak but could only manage a series of incoherent grunts. Melvin stepped forward and ripped the duct tape from his mouth. Collins let out a sharp groan of pain and chugged large mouthfuls of air.

'Water,' he said. His words were tinder dry and ripped at his throat like barbed wire. 'Please, water.'

Melvin gestured for Ronnie to get him what he wanted. As Ronnie shuffled off, Collins felt his lungs filling, his head clearing some. Breathing was good, but he needed to see these men; look into the whites of their eyes, consider their intentions.

'The blindfold? Can you?'

'You must be bloody joking,' Melvin said. 'You'll get water and food, that'll be it.'

Collins nodded. 'Small mercies,' he muttered, and he meant it. He did feel grateful to the man, Mel, the older sounding one. He'd take Mel's small mercies, as many of them as he could get.

Ronnie returned and shoved the plastic bottle to his lips. Collins swallowed and, like Oliver Twist, dared to ask for more.

'More? I'm not your fuckin' errand boy,' Ronnie barked.

Collins took a breath, found some words. 'You do want to keep me alive, don't you? For whatever it is you're planning? I'm sure I'm no use to you people dead.'

Collins couldn't see, but he guessed Mel had directed Ronnie to fetch more water 'What is it you want? Money?'

Melvin said nothing, just looked at the man standing in front of him; his expensive clothes covered in dirt, his face smudged with soot and dried blood. What did he want with him? It was a bloody good question. He'd never wanted this but with Collins their prisoner, he needed to figure out something fast. They couldn't let him walk. He'd seen their faces, heard their names, it wouldn't take the police long to track them down, especially on this island.

'Keep your mouth shut, unless you fancy dying in there,' Melvin said – a death threat was as good a distraction as any from answering his question.

Collins swallowed. 'And are you planning to kill me?'

Melvin felt his patience wearing thin. 'Yeah. Yeah I bloody well might if you don't stop fuckin' talking,' he said, lunging forward and grabbing Collins' shirt collar.

'Good idea, rough him up a bit,' Ronnie said, when he returned. 'Bastard deserves what's coming.'

Melvin watched as Collins drank desperately from the bottle. Good ideas? He was short on those, but he wasn't stupid enough to let Collins in on the fact. 'Lock him up,' he said.

Collins protested. Ronnie put a swift end to that by ramming a fist into his solar plexus and stood back grinning as Collins vomited most of the water he'd just drunk onto the floor.

'Where you off to?' he asked, as Melvin grabbed his car keys.

'Calling someone,' he said. 'Don't want him listening in.'

Throwing himself into the driver's seat of his car, Melvin felt a deep paralysing shock. It was as if his chest was collapsing in on him, followed by a pain that clawed his insides like a grappling hook. The doctor had warned him about this; a severe bout of pain that would arrive without warning and leave in much the same way. He prayed the doctor was right, that the pain would leave, and soon.

He breathed slowly and deliberately, hoping it might ease the agony. It didn't, and made Melvin more conscious of what he was sure was the cancer's intention: to remind him he had no dominion over the disease. Eventually, the pain eased to a dull throb that transmitted pulses of electricity through his stomach; he might have called them butterflies, but that was too pretty a word. They were more brutal; more like bat wings, thousands of them, baffling and beating, trying to find a way out.

He called the number he'd intended to call some ten minutes ago before the blunt reminder of the cancer sucker punched him. The call was picked up on the second ring.

'Hi, love, it's me. Yeah, that help you offered? I might take you up on it after all.'

Chapter 38

Mohsin Sadiq lived on one of the less desirable housing estates on the outskirts of Bangor. As Manx turned into the dour estate – even the sunlight struggled to grace the houses and lawns with any semblance of warmth – his neck-hairs pricked to attention. It wasn't the sort of place that took to coppers turning up in the middle of the day. The vacant stares from the teenagers drinking their way through the summer holidays reminded Manx he was a visitor here, and the car was hardly helping him blend in. The kids' jaws slacked open as he drove: they were either impressed at the sight of forty-year-old British coachwork entering their territory; or a car with functioning wheels and not sitting on its chassis supported by bricks was a rare sight in the neighbourhood.

Mohsin's house was the best kept in the cul-de-sac; lawn groomed, rose bushes trimmed, flower baskets well-watered. Manx parked outside the living room window where he could hopefully keep an eye on the car. The kids may have looked impressed, but that didn't mean a butterfly's bollocks in a place like this.

'I don't know what this has to do with us,' Mohsin said, grasping for his wife's hand as they sat. Mohsin and Rida were in their late sixties and as neatly put-together as their front garden: perfectly pressed slacks and ironed short-sleeved shirt for him, a deep green and gold sari for her. They looked at each other, each hoping the other had an answer, and when coming up empty-handed, returned their communal gaze to Manx.

'I understand. But it's our job to follow up on a criminal accusation.'

'What criminal accusation?' Mohsin snapped. 'Who made this accusation?'

'Ali Kalpar. He thinks you were involved in the theft of his van, which was subsequently used in a violent crime.'

Mohsin flipped open his palms and shrugged. 'Why would I steal a van that I already sold to him? It makes no sense.'

'I told you,' Rida said. 'Didn't I say only trouble will come from doing business with that man? So stubborn, you never listen.'

Mohsin patted his wife's hand. 'Hush now, water under the bridge. What's done cannot be undone.'

Outside, Manx heard a cacophony of voices. He glanced through the window; the Jensen was still on four wheels, unmolested. He continued. 'Can you tell me your whereabouts on the evening the van was taken? Wednesday July the twenty-third?'

They looked at each other, a nervous flicker dancing between their eyes, then glanced to the floor.

'Mr Sadiq?' Manx urged.

Rida slowly rose from the sofa and walked over to a cabinet packed end-to-end with photographs slipped into ornate picture frames. She carefully took one in her hand, sat back and handed it to Manx. 'Our son, Danvir,' she said, folding her hands to her lap.

Manx checked it out. A chubby-faced young man wearing John Lennon-style glasses and a huge smile – the kind of smile that told the world he was coming, and the world had better take notice.

'He was killed, last year. He was a medic in the RAF.'

'I'm very sorry—' Manx began.

'Yes, everyone is very sorry, so many apologies,' Rida interrupted, a weary steeliness woven into her voice. 'Wednesday was our son's birthday. He would have been thirty-six. We promised to honour him by celebrating his life, not his death.'

'Well, he died for something important,' Manx said, struggling for words. 'Serving his country.'

'Oh?' Rida said. 'What did he die for that was so important?'

'Rida,' her husband chided, with a low sigh.

Rida paid no heed. 'Oil? Money? Revenge? I loved my son with all my heart, but I cannot pretend he died for something good. I have many relatives who have witnessed this war on terror. I never thought Danvir would…'

She quickly caught herself, working hard to keep the tears dammed in. 'To answer your question, on Wednesday we were here with our family, remembering our son who died for nothing. That, Inspector, is what we were doing the night that bloody fool Ali Kalpar says we stole his van. Shame on him. Shame. On. Him.'

Manx wasn't often stuck for words, but Rida had rendered him speechless. She was crying softly, weaving her fingers over and through themselves. Manx rose and returned the photograph to the cabinet. As he did so, he noticed another photo; Danvir's wedding day. The woman standing next to him, his bride, compelled him to look closer. Max had stood by her hospital bed not three days ago.

'I assume this is Danvir's wife?' he asked.

Mohsin looked up. 'Yes. Bobbie. She's a good daughter-in-law, always comes to visit, even though…' Mohsin's thought trailed away, evaporating like jet vapor in the air.

'Would it be okay if I took this for a while?' Manx asked.

'Why? Why would you need that?' Rida asked. 'Bobbie's not involved with this. No, you cannot take it.'

Manx pulled out his mobile phone. 'Is this okay?' he asked, switching on the camera function. 'It's just routine, that's all, eliminating people from our inquiries.'

Rida shook her head. 'I suppose I can't stop you. Mohsin, you can see the policeman out,' she said, then left the room.

Chapter 39

'You're late,' Bobbie said, as Call Me Andy walked towards her. She'd been standing outside his office on the second floor of the RAF Valley welfare hub for the past ten minutes.

'Sorry,' Pierce said, struggling to balance a ream of papers in his hands. 'My meeting with Commander Boyd ran over. Can you hold these?'

Bobbie took the papers and watched carefully as he entered the five-digit code, taking note of each number as he pressed on the keypad.

Inside, the office air was stagnant and hot, and the desire to run a finger under her shirt collar was strong. But that would have been too much of a 'tell', more than Bobbie was willing to surrender. 'It was you, wasn't it?' she said.

Call Me Andy looked up from his notes. 'It was me what, Bobbie?'

'You found me, drove me to the hospital.'

'Do not pass a man in need, for you may be the hand of God to him.'

'I don't really relate to fairy stories. What were you doing on the road at that time of night? Awfully late for you to be out driving.'

'Are you interrogating me?'

'No, just curious. Seems like a coincidence, my therapist finding me out there.'

'Lucky I did find you. If it makes you feel better, I was counselling at an AA meeting in Holyhead. I took the back roads back to the base housing.'

'Must have been my lucky night.'

Pierce calmly sat back. 'All this resentment and anger. It's counter-productive to your healing. You're in a very vulnerable place right now. You need to let someone help you.'

'You know me, Andrew, I don't do vulnerable.'

'Remember what I told you a few months ago when we first talked?' Pierce said, leaning forward.

'You said a lot of things.'

'Specifically, about your shadow soul, how it can serve as a vessel for all your repressed negative emotional reactions to your trauma. Fear, resentment, rage, guilt, depression, shame, paranoia—'

'Aren't we paranoid ones the only ones who really know what's going on?' she interrupted.

Pierce continued. 'That kind of darkness can be overwhelming, Bobbie, it can be hard to fight against if you don't have the necessary mental tools. Have you felt anything like that? I liken it to brain fog, but it's darker, like you'll never find your way through it.'

Bobbie thought on the question. Call Me Andy could have been describing any hours in her life between waking and sleeping over the past twelve months. 'If that ever happens, I'll let you know,' she said.

'Good. Good to know, Bobbie,' he said. 'Oh, I thought you might like this back.' He reached into his briefcase and placed the headset she'd given him a few days ago on his desk. 'I noticed some of the gems were loose, so I glued them back on.'

'Why? Why did you do that?' Bobbie said, standing. 'I didn't ask you.'

'Just a gesture, that's all. I thought it might help.'

'You thought wrong. I told you, it's no use to me now.'

* *A few minutes after she left, Bobbie's words still smarting like nettle stings, Pierce ran his hands along the crust of gems. In two weeks, Bobbie Matthews would be out of his sphere of influence. The thought carved a deep hole in his stomach. He'd been naïve to think Flynt would have kept Bobbie on the base, but what pinched his heart most was that he'd failed Bobbie; failed a woman who he'd loved since they'd first met, though had never found the courage to

tell her. Bobbie wasn't lost to him yet; he still had time. Time to prove to her that if she couldn't accept God as her saviour, then she'd have to accept him as her saviour.

He looked out to the airstrip, the thud of helicopter rotors cutting through the warm air, and ground his palms into the headset, his thumbs edging under the gems until they began to shed like confetti onto his desk.

Chapter 40

Byron Gates had checked into Rose Cottage bed and breakfast earlier that day. After setting up his laptop, he logged into his private IP wireless connection and checked his messages; nothing since yesterday – good news, it meant Reaper was still committed to meeting.

After unpacking, he drove to a nearby pub, ordered a shandy and scarfed down a ham and cheese toastie, before heading to the meeting point; a café called Tide, on the Halen Môn sea-salt plant.

When Byron arrived, a cluster of be-shorted tourists were being led around the Saltcote visitors' centre. He ordered himself a cappuccino from the coffee truck and found himself a quiet table far from the crowds.

As he made himself comfortable, he took in his surroundings. The Saltcote was perched on the banks of the Menai Strait with a breath-taking vista across a green-blue ribbon of water. Byron was struck by the majesty of the view: a bucolic setting of lush fields with speckles of sheep, like cotton-wool puffs, set against the green. Above the green, the sun anointed the knotty spine of the Snowdonia mountains with a hazy glow, and at the shallowest points of the strait the water rushed in white flurries.

As he sat, his mind cleared. He'd been far too tense over the past few days, spent too many hours with his eyes focused inches from his screen. It took his mind some minutes to adjust, as if the real world was too overwhelming, its panoramas too wide, its colours too vibrant and saturated, requiring his brain some time to recalibrate.

He glanced at the crowds and wondered if Reaper was watching, or even if someone might be following him. He'd suffered a severe paranoid episode several months ago when he was certain he was being watched. He had no proof, but what was it they said about paranoia – that it's the realisation that everything around you is alive and urgent? That's how he felt now; as if everything around him was dialled up a notch, tweaked to the maximum setting.

Reaper had asked him to send a photograph. Initially, he'd refused, but relented when Reaper threatened to back out of the meeting. He'd taken a selfie and sent it via a double-encrypted website he used for transferring documents. Reaper had obviously wanted to make sure Byron knew who was in control. All he could do was wait for him to make the first move and introduce himself.

He didn't need to wait long.

He was barely three sips into his coffee when someone pulled up the chair across from him and sat. Byron's face must have betrayed his surprise.

'Expecting someone else?' Bobbie Matthews said, pulling the bill of her baseball cap low over her forehead.

Chapter 41

After attaching the photograph Logan Collins' wife had given him to the incident board, Manx turned to the team. 'No communication, no ransom, no clue as to where he's being held and who's holding him. We're relying on witness testimony and luck, both notoriously unreliable and illusive.'

'All the witnesses say the same thing, boss,' Nader said. 'The bloke was wearing a face mask and sunglasses. He kicked and punched Collins then led him off with some kind of weapon, maybe a knife, to his neck.'

'That tallies with the surgeon's report on Vera's wound,' Manx said. 'Any updates on the witness footage?'

'Eight people filmed the incident on their cell phones. We looked at all the footage. Nothing that contradicts the witness statements, but this one was interesting.' Priddle turned his computer screen to face Manx. 'It was taken just before it happened.'

Manx watched the brief, shaky video. The white van hurtling down the hill, its nose aimed directly at the food slam entrance. The loud squeal of brakes, tyre skids, and the van almost jack-knifing before coming to a stop, the front wheels mounting the kerb. The silhouette of a man running into the crowd.

'No doubt in my mind,' Manx said. 'Collins wasn't where he was meant to be, the driver notices and deviates from the plan. Now he's lumbered with a hostage he doesn't know what to do with, which is why we're still waiting for the bloody ransom demand. Collins has probably seen his kidnapper's face, so he can't just let him go. He's still figuring out his next move. We're in a waiting game.'

'The witnesses only saw one man,' Priddle said. 'Maybe someone else was waiting for him down a side street.'

Manx gestured to the scene-of-crime photographs. 'The CCTV footage has been analysed from every angle. Unless he knew exactly where the cameras were positioned, then made a point of avoiding them, he vanished into thin air.'

'What if he didn't have a car?' Morris said, almost leaping from her chair and marching over to the incident board.

'Meaning?' Manx asked.

She traced a finger along one of the aerial photographs, following the outline of houses on the Anglesey side of the strait. 'There's all these private slips between Menai Bridge and Beaumaris. Someone with a boat could have been waiting for him.'

Manx considered her theory. 'Knock on some doors first thing tomorrow, see if anyone had their slip used without their permission in the last few days.'

'Sir,' Morris said, unable to resist a small smile as she returned to her seat.

'Priddle, any luck with that hit-and-run incident?'

'Right, almost forgot, what with all this going on.' He flicked through his notebook. 'Spoke to all the garages on the island. Nobody's worked on a driver's side wing mirror repair in the last two weeks. I'll extend the search to Bangor and Caernarvon. Don't think they're connected do you, boss?'

Manx pinned the print of Danvir and Bobbie to the board. 'Bobbie Matthews' husband, Danvir Sadiq, died last year on a tour of duty in Syria. His parents, Mohsin and Rida Sadiq, used to own the Halal abattoir in Gaerwen until they sold the business, including the delivery van, to Ali Kalpar several months ago. This van is the same one used in the kidnapping and the attack on Vera Troup. It's a tenuous link to Bobbie Matthews, and as far as we know she had no connection to Collins.'

'How's Vera doing, boss?' Nader asked.

'Still critical. But don't let that be a distraction. Vera wouldn't want us sitting around twiddling our thumbs and worrying about her. Go out there, do your jobs, solve the case.'

His words were met with a thoughtful nodding of heads. They all understood the subtext. Whether she survived this or not, they had to do Vera Troup proud. They owed one of their own that much, at the very least.

Chapter 42

Byron Gates wiped a smudge of foam and chocolate powder from his lips. 'Reaper?' he said, taking stock of the woman. Build: slight and wearing too much clothing for the warm weather. Face: sharp and angular, a blot of a birthmark above her right eye and a series of minor scratches – which looked recent – across her cheeks and brow. Eyes: well, those were hidden behind the polarised sheen of aviator shades tinted so dark, all he could see was his reflection in the lenses.

'I'm going to make this brief, Byron.'

'Yeah, all right, brief's good.'

'The official report they released about Operation Vanguard. Do you think it's a cover-up?'

Byron took a short sip of coffee and made a serious effort to appear nonchalant, leaning back and folding his hands into his lap. 'Could be. Not that anyone gives a shit.'

'I was there. I give a shit,' Bobbie said.

Byron gestured to the papers he'd laid out on the table. 'After the initial strike, there was a counter-attack by insurgents that left six RAF medics dead. You have proof that's not the case?'

'Who sent you that report, Byron?'

'I couldn't tell you even if I knew. Most of the information I receive is anonymous, obviously.'

'And why did this one make such an impression?'

Byron stroked his beard. 'It didn't, not at first. But when I published it, the web traffic went off the charts, and then…' he hesitated, glancing nervously towards the patio as a woman stumbled over one of the chairs, knocking over a coffee cup.

'Then what, Byron?' Bobbie urged.

He lowered his voice to just above a whisper. 'I couldn't prove anything, but you know when you get that feeling that someone's watching you? I'd get that every time I left the house. I don't know, maybe I was just being paranoid or something.'

'It's likely you were being followed, or at least watched.'

'Do you think they're watching now?'

'Watching who? Me or you?'

Byron twisted his coffee cup around. 'Erm… both I suppose.'

'I scouted the area a few hours ago and checked out that Toyota Prius of yours for tracking devices.'

Byron's mouth slacked open.

'Don't worry, nothing to report. But the question I'm asking myself is, are you the person I should be talking to about this? Are you a safe harbour?'

'Oh, yeah, no worries there.' Byron straightened his back. 'My site's triple-encrypted, non-static IP addresses, military-grade firewalls, the works. No one's hacking into that without tripping a series of alarms that'll shutter down the whole site.'

'Good to know. Now, Here's the deal, Byron, I tell you the whole story. You post it. But you need to do something for me.'

He hesitated. 'Like what?'

'You need to take this story to one of the national newspapers, one of the more respectable ones.'

Byron grimaced. 'It's risky, leaves me exposed. I'm not sure–'

'You're not sure?' Bobbie interrupted. 'I'm handing you one of the biggest stories on our government's drone programme you've ever had access to and you're not sure?'

Byron tugged sharply on his beard. 'I don't even know if you're legit, you could be setting me up.'

Bobbie reached into her bag and took out a copy of the *Daily Post* from three days ago, making sure he could see the headline.

RAF Officer Found Dead on Popular Anglesey Beach

'Do you recognise the name?' she said, pointing at the paper.

Byron glanced at James Flynt's name, shook his head.

'Flight Commander Flynt was the overseer, what we called the boss-auth, in the station that day.'

Byron sensed an arc of electricity pulsing through him. 'Do you think they killed him, to keep him quiet?'

'It's possible. It's also possible they might kill me, which is why the urgency in getting this story out there, Byron.'

'Jesus,' he said, sitting back as if he'd been walloped in the sternum. 'If they knew I'd talked to you—'

'You haven't signed the Official Secrets Act. I'm exposed here, not you.'

Her words were some comfort to Byron, but he still felt uneasy. There was a detached coldness about her that unsettled him.

She continued. 'What is important is that you tell this story and tell it correctly. Those medics were not killed by an enemy strike. A secondary battle damage assessment was conducted after our drone left the strike zone, but that report never came to light. After an official hearing, everyone involved with Operation Vanguard was cleared of any blame, but the command saw fit to permanently suspend my combat-ready status. That, Byron, is not acceptable.'

'Yeah, I can see that,' Byron said, sensing a surety in her tone that made him think she'd spent too many hours churning this over in her mind – the signs were familiar. He reached into his backpack and retrieved a small voice recorder. 'Is this okay?'

She stared at the antiquated device. 'Bit analogue, isn't it?'

Byron huffed. 'I'd like to see some black hat attempt to hack their way into an off-the-grid strip of magnetic tape,' he said, checking the micro-cassette was fully rewound.

'Off the grid? If you say so,' she said. 'I'd go and grab yourself another coffee: this could take a while.'

Byron's tape stopped recording fifty-eight minutes and thirty seconds later; his coffee untouched. Reaper had been good to her word, relayed everything that had happened that day, albeit with an eerie tone of detachment. When she talked about the explosion that took out the medics' convoy, her tone shifted, a perceptible crack in her voice. 'Imagine the worst day you could possibly have, then multiply it to the power of ten and you might just begin to get close.'

'Aren't you risking everything?' Byron said. 'Telling me this? They'll figure out it was you eventually.'

'I've already lost everything that ever mattered to me. There's nothing left for them to take away.'

Byron clicked off the recorder. He had no idea how to respond to her words, other than avert his eyes and make himself look busy stuffing papers back into his backpack.

'If you've got what you need,' Bobbie said, running a finger under her shades.

Byron guessed she was wiping away a tear but couldn't be sure. 'Yeah, yeah, it's great, really good stuff.'

Bobbie didn't offer her hand and Byron didn't offer his. They were strangers who had met at a table, talked, then gone their separate ways.

As she slipped through the crowd, Byron sipped his coffee and winced; it was stone cold. He'd been so engrossed in Reaper's account that he'd failed to notice the sun had been beating down hard for the past hour; his face felt as if it had been seared in a hot pan.

He passed the back of his forearm over his brow. Several hundred metres away, a powerful telephoto lens framed Byron's sun-reddened face in extreme close-up. It was file sixty-three taken that afternoon, and would become file number six hundred and fifteen in a folder labelled *Byron Charles Gates*, residing on a secure hard drive deep in an RAF Intelligence server room.

Chapter 43

Manx arrived at the cottage just after midnight. His sister greeted him at the door, her face pale, eyes bloodshot. Sara had called him thirty minutes ago. Late-night calls from his sister were rarely good news; in fact, most phone calls he received in the early hours of the morning were rarely harbingers of anything good.

'You'd best come in, they're waiting.'

Manx kicked the mud off his boots and entered.

'This is my brother, Tudor,' Sara said, as Manx followed her into the kitchen of the holiday cottage, located two fields west of his mother's house.

A thin man with a dark beard shook his hand. 'Barry Coleman. This is my wife Diane and our daughter, Juliet.'

Manx nodded and sat. Juliet was around nine years old, and was spread across her mother's lap, half asleep. Diane, a bookish-looking woman with an air of calmness stroked her daughter's brow. 'Is your mother okay?'

'As okay as she'll ever be,' Sara said.

'So, what's going on with Mam?' Manx asked, his eyes bleary and his breath still smelling of the scotch he'd drunk before bed.

'Went off wandering, again,' Sara explained. 'Came over here and scared the living daylights out of this little girl. Just stood outside her window, staring. I didn't even know she'd left the house.'

'Your sister explained the situation,' Barry said. 'I went through it with my own father some years back. It's not easy.'

'So, Mam left the house in her dressing gown, walked over two fields and stood outside a little girl's bedroom?'

'That's what I just said,' Sara said, impatiently.

'Just making sure I've got all the facts.'

'As you can tell, my brother's a policeman,' Sara snipped. 'We only get to see him on holidays and family emergencies.'

Manx ignored the obvious barb. 'You're renting the cottage?'

'Just for the week,' Barry confirmed.

'Any idea why my mother would wander over here in the middle of the night? Did you meet her or speak to her?'

'She was walking on the side of the road when we drove in. She waved at us, I think,' Diane said.

Juliet stirred on her mother's lap. 'Miriam,' she said. 'The scary woman kept saying 'Miriam'.'

Manx and Sara looked at each other, eyes wide, each sensing a similar cold shiver pass through their bones.

'Are you sure?' Sara asked, bringing a hand to her throat.

Juliet nodded. Manx and Sara both studied the young girl. They hadn't noticed it before, but as they looked closer the resemblance was uncanny enough for them both to catch their breaths.

'Who's Miriam?' Diane asked.

Sara spoke. 'Our sister. She died–'

'Disappeared,' Manx interrupted. 'Thirty years ago.

'And she looked…?' Diane asked, glancing at Juliet.

'Show her the picture.'

Manx pulled out an old faded photograph of Miriam from his wallet. 'She could be her sister,' Barry said, studying the bright-eyed young girl, hair parted in the middle, a smile so eerily similar to his daughter's it made him shiver.

'We're so sorry,' Diane said, softly. 'It must have been awful.'

It was, Manx thought, but 'awful' didn't even come close. 'Where's Mam now?'

'I put her in the car. She won't move: she likes the heated seats.'

'Good enough,' Manx said, standing. 'Thank you, both. I'm very sorry this happened. It won't happen again, I promise.'

Sara threw him a look that could have curdled milk.

‘Honestly, no harm done,’ Barry said, seeing them out. ‘Juliet will have forgotten all about it by the morning, I’m sure. Best of luck with everything,’ he added, closing the cottage door.

Outside, Sara leaned against the car and lit up a cigarette, her hands shaking as she brought the lighter to the tip. ‘Promise? Who the hell are you to make promises, Tudor?’ She took a deep inhale.

Manx looked at his mother in the passenger seat. She glanced back at him and pulled her grey hair away from her face. There was a flicker of recognition, but not enough to keep her interest.

‘What was I meant to say?’

Sara crossed her arms and dragged the heel of her slippers along the gravel. ‘I don’t know, Tudor. I don’t fucking know.’

‘You need new locks. I’ll send someone over tomorrow.’

‘Thanks, but I can call a bloody locksmith,’ she said, exhaling a thick trail of smoke. ‘Any other bright ideas?’

‘Motion sensors, so you’ll know if she leaves the house.’

‘Brilliant. Motion sensors. You’re a godsend, Tudor, so glad you’re back.’

Manx was about to protest when Sara raised her hand to stop him. ‘By the way,’ she said. ‘I’m having a clear-out, getting rid of some old stuff, got a box with your name on it. If you want it, come by before the weekend.’

‘Not much of a one for souvenirs.’

Sara shrugged and yanked open the car door. ‘Right. I’ve told you, so there, job done.’

As his sister drove off, Manx looked across the pasture towards Alice’s house, which under the soft glare of the moonlight, looked misshapen, like the cruel curvature of an old lady’s stoop.

Cwm Tawel – Peaceful Valley – the name of the house had more than a hint of irony. Manx had never felt anything close to a sense of peace within its walls. What he did sense, with every bone in his body was the presence of ghosts, waiting for him in the rooms and hallways.

He could feel the dead weight of their greeting each time he walked in, as if they’d missed him and were waiting anxiously for his return.

Chapter 44

PC Morris stood at the end of the long garden that ended at the slip on the banks of the Menai Strait. Across the water, sunlight broke the surface in sparks of bright white. She looked back at the huge mid-century house behind the shade of oak trees; this, she guessed, was what was known as 'a multi-million-pound property', one of many constructed along the Anglesey side of the strait.

'I haven't had a boat since Martha died,' Peter Whinstone said, as they walked. Peter was in his late seventies, thin, with a severe stoop. 'I never was one much for the water myself; dickie tummy. Tried everything, ended up with my head over the side most of the time, put a real dampener on a day out on the water.'

Morris gestured to the slip. 'What makes you think it's been used recently?' she asked, with a tone of hurried expectation. She'd been knocking on doors all morning with no luck. When, at 12.10 pm, she'd knocked on Peter's door, the shine of the gleaming idea she'd had yesterday was already fading.

As they reached the rim of the decking, the water slapping lazily against the stanchions, Peter pointed. 'See the cleats?' he said, directing a shaky, liver-spotted finger at the steel teeth protruding from the timbers. 'The ropes were still wrapped around them from when I sold the boat. Couldn't get the buggers off to be honest, so I just kept them. I thought they might protect the cleats.'

Morris squatted and examined the metal. The centre bias of the cleat was considerably less corroded than the prongs, which had been left exposed to the elements. 'When did you notice this?'

‘A few days ago. I didn’t think much of it. I thought they’d maybe come off in the winter storms.’

‘Be a pretty fierce storm to rip ropes off a cleat.’

Peter kicked a loop of rope lying on the deck. ‘You think this is connected to that business over at Menai Bridge?’

Morris focused on an unusual pattern of red spots on the deck. ‘What colour was your boat?’

‘*Martha’s Pride*? White and blue. Why, is that important?’

‘Not sure yet,’ she said, standing. ‘Any other access points to the slip other than the garden?’

‘There’s a pathway down to the cove, then it’s a bit of a climb, but a cakewalk for someone half my age and no arthritis.’

‘Did you notice anything or anyone suspicious on or around last Thursday evening?’

Peter wagged his finger. ‘So, you do think it has something to do with what happened at the food slam,’ he said, puffing out his chest as if he’d just succeeded in getting one over on the young PC.

‘You never know. Did you see anyone?’

‘Not that I recall. But it wouldn’t be me who saw anything.’ He gestured to the side wall of the house.

Morris noticed them immediately. Two security cameras pointed directly at the slip. ‘Do they still work?’

‘Better had. They cost me a bloody arm and a leg every month for the monitoring,’ Peter said. ‘I expect you’ll want to look at the footage, then?’

Chapter 45

'So, are you going to tell me what that's all about?' Tammy asked, sliding a coffee mug across the table and gesturing to the bloodied cuts on Bobbie's face.

Bobbie hesitated. 'I was in the hospital. Just overnight.'

'Why didn't you tell me? What the hell happened?'

'Don't fuss. I was out running, a car hit me then drove off.'

Tammy shook her head. 'Out running at night again? I don't know why you just don't get some sleeping pills.'

'They don't work.'

'Tell me you at least went to the police.'

'Of course I did.'

'Christ, Bobbie,' Tammy said, sitting back and folding her arms. 'You and your bloody secrets.'

'I'm telling you now, aren't I?'

'If anything like this happens again, promise you'll call me.'

'Promise,' Bobbie said, pulling out a ream of paper from her backpack and placing it on the table. 'Listen, Tam, in two weeks I'm being transferred to a veteran's hospital near Liverpool—'

Tammy let out a breath and grabbed her sister's hand. 'Honestly, that's the best news I've heard for ages, love. After what you did to that bloke in the pub, I was beginning to worry. This will be good for you; you'll get some proper help. And you don't need to ask, I'll visit you every weekend, if that's what you want.'

Bobbie slipped the papers towards Tammy. 'I had to name a

beneficiary, now that Danvir's gone. You know, if something happens to me. It's just some savings and my RAF pension.'

'I don't like you talking like this,' Tammy said, moving back, as if wanting to put as much distance as possible between her and the papers.

'It's just a formality. RAF protocol.'

As Tammy considered her sister's words, Bobbie's mobile rang. She checked the area code – Waddington. 'I'd better take this, might be important.'

Bobbie stepped into the garden. A woman's voice identified herself as Sophie Dawson. Before she said another word, Bobbie felt a sickening premonition like a wave of nausea flood through her.

Officer Cadet Cole Dawson had been found in his garage, hanging from the rafters by his belt, wearing full RAF service dress. A simple three-line note, *Sorry. I love you. It's not your fault* was stuffed into his pocket.

Bobbie's whole body shook as she hung up. She leaned against the patio table, knocking over a vase of flowers. As she watched Tammy through the patio window flipping through the papers, one thought thundered in her head.

With Flynt and Dawson both dead, would she be next?

Chapter 46

While the CCTV footage from the slip hadn't provided the case-breaking evidence the team had hoped for, it did prove there were two men working together.

'Anyone recognise these two?' Manx asked, freezing the video. The footage was grainy: the cameras had been installed before high definition recording equipment was the norm and the lens was foggy.

'Those bastards could be anyone,' Nader huffed.

Manx let the footage play to the point when the vessel left the slip and motored towards Beaumaris, disappearing left of frame.

'No name on the boat, either,' Nader said.

'At least we can confirm we're looking for two suspects.'

They all turned as PC Priddle bounded through the doorway with the enthusiasm of an excited puppy.

'You took your time,' Manx said. 'Stop off for a bacon bap?'

He waved a slip of paper he was holding like a trophy and sat down in the nearest chair. 'DNA results from the blood Morris found on the dock.'

'Make my day and tell me it's a match for Collins.'

'Not Collins. They ran it through the national database, no matches either.'

'Then why do you look like the cat who got the bloody cream?' Nader asked.

Priddle leaned back casually in his chair. It tipped slightly too far back as he sat. He caught himself before gravity got the better of him and planted his boots to the floor. 'I had an idea,' he said.

'Bring on the dancing girls,' Nader grunted. 'The lad's had an idea.'

'I asked Bevan to check on any familial DNA.'

'What's that, then?' Nader asked. 'Familiar DNA?'

'It's familial, not familiar, Sarge,' Morris corrected him. 'We learned about it in basic training. It's how they caught the Golden State Killer, that sicko who killed thirteen people in the 1980s.'

'A bit of light bedtime reading, eh, Minor?' Nader quipped.

Morris paused for only a second; she was becoming well-practised in the fine art of not rising to DS Nader's bait, though at times it took a large chunk of her willpower to hold her tongue. 'They took DNA from one of the crime scenes. There were no matches, so they reckoned it was a dead end; whoever the killer was hadn't been arrested for any other crimes. So, they checked to see if a close relative with a DNA match had been arrested. Turns out his uncle was in the system, so they created this family tree and arrested the sick bastard a few weeks later. Turns out the killer was a copper, a sheriff.'

Nader folded his arms. 'Right, so if this bloke's brother, uncle or grandmother's DNA's in the database we could find a match?'

'Not his grandmother,' Manx said. 'Familial DNA only works with Y chromosomes, men.' He turned to Priddle. 'So, did Bevan find a familial match?'

'Em, no,' Priddle said. 'Said it was going to take a few days, went on about his reputation, due diligence and that, but here's the good part. He confirmed the DNA from the joint we found in the van is from the same family as the blood Morris found on the slip, which probably means the men are related.'

'That's something, I suppose,' Manx said. 'Did Bevan give any indication of when he'd have the results?'

'To hell with that, we'll be waiting ages for Bevan to pull his finger out,' Nader snapped. 'We should be out there, rattling cages, not waiting for bloody handouts.'

'No reason we can't do both,' Manx said.

Nader shook his head. 'Waste of bloody time, if you ask me.'

'You have a better idea?'

'Yeah, I do,' Nader said, his face flushed. 'Round up all the nasty bastards we know who wouldn't give two shits about knifing a copper. Got a few I'd like to question outside the interview room.'

'Excellent example you're setting,' Manx said. He gestured to the rest of the team. 'You lot, get back to work. Nader, you stay.'

As the team left, Manx dragged a chair and sat across from Nader. 'What the bloody hell was that about?'

'Just saying, like, they're brutal bastards whoever did that. Didn't take to the woman much myself, but she was the boss.'

'Still is the boss,' Manx reminded him.

Nader's skin tightened around his knuckles like the taut head of a snare drum. 'I want to catch 'em, boss, that's all.'

'You're not special, Nader, we all want that.'

'Yeah, but the courts these days? Too many bastards get off on some technicality. We spend all this time investigating then something gets fucked up and they're back on the streets cocky as you like bragging how they got one over on the system.'

'You, talking like this. That's what'll fuck things up, compromise the case we're building.'

'But still, one of our own…'

That phrase again – the one that settled like cold stones in Manx's gut. Problem was, he knew where Nader's head was at, had felt the same emotions after reading the report on CeeCee Cartwright's death; suicide. Manx's less official version? Not. Bloody. Likely. CeeCee wasn't the suicidal type, never had been.

'Don't do anything that's going to make me regret not taking you off this investigation. Your record on this kind of thing hasn't exactly been squeaky clean.'

'Why keep me on it, then, if I'm such a bloody liability?'

'Because, Nader, I need every officer we can spare, even a hot-head like you. You're angry about Troup, we all are, but this case gets closed by the book. We do things the right way.'

Nader stood, hitched up his trouser belt. 'Yeah, and you've always done things the right way, boss?' he said. 'That why you're back here and not still down in London, cracking the big cases?'

Manx sensed his own rage stirring but kept it on a low simmer; there was enough tension in the room without adding to the mix.

'Just ask yourself this question,' he said. 'When DCSI Troup recovers, how are you going to look her in the eyes and tell her you went off on some maverick crusade that compromised the whole investigation and her attackers are walking around, like you said, 'cocky as you like'? Tell me that.'

Nader took a deep breath. 'Dunno, boss,' he said, leaning his hands on the desk. 'How are you going to look her in the eyes if we don't catch the bastards?'

As Nader walked out, the duty sergeant walked in. 'Got a woman in reception,' he said. 'Says her name's Bobbie Matthews. Insists on talking to you. Says she'll wait as long as it takes.'

Chapter 47

After Bobbie finished speaking, Manx gathered his thoughts. The woman has been lucid, laid out her suspicions in an organised fashion, but still something troubled him. Maybe what her psychologist had told him at the hospital concerning Bobbie's trauma was colouring his attitude. Or maybe it was her emotional detachment, as if all this were happening to someone else, and how her eyes locked with his as she spoke; they were the eyes of someone haunted by something, something Manx couldn't begin to fathom, at least not yet.

'What am I meant to do with this information?' he asked. 'There's no evidence to support what you've implied. Commander Flynt's death is still under investigation. This Cole Dawson you mentioned? Cause of death hasn't been determined, and even if it does turn out to be suspicious, Lincolnshire is out of my jurisdiction.'

'What about the car that ran me down?'

'We're still investigating. Could have been someone with a bellyful of booze. If that's the case, we'll track them down and they'll be arrested.'

'Commander Boyd? He didn't tell you I'd talked to him.'

'We'll be addressing that with the commander when he returns our calls,' Manx said, an irritated edge to his voice. He'd already left several messages with Boyd's assistant with no response. He was beginning to feel like the desperate, dumped boyfriend.

'They're lying, you know,' she said.

'Who? Who's "they", Bobbie?'

'All of them. Flynt, Boyd, RAF Air Command… the government.'

'The government?' Manx said, his eyebrows arching. 'You'll need to be a bit more specific. Names. Titles. Any previous form.'

Bobbie stiffened. 'I can see you're not taking this seriously. I'm wasting my time. I should take this to a more senior officer with experience in more complex cases.'

Manx met Bobbie's defiant stare with a steely glare of his own. 'My seriously understaffed team is currently investigating a suspicious death and dealing with the aftermath of the vicious stabbing of a colleague, who is still in a critical condition. And let's not forget some nasty little toe-rag kidnapped a local politician and we're in the process of turning over this whole island looking for him. So yes, your conspiracy theories are a bloody waste of time; mine not yours. Now, before you leave, there's one question you can answer for me.'

Manx slid the print-out of the photo he'd taken at the Sadiqs' home. Bobbie's hands gave a momentary tremor as she looked at the photo of her and Danvir on their wedding day.

'How? How did you get this?'

'Were you aware the van once owned by your father-in-law, Mohsin Sadiq, was used in the attack at Menai Bridge?'

'No. I was not. And I don't see the relevance or why you would ask me about something I have no connection to.'

'Your husband, he was killed last year. I'm very sorry, that must have been terrible for you. But you can understand why I have to ask the question.'

'No, I really don't,' Bobbie said, folding her arms.

'Here's another question. The night of Commander Flynt's death. Did you follow him to Benllech?'

Bobbie quickly pushed back her chair and stood. 'I came here to give you information about a serious military cover-up, and now I'm the criminal? I'll see myself out,' she said, turning her back on Manx and slamming the interview room door as she left.

Running down the station steps, muttering to herself, her anger reaching peak boiling point, Bobbie checked her phone: several missed calls and a voice message from Tammy. She listened to the message three times, the words failing to sink in. By the time she'd reached the cemetery, the words had sunk in with horrifying clarity.

'Who would do this?' Bobbie said, kneeling at Danvir's gravestone, the words *Paki Scum* spray painted across the marble in red. At the base of the stone, the flowers that Bobbie made sure were fresh each week had been thrown from their vases and trodden into the gravel.

'I don't know, Bobbie,' Tammy said. 'Sick, that's what they are, just sick.'

Bobbie traced her finger along the engraving; *Danvir Sadiq. Dedicated son. Loving husband. Died serving his country.*

Died serving his country. That epitaph crawled its way under Bobbie's skin. It sounded as hollow and meaningless as the cruel words sprayed across it.

Tammy began to clear up the flowers, setting the less damaged back into the vases.

Bobbie grabbed the flowers from Tammy's hands. 'Leave it. He was my husband, not yours.'

'I was only—'

'Give me some space, Tammy, for God's sake,' Bobbie said, her voice raised, face flushed and close to tears.

Tammy laid down the flowers and backed off. 'Yeah, of course. Call me later, eh?' she said, walking back to her car, leaving Bobbie kneeling at the graveside.

That night, sleep came to Bobbie in fits and starts, interrupted by fragments of dreams, memories and wild leaps into her subconscious, where she waded, knee-deep, through a thick marsh that seemed as endless as it was deep.

On the ceiling figures, like shadow puppets, took to the stage, played out their scenes then exited. Danvir, James Flynt, and Commander Boyd flickered like old film, their features distorted and blurred as if the celluloid were melting as it passed over the projector's worn teeth creating spectral blooms that floated around her bedroom. Cole Dawson, though, came to her in brilliantly rendered colour; lips blue, face pale, wounds around his neck red and raw, body swaying like the pendulum of a grandfather clock; leather creaking against wood as it brushed against the rafters.

The dull thud of his body cut from the belt and falling to the floor startled her awake. She lay there for several minutes, limbs rigid, eyes wide open in the darkness. Call Me Andy had been right about one thing. She could sense it now, her shadow soul, could almost reach inside herself and touch it. But it wasn't a shadow; not anymore. It had matured into something greater. It was a sky full of thunder clouds with no cuts of blue or breaks of sunlight, just blackness; dense and relentless. And like thunder, the breaths in between its beats were becoming shorter and shorter, until there were no breaths anymore, just a darkness that swallowed all in its path.

At around 5.00 am she stepped out of her bed, expecting the heaviness that had greeted her most mornings. Instead, she had a clarity and focus that was as close to a religious experience as she was ever likely to get. With the sunrise flickering behind the tree branches in her garden, she made herself a coffee, sat at the kitchen table, and thought about making a start on the papers she'd brought home from the base. One of the press releases she'd been editing, red-lined with Commander Boyd's suggestions, fell to the floor. She picked it up. As she glanced at the contents, another moment of clarity seared clean across the morning.

This is it. The sign she was sure would reveal itself. The starlings, Flynt's death, the bull in her path, the car running her off the road, Cole Dawson's apparent suicide, the vandalising of Danvir's gravestone; they were all signposts along the way, guiding her here to this moment.

Bobbie picked up her phone and dialled.

'I'm ready to help you,' she said, her voice barely above a whisper. 'But we do things my way.'

Chapter 48

If Manx could have bothered himself with the concept of a to-do list, that morning it would have included three action items: a meeting with the North Wales coroner, Richard Hardacre; a long-awaited meeting with Commander Boyd; and, at the end of the day, dinner at his mother's house. His sister had called last night to remind him she still had a box of his 'stuff' and if he wanted any of it, this was his last chance. He couldn't imagine what 'stuff' Sara referred to; it had been over thirty years since he'd left home. Out of curiosity, he agreed to drive over. He'd at least get a decent meal; no doubt served with a side-order of guilt and a slice of humble pie for dessert, which he'd be required to swallow without complaint.

At 11.30 am, Richard Hardacre sat in his garden. He wore a Panama hat and was sipping a gin and tonic from a large, bulbous glass, nibbling on a cut of cheese and looking as if the troubles of the world were far from any of his concern. Manx walked across the lawn. He was greeted with a subtle tip of Hardacre's hat.

'Hatching your evil plan for world domination, Hardacre?'

'As usual, Manx, you've lost me.'

'The Bond villain look? All you need is a cat and a bad accent, and you'd have had me at 'I've been expecting you, Mr Manx'.'

'Droll. Take a seat.'

'So, why the summons to the lair?' Manx asked, pulling up a chair and shuffling into the shade.

Hardacre poured more gin over the ice in his glass. 'Day off from the cold slab of the morgue, Manx. I'd offer you a drink, but I suspect you'll say you're on duty.'

'I'm not the cocktail type.'

'Why doesn't that surprise me? Listen,' he said, putting down his cheese knife and laying a folder on the table. 'My friend, the geologist? She's put the cat amongst the pigeons, Manx.'

'Do geologists do that? Wouldn't they be more likely to throw rocks at glass houses or something?'

'Strained metaphors aside, Manx, take a look at this.' Hardacre placed two photographs on the table. 'Exhibit one. The rock fragments found under our victim's fingernails contain the expected amount of limestone, native to the cliffs around Benllech.'

He laid down another photograph. 'Now, the fragments I excavated from said victim's head wound. Turns out they're not native to that area. My geologist friend confirmed these fragments are from blueschist rocks. A few hundred million years old, mind you, but widespread all over Anglesey.'

'But not at Benllech beach?'

'Unlikely.'

'Does she know where?'

'Like I said, blueschist is one of the most common rocks on the island. However, simple deduction suggests—'

'Flynt couldn't have struck his head on the rocks at Benllech,' Manx interrupted. 'Killed elsewhere, then driven there, maybe?'

'Or the killer was already in possession of the murder weapon, and chose to batter our victim's skull close to where we found him. It would have been my preferred modus operandi, spares the effort and mess of transporting a dead body in the boot of the car.'

Manx stood, and rolled up his shirt sleeves. 'I was right, you're a criminal mastermind, Hardacre. A real-life Scaramanga.'

Hardacre squinted. 'Just don't tell the wife, she'll be wanting to know where I stashed my ill-gotten gains.' He took a sip of gin. 'Good luck with all this, Manx. I suspect with this, and that kidnapping situation, your summer holiday's on hold for a while.'

'I'll live it vicariously through you, Hardacre,' Manx said, heading back to his car.

Commander Boyd had requested to meet off base. Manx had reluctantly agreed – he wasn't going to hand him another excuse to delay. He pulled the Jensen onto several hectares of freshly cut fields just off the A55, passing three large billboards welcoming him to this year's Anglesey Agricultural Show. He drove past a crew of men ramming fence posts marking out the show perimeter, while a few hundred metres away a large crane lifted the poles supporting the main show pavilion. He parked and walked to the only other vehicle close by, a black Range Rover.

'Don't want me snooping around the base, Commander?' Manx said, making himself comfortable in the passenger seat. 'If I was the suspicious type, I'd think you'd have something to hide.'

'I thought you lot thrived on suspicion,' he said, pronouncing the words 'you lot' as if they tasted sour in his mouth. 'I'm told RAF Valley has always been heavily involved with the Anglesey Agricultural Show, hence my presence. What can I help you with?'

'One of your officers, Bobbie Matthews. She told me she'd informed you several days ago she'd seen Flynt driving from his home the night he disappeared, and here I am having to chase you down to verify those facts.'

The commander tapped his fingers on the steering wheel. 'Flight Lieutenant Bobbie Matthews is… how shall I put this delicately? Mentally unstable.'

'That was delicate?' Manx said.

'I assume she informed you she's being transferred to a psychiatric hospital at the end of the month?'

'She neglected to mention that, but I'm still curious. Did she tell you about seeing Flynt that night or not?'

'I have no recollection of such a meeting.'

'So does that mean it didn't happen, or you just forgot? Busy man like you, I expect you're in meetings all day.'

The commander pursed his lips. 'No recollection means it never happened. Now if there's nothing else, I've got a security audit to conduct,' he said, gesturing at two RAF officers walking from the showground. 'What with the Duke and Duchess opening the show this year, the pressure's on to oversee their safety.'

'Heavy lies the crown, right?' Manx said. 'Do you know why Bobbie Matthews wanted to speak to Flynt that night?'

'Not a clue. Now, if that's all,' the commander said, checking his rear-view mirror and starting the engine.

Stepping out over the running boards, Manx turned to face the commander. 'Oh, you should probably know, new evidence came to light today that strongly suggests Commander Flynt's death wasn't an accident. We'll be stepping up our investigation a gear or two. Expect a visit from myself and my team in the next few days.'

Commander Boyd waited for Manx to reverse out of the grounds before selecting the Bluetooth function on his dashboard and calling the number he'd stored simply as *JC* in his contact list.

He coiled his fingers tight around the steering wheel as the call connected. 'Seems Bobbie Matthews is a bigger problem than we imagined,' he said, giving the two RAF officers the two minutes hand gesture. 'I wouldn't book your ticket back to London just yet.'

Chapter 49

The sun was leaning low over the horizon, with dusk yet to descend, when Manx arrived at Alice's house. He sat at the kitchen table, picking at his tofu stir-fry as if hoping to unearth something meatier amidst the greenery: Sara had apparently committed to No Meat Mondays, so it was bad timing on Manx's part.

His mother spoke. 'Nice of you to come, Tudor. We don't see enough of him, do we, Sara?'

'No, no we don't,' said his sister, spearing a chunk of tofu as if it were prey and throwing Manx a short snip of a smile.

'No more late-night wanderings I hope, Mam,' Manx said.

Alice looked at Sara, confused. 'I don't know what you mean. Sara, what is he talking about?'

'She doesn't remember a thing,' Sara said.

'All for the best, huh, Mam?'

Alice drifted for a moment, her gaze floating through the kitchen window to the cottage two fields away. It was as if she remembered fragments but couldn't attach them to her memory in any meaningful way.

Manx noticed his seven-year-old nephew, Dewi, gawking intently at him from across the table.

'You don't look like my dad,' the boy finally announced.

Manx glanced over to his sister.

'He wouldn't, would he?' Sara said. 'Uncle Tudor is my brother, not your dad's brother, so he's going to look like me, not like your dad.'

Dewi took in the information and studied them both through squinted eyes. 'He doesn't look like you, either,' he said.

Dewi wasn't the first to make that observation. Manx had the leaner, taller bearing of his mother. Sara took after their father; shorter and stockier. They did share the same colour eyes; slate grey, steely, untrusting.

'Of course, they do. I gave birth to them, I should know. But your aunty, Miriam…' Alice said, leaning closer to the boy. 'You never met her; she was the best-looking out of all my children. She was a gift, you know, a gift from God.'

Manx and Sara looked at each other and shrugged. There was no competing with ghosts; they'd given up trying decades ago.

'You'll get to meet her when she comes home,' Alice said, snapping her napkin tight in her lap.

'Where is she?' Dewi asked.

'A beautiful place.' Alice's eyes drifted. 'A paradise,' she confirmed, satisfied that it was indeed true.

Dewi thought for a moment 'If it's that beautiful, why would she want to come back here?' he asked.

Silence lay heavy across the table. Some questions were just too hard to contemplate, let alone answer. Sara collected the dishes solemnly, as if retrieving church collection plates, while Manx rolled up his sleeves and stacked the dishes into the sink.

Just after 7.30, dishes cleaned and dried, Manx said his excuses and headed upstairs to examine the box of 'stuff' Sara was so eager to offload. As he walked along the landing, he passed Miriam's room. He hesitated, then slowly opened the door. Alice had kept the room just as Miriam left it, as if she expected her daughter to return. Manx doubted his mother had even stripped the bed and laundered the sheets since that day. He hovered around the door, unable to raise the willpower to enter; maybe his mother was right, some things should remain undisturbed. He clicked the door back into its frame.

In Sara's bedroom, he tore the masking tape from the top of the box. The artefacts were a time-capsule from the last three years Manx had spent at Cwm Tawel; ages fourteen to seventeen. A faded collection of beer mats; a pack of custom-gauge steel guitar strings, unused; a stack of old school notebooks and a copy of *New Musical Express* with The Specials gracing the cover. However, two objects did pique his curiosity; a scuffed Pentax thirty-five millimetre camera and a RC 2500 radio with a built-in cassette recorder, which seemed like a relic from a long-lost civilisation.

He reached for the camera; it felt sticky, as if coated with dried saltwater. When he placed his thumb over the advance clicker, it made a grinding sound. He flipped the camera over, shook out the grains of sand and tried again. The plastic gave one final click, then stopped. He wound the spindle tight, opened the back and retrieved the roll. If there were any place on the island that still developed film, he'd take it in; he was curious to see what was on there, but equally hesitant. Maybe thirty years on, the images had dissolved to mere ghosts on celluloid; he'd amassed enough ghosts in the past few decades and wasn't looking to add to his collection.

He pocketed the roll and plugged in the recorder. The Memorex C90 cassette was nearing the end of its life expectancy; he could almost see through the thin magnetic tape as he held it to the light. He clicked the tape into the spindles. 'Chuck E's in Love' by Rickie Lee Jones was reaching its final chorus. From 1979, Manx guessed. The year Miriam was lost to them.

The following song was a disco-infused version of 'Light My Fire'. Time hadn't been kind to the remix; the production sounded paper-thin, propelled by a monotonous, manufactured drumbeat. He was about to press fast forward when the song abruptly ended. It was followed by a rustling noise, then a girl's voice that sent a shiver so deep down Manx's spine he doubted he could have stood up straight even if he willed himself.

Miriam. She'd likely found the cassette recorder in Manx's hiding place; an old shoebox slid under his bed. She began to sing. He remembered the track; she'd been singing it the whole summer: 'I Don't Like Mondays' by the Boomtown Rats. It was a blast of nostalgia that sucked the wind right out of him. It was as if she were here in the room, singing just to him. He secured his back against the wall.

Miriam's voice took him right back to that day. The day Manx had one job to do – look after his sister – and he'd failed. Failed her in the worst way possible.

And it was all because of a girl. Nothing, at the age of sixteen, was more important than a girl, certainly not watching his younger sister. The girl's name was Frankie; large, trusting brown eyes, skin that tanned like some exotic plant in the summer and a smile that sent Manx's heart fluttering some three feet above his chest. He'd been infatuated with Frankie since she had arrived as the new girl in school one year previously. Her family had moved from Liverpool to Anglesey when her father was transferred to the Wylfa Nuclear Power Plant. Frankie had a cool, alternative edge; everything the girls at his school aimed for, but for the most part, failed to achieve. Frankie and Manx had bonded over a mutual love of the Patti Smith Group and anything released on the Two-Tone record label. Frankie was also a committed fan of black; black clothing, dyed-black hair and black eyeliner – the darkest she could find in Woolworth's cosmetics aisle. Manx thought Frankie the coolest girl, outside of Debbie Harry, that he'd ever set eyes on. Looking back some years later, Manx would have admitted Frankie was his first love; the kind of first love that never fails to leave a scar somewhere on your heart.

That day, Manx had driven Frankie and his sister to the beach in his mother's ageing Ford Anglia, which he'd taken without her permission. When he picked up Frankie from her local bus stop, the day was brimming with sunshine and promise. Miriam sat in the back, her bucket and spade resting on the beach towel in her lap, singing 'I Don't Like Mondays' as if trying to commit it to memory. Manx and Frankie sat up front, holding hands and stealing glances at each other as the tilt of sunlight shone through the car windows.

Sometime during the heat of the afternoon, he and Frankie had wandered off into the shaded privacy of the sand dunes. On a Wednesday, the beach was all but deserted save a couple of families picnicking nearby. Miriam had made friends with one of the children, a boy called Martin.

The family had never come forward when the alarm was raised later that evening; maybe they never heard it or had their own reasons for not talking to the police.

When Manx and Frankie returned, Miriam was gone. Manx doubted he'd ever felt anything so sickening as that sensation before or since; his world had shattered around him and there was no way to pick up the pieces and fix it back together again.

It had been over thirty years; it was as if the air itself had taken her. Barely a day passed when Manx didn't think about Miriam and, if he was offered the chance to do it all again, how he'd never take his eyes off his sister that day; not for one second. But he'd learned that life rarely offers do-overs, and the best he could hope for was to someday find some answers that would bring closure to his family. He guessed that life didn't owe him that sort of guarantee either, but it wouldn't stop him from trying.

'She always had a good singing voice,' Sara said, leaning against the door frame. Manx wasn't sure how long she'd been there. 'National Eisteddfod material, Mam always said,' she added, a hairline crack breaking through her voice.

'Did you know?' he said, gesturing at the recorder.

Sara shook her head and reached for her pack of cigarettes. 'Christ, it's like she's here in the room with us.' She shuddered.

Manx wiped his hands over his face. 'We can't tell Mam; she won't be able to cope.'

'That'll be the first thing we've agreed on for a while,' Sara said, throwing open the window and lighting a cigarette. Over the Snowdonia mountains the sky was turning colour, thin strips of orange peel littering the low clouds.

'Can I hear it? All of it?' Sara said, sitting on the edge of the windowsill and blowing the smoke into the blue twilight.

Manx pressed rewind. They both sat in silence as Miriam sang, neither of them wanting to break the spell. They replayed the tape five more times, hoping they'd catch some clue, or some answers. There were none to be found.

As Manx left, he felt more tired than he had in weeks. Spending time at his mother's house always had this effect on him, but tonight it was infinitely more pronounced as if the ghosts in the house had finally found a way to latch on to him and were intent on tightening their grip. There was only one cure for those kinds of feelings, and it came in a non-prescription bottle of single malt, Isle of Islay scotch, preferably room temperature with a single ice cube.

The thought of a few stiff drinks before bed fortified him as he drove the twenty-minute journey back home, the familiar turns and twists of the roads blurring past, canopies of ancient oak trees swaying overhead. He imagined, if he drove fast enough, he could avoid the grasp of their branches. Or maybe that, like hoping to one day find the truth about Miriam and finding closure, was also nothing but wishful thinking.

Chapter 50

As Logan Collins was dragged from the coal shed, something sharp and cold was thrust into his lower back; a gun, or a knife maybe? Something that nicked into his flesh and hurt like hell, that was for sure. His eyes burned as sunlight burst through the fabric of his blindfold. He stumbled, legs weak, as Melvin urged him over the cobblestones. The loud creak of a door opening, and Collins found himself in another room. This one he sensed was larger with more light and air circulating around the space. Colder, too.

'Sit,' Melvin grunted, pushing him onto a chair.

He took the chair; it felt good to rest against something other than bricks. In one swift motion, the tape was ripped off his mouth.

'Water?' Collins asked, his lips dry and stinging. 'Please.'

His request was met with the sharp rim of a plastic bottle at his teeth and the sweet relief of water slipping easily down his throat. 'And the blindfold?' he croaked.

'All in good time.'

A new voice? A woman's voice.

She spoke again, clear and precise. 'Mr Collins, you're going to do exactly as we say. Do you understand?'

He nodded.

'No,' she said, voice slightly raised. 'I need to hear, verbally, that you understand my instructions.'

Collins cleared his throat. 'Yes. Yes, I understand.' His voice was dry and cracked. Although he could feel the words form in his mouth, they sounded as if they were spoken by a stranger.

'In a few minutes we will remove your blindfold. In front of you there will be a camera and below the camera a sheet of paper. On that sheet of paper are words that you will read out.'

Collins swallowed hard. 'What words?'

She ignored the question. 'We will give you exactly two minutes to look over the words then you will speak them. Is this all clear to you?'

Collins nodded.

'I need–'

'Yes. Yes, it's clear. I read out the words, you record me. What are they, your ransom demands?'

No reply, just footsteps, the smell of sweat and the reach of thick fingers working to untie the knot. The relief of the blindfold's release was short-lived. He caught a glance of the woman's face, barely enough time to make out her features, before she was set into shadow behind the beam of a dazzling spotlight. He squinted, trying to make sense of the words printed below the camera lens.

'Can you move the light?' he asked.

The woman tilted the beam a few degrees and stepped to her left. It was a smart move. Even as Collins craned his neck, attempting to make some kind of eye contact, she was still cast in shadow; an amorphous form looming behind the beam.

As his eyes grew accustomed to the light, he focused on the words – four paragraphs that killed whatever hope he had remaining. 'I… I can't read this,' he stammered.

The woman spoke. 'You're mistaken. You seem to think you have some leverage in this situation. I assure you, you do not.'

'No one will agree to this, it's madness,' he muttered.

'Then you'll die, here. Alone.'

'Can I at least see your face?' We can talk, maybe figure out a way we all come out of this thing without anyone getting hurt. Surely, you must understand this won't end well for you.'

'Typical bloody politician, can't stop fucking talking.' That was Melvin's voice. He'd stepped closer, dragging the weapon he'd held earlier across the soft tissue around Collins' neck.

'If I read this, I'm signing my own death warrant,' he said, his neck muscles taut, wire tight. 'I refuse.'

Melvin took a few steps back, placed his foot in the crossbow's stirrup, cocked the mechanism, slid the twenty-inch four-hundred-grain carbon fibre bolt into the rail, and steadied himself to take the shot.

A stiff twang echoed off the walls as the crossbow limbs released their pent-up energy and propelled the bolt at 300 feet per second from the tiller.

Pain was too soft a word for what Collins felt next; it was pure agony, and it radiated in thick swathes of nausea through his body. As the initial shock wore off, he looked down. The bolt had made clean entry through his foot and into the floor. He felt the salty spill of tears as he watched blood pool inside his loafer.

'Now we understand each other, Mr Collins, I recommend you read the words. Unless, of course, you'd prefer Melvin to reload and continue firing until you comply.'

Despite the searing shock of pain pulsing up from his foot to every cell in his body, Collins read the prepared script. The woman made him repeat it another three times until she was satisfied with the conviction of his performance.

'You'll never follow through with this,' he said, sitting back.

She stepped forward, her face still silhouetted against the blast of light, and knelt by his feet. 'People die all the time. You'll be missed, but in time forgotten,' she said, grabbing the nock and yanking the bolt clean from his foot.

Collins' scream was feral; a guttural wail that seemed to emanate from some deep, primal place.

'Your death will simply redress the balance.'

Back conversing with the dark night of his soul in the coal shed, Collins thought on her words. She sounded seriously disturbed, operating on a far more dangerous level than Ronnie and Melvin. They were in over their heads, given time he could have maybe pitted them against each other, persuaded them to let him go. But the woman? She had an agenda; an unwinnable one as far as he could tell. He was no longer an irritant in the hands of a couple of opportunists. He was now a hostage with a price on his life; a price he was sure nobody would be willing to pay.

Chapter 51

Byron Gates had spent the day transcribing what Reaper had told him and cross-checking the information against the redacted papers sent to him several months ago. He was running through the events in his head when something Reaper had said made him sit up; about having 'taken everything from her'. It sounded as if she were talking about more than her career – a lot more.

He wondered if she had been completely honest with him. Did she have an alternative motive, or a personal axe to grind? He was no stranger to some personal axe grinding of his own, but she'd also insisted he approach the media, which would leave him exposed. He'd agreed to her terms – the story was worth the risks – but just over twenty-four hours later he was having second thoughts. There were too many anomalies, too many questions he'd failed to ask.

He logged on to his secure browser and searched for an article he recalled reading when the incident was first reported. It was deep in the hyperlink hierarchy by now, but after some digging, he sourced the original article on the *Mirror*'s website. The headline had the hallmark of the publication's expected jingoistic outrage; *IS Murder Our Boys!* He looked closely at the names of the six men killed that day, searching for clues. One of the names on the mournful rollcall of young, dead men caught his attention; Danvir Sadiq, along with his photograph and an obituary stating that he was survived by a thirty-eight-year-old wife, also a serving RAF officer, and his parents, who lived in Bangor, North Wales.

He took a minute to check his map application. Bangor was less than ten miles away from where he was staying; he remembered seeing the road signs as he drove here. A kernel of an idea began to form. He searched for Danvir's Facebook profile. It had been, as he expected, memorialised, with a single photo of Danvir's face and the word *Remembering* preceding his name. He scoured it for any reference to the legacy contact who had frozen the profile in time; there was none. Instead, he searched through the messages left on the page, and cross-referenced the names with another Facebook search in a new tab. He got a hit on one of the names, Tammy Povey, a Facebook friend of Danvir's who lived on Anglesey.

He searched through Tammy's feed. She was an avid poster, at least three times per day, and mostly photographs taken at some new restaurant or expensive-looking wine bar. Clicking around for several more minutes, he finally found the needle in the haystack; a wedding photo with the caption; *Danvir and Bobbie finally tie the knot!* written under. It was taken underneath the gables of a church, the camera catching the storm of confetti as it swirled around the bride and groom. Byron dragged the photo to his desktop, opened his editing app, and enlarged the image. It lost some detail in the process, but he was nearly one hundred per cent sure this was the same woman he'd met with two days ago. The angular features, the slight build, the small, circular birthmark above her right eyebrow.

On the bedside cabinet, his phone pinged. He checked the incoming message. Reaper was requesting a second meeting: she had some additional information she was sure he'd want to hear. *Good*, Byron thought, typing his reply, he had some information of his own he was keen to ask her about. The meeting was set for later that day, at the Porth Wen brickworks, on the northern lee of the island. He confirmed he'd be there, 7.00 pm.

During the three hours before then, Byron made his preparations. As he structured his theory – things always seemed to make more sense once he put fingers to keyboard – the pieces fell into place, though he still had one unanswered question. Was Bobbie, if that was even her name, a grieving widow looking for someone to blame for her husband's death? Or had she ventured beyond that now? And people like Byron would become collateral, sacrificed for Bobbie's mission.

The troubling thought was still at the back of his mind as he drove to the meeting point.

Chapter 52

The beehive kilns were circular in design, covered with domed roofs, and supported with brick and iron bands. They'd been constructed in 1852 when Porth Wen's sole function was to manufacture silica bricks that could withstand the vast heat generated by the furnaces powering Britain's steel production. Less than a hundred years later, the plant had shipped its last cargo of brick and was abandoned to the vagaries of the Anglesey weather and the Irish Sea's caustic bite. It was now a scheduled historic monument, but because of its remoteness received few tourists. Was this why Reaper had wanted to meet here? She either suspected they were being watched or else she wanted to meet Byron far away from any witnesses. Neither alternative was of any comfort.

He was standing in the belly of one of the kilns, peering through an archway looking out to the ocean. Several metres below, the waves cymbal-crashed into the slick, black rocks, while a salt-tinged breeze whistled through the cracks in the stonework as if calling out to lost souls.

Byron leaned against the kiln wall. He was glad of the rest: his knees were complaining from the cross-country trek; at least forty-five minutes from St Patrick's Church in Cemaes over a rough, stone-strewn pathway that hugged the coastline. Dusk was already bearing down, casting its dim light over the crumbling winding house and old crushing sheds. Rising from the small crescent-shaped bay, the lines of the funicular, which was used to transport the raw silica from the docks to the plant stood out like scars of an old addiction in the overgrown dirt. To his left, the tall chimney seemed perfectly preserved in time; a testament to the skill of its Victorian engineers. It cast a shadow, like that of a long finger, pointing over the wild scruffs of grass.

Byron took a sip of tea from his flask and checked his watch. 6.58 pm – she'd be here soon, Reaper seemed like the punctual type. Unless, of course, she was already here, observing. The thought produced his second shiver of the night. He wondered if it was wise, coming here. But he was a journalist, at least of sorts, more of a truth-seeker, and Byron Gates didn't turn his back to the truth, no matter how uneasy it made him feel.

He turned as he heard footsteps scrambling down the bank behind him. He screwed the top back onto his flask. Reaper walked towards him, dressed as she was when they first met, but without her shades. As she drew closer, he was one hundred per cent sure it was the woman he'd seen in the wedding photograph.

'Byron,' she said, moving closer. 'I have a task for you.'

'What kind of task?'

She reached into her jacket pocket. Byron stiffened, backed away a couple of steps.

'What? A gun? Is that what you were thinking?'

'Um, no, it's just...'

'What I have is far more compelling than a gun to your head,' she explained, holding a USB thumb drive between her fingers.

Byron glanced at it. 'Yeah? Like what?'

'I have some communication that requires distribution. Communication we can't risk sending through the usual channels.'

'Usual channels?' Byron's mind had already jumped to the word 'we'. Who the hell was 'we'? The question would have to wait.

'YouTube will provide us with wide exposure, but we can't risk the North Wales Constabulary tracing its origins.'

Byron's mouth ran dry. 'The police? I'm not sure...' he began.

'Yes, you are sure, Byron,' she insisted.

He collected his thoughts. 'You want me to post whatever's on that thumb drive so no one can detect where it came from?'

'You did assure me your network was, I think your words were, "military-grade"? Multiple VPNs and non-static IP addresses?'

Byron squared his shoulders. 'Only amateurs use VPN socks,' he said, cockily. 'If I want to send something undetected, I use a pwned system, hijack at least four devices all over the world, make them zombie machines, no way to detect where it originates from.'

'I knew you were our man,' she said, stepping closer and handing him the USB.

He turned it over in his palm. 'What's on it? Some kind of malware code?'

'Nothing that complex. Just a short video.'

'I-I don't want to get into any trouble,' he stuttered.

'Oh, you don't know?' Bobbie said. 'You're already in trouble. There's a significant digital dossier on Byron Charles Gates in RAF Central Intelligence. Photographs, documents, everything ever uploaded to your website. I'd call that trouble.'

'Old news,' he said, trying to sound nonchalant. 'If they were going to prosecute me, they would have done it by now.'

'Prosecute?' Bobbie said. 'Far more efficient to have you eliminated. You do this for me and I can point you to the location of that digital file and you can destroy it like it never existed.'

The wind chose that moment to pick up, baffling around the kiln's stonework with an urgent menace. The flask in Byron's hand was shaking. He laid it down. 'And if I don't do this? This task?'

Bobbie looked behind her. From the shadows a man appeared, his crossbow primed. She nodded. The bolt cut through the air at speed, landing millimetres from Byron's boots and scattering a handful of dirt in the air as it made contact with the soft earth.

Byron jumped back, contemplated running, but saw the man had loaded another bolt into the tiller and raised the weapon a few feet higher, so it was now aimed directly at Byron's chest.

'Tonight,' Bobbie said. 'Do it tonight, or we'll make a visit to the

Rose Cottage bed and breakfast. If for some reason you're not there, we'll make a house call on your mother at 31 Burlington Avenue, Waddington. Is this clear to you, Byron?'

He nodded. She couldn't have been any clearer.

'No,' she said. 'Tell me, in words, that this is clear to you.'

Byron wiped an arm across his forehead. 'Yes. Yes, it's clear.'

'Good work,' she said. 'We won't meet again, but if we do, you can be guaranteed my partner's aim won't be so generous.'

As Bobbie turned to leave, Byron steeled himself. 'I'm sorry,' he said, blurting out the words.

Bobbie turned, her eyes seeming to scan right through him.

'About your husband, Danvir. It was a terrible accident.'

She stood for a moment, processing the information.

'But I don't think it's fair you're taking it out on innocent people, like me, Bobbie,' he said, heavily stressing the last word.

She smiled, tight and controlled. 'Innocent? A man I know would have an answer to that,' she said. 'Let he who is without sin cast the first stone. I'll look forward to your decision.'

She turned to leave, the man following close in her shadow.

Byron immediately regretted saying anything. Had he shown his cards too early? Admitting he knew her name and her motive? He imagined the information would have given him some currency to negotiate with. He was wrong. She wasn't the negotiating kind.

As he staggered over the path back towards his car, the twilight was quickly obliterated by darkness. He used the flashlight on his mobile to guide him along the narrow path, stumbling a few times over the rocky outcrops. He took a break at one of the benches along the way, felt the USB drive in his palm and contemplated throwing it into the ocean. It was a stupid idea; another Byron Gates fantasy doomed to failure. This wasn't programming code, hacking around servers or posting anonymous documents anymore. He'd walked into a situation where he was way out of his depth and he'd been confronted with a choice, which was really no choice at all. If he wanted to live to see his home again, his mother, his friends, he'd have to do as she demanded.

The thought churned his stomach as he looked over the blackening landscape, the sound of the ocean crashing like broken bones onto the rocks behind him. Reaper, Bobbie, was out there, somewhere, watching his every move.

He'd never been more certain of anything in his life.

Chapter 53

'My name is Logan Collins. I've been asked to speak these words by the Welsh Nationalist Movement, Meibion Glyndŵr. To ensure my return, they have two demands which, if not met, will result in a swift and violent response.

'Eighteen months ago, the Royal Air Force launched a drone strike, Operation Vanguard, on a convoy of insurgents travelling south of Mosul, Syria. In the aftermath of this attack, six RAF officers were also killed. The official report on this incident cites the second explosion as an attack by enemy combatants. This is not true. The report was falsified. Our demands are simple. A redaction of the validity of the report by the RAF, with full disclosure of the events. Truth and transparency.

'Our second demand is for the Anglesey County Council and the National Assembly for Wales to write into law safeguards limiting the sale of homes as rental properties for all of Wales.

'You have seven days to comply. If after seven days, these demands are not met, I will be executed. I know the police will attempt to locate me, but the longer you waste your time, the more lives will be put in danger. Act now, swiftly, and no one else needs to die.'

Manx froze the video just before Logan Collins' terrified expression faded to grainy black. The incident room fell into silence as the officers absorbed the information. At 10.30 pm, the core investigation team may have been bleary-eyed and beat from their day shift, but Collins' words were like a jolt of caffeine to their system; they were now attentive, primed and anxious.

'Looks like he's half-dead already,' Nader said.

'A dead man talking,' Manx agreed, wiping a hand over his face. 'Right, what do we know about this Meibion Glyndŵr outfit?'

'Active in the late eighties and early nineties,' Nader said. 'They were named after Owain Glyndŵr who led the Welsh rebellion against the English. Died in 1530, or something.'

'Yeah, and that's their flag,' Priddle said, pointing at the four lions outlined on red and yellow squares serving as Collins' backdrop.

'I'm not the most patriotic Welshman in the room,' Manx said, 'but doesn't the Welsh flag have a red dragon?'

'The red dragon on green and white wasn't officially recognised as the Welsh flag until 1959,' PC Priddle explained. 'And Owain Glyndŵr died in 1415 Sarge, but nobody's really sure because there were no records of him after 1412. Vanished, apparently, or went into hiding.'

'Oh, right you are, Professor Priddle,' Nader said, chuckling. 'Got a cold case you want to chase up, then? The vanishing of Owain Glyndŵr. Last known sighting on a battlefield back in 1412. We're appealing for witnesses anywhere in the vicinity.'

'No, just interested in history, that's all,' Priddle said.

'How the hell does this help us find Collins?' Manx asked.

'It makes sense, though, doesn't it?' Morris said. 'They set holiday homes on fire back in the day too.'

'They did a bloody lot more than that.' Priddle's voice rose an octave as he talked. 'They sent letter bombs to English MPs, planted bombs on power lines and water plants. Fire-bombed over two hundred homes owned by the English, and estate agents all over England, too. I don't think they killed anyone, though.'

'More through luck than judgement, maybe,' Manx said. 'If we've got a resurgence of Welsh nationalist militants burning down holiday homes, how the bloody hell is this connected to the RAF and this Operation Vanguard?'

'If what Hardacre says is right and Flynt was killed, he could be the connection,' Priddle offered.

'I'm not seeing it,' Manx said. 'Let's assume the two men on the slip are members of Meibion Glyndŵr.' He pointed at the CCTV print-out. 'Originally, they'd planned to use the go-to terrorist-approved move of ramming a moving vehicle into their target. The plan changed, they kidnapped Collins, we hear nothing for five days, then they post this video. I'd expect the demand for the change in housing laws, but the second demand, Operation Vanguard, it's not fitting the motives.'

'It's like two birds, one stone,' Nader said.

Manx turned to the board. 'We're looking for a connection between the RAF and Meibion Glyndŵr. Flynt is dead, Commander Boyd's only been here on the island for less than a week. Which leaves us the only other serving RAF officer who's involved, Bobbie Matthews.' Manx pointed to the photo of Bobbie and Danvir. 'She saw Flynt the night he disappeared. When she came to see me, she was very agitated, on edge.'

PC Morris searched her notes, then spoke. 'Sir, I didn't think anything of it at the time, but when I was researching Bobbie Matthews, that name 'Operation Vanguard' cropped up. It's when her husband was killed. The dates line up.'

'Good. That's the connection we've been looking for,' Manx said. 'If Bobbie Matthews blames the RAF for the death of her husband, then that's a bloody big motive. And, if we can tie Flynt to Operation Vanguard, that's another motive. Either Bobbie Matthews was right in what she told me, or she's very clever at covering her tracks and she killed Flynt and kidnapped Collins.'

'She's got to be working with someone, someone from the island,' Nader offered.

Manx wrote the words Meibion Glyndŵr on the board. 'We need records on this lot from back in the day,' he said. 'Arrests, anyone under suspicion or affiliated.'

'Aye, good luck with that,' Nader said. 'We weren't exactly high-tech back then, and the archives got moved, twice. Who knows what the hell got lost?'

'Evidence, witness statements, DNA, we need the lot.'

'Won't be any DNA,' Nader said. 'Not back in the day.'

'None that was tested. But any physical evidence might still contain some residue. If we get a match with the two samples we've already analysed, the closer we are to finding who did this.'

Manx was about to extend the team one of his end-of-briefing pep talks to keep them focused, when DCI Canton entered the room. 'Ellis,' Manx said, looking up. 'Good news about the extra officers I requested, I hope?'

Canton forced a thin smile. 'Couple of gents requesting to speak to you. They don't look like the types who take too kindly to "come back later".'

Chapter 54

As Manx and Canton walked into the station conference room, Commander Boyd looked agitated, eager to dispense with pleasantries and get down to business. 'Obviously, these demands are ridiculous,' he said, looking over at Jack Carlisle. 'The RAF will not be releasing any documents pertaining to this or any other incident.'

'Completely out of the question,' Carlisle agreed, as he leaned back and smoothed down his tie.

'But you know the incident the kidnappers are referring to, this drone strike? Operation Vanguard?' Manx asked.

The commander's posture stiffened. 'I wasn't directly involved, but yes, I have been briefed.'

'Right you are,' Manx said, fixing his gaze on the commander's eyes which struggled to meet his own. 'But why here? Why is all this happening at RAF Valley? The only obvious connection is James Flynt, but he's not likely to come forward with any new information anytime soon.'

The commander glanced at Jack Carlisle, who, with a subtle nod of his head, assured him he had permission to speak further.

'I can only confirm what's already in the public domain. James Flynt was transferred to RAF Valley. Before that, he was an overseer at the unmanned aircraft ground control station at RAF Waddington, Lincolnshire.'

'Was he connected to Operation Vanguard?'

'Disclosing that could put our servicemen in danger.'

'Of course,' Manx said, wearily. 'And was this the same incident that an RAF medic…' he rechecked his notes. 'Danvir Sadiq was killed?'

'I couldn't possibly—'

'No need,' Manx interrupted. 'These online news archives are a godsend, saves us a lot of wasted man hours.' He dumped a thick wad of printed articles on the table. 'I visited Danvir's parents on a related matter. Nice couple, heartbroken as you can imagine. As it turns out Danvir's widow is Bobbie Matthews, who we've already talked to. She's big into her conspiracy theories.'

'Which is why her transfer to the VA facility is being fast-tracked,' Boyd said. 'The sooner she receives help, the better.'

'Bloody big coincidence, though, isn't it?' Manx said. 'Flynt killed, Bobbie Matthews in a hit-and-run, and now a ransom demand relating directly to the RAF and her husband's death? But here's the thing, I'm not a big believer in coincidences. Now, facts and hard evidence, those are the kinds of things I can put my faith in.' Manx opened his palms. 'Commander, do you have any of those you can share with myself and DCI Canton? Because we're running against a deadline and I have no doubt these people will follow through on their threat. Do you have any information that might help me stop those threats before we're sending out a coroner's van to pick up Logan Collins' body from a ditch somewhere?'

Boyd was set to speak when Carlisle, who'd been silent for the past few minutes, spoke. His tone was icy, controlled. 'It appears we've reached an impasse, gentlemen,' he said. 'Commander Boyd is bound by the Official Secrets Act. Both of you have a serious hostage situation and its aftermath to contend with. Maybe there is some information we could share that would help in your investigation.'

Manx folded his arms across his chest. 'I'd have preferred to hear that a week ago, but I'm listening.'

'The person you should be interrogating,' Carlisle said, reaching into his briefcase and laying a folder on the table, 'is Byron Charles Gates.'

Manx glanced at the photo. A surveillance shot of an overweight, bearded man with a bad sunburn. Sitting next to him, Bobbie Matthews.

'Byron Gates?' Canton said, scanning the file. 'Says here he lives in Lincolnshire.'

'His primary residence, yes, but our intelligence confirms Gates has been here on Anglesey for several days.'

'Why is he important to you?' Manx asked. 'Has he made any threats?'

'When an enemy of our country moves within five miles of the people I'm tasked with protecting, I get twitchy.'

Manx doubted if Carlisle got twitchy about anything. 'What's his connection to my case?'

Carlisle flipped over one of the pages. 'Byron Gates operates a website called DronewatchUK. He's a ghost in the machine. He receives sensitive military documents from service personnel who think nothing of betraying their country, then publishes said documents on his website.'

'You're the military, can't you just shut him down?'

'We have, many times, but fifteen minutes later the site's back online, masked behind a wall of non-static IP addresses and hijacked devices.' Carlisle paused, directed a frosty look in Manx's direction. 'The same technical expertise it takes to upload a video and make its origin untraceable.'

Manx processed Carlisle's words. His theory was plausible, but he remained unconvinced. 'Just so I understand this. You think Byron Gates kidnapped Logan Collins and is now holding him hostage to force the RAF to release information about a drone strike that happened thousands of miles away, over a year ago?'

'People like Gates find it hard to move on.'

'Has he made any credible threats?'

'You know as much about his threats as we do,' Carlisle said, 'but we do have his location.' He handed over a handwritten note.

'You won't mind if I take the file?' Manx asked.

'Not at all. We have copies.'

'If you know his whereabouts, why don't you just pick him up yourselves?' Canton asked.

Carlisle nodded. 'Gates is still a civilian, in the eyes of the law he's done nothing illegal. We can't prove he uploaded the documents: he's a master of obfuscation. The North Wales Constabulary has enough evidence to pick him up and question him for twenty-four hours at least. We would, of course, also need to question him once he's in your charge.'

'Of course you would,' Manx said. 'Maybe you'd want to haul him off to Guantanamo too, while you're at it?'

Canton quickly jumped in. 'Inspector Manx will personally take care of it. If this Byron Gates character's our man, we'll know soon enough.'

Carlisle tugged down on his jacket sleeves. 'You should also know Gates has become increasingly desperate of late. Multiple postings, ranting blog posts.'

'Big jump, though,' Manx said. 'Blogging to kidnapping.'

Carlisle's eyes narrowed. 'We suspect Gates is on medication – or maybe even off his medication, to escalate matters to this severe a level. We are not prepared to gamble with the life of the second in line to the throne. Neither, I suspect Inspector, are you.'

Manx internally flinched at the implication. Carlisle's world view was solidly black and white; you were either with him, or you were against him. Manx was still debating on which side he'd fall.

'Oh, one more thing,' the commander said, gathering his cap. 'Valley is on lockdown until this is resolved. We've informed the commercial airlines that share our airstrip of our decision.'

'Can you do that?' Manx asked.

'It's the Ministry of Defence,' Carlisle confirmed. 'There's little they can't do. Bottom line, there really is no value in having the local police coming and going from the base as they please. It's simply not practical.'

'And what about Bobbie Matthews?' Manx asked.

'We suspect they may be working together,' Boyd said.

'Matthews and Gates? How so?'

'A picture paints a thousand words,' Carlisle said, nodding at the photograph.

'If that's the case, I'd like to speak to Bobbie Matthews immediately, base lockdown or not.'

'So would we,' the commander said.

'Ah,' Manx said. 'One of your own gone AWOL?'

'I'm sure with the efforts of the North Wales Constabulary it won't take long to locate her,' Carlisle said.

'We're a little busy right now, what with this kidnapping and a few other ongoing investigations.'

Carlisle's eyes were two grey ice-blocks set against cold white. 'I suggest we all leave here on good terms, our goals aligned.'

'Our goals?' Manx asked.

'Neutralising the threat to our country's security.'

'And finding Collins before they put a bullet through his head,' Manx said, throwing Carlisle a cold, hard stare of his own.

'Of course, same goals,' Carlisle replied, easing out of his chair and extending his hand. 'Best of luck.'

Manx and Canton watched the black Range Rover HSE pull out from the station car park, its metallic paintwork gleaming.

'You buy all that?' Canton asked.

'Buy it?' Manx said, glancing at Carlisle's dossier. 'I buy that it's a distraction, but that's not what they were selling us.'

'Worth following up.'

'I'll send someone to check out Gates.'

'Good man. Same place tomorrow, early?'

'No other place else to be, Ellis.'

Manx lifted the thin dossier from the table. It felt weightier than it should, as if its pages were bloated with the same doubts and reservations that had settled heavy on Manx from the moment Jack Carlisle opened his mouth and spoke. He suspected a restless night was in store. Seven days? The silent ticking of the clock was already counting down, he could sense it deep in his bones.

Chapter 55

Andrew Pierce drove back from the RAF housing in a daze. He'd headed over to Bobbie's house as soon as he heard the news reports and saw Logan Collins' terrifying video. The house was deserted, locked up as if she'd never been there. He'd knocked on a few neighbours' doors; nobody had seen Bobbie for days.

He headed south east along the A55, turned on the A545 into the town of Beaumaris, and pulled up in the car park overlooking the Menai Strait, the ruins of the old castle behind him. He passed the small turret-like entrance at the pier and walked the whole length before resting at an empty bench.

The day was thick with tourists enjoying the sunshine and career-opportunist seagulls cackling above, ever on the scrounge for their next meal. This was the cadence of the everyday world, and Pierce felt three steps out of sync with its rhythm. He'd failed Bobbie, and that burden lay like cinder blocks across his heart. The demands Logan Collins had spoken came back to him as he looked over the green ribbon of the strait. 'The truth about Operation Vanguard'. It was all Bobbie had ever wanted; what she deserved. Maybe he could still help her; save her, even. But for that he required a large, unambiguous gesture.

He reached for this mobile and searched for a number. After several rings, it was answered. He explained the situation clearly and precisely. Several moments of silence were followed by a deep resigned sigh, and clear instructions on the time and place to meet.

Chapter 56

Byron Charles Gates had been a conscientious child, quick to defend others against perceived injustice. Some might have called him a snitch; Byron would have simply called it redressing the balance of justice. In the playground, he'd caught enough beatings for his tattletale leanings. Not that a black eye or bloodied nose had deterred him: if anything, it had strengthened his resolve. But by the time Byron had entered upper school, he towered several inches above his peers and had filled out like a prop-forward. He suffered little bullying after that summer-long growth spurt.

The kids simply ignored Byron now, called him 'Wacko Byro' behind his back. It never bothered him; he was happy keeping to himself, spending hours alone mastering every video game he could set his thick thumbs around. Bored with playing, he began programming his own games, writing code, then when in college, collaborated with a group of like-minded misfits who taught him the basics of cyber hacking. After that, his course was set. Not that he'd done any of it for the money. Byron had loftier goals than holding peoples' computers for ransom or selling stolen credit card numbers for a few quid a pop. His targets were the multinational corporations which acted with impunity when it came to paying their corporate taxes, dealing in illegal arms trades or funding terrorist organisations. It was around that time, the early 2000s, that Byron had launched DronewatchUK. He had a new enemy in his sights now, the industrial, technology and military complex.

In Byron's mind, the drone strikes sanctioned by the RAF were no different to the mass carpet bombing of Berlin and Dresden during the Second World War. Back then, tens of thousands of innocents had suffered at the hands of the military gods. People were still suffering their wrath, albeit thousands of miles away in remote villages across the middle east and Pakistan. He had a duty to tell the world the truth: if only the world was listening.

Watching the video, he'd been conflicted. There was an insane bravado in forcing the RAF's hand, but the hollow look in the politician's eyes, the way he talked as if he were already dead and had found himself in hell, had shaken Byron. Not that he had much choice, Bobbie had made that clear.

After he'd uploaded the video – fake Gmail account, several highjacked devices in Macau, Odessa and Lagos, and eight different IP addresses pinging across three continents – he'd conducted a far simpler hack; locating Tammy Povey. If he could speak to her, gather some intelligence, he might gain some leverage, something he could use to bargain for his life if the time came.

He wrote down her address on the stationery in his room: those kinds of records were best kept analogue. He left fifty pounds on the bedside table, plus a five-pound tip. After stuffing his clothes into his backpack, he flipped open his laptop, logged onto his TOR browser. Bobbie had already threatened his life and, as she'd told him, the RAF possessed a hard drive full of evidence against him. What if they had eyes on him now, were tracking every mouse click and keystroke? The words 'rock and hard place' came to mind. He needed a failsafe, a backup if the worst happened.

He clicked to the Duck Duck Go search engine, scanned the *North Wales Daily Post* online edition for the past week and found the officer leading the investigation: Detective Inspector Tudor Manx. Next, he accessed the public-facing website of the North Wales Constabulary. Manx was stationed at Llangefni, no personal email address, but there was a general email where members of the public could send in questions. The subject line, it informed him, should include the officer's name and the words, 'Just Ask a Copper.'

Byron laughed. Just ask a copper for what? Protection from Bobbie? Immunity from prosecution if the RAF were tracking his every move? No, he needed to be smarter, several steps ahead.

He pasted what he'd written earlier; everything he suspected about Bobbie, her threats, how she forced him to upload the video, how he feared for his own life. Before sending, he hesitated. Was he showing his hand too early again? If Bobbie found out, he was done for. Clicking back to his TOR browser, he pasted the contents to his secure email server, adding a specific time and date for the email to be sent. He just needed to stay safe a few more days, then this would all be over, and he could go back home. If not, he'd have something to use to bargain for his life.

Live long enough? Bargain for his life? How in God's name had it come to this? Three days ago, he was at home, minding his own business, playing pinball; his only concerns were generating extra income from his computer repair business, and his mother's health. Today, he was putting a plan in place in the event of his death; or more specifically, his murder. He pushed the grim thought to the back of his mind, grabbed his backpack and drove into the warm Anglesey night.

Chapter 57

Melvin's day had started badly. He'd woken up at 5.00 am. During the night, a knife blade had somehow twisted a path inside him and was carving up his lungs like meat on a butcher's block. The thick phlegm of blood that he'd coughed up while sitting on the toilet seat had seemed unreal to him, as if it had been exorcised by someone else, someone weaker, someone who wasn't Melvin Powell, Gwynedd County Welterweight Champion; the Great Welsh Hope. He'd had a good laugh at that word, hope. When hope was just about gone, what else was there left other than to laugh at how ridiculous the word sounded on his lips?

At the kitchen table, Lydia had laid into him about how he looked thinner, paler. Was there something wrong? Something he needed to tell her? It riled Mel, being questioned about anything before he'd finished his first mug of tea of the day. Lydia's questions had made him edgy and defensive – Lydia didn't do subtle. He'd left the flat before finishing his breakfast, thrown half a glass of juice at the wall, he wasn't proud of that, but the woman could really push his buttons when she set her mind to it.

Adding to his dark mood, a paint job he'd bid on for an office building in Holyhead had fallen through. Someone had undercut his quote; no doubt one of those cowboy operations that had sprung up on the island recently, Polish or Ukrainian lads, scruffy, homeless-looking sods, knocking on doors, offering to work – any kind of work – for a few quid an hour, or shining tyre walls at the local car washes. They were likely trafficked in through Holyhead and living ten-to-a-room in a half-demolished farmhouse out in the middle of nowhere, where the coppers wouldn't come knocking.

With nothing better to do, he'd driven to Cemaes Bay to work on his boat. She needed a fresh coat of wood varnish and the motor needed cleaning out if he had any hope of selling the vessel. He was crouched over the engine, cleaning between the thin grooves of the spark plugs when he heard someone calling his name. He looked up, lifting the bill of his cap to see the bulky, anxious figure of Stan Thomas standing at one of the mooring cleats.

'All right, Stan, bit early for you, isn't it? Bookies don't open till eleven, or do you do all that online gambling these days?'

Stan looked around as if he suspected someone had followed him. He took out a late-morning copy of the *North Wales Daily Post* from his pocket 'Is this you, then?' he said, waving the paper at Mel. 'You and that lapdog nephew of yours?'

'Don't know what you're talking about, mate,' Melvin said, widening his stance on the boat's floor to steady himself.

'Come on, I wasn't born yesterday.' Stan edged closer to the dockside. 'Step too far this is, mate. Setting fire to a few houses to make a point, that's what we signed up for, but kidnapping, death threats? We all agree, it's too far, too bloody far. We've got wives, kids – grandkids some of us. What the hell are you thinking?'

Melvin looked down, ran an oily rag through his fingers. 'Liberation or death, brothers till the end?'

Stan laughed. 'We're not bloody kids anymore. Grow up, eh?'

Melvin threw the rag to the floor. 'What are you doing here, Stan? I'm busy,' he said, his anger swelling, but he wasn't going to show that, not to Stan Wilson. He held it back, kept it locked down, waited to see how the conversation played out.

'Came to tell you it's done, mate. All that Meibion Glyndŵr stuff, all done with. If you don't stop, we're all agreed, we're going to the police, tell them everything.'

Melvin stretched out his arm. 'Give us a hand up.'

Stan hesitated.

'What? You think I'm going to drag you into the fucking water? Come on, help me up.'

As he reluctantly stretched out his arm, Melvin grabbed Stan's wrist and hoisted himself from the boat and onto the dockside. The moment his boots hit dry land, he snatched back his arm and pummelled his fist hard into Stan's solar plexus.

Stan felt his stomach push into his backbone, his legs buckling. He fell, his knees taking the brunt of the landing. Setting his hands either side of him, he vomited a pool of clear liquid onto the dockside.

'Listen,' Melvin said, speaking calmly into his ear. 'You start mouthing off, any of you, there's going to be trouble. Go home and I'll forget you threatened me. Can you do that, Stan? Or do you need reminding what I was like in the ring, back in the day?'

'You're not right in the head, Mel,' Stan said, barely exhaling his words. 'Bloody mad, off your rocker.'

'Aye, you might be right, there,' Mel said. 'Now, you go back and tell the rest of them, if I go down, they all go down, and not just for the fires. That clear enough for you, Stan?'

He nodded and hauled himself up, his legs barely supporting his body. 'It's not going to end well, Mel, none of this, I can tell you that now.' He spat on the ground and turned his back.

As Stan walked away, his gait slow and pained, Melvin climbed back onto his boat. End well? Of course none of this was going to end well, not for him at least. Not that it mattered. Best to go out with his arms high, fists raised, not pissing in a hospital bed, his dignity ravaged to nothing, his body and mind numbed solid by painkillers.

He pressed the start button on the engine. After a few sputters it cracked to life. *Fuck Stan and the rest of them*, he thought as he threw off the casting rope and headed towards the open ocean. He had a true cause to fight for now. He'd made a promise to Bobbie, one he wasn't about to break just because Stan Thomas was crapping in his knickers. If there was a bitter end, he'd see it all the way through to that final destination. He owed her that much.

Chapter 58

DI Tudor Manx's morning had started at 2.15 am with a head full of theories that dead-ended at every turn, and the relentless ticking of a time bomb counting down at the back of his mind. The day was made worse by a visit from the North Wales Constabulary's chief press officer, demanding a statement and a time and date for a press conference with himself and Canton. Manx had given her the brush off; he could delay the request a few days, and right now he'd take any breathing space he could get.

'Papers are having a bloody field day,' Nader said as Manx walked into the incident room. 'What with those dead starlings – by the way, my money's still on the jet fuel – and Collins' kidnapping. They're quoting all these old Welsh academics, even got an interview with Dafydd bloody Iwan.'

'That'll boost his record sales,' Priddle offered.

'Always a silver lining,' Manx said. 'Anything on Gates, Priddle?'

'He checked out of the bed and breakfast.'

'When?'

'The landlady, Mrs Rose, went up to his room yesterday evening, his door was wide open, no sign of him. Said he left fifty quid and a fiver tip on the bedside table.'

'Conscientious type, then?'

'How do you mean?'

'People doing a runner don't usually leave payment plus tip.'

'Yeah, I suppose,' Priddle said. 'Oh, Mrs Rose took his car registration. He was driving a Toyota Prius.'

'Make sure we get that number to dispatch. Send it out to every station and patrol car on the island.'

'Do you think Gates is responsible for this?' Morris asked.

'The RAF and Carlisle are hot under the collar for us to apprehend him, but we have no evidence other than he has the technical skills to anonymously upload a video to YouTube, which most teenagers with half a brain cell could probably pull off.'

'Do we have any other suspects?' Morris asked.

Manx turned to the incident board; it made for dismal reading. Two weeks after the discovery of James Flynt's body, they should at least have a prime suspect, but every lead had fizzled to nothing, and with RAF Valley now off limits Manx felt he was investigating with two hands tied behind his back and his feet stuck in quicksand.

'I could rattle a few more cages,' Nader said. 'Been on this island long enough to know most of the nasty toe-rags out there. Bring them in, turn them upside down, see what shakes out.'

Manx conducted a mental count to ten. He didn't need this from Nader, not today. 'I want you focused on what I asked you to focus on, Nader: the archives on that Meibion Glyndŵr outfit.'

Nader cocked his head towards the corner of the room.

'That's it?' Manx asked, looking at the three thin cardboard boxes stacked on top of each other.

'The archives flooded a few years back. Lost boxes of evidence to water damage, that's when they moved the record-keeping over to Colwyn Bay.'

'I looked through it already,' Morris said. 'I can start tracking down some of the names this morning.'

'Yeah, good luck with that, Minor,' Nader said. 'Probably moved away years ago, or dead and buried by now.'

'Or they might not have done anything,' Priddle said, a hesitant edge to his voice.

'Oh, aye, know that for a fact, do you?' Nader snapped.

Priddle shuffled awkwardly in his seat. 'Some people reckon the whole thing was a set-up, by the government.'

'Oh, classic Priddle, this is,' Nader chuckled. 'Can't wait to hear the professor's latest bloody theory. Go on then.'

Priddle pushed against his chair and pulled back his shoulders. 'It's not just a theory, Sarge,' he said. 'The English government paid these blokes to stage the attacks, so it made the Welsh look bad, like we were all terrorists, like the IRA.'

'That right?' Nader said, chuckling. 'And I heard the Titanic hit an iceberg planted by the Germans and Owain Glyndŵr was seen having a pint down the pub last week with Princess bloody Di.'

'That's as barmy as starlings killed by jet fuel and soundwaves,' Morris said, with a smile.

'Fascinating as this is, conspiracy theories from forty years ago are not top of my list of priorities today. What I need from you, Morris and PC… sorry, what was your name again?'

The young constable, red-faced with the wisp of a ginger goatee, sat up straight. 'Pritchard. PC Bryn Pritchard.'

'What I need is for you to sift through those evidence boxes like you were panning for gold. The big shiny nugget you're searching for is any forensic evidence with a high probability of containing DNA – clothes, blood stains, fibres, weapons found at the scenes – and send them over to Bevan's team for analysis.'

Manx directed his next question at Priddle. 'Any updates from Bevan on that familial connection we requested?'

'Nothing yet.'

'Lurk outside his bloody door if that's what it takes. The clock, Priddle, and the rest of you, is ticking.' He took his pen and pointed to the board. 'We need to find Bobbie Matthews, quick.'

'Is she connected to this Byron Gates?' Priddle asked.

'The RAF seem to think so.' Manx pinned up the surveillance photo of her and Gates. 'With RAF Valley on lockdown until this blows over, our hands are tied.'

'If she lives in the RAF housing, not in the barracks, then it's not on the base,' Nader said. 'Fair game.'

'Then, move on that. Search the electoral register for her address.

Ask around, maybe the neighbours saw something.'

'Got it, boss,' Nader confirmed.

Manx turned to the seven-day calendar and timeline he'd scribbled onto the incident board late last night: in the cold light of day, it looked as if it were drawn by a drunk. 'For the next six days, we live and breathe this timeline. All leave is suspended, we'll be working long shifts, and before you ask, yes, Canton has approved all overtime.'

Looking over the already exhausted team, Manx imagined they'd need every reserve of stamina and fortitude before this was all over.

Chapter 59

Andrew Pierce had opted for casual civilian dress that morning: trousers, an open-neck shirt and a blue linen blazer. The outfit was designed to attract as little attention as possible: just another passenger boarding the 9.05 am Bangor to London train, with a change at Crewe, final destination, Lincolnshire.

At 1.35 pm, he sat at the Costa Coffee at Lincoln station, ordered an extra hot flat white and waited for his contact to arrive. He sensed a flicker of nervousness. This wasn't his style – setting up clandestine meetings to procure classified information – but these were extenuating circumstances. The unnerving sensation that he was close to losing Bobbie for good was like a deep, gaping hole in his chest.

Turning the screws on an old colleague had been more challenging than he expected. After several reminders of how far he'd stuck his neck out for him, and a not-so-subtle hint that Pierce had kept a record of 'certain evidence you wouldn't want to come to light', eventually William Baker had agreed to meet.

Baker was a commissioned officer before moving to the MoD, where he'd made fast progress climbing the Whitehall career ladder; Pierce recalled he'd always had a nose for the way the political winds were blowing. Early in their careers, Pierce and Baker had been stationed together and had become close friends. Baker was a hard drinker; the Oliver Reed level of drunk but without the charm or charisma. Baker was driving home late one night after an afternoon-long bender in the local pub when he hit a cyclist; a young lad no more than twenty-three;

one of the civilian contractors at the base. Baker hadn't even stopped, just continued as if he'd hit a stray badger or fox. The lad had suffered through a long, drawn-out coma before his heartbroken parents signed the paperwork and his vital organs were removed and helicoptered out.

Baker began to fall apart soon after and had come to Pierce for guidance, either spiritual or mental; it made no difference, Pierce was still training, not yet ordained as a chaplain nor fully qualified as a clinical psychologist. But the prospect of trying to 'fix' Baker was too much of a temptation to resist. After all, it was the reason God had put him on earth; to heal the wounded.

Pierce had recorded all of their conversations, mostly for his own training. As the sessions progressed, Baker formed his own, warped, narrative around what happened; a narrative that absolved him of all blame. It was then, his morality already compromised, that Pierce realised the recordings could be useful in another way. He wasn't yet qualified to treat anyone, so any idea of patient–doctor confidentiality was irrelevant. If he confessed to the base commander how he'd got the recordings, he'd face disciplinary action which could see him drummed out of the service along with Baker. Instead, he kept seeing Baker and recording their sessions until one day Baker declared he'd found salvation in God's word, and God had chosen to forgive him. Pierce's counsel was no longer required. He doubted Baker had found any kind of salvation, divine or otherwise, but Pierce had kept the recordings for over fifteen years, figuring some day they might be used as leverage. Today was that day.

Baker, as expected, was punctual. He sat across from Pierce with a grunt and a look that suggested his attendance was only marginally less unpleasant than root canal surgery.

'You look older,' Pierce said. Baker's hair, what remained of it, was a dirty shade of grey. His pallor was of someone who had spent long, tedious hours under the artificial glow of fluorescent strip lighting in some dank basement office.

'Let's dispense with the pleasantries, shall we?' Baker said, taking a small USB drive from his trouser pocket and looking around him before placing it under a napkin on the table. Pierce palmed the object, slipped it into his jacket pocket and handed Baker an envelope containing the session recordings.

Baker got up to leave.

'No catch-up, Bill?' Pierce asked.

Baker shook his head. 'Some other time. Maybe never. Is never good for you, Pierce?'

'Why meet here? It's a long train ride from Whitehall.'

Baker sighed, eyes rheumy and narrowed. 'Confidential Air Command matters to attend to. Way above your pay grade.' He stood, placed his palms on the table and loomed over Pierce, his top lip moist with sweat. 'If this ever gets out, I'll make it my personal mission to destroy you. With any luck, I'll never see your face again, and you best hope you never see mine.'

'That Whitehall job's made you paranoid,' Pierce said. 'Still accepting God as your saviour, Bill? Or are your allegiances more secular these days?'

Baker emitted a short grunt. 'You always were an insufferable prick, Pierce,' he said, before turning his back and scurrying out like a dog with its tail between his legs.

By 7.00 pm, Pierce was back at his office. He slipped the drive into his PC. He clicked on the folder titled simply *_VG* and waited for its contents to reveal themselves.

A single PDF document opened up. The name *Operation Vanguard* was typed across the top and the government protective marking, *Top Secret* – suggesting it contained information which could cause serious harm if compromised – was stamped in large block lettering across the front.

Before reading, he looked up as the lights from an incoming aircraft illuminated the office. Something wasn't right. He glanced at the back of his office door where he always kept his chaplain's vestments and clerical collar; they were missing. He could have sworn he'd hung them there after his service last Sunday… or perhaps he was mistaken, and he'd left them back in the vestry at Valley church. No matter, he'd go over there tomorrow and make sure.

He returned his attention to the document, and began reading.

Chapter 60

Byron Gates had spent the night in his car. It wasn't the first time. The afternoon he spotted a black Range Rover parked across from his house, he'd made a rapid escape and headed for a secluded spot near Lincolnshire Wold. He'd hidden out there for three nights; it was all his body could handle. His back was sore for a week after. When he returned, the Range Rover had gone; if it was ever there in the first place. Sometimes Byron's mind liked to play tricks like that; little pranks to keep him on his toes.

Today, when he woke, he was greeted with a similar twinge of pain, but this time accompanied by a spectacular sunrise streaming like a wash of yellow corn through the windscreen. He'd parked at Dinas beach, a sheltered bay, accessible only by a one-track road. At 7.00 am, the car park was deserted, save the chorus of cormorants and seagulls cracking the dawn wide open with their cries.

He switched on the radio. The news was still broadcasting coverage of Logan Collins' video. He felt guilty, as if he were somehow to blame. He chided himself for feeling that way; this was all Bobbie's handiwork. If nothing else, it confirmed he'd made the right decision to stay off the grid – Bobbie wasn't one for idle threats, that was for sure. After pouring himself a few tepid mouthfuls of coffee from his flask, he entered the address he'd copied to his mobile and headed towards Beaumaris.

When he pulled up outside Tammy Povey's home, a large detached house with a wide driveway and what looked like a brand-new Mercedes C250 parked outside, the sun was in full bloom, a scattering of benign white clouds floating high in the blue. He knocked three times, rang the bell twice. He was set to leave, call back later, when the door was pulled sharply open. Tammy, hair tousled, eyes half-closed, stood in the doorway. She tied the belt of her red dressing gown around her waist.

'This better be bloody good, waking me up on my day off,' she said, barely registering Byron's face. 'Where do I sign?'

'Erm…' he began, scrunching his brow in confusion.

Tammy tugged the lapels of her dressing gown across her chest. 'No package? I don't get my new oil delivery until September. Who are you?' She stepped back, shook her head. 'Oh, not with the God Squad, are you? Jehovah's bloody Witness or something?'

'Huh? Um, no,' Byron stammered.

'No,' she confirmed, studying Byron. 'Too bloody scruffy.'

'I'm a friend of Bobbie's.'

'Yeah,' she said, checking out Byron's dishevelled, nerdy appearance. 'You look like you might be, but why are you here?'

Byron hadn't anticipated this question. In fact, he hadn't anticipated much of anything, least of all questions. It was a spur of the moment decision, coming here; he could have kicked himself for not being better prepared.

'Well?' Tammy pressed.

'I was wondering if you knew where she was?'

Tammy shrugged. 'Home. Or working, all she ever does.'

'And where does she live again?'

Tammy folded her arms across her chest. 'If you were her friend, you'd know that.'

'We lost touch, a while ago.'

'What did you say your name was?'

'I'm just trying to reconnect with Bobbie.'

Tammy set both her palms against the door, pushing it closed. 'Try Facebook, like a normal person.'

Byron wedged a boot in the doorway. 'I don't mean to scare you, honest, but I think Bobbie might be in trouble. I'd really like to speak to her.'

'Trouble?' Tammy smiled. 'If anyone can handle trouble, it's my sister. Now, if you don't get your foot from my door, I'm calling the police,' she said, slipping her mobile from her pocket.

'Sorry to have bothered you,' he said, pulling his foot away. He felt the draught on his face as Tammy slammed the door. No matter. He'd obtained one vital piece of information he wasn't expecting. Bobbie was Tammy's sister.

It was a start. He'd uncovered a small nugget of hope, some leverage he could use when the time came. The thought gave him some comfort as he started the engine and searched for his next hiding place. Someplace isolated. Someplace Bobbie wouldn't find him.

Chapter 61

After several heavy fist pummels on the front door, DS Nader walked around to the back of the house. There were two ground floor windows, one looking into the kitchen, the other looking into the dining room. Both had the curtains drawn tight as blindfolds. The garden was small with a square patch of lawn and flower beds framing the edges. The Indian stone driveway was also empty, save a wet pool of engine oil. He crouched down, touched the thick black solution. Fresh; maybe a recent engine leak.

'She's not buried under the driveway, if that's what you think.'

Nader stood, his knees creaking like a pair of rusty door hinges. 'And who are you, love?' he asked, looking over to a woman speaking to him from behind the white sheet she was pegging to the washing line.

'Bloody neighbour, aren't I? Who do you think?' she said, nodding towards the house. 'Candice. Everyone calls me Candy.'

Candy was in her mid-thirties, Nader guessed, hair colour straight from a bottle, outfit courtesy of Primark; attitude honed on the council estates of Valley.

'You know the woman who lives here?'

'Depends on who's asking, don't it?'

'Detective Sergeant Mal Nader, North Wales Constabulary,' he said, taking out his badge.

'Closer,' Candy said, beckoning him with her hand.

Nader stepped forward.

Candy leaned her thick forearms across the hazel hurdle fencing. 'Yeah, I know her,' she said, wiping her hands down her oversized pink Juicy

Couture T-shirt. 'Bobbie Matthews. Why? What's she done? Already had some bloke asking about her a few days back.'

'Oh, aye, who was that then?'

'RAF type, from the base. Didn't tell me his name.'

'Did you ask?'

'Mind my own business, I do.'

'That right?'

'Yeah, it is. But I feel sorry for the young girl, yeah?' she said with a solemn shake of her head. 'Widowed at her age. Thank God mine's out of active service.' Candy leaned forward, lowered her voice. 'Mind you, some days I wish they'd deploy the useless lump a few thousand miles away, leave me in peace.'

'Did you know Bobbie Matthews well?' Nader asked.

Candy shrugged. 'She wasn't the get-to-know-you-well type, if you know what I mean. Kept herself to herself, bit miserable if you ask me. Mind you, I bet it weren't easy for her, settling down here in RAF housing after what happened. Most of us wives have been here for years. We stick close, like. Not that we didn't invite her over – drinks, cards, that kind of thing – but she was always too busy. Well, after a while you stop asking, don't you?'

'Have you seen her recently?'

'Her car's not been there for a couple of days, and I've not caught sight of her around the village for a week now.'

'See her down the local?'

'Like I said, she wasn't the "meet me down the pub" type.'

'Anywhere you know she might have gone?'

Candy thought for a moment. 'She kept herself to herself, and I'm not one to pry. But she did mention she had a sister over in Beaumaris.'

'Did this sister have a name?'

Candy paused. 'Tammy. Yeah, Tammy, that's it.'

'Good, Candy,' he said. 'Thanks for your time.'

'You lot going to find that bloke before they kill him? Not much for politics, but he's got a wife and kids,' Candy asked, her voice raised as if she wanted the whole housing estate to hear.

'We're doing the best we can.'

'And those dead birds. Want to know what I think?' she said, crossing her arms across her chest. 'All the radiation from those mobile phones, got to be.'

'Well, when we know you'll know,' Nader said, turning his back and walking back to the service car.

'Oh, yeah? Great bloody comfort that is,' Candy said, shaking her head and pegging her sheet firmly to the washing line. 'Radiation. Hot tip, that is, mate.'

Nader continued walking.

'Hey! You're bloody welcome,' Candy called out.

Chapter 62

Tammy opened the door to her sister earlier that evening. Bobbie had stood under the porch light, kitbag flung over her shoulder. Bobbie would often turn up on Tammy's doorstep, stay for a couple of nights then leave without a word. She'd learned to live with it by now; well, not exactly live with it, more like roll with it. That kind of attitude became second nature when you were Bobbie Matthews' sister.

'You can use the spare room, but you're making your own bed, mind.'

Bobbie had agreed to the terms with a sharp nod and walked upstairs. By the time Tammy had turned from the doorway, Bobbie had already closed the bedroom door. It was another three hours before she emerged to join her sister in the kitchen.

'You look like you need a stiff drink,' she said, as Bobbie threw herself onto one of the kitchen chairs.

'Tea's fine, thanks.'

'Yeah, of course it is,' she said, flipping down the switch on the kettle. 'Want to tell me what this is all about?'

Bobbie stretched out her legs and shoved both her hands deep into her hoodie pockets. 'Not now, Tammy, I'm knackered.'

'Suit yourself, but if you're kipping here you need to talk to me. I've had it with this sulky teenager act.'

Bobbie shrugged. 'Yeah, just give me time, okay?'

'Is this about Dani? Having one of your bad days?'

Bobbie shrugged.

'You can talk to me, you know, about what happened.'

'Been there, tried that.'

'Yeah, I'm not talking about some grief counselling thing. We're sisters. We grew up together. Remember, we used to tell each other everything. No secrets.'

Secrets. The word made Bobbie want to laugh. Tammy might have thought Bobbie was still the sullen teenager she remembered growing up, but Tammy hadn't matured that much either. She still believed in some adolescent fantasy of a girlish sisterhood that had never existed; at least not that Bobbie remembered. Truth was, neither of them had been the sister the other needed. They were sisters in name only, separated by the genetic traits of two different fathers. It should have drawn them closer, but instead those differences had thrust a sharp wedge between them.

'You heard about that poor bloke who was kidnapped?'

'Hard not to.'

'I always thought this place was too bloody quiet; now I could do without all the stress to be honest.'

'Careful what you wish for, right?' Bobbie said.

A few seconds of silence was broken by a sharp kettle whistle. 'Oh, I almost forgot,' Tammy said, sloshing hot water over the teabag. 'Some bloke called round this morning, looking for you.'

Bobbie stiffened, but kept her composure as Tammy sat and slid the mug across the table.

'What bloke?'

'Didn't say. Said he was a friend of yours. Scruffy-looking sod, big beard, nervous too. Looked like he didn't socialise much.'

Bobbie straightened her back. 'What did you tell him?'

'Didn't tell him anything, just sent him packing.'

Bobbie pushed back her chair and stood, wiping her hands down the front of her hoodie.

'Where are you going? You just got here.'

'Sorry, I've got to—' she said, cutting her sentence short before rushing upstairs.

Bobbie slammed the bedroom door and stuffed the clothes she'd just unpacked back into her kitbag.

Tammy flung the door back open. 'Who was he?' she demanded, stepping into the bedroom. 'What did he want?'

'He's a nobody, just a creep.'

'Oh, like a stalker you mean? Had one of those myself, once.'

'Yeah a stalker, just like a stalker,' Bobbie said, hauling the kitbag over her shoulder.

'He said you were in trouble, Bobbie. Is that true? Are you?'

Bobbie's stomach snarled into a stiff ball of wire. More questions. Tammy had more questions than Call Me Andy. Didn't they realise she was tired of talking, tired of being lied to? She took a step forward, ready to shoulder-charge her sister if necessary.

'No,' Tammy said, blocking the door and folding her arms. 'Not until you speak to me. Why did he say you were in trouble? Is it about Dani? How he died?'

The sound of her husband's name on her sister's lips was like the twist of a knife in Bobbie's chest. Tammy had always called him Dani, as if she were too lazy to take the time to learn how to pronounce his name correctly. Bobbie snapped out her arm, wrapped her sister's wrist in her hand and pressed hard with her thumbs. Tammy groaned with pain.

'Jesus, Bobbie!' she said, stepping aside and rubbing her wrist. 'If you want to go that badly, just go. But you don't get to come back. This is the last time.'

Bobbie dropped her kitbag, turned to face her sister and stood to attention as if presenting herself on the parade square. 'Danvir. My husband's name is Danvir Mohsin Sadiq. He died in a missile attack in Mosul, Syria, but I don't know if that's true or if it's a cover-up, or if I killed him. I've been relieved of my duties and will be sent to a VA psych hospital for rehabilitation for as long as they see fit to keep me there. Everyone else involved in Operation Vanguard is now either dead or lying about what really happened. It has fallen on my shoulders to exact the punishment and redress the balance of justice. Necessary killings in a necessary war.'

'What the hell are you saying, Bobbie?' Tammy asked, the pain in her wrist replaced by a more unsettling feeling; fear.

Bobbie lifted her kitbag. 'I am not in denial, Tammy, I'm living with the echo of what I did every single minute of the day. My house reminds me of Danvir. My job reminds me of him, the base, the uniforms, the bloody wives in the housing, everything. There has to be justice, right, Tammy? A balance? I wanted to explain this all to you later, when I'm in a better place. All I asked for was time, but you're just like Maggie – Keep calm and carry on, get over it, Bobbie, move on, Bobbie, cheer up, Bobbie, it might never happen, Bobbie. But you know what, Tammy, it *did* bloody well happen.'

'Jesus—' Tammy began before Bobbie interrupted.

'Happy? Good conversation, sis?'

Tammy's words were stuck somewhere deep in her throat. If she'd managed to speak, she was sure her words would have tumbled into a mess of incoherent noise.

Bobbie bolted down the stairs, pulling the door hard into its frame as she left. In the resonance of the slam, Tammy had the unshakeable feeling that her sister was heading into something dangerous; something there was no coming back from. The sensation sent a sudden chill pulsing to her core.

Chapter 63

The following day, Manx pushed through the mob of reporters, microphones and news cameras blocking his way up the station steps. The questions were the same as yesterday and the day before:

Have you located Logan Collins yet?

Has anyone been arrested?

Will the RAF release the Operation Vanguard documents?

Is the North Wales Constabulary failing in its duties?

When will there be an official press briefing?

How is Logan Collins' wife dealing with the stress of her husband's kidnapping?

That last question was a new take, Manx thought as he shoved open the station door. Entering the reception, the question suddenly made sense. Danica Collins – back pin-straight, hands fixed in her lap – sat on one of the chairs. She was composed, but had the pallor of a woman who was a stranger to sleep. She stood, smoothed down the front of her jacket and looked directly at Manx; her eyes had the same other-worldly clarity he'd noticed when they'd first met.

He turned to the duty sergeant. 'Interview room two free?'

The sergeant checked the monitors and nodded.

'Follow me, Mrs Collins,' Manx said, buzzing open the door and leading her into the brightly lit corridor.

'Just so you understand, I did not come to hear platitudes,' Danica said, gracefully easing herself into the chair.

'Truth is, I have none to give you, Mrs Collins,' he said, sitting across from her.

'Do you still think my husband is being held on the island?'

'Most likely, yes.'

'It's not that large.'

'One person, two hundred and sixty square miles, and limited police resources—' Manx began.

'So, what are these resources actually doing?' she interrupted.

'Our job, Mrs Collins. Investigating.'

Danica dropped her hands to her lap. In that moment, she looked fragile; a woman navigating her own personal hell. 'When my husband was first taken, do you remember what you told me?'

She didn't wait for Manx's reply.

'You told me most of these situations are resolved. The victims are returned, unharmed. Nobody gets killed.'

Manx had a vague recollection. It was only a few days back, but it already felt like weeks ago.

'So, let me ask you,' she said, leaning forward. 'Do you still believe that's true?'

Manx's hesitation was the only answer Danica Collins required. She held herself stiffly, as if she was controlling every muscle in her body and if she relaxed any of them, she might fall apart at the seams. She dragged back her chair and stood.

'Mrs Collins—'

'Words don't interest me, Inspector,' she said. 'Actions. Finding my husband, bringing a father back to his children, those are the only things that matter now.'

As she pulled the interview room door closed behind her, Manx leaned back. 'Jesus Christ,' he muttered to himself.

Back in reception he glanced through the window at the commotion outside. Danica Collins was addressing the cameras. Manx couldn't hear what she was saying, but he was damned sure she wasn't thanking the North Wales Constabulary for the sterling job they were doing in locating her husband. As he turned to head into the break room to pour himself a tepid coffee before digging through the evidence again – his life was turning into a macabre version of

'Groundhog Day' – DS Nader rushed in from the incident room.

'Boss!' he said, waving a slip of paper in his hand. 'Bobbie Matthews' sister's address. Got her photo off Facebook. She's a bit of a looker, too. Wouldn't have to ask me twice. I'll head over there now.'

Manx took the paper. 'No,' he said. 'I'll go. Could do with some fresh air and a change of scenery.'

Nader's face fell a few millimetres, then he smiled. 'Maybe for the best. The woman probably wouldn't stand a chance, once I turned on the old Nader charm.'

'Nailed it, as usual, Sergeant,' Manx said. 'Now maybe you use some of that charm to solve these bloody cases. Call me with anything new.'

Chapter 64

Tammy Povey was having none of it. She sat at her breakfast bar, arms folded tight. 'Don't know why you're asking about Bobbie, I hardly ever see her,' she said, staring defiantly at Manx.

'When did you last see your sister?'

'Half-sister,' Tammy said, snapping her dressing gown cord tighter around her waist.

'Your half-sister. Have you seen her recently?'

'Is she in trouble or something?'

'How well do you know her, Tammy?'

'What kind of question is that? We've known each other all our lives.'

'That's not what I asked,' Manx said, sensing her unease as she shuffled and brushed a length of hair from her face. It was early in the morning and Tammy Povey had obviously had no time to attend to her typical make-up routine, but Nader had been right. Tammy was a looker, striking even; sparkling blue eyes that locked onto his when she talked; high, perfectly sculpted cheekbones; skin that seemed to glow in the morning light streaming in through the kitchen window. She had the sort of energy Manx found himself drawn to; a natural confidence he'd always found attractive. Tammy had it in spades, and he could sense it sparking across the table as she crossed her legs, revealing a sliver of thigh, and looked at him as if she was waiting to be impressed.

'You can live with someone all your life and still not know them,' he finally said.

'Oh, like those women married to serial killers you mean?' she said, pointing her coffee cup at Manx. 'Don't buy it, myself. I'd sniff that out in a heartbeat and any woman who tells you otherwise is lying. There, you can have that insight for free, Inspector Manx.'

'I'll remember to include it in my memoirs,' Manx said, laying out the print-out of Bobbie and Byron Gates on the table. 'Do you know this man?'

Tammy picked up the photo. 'Yeah. Well, I don't know him, but he called around here looking for Bobbie a couple of days ago. He looked shifty, so I sent him packing, almost called you lot, actually. Who is he?'

'His name's Byron Gates. We have reason to believe he and Bobbie are working together.'

Tammy narrowed her eyes, causing her nose to scrunch in a way that made Manx smile. 'How do you mean, working together? And why are you smiling like that?'

Manx continued. 'Logan Collins' kidnapping—'

'No. No,' Tammy interrupted. She stood and walked to the opposite end of the kitchen. 'Bobbie's been upset recently, but she's getting help. She's checking into a psychiatric hospital in a couple of weeks. You're barking up the wrong tree. What about that Gates bloke? He looked the shady type to me.'

'Do you know where she is, Tammy? A place she might feel safe? Friends she's close to that wouldn't hesitate to help her out?'

'Friends?' Tammy said, shaking her head. 'This is Bobbie we're talking about.'

'No friends?' Manx said. 'Seems unlikely.'

'Then, you don't know Bobbie,' Tammy said.

'No,' he agreed. 'I don't, but you do.'

He stood and handed Tammy his card. 'If she contacts you or you think of any place she might be hiding, call me. We want to find her before anything bad happens. I want to keep Bobbie safe. Whatever she's done, we can work through it, make sure she gets the help she needs. Do you understand, Tammy?'

'I think so.' She twirled the card around her fingers. 'Thank you,' she said, flashing another dazzling smile his way: one he'd happily have pocketed and taken home with him, if he could. 'You're all right, you are.'

'Nicest thing anyone said to me all week,' he said.

'For a copper,' Tammy clarified, this time her smile wider, a playful glint in her eyes.

'For a copper,' Manx muttered to himself, shook his head and saw himself out.

Chapter 65

Collins was running, or was he dreaming he was running? He could no longer discern what was real and what his imagination had cooked up to keep him sane. All he knew for sure was that the ground under his feet was soft and someone was calling out to him from behind a beam of light. The smell of slurry was potent, the sky dark but clear – it seemed bigger than he remembered it, as if it had expanded in the days he'd been blindfolded.

As he ran, Collins' foot sent a shock of pain searing through to his bones – a stark reminder of the bolt Melvin had fired into his flesh. The bandage they'd provided to wrap his foot and the disinfectant they'd poured over the wound to stop it festering wasn't working; he could tell by the stench and the blackening skin that it was already infected. For a glorious moment, he wondered if this was all just some nightmare and the agony, the shock, the sheer terror, were all being played out in his imagination. But, if that were true, wouldn't he have woken by now, safe in his bed, his wife sleeping beside him? As the voice shouted at him to run faster, it didn't seem to Collins he'd be waking up anytime soon.

Melvin Powell wasn't one for dwelling on regrets, but what he'd done in the snug of the Lantern Arms less than an hour ago? That, he did regret. Not that the bloke wasn't asking for a slap in the mouth; he was, and then some. It had begun innocently enough, some light-hearted banter then the man, who was old enough to know better, latched his attention on to Lydia with a crock of half-arsed compliments and a mouthful of filthy jokes he must have heard in one of the rougher pubs around Holyhead docks.

As the evening slipped into night, the man began downing whisky like water. At around what must have been his seventh or eighth double, a switch seemed to have flipped in his brain. When Lydia walked around the front of the bar, he grabbed her around the waist, pulling her in for a full-on lip kiss. Melvin knew Lydia could handle herself but had kept an eye on the situation just the same, twisting a damp beer towel around his fist as he watched. When the bloke pawed at Lydia's blouse buttons, asked her to show him her tits, then called her an old tart when she refused, Melvin's patience had finally snapped. He'd climbed over the bar, grabbed the bloke by the shoulder, span him round and looked him directly in the eyes so the man understood exactly what was coming his way, then ploughed his fist into his face.

The bloke didn't talk much after that.

Instead, he'd swayed for a second as if he were processing the hammer that had just pummelled his jawbone, fallen backwards and landed on a table of empty glasses which had shattered to the floor. Lydia had screamed at Melvin, shoved him out of the pub, shouted something at him he couldn't hear because by that time the blood in his ears was roaring like thunder.

That was an hour ago. He'd cooled down since then – the joint had helped ease the dull thud of his pulse against his skull. He leaned against the wall behind the pub. He was letting the pressure get to him – that wasn't smart, not when things were still in motion.

His sickness was harsh enough to contend with, but the situation with Logan Collins wasn't helping. The video had been Bobbie's idea, a good one too, better than having to kill the bastard. He couldn't deny punching that bloke's lights out earlier had made him feel more alive than he'd done in months, but it wasn't fair to Lydia. The pub was her livelihood, it would be all she had, and he had no right to lay into one of her customers like that. Lydia would have calmed the man down, put a lid on the situation without raising a hand. Regrets? Yeah, he had a few. He heard voices coming from the field near the coal shed. He stubbed out his joint and walked over.

The padlock was hanging off the latch, the door knocking lightly against the frame in the slight breeze. He peered inside; no sign of Collins. Looking over the field behind the pub, he noticed a light breaking through the darkness. He pushed open the gate and called out to his nephew – no reply. He called out again, this time louder. He heard a faint 'Yeah?' in the distance.

'What the fucking hell are you up to?' he asked, marching towards Ronnie.

Ronnie held the crossbow low at his hip, directing the beam towards a dark figure wandering aimlessly in the distance. 'He was complaining he was getting cramps. Wouldn't fucking shut up, so I told him, ten minutes, but you stay where I can see you.'

'We discuss these things, Ronnie,' Melvin said, poking him in the shoulder.

'Oh, yeah? Like Collins' fuckin' YouTube video? Don't remember much discussion 'bout that.'

'That was different: someone had to fix your fuck-up.'

Ronnie ran a sleeve under his nose. 'Yeah, you and her come up with that idea, did you? Bloody stupid, if you ask me. You're no better than her errand boy.'

Melvin's blood thundered in his ears. It would have been easy to floor his nephew, but he'd already made one mistake tonight. He was about to direct Ronnie to shove Collins back in the shed when he heard the ground rustle behind him. He turned.

'What's all the noise about, Mel?' Lydia said, squinting in the intense beam of the lamping light.

As Logan Collins stumbled back across the field towards them, Lydia gasped. 'Jesus, Mel, is that…?'

Mel debated lying, but there was really no use, not now. 'So now you know,' he said. 'Ronnie, get him back in the shed.'

Lydia took a few seconds to process. 'What the hell have you done, Mel?' she said, her voice straining.

'Kept your nose clean and out of this, that's what,' he said, stabbing his index finger in her face. 'And I can still do that, if you keep quiet, forget you saw anything.'

Lydia brought a hand over her mouth and watched, eyes saucer wide, as Ronnie shoved the crossbow into Collins' back and led him back to the shed. 'I don't know. This isn't making any sense, Mel. This was all you? You and Ronnie?'

'Now you know, nobody's going to do something stupid like call the coppers.'

'You've got him locked up in a bloody shed, for God's sake, Mel,' Lydia said, turning back to walk towards the pub. 'It's not right, none of this. I'm calling the coppers.'

'You're not going anywhere,' Melvin snapped, grabbing her wrist in a tight grip.

Lydia spun on her heels. 'Oh, going to clock me one too, like you did that bloke?' She stepped close, her face inches from Mel's. 'I knew you lot were up to something, but this? Takes the bloody biscuit. I don't want any part of it. I've got the pub to think about.'

'Aye, and that's why you'll keep your mouth shut. If the brewery finds out, they'll throw you out on your arse, get someone else in to run the place.'

'I can't, Mel, I just can't…' Lydia said, sensing the pull between what she knew was the right and the cold, barren truth of Melvin's words. A voice to her left startled her from her thoughts.

'I really recommend you revise your position, Lydia.'

Lydia shook her wrist free and looked at the woman, who she was sure she recognised; a customer but not a regular. The woman slipped her kitbag from her shoulder, letting it drop on the grass.

'Do you understand what Mel just told you?' Bobbie Matthews said, walking towards Lydia. 'What that implies?'

'Mel?' Lydia said, turning. 'What the hell is going on?'

A swathe of light crossed the three of them as Ronnie returned from the shed. He stopped and shone the beam directly into Bobbie's face. 'What the fuck's she doing here, Mel?'

Bobbie brought up a hand to shield her eyes. 'Put down the light, Ronnie.'

'Not even a please?' he said, waving the beam across her face, as if searching for something in her features that would give him some clue as to the hold he was sure this woman had over his uncle.

'I've had enough for one night, Mel. Who is she?' Lydia said. 'Coming here, telling me how to behave on my own doorstep.'

There was a momentary glance between Bobbie and Melvin, an understanding that now was as good a time as any.

Melvin took a breath. 'Her name's Bobbie Matthews,' he said, his voice low, almost a murmur swallowed by the night.

'And?' Lydia pressed – there was more to her than just a name; she could tell by now when Melvin was holding back on her.

'She's…' he looked to the ground, then pulled back his shoulders as if to give the words more emphasis.

'She's my daughter.'

'Shit!' Ronnie said, shining the beam directly in Bobbie's face, this time looking for something more tangible, some familial similarity. 'You told me you didn't have any kids.'

Melvin pressed his hand on the crossbow lamp, directing the beam to the floor. 'Well, shows how much you know. And before you say anything else, Bobbie needs a place to stay, I told her she could have the spare bedroom in the cottage.'

'As if,' Ronnie said, spitting. 'That's my home. I get to say who stays there or not.'

'You start paying rent, you can call it home. Until then, Bobbie stays in my cottage, no arguments.'

'For how long?' Ronnie asked sulkily.

'As long as she bloody well needs,' Melvin confirmed. 'Now, let's go inside, I need a bloody drink.'

Chapter 66

Lydia dragged a chair to the head of the kitchen table and sat.

Bobbie and Ronnie positioned themselves on either side of her, with Melvin sitting five feet across the stretch of old pine. He seemed like a stranger to her now; a stranger with his feet under her table and a space in her bed. *Not for much bloody longer*, she thought as she lit up a joint, tapping her fingertips on the table.

'Right, who wants to start?' she said, inhaling a dense plume of smoke.

Silence, save the shuffle of feet over a hardwood floor.

Lydia waited, looked each of them in the eyes. They all avoided her gaze, except for Bobbie, who met her eyes with an equally resolute stare of her own. It unnerved Lydia – it was the sort of look that seemed to penetrate through to someplace she wasn't prepared to have exposed.

'No one?' she said a few moments later. 'Right, then I'll start. You kidnapped that politician, locked him up, and now got him to say all those things on camera. How's that for my starter for ten?'

'Correct,' Bobbie confirmed.

'And you,' Lydia said, pointing. 'Are you Mel's daughter?'

'Also correct.'

She took another drag. 'So, any other kids you haven't told me about, Mel? A second family somewhere?'

'It's not like that,' Melvin protested.

'Oh, what is it like? Spill the beans, eh.'

Melvin opened his palms. 'It was a lifetime ago, Lyd,' he said, sitting back. 'I knew Bobbie's mother, Maggie.'

'Seems you did a lot more than bloody well know the woman.'

'Maybe I can help,' Bobbie said. She reached into her kitbag and took out a pile of letters wrapped in an elastic band. 'These were my mother's,' she said, setting the bundle on the table. 'They're letters between her and Melvin. It took me a few months to figure it all out, but Melvin is my biological father.'

Lydia turned the letters in her hand. 'Tell. Me. Everything.'

Bobbie relayed as best she remembered what her mother had told her and what she'd read in the letters. Melvin added his own punctuation of the odd head nod and low grunt as Bobbie spoke. After she finished, Lydia shoved the letters back across the table.

'Bloody closed book you are, Melvin Powell,' she said, shaking her head. 'But it's all water under the bridge, none of us were angels back in the day, but that bloke you've got locked up? You're letting him go, tonight. No argument.'

'We can't do that,' Bobbie said.

Lydia slapped her hand on the table. 'You will bloody well do it, or I'm calling the police, no two ways about it. Understand?'

Bobbie leaned forward. 'I don't think you understand, Lydia. Our mission is incomplete, and don't forget you've implicated yourself just by talking with us.'

Lydia looked at Melvin. 'What does she mean? Tell me what she means.'

Ronnie drummed his fingers on the table. 'Don't be fucking stupid,' he said, shaking his head. 'She means you're just as fucked as the rest of us if the cops find us.'

Lydia took a moment, leaned close to Ronnie. 'I wasn't asking the monkey,' she said, blowing a thick plume of smoke in his face. 'I was asking the monkey's uncle.'

Melvin spoke through gritted teeth. 'If the police come, they'll say you're part of all this, probably lose your licence. It's like you keep saying, this pub's all you've got.'

'And,' Bobbie said, leaning back, 'you'd need us to back up your story that you were innocent in all this.'

Ronnie exhaled a loud whistle. 'Fucking hell! Cruel bitch, you are. No doubt you're a Powell through and through, yeah?'

'I didn't ask for this. None of it,' Lydia said, running a hand through her hair.

'You've got Ronnie to thank for that,' Melvin said. 'My nephew, the criminal mastermind, left us no choice, did he?'

'Oh Christ!' Lydia said, her eyes wide, a hand shooting to her mouth. 'That copper, the one that was stabbed? That was you?'

Ronnie couldn't resist a faint smile of pride. 'She was asking for it. The bitch pepper sprayed me. She got what was coming.'

'That does it,' Lydia said, reaching for her mobile.

Bobbie placed her hand over Lydia's wrist. 'Not the smartest strategy for you right now, Lydia, trust me.'

'Oh yeah, what are you going to do, tie me up? Shove me in the coal shed along with that other bloke?'

'If necessary,' Bobbie said, pressing her thumbs down hard on the veins on her wrist.

It wasn't the answer Lydia was expecting. 'Mel?' she said, a creeping sense of desperation in her voice.

'Sorry, Lyd, she's right. We've come too far.'

'Jesus,' she snapped. 'All this over the English buying holiday homes? You're no better than those bloody Muslim terrorists.'

Bobbie exerted a heavy and sustained pressure on Lydia's carpal muscle. 'This is different,' she insisted. 'Very different.'

Lydia stared into Bobbie's eyes, hoping to find some kindness in there, an ounce of female bonding, but there was none, just a blank, cold emptiness. 'What happened?' she asked. 'What happened to make you like this? So... I don't know, cruel?'

'When you've lost everything that mattered to you, then you're qualified to ask me that question, not before,' Bobbie said.

'Look, I don't know what happened, love, who made you like this, but I can't let you destroy my life, Mel's too. It's not right.' She turned to Melvin. 'Why? I just don't understand, why?'

'She needed a father's help,' Melvin said, nodding in Bobbie's direction. 'I wasn't around for her growing up.'

'Help for what, for God's sake?'

'She's family. She needed my help, end of story.' As he spoke, Melvin's chest tightened, a hard fist bunching around his lungs, squeezing the life from them. He gripped his fingers around the table and attempted to inhale, but all he could do was cough; cough as if his whole insides were rattling loose. He wiped a napkin across his mouth and coughed large globules of blood onto the white.

Lydia's face paled, the pieces falling like shrapnel, into place. 'It's to do with all this, isn't it? Whatever it is that's wrong with you.'

'Melvin has stage four small cell lung cancer,' Bobbie said, flatly. 'His condition is terminal.'

'Oh God,' Lydia said, her chest suddenly heavy and tight. 'I knew it, I knew something was wrong. Why didn't you tell me? You should be in hospital, chemotherapy or something.'

'No,' Melvin said, finally wrestling his coughing under some control. 'I do this my way, my rules.'

For the past few minutes, Ronnie had remained silent, absorbing the information. Now he stood, pulled back his chair and walked towards the kitchen door. The three of them watched as he slammed shut the door.

'He didn't know, did he?' Lydia said.

'It's how Mel wanted it,' Bobbie explained.

Lydia's anger rose to a sharp boil. 'You should be ashamed of yourself. He should be resting, not messing around with whatever you've got him involved in. You just told me you were his daughter, for Christ's sake. You're using a sick man for your own ends.'

'Enough, Lyd,' Mel snapped. 'I'm my own man, nobody forced me into anything. I'm doing this for me, understand?'

'No, no, Mel, I don't understand, none of it.' Lydia's eyes were moist, stinging from the effort it took to hold back the dam of tears.

'I'm a fighter, it's in my blood.'

'But cancer, Mel, you can't punch your way out of that.'

'I'm not going down without a fight.'

'So, this is what this is all about? Well, let me tell you, Melvin Powell, you're fucking delusional. What's the plan? Go out in a blaze of glory like some kind of bloody hero?'

Melvin wiped a hand across his lips. 'Better than the alternative. Everybody pitying me, looking at me like I'm already dead. Leave it alone now, what's done is done.'

Every bone in Lydia's body wanted to reach over, shake Melvin, slap his face; wrap her arms around him like she'd never let go. She did none of this; she was wasting her breath, that was clear. She knew by now when to let a thing go. But there was still the matter of Collins; that she wouldn't let go so easily.

'That bloke you've got locked up, you're letting him go, tonight,' she said, staring at Bobbie.

'I've already told you, that's non-negotiable.'

'You bloody well will, or I'll call the police myself.'

'No. No you won't,' Bobbie said, grabbing both of Lydia's wrists as if she were about to lead her in prayer. She embedded her thumbs deep into the veins. 'In a few days, this will all be over. We'll move Collins, no one will ever know he was here. If you call the police, I can't guarantee you won't be implicated. If you still refuse to co-operate, you will force my hand, which will not end well for you. Do you understand what I'm telling you, Lydia?'

Lydia looked at Melvin, her eyes pleading; pleading for something he was unable, or unwilling, to grant her. It was the moment she knew it was over; Melvin, her protests; everything. She wasn't one to cry, hadn't cried for years, decades even, but the sheer hopelessness of her situation hit home, hard. She nodded, the spill of tears running down her cheeks, cutting rivers through her concealer and through to her foundation.

'No, Lydia,' Bobbie said, pressing harder, looking harder into Lydia's eyes. 'Tell me, in words, that you understand my instructions.'

'I… understand,' Lydia whispered. 'I understand.'

Chapter 67

'"Stand By Your Man", "Apartment Nine", "D.I.V.O.R.C.E", which is probably her most ironic song as she went through five husbands,' Manx said, forking a chip from a shallow pool of malt vinegar.

'Impressive,' Tammy said. 'And Bobbie Gentry?'

Manx paused. '"Ode to Billy Joe", "Mississippi Delta", and she recorded a blinding version of "Gentle on My Mind".'

Tammy wiped her hands on a napkin, applauded and reached into her purse to hand Manx a fiver. 'You named three songs by each of them. You win, Inspector.'

'Keep it,' Manx said. 'Buy me a pint next time.'

'Next time?' Tammy said. 'You're confident.'

Manx forked another chip and smiled. They were sitting at Red Wharf Bay watching the retreating tide as twilight fell over the boats anchored like toys in the sand. Behind them, the Ship Inn was bustling with tourists clamouring for space at the outside tables, the bar four deep, the young waiters struggling to keep up with the orders. Manx stole a glance Tammy's way; she looked even more striking than the last time he'd seen her. Her jeans, skin-tight; the black leather boots, expensive; the beige cashmere hoodie which she'd zipped up to just under her neckline, hugging every curve from her hips to her chest.

'So, what do you do when you're not trying to con impressionable men out of their money?' Manx asked, fixing his attention back to why they were here in the first place.

'That's just my hobby,' Tammy said, laying down her fish and chip dinner on the bench. 'I'm a regional manager for a well-respected bank. Loans, financial products, fraud; all very exciting. Youngest regional manager and first ever woman to supervise the whole north west territory, by the way.'

'My turn to be impressed.'

'You should be,' she said. 'You're on a date with a very powerful woman. Some men get very intimidated. Are you intimidated, Inspector?'

'By the fact you just said we're on a date, or that you're a powerful woman?'

Tammy smiled. 'I'll have to be on my toes around you.'

'Top of your game,' Manx agreed, taking a swig of beer, then asking the question he'd been waiting to put to Tammy all evening. 'Tell me about Bobbie.'

'I knew you had an ulterior motive for asking me out.'

'Call it two for the price of one, in my advantage,' Manx said.

'You already know the important stuff. Bobbie transferred back here last year after her husband, Dani, was killed. She wasn't the same after that. Not that she was ever the life of the party, but she really withdrew into herself. She had all these counselling sessions, they helped a bit, but I couldn't see her getting any better. Then there was the incident at the pub.'

'What incident?'

Tammy explained how Bobbie had turned on the young RAF auggie and forced him to apologise. 'Not that he didn't deserve it, mind, but it was like she snapped or something.'

'Does she have many friends?'

'She's always been a loner, private. Our mam, she drilled it into us, 'don't depend on a man, they'll only end up disappointing you.' Probably the best thing she ever did for us, but I think Bobbie took it too far, she was too bloody independent. That's why we were so surprised when she got married. It was like the two of them against the world: her and Dani.' Tammy took a deep breath. 'What happens when you find Bobbie?'

Manx took a swig of beer. 'That all depends. The longer she puts off turning herself in, the worse it gets. Do you know where she is, Tammy? Any ideas at all?'

'I wish,' Tammy said, shaking her head. 'I wish I bloody well knew. I can't believe she'd do something like this, she's always been so dedicated to the bloody RAF, it's not like her. I just want this to be over, I want Bobbie to be safe, get the help she needs.'

'We all do,' Manx said. As he spoke, he recognised a familiar voice from the opposite side of the car park: Ashton Bevan calling after his wife, Sherry.

'Shit,' he said, throwing the remainder of his cod and chips into the nearby bin. 'Let's go.'

'Go? Go where?'

Manx didn't answer, took her hand and pulled her from the bench.

'Okay, mister take bloody charge all of a sudden,' she said as he guided her to a small hidden area to the side of the pub where the narrow footpath leading from the town of Pentraeth ended.

'Christ,' Tammy said, settling her back against the wall and looking out to the car park. 'What was that all about?'

He watched as Bevan and Sherry walked arm in arm along the seafront. 'Someone I'd rather not bump into right now.'

'Wife? Jealous ex-lover?' she asked, looking to the car park.

'Neither. Just the local town bloody crier.'

'So, you're embarrassed to be seen with me?'

Manx turned, realised there were just a few inches of air between them: that and a thick crackle of electricity that he could almost run his fingers through. 'Correct,' he said, looking into her eyes. 'I'm ashamed to be seen in public with an attractive woman.'

Tammy tilted her head slightly. 'Attractive?' she said, hooking her fingers around his jean pockets and pulling him closer.

'If that doesn't offend your whole independent woman thing.'

'No. I'm not offended,' she said, lifting her lips to meet his.

Manx ran his hands over Tammy's waist, her hoodie rising until his fingers caressed soft skin. She drew a hand around the back of his neck and pulled him closer, kissed him like she had no intention of stopping. For a few minutes it was all there was in the world: him, Tammy, the warm summer air on their skins.

After a few minutes, Tammy pulled back and flicked a strand of hair from her cheek. 'You forgot one,' she said and began to hum a tune. Manx immediately recognised it from the first three bars.

'Written by Bacharach and David,' he said, kissing her neck. 'UK number one for Bobbie Gentry, 1969.'

'Bingo,' Tammy said, smiling as she hummed the first few lines of 'I'll Never Fall in Love Again'.

'Am I meant to read something into that?' he asked, moving to kiss the nape of her neck.

'You're the copper, you tell me,' Tammy said, pulling Manx's face closer.

Chapter 68

That morning, it was neither a corn-yellow sunrise nor the cormorants' hungry cackle that woke Byron Gates. In fact, the sun was yet to break the back of the Irish Sea when he was woken by an urgent clanking noise; something heavy and metallic falling in a steady clank, clank rhythm against the glass. His eyes finally gaining focus, he looked through the windscreen to the sunrise casting an orange glow over Aberffraw beach, a half-mile long stretch of sand protected by a ridge of dunes sheltering the bay from the main road. The beach was rarely busy and, a few minutes after dawn was populated only by a group of hardy windsurfers floating like bait bobbins as they waited for the wind to fill their sails.

Byron barely had time to register the metal clanking at the glass was the tiller of a crossbow, before a blast of light filled the car with a cold, white glow followed by the urgent pull of the door handle and a simple command.

'Byron, exit the car. Now.' The voice was chillingly familiar. That curt, military tone that left no space for misinterpretation or reading between the lines – Bobbie Matthews rarely used more words than were necessary.

He lifted his hand to his brow. 'Why? What do you want?'

Byron could have sworn he heard Bobbie's impatient sigh from behind the glass. 'Just exit the vehicle, Byron, like I requested.'

The vessels in Byron's head thumped. These were the commands of a bully; a woman who used others to get what she wanted, wielding her own brand of justice. He folded his arms across his chest, shook his head and kept his gaze fixed through the dirt-ridden windscreen. He heard the muffled speech of two people debating next steps, followed by a tense, uneasy silence where Byron wondered if they'd maybe given up and left him the hell alone.

He should have known better.

Seconds later, the silence fractured as a crossbow bolt shattered the driver's side window and embedded itself with a sharp twang in the innards of the car's navigation screen.

Message received, Byron brushed the shards of glass from his lap, exited the car and waited, shivering in the cold dawn air, his feet clad only in his socks. Bobbie Matthews stood a few feet in front of him. To her right, the same man he'd seen that night at the brickworks slipped another bolt into the tiller.

'Now we understand each other, we need to talk,' Bobbie said. Kneeling at the right wheel arch, she reached inside and extracted a metal object. 'If you were wondering how I found you,' she said, turning the object in her palm. 'That day we first met, and I informed you I'd checked out your car to make sure you weren't being followed? That was a lie. Well, more of a half-truth. You were being followed, but not by who you thought.'

Byron shivered, felt his throat coat with sand as Bobbie dropped the tracking device and slammed the heel of her boot down hard on the thin metal casing, crushing the internal circuitry.

'Why can't you leave me alone? I did what you asked.'

'Correct,' she said, leaning against the car's bonnet. 'But you overstepped your mandate. What do they call it, overachieving?'

'I–' Byron began.

Bobbie moved closer, stepping the full weight of her boots onto the toes of his right foot. Byron exhaled a sharp groan as his metatarsal bones bent under the compression. 'You visited my sister. I don't remember that being part of your mission, in fact, I'd say you went rogue on me, Byron. Snooping around my private life. What were you hoping to achieve? Leverage you could use to find me, then what? Threaten me? Blackmail, maybe?'

Byron clenched his teeth, felt the cold metal of the crossbow urging into the nape of his neck.

'I thought we had an understanding, but I see now I was wrong. Who knows who else you've spoken to – the police? Should I expect a knock on my door soon, Byron? Should I?' Bobbie pressed down harder on his foot.

'No, I… I wouldn't,' Byron stammered.

Bobbie looked Byron up and down as if sizing him up to ensure the correct dimensions for his coffin. 'I can't trust what you tell me, and that's unfortunate.' She stepped back, releasing the pressure. 'People always disappoint you in the end, don't they? But no matter, for every cloud a silver lining, right? It just makes the decision to terminate you that much easier.'

Byron's hands trembled. He had words, things he wanted to say, but sentences failed to form, thoughts resisted any attempt to render them coherent.

'I see you're upset, Byron, that's only to be expected, but I'm not completely without mercy.' She stuffed her hands in her pockets. 'Are you aware of what we call those enemy combatants who escape a missile attack?'

Byron shrugged. 'Lucky?' he said.

Bobbie smiled. 'Good one, Byron, but no. They're called squirters. These men, these terrorists, would hear the sonic boom from the missile launch some thirty thousand feet above them, or notice the red laser point reflecting off their truck window, and they'd realise they had twenty seconds to get the hell out of the blast zone or get blown to a thousand body parts.' She paused, allowing him to take in the information. 'I'm going to extend you the same courtesy, but in your situation, let's make it forty seconds: you don't look like you're in much shape for sprinting.'

She nodded to Melvin, who flipped on the spotlight and shone the beam directly into Byron's eyes.

'Forty seconds,' she said, gesturing to the long ridge of dunes stretching like the spine of a sleeping dragon along the beach. 'Who knows, we may never find you, and you get to live. Either way it's the best option you've got right now. A forty-second head start.'

Byron looked at Bobbie, hoping to find some trace of humanity in her eyes; there was none. She may as well have been wearing the same sunglasses she wore on the first day they met; her eyes seemed tinted with a similar darkness. His options, he figured, were as limited as they came, but maybe there was a chink in Bobbie's armour, a gap where some light could penetrate.

'You and me, we're the same.'

'Really?' she said, with a slight cock of her head.

'We both want justice. It's all I've ever wanted. You, forcing the RAF to release the truth behind Operation Vanguard – it's the same, can't you see that? We're on the same side, Bobbie, we want the same thing, it's just our methods are different, that's all.'

Bobbie studied his face for a moment: a moment when Byron thought a glimmer of light might have snuck in. He was wrong; no light was strong enough to penetrate that darkness. Bobbie was a black hole, a place where energy came to die and, alongside it, hope.

'I can see how you might think that. But the difference is you haven't lost everything that mattered to you. So no, this is not an even playing field. I have nothing left to lose; you, however, do.'

'I know the truth,' Byron lied. 'What really happened that day. Let me go and I'll show it to you, all of it.'

Bobbie stepped back. 'I wish I could believe you, Byron.' She checked her watch and began to count.

Her voice was like the boom of a starting pistol. Byron looked quickly around him, then ran. As he stumbled through the wet sand, heading towards the dunes, Bobbie Matthews' voice was thick and precise, counting down to Byron's fate.

'Thirty-nine. Thirty-eight. Thirty-seven…'

Chapter 69

There was something about skirting so close to death that made every nerve in his body pulse with life. The irony wasn't lost on Byron Gates as he scrambled over the marram grass sprouting from the sand dunes. He could shelter there for a few minutes before the cruel shaft of the spotlight caught him, compelling him to run across the no man's land that led to the next sheltering point.

They were gaining fast, footsteps crushing the undergrowth beneath them, every splintering twig seeming to echo closer, then closer still. His breathing was laboured, his lungs squeezed of air. Bobbie was right, he was in no condition to run, not for this long and this fast. His body, never a loyal friend, was failing him just when he needed it most; needed it to keep him in motion, keep him alive.

He scrambled up the dune on his hands and knees. Grains of sand burrowed like ants under his fingernails. With one final wrench on a stub of marram grass he made it to the peak, lay face-down across the sand and took a moment to regulate his breathing, which seemed like swallowing razor blades as he took in the morning air.

The top of the dune gave him a good vantage point to scour the landscape. The light was changing fast, sunlight falling across the terrain in uneven shafts through the low foliage of cloud. The dull greens and browns of the terrain were awash in a glow of orange, making it harder to discern shapes, especially any human forms stalking over the undergrowth. For a moment, he imagined that maybe they'd given up on the chase, would let him live.

It was the second error of judgement concerning Bobbie Matthews that Byron had made that morning.

He turned to face the open sea as the sun struck down on the ocean's broad shoulders in stark white rays. If he ran fast enough, dug deep into that reserve of fuel, he could make it to the ocean. He'd always been a strong swimmer, maybe he could swim along the coastline, drift far from the beach to some hidden cove. What was it that Bobbie had said? A head start? A chance to live?

He rolled down the dune, sand grains filling his eyes. At the beach level, the ground was damp but solid. He stood, rubbed the back of a hand across his eyes.

As he looked out to the ocean, contemplating the hundred-metre hinterland between him and the water, a thought occurred to him; he would have liked to have tried windsurfing. It seemed the kind of pastime that compelled you to go with the flow, surrender to the forces of nature. All his life it seemed he'd been doing the opposite, pushing back against forces more powerful than himself. All that resistance seemed futile now, a waste of a life. But if he could make it to the ocean, maybe he'd be rewarded with some kind of redemption, a second chance.

As he ran, his feet sinking into the sand, the sunrise burst through the clouds in a magnificent coat of orange. But that kind of beauty was not Byron's to enjoy. Not today.

His pain was sharper, more immediate than any perfect sunlit Anglesey morning, cutting through the splendour with the precision of a perfectly-aimed crossbow bolt burying itself deep into his neck.

Chapter 70

The ratcheting of the zip around Byron Gate's face was a fitting punctuation mark for the morning's events. His body had been discovered by windsurfers after they'd noticed plumes of black smoke rising from behind one of the sand dunes. By 11.00 am, Byron had been zippered into a body bag, hauled into the back of the coroner's van and driven to the morgue. Surrounding the burned-out remains of his Toyota Prius, several CSI techs in body suits were gridding the scene and combing diligently through the evidence left behind in the ash and tangled metal.

Lead CSI Ashton Bevan walked towards Manx and presented him with a clear, plastic evidence bag. 'Pretty cut and dry on cause of death,' he said. The bag contained a single blood-stained crossbow bolt. 'Did you know the victim?'

'Only by reputation.'

'One of Anglesey's most wanted?'

'Someone obviously thought so,' Manx said, looking over to the vast expanse of rolling ocean and glistening sand. Aberffraw never failed to leave a Miriam-sized hole in his gut. She'd disappeared close to the spot where they'd found Byron Gates. His mind flashed back thirty years to a day as warm as this one, the tide retreating; a girl who was there, then suddenly she wasn't.

'Bad memories, Manx?' Bevan said, his eyes scanning the inspector as if looking for clues.

Manx said nothing.

Bevan pushed a little more. 'This is where she disappeared, right? Your sister?'

Manx sensed the familiar pangs of irritation that appeared whenever Bevan was within striking distance. This was Bevan's go-to interrogation technique: throw some seemingly off-hand remark with the implication that he knew much more than he was letting on, in the hope Manx would fill in the blanks. Manx was too tired, running too low on patience to engage. He was about to walk away, talk to the techs busying around the carcass of the car when he noticed DCI Canton stumbling towards them over the uneven terrain, his forehead already glistening with sweat.

'Morning, Bevan,' Canton said, wiping a handkerchief across his brow. 'Busy enough summer for you lot?'

Bevan exacted a thin, forced smile. 'I'd best be off,' he said. 'Idle hands and all that.'

'Before you leave, any luck on that familial DNA we requested, what was it, three days ago now?' Manx asked.

Bevan pursed his lips. 'I understand you're under an immense amount of pressure, Manx, what with that kidnapping and all these fires and still no results to speak of, but—'

'Simple question, Bevan. Do you have the results or not?' Manx interrupted, sensing his fists clench under their own will.

Canton noticed and put a hand on Manx's arm. 'Easy,' he said. 'We're all on the same side here, isn't that right, Bevan?'

Bevan squinted, as if debating the veracity of Canton's remark. 'Should have something for you tomorrow.'

'Fair enough,' Canton said. 'Right, Manx?'

'Am or pm?' Manx pressed.

'If, and when, we get a match, you'll be the first to know,' Bevan said, before turning and heading back to his van.

Canton guided Manx several metres away and spoke in a low whisper. 'I just left the hospital half an hour back.'

Manx's stomach flipped. He'd had enough bad news for one day.

'The consultants reckon she'll pull through, but it's going to be a long haul. Several months of rehab with no guarantee she'll return to duty at the end of it.'

'Vera was lucky.'

'I prefer to think someone's looking over the good ones,' Canton said, with a soft smile.

Manx debated arguing with his DCI – there was sure as hell no one watching over Miriam the day she vanished – but let Canton's remark drift off on the morning breeze.

'Any thoughts on all this?' Canton asked, waving his arm across the beach as if he were trying to wipe it clean.

Manx had thoughts, plenty of them, but none that added up to anything solid. 'We can rule out Byron Gates as the kidnapper.'

'Which leaves us with no prime suspect.'

'He was never top of my list.'

'Tell me you do have someone you're looking into, Manx?' Canton said, with an edge of concern.

'Bobbie Matthews. This all leads back to Operation Vanguard and her husband's death.'

'And the attack on Vera?'

'It's connected, but Bobbie Matthews can't be working alone. Friends, family; who the hell knows? She's somewhere here on the island; someone's providing her refuge.'

'What about that familial DNA?'

'It's a long shot. Even if the database throws up a connection it could take weeks to comb through all the relatives.'

'We don't have weeks, Manx. We've got a few days at best.'

'Four,' Manx confirmed.

'Then you're putting a lot of faith in Bevan turning up something with that DNA match. You hopeful he'll deliver?'

'If it's what you want to hear, Ellis, yes I'm hopeful we'll find a match. Feel better now?'

Canton shook his head. 'Not remotely.'

'No, me neither,' Manx said, and trudged away past the smouldering wreckage of Byron Gates' car.

PART III

KILL SHOT

Chapter 71

Police work, or 'coppering' as Manx often called it, frequently threw up days like this. It wasn't like the movies or TV police dramas where the clues came in neatly, perfectly timed sequences. Real coppering was far more unpredictable and looser around the edges. Days like this, when the investigation hit a dead end, when the evidence trickled in or stopped completely, when promising leads fizzled to nothing (though he noticed the hotline received plenty of calls proffering theories on the demise of the dead starlings), those were the days that tested your mettle not only as a police officer but also as a human being. The frustration and long hours were by now etched deep into the faces of the investigation team. Manx likened it to having all the pieces of a jigsaw puzzle but with no reference picture to help figure out where the pieces belonged.

Long days were punctuated by pub lunches scarfed quickly, errands run to pass the time in the hope distraction might trigger some new insight; it hadn't. Manx had taken several trips to Benllech beach just to walk the scene, had come back with nothing but a headache from the sun's reflection beating off the ocean.

He'd taken the opportunity to visit the chemist and drop off the film he'd found at his mother's house. The young girl behind the counter had looked at the roll as if it were a curious museum piece and told him to come back in two weeks. *Those were the days*, he thought as he headed back to the station.

The team continued to comb through the evidence in the Meibion Glyndŵr cases looking for connections and any glaring red flags. There were none; at least none that were obvious. They'd tracked down three of the original members still living on Anglesey and brought them in for questioning. They all had solid alibis for the nights of each of the holiday home fires and the evening Collins was taken hostage. The remainder were either deceased or had left the island decades ago.

Manx considered petitioning for a warrant to search RAF Valley, but that required permission from the MoD, which he was unlikely to secure. He'd even contemplated turning up at the base without an appointment, but imagined he'd be turned away at the checkpoint with nothing to show for it but a wasted couple of hours and several gallons of petrol drained to fumes. His discussion with his DCI had been equally fruitless. Canton reminded him that 'being an arrogant prick' wasn't sufficient evidence for a warrant. A fair point. Flynt had died off base and Manx's team had interviewed, twice, all the personnel the commander had given them access to. Boyd was under no obligation to furnish them with any further information.

Manx had spent the last two evenings sitting on the patio of the Pilot Inn until it became too cold, then headed inside for a nightcap, followed by several more malt-coloured nightcaps back home, accompanied by his John Prine playlist; it was always John Prine when an investigation took this kind of downturn. Prine's lyrics had always cut to the quick, were more like mini movies than they were songs. Manx was hoping he might be blessed with a similar clarity, a flash of incisor-like insight. It hadn't happened.

The one bright spot was the call he'd received from Tammy. She'd wanted to talk about Bobbie. It was past closing time and Manx suspected she might have been a little tipsy. *Pot, kettle, black*, he'd thought as he put her on speakerphone and poured another drink of his own. Tammy hadn't given him much more information than he already knew, but the desecration of Bobbie's husband's grave was news to him. She'd also related the story of having to sneak Bobbie into the house on the evening of her seventeenth birthday, worse for wear after downing one too many rum and blacks. It was the only time she'd ever seen Bobbie drunk. 'I liked Bobbie like that,' she said. 'She should have been drunk more often.'

He figured Tammy had wanted to talk, and he was happy to let her do so.

'You're a good listener,' Tammy had said, some hours later.

'For a copper?' Manx had replied.

'For a copper,' she'd agreed, before hanging up.

As Manx walked into the incident room the following day, the smell of sweat, cheap cologne and desperation hit him fat in the face. Five additional constables had been recruited, along with several community support officers who were given administrative tasks and were expected to keep the core investigation team fed and watered. When he received a call from Ashton Bevan requesting a meeting at the Bull's Head, Manx would have typically told Bevan to get off his arse and drive over to the station, but after a morning trawling through the same evidence for what felt like the hundredth time, he was ready to blow off the cobwebs.

'You look like something my cat threw up,' Bevan said, as Manx pulled up a stool next to him at the bar.

'You're a born charmer. Did you get a match on my DNA?'

Bevan took a sharp sip of his lager shandy. 'Can't rush these things. I'm not about to put my reputation on the line for you, no matter how desperate your investigation.'

Manx ordered a pint of the local cask ale. 'If this is another quid pro bloody quo tactic, I should warn you I'm running on three hours' sleep, a headache that could down a horse and an itch to punch a hole in the nearest wall. Just so you know.'

'Got it,' Bevan said. 'I'll cut to the chase. The DNA from the blood found on the slip at Menai Bridge threw up an interesting match.' He took a piece of paper from his jacket pocket and laid out the DNA analysis. 'A familial match to someone already in the database, very probably a close relative.'

'And?' Manx asked, taking a gulp of beer.

'One Dafydd Merion Powell. Sentenced to four years for arson on a holiday home near Trearddur Bay back in the early eighties.'

Manx took the paper in his hand. 'Bit early in the decade to be collecting DNA samples, wasn't it?'

Bevan smiled, pulled, like a magician from a hat, a plastic evidence bag, inside a black leather glove. 'Thanks to some stellar work from my team, we located a splinter of fingernail in the right index finger cavity. Normally, the hard cuticle contains little useable DNA, but today must be your lucky day, Manx.'

'I'll head off to the bookies, then, wager a tenner on a hundred-to-one outsider while you get to the bloody point.'

Bevan pursed his lips and continued. 'There was still some soft tissue attached to the nail, along with several spots of dry blood on the inside of the glove. Best guess, he tore off his fingernail on a wall or barbed wire, put on his gloves to protect the finger then dumped them soon afterwards, the nail still inside. When we ran the DNA through the database, it threw up a match. This Dafydd Powell character was involved in an altercation—'

'Altercation?' Manx interrupted, taking a long sip. 'What's that a euphemism for these days?'

'Aggravated assault. He sent some unlucky bugger to the A&E with a ruptured eardrum and a serious mandibular fracture; broken jawbone to you, Manx.'

Manx let the insult roll off his back, this time. Bevan had delivered him the first glimmer of light in a case that had had him stumbling around in the darkness for days.

'The victim refused to press charges, no doubt scared he'd come back to finish the job, but Powell was required to provide a DNA sample, hence the match.'

'So, the DNA from the slip is a relative of Dafydd Powell?'

'Yes, but don't go hanging out the bunting just yet. This is familial DNA. I did some cursory research and it seems the Powell family bred like Catholics.'

'Bred like Catholics? Christ, don't go surrendering your seat at the peace talks just yet, eh?'

Bevan ignored the barb and continued. 'It would take some time to trim down the whole family tree, time that I suspect you don't have.'

Manx quickly downed the remainder of his pint. 'Then we go directly to the source,' he said, picking up the bag and resting his empty glass on the bar.

Bevan laughed. 'You think a convicted criminal is about to surrender one of his own family to the police force who got him four years jail time? Good luck with that.'

'All I need is a little luck, Bevan. The rest I can handle.'

Chapter 72

Ronnie Powell had perfected the art of sulking; could have won a gold medal for it if it were an Olympic sport. He'd spent the day riding his quad bike across the fields, determined to put as much space as possible between himself and Bobbie who'd moved into the spare room in Melvin's cottage: his cottage. He couldn't bring himself to call her Mel's daughter – he would have choked on the words. But it was nothing compared to the anger he felt at Mel's betrayal. *Cancer? Terminal?* He couldn't shake the weight of those words. They were terrifying. There was only one other word that followed those, and that was *death*.

Cancer. Terminal. Death.

He came to a sharp stop at the peak of a hill and cut the engine. Why hadn't Mel told him himself? Why confide in her and not him? He lit a joint and looked over the fields. It reminded him of the days he and Mel would greet the dawn together after a night's lamping. Two men against nature, relying on some primal instinct that was strong in them both; a bonding as powerful as father and son; stronger because Mel had chosen him, chosen to raise Ronnie as his own. All that was good as gone now, what with Bobbie on the scene and Mel's diagnosis. He still couldn't comprehend it. His uncle was a bull; stronger than anyone he knew, could down any man he wanted with a single punch. How could energy and power be snuffed out so easily, laid to rest? But he'd witnessed the very same last night, Mel's strength flooding out of him as he coughed blood into his handkerchief.

He wiped the sleeve of his camouflage jacket across his eyes, looked down at the damp spots on the fabric. Tears? The last time he cried was that afternoon when Mel rescued him from the beating Dafydd Powell was inflicting on his son. Ronnie had made a promise to himself that night, one that he'd kept ever since. He wouldn't give anyone the satisfaction of making him cry; not ever again. His father would have been proud, he thought; proud that his fists had done their intended work.

As he felt the tears sting the back of his eyes, he let them drip like raindrops onto his jacket. If his father could see him now, he'd laugh at him, give him the beating he deserved. But maybe he could do that himself, take away the pain.

He clenched his fists, raised his arms, began pummelling his forehead until his head swam and ghostly orbs floated in front of his eyes.

The pain felt good, though, felt it was what he deserved. An old familiar friend come back to visit.

Chapter 73

Dafydd Powell was a rough sort, hewn like a tree trunk, his face wizened like old bark. His face bore the scars of blows that had found their target once too often. At ten that morning, he either reeked of the scotch from the night before, or the chaser he'd had with this morning's coffee, Manx couldn't decide.

'I'm innocent,' Dafydd said, slotting a cartridge into his Beretta S686 twelve-gauge. The gun had seen better days; the wooden barrel was chipped, the chrome receiver scratched. He raised the sight, aiming at a paint can at the bottom of the garden. He drew back the trigger. The can ricocheted off the wall with a dull metallic thud.

'I haven't accused you of anything,' Manx countered.

'Not yet you haven't.' Dafydd dropped the gun to his waist and unlocked the barrel. 'Been a pillar of the community since I moved out here,' he said, gesturing to the miles of wilderness stretching out from his back garden to the foot of the Snowdonia mountain range. 'Don't get into any trouble.'

'Don't expect there's much trouble to get into,' Manx said, scanning the rolling green fields and craggy outcrops of slate, which even in the heat of a summer afternoon held on to a cold and inhospitable chill.

'Why the house call?' Dafydd asked. 'The shotgun's legit. You can ask the missus.' Dafydd had a defensive way of talking, as if he were trying to pre-empt any questions about to be hurled his way.

Manx decided on the direct approach. 'Meibion Glyndŵr,' he said, allowing the words to hang for a few seconds.

Dafydd settled the shotgun on the table next to him. 'Another bloody lifetime.'

'Was it?'

'I served my time, no more to be said.'

'No stirrings of the old patriotism, Dafydd? One last fight for the great cause? What did they call it at the time? Wales Rising?'

Dafydd stabbed his finger at Manx. 'Oh, I get,' he said, nodding. 'The answer's no fucking way. I haven't been back to the island for years. You're wasting your time, mate.'

Manx took the plastic evidence bag from his pocket. 'Recognise this?'

'A glove? Christ, you lot must be desperate.'

'Your glove,' Manx said, laying the bag on the table.

'Never seen it before.'

'It's evidence from that holiday home fire you were convicted of in Trearddur Bay.'

'Like I said, mate, I'm a reformed character.'

'No doubt, except for that aggravated assault charge two years ago. Where was it again? Caernarvon?'

'The bloke made it all up, dropped the charges.'

'But you provided a DNA sample.'

'Had no choice, did I?' Dafydd said, his fists bunching. 'Look, are you getting to the bloody point anytime soon?'

'All right, Dafydd, let's do that,' Manx said, poking the evidence bag. 'Your DNA, which we obtained from the soft nail tissue inside this glove was a match to the sample you provided at the Caernarvon police station.'

'So what? Can't be convicted of a crime twice now, can I?'

'But here's the thing, Dafydd. We found further DNA evidence at a more recent crime scene on Anglesey.'

'Well, that won't be mine. Unless you lot planted it.'

'It belongs to a relative of yours. A very good match according to forensics. I need to know who that relative is, Dafydd. Problem is, you've got a big family. It's going to take us a while to interview the whole clan, time we don't have.'

'Oh, takes the biscuit, that does. You, coming up here asking me to snitch on my own family.'

'Expedient, that's all. Cards on the table, anybody spring to mind?'

Dafydd stroked his chin in a mock-thoughtful manner. 'My old gran,' he said. 'Bit of a hell-raiser in her time, she was. Ninety-three now, mind you. Lives over in the old people's home in Menai Bridge. Got her number inside if you want it.'

Manx reached down and picked up Dafydd's shotgun. 'Nice piece, looks vintage.'

'She's a few years old, aye.'

'So, how long was it you served at her majesty's pleasure?'

'Four years. They let me out after three for good behaviour. But you already know that.'

'Can't get much past you, Dafydd,' Manx said, turning the shotgun in his palm. 'Now here's another question. How did you obtain the licence for this?'

'Applied for it, like anyone else,' he said, tugging at the front of his T-shirt.

'That right?' Manx said, laying the shotgun back on the table. 'As far as I recall, and I might be wrong as I'm a little rusty on the details, but Section 21 of the 1968 Firearms Act prohibits anyone from owning a firearm if they served a sentence longer than three years. Are you aware of that?'

Dafydd jerked his shoulders back.

'Wouldn't take more than a phone call,' Manx said. 'Have an officer come over, confirm you obtained that licence under false pretences; if you even have a licence. That's another jail sentence, maybe a big fine to go with it. So, what do you say, Dafydd? One name and I'll be out of your hair.'

'You coppers are all the same,' he said, slamming two shotgun casings on the table. 'Fucking bastards, the lot of you.'

'I've been called worse, and from people a lot scarier than you. Now, give me a name, Dafydd, one name and you can keep shooting tin cans off a wall until the cows come home.'

Dafydd bit his lower lip, raised his finger to his left eye which Manx had just noticed didn't move in its socket, as if it were stuck in a single focal plane. 'Twenty per cent vision,' he said, gritting his teeth. 'Doctor reckons I'll be blind in five years.'

'What's that got—' Manx began, before Dafydd interrupted.

'Fuckin' family,' Dafydd said. 'Tough love they call it, yeah?'

'Who, Dafydd?' Manx said, sensing he had Dafydd on the back foot, and was about to leave himself wide open.

'My brother,' he said, spitting on the floor.

'You had a falling out?'

'You're a sharp one.'

'Name?'

Dafydd clenched his fists. 'Melvin. Melvin Powell.'

'Address?' Manx asked.

'No idea. Haven't spoken to him for over twenty years.'

'It's a start,' Manx said, turning to leave.

'Oy!' Dafydd called out as Manx walked towards his car. 'If you find him…,' he began.

'He doesn't need to know it was you,' Manx said.

'I don't give a fuck, tell him if you want. I've waited long enough to get payback for what he did.'

'Then what?'

'If he's got a lad there with him – he'd be in his twenties by now – go easy on him, eh?' Dafydd slipped two fresh cartridges into the barrel. 'Melvin likes to be top dog, has to be in control. God knows what the hell he's turned that boy into by now.'

Dafydd turned away, brought the shotgun to his good eye and fired at some phantom target deep in the countryside. The shot ricocheted like the resonant toll of a bell echoing off the thick slate mountains.

Chapter 74

Ronnie watched Bobbie from the old, battered armchair in the corner of the kitchen. He hadn't spoken to her yet, at least not properly, other than a grunt or mumble when he passed her in the hallway or waited for her to get the hell out of the bathroom so he could take a shit.

For the past hour she'd been assembling a quadcopter drone, the sort Ronnie had seen on YouTube. As she slipped the propellers from their protective cover and laid them carefully on the table Bobbie spoke. 'Are you going to sit there watching?' she asked, directing her focus to attaching the propellers to the four motors positioned at each corner of the rig. 'Or are you going to help?'

Ronnie shrugged. 'Suppose I could,' he said, looking around as if he expected someone to chide him for offering. He put down the strip of wood he'd been whittling and joined her.

'Hold on to the main body while I attach the pushers.'

Ronnie did as he was asked while Bobbie reached for the smaller propellers and secured them at opposite corners of the drone.

'DJI Inspire Quadcopter,' she said, noticing Ronnie's interest in the packaging.

'Yeah, I can read,' Ronnie mumbled.

'Commercial grade,' Bobbie continued. 'Twenty-seven-minute flying time, dual-frequency signalling, maximum speed fifty-eight miles per hour, four rotors, auxiliary battery pack and capable of carrying several pounds of extra weight.'

'That meant to impress me or something?' Ronnie said. 'Just a big bloody toy, isn't it? Uncle Mel won't be happy you're wasting time playing around.'

Bobbie leaned over and tightened the final screws on the landing gear. 'You're close with Mel, right?' she asked.

Ronnie sniffed, ran the back of his hand under his nose. 'Brought me up like I was his own.'

'Must have been nice,' Bobbie said, double-checking all the components were secure. 'Was he a good dad?'

'Better than my own, but he was a right fucking bastard, so I don't have much to compare, really.'

Bobbie nodded, grabbed the drone around its belly and lifted it so the sunlight streaming in from the window reflected off the silver casing. 'Ever flown one of these, Ronnie?'

'Nah. Seen them on the internet, like.'

'Come with me,' she said, heading towards the front door. 'Let's get you in the pilot's seat.'

It took Ronnie around twenty minutes to get the hang of keeping the drone airborne and landing without crashing. Bobbie had taught him the basics; how to focus on the navigation screen streaming the live video while at the same time directing the drone's flight path and pitch with the buttons and small joystick on the slave controller.

'Just like a video game, this is,' he said, unable to resist a smile as he manoeuvred the quadcopter several hundred feet skywards, then swooped it down low over the outbuildings and the old stable.

'The military ones aren't so different,' she said, looking up.

'Yeah? You flown them, like?'

'I was an unmanned aircraft pilot,' she said. 'Flight Lieutenant in the RAF.'

'Why did you leave, then? Cool job like that.'

'Long story.'

Ronnie looked down at a red flashing alert on the screen. 'What's it doing?'

She looked over. 'The battery's about to run out.'

'Should I land it?'

'No need,' Bobbie confirmed. 'It senses when it's low on power and returns to its base location before it runs out. Take your fingers off the buttons and watch.'

Ronnie watched nervously as the quadcopter descended, carving a slow, graceful path back to him before landing itself softly at his feet, the propellers coming to a gradual stop.

'Brilliant, that is,' he said, squatting as if he were about to pet the drone like a good dog for returning to its master.

'Few more hours of flying time and you'll be fully prepared.'

'Prepared? Prepared for what?'

Bobbie picked up the drone and flipped it belly side up. 'The insurgents we attacked with our Reaper drones,' she said, removing the ancillary battery pack from its housing. 'They eventually took to giving us a dose of our own medicine. All they needed was a drone, a strong phone signal and a forty-millimetre grenade stuffed into a small plastic bottle. They'd fly them as close to the target as they could, usually an allied convoy or small military base, and drop the grenades from as low as they dared to fly. The damage was never that significant, but that wasn't the point. Their goal was to spread fear, keep their enemy guessing. When you think about it, that's the true definition of terror, isn't it, Ronnie? You never allow your enemy to relax, not for a second.'

'Couldn't you just shoot them down?'

'Good question,' she said, screwing the cover back on the battery housing. 'They could, but there was always the possibility of civilians being caught in the explosion. Eventually, we developed drone hunters; guns that fired out nets to drag the drones someplace safe before destroying them.'

'Makes sense, I suppose,' Ronnie said, shrugging. He fidgeted with the controller, flicking the thin joystick with his thumb. 'So, why are you telling me all this?'

'It's obvious Mel is in no condition to partake in a plan requiring this level of focus.' She looked Ronnie directly in the eyes. 'But you, Ronnie, you're a natural. All those video games you've been playing? You can finally put those skills to good use.'

'Is this to do with Logan Collins?' he asked.

'A large, unambiguous statement is required. The RAF has chosen to hide certain truths. They need encouragement to release that truth into the light. Do you understand?'

'Aye, maybe,' he said.

Bobbie placed a hand on Ronnie's shoulder. 'I know this has all been a shock to you; me, Mel's cancer, it's a lot to take in. But you can do this. You might not like me much, Ronnie, and we can work on that, but that doesn't mean we can't work together to make your uncle proud. I hate to say this, but it might be the last chance you get to make that happen.'

Ronnie thought for a moment, took in everything Bobbie was telling him. Maybe Bobbie was right, this was the way to make Mel proud, pay him back for all he'd done for him.

Bobbie smiled. 'I'm leaving this in your charge now, Ronnie,' she said, handing him the drone. 'Keep it somewhere safe, not here. When I'm done, I'll give you the package it's going to be carrying. Are you ready for this, Ronnie? Can I count on you?'

Ronnie looked down at the quadcopter and nodded.

'No, Ronnie,' Bobbie said. 'Tell me in words that you are ready and willing to carry out your mission.'

Ronnie looked up. 'Ready?' he said. 'I was born fucking ready.'

Chapter 75

Manx attached the Google earth photograph to the incident board. 'Tŷ Gwyn, cottage in Church Bay, home address of Melvin Powell. One of three Melvin Powells on the island, the only one related to Dafydd Powell.'

DS Nader huffed and threw his copy of Melvin's briefing document on the desk. 'No priors, no link to Meibion Glyndŵr. You sure he's our man?'

'Maybe he was never caught,' PC Morris said. 'Got lucky.'

'Lucky or not, here's what we do know,' Manx said. 'Dafydd Powell was an active member of Meibion Glyndŵr from '81 to '87. He served a four-year sentence in Wrexham prison for burning down a home in Trearddur Bay in 1987. On his release, he moved a few miles outside Llanberis, where, he assured me, he's lived the life of a hermit ever since.'

'So he says, yeah?' Nader snarled.

'Powell senior is not our man,' Manx said, pinning a photograph of Melvin on the board; a low-resolution portrait taken several years back for the 'About Us' page on the Mel's Paint and Plaster website. 'Our person of interest is his younger brother, Melvin Powell. According to the reports, back when people actually read newspapers, Melvin was your regular teenage troubled child until he found his salvation in boxing.'

Manx pinned up another photograph; an old black and white print of Melvin, gloved fists raised high, scowling at the camera, eyebrows raised, one side of his mouth curled into a menacing snarl, and the headline *the Great Welsh Hope* running across the lower third of the frame.

'Unfortunately for Melvin, that career path ended at the age of twenty-two when his motorbike lost an argument with a tractor reversing into the main road. A year later, he set up Mel's Paint and Plaster, which he's been running ever since. Now, let's play out this Powell family drama for a minute. Melvin's twenty-two years old, all his dreams just crashed and burned into the rear end of a Massey Ferguson. He's angry, pissed off. Boxers at Melvin's level don't just lose that fighting instinct. He needs to find another outlet for that energy and I'm betting house painting's not going to cut it.'

'He joined Meibion Glyndŵr!' Morris said.

'It's highly probable Dafydd Powell recruited his younger brother. Melvin's young, idealistic, and more importantly he wants to prove that he's still got it, that he's still the 'Great Welsh Hope'. As Morris pointed out, it was probably dumb luck that he was never caught, but he'd have learned the best way to start a fire and how to leg it out of there without being caught.'

Manx continued. 'Take a close look at the house,' Manx said, pointing at the aerial photograph. 'Two miles off the nearest main road, hidden behind a copse of oak trees, several outbuildings'

'That's where they're holding Collins!' Morris interrupted.

'Bloody hell!' Priddle said. 'We've found him.'

'Don't go planning the celebration beers just yet. It's a good lead, but as of now it's still unconfirmed.'

'So, what's the plan?' Nader asked.

'We probably have three people hiding out in that house. Melvin Powell, Bobbie Matthews and an unidentified male, the one captured on the CCTV from the slip at Menai Bridge. We'll enter the property three hours from now. No sirens, no flashing lights, no helicopters. We don't extend them the courtesy of an early warning. The authorised firearms officers will do the door breaking and general scaring the holy crap out of the occupants; we'll follow behind and make the arrests. We'll position several officers around the perimeter of the property, including the back door, side entrance and outbuildings. The only way anyone's getting out of that house is in the back of one of our armed response vehicles.'

As Manx gave the team the remainder of the itinerary, the incident room door swung open. 'Someone to see you, boss,' the desk sergeant said, standing in the doorway.

Manx looked up. 'Is it important?'

'Bloke reckons so. Works over at the RAF base.'

Chapter 76

Andrew Pierce slid the folder across the interview room desk. 'What Bobbie Matthews is demanding,' he said, sitting back.

Manx slipped out the paperwork and read the headline: *Operation Vanguard, Top Secret*. 'How did you get this?'

'It's not important. What is important is that Bobbie sees this and that you don't tell anyone how you got your hands on it. Not ever.'

'How long have you been holding on to vital evidence, Mr Pierce?'

He shrugged. 'I didn't know what to do. If I took this to the press, then I may as well paint a big target on my back. I thought this was the safest option.'

'You're risking a lot for a patient.'

'Bobbie's more than a patient,' Pierce said, blushing slightly. 'She's a friend, a good friend, and she deserves to know the truth.'

'And the truth sets us free?' Manx said.

Pierce leaned back, steepled his hands. 'Let us not love with words or speech but with actions and in truth.'

Manx failed in his attempt to resist a heavy sigh. 'Are you sure you don't know where Bobbie Matthews is hiding? You two seem close and you obviously risked a lot to obtain this classified information.'

'If I knew, I'd tell you. Don't you think I'd have taken this straight to her so she could stop all this. I only ever wanted to help her. I'm not stupid, I know what can happen, she'll spend most of her life locked away for what she's done. But she deserves to know the truth.'

Manx thought. The man seemed genuine enough, his reasoning

plausible, but still there was something about him, something that Manx couldn't put his finger on.

'She's your patient. How likely is she to go through with her threat to kill Collins?'

Pierce thought for a moment. 'Honestly, it makes no sense. Her trauma is directly related to the death of her husband and her obsession with getting to the truth of Operation Vanguard, which, when you read the report, you'll see she was right to pursue. It's the RAF she's angry with, not some local politician.'

'So why threaten him?'

'Her judgement may be clouded. Trauma can severely damage the mind, rational thinking takes a back seat.'

'Isn't it your job to treat that kind of thing?'

Pierce flinched. 'These things take time. James Flynt was impatient to have her shipped off to one of our veterans' hospitals. She should have stayed with me; I could have helped her. Read the report,' Pierce said, standing. 'But you'll never be able to tell anyone what you've read. It's a burden you'll have to live with.'

'Any other words of wisdom? More evidence you haven't told me about?'

Pierce thought for a moment. Manx guessed he was debating whether to keep talking or not.

'One thing,' Pierce said. 'It's probably nothing, but I noticed something was missing from my office.'

'What thing?'

'My clerical garments. I always hang them behind my door. I think maybe Bobbie saw me enter the keypad code and remembered the number. I should have changed it, but I didn't imagine…'

'Seems like a strange thing to take. Did she have a religious conversion or something? A come to Jesus moment?'

Pierce shrugged. 'We can but hope. Anyway, I thought you should know.'

Manx looked at the folder in his hand. 'No plans to leave the island any time soon?'

Pierce shook his head.

'Keep it that way,' Manx said.

'And the report?'

Manx felt its weight in his palm. 'Leave it with me,' he said.

After Pierce left, Manx took his time. He read the report three times to make sure all the details had sunk in. Pierce was right; he couldn't show this to anyone. The consequences would be too great; way above Manx's pay grade.

In a way, he wished he hadn't read it. If they did find Bobbie before the deadline, could he even hand it over? And if he did, what would be the repercussions for him? For Pierce? If Bobbie didn't read it before the deadline, the consequences could be equally dire.

Devil. Deep blue sea, he thought. *Manx caught somewhere in between.*

Chapter 77

Bobbie, by now, had learned to trust her instincts. They'd been honed over the years, sharpened and battle-ready, like a constant surge of electricity to be accessed at will.

As she stepped from the cottage for some air, she was overcome by a sensation similar to that she'd felt on the day she'd entered the ground control station for the last time. She should have trusted her instincts that day. Tonight, she wouldn't make the same mistake.

She looked to the sky. The moon, a half-opened eyelid, seemed to be watching her. Speckled around the moon, the clusters of stars were like peepholes where more eyes were watching. Somewhere in the highest branches of the oak trees, the hollow call of an owl. Behind her the restless rustle of a fox or badger burrowing through the nearby hedges. A light wind scattered a litter of leaves along the driveway, then settled again as if it were just in rehearsals for its main performance at some later date.

There was something else out there, too. This wasn't the nocturnal clock awakening the night's predators, it was man-made, not nature born. There were eyes all over her, she could sense them.

Three hundred metres to her right, something caught her attention. Not a sound, more of a glint, like the soft glow from a mobile phone screen high in the trees. Or maybe it wasn't in the trees at all. She traced her eyeline across the canopy of branches. As the light extinguished, she concluded it came from the top of one of the poles carrying electricity into the cottage. Whatever the source of the light was, it was nothing natural, that was for sure. And every instinct told her it was coming for her.

Chapter 78

'We're leaving,' Bobbie said, running back into the cottage, gathering up all her clothes and throwing them into her kitbag.

'Leaving? Where to?' Melvin asked, groggily. He'd been dozing for the past hour, his reactions slurred and blunted by fitful sleep and alcohol. They'd all decided that Mel's cottage was the safest place for the next few days, and besides, Lydia had thrown Melvin out on his ear the night he'd confessed. Bobbie had made a point of visiting Lydia the following day. It was just a precaution; a reminder of the consequences of blabbing her mouth to anyone, especially the police.

'Someone's out there,' Bobbie said, slipping her arms through her jacket sleeves. She reached into the pockets, took out her black beanie hat, pulling it tight over her head. 'We need to move, now.'

'Paranoid, you are,' Ronnie said, turning his attention away from the TV; another one of those reality shows that was pretty far removed from any reality Ronnie had ever encountered. 'We're in the middle of nowhere, there's always something out there this time of night. It's nature, yeah?'

'No, you don't understand,' Bobbie said, throwing Ronnie the hoodie he'd left dangling on the kitchen chair. 'We're leaving, now. Someone's out there.'

'What do you mean, someone?' Melvin asked, looking through the window into the thick darkness. 'Looks clear to me.'

'Trust me,' Bobbie urged. 'I saw a light, something.'

'Probably lampers,' Ronnie said, increasing the volume on the television as the presenter revealed the unlucky contestant leaving tonight's show. 'Bastards hunting on our patch.'

'Too early for lampers,' Melvin said, an edge of concern in his voice. 'Not much to kill this time of—'

Melvin's sentence remained unfinished.

It was punctuated by the clatter of fifteen kilograms of steel pummelled against wood. Mel span around. The front door buckled as the steel enforcer made easy work of the frame. That was followed by a loud voice instructing them to fall to the floor, hands on heads, eyes closed, any weapons dropped and shoved towards the door.

Before they could comply, the house was plunged into darkness.

Bobbie and Ronnie fell to the floor and crawled towards the back door. Melvin's reactions were running slower. He put it down to the five cans of beer he'd drunk earlier, and maybe the cancer. Yeah, he'd blame whatever happened next on the cancer.

Chapter 79

Ronnie followed Bobbie's lead, scuttling along the floor. A bright strobe of light, pouring from a torch, skimmed the kitchen window like a searchlight.

'Is there another way out?' Bobbie asked.

Outside, the commotion was building. The anxious barks of dogs, the scent of prey heavy in their nostrils.

'Yeah,' he said. 'Up the back stairs. The window opens to the old stable roof. We run across, jump down on the other side.'

'You're sure?'

'Did it all the time when I was younger. Piece of piss.'

Bobbie weighed up her limited options, then agreed.

They rose from the floor, crouched low like panthers, and ran. Ronnie stopped at the foot of the stairs. 'Mel? Where's Uncle Mel?'

'I thought he was behind you.'

'We can't leave him.'

Bobbie debated. Going back was a suicide mission. She knew it, Ronnie knew it. Not that it made the decision any easier.

'Mel will be fine,' she said.

'But—'

'Ronnie!' Bobbie snapped. 'Mel can look after himself, he's probably found another way out. Now, come on, let's go.'

Ronnie hesitated, debated with himself. *Yeah, Mel has probably got out already*. He'd see him when this was all over. He was a hundred per cent sure of it. Maybe ninety per cent. Maybe a little less.

Chapter 80

Melvin Powell had never considered himself the sacrificial type. He was barely religious: what with having his dreams crushed at the age of twenty-two, then forty years later having his life cut short by cancer, and with nothing to show for the years in between, it tended to blunt belief in any kind of god.

All Mel had really understood was fighting. In the ring there was no grey area. You fought to win, and to win you had to surrender to your instincts. In a fight, he'd have a split second to predict the punch his opponent was about to unleash, where it would land and how to defend against it. He'd been good at that. On his best days, he could almost see his opponent's glove move in slow motion, catch the tell in his eyes that signalled Melvin to expect an uppercut, right hook or body blow before his opponent had decided himself.

Tonight, that kind of primal instinct was beyond him.

He heard the ominous rolling of a CS tear gas grenade scraping across the floor, then exploding in a plume of grey, foul-smelling smoke. He drew his arm across his eyes as the gas escaped, seeping under his eyelids. Seconds later, the specialised firearms officers team rushed in, bodies crouched, helmet visors pulled low.

'On the ground! Now!' The voice was loud, but somehow lost in the distance, as if it were calling Melvin from beyond the sea. His ears were ringing, noise swirling and roaring. He looked for Ronnie and Bobbie through the dense smoke. Nothing. Maybe they'd made it out. He hoped they'd made it out.

As one of the men moved closer, Mel lashed out with his fists. But the strength wasn't there, never would be again. His fist landed somewhere in the officer's upper arm, barely making an impact through the Nomex suit.

Melvin felt a strong grip on his shoulder, pushing him to his knees. He coughed, the gas stinging his eyes and seeking a way into his lungs, coiling around them like a snake.

By the time the smoke finally cleared, he had been dragged by his collar from the cottage and into the brittle night air. Around him a sea of blue lights twitched nervously. The man holding him hauled Melvin to standing, shoving him towards one of the police vehicles.

'This your man?' the AFO asked, slipping off his visor.

DI Manx took his time to study Melvin Powell. 'It's him,' he said, stepping forward. 'Logan Collins. Take us to Logan Collins.'

Mel looked up at the tall, lean copper demanding something from him he was not ready to surrender, at least not without a fight.

'Don't know what the fuck you're talking about, mate,' he said. 'And before you ask me anything else, I want a bloody solicitor.'

Chapter 81

The police dogs stalked the perimeter of the cottage, stopped in their tracks, raised their heads and barked furiously at the stable roof.

'Shit!' Bobbie muttered, looking down at the swarm of blue and white lights and the sheen of anxious fur stalking below.

Ronnie inched his way towards the far gable.

'No, Ronnie!' Bobbie grabbed his belt.

He reached into his pocket, pulled out a set of keys. 'I'll distract them, you jump down, meet me at the gate by the far field.'

Before Bobbie could protest, Ronnie had flipped himself over the guttering and was gone. A cacophony of raised voices was followed by nervy spotlights scanning the cottage walls and yard. Then, the sputter of a four-stroke engine peaking to maximum revs.

Bobbie scuffled the length of the roof, hesitated only briefly before jumping and landing in a crouched position on the grass, then made her break towards the iron gate that led to the fields beyond the cottage. Ronnie was waiting, engine ticking over, lights killed: he knew this terrain like the back of his hand.

Bobbie mustered all her strength and sprinted. Her scent caught in their nostrils, the dogs pursued her like wolves hunting their quarry, snapping in the darkness; she could almost sense their hot breath on her neck. They were close, but she'd make it.

She jumped on the back of the bike, wrapped her arms around Ronnie's waist. One of the dogs had made fast progress, teeth nipping at Bobbie's heels as she secured her feet on the footplates. 'Go. Now! Go!' she shouted.

Ronnie slammed the throttle. The tyres churned up splatters of mud as they dug into the soft ground. The dogs' barks faded into the night as they sped across the fields.

'Where?' Ronnie asked. 'Where the fuck do we go?'

Bobbie didn't hesitate. 'Lydia,' she said, brushing the hair from her eyes. 'She set us up. She needs to face the consequences.'

Chapter 82

Manx, Nader and DCI Canton observed Melvin Powell and his court-appointed solicitor through the interview room mirror. After several minutes, Melvin stood, walked to the glass, checked his reflection, and adjusted the top button on his shirt.

'Looks like the bastard's getting ready for his bloody close-up,' Nader said.

'Or preparing for his performance,' Manx said, studying Melvin's mannerisms. They were deliberate, nonchalant even, as if he were preparing to enjoy himself as tonight's main event.

'We've let him stew long enough, lads,' Canton said, checking his watch. 'And no deals without authorisation,' he warned.

'Got it.' Manx picked up his coffee mug and watched as Melvin ran a hand backwards over his hair, tightened the elastic around his ponytail and nodded in satisfaction.

'Right, Nader you're with me. Let's see what My Little Pony has to say for himself.'

Chapter 83

Bobbie shoved Lydia Jones onto the kitchen chair and leaned in close. 'We all have one big regret in life, don't we?' she said, slipping the sleek crossbow bolt from her jacket and setting it on the table. 'Something we'd like to go back and change. What do they call it, a re-do? What you did, Lydia, I suspect that will be your life's biggest regret, don't you think?'

'You know nothing about me, love, nothing,' Lydia snapped, twisting her cordless phone in her hand. She'd been trying to call Melvin for hours, must have left him twenty messages, each one more desperate than the last. But she wasn't about to put that desperation on display, not to her.

'I know you called the police, gave them our location.'

'Where's Mel?' Lydia asked, looking to the door as if she expected him to barge in and end all this. But she knew better, knew by now that knights in shining armour were in short supply for women of a certain age, if they'd ever existed at all.

'Mel had things to arrange, isn't that right?' Bobbie said.

Ronnie lifted his head from the crossbow he was spit-polishing with his sleeve. 'Yeah, he'll be here later,' he confirmed. 'Soon as.'

Lydia looked at them both. She'd been lied to often enough that she could almost smell it on people – and these two, thick as thieves, feet under her table gave off a rotten stench. She gripped the phone. 'Maybe I'll call Mel, see what he's got to say for himself.'

'Not recommended,' Bobbie said, laying the phone on the table and driving the bolt into the flimsy plastic casing.

'You ruined him,' Lydia said. 'God knows he was no angel, but you? There's something dark in you, love, dark and cold.'

'Like the grave?' Bobbie said, extracting the bolt from the innards of the phone. 'You don't like me much, do you? I suppose I'm what they call an acquired taste. Isn't that right, Ronnie?'

Ronnie nodded. 'Aye, mates now though,' he said.

'Go to hell,' Lydia snapped.

'Been there, done that.' Bobbie lifted the bolt and caressed it gently down Lydia's cheek, then placed the tip on her lips, parting them slightly. 'You alerted the police, gave them Mel's old address. Did it feel sweet on the tongue, Lydia, exacting your revenge?'

Lydia exhaled an anxious chuckle. 'I haven't known you long enough to miss you, love, so get off your bloody high horse. Don't you think the police would be here now, waiting, if I'd told them?'

'You were the only person who knew where we were. Logic concludes it must have been you.'

'I don't know how many times… it wasn't me.'

Bobbie nodded, stood, buttoned her jacket.

'Leaving, are you?' Lydia said, a tremor of relief in her voice. 'Be on your way. I don't want to see your face round here again.'

'Leaving?' Bobbie said, reaching for the rope she'd asked Ronnie to bring from the quad bike. 'I'm not the one who's leaving, Lydia.'

Chapter 84

'No. Bloody. Comment.'

Two hours into Melvin Powell's interrogation, those three words were beginning to set Manx's teeth on edge; punching into his nerves like a dentist's drill. *No. Bloody. Comment.*

'Come on, man,' DS Nader said. 'Change the bloody record, for Christ's sake.'

Melvin smiled. 'No. Fucking. Comment.'

Nader shook his head and kicked the table leg.

'I'll ask you again, Melvin,' Manx said. 'Where are you holding Logan Collins?'

Melvin shrugged, offered another cocky smile which instantly reminded Manx of Dafydd Powell – the same slight upturn to the right of his lips, like a lopsided snarl.

Manx sat back, decided on another approach. 'Do you know how we found you, Mel?'

'Yellow pages?'

'Your brother, Dafydd. Couldn't wait to shop you, some family dispute back in the day he wanted pay back for. Know anything about that?'

For the first time, he observed a small tell: a flicker of a twitch in Melvin's right eye, as if he were flinching from an incoming punch. 'Can't choose your family. Haven't seen him in years, surprised he's not dead. Thought his liver would have given up on him by now or someone put a knife in his back.' Melvin exhaled a loud cough that rattled his ribcage.

Mel's solicitor, Ffion Owens, spoke. She was in her late forties, all business, slightly overweight and had an attitude that had immediately raised Manx's hackles. 'My client requires water before answering any more of your questions, which, I don't need to remind you, you are legally obliged to provide him with.' Ffion was an old hand at this, had been on the circuit for a couple of decades representing the likes of Melvin Powell.

'No, you're right, you don't need to remind me,' Manx said, nodding towards the two-way mirror. Melvin coughed again; Manx wondered if it was all part of the act. He had his solicitor convinced, that was for sure. Manx sat back and adopted a tone a shade more compassionate. 'Mel, you don't look the picture of health. Not the Great Welsh Hope you once were, eh?' He shoved the old newspaper clippings towards Melvin. 'Are you sure we can't get you something else? A towel maybe, so you can throw it in before you fuck this up, too?'

'Fuck off. I'm not talking.'

The incident room door opened. PC Morris walked in, handed Manx a slip of paper and placed a cup of water on the table.

'Good news, at least for us,' Manx said, glancing at the paper. 'The DNA we found at the boat slip is a 99.9 per cent match to yours. Want to enlighten me as to how it got there, Mel?'

Melvin took a slow sip of water. 'What boat slip?'

'The one owned by Peter Whinstone. Ninety-seven Beaumaris Road.' Manx turned his laptop screen and played Melvin a repeat performance of the security camera footage. 'That was the same evening my detective chief superintendent was stabbed. You were less than a quarter of a mile away from where it happened.'

Melvin shook his head. 'Nah. Shadows, mate. All you've got there is shadows.'

'So why is your DNA all over that slip?'

Melvin looked at Ffion. She thought for a moment, then nodded. 'Painted the bloke's conservatory. He asked for a quote for refinishing the wood on the deck. I looked it over, gave him a quote, end of.'

'We'll check it out. Morris, if you wouldn't mind,' Manx said.

As Morris left, he sat back. 'Okay, let's play this out. You knew the slip was unused because you'd been there a few weeks before, but your grand plan went tits up, didn't it? Whoever was driving the van you stole from Ali Kalpar decided to take Collins hostage. Is that what you and Bobbie were arguing about on the slip?' Manx gestured at the screen. 'What you were going to do with the bloke?'

Melvin's right eye repeated the same twitch it had betrayed a few minutes ago.

'Didn't think we knew about Bobbie, did you? How did you persuade her to get involved in all this? You can't be lovers, that would be an image I'd find hard to unsee. Friends, maybe? Though God knows why she'd be hanging around with a low-life like you.'

Manx saw Melvin's fists tighten, noticed how dense they were, pale, as if no blood was reaching the knuckles.

'If not friends, definitely not lovers, then what?' Manx stood, paced the room, hands in his pockets. 'Must be family, right? Somehow, some way, you and Bobbie are family? Am I warm?'

'Stone, fucking—' Mel began. Before he could finish, another kind of fist formed. This one was vice-tight, grappling around his insides, choking the bronchi and lobes into narrow passages where the air struggled to fill his lungs. He brought a hand to his chest, his breathing now more of a crippled wheeze.

Manx sensing an advantage pushed harder, reached for a tissue from a box on the table. 'Come on, Mel. All this holding stuff in, it's not doing you any favours, let it all out. Tell me where you're holding Logan Collins, I guarantee you'll feel better.'

Mel slapped a hand on the table, grabbed the tissue and coughed a thick wedge of blood onto it.

'Where is he, Mel? Logan Collins? What's your connection to Bobbie Matthews? How did you murder James Flynt? Why stab Vera Troup, then kidnap Collins? Was it you who put a bolt through Byron Gates' neck?'

Mel was doubled over, slipping off the edge of the chair, using the table to support himself. 'Fuck you,' he wheezed.

'Inspector Manx!' Ffion shouted, standing and putting her arm around Mel's shoulder. 'I can't tolerate this—'

'Not acceptable,' Manx said, walking around the table, squatting next to Melvin, whispering in his ear. 'Come on, Mel, it's over for you now, you know it. Spit it out. Where are you holding Collins, Mel? Where. Is. He?'

Melvin did spit it out. Coughed a thick chunk of blood-tainted phlegm over Manx's shirt. 'Christ!' he shouted, stepping back and grabbing a handful of tissues to wipe himself down.

By the time Manx had turned back around, the Great Welsh Hope was regaining his strength; at least for now. 'Don't worry, I'm not contagious,' he said. 'And fuck you and your stories. I know nothing.'

Manx shoved his chair hard against the table. 'Pausing interview with suspect Melvin Powell at 9.16 pm. Inspector Manx leaving the interview room.'

Manx flung open the gallery viewing room door, slammed it behind him and grabbed another handful of tissues to wipe the blood.

'All going to plan then?' Canton said, turning from the screen, his face three shades more flushed than usual. 'What the hell were you doing in there? Trying to get the whole case thrown out?'

Manx flung himself onto the nearest chair, then scooted back as Morris and DS Nader made their way in.

'Powell's right. He did a paint job for Peter Whitestone back in early July,' Morris said. 'And Whitestone did ask him to quote for refinishing the slip. Sorry, sir.'

Manx stood, placed his palms on the two-way mirror and shook his head. 'He's lying. That cocky little shit is lying his arse off.' He slapped hard on the glass.

'You need a confession, Manx,' Canton said. 'The DNA only confirms he was on the slip at some point, which he's already admitted to. The CCTV footage is worthless. If Bobbie Matthews was hiding out in that cottage, then she's long gone by now, and unless we find the words *Bobbie Matthews was here* finger-painted in one of the rooms, there's no way to prove she was even there; neither her DNA nor prints are in the system.'

'What about the other bloke?' Nader asked. 'He's got to be helping Bobbie Matthews.'

'Got away on a quad bike,' Manx said, leaning his back against the glass and taking a deep, calming breath.

'Here's the deal, Manx,' Canton said. 'And I'll tell you this before Ms by-the-book human rights solicitor in there reminds you. You've got twenty-four hours to either release him or charge him. With the evidence you've got, I doubt you'll secure an arrest warrant. I don't like it any more than you do, but if by nine o'clock tomorrow night Melvin Powell's still giving you the "no bloody comment" line, and we haven't found any credible evidence to charge him, he walks.'

'We ask for an extension,' Manx said. 'Kidnapping and attempted murder of a senior police officer, they've got to grant us more time to secure the evidence.'

'Give it your best shot, Manx,' Canton said. 'You might get thirty-six hours, if you're lucky.'

Manx looked through the mirror as Melvin Powell strutted the room and checked out his reflection.

He didn't look like the confessing type. Not even close.

Chapter 85

Manx stared at the bottle of Springbank as if it were his mortal enemy. What was it they said? Keep your friends close and your enemies closer? Manx pushed the temptation of his enemy to the farthest end of the breakfast bar. It was far too dramatic a gesture; the bottle was still easily within arm's reach, his name floating flirtatiously in the scotch's honeyed depths.

It was 11.45 pm. Manx had thrown in the towel with Melvin Powell an hour before, decided to tackle the weaselly bastard first thing tomorrow morning with a fresh head and a few hours of sound sleep. He'd kept his drinking to his rationed two fingers of scotch, one ice cube, repeated three times; a ratio he'd worked out over the years that would help take the edge off and still avoid the foggy mire of a hangover. He quickly sorted through his post; two bills, three new credit card offers, a request for a donation to the RNLI, and a flyer for Thursday's Anglesey Agricultural Show.

Most of his mail dumped, donation envelope filed for later, Manx flipped open his laptop and searched his music library, opting for the shuffle feature; tonight, he'd let fate roll the dice. 'Hard Luck Story', a track from one his favourite alternative country bands, Whiskeytown, played over the speaker. The irony didn't pass him by as the song's propulsive, freight-train rhythm filled the tiny kitchen. 'I gotta bucket full of tears and a hard-luck story,' Ryan Adams sang as the song reached its chorus.

'Amen to that,' Manx mumbled, raising his glass to the ghosts, present, past and future, who had suffered the same biting sting of failure. The raid on the cottage had barely been rescued from total disaster by the capture of Melvin Powell, but two other suspects, one of which had to be Bobbie Matthews, had escaped. That wasn't what he'd call 'mission accomplished' by any means.

At precisely 11.59 pm, as he nursed his last ration of scotch, a loud ping from his computer interrupted his playlist. He clicked on his email app. There was a forwarded email from the North Wales Constabulary Just Ask A Copper account; the first and only one he'd ever received. He checked the sender's address: ByronGates@dronewatch.uk.

The hairs on Manx's neck spiked. It wasn't often he received emails from a dead man. He read the first few lines:

For the attention of Detective Inspector Tudor Manx.

If you're reading this email, I'm more than likely dead. The cause will be murder, and the person who killed me will be Flight Lieutenant Bobbie Matthews. If you're investigating her already, this won't surprise you, if you're not, then I'd recommend finding her as soon as possible. Here's what you need to know about Bobbie Matthews…

Manx read the rambling dissertation. Much of it Manx already knew; Operation Vanguard, the kidnapping of Logan Collins; Byron had obviously spent hours formulating conspiracy theories of his own. He went on at length about how Bobbie had forced him to upload the video, how he'd searched her, found the motive to her actions, how he'd visited her sister Tammy.

Reading Tammy's name, Manx almost resisted the urge to call her, but the scotch was making him feel more cavalier than usual. Tammy answered on the third ring, pretended to be annoyed, but then agreed that she too was finding it hard to sleep and yes maybe she could come over, talk, pass the time.

Thirty minutes later, Tammy sat in his kitchen, pouring the gin she'd brought with her into a glass, having guessed correctly that Manx's larder would be woefully bare of her drink of choice.

'Did Bobbie ever mention anyone called Melvin Powell?' Manx asked, watching Tammy bring the glass from her lips: lips he was desperate to reacquaint himself with, but he resisted temptation, at least for the moment.

Tammy shook her head. 'Why? Is he important?'

'Just a name, that's all.'

'I can't get my head around all of this,' she said. 'I keep thinking if there was something I could have done differently or said differently. If I'd been a better sister, then she wouldn't have done any of this.'

'There was nothing you could have done. Bobbie set her own course.'

'And you really think she killed Byron Gates?'

'Or had him killed,' Manx said.

'Christ, I don't know which scares me the most,' Tammy said, putting down her drink. She took a deep breath and wiped her hands across her eyes. 'I'm sorry,' she said, composing herself. 'Bobbie was always a little strange, you know. When we were kids, she had to win every game we played, she'd get into a huge strop if she lost. In the end, I'd just let her win, just for some peace. I didn't care, it made her happy, anyway it was just a game, no harm done.'

Tammy placed her palms flat on the table, looked at the wall clock; 12:53 am. 'I should go,' she said, screwing the top back on her bottle of Aber Falls botanical gin.

Manx sensed the gesture was at best half-hearted. 'Stay,' he said, almost without thinking.

Tammy sat back and smiled. 'Stay? The night? With you?'

'No one else here.'

Tammy thought for a moment. 'It is a bit late to be driving home, I suppose,' she said, leaning across the breakfast bar.

Manx leaned in to meet her gaze. 'Can't be too careful these days, maniacs on the road,' he said, moving his face closer to hers.

Her lips parted slightly, shaping a seductive smile. 'You'd think the police would do something about that.'

'I have connections,' he said, running a finger down her hair to her neck. 'I could have a word.'

'Then there's the gin, probably over the limit by now.'

'I hear there's patrols all over the island this time of year.' Manx breathed in the heady bouquet of her perfume and pressed his lips against her cheek. 'I'd hate to have to come and bail you out.'

'Well, that settles it,' she said, her lips brushing his. 'I expect you have a spare bedroom I can kip in?'

'Single bed, very uncomfortable, you wouldn't sleep a wink.'

Tammy nodded. 'Is that right? And the sofa?'

'Lumpy as hell. You'll have back problems for weeks.'

Tammy sat back, dragged the hair from her face and placed her palms on the table. 'I don't usually do this on a second date, just so you know.'

'Technically, it's a first date,' Manx said. 'That evening at the Ship Inn was you helping the police with their inquiries.'

'And tonight?' she asked.

'If you continue to resist, I might need to keep you here overnight, continue the interrogation.'

Tammy stood. 'Well then, Inspector Manx, I'd hate to disappoint the North Wales Constabulary.'

Most of their clothes were torn off and discarded to the floor before they'd reached Manx's bed. There was little talking. Skin pressed against skin; fingers entwined in fingers; limbs wrapped around limbs. Faint moonlight spilling in from the window shone across Tammy's body, casting a milky aura over her skin. In that moment, Manx doubted he'd ever seen anything more beautiful, and if he had, it was so long ago the memory had by now faded to dust.

Forty-five minutes later, their bodies recovering, a sheen of sweat covering their skin, Tammy shuffled close to Manx and draped her arm across his chest. 'There's a problem,' she said.

'I'm open to most requests,' he said, drawing her closer.

Tammy lightly slapped his chest. 'If we're going to do this again, I can't keep calling you Inspector.'

Manx smiled. 'Tudor,' he said. 'Tudor Manx-Williams.'

'Tudor,' Tammy whispered. 'Very regal.' She said his name again. Then there were no sounds, just the steady breathing of deep and satisfying sleep.

Manx was maybe three hours into the best sleep he'd had for weeks, months even, when he woke with a striking thought that had made its way into his subconscious while he slept.

He slipped quietly from the bedroom, headed to the kitchen and opened his laptop. He replayed, at low volume, the video of Logan Collins reading out the demands, scrubbing to the section where he said 'no one else needs to die'. He replayed it several times. He hadn't noticed the significance before. Why reference other people dying when the only threat had been to murder Collins?

He recalled the conversation with Andrew Pierce. 'Bobbie was angry with the RAF; it makes no sense for her to kill Collins.' *No, of course it made no sense*, Manx thought as he sat back and ran a hand across his mouth, which still tasted of Tammy's skin and lipstick. What if threatening Collins wasn't all Bobbie had planned? He looked to the wall opposite at the Moelfre Lifeboat calendar he'd bought for half-price a few months back. He checked out the month of August and scanned backwards through the days.

Summer Bank Holiday, August 26th; RNLI Open Day, August 14th; August 7th – the day after tomorrow – *The Anglesey Agricultural Show*. He remembered his father, Tommy, taking him there one year. Or, more precisely, dropping Manx off then picking him up several hours later stinking of beer, fags and pig roast.

Manx thought for a moment, his brain slowly catching up with the tingling sensation he always felt in his neck when he was close to finding a breakthrough in a case; it was like the slow drip of water seeping through cracks in a wall.

He reached behind him into the bin and pulled out the flyer for the Anglesey Show he'd thrown in there earlier. He flattened it on the table, flipped it over, and read the list of events. One caught his eye. The official opening to be performed at 11.30 am by their Royal Highnesses the Duke and Duchess of Cambridge.

Manx sat back down, reached for the bottle and took a hearty mouthful. That tingling he felt earlier was now a fully-formed tsunami of certainty. The threat to Logan Collins was real, but it wasn't the only threat. Bobbie Matthews had something else planned. Collins had been a convenient coincidence, a decoy.

If he was right, and he hoped to God he wasn't, he had twenty-four hours to find out what Bobbie Matthews had planned and stop her. But right now, at 3.33 am, the night still thick, the sun two hours away from rising, he had no shadow of a doubt the odds were stacked firmly against him.

Chapter 86

How Melvin Powell could hold in his smile a curl of menace and a kind of lopsided goofiness was a mystery to Manx. But there it was, staring him right in the face at eight in the morning, along with the refrain that was beginning to loosen the nails from Manx's fingers:

'No. Bloody. Comment.'

Manx pressed his palms on the table and towered over Melvin. 'Just tell us. We know Bobbie's planning something at the Anglesey Show. Tell us what it is, and maybe we can talk to the CPS, get you a deal.'

'I don't think you can promise anything, Inspector Manx,' Melvin's solicitor, Ffion Owens, said as she walked in. She took the chair next to Melvin and threw her briefcase on the desk as if throwing down a gauntlet. 'And you don't have the right to question my client without me in the room. Anything he told you will be inadmissible in court.'

'That's a relief,' Manx said. 'Because if I hear 'no bloody comment' one more time I might lock myself up in one of our cells. Now, I'll ask you again, what's Bobbie Matthews planning?'

'No—'

'Bloody comment. Got it,' Manx said. He stormed out of the room, slammed the door behind him, and joined Canton in the viewing gallery.

'It's a bloody stretch, Manx,' Canton said as Manx walked in. 'Even for you, I'd say this is a big leap of imagination.'

'Not that big,' Manx said, sitting. 'Collins has no real value for Bobbie. He's a means to an end. She kills Collins, she's gained nothing, just taken the life of some local politician. Her target is the RAF, always has been. If she launches some kind of attack tomorrow, the day the royals open the Anglesey Show, that's going to make the RAF look like a bunch of incompetent fuckwits. If she can't get the truth she's looking for, then she's going for full-on humiliation.'

'Do you think she's capable of this?' Canton asked, his tone indicating that he was slowly coming around to Manx's theory.

'Her clinical psychologist seemed to think so.'

'Shit,' Canton said, shaking his head. 'We can't go to the press with just a bloody hunch. Imagine the panic, and don't even think about the RAF being embarrassed. If you're wrong about this, we'll both be hung out to dry like this morning's washing.'

'We don't start with the press,' Manx said, grabbing his coat and car keys. 'Well, are you coming or not?'

'You are pulling my bloody leg, aren't you?' Morgan Lloyd, chairman of the Anglesey Agricultural Show, said, throwing himself into the leather chair parked behind his obscenely large mahogany desk. 'This is a joke? A prank?'

'I believe the threat is genuine,' Manx said.

'What threat?' Lloyd asked, rubbing a palm over his broom-bristle moustache and pointing a stubby finger at Manx. 'This sounds like something you've just pulled out of your arses.'

'Could we quote you on that?' Manx said. 'I'm sure Collins' wife and the local press would be over the moon.'

'This Anglesey Show,' Lloyd said, 'we're expecting 60,000 people. I've got farm machinery manufacturers from all over the country already here, including Massey bloody Ferguson who are sponsoring the opening night dinner.'

'I understand—' Manx began, before he was interrupted.

'Let me tell you, Inspector, unless you can present me with a specific threat, there is no way in hell I'm cancelling my show. But, if you're offering to add a few more coppers on the field, I'd be happy to take them. God knows the North Wales Constabulary hasn't offered up anything much in the past.'

Manx's blood pressure rose a couple of notches. 'Some co-operation wouldn't go amiss.'

'Other than cancelling the show, how can I help you?'

'We want to search the showground tonight, when it's quiet so no one gets wind.'

Lloyd nodded. 'Anything else?'

'Increased surveillance on the day. Undercover officers.'

'Still on the hush-hush,' Lloyd said. 'I won't have any of my exhibitors spooked.'

Manx and Canton agreed.

'Good,' Lloyd said, standing and gesturing it was time for them to leave. 'Now, as they say, gents, the show must go on.'

Chapter 87

After dropping Canton back at the station, Manx made a quick call, briefed the team on the morning's events, and put Nader in charge of organising the explosive-detection dog team to search the showgrounds. Half an hour later, he was back in the Jensen, coasting the A55.

He pulled into the showgrounds. The fields were bone dry, the earth hard, grass yellow-tipped and brittle. As Manx and Carlisle walked, several articulated lorries the size of tanks off-loaded their heavy-metal: row-crop tractors, combine harvesters, rotary tillers, earth movers and the like were driven off their semi-trailers and reversed, engines spluttering, into their pre-assigned lots.

Carlisle waved away a blue bottle buzzing near his face. 'I'd say it's wild speculation, Manx. Our intelligence hasn't picked up any chatter, and you're not in possession of a specific threat.'

'You're not the first one to point that out.'

'Then maybe the universe is trying to tell you something,' Carlisle said, stopping at one of the fence posts. 'What makes you believe the royals might be targeted?'

Manx didn't have a concrete answer for that, he was running on instinct; but that trickle of static at the back of his neck that told him he was right. 'Prince William? He's an honorary air commandant as well as a lieutenant commander, correct?'

'Amongst other military ranks from the navy and army.'

'Take that to its logical conclusion. Bobbie Matthews is demanding the release of highly sensitive military information–'

'Which will never see the light of day,' Carlisle interrupted.

Manx continued. 'She's issued a threat timeline that ends on the opening day of the Anglesey Show – tomorrow – which the royals are scheduled to officially open.'

'Could be a coincidence, completely unconnected.'

'I don't think you really believe that, otherwise you wouldn't have agreed to meet me. If the end game is to make the RAF pay, or embarrass them in some way, then there's no better target than a senior member of the royal family serving at Valley.'

Carlisle looked towards the expanse of land that stretched in a carpet of wide, uninterrupted green. 'And if you're right?'

'Believe me, Carlisle, I'd be happy if I was wrong, but there's a bloody good chance I'm not.'

Carlisle let Manx's words simmer for a few moments. 'I've known them long enough. They don't like disappointing their public. Building goodwill here on the island is important to them.'

'You need to make them listen.'

Carlisle swatted another fly buzzing near his face. 'I don't *need* to do anything, but I'll take the information into consideration. Without a specific threat, there's nothing I can do. Unless, of course, you lock this down and make an arrest before tomorrow.'

'There's always that,' Manx agreed.

'Settled, then,' Carlisle said. 'I'll pass on your concerns. If the North Wales Constabulary neutralises the threat before the Anglesey Show, then situation normal, we move ahead as planned. If, by the end of today, you're no further on in your investigation, I'll insist they cancel their appearance.'

Manx considered pushing him further, but figured he'd reached as close to a compromise as he'd get from the man.

'It's my best offer,' he insisted.

Manx shoved his hands in his pockets and agreed.

'Good man.' Carlisle tugged on his shirt cuffs. 'Seems you were right about Byron Gates,' he added.

'Lot of good me being right does him now,' Manx said.

'We work with the intel we have, not the intel we wish we had,' Carlisle said. 'Threats to our national security need to be neutralised, I'm sure I don't need to remind you of that. I'd wish you luck, but it seems we're well beyond relying on luck by now. I'll expect your call when you've found Bobbie Matthews.'

Manx watched Carlisle climb into his Range Rover and drive off. Several hundred metres away, the deep rumble of heavy farm machinery engines sent a shudder through the ground and into Manx's boots. It was like the tiniest of earthquakes, faint enough to be of no consequence, yet held within it a sober reminder of its power and the destruction it was capable of unleashing.

Chapter 88

Logan Collins imagined he must be veering close to delirium, maybe even a razor's edge away from insanity. He had probably only been here a few days, a week at most, but it felt like this was all there ever was; all there had ever been.

He was thinking on this when a thin shaft of light cut through his blindfold. 'Melvin?' he asked. He hoped it was Melvin, not that cruel kid, Ronnie. But hope was a fleeting thing, engineered to take flight in an instant. That instant came with the sound of Ronnie's voice.

'Got you some company, mate,' he said, yanking down Collins' blindfold. Ronnie shoved the woman, forcing her to sit. 'No touching, mind you, she's Mel's bird. He'll put another bolt right in your bollocks if you start feeling her up.'

Ronnie's giggle was childish and cruel as he left. But at least there was one saving grace, he'd neglected to pull Collins' blindfold back in place. Collins blinked a few times, his eyes adjusting to the light. He looked at the woman. She didn't look scared, she looked defiant; more than defiant, angry – top of the boil, furious angry.

'What the bloody hell are you looking at?' Lydia snapped, kicking to loosen the ropes which were wrapped tight around her ankles.

'Erm, nothing,' Collins said, his voice dry, barely audible.

'Good,' she said. 'Got any ideas on how to get out of here?'

Collins shrugged, showed her his hands, bound tight with duct tape and rope.

'Typical bloody politician,' Lydia said. 'Not one decent idea between the lot of you.'

Chapter 89

It was a probability Bobbie had to consider, no matter how grubby or disloyal it made her feel. Melvin had now been in custody for over twenty-four hours and she had no idea what he might be telling the police. She was sure he wasn't the kind of man to betray his family, but what did she really know about him?

What she did know was this. The man hadn't hesitated when she told him she suspected she was his daughter. He'd smiled, said he could see the family resemblance in the sharp, angular features of her face and the way she held herself proudly. 'You hold herself like a fighter, Bobbie,' he'd said. She did wonder if it weren't for his terminal diagnosis if Melvin would have risked so much. But that was a question she couldn't dwell on. She was resolute now, determined to ensure Danvir hadn't died in vain and that someone would pay for his death.

She walked into the kitchen of Lydia's flat. Ronnie was at the kitchen table flipping through an old photo album. Bobbie passed behind him. 'You both look young in that one,' she said, pointing at a picture of Ronnie and Melvin standing at the cottage gate, crossbows cradled in their arms.

'First time we went lamping,' he said. 'Shot three rabbits and a fox that night.'

Bobbie placed a hand on his shoulder; it felt like the right thing to do, even though that sort of gesture made her uncomfortable these days, as if whatever shadow cast within her grew weaker with human contact. Tomorrow that shadow needed to be strong, stronger than ever; stronger even than her.

She pulled her hand back. 'We should run through tomorrow's strategy.'

'No need. Got it all in here,' he said, tapping his forehead.

'And the quadcopter?'

'Stored it in the back room where we had the meetings: no one ever goes in there.'

'Is the battery fully charged?'

'Will be by tomorrow morning.'

'And the vehicle?'

Ronnie sighed. 'Nicked one. Old Ford Transit from outside a chippy in Bangor.'

'Good,' Bobbie said, pacing the room like a caged animal.

'Sit down, you're making me nervous.'

'There's a lot to be nervous about.'

'Nah,' Ronnie said, raising his right hand, making a fist, then circling it in sweeping motions before releasing the fist and emulating the sound of an explosion. 'Piece of fuckin' cake.'

Bobbie left him to his memories and walked into the bedroom. She took out her combat flying suit from her kitbag and laid it out on the bed, smoothing out the creases with her palm. Next to the suit, she placed the medal she'd earned for her role in the RAF's Operation Shader in Iraq and Syria. She should have been awarded more medals, a lot more, but the RAF had only recently begun awarding the operations service medals to drone pilots: this after years of lobbying. It was yet another example of how the RAF had treated drone pilots like herself, and another reason the RAF should be held accountable. Successful kill strikes were still kill strikes, no matter if you made them from three feet away with a rifle, 10,000 feet above from the seat of an F150, or three thousand miles away from the flight deck of a ground control station. Taking out the enemy was still the objective, and she'd done her job better than most. The service had chosen to repay her with one token medal and the suspension of her combat-ready status; for that, they needed to pay. Holding the silver medal between her fingers, the queen's face rendered in profile, it suddenly seemed less like a medal and more like a fairground consolation prize; the plastic toy when she'd failed to hook the duck and win the goldfish.

She shook, tossed the medal into her bag, stepped into her flying suit and pulled up the zipper. She hadn't worn it since that day in Waddington. It felt heavier on her now and it was still thick with the smell of the ground station. That was over a year ago, her ground zero, and now that journey was coming to its conclusion.

When she'd forced Collins to speak those words, she hadn't imagined this day would finally come to pass. She'd been convinced – or maybe had just convinced herself – the RAF would give in to her demands, but they'd offered nothing. That decision had left her no choice. Pointless deaths had to be avenged, injustices redressed. Maybe, as Byron Gates had suggested, they weren't so different. They were both seeking justice, both fighting a power far greater than themselves. But Bobbie wasn't different from Byron because she had nothing left to lose, she was different because she'd sought to redress that injustice and not just posted documents on a website that mattered to no one. Byron Gates had been nothing more than a messenger, and the fate of messengers had been written in cliché for hundreds of years.

The same was true of Call Me Andy. He was a messenger of a different sort; one who was there to merely rubber stamp the decisions made by the command. Unlike Byron Gates, who'd betrayed Bobbie, Call Me Andy had at least tried, and for that his life could be spared. Before she left the base for the last time, she'd gone over to his office with the intent of giving him at least the courtesy of a goodbye, but he was out for the day according to his calendar. Before she left, she'd noticed his chaplain robes and white collar hanging on the back of the door.

Now, she took them out of her kitbag and laid them out on the bed before trying them on for size.

Chapter 90

The following morning, a thick layer of grey, soupy mist had settled over the showgrounds, stretching across the fields and farmland on both sides of the A55 artery. The earth underfoot was firm to the shoe, the dampness of the dawn tweaking the saturation of the grass and rendering it a brilliant green. Twenty-five miles south east, rising three thousand five hundred feet, Mount Snowdon's jagged peak was set clear against the blue. Behind the peak, a belt of low morning cloud brushed with the barest hint of a flame-red sunrise sketching its way into the day.

The showground was already a bustle of activity. Prize bulls, magnificent and proud, were led from their trailers to holding pens. In the animal enclosures, farm hands applied the final touches to the show horses, looping brasses over manes and brushing coats to a show-quality shine. To the north of the main arena, the salespeople added the finishing polish to the already sparkling metal of the farm machinery they'd been sent here to sell.

Around the perimeter, the explosive-detection dogs, noses to the ground, tugged hard on their leads. Meanwhile, Manx's team combed the food tents and craft stalls, paying specific attention to the main stage, where the royal couple were set to appear in a few hours. Each officer carried a photograph of Bobbie Matthews with strict orders not to approach and to alert Manx if she was spotted.

As Manx walked into the administration tent, Jack Carlisle was already there; had been for some time it seemed, sipping tea with the show chairman Morgan Lloyd, who was flipping through a thick wad of tickets.

'Counting your chickens?' Manx asked.

Lloyd sat back, hoiked up his trouser belt. 'Best year yet, I reckon. Seventy thousand, give or take.'

'Let's hope that's all it's memorable for,' Manx said.

Lloyd huffed and went back to flipping through his ticket receipts like Fagin tallying his takings after a fruitful day's pick-pocketing.

Carlisle settled his mug on the table. 'A word, Manx?' he said with a subtle nod. 'Outside.'

'If you're about to ask me if we've received a credible threat, I'm not in the mood. I'm knackered and my team's worn down to a nub.'

'I'm not saying you're right, Manx, but we have strengthened security,' Carlisle assured him. 'The royals will arrive in the first Range Rover, myself and my security detail in the other. We'll be in communication as we approach, and I've placed three undercover officers ready for when the gates open at zero nine thirty hours. They'll only be in communication with myself and my team. Arses well and truly covered. And one thing, Manx, this all better be more than a hunch, or you'll have the whole damn royal security detail wanting your head on a silver platter.'

'I'd feel a hell of a lot better if they'd cancel the appearance altogether,' Manx said. 'Save us all the headache.'

'If we allow the terrorists to dictate the rules of the game, they win, Manx,' he said, turning to leave.

'One question, Carlisle,' Manx said. 'What does a win look like, in your book?'

Carlisle turned back, paused. 'Easy, Manx, it looks like this.' He motioned across the breadth of the showground towards the crowds shuffling through the entrance gates.

Manx got his point; business as usual, living in freedom, only gets to happen because of people like Carlisle, and in his world, there were no grey areas. You either understood that or you didn't.

Chapter 91

Ronnie pummelled his fists against the wall of the Transit van and shouted. 'Stop fucking kicking, or I'll put another bolt through you myself!'

Silence followed as Logan Collins complied.

Ronnie was parked on a hill overlooking the showground. At 9.00 am, a long tail of traffic was backed up to the town of Gaerwen, three miles east. The warm weather meant big crowds for the show this year. Ronnie almost felt envious. *Yeah, it would have been champion on a day like today, walking the showground with Mel, checking out the big farm machinery and trawling the beer tents until closing time. Next year.* There was always next year.

Kneeling, he carefully unwrapped the package Bobbie had given him last night; a steel pipe bomb, eight inches in length, three inches in diameter and sealed at both ends with brass caps.

'This is very volatile, Ronnie, don't fuck about with it,' Bobbie had instructed him. 'Handle it the wrong way and it will blow your head off and scatter your limbs in all directions.'

His hands were calm, still as rocks, as he attached the device to the auxiliary battery compartment. He ripped off two strips of duct tape with his teeth, then fixed the pipe to the drone. The final step was the trickiest. In the centre of the pipe was a narrow hole filled with two, four inch long fuses which Ronnie connected to the motherboard of the quadcopter via two wires; one to carry the signal from the control panel to the drone, the other to detonate the five pounds of tightly packed explosive material stuffed with masonry nails. Once that was complete, he took the screen from his backpack and secured it to the A-frame above the control panel.

Stepping back, he fired up the main motor. The four propellers oscillated slowly at first, then quickly gained velocity. As he hovered the drone a few feet above ground, an alert beeped on the screen. He checked the message. Something about a low battery. That couldn't be right. He'd had it on charge all night. He was certain he'd plugged it into the correct socket – the one Melvin told him to always plug the kettle into – the only working socket in the old building.

Yeah, he thought as he navigated the quadcopter fifty feet skywards, he was a hundred per cent sure he'd plugged it into the right socket.

Or maybe ninety per cent sure. Or maybe a little less.

Chapter 92

'Any sign of Bobbie Matthews?' Manx called out over the radio as he walked the grounds. A chorus of 'negative', 'no boss', and 'no guv' came back over the radio.

As he clicked off, DCI Canton, his bald head shimmering in the heat, walked over. 'Christ, Manx,' he said, taking out a handkerchief and dabbing his brow. 'Are you sure about all this? We've been here two hours and no sign of the woman.'

'Don't you start, Ellis. Carlisle's already laid into me.'

'Maybe he's right. What if Bobbie Matthews is halfway to the bloody Algarve by now, laughing her arse off?' He took out her photograph. 'We've got twenty officers patrolling the grounds, plus Carlisle's lot. If she was here, someone would have spotted her by now. She's not a master of bloody disguise.'

Disguise. The word triggered a flash in Manx's mind. He nudged his brain into reverse gear. Andrew Pierce. The interview room. Three days ago. What the hell was it? It seemed like an off-hand remark at the time. Then it hit him, square in the eyes.

'A vicar,' he said. 'Bobbie Matthews stole the chaplain's uniform, or whatever they call it.'

'Vestments,' Canton said. 'A clergyman's vestments.'

Manx clicked on his radio and alerted the team on the updated description for Bobbie Matthews.

Chapter 93

People trusted vicars, priests, men of the cloth, which made it a lot easier for Bobbie Matthews to pass through the heightened security cordon that morning and into the showground.

Officers charged with searching for persons matching Bobbie's description would have passed her by without a second glance. She resembled a man of God; briefcase in hand, as if off to conduct some emergency exorcism, her hair scrunched under a hat and black robe flaring behind. The white clerical collar was the finishing touch that left no doubt Bobbie was who she claimed to be.

Along with Call Me Andy's Sunday best, she'd also taken an RAF radio comms device. That sort of hardware was easy to smuggle out of the base. Weapons, on the other hand, required signing out, paperwork filled in, permissions granted. No matter, she was resourceful. Building a home-made explosive device was hardly brain surgery these days; there were hundreds of pages dedicated to the subject on the dark web. She'd presented the finished device to Ronnie late last night.

Bobbie had then driven by the showgrounds to conduct a final scout. When she arrived, her gut had told her something wasn't right. There were too many cars parked for that time of night – specifically, too many police cars. She'd driven past, decided it was too risky, and headed back to the Lantern Arms. The same unsettling thought she'd had last night came to her this morning as she passed a stall selling Welsh dragon belt buckles, similar to the ones Melvin wore. Had he confessed? Given the police the time and location? Or had the police, smarter than she'd given them credit for, figured it out for themselves? Of both scenarios, the latter seemed most likely – Melvin was a lot of things, but he wasn't a traitor. Either way, she'd need to be vigilant; she still had work to do, elements to lay in place.

She headed to where the royal couple would be addressing the crowds later. Several dogs were sniffing around the stage. She waited for the handlers to pull them away, then slipped her briefcase under the stage, making sure it stuck out enough for someone to notice. She snapped some photos with her phone and texted Ronnie. They would give him some solid visuals for his mission.

Ronnie had been a fast and eager learner, but he'd be anxious by now, which is why Bobbie had secured a timing device to the drone. Instead of triggering the explosives manually, Bobbie would send a text when the target was in range. Ronnie would set the countdown for ten minutes, pilot the drone fifty feet above the target and hover it in place until the timer hit zero. It was a failsafe mechanism, she'd told him, in case the digital trigger she'd rigged onto the control board failed to engage.

Her explanation was half true. Manual triggers could be unreliable, especially if the signal was corrupted between the control panel and the quadcopter, but the key reason was Ronnie himself. If he was compromised, or bottled out at the last moment, this ensured the mission would be completed, with or without him.

Chapter 94

Five miles away, at Llangefni police station, Melvin Powell's solicitor Ffion Owens was arguing with PC Bryn Pritchard, a sickly-looking young man, still six weeks away from completing his twelve-week mandatory constable tutoring programme. Canton had assigned him to manage the reception while he and the senior officers patrolled the showgrounds.

'The North Wales Constabulary has a legal obligation,' Ffion stated. She checked her watch. 'In ten minutes, the thirty-six-hour detention ends and you'll have to either arrest or release my client.'

'To be honest, I'm not really familiar with the case,' Pritchard said, tapping his pen on the desk, trying to recall if he'd studied anything similar in classroom training a few months back. His mind drew a blank. 'I don't think I can just release him,' he said – more of a question than it was a statement.

'Listen,' Ffion said, checking his name and number. 'When I inform the Crown Prosecution Service that PC Bryn Pritchard, collar number ID 1271, failed to release a member of the public after the statutory, legally-permitted, time, whose feet are they going to hold to the fire? DI Manx's? DCI Canton's?'

'I wouldn't know anything about that,' Pritchard mumbled. 'They only brought me in today, I'm usually over at Beaumaris. Don't get many arrests over there like, pretty boring actually, get the odd drunk, tourists lost their wallet or something—'

'PC Pritchard,' Ffion interrupted. 'Unless you want to trigger a lawsuit, I recommend that within the next eight minutes you release my client.'

'Erm...' Pritchard muttered. 'I should probably call my DI, just to make sure, like.'

'You do that.'

Ffion checked her messages as Pritchard dialled Manx's number, mentally crossing his fingers he'd pick up. The call went straight to voicemail.

'No reply,' he said, hanging up. 'Probably busy.'

'Great detective work. I can see why the force snapped you up. Now, let me help you out here, Constable,' Ffion said. 'You can legally release my client under a "released under investigation" document. You are familiar with the procedure?'

Pritchard cast his mind back several months to a lecture on arrest and release procedures. 'Yeah, I'm not bloody stupid.'

'Let's leave that open for discussion,' Ffion said, smiling. 'You sign the document and my client is released within the thirty-six-hour window. The North Wales Constabulary is still within its power to bring my client in at any time for further questioning. And, you've seen the state of the man, he's hardly a flight risk.'

'Aye, I suppose,' Pritchard agreed.

'It's the morally right thing to do. That's something they wouldn't have taught you in training,' Ffion said, with a slim smile.

Pritchard sighed. 'Wait here,' he said, and trundled out of the reception area, wondering where the hell they kept the 'released under investigation' paperwork.

Chapter 95

By the time the news of Melvin Powell's release reached Manx, the metaphorical horse had bolted the metaphorical stable: Melvin could have legged it anywhere, but Manx's instincts told him he would want to be wherever the action was. Rather than spend the next five minutes giving Bryn Pritchard the mother of all bollockings, Manx hung up and focused on his next steps.

With all his key officers patrolling the showground, he'd left the station woefully undermanned; it was like he'd pushed all his players forward, leaving no one in defence and the goal mouth wide open. He was in no doubt Melvin was heading over here and was about to alert the team when Nader's voice bled in over his radio.

'Boss, I think we've found something,' he said, his words tripping out fast and anxious. 'There's a briefcase under the stage. Weren't there when we looked twenty minutes ago. I've got a bad feeling about this. Me and the lads—'

'Secure the area, right now!' Manx instructed. 'Move the crowd as far away from the stage as you can.'

'I'll try my best.' Nader's breathing was hurried. Manx could almost picture the clammy sheen of sweat forming across his DS's upper lip.

'Keep a lid on any panic. And Nader, I've just been informed Melvin Powell's been released from custody. If he's making his way here, keep a look out, and tell the rest of the team.'

Nader clicked off the airways without responding. Scanning the area, Manx was suddenly and acutely aware of the large crowds now congregating. The voice of the show announcer booming over the PA system gave him an idea. He ran, elbowing his way through the crowds. A crackle of static broke through the radio, followed by Jack Carlisle's voice.

'Danny Collins and Daphne Clark en route. ETA five minutes.'

Manx responded. 'We have a level critical threat situation. Advise driving Danny and Daphne back to home base.' Manx chose his words carefully. He was certain Carlisle would understand and react to the phrase 'level critical' – an attack was imminent.

A brief moment of silence was followed by Carlisle's measured tones. 'Negative. Vehicles are stuck in traffic, no way to execute a safe retreat.'

Before replying, Manx recalled a back road the team had identified last night, that ended where the animal transporters and trailers were parked. He gave Carlisle the directions, picked up the pace and made a direct line to the announcer's stage.

Winking Wynn Williams, a local celebrity with a predictable line in corny patter, jumped out of his seat as Manx bounded onto the stage. 'Hey, steady on,' Wynn said, his laughter forced. 'Seems we've got someone looking to take over my announcing duties. Are you in the union, son?' Another nervous chuckle.

Manx shoved his police ID in his face, cupped his hand over the microphone, and spoke to Wynn in a low, urgent tone.

Winking Wynn Williams nodded slowly, his face now three shades redder, and cleared his throat. 'Erm, ladies and gentlemen, no need to panic, like, but the North Wales Constabulary have asked me to make this very important announcement…'

Chapter 96

Danny Collins and Daphne Clark? The code names were almost comical, Bobbie thought, as she adjusted the volume on her RAF radio. She'd overheard the airmen mention the code names in the canteen. Danny Collins and Daphne Clark. The royal code names were always based on the initials of their titles; Duke and Duchess of Cambridge: DC. *That will need to change after today*, she thought, *or be nixed all together if Ronnie has his shit together.*

The sound of the announcer's voice over the PA system caught her attention. The police had obviously found the briefcase. She smiled and texted Ronnie: 'Danny and Daphne on the road.'

As Bobbie walked towards the livestock carriers and horse trailers at the western side of the showground, she had the distinct sense someone had eyes on her. By now, she'd learned to trust that instinct, embrace it. She continued, her pace unchanged but her senses on high alert, her mind already set on a strategy.

Chapter 97

Detective Sergeant Mal Nader didn't have a strategy, it wasn't his style. What he did have was a scorching anger, like a severe, unquenchable heartburn raging in his belly. Melvin Powell had been released. What he'd predicted to Manx had come true. He could just imagine Melvin Powell strutting out of the station doors, pleased as punch with himself. If he saw him now, he wouldn't hesitate to punch the bloke's lights out or zap the bastard with his taser, to hell with the consequences.

When he spotted Bobbie Matthews a hundred or so metres away, dressed in a black robe and clerical collar, he was in no doubt that she and Melvin Powell were the reason DCSI Troup was in hospital holding on to life by a fingernail. She wasn't just his DCSI; she was a wife and a mother. His anger burned brighter and fiercer as he thought of her daughter; that poor kid, having to watch her mother suffer like that.

As he watched Bobbie Matthews slip behind the line of animal transporters, he clicked the talk button on his radio, held it down, was about to inform Manx and the team, then decided otherwise.

No. He could handle this without calling in the bloody cavalry. A slip of a girl dressed like a bloody vicar? No two ways about it, he could take care of that problem.

He released the talk button and followed Bobbie Matthews; his fingers gripped tight around his baton.

Chapter 98

After initiating the countdown, Ronnie navigated the drone east towards the showground, gradually increasing the elevation as it flew. He checked the screen as the drone glided, effortlessly it seemed, over the fields. For a moment, he was lost in the high definition, brilliant greens of the island where he'd spent all his life. Watching the live feed from this perspective, he realised how special this place was. He could never imagine living anywhere else; it never even crossed his mind. He was deep in this thought when he heard a voice behind him calling his name.

He froze, turned slowly around. 'Christ, Mel,' he said, with a tremor of relief. 'I nearly shit myself. When did they release you?'

'About an hour ago.'

'You should be resting. Me and Bobbie, we've got this.'

'I'll rest when I'm dead,' he muttered, as if he were making a promise to himself.

'Nah, you should be resting now, Mel. Save your energy for the celebrations, yeah? Few pints, open a bottle of Penderyn.'

Mel walked towards Ronnie. 'Give me the controls, boy. That's my job.' He coughed, straining.

'You're in no fit state, Mel,' Ronnie said, glancing nervously at the screen. The warning had appeared again; low battery. 'Just hang back. Me and Bobbie, we've got this under control.' He turned the screen towards Mel 'See, six minutes, then it's done, we made our point. Six minutes, we'll be legends, Mel, bloody legends.'

But Melvin wasn't listening. As he stepped closer, the familiar look in his eyes made Ronnie's blood run cold. It was a look that said he wasn't going to take no for an answer. A look that had all the chilling hallmarks of another family member, his own father, Dafydd Powell.

When the punch struck, Ronnie didn't even see it coming.

Chapter 99

Leaving Winking Wynn Williams in a state of agitation, Manx headed across the showground. He hoped Carlisle had taken the back road and was safely parked. If the briefcase contained any kind of explosive device, they'd be well protected behind the wall of livestock transporters and trailers.

As he walked, a loud buzzing sound, like an angry swarm of bees, stopped him in his tracks. He brought a hand to his brow and looked skywards. A deep pit hollowed out in his chest as he tracked the bright glint of metal circling as if it were searching for its target. He grabbed his radio. 'Carlisle, find a way out of there, now!'

'Negative, Manx, the access road's blocked.'

'Then head towards the showground.'

'Are you serious? You just informed me there's a bomb there, and you want me to drive right to it?'

'It's a decoy. Bobbie Matthews planted a decoy.'

'What the fuck is going on Manx?'

'There's a drone circling the showground. I don't think it's here taking footage for tonight's news.'

A short pause of static over the airwaves, then Carlisle spoke. 'Thanks for the intel, Manx.'

'Thanks for the intel?' Was that it? It seemed like a gross underreaction, Manx thought as he kept eyes on the drone. The good news was it was heading away from the crowds. The very bad news was that it was travelling at high velocity directly towards Carlisle and the Royal Protection Squad.

Chapter 100

DS Nader trod carefully at the rear of the livestock trailers, the stench of fresh slurry in his nostrils. He'd lost sight of Bobbie Matthews, but he was sure she was here, hiding. His hunch was confirmed when from inside one of the trailers the troubled neighing of a horse caught his attention. He moved closer, squatted, and checked out the pile of clothing left on the trailer's ramp; a black robe and a clerical collar.

He felt suddenly vulnerable, as if he were being watched. Back in his army days he'd have his nine millimetre LA91 Browning close to hand, but today he was armed only with his collapsible baton, a can of CS incapacitant spray, and the X26 taser that all team members were issued with last night. If it came to it, he'd use them all.

That chance never came.

Before he sensed somebody had crept up behind him, he felt the cold sting of a steel bolt into his neck and a hand pulled back on his hair.

'One wrong move and this ends up severing your jugular. Understand?' Bobbie Matthews said, urging her point further into his neck.

Nader nodded.

'No,' Bobbie said. 'Say the words. Say you understand.'

'I… I understand,' Nader confirmed. 'I understand.'

'Good. Let's walk,' Bobbie said.

Chapter 101

Ronnie wasn't sure how long he was out, but it couldn't have been more than a minute. His cheek was sore as hell, his mouth sodden with the metallic taste of blood. He lifted himself up.

Melvin now had control of the drone. He seemed lost in his own world. 'You better stay there, unless you want another smack in the mouth,' he said, barely turning to look at his nephew to confirm he'd comply; that was a given.

Ronnie leaned on the front of the van and wiped the blood from his lip. 'You know what you're doing with that thing?'

'Bobbie showed me,' Melvin said. 'Who'd have thought it, eh? A kid that smart in the Powell family.'

Ronnie craned his neck to study the screen. The countdown clicked down to four minutes.

'What's that sound?' Melvin asked as the control panel emitted three urgent, short beeps.

'Low battery, I think,' Ronnie said. 'But I charged it up yesterday, so it's probably just on the blink.'

The beeps stopped. Melvin smiled. 'Going out fighting, yeah? Just like I always said I would.'

'Yeah,' Ronnie agreed. 'Like a champ, Mel,' he said, spitting a glob of blood on the ground. 'Go out like a champ.'

Chapter 102

Manx ran to where Carlisle had positioned the Range Rovers. They were parked to form a point, like the apex of an arrow, engines running, primed for either a rapid escape or the back seat occupants were demanding their creature comforts of air conditioning; not that he could see beyond the tint of privacy glass.

Carlisle stood in front of the vehicles talking into his mobile, nodding, as if confirming a command he was confident he could follow through on. Set around him were four of his men, Glock 17s in hands, eyes scouring back and forth between all compass points.

'Standing your ground, Carlisle?' Manx shouted. 'Your call, but I think it's the wrong one.' He looked up. The drone was barely a pinprick of light in the blue, but the sound was still there; a menacing, insistent hissing of rotors.

Carlisle ended his call and fastened the middle button of his suit. 'We'll take it from here, Manx. Thank your officers for all their support. I'll make sure the royals are aware of your dedication to their safety and well-being.'

Manx was still processing Carlisle's words when a sudden movement to his right made him turn – Bobbie Matthews, dressed in her combat flying gear. To her left, DS Nader, his face pallid, eyes wide open; a crossbow bolt secured at his jugular.

Carlisle's men turned with a speed and efficiency that took Manx by surprise and trained their weapons on Bobbie.

'If you think you can shoot faster than I can stab, go ahead,' she said, standing her ground some ten metres away.

The security detail gripped their fingers firmer around their weapons and waited for Carlisle's order – a barely visible shake of the head. A non-verbal signal they'd no doubt rehearsed for these kinds of emergency situations. The men relaxed their stance a degree.

'What do you want, Flight Lieutenant Matthews? What are your demands?' Carlisle's voice was calm, precise.

'Now you ask?' Bobbie said. 'The RAF had their chance. The deadline has passed.'

'I'm not RAF, neither is that officer you're holding hostage.'

'Leverage is leverage,' she said, urging the point of the bolt deep enough into Nader's neck to draw a trickle of blood.

'Boss?' he mumbled. No pre-arranged signals required; his face told all the story Manx needed to know; Nader was terrified.

With her free hand, Bobbie checked her mobile and permitted herself the luxury of a thin smile. 'In precisely four minutes, a quad-copter drone will drop a hundred feet and detonate five pounds of explosives, wrapped in a pipe bomb, directly onto those two shiny Range Rovers over there. I expect the collateral damage to be significant, especially to that precious cargo you're carrying in the back seats. You could attempt to get away, but what with that security incident in the showground and the line of cars bottle necking all the escape routes, I doubt you'd get far. Oh, and of course, this police officer would see none of that because he'd be too busy trying to stem the flow of blood from his neck. He'll do this for around a minute before realising he's going to die.'

Carlisle slipped his phone into his jacket pocket. 'Five pounds of explosives?' he said, his tone calm and considered. 'Anything within a hundred metres off the blast radius will be destroyed, including yourself.'

Bobbie smiled. 'My death is of no consequence. I have nothing left to lose.'

Manx was taking all this in, his eyes darting around from Carlisle to Bobbie, to Nader, to the security detail who were becoming twitchy, stances no longer relaxed, Glocks primed. Manx observed that their hands were rock-steady, holding not a tremor of doubt that if the order came, their triggers would be pulled. The stand-off continued for another minute. Manx broke the silence. Maybe there was a way to end this; lives saved, no one killed.

'Don't you want to know what happened, Bobbie?' he said, reaching into his jacket pocket to retrieve the printed copy of the report Andrew Pierce had left with him. 'Operation Vanguard? The truth?'

'Manx, what are you doing?' Carlisle said, his voice wire tight and fringed with caution. 'I thought we requested you to leave.'

'He's not going anywhere,' Bobbie said, urging the steel another few millimetres deeper into Nader's neck. Another slow ooze of blood.

'It's all in here,' Manx said. 'What happened after the strike, how your husband died.'

'You're lying,' Bobbie said, her eyes narrowing, her hands betraying the slightest tremor.

Manx could see she wanted to believe. Wanted to know that all this had been worth something. 'You didn't kill Danvir, Bobbie. It wasn't you.'

The sound of her husband's name was like ice dripped down Bobbie's spine. Before she could make sense of Manx's words, the drone plunged downwards, reappeared fifty feet above them, propellers slicing through the still morning air. Three of Carlisle's men quickly trained their Glocks on the quadcopter, the other man keeping his aim sure and steady on Bobbie's upper body.

'You shoot, you still lose,' Bobbie said, checking the countdown. 'It blows, we all blow.'

'You don't need to do this, Bobbie,' Manx said, his throat tight, neck muscles tensing. 'Fly the drone into the fields and I'll read you the report. If, after that, you still want to kill us all, go ahead, do it.' He showed the first page of the report to Bobbie.

'You're out of order, Manx,' Carlisle said. 'You have no authority to negotiate.'

'Neither do you,' Bobbie snapped back.

Manx could see Bobbie was debating, deliberating her choices as the drone gained altitude and veered back over the showground.

'Good. Good, Bobbie,' Manx said. 'Fly the drone as far away from here as you can, and we'll talk. I'll read you everything that's in here. Everything.'

'No,' Bobbie said, glancing nervously at her mobile, trying to get some clarity on the situation. 'It's not… it's not me. I don't have control. It's flying itself.'

Chapter 103

Ronnie turned as he heard the hiss of propellers travelling closer. The drone was sweeping in at high velocity back to its base. That wasn't the plan. Mel must have got confused, messed up the controls. He ran over.

Melvin was lost in his own world; unaware he was piloting the drone back to its launch point.

'Mel! What the fucking hell are you doing?'

Melvin seemed hypnotised by the screen, watching the fields rendered in brilliant high definition as the drone flew above them.

Ronnie made a grab for the control panel. Melvin's elbow pummelled him hard in the ribs, sending him reeling. He stumbled back up, checked the countdown and felt his stomach lurch.

Twenty-nine seconds. Twenty-eight...

Bobbie's words came whirling back to him, loud and clear. 'Five pounds of explosives, Ronnie. Enough to scatter your limbs in all directions, Ronnie.'

Mel turned to his nephew, his brow creased in confusion. 'What the fuck is it doing?' he said, stabbing the screen like a frustrated child trying to get a device to do its bidding. 'It's not listening, and it's beeping again.'

A bolt of realisation hit Ronnie between the eyes. Mel wasn't piloting the drone. He'd ceded control some two minutes ago when the last bar of power had dipped under three per cent.

His mind raced back to the afternoon Bobbie had taught him how to pilot the quadcopter. *When the battery pack runs low, it automatically takes its feed from the auxiliary battery pack.* But there was no auxiliary battery pack. That had been removed and replaced with explosives. With no power source, the drone would pilot itself back to the base station like a faithful dog fetching a stick.

'Mel! We've got to get the fuck out of here, now!' Spit sprayed from Ronnie's mouth as he screamed. 'Now, Mel, drop the fucking screen!'

Fifteen seconds. Fourteen seconds.

Ronnie lunged at Melvin, managed to grab a handful of his T-shirt before his uncle struck his fist like a hammer across Ronnie's cheek. Ronnie felt the teeth rattle in his mouth, the familiar rust of blood on his tongue. He stumbled backwards, just managing to keep his balance. Through the floaters and popping points of light fogging his vision, he glanced at the screen:

Ten seconds. Nine seconds.

'What's going on, Ronnie? What the fuck's going on?'

Those were the last words Ronnie heard from his uncle. Melvin was still poking at the screen as Ronnie made his decision. He could stand there, alongside Mel, have his limbs blown from his body, or he could run.

Six seconds. Five seconds.

Before Ronnie turned his back, he watched the drone land perfectly at Mel's feet, the whir of the rotors slowly fading. This was it. The twelfth round, the final bell; Mel refusing to back down, prodding the screen as if his strength alone could will it into submission.

Ronnie almost tripped over his feet as he ran. He hurled himself against the rear of the van, as petrified as the day his uncle had rescued him from Dafydd Powell, except this time there would be no saviour. He clenched his fists, brought them to his mouth, tried without success to stop the skin on his bones from shaking.

Chapter 104

The explosion was a sonic boom of heavy thunder on the horizon. A thick cloud of grey smoke mushroomed into the blue. The Transit van seemed like something spat up by the ground as it catapulted skywards, its metal catching the sunlight before it landed on its side, doors and windows blown out, wheels spinning uselessly in place.

Bobbie turned to the chaos, attempting to make sense of what the hell had just happened. In that split second Manx noticed a red laser dot float across her forehead like a freshly bloomed blemish.

'No!' Manx shouted. 'Don't–'

His protest was too late, and futile. From the rear window of one of the Range Rovers, a long-range rifle took the kill shot. It struck its target with absolute precision.

Bobbie Matthews' head snapped back. Blood sprayed from the single bullet hole. Her fingers flexed open, releasing the bolt. She crumpled to the ground, her combat suit seeming to deflate as she fell. Beside her, DS Nader dropped to his knees, wiping Bobbie's warm blood splatters from his face.

'Nader! Are you all right?' Manx said.

'Never been better, boss,' the DS said, rubbing a warm smear of blood off his shirt.

Confident Nader was safe, Manx turned his attention to Carlisle. 'You didn't need to–'

'Yes. Yes, I did,' Carlisle confirmed, taking out his cell phone to relay the message that his mission was complete; orders carried out. 'My job is to protect. I did that job. The world is a safer place without Bobbie Matthews in it.'

As he spoke, a flash of realisation burned bright in Manx's mind. Carlisle was far too careful and calculated to take this level of risk. He threw down the report and rushed towards the Range Rovers.

'Manx! Do not–' Carlisle warned.

'I don't take my orders from you,' Manx said, pulling open one of the back doors. He stepped back as he came face to face with the muzzle of a SIG SG 550 assault rifle. He looked down. A red laser point hovered over his shirt, directly above his heart.

'Manx!' Carlisle shouted. 'Do not give me a reason.'

Manx ignored him and flung open the back doors of the other vehicle. The back seats were pristine; empty.

Carlisle took a deep breath and signalled for the marksman to stand down. He complied, pulling the door shut.

'Did you really think I'd endanger the life of the royals?'

'So, you lied?'

'Loose lips and all that. I couldn't reveal any intelligence that would have jeopardised our operation.'

'What operation?'

Carlisle leaned his back against the front wing of the Range Rover. 'What people like you will never understand, Manx, is that our country is at war, and will be for the foreseeable future. There won't be any victory day parades when this is all over, and do you know why, Manx? Because it won't ever be over. These fundamentalists don't just wave a white flag, surrender and shuffle back to whatever hut they crawled out from. Fighting is all they know; all they'll ever know. This is the new reality of war; poor, uneducated jihadists sending women and children strapped with explosives to their deaths with no notion of what victory looks like beyond a vague notion of the world kneeling in terror at their feet. I, for one, am not willing to let that happen, neither was Bobbie Matthews. She'd been on the front line of that war, seen more death in a few short years than any of us will see in a lifetime.'

‘Then why kill her? She would have stood trial, been put away for life on the evidence we had.’

‘You’re forgetting one thing, Manx,’ Carlisle said, gesturing at the Operation Vanguard report. ‘She would never have stopped searching for answers, and once she found those answers we couldn’t risk her leaking them to the press or whoever. We need the public and the press on our side if we’re to make any progress in ending this.’

Manx gestured to Bobbie’s lifeless body. ‘So, you used us to bring Bobbie out in the open so you could kill her? That makes you no better than the bloody terrorists.’

Carlisle spoke deliberately as if he were explaining a difficult concept to a child. ‘In my experience, traitors rarely repent for their sins; there was no cure for what ailed Bobbie Matthews. Prison would have been little deterrent to someone of her persuasion, let alone a low security psychological hospital. I’m sure you’re more than familiar with how lenient our justice system has become, what with the Courts of Human Rights and the hurdles we have to jump over to make any charge stick. It’s a sad reflection of the times we live in when the people who threaten our freedom are granted the same protection as everyone else.’

‘All equal in the eyes of the law,’ Manx protested. ‘And what about Flynt? Did you silence him too?’

‘There was no need to. He got the promotion he wanted; we gained his loyalty. You should look closer to home if you’re looking for who killed Flynt,’ Carlisle said, gesturing towards Bobbie.

‘And Cole Dawson?’ Manx asked.

‘I believe the official cause of death was suicide. Hardly a surprise, the man was a drunk with severe battle trauma. We tried, but he wasn’t ready to accept our help.’

Carlisle directed his men to fall back. ‘We did good work here today, we neutralised a terrorist, a danger to our country, we should be proud of that.’

‘Proud?’ Manx countered. ‘She was a widow looking for the truth and you killed her.’

‘And now, no doubt, she’s found whatever truth she was seeking,’

Carlisle said, stepping onto the Range Rover's running boards. He took one final look over the fields, the spirals of grey smoke rising over the horizon.

'Looks messy,' he said with a grimace. 'Good luck with the clean-up.'

Chapter 105

Five days after Bobbie Matthews' death, the summer heatwave broke, bringing with it a heavy downpour that soaked the island for several hours. The rain fell hard on the fields where the Anglesey Show, for that year, had been cancelled. Afterwards, the air seemed fresh to the touch; a presage of a new beginning. At least for some. For others, the time for new beginnings had passed.

Manx gazed through the window of Gwynedd Hospital, watching the last of the grey clouds scuttle west as if being pursued by the incoming blue. Three floors below, the media presence had dwindled to a single BBC Cymru crew. After the initial flurry of media attention, the news cycle had moved on.

People, as they were often compelled to do, had also moved on. In a few weeks, the memory of Bobbie Matthews and the 'Showdown at the Showground' as the newspapers had christened the incident, would begin to fade. Six months on, few people would be able to recall the name of the other victim, nor the name of his nephew who had barely escaped with his life and was now waiting for his trial date, cuffed to a bed inside the Ashworth high security hospital on Merseyside.

The names Melvin and Ronnie Powell would, however, remain present and clear in DI Manx's memory for years to come, as would the name Logan Collins.

Collins himself had been lucky; a word he would keep returning to as he ramped up his political ambitions come the autumn. The rigid structure of the Transit van had functioned like a steel cage, protecting

Collins from the worst of the explosion, though he hadn't escaped unharmed. He was bounced around the van like a human pinball as the shockwaves struck the metal. The Transit's gear lever, shorn from the transmission, had buried itself into Logan's right thigh. His left leg had fared far worse, crushed under the heavy weight of the front seats as the van flipped and landed on its side.

Manx had spoken to Collins' wife, Danica. The conversation had not gone well. Danica remained calm and listened to Manx, before turning those narrow, feline eyes on him in a manner that suggested Manx could burn in hell for all she cared.

'You are the reason my husband will never walk again. You are the reason he's in a wheelchair; a cripple. You assured me these things rarely happen, victims return unharmed. You were wrong. I believe you and your team did not do enough to find my husband. We will make sure you pay for that, no matter how long it takes. Remember, Inspector Manx, you have blood on your hands.'

Days later, those words were dark echoes in the back of his mind. *Blood on your hands*. Maybe she was right, but Danica Collins was not in possession of the full facts, never would be.

Hours after the explosion, a man had been flown by helicopter from Whitehall to RAF Valley and was driven directly to Llangefni station. The grim-faced civil servant, William Baker, several pay grades elevated from Jack Carlisle, had sat Manx and Canton in one of the interview rooms and laid out in no uncertain terms what they could or could not release to the public. As Manx expected, Carlisle's name and any reference to the Royal Security Squad were to be kept out of all and any press releases. 'This falls on you,' Baker had explained. 'The North Wales Constabulary takes full responsibility. That, gentlemen, is how it will be.'

Baker had also demanded they hand over any copies, both digital and printed, of the Operation Vanguard report. 'I suspect you won't want to perjure yourself, so I won't ask how you came in possession of these,' Baker had said, slipping the papers into his briefcase.

Manx had accepted the demands with little protest. Hours after the incident, his emotions were raw; capitulation came easy. As Danica Collins had said, he had blood on his hands. He couldn't see or touch it, but he could sense it, like an invisible film across his skin.

Lydia Clarke; her name had come across his desk a day later when she was found in the coal shed behind the Lantern Arms. The driver from the brewery had heard her screams as he was hauling beer kegs off the back of his lorry. She was Melvin's lover, she'd told Manx; she'd told him a lot more too, happy to keep talking to save her own skin. When she revealed, almost in passing, that Melvin was Bobbie's biological father it was the final piece of the jigsaw falling into place. Melvin wasn't only on a mission to go out in a blaze of glory, he was expecting some kind of redemption by helping his daughter uncover the truth she was so desperate to find.

When the dust had settled, and memories of that day began to fade like the last faint ripples across a pond, the name that would haunt Manx the most was that of Bobbie Matthews; the young widow searching for truth. She never got to hear that truth; unless what Carlisle had hinted at was true, and wherever Bobbie was now all would have been revealed and she would be at peace. As comforting as that thought was, it took more faith than Manx had the capacity for.

To hint that Bobbie Matthews was as much of a victim, as some of the more liberal-leaning papers and online commentators had suggested, was a stretch too far in Manx's book. If nothing else, her death had pointed a glaring light on the trauma suffered by military personnel who may have been thousands of miles away from the line of fire, but their trauma was no less real than if they'd stood eye to eye and taken a life.

Some weeks later, the BBC broadcast a *Panorama* documentary 'Behind Friendly Lines' about that very subject, along with interviews with former drone pilots, their faces obscured under shadowy lighting. If he could have seen their eyes Manx wondered if they'd be haunted with the same emptiness he'd seen in Bobbie Matthews' eyes? Manx could never condone her actions, but at the same time, he couldn't condone her murder. She should have stood trial, where the truth would have come to light. But that was Carlisle's objective when he ordered the kill shot; to keep that truth hidden, locked away for good.

There was plenty Bobbie Matthews didn't know about what had happened after she left the ground control station that day. Flight Commander James Flynt had immediately called the Waddington Base Commander, who in turn had contacted the Chief of the Air Staff, the highest ranking official in the RAF. His call to the Defence Secretary, head of the MoD, had escalated the situation to the highest level of government. Within thirty minutes of the strike, a strategy was formed, a plan put in place; orders carried out without question.

A secondary, more detailed, battle damage assessment conducted by British ground troops had found the cause and origin of the secondary blast. There were no enemy combatants in the vicinity and none of the debris had the markings of usual IS weaponry. What they did find was the blown-out remains of three large propane cylinders buried seven feet underground, packed solid with explosives. The destruction was so complete it was impossible at the time to discern if they'd been stored by insurgents or planted by the allied forces for use later as a massive IED in an attempt to beat the enemy at their own game.

It wasn't until the formal forensic report came back the following day that the provenance of the explosives was verified. The debris contained traces of RDX nitroamine and dioctyl sebacate; two of the core components and a binding agent found in most United States Armed Forces explosive devices. British-made explosives typically contained cyclonite and lithium grease.

Several days of tense negotiations followed between the MoD and the United States Joint Operations Command. If the findings were leaked, it would have looked bad for both sides; made them look at best careless, and at worst incompetent. Neither was a good option when trying to win the hearts and minds of the public in the war on terror. What did win hearts and minds was outrage. Outrage directed through the right channels to sympathetic newspaper editors.

It took a few days at most for the British tabloids to attach themselves to the story of six young RAF medics blown up by Muslim terrorists. It was the kind of spin that sold papers and bolstered the government's position on utilising drones in the fight against terror.

Manx remembered Byron Gates had used the phrase 'false flag' several times in his rambling communication; he was half right. The RAF hadn't deliberately killed their own men to further their cause, but they had used a tragic accident to their advantage, with no thought as to the lives ruined in the process.

If Bobbie Matthews had been furnished with the truth at the beginning, then maybe none of this would have come to pass. James Flynt and his wife would be enjoying retirement; Logan Collins would be standing at the podium, not in a wheelchair, as he delivered his campaign speeches; Byron Gates would have continued his fight against injustice; and Bobbie Matthews would have lived, given herself the chance to properly grieve for her husband and, over time, may have come to forgive herself for something that was never her fault.

Manx turned from the window, the burden of the last two weeks still bearing down on him, and looked into Vera Troup's room. The hospital auxiliary staff were busy stripping sheets and blankets from the bed, preparing the room for the next occupant.

'She'd like to talk to you,' DCI Canton said, walking into the waiting room. Five days on, he still looked ragged and worn out; Manx guessed he'd fared no better himself, but there was something more serious in the way Canton held himself. The slump in the shoulders, the weariness in his voice, made Manx think there was something more at play than just exhaustion. His mentor and friend looked older; perhaps the job was finally taking its toll on him.

'She's asking for the name of that St John ambulance volunteer,' Canton said, sitting down with a groan. 'Reckons he saved her life; she'd like to personally thank him.'

Manx nodded. *Hugh Jones deserves that recognition*, he thought. The man had stepped up, done his job without complaint and saved a life. He should be damned proud of that, certainly a lot prouder than Manx was feeling about himself right now.

'How's she doing?' Manx asked, sitting in the chair opposite.

'Weak, gets tired quickly, but there's one thing for certain, her days as a DCIS are over.'

'She said that?'

'Not in so many words, but when something like this happens your priorities change.'

Manx nodded. 'And you, Ellis? Stepping up?'

'I daresay that ship's sailed,' he said, his voice betraying a slip of resignation. 'I'll hold the fort, but they'll want someone with some juice still left in them. They've already retained a talent recruitment company and I doubt my name's on their radar.'

'Everything changes,' Manx said with a resigned smile.

'We all jump back on the merry-go-round and just hope we get off at a better place than we got on, right, Manx?'

Manx thought for a moment. 'Problem is, Ellis, I don't remember ever getting off the bloody ride in the first place.'

Chapter 106

One month later

The short service for the scattering of Bobbie Matthews' ashes was an intimate affair conducted at Cable Bay beach in the late afternoon. Manx stood next to Tammy; Mohsin and Rida Sadiq stood to his left. Rida seemed to tolerate his presence but arched her eyebrows and glanced at her husband when she saw Tammy slip her hand into Manx's.

Few words were spoken. Tammy set a small speaker on a rise of marram grass and took out her phone. "(What's So Funny 'Bout) Peace, Love & Understanding" by Elvis Costello and the Attractions drifted on the early evening breeze. It seemed like a solid choice, Manx thought. He hadn't got to know Bobbie, but he imagined she wasn't the kind of woman who would have approved of an overly sentimental pop song to mark her passing. After the track faded out, Tammy reached into the urn, took a handful of ashes and let them fall from her palm. They floated away on the cool evening breeze; a life scattered to the winds.

Tammy and Manx headed back, taking the pathway leading to the car park. As they walked, Manx noticed a lone figure in RAF service dress standing at the edge of the beach. He told Tammy he'd call her later that evening and made his way towards the man.

Andrew Pierce shuffled uncomfortably as Manx approached. 'They didn't have to kill her,' he said, looking over the white caps skimming the ocean surface. He had Bobbie's headset in his hand, his fingers rubbing over the cheap gemstones.

Manx had no response; at least none that had any merit or one that didn't contradict his own feelings about Bobbie's death. He turned up his jacket collar as a gust of wind blew up from the beach, bringing with it a smattering of sand.

'You always imagine there was something more you could have done, an extra mile you could have walked,' Pierce said, wiping away an errant grain of sand caught in the corner of his eye.

'Bobbie made her own decisions. She chose a bad road to go down. It was never going to end well for her. I think she knew that,' Manx said.

'She deserved to know the truth. It would have set her free, I'm sure of it.' Pierce exhaled loudly, barely holding back his tears.

'Do you believe the truth sets any of us free?'

'I have to believe, or what else is there left?' Pierce looked at the headset and began picking off the gems one by one. The rainbow of colours caught the light for a moment before they fell to the ground and were lost in the beige carpet of sand.

When Manx reached the car park, two cars remained; the Jensen and what he assumed was Pierce's Mitsubishi Outlander. Walking past, he noticed a thick wedge of masking tape wrapped around the driver's side wing mirror. He ran his finger along the edge. The mirror toppled to the right, the tape pulling at the seams. He peered inside; Pierce's cap was set on the passenger seat.

He reached for his mobile, called the station and asked Nader to meet him here as soon as. Then he called Ashton Bevan. 'James Flynt's cap? Did you check it for any DNA other than Flynt's?' he asked, peering through the rear windscreen and at the fleece jacket in the boot.

Bevan replied they hadn't.

'Do it,' Manx said. 'And while you're at it, look for any blood traces.'

He hung up and looked over at Pierce, still plucking at the headset as if he were picking out daisy petals: *she loves me, she loves me not.*

Chapter 107

Andrew Pierce was calm, resigned almost, as he sat in the interview room. He'd agreed to come in and 'help with our inquiries,' as Manx had informed him. 'You're not under arrest, but any information you have could prove to be useful.' Pierce attempted to be evasive, but Manx could tell his heart wasn't in it. Unlike Melvin Powell a few weeks back, Pierce looked the identikit picture of the confessing type. It was only a matter of time before he folded. That was fine by Manx, he was in no rush, Bevan's team was still combing over Pierce's car for the evidence Manx needed to hammer home the final nail on Commander James Flynt's murder.

'How long had you been in love with Bobbie Matthews?'

'From the moment I met her,' Pierce said, matter-of-factly.

Manx slid the print-out of Bobbie's wedding photograph across the desk. 'When her husband died, I'm sure a small part of you saw that as an opportunity to make the moves on Bobbie. A familiar shoulder to cry on?'

'It wasn't like that.'

'Tell me, what was it like?'

'Bobbie was special, I'd never do anything to hurt her.'

'But you did hurt her, Pierce. You ran her down in the middle of the night. Lucky for her you were there to pick up the pieces.'

Pierce shrugged. 'Are you going to charge me for that?'

'What was your end game, here? You'd be her guardian angel? Her protector? Someone she couldn't live without?'

'Bobbie never needed a protector.'

'That must have hurt, the rejection?'

Manx turned as the door swung open. PC Priddle walked in, handed Manx a Manila folder, then scooted out.

'Let's talk about James Flynt. You didn't agree with his decision to transfer Bobbie to a psychiatric facility?'

'We were making progress; it would have been like starting all over again for Bobbie. She didn't need to go through that.'

'Is that why you killed him?'

Pierce's Adam's apple rose and fell like a sewing machine needle, his breathing shallow and hurried. 'I didn't–'

'The tyre prints we found next to Flynt's car are a perfect match to your Mitsubishi Outlander.'

'There must be hundreds of cars with the same tyres.'

'Thousands,' Manx confirmed. 'But that's not the evidence that's going to put you away, Pierce.' He pulled out a plastic bag from the folder. 'We took these rock fragments from the fatal wound you made in Flynt's skull when you struck him with the rock you were carrying in your jacket pocket.'

'I'm not sure what–' Pierce began.

'We're sure, and we've got the science to prove it.' Manx flipped over a signed document from Mary Bedford, Department Head, Geological Oceanography at Bangor University. He took his time to explain to Pierce how the fragments in Flynt's skull couldn't have come from Benllech beach. 'So, how did fragments of blueschist rocks get into his wound, Pierce? Any idea?'

Pierce's brow glistened with a layer of slick sweat.

Manx leaned forward, held Pierce's gaze. 'I'll save you the time and energy of coming up with a lie. You called Flynt, made up some specious reason for meeting that time of night. You knew it was a long shot, persuading him to change his mind about Bobbie, but you had a backup plan. A murder weapon you picked up somewhere. Maybe from your back garden? The base? Who the hell knows? That's not important. What is important is that once you put that rock in your pocket with the intent of killing Flynt, that's as close a definition to premeditated murder as it gets.'

'I… I think you're reaching,' Pierce muttered.

'We also found blueschist fragments all over the passenger seat of your car. And the fleece jacket you kept in the boot? In the right-hand pocket, we found the exact same fragments. I think you carried the rock on the front seat, then put it in your jacket pocket when Flynt arrived. Again, premeditation.'

'That doesn't prove very much,' Pierce mumbled.

'Not by itself. But that's not how evidence works. We like to package it all up, so the CPS has a very clear understanding of why you should be arrested.'

Manx turned his laptop to face Pierce and pressed play on a short video clip. 'This is CCTV footage of your car leaving Breeze Hill public house in Benllech at 9.45 pm. You also have no alibi for the remainder of that evening, other than sitting at home alone. Now, you can see for yourself how my case suddenly becomes very persuasive. I have motive; traces of what we believe is the murder weapon in your car and on your clothing; and you were in the vicinity of the murder when it happened with a paper-thin alibi that's not going to hold water in front of a jury.'

'I think I'd like a solicitor,' Pierce said, shuffling like he'd just found something sharp sticking out of his seat.

'Good idea,' Manx agreed. 'Once they're briefed, we can legally request that you provide us with a DNA sample.'

'I'm not saying anything else until my solicitor gets here.'

'Fair enough,' Manx said. 'But here's what we did figure out. Flynt was wearing his cap when you struck him. Do you know how we know that?'

Pierce shrugged.

'Our forensics lads found traces of blood splatter on the outside rim of the cap, which means he must have been wearing it when you delivered the fatal blow. You then returned the cap to Flynt's car to make it look like he'd gone for a late evening stroll with every intention of returning. Now, when we collect your sample, what do you think are the chances we'll find some trace of your DNA on that cap? A skin flake, blood; a strand of hair? Or you could just save us all the time and confess. Your call, Pierce.'

Manx gathered his things, stood and turned to face the door.

Pierce sniffed loudly, ran the back of a hand under his nose. 'Bobbie just needed someone to care for her. She needed a friend,' he said, looking off into the distance, as if trying to convince himself.

Manx turned. 'With friends like you, eh,' he said, and left the room.

Chapter 108

When Manx arrived back home later that evening, daylight was still in bloom. It would be another thirty minutes before darkness fell completely, but for now the sky was a ribbon of dark blue etched with deep orange. As he reached his doorstep, he noticed a small package with a note attached.

Thought you were probably too busy to pick up your photos. Pay me next time. He glanced at the signature – *Gina Roberts, Benllech Chemist* – and looked out over the roofs of the small housing estate towards the fields. To the east, a flock of starlings flitted, swooped, and spiralled in an impossible, intricate dance. The old farmer, Walter Edwards, had been right; the murmuration was beautiful, and at the same time hauntingly unfathomable. The deaths of the hundred starlings had been equally enigmatic, but six weeks on, the experts had concluded the flock had probably entered a dive murmuration to avoid a severe weather incident or a raptor, and were unable to pull back quickly enough to avoid hitting the ground. When Manx had read the findings, his thoughts immediately turned to Bobbie Matthews. That had been her fate, too. The last year of her life had been one long, free-falling tailspin that she was destined never to pull back from and recover. For that, she'd paid the ultimate price. Before heading inside, Manx watched the remainder of the starlings' performance until the flock extended its final curtain call, bowed, then vanished like a brush stroke into the watercolour complexion of dusk.

In the house, he peeled off his jacket and slipped off his shoes, exhaustion and hunger hit him like two trucks at once. It was only an hour later, after nuking and devouring a lamb biryani he'd excavated from his freezer and chugging several bottles of Kingfisher, that he found the courage to open the package. Part of him hoped the roll of film would be completely blank; nothing to see here, no gut-churning reminders of that day, but he doubted Gina would have gone to the trouble of hand-delivering an envelope of black prints.

He stacked his plates in the dishwasher, shoved the plastic container into the bin, twisted the top off another beer and called Tammy. Their conversation was subdued, gentle even, both too tired to talk long. They hung up after about ten minutes, both agreeing that grief was sometimes best shared alone, in reflection. He promised to call her tomorrow.

He walked to his spare bedroom, slipped the brightly coloured envelope from its plastic and flipped through the photographs. His initial suspicions were correct. There were neither date stamps nor geo-tag information back then, but there was no doubt they were all taken on the day Miriam had vanished. Most of the photographs were of a seventeen-year-old Frankie, his girlfriend at the time, smiling and mugging to camera. Most would have been instantly relegated to the trash icon in today's Instagram-filtered world, he imagined. The other thought he had glancing at Frankie's youthful, almost childlike face, was far more visceral. *Where the bloody hell did the time go?*

He took a swig of beer, wiped his mouth, and shuffled through the photographs. The remaining shots were all scenic; a teenage Tudor Manx's sorry attempts at art, no doubt trying to impress Frankie. They looked humorously forced: a discarded Coke can set into the sand, the ocean blurred in the background; a blade of marram grass, bright green and mostly out of focus; a close-up of Frankie's black polished fingernail resting on her choker necklace. He'd always tried too hard around Frankie, imagining he was never cool enough for her. He wondered if Frankie, like him, had left at the first opportunity? Or had she hung around, married, found herself with three kids, a dog and a mortgage? Frankie never seemed the family type, but then again, people change.

He flipped quickly through the remaining pictures, hoping that maybe he'd taken one of Miriam that day, but he hadn't. One photo, however, caught his attention. A wide shot of Aberffraw beach, a car parked on the old stone bridge crossing the river. He pulled the image closer; a midnight blue Jensen Interceptor, he was sure of it. Someone was leaning on the bonnet. It must have been his father, but the face was too blurred to be sure. Why would Tommy have been at the beach that day? His father never mentioned it, not once, as far as he could recall.

Manx taped the photograph to the whiteboard on the bedroom wall; it had now become his personal incident board. He'd created the collage of clippings soon after he'd been transferred to Anglesey and begun receiving cryptic text messages concerning Miriam's disappearance. Ten months later, the wall was a jumble of old newspaper clippings, faded photographs of his sister, and texts he'd screen-grabbed and printed out – origin unknown and sent via a cryptophone; anonymous and untraceable. He was convinced someone on the island was sending the messages, but were too scared to come forward, preferring to leave clues, like breadcrumbs, for him to follow or maybe to drive him into some kind of obsessive madness; Manx was still debating.

He took another slug of beer. The photograph made no sense. Was it taken on a different day? Not likely. Why didn't Tommy mention he was there? Manx had combed the cold case files often enough to know his father had never mentioned it. So, what was he doing at Aberffraw beach the day his daughter vanished, and why hadn't he provided the police with a statement to that effect?

Manx slid down from the bed, sat on the floor, and pressed his head back against the mattress. He hadn't spoken to Tommy in years. The last he knew, his father was living outside of Cardiff. He'd always made a point of keeping tabs on Tommy; nothing too overt, just a subtle check-in via the police database every few months. Now, it seemed to Manx, would be the time to reconnect. But not tonight, nor tomorrow; next week maybe. Tommy wasn't going anywhere, hadn't moved for years, and besides, he was sure answers as important as these were worth waiting for; worth taking the time to prepare the right questions that could bring him a step closer to the answers he was searching for.

Whether those answers would provide him the closure he wanted, of that he was less sure. He knew from experience the wide gulf that existed between the answers you assumed were the truth and the truth itself. Sometimes they met in the middle, more often than not they were miles apart.

THE END

Acknowledgements

A huge thanks as always to my wife, Laura, for her unwavering support and patience. A massive thanks to my dear friend Gloria for her insight and attention to detail. And for saving my arse on numerous occasions, a big thanks to my diligent and eagle-eyed editor, Clare.